D0464903

THE
KNOWN
CITIZEN

THE
KNOWN
CITIZEN

A HISTORY OF PRIVACY

IN MODERN AMERICA

Sarah E. Igo

Harvard University Press

Cambridge, Massachusetts
London, England
2018

Library of Congress Cataloging-in-Publication Data

Names: Igo, Sarah Elizabeth, 1969– author.
Title: The known citizen : a history of privacy in modern America / Sarah E. Igo.
Description: Cambridge, Massachusetts : Harvard University Press, 2018. |
Includes bibliographical references and index.
Identifiers: LCCN 2017050085 | ISBN 9780674737501 (alk. paper)
Subjects: LCSH: Privacy—United States—History—20th century. | Privacy—United States—
History—21st century. | Self-presentation—United States—History—20th century. |
Self-presentation—United States—History—21st century. | Privacy, Right of—United States—
History—20th century. | Privacy, Right of—United States—History—21st century. |
Information society—United States—History—21st century.
Classification: LCC BF637.P74 I38 2018 | DDC 323.44/80973—dc23
LC record available at https://lccn.loc.gov/2017050085

for my daughters:
Eleanor, Greta, and Harriet
and for Ole, again—
beloved invaders of privacy, all

Contents

THE
KNOWN
CITIZEN

Introduction

In a sardonic poem of 1940, composed just after his migration to the United States from Great Britain, W. H. Auden memorialized an "Unknown Citizen." Written in the form of an epitaph for an "unknown" and yet all-too-knowable citizen, the poem offers a capsule biography of an unnamed individual from the point of view of the social agencies charged with tracking and ordering his affairs. The citizen it commemorates is identified by a string of code similar to a U.S. Social Security number—"JS/07/M/378"—and his life amounts to a compendium of details gathered by employers, hospitals, schools, psychologists, market researchers, insurers, journalists, and state bureaus. The poem's final lines point simultaneously to the hubris and the limits of society's knowledge of this man. "Was he free? Was he happy? The question is absurd: Had anything been wrong, we should certainly have heard."[1]

If seldom as eloquently as Auden, contemporary Americans raised similar questions about those who sought to know them, whether for the purpose of governance or profit, security or convenience, or social welfare or scholarly research. Indeed, the proper threshold for "knowing" a citizen in a democratic, capitalist nation would become in the twentieth century one of Americans' most enduring debates. How much should a society be able to glean about the lives of its own members, and how much of oneself should one willingly reveal? What aspects of a person were worth knowing—and to whom—and which parts were truly one's own? Where and when could an individual's privacy be guaranteed? As the century advanced, the questions became more insistent. Were private spaces and thoughts, undiscovered by others, even possible under the conditions of modern life? What would

1

an ever more knowing society mean for the people caught in its net—and for the individual liberties that Americans supposedly prized? To wit: Could known citizens be happy? Were they, in fact, free?

This book borrows the poet's questions to pry open the contentious career of privacy in the modern United States. Individual privacy first surfaced as a sustained political issue only in the late nineteenth century, but it would swiftly become a fixture—even fixation—of U.S. public culture. As corporate industry, social institutions, and the federal government swelled, so too did disputes over what sort of prying and how much probing into citizens' lives were acceptable. These debates emerged alongside an increasingly impersonal, urban society: its techniques for maintaining social order but also its mass media, its scientific technologies as well as its styles of selling. Privacy talk waxed and waned, following no predictable path. But it closely tracked public attention to the perils—and the promise—of being a known citizen.

Modern privacy sensibilities were honed at the crux of a contradiction. Even as Americans grasped at wider freedoms in the twentieth century, they, like Auden's protagonist, were becoming ever more intelligible to an expanding array of parties: state bureaucracies and law enforcement; the popular press and marketers; financial institutions and private corporations; scientific researchers and psychological experts; and, eventually, data aggregators and proprietary algorithms. A knowing society impinged on individual liberties in unsettling ways. Being known could bring punishment from the state or destroy a reputation crafted for peers; it could raise one's insurance rates or cost someone a job. It could even compromise one's free will and sense of authentic personhood. Because they possessed this capacity to know, modern social institutions raised Auden's questions quite directly. Emerging technologies and media, novel modes of expert and corporate surveillance, and new practices of official documentation all propelled the problem of individual privacy to the foreground of U.S. public culture. There it would remain, becoming more and more central to citizens' assessments of their state and social order.

Americans turned to privacy talk because it helped them navigate the pull and push of a knowing society, one that sought to apprehend, govern, and minister to its members by capturing them in fuller and finer detail. Such a society carried rewards as well as risks. The proliferation of techniques for rendering citizens knowable, from credit reports and CCTV cameras to psychological testing, promised opportunity and security, even self-understanding. But being known too well—through the monitoring of one's sexual or consumption habits, for instance—could threaten personal autonomy, undermining the notion of a free-standing individual so foundational to U.S. politics and culture. In like fashion, to remain unrecognizable was in certain contexts a sign of privilege, but in others a form of disempowerment. Being traceable in a national criminal or DNA database was a different matter than being identifiable to a benefits-granting program like Social Security. It was possible, that is, to suffer not only from too little but also from too much privacy. Invisibility to service providers or census takers could sharply limit one's social opportunities and legal rights.[2] Whereas one's individual dignity might require being shielded from public view in some contexts, in others it could demand just the opposite: the validation of being named and seen. A longing for public recognition could oscillate with a desire for obscurity, even within the same person. And so, whether one could be known accurately and authentically—and on one's own terms, rather than the larger society's—was yet another question animating privacy's presence in American public life.

Arguments about privacy were really arguments over what it meant to be a modern citizen. To invoke its shelter was to make a claim about the latitude for action and anonymity a decent, democratic society ought to afford its members. Responses to that claim exposed the fault lines of civic membership. Which citizens, after all, could be entrusted with privacy, and therefore be liberated from official scrutiny? Because privacy could both foster intimacy and nurture vice, it came packed with assumptions about the kind of person entitled to it. And so, although privacy was obviously not the only way to talk about citizenship in the twentieth century, any conversation about privacy was already entangled with ideas about one's status in the broader society. How much privacy, for example, ought to be allotted to prisoners, soldiers, patients, or teenagers? When could different sorts of sexual subjects—male, female, straight, gay, married, unmarried—claim its mantle? Under what social and economic conditions could a person be said genuinely to have privacy, and how on a daily basis did one's class and race shape access to it? More generally, who had the ability to keep parts of their lives secret? Conversely, who could be recognized and appraised for who they truly were? The degree and nature of privacy that individual Americans enjoyed—including who could demand it and under what circumstances—were ways of defining, and divvying up, civic membership. No wonder, then, that privacy would become a dominant theme of twentieth-century politics.

To conceive of privacy as a social benefit and a mark of belonging enlarges the standard meaning of citizenship as a status conferred and regulated by the state.[3] Auden's anonymous subject, after all, was defined not simply by his nationality but also by his many other quasi-civic roles: employee, union member, father, neighbor, and consumer. "The Unknown Citizen" points us to the ways that full inclusion in an industrial democracy was a matter of one's capacity to move relatively freely through a force field of social institutions, private as well as public. For citizens themselves, it is clear, "citizenship" was never merely a juridical status, but instead a looser, more expansive marker, gesturing to one's ability to exercise choice and autonomy in the many realms of social life.[4] Like them, this book employs the term "citizen" in its most capacious sense. Privacy, understood as freedom from intrusion or scrutiny, could by these lights sometimes act as a substitute for explicitly enunciated rights. Its absence—via formal law or informal circumstance—could work to deny even full citizens equal social standing. Asserting how one could be known in the workplace or the marketplace, on a city street or in a suburban bedroom, was a claim to self-determination as well as social power. Americans in the twentieth century thus made of privacy much more than a legal right. They made it foundational to their sense of personhood and national identity.

Privacy has played a vital political and cultural role in the modern United States. But it has largely eluded scholars. This book pursues its history from a new vantage point: the question of how Americans would, and should, be known by their own society. Across the last century and a half, tabloid journalism and new technologies, welfare bureaucracies and police tactics, market research and personality testing, scientific inquiry and computer data banks, tell-all memoirs and social media all posed this question. In response, jurists and philosophers but also ordinary citizens weighed the advantages and hazards of being known. They would, in the process, remake conventions about access and intimacy, redrawing the borders separating the private from the public self. Trained on how citizens approached unfamiliar practices of identification and intrusion, record keeping and revelation, this book illuminates the deeply personal—but also profoundly social and political—meanings they attached to private matters. Spanning the long twentieth century, from the era of "instantaneous photography" to our own age of big data, it offers a wide-angle view of privacy as Americans have argued and imagined it.

Privacy, it scarcely needs saying, looms large today. If the drumbeat of headlines and bestsellers is to be believed, Americans are in the midst of an unprecedented privacy crisis—under "relentless surveillance," on the road to a fully transparent society, and with "no place to hide."[5] The ingredients of this crisis are well known to us. Data mining and NSA spying, recommendation algorithms and electronic footprints, biometric identification and extensive information sharing on social media platforms have raised fears about government and corporate surveillance to a high pitch. That a certain standard of protection from the gaze of others is routinely violated, and perhaps unrecoverable, is widely decried.

In this climate of worry about any number of parties and techniques that expose us against our wishes, privacy seems self-evidently a political matter. Despite privacy's starring role in contemporary diagnoses of U.S. culture, however, we have a surprisingly poor grasp of how it arrived there. Certainly, privacy has figured for centuries as an essential ingredient in theorists' formulations of liberal selfhood. Almost endlessly elastic, the term has, since its first appearance in English in 1534, accrued religious, philosophical, social, political, legal, and psychological dimensions.

Yet privacy was not always a matter of public import for Americans. As a topic for widespread popular debate or as a common public language, it is a creature almost entirely of the late nineteenth century. Born of disquiet about the status of the private person in the post–Civil War United States and an age when the contents of citizenship were under reconstruction, modern privacy arrived on the scene simultaneously prized and endangered. A new form of privacy talk took hold in this era, with mounting numbers of citizens both claiming a right to privacy *and* believing their privacy to be under siege. Only in the twentieth century did privacy emerge as a central concern of American life, with some commentators going further, tagging it an obsession or a "cult."[6] And only then was it vigorously pursued as a public, and sometimes collective, claim. "Privacy" gained an unusual capacity to frame Americans' discussions about the state, their social institutions, and even themselves. This is a story that is still unfolding, of course.

Privacy may have made a late entrance into U.S. politics and public life, but its staying power has been impressive. Nearly every major development in the United States since the Civil War—public health campaigns, media and communications technologies, military mobilization, social welfare legislation, workplace innovations, therapeutic methods, urban planning and suburbanization, social movements, criminal and terrorist threats—has been assessed in terms of its implications for citizens' privacy. Privacy talk has coursed through realms as different as bioethics and celebrity, national security and architecture, social etiquette and professional codes. At least since the turn of the twentieth century, it has also been democratic: just about anyone can demand privacy, if not achieve it. Immigrants, laborers, schoolchildren, and prisoners have all laid claim to the concept. It has featured as regularly in science fiction as in scholarship, in poetry as in political commentary. Invoked as an essential freedom and even a human right, yet worried over as a fragile and perhaps dying value, privacy became in the twentieth century a dominant concern of modern publics around the globe.[7] In the post–World War II United States, concerns over its status gathered enough momentum to launch a new constitutional right. Since then, it is safe to say, privacy's role in the American public sphere has only intensified.

Privacy in the modern United States thus has not been "private" at all. Rather, it has functioned as a crucial category of public life and a durable feature of partisan politics, even as its availability—or absence—has shaped countless personal choices and relationships. Highly visible contretemps over what should be kept out of the public eye across the last century fundamentally shaped U.S. political culture. The same is true today, even as a large body of writing declares that privacy is dead and gone.[8] In fact, privacy has never been more present in American life. It informs pundits' and citizens' discussions of topics ranging from the social behavior of youth to airport screening procedures, and from online search tracking to state intelligence operations. It regularly punctuates public life as a policy concern, a legal claim, and an individual hope.

The modern concept of privacy, as even this brief sketch makes clear, is sprawling. It has for good reason prompted voluminous scholarship in law, philosophy, literature, communications, design, technology, and the newer field of surveillance studies. Yet inquiries into its past have been curiously confined. As I worked on this book I kept arriving at a paradox: privacy is everywhere in modern America and yet hardly anywhere in modern American history. Arguably one of the most charismatic words in the national lexicon, privacy is missing from the indexes and headings by which we organize our understanding of the past. Key episodes in the legal history of privacy are well charted, as are specific controversies. But the scholarship remains heavily state- and rights-centered, neglecting privacy's significance as a cultural sensibility and public value. Historical works that examine the idea of privacy in all of its unruliness, or even some of it, are scarce, especially for the twentieth century—the period in which it entered national life with force.[9]

Existing histories of privacy are typically narrower affairs: explanations of the emergence of privacy *rights*, trained on doctrine, precedent, and policy. Legal scholars have devoted much attention to the first widely recognized demand for a "right to privacy" in 1890, the codification of state privacy laws over the ensuing decades, and the enunciation of privacy as a constitutional right in 1965.[10] These works treat the evolution of jurisprudence as a proxy for less neatly contained shifts in Americans' thinking about intimacy and intrusion. But such studies do not dwell on changes in citizens' sensibilities or on the reasons behind them. Scholarship on privacy's technical, juridical career has thus made little impact on our understanding of the politics and culture of modern America. Privacy as such makes only a brief—if dramatic—appearance in standard textbook surveys, usually beginning in 1965 with *Griswold v. Connecticut* and cresting in 1973 with *Roe v. Wade*. It bursts on the scene as a political problem, is transformed into a constitutional if controversial right, and, thus dealt with, promptly vanishes again.

There are excellent accounts that take up aspects of the history of privacy, especially concerning sexual regulation, the popular press, and state spying.[11] Each of these is a massive and complex topic in its own right. But fixing on a single strain of privacy's history can be misleading. For example, the two leading narratives about privacy in the United States—its eradication through state, workplace, and electronic surveillance, on the one hand, and its gradual, if tenuous, triumph through hard-won criminal or reproductive rights, on the other—point toward radically opposed conclusions.[12] Important as such scholarship is, it cannot do justice to privacy's wide-ranging, generative role in U.S. public culture. It cannot explain why Americans have so regularly turned to privacy to talk about such unlike things: their intimate relationships, their living spaces, their personal data, their political rights, and even their psyches. And it cannot account for why citizens' understandings of and feelings about privacy have evolved over time. Yet precisely what we require is a history of privacy's persistent, pliable appeal. Only by attending to its arrival in disparate spheres—law and technology, medicine and media, literature and architecture—will we be able to fathom how privacy came to sit at the very core of American politics and social life.

My panoramic approach attempts to overcome what is thus far a patch-work history. This book deliberately peers into otherwise unrelated domains in U.S. society in order to piece together a new picture of how and why privacy came to matter so much to modern Americans. Rather than lament privacy's disappearance, as do so many recent commentators, I track privacy's *appearances* in the U.S. public sphere, asking: When and why did privacy make its claims on citizens' attention? In what terms, and with what consequences? How, in the process, were Americans' expectations of privacy not simply diminished but transformed?

What, indeed, made privacy such a compelling idiom, brought to bear on topics as varied as intelligence gathering and confessional memoirs? Privacy talk, I argue, has been a response to, and sometimes a resolution of, an inescapable impasse of modern life: the fact that, even as U.S. public culture purported to honor the will and choices of individual citizens, its agencies pressed in new and forceful ways on the private person. "Privacy" rarely referenced a thing with definite contents; rather it served as an index to changing ideas about society itself.[13] Legal scholar Lawrence Tribe captures this sense of privacy when he describes it as "nothing less than society's limiting principle."[14] And indeed, citizens enlisted it, time and time again, to fix the line between the modern person and the collectivities to which she or he belonged.

To call something private, an option more and more Americans exercised in the twentieth century, was almost never to make recourse to an agreed-on definition. It was to make an argument about the proper relationship among citizen, state, and society. Sociologist Christena Nippert-Eng puts it this way: "privacy is about nothing less than trying to live both as a member of a variety of social units—as part of a number of larger wholes—and as an individual—a unique, individuated self."[15] The topic of privacy invited, even incited, grassroots social theorizing about power and intimacy, surveillance and subjectivity. It was the public vocabulary citizens reached for to debate the scope of the state, the conduct of social relations, and the very borders of the self.

More specifically, privacy was the language of choice for addressing the ways that U.S. citizens were—progressively and, some would say, relentlessly—rendered knowable by virtue of living in a modern industrial society. Given the number and range of parties that aspired to know them, Americans rightfully wondered what aspects of one's body, personality, identity, biography, and data an individual had ultimate claim to. In different ways, a candid photograph, a financial record, and a psychiatric diagnosis each raised this question: How distinct from the mesh of institutions, practices, and norms that constituted social existence could a person actually be? Privacy talk attempted to bridge the tension between expanding claims to personal inviolability and more sophisticated methods of infringing on it. It mediated, too, between the desire to be "let alone" and the urge to *be* known. These tensions created special problems in a national culture staked on personal autonomy. Invoking privacy was one of the chief ways that Americans of all stripes weighed in on an enduring political and philosophical quandary as to what separated self from society.[16]

And yet, as we would expect, privacy was not a shared or unitary concern, but was experienced and summoned in markedly uneven ways in the American twentieth century. Citizens viewed and wielded privacy differently depending on their status and circumstances, and some could barely access it at all. As a general rule, those excluded from full political citizenship because of their class, race, gender, age, nationality, able-bodiedness, or sexuality—or combinations thereof—also suffered most from a lack of privacy.[17] Prisoners and other institutionalized populations, but also the young, the poor, and the infirm, had few defenses against the intrusive monitoring of their lives. Racial minorities, immigrants, and noncitizens were subject to far higher rates of police and bureaucratic surveillance than were white native-born Americans; intensely scrutinized, they were perhaps always less deeply known by agents of the dominant society.[18] Women and sexual minorities were presumed to have a lesser claim on privacy than heterosexual men, and as a result they came first to the recognition that altering privacy's terms through disclosure and confession might be the path to a more inclusive public sphere.

In contrast, owning a home, making a comfortable living, and conforming to dominant norms of respectability all decidedly increased one's chances of evading society's gaze. And yet it was often white middle-class citizens who denounced privacy invasions most vociferously. This has led some to consider privacy talk a bourgeois pastime, the preoccupation of a select part of the population.[19] Elite Americans have sometimes embraced that characterization; privacy, noted the prominent nineteenth-century editor E. L. Godkin, was "one thing to a man who has always lived in his own house, and another to a man who has always lived in a boarding-house."[20] It is undoubtedly the case that privacy debates in the United States came with a class profile. As privileged citizens felt the press of social institutions on their own lives and liberties, their particular worries became the fodder for media coverage, congressional hearings, and public policy. But it is also evident that privacy's promise beckoned, if in a variety of registers, to a wider swath of Americans, including juveniles, patients, soldiers, union members, research subjects, and welfare recipients. As W. H. Auden—an immigrant to the United States and a gay man—well understood, the extent to which an individual could be rendered knowable was full of consequence in a modern nation.[21] The efflorescence and democratization of privacy talk over the course of the twentieth century were testament to that fact.

Precisely because privacy in the United States has been billed as a personal possession, outside the realm of the state or politics, its history opens an illuminating window onto the social strains of modern citizenship. Across the last century privacy was increasingly linked to that most public of identities, the rights-bearing citizen. Privacy talk thus became a potent avenue for claiming *and* circumscribing the social benefits of a modern industrial democracy. At the same time, insisting on recognition—as a citizen, a holder of a specific identity, a person out of the shadows—was basic to enacting one's membership in society. How well known a citizen would be was a sensitive marker of status and power, a fissure like any other cutting across professions of equality and opportunity in American life.

Charting the travels of something as abstract, but also as intimate, as "privacy" has its challenges. To begin with, the question of what privacy *is* has long bedeviled legal and philosophical discussions. In the course of researching this book it was amusing, if also sobering, to come across other observers' frustrations with how ungovernable a subject it is. "Few values so fundamental to society as privacy have been left so undefined in social theory or have been the subject of such vague and confused writing by social scientists," charged legal scholar Alan Westin in 1967.[22] Forty years later, Daniel Solove, a leading theorist of privacy, branded it "a concept in disarray."[23] Like the weather, concluded a sociologist in 2016, privacy is "much discussed, little understood, and not easy to control."[24] A large body of work nevertheless offers ever-finer taxonomies of privacy's "spatial," "decisional," "aesthetic," "proprietary," and "informational" dimensions.[25] But these efforts have considerable limitations for the historian. If we want to understand how Americans in varied contexts and times understood privacy, we need to abandon the notion of it having a stable definition. We cannot treat the bundle of ideas that inform modern privacy as transhistorical or ahistorical, a timeless principle waiting to be discovered, as in the abstract "right" to privacy—itself a puzzle since no such right was enunciated in formal legal terms in the United States until 1890.

The history offered here undercuts assumptions that there is something essential, even constitutional, about the concept. I argue that "privacy" has served in the United States as a catch-all for concerns about modern life and social organization, from new forms of media and technology to new state projects, new kinds of expert intervention, and even new living arrangements. As Americans reckoned with these developments, and particularly what they entailed for personal boundaries and individual rights, privacy itself—as an idea and a practice—evolved. In entertaining novel understandings of what could be asked and what could be said, what could be exposed and what should be disclosed, citizens shifted the very contents of "public" and "private," even as they regularly treated those categories as a fixed feature of social life.

In contrast to virtually every recent book on the subject, then, mine is not an account of what happened to the privacy Americans once, and seemingly straightforwardly, enjoyed. Instead it recounts what has happened to citizens' *thinking* about privacy—and, just as significant, what privacy has allowed them to think about. Threats to Americans' solitude and security changed dramatically over the last century. Their expectations about privacy shape-shifted in response. In certain eras, privacy debates focused most intently on incursions into personal space; in other periods, on violations of individual bodies, psyches, data, or peace of mind. Although citizens at times seemed to crave privacy, at others they were insensible to its importance or deliberately repudiated it. In the name of personal dignity—or autonomy or liberation—some wrapped a cloak of privacy around themselves, whereas some tore it off or tried to strip it from others. Americans never all conceived of privacy in the same way, of course. Nor did they all attend to, or participate equally in, such debates. What remained remarkably consistent, however, was their recourse to privacy as a way of arguing about their society and its pressures on the person.

Here, the same imprecision that vexes theorists proved to be privacy's true political value. Privacy, it turns out, has been a highly flexible container for social thought. The various domains in which Americans invoked privacy had little in common. But the questions that provoked the claim—who had the right to know, what ought to be publicly known, and who and what should remain unknown—were surprisingly stable, linking debates over print journalism in the 1890s to debates about confessional memoirs a century later, and contests over state filing systems in the 1930s to those over commercial algorithms in the present. Privacy may have been an inadequate vocabulary for that range of concerns, as a number of observers pointed out along the way. But the fact that so many items huddled together under its umbrella suggests privacy's indispensability as a mediator of modern social life.

Privacy is, finally, a tricky historical quarry because it refers to those matters one hopes to keep out of the public eye, to those corners of life that are off-limits or beyond scrutiny. And yet, at many points across the last century, privacy went public as it were, suddenly becoming visible in editorial pages, congressional hearings, and popular protests. To get at its changing contours, I take my cues from major controversies that had privacy at their core, whether in the form of "instantaneous photographs," Social Security numbers, or reproductive rights. A focus on public debates naturally leaves much hidden. This book cannot speak to the irreducible diversity of the ways Americans experienced privacy in their daily lives. Yet national debates can hint at more intimate ones, and what these disputes disclose is how regularly private matters have reshaped the public domain. Moments of uncertainty over the borders of public and private threw the concepts themselves into sharp relief, rendering cultural norms, and their transformation, visible. Attending to those moments moves us beyond elite commentary and legal arguments, getting us closer to the complex texture and meanings of modern privacy.

When did Americans call for privacy or give it up, and how did this depend on the setting: a bedroom, a laboratory, or a government office? Which citizens felt privacy's lack—or publicity's glare—most keenly? With what words did they defend their claims to privacy or argue about its violation? How were such beliefs, even deeply cherished ones, revised? Examining what a diverse array of Americans made of privacy, I document how conventions about access, intimacy, and disclosure were built but also dismantled. And I replace a now-familiar narrative about the "end of privacy" with one that recognizes both the curtailing of old privacies and the invention of new ones over time. That history cannot be told in linear fashion. And so I pick up the threads of particular privacy debates when they first appeared and let them go when others gained ground, without carrying each story to its conclusion. Rather than retell the history of photography, policing, research ethics, or "outing"—although portions of each of those histories appear here—I have sought to follow in the tracks of the known citizen.

No one book could capture the whole of this story or every angle of U.S. privacy debates. But by alighting on a series of critical episodes, this one aims to illuminate both the prominence and the significance of privacy talk in the modern American public sphere. That story begins in new understandings of the "inviolate personality" in the late nineteenth century and culminates—though does not end—with the emergence of a national "confessional culture" in our present. In between, I showcase pivotal moments when privacy talk became concentrated and consequential.

The first such moment came in the 1890s, when Victorian norms of propriety and respectability collided with mass-media technologies and prompted the first modern call for a "right to privacy." The second was occasioned by the rise of the administrative state in the early decades of the twentieth century, which heightened anxieties about the government's capacity to catalog and monitor its citizens. By mid-century, the intersection of a full-blown national security apparatus with more intimate forms of prying—in suburban communities, therapists' offices, the white-collar workplace, the public school, and the consumer market—riveted public attention on the invasiveness of American culture itself.

In the 1960s, in response to this series of technical and cultural developments, privacy gained new status as a constitutional right, becoming a cornerstone of Americans' popular lexicon of entitlements. Yet the fragility of that right in an era of advancing social and scientific research, government surveillance, and computer data banks meant that privacy concerns did not fade away. Instead, they were aroused anew, ushering in altered norms around confidentiality, consent, and access. In the 1970s and beyond, political demands for transparency, exposure, and disclosure—by one light privacy's opposites—redrew the borders between society and citizen. By the end of the century, the commercialization of surveillance along with the outflow of confessional talk would prompt many to conclude that there was no longer any privacy in the United States, nor even any desire for it.

Yet privacy talk erupted with force once again in the twenty-first century, triggered by the arrival of social media, big data, and startling exposés of just how well corporations and the state could know individual citizens.

The ways Americans debated the fate of personal privacy in the late nineteenth century can sound strangely familiar in the twenty-first, especially citizens' conviction that threats to privacy were new and uniquely compromising of individual liberties. Important continuities do in fact mark this history. Yet there have also been striking transformations, which we can only understand by reference to the problem of the known citizen.

One was Americans' turn from an emphasis on tangible claims to privacy—in the form of property rights and physical space—to intangible ones centered on psychological freedom, decisional autonomy, and personal identity as a more knowing society took root. Another transformation was in the shifting sense of who was entitled to privacy's refuge. The person imagined to be deserving of privacy, from the man of reputation in the 1890s to the "data subject" in the 1980s, did not stand still; the expansion of formal privacy rights and regulations across those decades testified powerfully if insufficiently to the felt need for protection from those claiming a right to know. But perhaps the most unexpected development was the way in which the closely guarded secrets of the Victorian era moved out into the open after the 1960s, whether in political, psychological, or pop-cultural form. Although never completely or finally, an older fear of exposure gave way to an embrace of disclosure, an age of discretion supplanted by an age of self-broadcasting. The yearning for recognition and authenticity that would take hold in many corners of American society in the 1970s confounds conventional narratives of privacy's twentieth-century career. It too is tightly bound to the career of the known citizen.

Although this book takes a broad view of privacy's history, its omissions may surprise. Today's commentators on privacy tend to gravitate to the most brazen instances of overreach and invasion, whether illegal federal wiretaps or covert social media profiling. My own search for bearings in more than a century of privacy talk has led me down a different path, alert to the manifold ways that Americans have managed their relationship to those who would know them. This has led me to spend far more time thinking about Social Security numbers, subliminal advertising, and public restrooms than I could have anticipated when I set out to write about privacy. *The Known Citizen* is, as a consequence, neither a history of the surveillance society nor of the national security state, two of the most common frameworks for thinking about privacy in the early twenty-first century (for perhaps obvious reasons).[26] Without a doubt, surveillance technologies and the demands of national security ratcheted up privacy talk in the twentieth century, as did innovations in commercial data mining at the turn of the twenty-first. But it is also the case that these developments—if and when Americans became aware of them—intersected with and amplified public debates that were already well underway. For this reason, Facebook surveillance and malware, as well as the headline-grabbing episodes of the Cold War and the War on Terror, show up here as bit players rather than the main event.

By trailing the known citizen, this book foregrounds less expected places where privacy talk percolated in modern America: scientific laboratories and family living rooms, marketing agencies and welfare bureaus, social movements and therapeutic encounters. Those conversations, I contend, were as critical to public debates over privacy as were revelations of state break-ins and massive data breaches. Scandals may have provided a clear focus for American privacy talk, but daily negotiations supplied the sensibility. Well-publicized privacy violations in this way obscure what might best be described as an ongoing skirmish over the demands of the modern social order and its many claims on the person. The encroachments of a knowing society—in the form of telephone lines or psychological exams, public records or credit cards—were often most keenly felt in the intimate rounds of personal life.

The potential rewards of such a society were evident too, with many people willing to live more openly by embracing new modes of exposure and disclosure. The domains of the household, the bureaucratic agency, and the talk show yield plentiful stories of those who simultaneously resisted *and* craved being known, who both pursued *and* dispensed with privacy. Writers focused on surveillance often neglect this crucial fact: that concerns about intrusion have often been accompanied by a desire for visibility. Citizens, indeed, have often sought to be better known by their state and society—whether in the name of security, convenience, or social recognition. If Americans were in the twentieth century increasingly sensitive to infringements on their privacy, they were also aware that the way they lived often depended on such invasions. That, in a nutshell, was the dilemma of a knowing society.

The history offered here also makes abundantly clear that the impetus for privacy claims in American society—stretching all the way back to the nineteenth century—has as often been the actions of private entities as those of the central government.[27] The notion that privacy talk in the United States has been animated primarily by governmental power is a byproduct of focusing on the legal right to privacy, generally framed as a defense against state action. Although aggressive journalists and photographers were a catalyst for modern American privacy arguments, it has been all too easy to neglect the central role of nonstate actors, whether corporations or private citizens themselves, in ushering in a modern sense of privacy's precariousness. The government could be both guarantor and violator of individual privacy. So too could the many other institutions of social life: workplaces, laboratories, schools, and homes.

Recent commentators often envision a giant ledger where privacy is slipping ever more swiftly into the deficit column. Yet we miss something important if we insist, as many do, that it has been on a steady and precipitous decline. Privacy in the modern United States has been less a thing with definite contents than a seedbed for social thought, a tool for navigating an increasingly knowing society. Recurring debates about intimacy and intrusion across the last century are a product of this society's dynamic, unavoidable tensions. This history explains why securing the boundary between one's private affairs and one's public identity has become such a routine, and yet urgent, task of modern life. A focus on the predicament of the known citizen—perhaps even more pressing today than it was when Auden wrote—will, I hope, help us better grasp privacy's significance for contemporary U.S. culture, politics, and law.

As such, this book allows us to listen in on a vital strand of social thought in the twentieth-century United States. Its goal is not to decry but to explore the multifarious forms of publicity, exposure, and disclosure that modern Americans have lived with either by choice or necessity. It acknowledges that individuals' search for privacy has always been complicated by their quest for recognition. It takes up the themes of secrecy and surveillance, recording and revelation, identity and identification that together constitute the danger but also the appeal of being known. It does its best to reckon with the knowledge problems at the heart of modern privacy—and of modern citizenship too.

1

Technologies of Publicity

Privacy is a distinctly modern product, one of the luxuries of
civilization.

—E. L. GODKIN, 1890

"One sketches one's age imperfectly if one doesn't touch on that particular matter: the invasion, the impudence, the shamelessness of the newspaper and the interviewer, the devouring publicity of life, the extinction
of all sense between public and private."[1] Novelist Henry James wrote these
words in 1888. His target was the new media of his time along with the
"invasion," "impudence," and "shamelessness" it brought in its train. At
the core of James's protest, however, was "publicity" itself, at once a set of
practices and a set of mind bent on eroding the once-sturdy line dividing
public from personal matters. His characterization will sound familiar to
Americans of a later day—so much so that we must pause to pin down the
specific conditions that rankled the novelist more than a century ago. For
James, the "devouring publicity of life" was inseparable from a host of
modern technologies that threatened to expose to common view all that
belonged to the private person. These ranged from the innocuous-seeming
postcard, which casually divulged a writer's secrets to anyone who could
read, to the formidable X-ray, which sparked fears that "walls could no
longer shield inhabitants from [its] piercing power" and that "the era of
privacy was at an end."[2]

Modern privacy was brought into being by these novel agents of "publicity." In 1888, there was no contesting that new tools were at hand for
rendering citizens more knowable to those outside their intimate circle.
Particularly dramatic were "instantaneous" photography, telegraphy, te-
lephony, sound recording, and the popular press, all of which flung open
private life to the curious eyes and ears of others. That exposure was all

the more unsettling for being virtual. While the intrusions of a "peeping Tom" or eavesdropper required physical proximity, the photographer and the wiretapper conducted their prying from a distance. These developments seemed to augur the "extinction of all sense between public and private." And they presented urgent questions: How private in fact *were* private citizens? What limits, if any, governed their exposure to the larger society?

Many Americans thrilled to the possibilities of modern communications and their newfound ability to peer into others' lives. Yet these same citizens often sought refuge from a culture intent on making public what had once been considered private. A knowing society would be defined in large part by this tension between the desire to see or be seen and the wish to evade society's gaze. For a man of James's milieu, the privileged class of America's gilded age, citizens appeared more open to view than ever before, but also more willing to place themselves on display.

The novelist aimed his outrage at professional purveyors of gossip, at the newspapers that unveiled private lives for public consumption. But he pointed to a broader transformation of public life—and with it, the conditions for individual privacy—in the post–Civil War United States. The changes were often first apparent to city dwellers, the vast numbers who migrated to urban centers from farms or small towns.[3] Those who had been subject to the close regulation of their families or local communities often welcomed the freedom from scrutiny that came from joining a "society of strangers."[4] The very gift of partial anonymity that city life offered, however, was being chipped away by new technologies and commercial interests. Technical leaps in the ability to peer into and record intimate scenes and a bolder, brasher journalism made private matters newly vulnerable. These practices—altering what individuals knew of others and how they themselves could be known—lifted privacy to a new status in American public culture.[5]

James's characterization of these developments as an offense to individual dignity and public decency had precedents.[6] But in the last decade of the nineteenth century his analysis resonated widely, entering political and legal discussions with fresh intensity. Even some far removed from James's upper-middle-class world grasped toward a right to be free of such intrusions. A modern answer to a modern problem, privacy emerged as a common language: one that women and men from many walks of life employed to parse, and sometimes protest, the knowingness of their own society.

This privacy was, in key respects, new. It was concerned less with an individual's immediate surrounds than with image, information, biography, and what Americans were beginning to call "personality." In James's complaint we can spy an older vision of privacy, one rooted in ownership and property lines, giving way to another. The novelist worried not about physical trespass or government officials pounding down the door, but—strikingly—about commercial agencies that delivered the news. In their aggressive uses of the camera and the pen, photographers and journalists mounted virtual rather than material invasions of citizens' affairs. These assaults on individual personality were the product of new machineries of exposure but also the modern sensibilities that accompanied them.

The shift from a property- to a personality-based form of privacy was never total: witness recent debates over police frisking and body scans at airports. But it was a harbinger of the way Americans would more and more invoke privacy in the century to come. Tracking when and where this new sort of privacy appeared illuminates the specific pressures a mass-mediated and information-based society placed on its inhabitants, unsettling the customary relationship between private citizens and the public world they inhabited. "Privacy" was, among other things, a counterweight to a knowing society, an attempt to calibrate the balance between the knowers and the known. It named a value that modern U.S. society deemed precious, but also, perhaps inevitably, made precarious.

The Beginnings of the End of Privacy

By some measures, Americans had from their earliest history enjoyed a good deal of freedom from the intrusions of state and society. Scholars have noted that a "substantial degree of personal privacy" obtained in the British colonies, the fruit of scattered settlement and light governance.[7] This description would not of course have applied to indentured servants, slaves, and other unfree laborers, nor to most women or youth. It was restricted to white adult male landholders and those of free birth. For this select group of colonists, property ownership, including the claim of self-possession, marked the borders of legitimate interference into one's affairs. Officially, the law of trespass and unreasonable search and seizure ruled, following the Anglo-American legal tradition in which the house and home were associated with "security against violent invasion." As the famed jurist William Blackstone had it, "The law of England has so particular and tender a regard to the immunity of a man's house, that it stiles it his castle, and will never suffer it to be violated with impunity."[8] This propertied conception of "immunity" would play a key role in the American Revolution and its memorialization, summoning up the specter of British soldiers forcibly quartered in colonists' domiciles.

This is not to say that early Americans were great respecters of each other's privacy. Eavesdropping, gossip, and other forms of meddling were part and parcel of life in small communities. Such interference may have been irritating, but it was commonplace. The watchfulness with which colonists supervised their neighbors' behavior and households, especially in the Puritan settlements, has been well documented.[9] Claims to privacy were suspect, even a threat to community values. Because "family and community, private and public life, formed part of the same moral equation," writes one historian of Plymouth colony, "the two realms became in a sense indistinguishable." Indeed, he concludes, privacy of the sort that contemporary Americans enjoy was inconceivable given colonists' tight living quarters and equally confining social strictures.[10] Privacy, at least as we now imagine it, was not "a highly publicized or articulated concept" in colonial America.[11]

The same was true in the new nation, where citizens had recourse to a number of bedrock legal protections to guard against intrusions into their homes, the reading of their mail, and the disclosure of confidential information.[12] These rights stood out against the utter lack of such safeguards for the marginalized and disenfranchised. The brutal controls on enslaved people in particular, imposed through slave passes and patrols, lantern laws, the branding of individual bodies, and the breakup of families, were the mirror image of the legally enforced entitlements that white property-holding Americans enjoyed.[13] And yet, before the Civil War, few discussed privacy as "a generalized legal, moral, or natural right."[14] This right was instead implicit, understood to belong to white men of land and wealth, including slaveholders, but also to small property owners, who reigned over their households and dependents: wives and children if not servants and slaves.[15] This kind of privacy, underwritten by property rights in land and people, the expansive sovereignty of the household head, and the denial of self-ownership to African Americans, was perhaps so assured that it did not require enunciation.

When "privacy" was invoked in the early United States, it was typically a more limited sort of claim, joined to the circumstances of one's immediate physical environment. Curiosity and outright prying were often billed as "democratic" American habits, but the conflicts they gave rise to were generally resolved through social sanctions rather than courts.[16] What legal discussions of privacy there were centered on shielding citizens' homes and papers from governmental interference.[17] But even these disputes were scarce. The Fourth Amendment guarantee of freedom from unreasonable searches and seizures was rarely invoked, cited just twice in federal court decisions between 1787 and 1865. Before the Civil War, summarizes one scholar, the legal understanding of privacy "had not expanded to encompass much beyond one's home and postal correspondence." Even the war itself, despite abundant telegram interceptions and some censorship of the mails, sparked "no organized public discussion" of the proper limits of official probing into citizens' personal affairs, nor calls for a "right" to privacy.[18] Until the last quarter of the nineteenth century—when growing corporate and state power as well as new citizenship claims would press the issue— privacy remained largely dormant as a public language.

At the same time, however, a more fulsome notion of the private sphere and its prerogatives was taking root. It trailed the evolving meaning of the word "privacy" itself. Privacy had once been considered a form of privation, implied by the Latin *privatus* and *privare*. Linked etymologically to selfishness—the love of one's own private interests—as well as deprivation, the concept was undergoing a slow metamorphosis.[19] Already by the turn of the nineteenth century, privacy carried far more positive connotations, unlike the similar terms of "alienation, loneliness, ostracism, and isolation."[20] Not simply the condition of being alone, privacy was coming to refer to a set of ideas about personal freedom and individual autonomy, an "inner uncoerced realm."[21] It denoted an interior sanctuary as much as an exterior, physical one.

This revaluation of privacy was linked to the emergence of the "home"— as distinct from the household or the physical house—as an idealized bourgeois realm of domesticity.[22] Private property and the "affective private life of the family" became tightly linked across the nineteenth century.[23] In architectural forms, prescriptive advice, and individual habits, there was new attentiveness to fortifying the borders between private and public arenas.[24] The walls of the family dwelling symbolized these divisions, physically as well as psychologically.[25] Well-off Victorians took active steps to guard their domestic affairs from prying, inventing back stairs for servants, for example. They also rejected an older Greek style of house that afforded little protection from the eyes of others, gravitating toward a

Gothic or "Picturesque" style that allowed for retreat and seclusion.[26] Etiquette manuals offered elaborate instructions for proper conduct on sidewalks and public thoroughfares, making an implicit but clear contrast to one's conduct in the familial, intimate sphere.[27] And young women's diaries testified to the labor involved in cultivating the private self, understood to be different from the roles one was called on to play in public society.[28]

Writing in the 1960s, sociologist Edward Shils concluded that the third quarter of the nineteenth century was the age of privacy's "efflorescence" in the United States. Finely tuned codes of respectability had by that point entered working-class as well as middle-class life, reinforcing "a sense of the inviolateness of what went on within the family." Domestic privacy, he suggested, was newly valued and socially enforced; curious neighbors— "Nosy Parkers"—were disparaged; and individuals erected barriers to being known by those outside the family circle. Legal protections for private property, along with the reigning ethos of economic individualism, Shils argued, underwrote and "helped stiffen a general regard for privacy."[29] This sort of privacy, very close to contemporary understandings of propriety, was not in any simple sense "private." It was a social good, keyed to dominant norms. Private life, properly ordered, was the very foundation of public morality. Privacy as such was coming to play a new role in public life, with "the potential to promote or betray one's moral self."[30]

Moralists of all kinds reinforced the message. The prominent minister Henry Ward Beecher, for example—his own alleged affair with a member of his congregation the object of avid press coverage in the 1870s— sermonized about the family's "sacred right to privacy."[31] Were by chance an outsider to glimpse domestic intimacies, the reverend advised, "honor would require him to turn from them"; if such knowledge were "forced" on him, it "should be locked in a sacred silence."[32] Victorians, British as well as American, invested enormous resources in the project of insulating private affairs from the knowledge and view of outsiders. Even the shames of the household gained new protection, as parents and siblings, cousins and aunts, guarded one another's secrets—including shocking ones like homosexuality or interracial liaisons—in order to preserve family respectability.[33]

Such respectability was found in its most distilled form in the good name of the head of the household. Legal scholar Susan Gallagher observes that much of the uproar about the popular press in the second half of the nineteenth century concerned less the behavior it exposed—sexual indiscretions in particular—than the "evil of public revelation" itself. This was because "command over public knowledge of a man's domestic affairs" had become the very marker of bourgeois masculinity.[34] Control over one's reputation—a right, even, to be known as one wished—was a privilege to which only some citizens were entitled, however. Long after the Fourteenth Amendment secured citizenship for African Americans in 1868, protection from public exposure in the name of one's dignity remained, in conception and in practice, a white man's right.

With reputation its sign and propriety its watchword, the bourgeois privacy of the late nineteenth century was exclusive and patriarchal. It was also corporate, the male-governed family its proper locus. As such, its liberties and protections were distributed unevenly across the household. The domestic ideal displaced pre-Revolutionary legal remedies that wives and subordinates had once possessed, including redress against physical punishments for disobedience.[35] Charlotte Perkins Gilman understood in her 1898 treatise on *Women and Economics* that honoring "private life" was not the same as honoring the rights of its participants, especially women and other dependents. She contended, "Such privacy as we do have in our homes is family privacy, an aggregate privacy; and this does not insure—indeed it prevents—individual privacy."[36] Nineteenth-century family and marriage law, two legal scholars concur, offered women "too much of the wrong kinds of privacy—too much modesty, seclusion, reserve, and compelled intimacy—and too little individual modes of personal privacy and autonomous, private choice."[37]

Because "aggregate" privacy was firmly aligned with the interests of the man of the house, a quest for individual rights within the family could easily be cast as a violation of his prerogatives. The woman's suffrage movement met opposition on exactly these grounds. One senator who opposed the franchise for women equated it in 1881 with breaking in "through a man's household, through his fireside . . . to open to the intrusion of politics and politicians that sacred circle of the family."[38] The U.S. Supreme Court in 1888 underscored the public benefits of this cordoned-off sanctuary for the male head of the household, tethering "the sanctity of a man's home and the privacies of life" to "his indefeasible right of personal security, personal liberty and private property."[39]

Privacy of this sort, profoundly marked by gender, class, and racial privilege, was by the late nineteenth century regularly depicted as "the crowning achievement of polite, liberal society."[40] It was, however, destined to be disrupted by that era's technological and commercial achievements. A newly aggressive journalism, as Henry James suggested, was at the very center of the disruption. The impulse to peer into others' affairs—an age-old feature of village life—had never actually subsided even during the high tide of domesticity and respectability.[41] In the waning years of the century, however, it found a formidable ally in the popular press.[42] Its bold intrusions, through the printed word and image alike, scrambled the neat Victorian compartmentalization of personal and public life, jeopardizing the careful management of reputation so valued by elites. New calls for legal rights to privacy at the end of the nineteenth century indicated that an established privilege in the form of mastery over one's own affairs was under strain. The privacy of elite white men, it seemed, could no longer be assumed.

Some citizens welcomed, even sought out, the breakdown of old proprieties that accompanied incursions into previously private places. Others resisted. But the conflict itself laid the groundwork for modern claims to personal, rather than domestic, inviolability. Privacy of a recognizably modern kind, built not on property but on personality, was born in this era—not fully possible, perhaps, until it had been both individualized and endangered. Only under the glare of new forms of publicity would privacy become an overt and explicit category of American public life: an object to be argued over and a gathering place for a wide variety of political and social concerns. Elite citizens who attempted to fortify domestic privacy, starting with control over their good names, were among the first to make privacy a public cause. In the process, however, privacy lost some of its propertied foundations and gained a more psychological profile. It also slipped from the exclusive grasp of "men of reputation," becoming the demand—if not yet typically the possession—of a wider band of citizens. Charges of privacy's "extinction" in the late nineteenth century in this way launched its public career. In announcements of its end were the beginnings of a modern political claim.

Privacy and Publicity in Practice

The immediate trigger for Henry James's warning about the "devouring publicity of life" was the outpouring of intimate details in popular broadsheets. But an inquisitive press was just one marker of a new culture of exposure. Publicity, like privacy, had many champions at the turn of the century. For every critic who insisted that publicity diminished its victims and public discourse alike, there was a social scientist or realist novelist convinced that stripping back the veneer of society to reveal it as it really was would enlighten and improve public life.[43] Indeed, many venerated "publicity" as a positive good and exposure as essential to social progress. Louis Brandeis, the American jurist most associated with the right to privacy, himself advocated passionately for what he termed "the duty of publicity."[44] For those who wielded publicity in the cause of reform—the social survey movement, the muckrakers bent on unearthing the evils of corporate malfeasance or political wrongdoing, newly professionalized journalists pledged to "objectivity"—scientific, fact-finding investigations were the solvent for all manner of social ills, from poverty to corruption.[45]

Historian Rochelle Gurstein has categorized these warring sensibilities as "the party of reticence" and the "party of exposure." To those in the camp of reticence, new forms of publicity were one piece of a larger assault on customary standards of propriety, the popular press collaborating with sex reformers and literary naturalists to undermine the sanctity of private life and the "high-mindedness" of public conversation. For those committed to exposure, on the other hand, discretion was the language of cover-up, repression, and prudery.[46] Centrally at issue was what properly ought to appear in public.

Thoroughgoing changes in information practices would interlace with these debates. Technological and commercial innovations in particular would present steep challenges to "reticence." Questions of privacy came to the fore in the post–Civil War decades as Americans reckoned with the massive private entities that "conveyed, broadcast, bought, and sold information—a commodity of growing importance in a more and more organized society."[47] Controversies over news monopolies as well as sensational reportage signaled the new power of this economic sector, as did the consolidation of the telegraph and newspaper industries in the form of the Associated Press wire service.[48] Railroad financiers and other corporate titans were keenly aware of the threat to their reputations—and bank accounts—posed by the quicksilver spread and international reach of damaging pieces of information.[49] These developments were disruptive enough to prompt some "to look to the law to control, not only what individuals could or could not do, but whether what they did would become generally known."[50]

When less prominent citizens took note of these trends, they focused on threats to privacy rather than to profits. For them, the communications revolution that picked up steam in the 1870s was experienced as a series of dazzling inventions. Among the most significant were the transcontinental telegraph and transatlantic cable of the early 1860s, laying the groundwork for the commercial telegraph in 1874. Right on its heels was the "Harmonic Telegraph," or telephone, in 1876.[51] Just five years later, the United States boasted the world's largest telephone network, soon to be incorporated as American Telephone & Telegraph. A flurry of other inventions—the commercial typewriter (1874), microphone (1876), and dictaphone (1889)—allowed information to be transferred still more accurately and efficiently. Meanwhile, the transmission of images was revolutionized through the introduction of photoengraving in 1881 and roll film in 1889.[52] Each of these technologies carried the potential to alter how news of both a private and public nature traveled. Words and pictures could be disseminated much more swiftly and smoothly through these means—but also less securely. As such, the new communications media of the late nineteenth century, much like today's, fascinated and perturbed their users in turn.

Conflicts over privacy grew up alongside new modes of communication. This was true even in the case of the postal system, one of the most familiar and trusted ways of transmitting news. Ralph Waldo Emerson had in the 1860s reflected admiringly on the confidentiality of the mails: "To think that a bit of paper, containing our most secret thoughts, and protected only by a seal, should travel safely from one end of the world to the other, without anyone whose hands it has passed through having meddled with it."[53] In fact, letter opening was hardly unknown, and in the 1870s, public moralist Anthony Comstock's campaign to root out obscenity in the mails further dented assurances of confidentiality.[54] A different sort of challenge stemmed from the introduction of the postcard, patented in 1861 but first authorized for sale by the U.S. Post Office in 1873. Postcards, inexpensive to send, were enormously popular with consumers: 200,000 were reportedly purchased in the first two hours they were on offer in New York City. Both the new method of sending words through the mails and its users, however, were vigorously critiqued for their role in changing the terms of personal disclosure.[55] In 1890, the editors of a literary magazine announced their contempt for the postcard as a means of personal communication: "We do not wish to have our affairs discussed publicly, nor do we care for servants and landladies to have the full benefit of our private matters." Even into the twentieth century, the *Atlantic Monthly* denounced the practice and, specifically, "a lady who conducts her entire correspondence through this channel," revealing "secrets supposed to be the most profound, related misdemeanors and indiscretions with a reckless disregard to the consequences." (The writer added that despite this woman's confidence "in the integrity of postmen and bell-boys," the latter "may be seen any morning, sitting on the doorsteps of apartment houses, making merry over the post-card correspondence."[56])

The postcard ruffled elite standards of privacy and propriety. But far more disruptive changes to communications were in the offing, and they would make social exposure a central conundrum of the day. The telegraph and telephone provided the most dramatic examples. Each increased the volume and circulation of all kinds of information. Private correspondence as well as news of public events now flowed more quickly and freely, communication no longer dependent on the physical delivery of messages.[57] The telegraph in particular, which came into general use at mid-century, helped "create modern expectations of timeliness and newsworthiness," altering the very "psychology of news consumption."[58] Both inventions would spark privacy questions, especially as they evolved from a form of "rich man's mail" to more widespread use.[59] The assumption that private messages would reach only their intended recipient would be seriously undercut by the penetrability of the new communication technologies. As one scholar observes, telegraph and telephone networks—precisely because they *were* networks—"made the personal lives and personalities of individuals increasingly accessible to large numbers of others, irrespective of acquaintance, social or economic class, or the customary constraints of propriety."[60]

The very cables by which telegraph messages sped through air put their users at risk. Wiretapping, a military art during the Civil War, found new uses by law enforcement agents, not to mention criminals, in the decades thereafter, prompting many states to enact laws banning the practice. According to an early court ruling, such legislation was necessary "to prevent the betrayal of private affairs . . . for the promotion of private gain or the gratification of idle gossip."[61] The telegraph network, dubbed the "Victorian Internet" by one scholar, posed a now familiar trade-off between privacy and convenience.[62] Telegram messages required the disclosure of their contents to a third party and companies retained copies of each transmission, meaning that ostensibly personal communications might exist in three or four separate locations.[63] Stored messages proved especially vulnerable to seizure by government subpoena, triggering political debate from the 1870s onward about the legal status of telegrams as compared to letters. The question, not to be resolved until well into the twentieth century, was as follows: Were communications via this means deserving of less protection than the mails *because* of the means?

Telephone lines, which proliferated after the first commercial exchanges were established in 1878, proved equally conducive to prying. Technically speaking, listening in on telephone conversations was even easier to accomplish than accessing information on the telegraph wires, with early experimenters impressed by "the rapidity and simplicity of the means by which a wire could be milked, without being cut or put out of circuit."[64] Urban police seized on the possibilities for virtually intercepting the plots of criminals and radicals.

Meanwhile, law-abiding citizens were subject to eavesdropping of a less systematic kind. The fact that the human operators of the phone lines were always liable to overhear was a common justification for treating telephone conversations as inherently unprivate by law enforcement.[65] Moreover, the structure of the network practically invited clandestine listening by curious neighbors. The earliest subscribers were connected on a single line to a central switchboard; later, it would be standard for four customers to share each "party line." As an Indiana woman later recalled, "When the ring occurred, everybody in the community would take down [the receiver] and would listen."[66] Their presence undetectable, multiple users could tune in to any conversation on the line, prompting one contemporary to denounce a dawning age of "electronic exhibitionism and voyeurism."[67] Concerns about unimpeded access to supposedly private conversations sent engineers scurrying for technical fixes such as selective ringing, introduced by the Chicago Telephone Company in 1896, and the "lockout system," which dashed the hopes of eavesdroppers with a busy signal.[68]

There were, naturally, two sides (at least) to this conversation: the listener and the listened-to, with their distinctly opposed interests. Also arrayed against each other were the avid users of new technologies and their detractors. Like postcard writers, telephone enthusiasts came in for plenty of censure. Against industry expectations that the new telephones would be used primarily as a business tool, consumers began to seek them out for personal conversation and what critics often branded as "trivial gossip," with some telephone companies even attempting to staunch the use of the wires for "visiting." The fact that women seemed to put the new device to this use much more regularly than men explains some of the resistance; one study finds that in the early twentieth century farm women in particular embraced the telephone to escape the loneliness of rural life. But telephones also seemed to promote improper conversations across gender lines, including "illicit wooing" and other indiscretions, which could now go unmonitored by parents or guardians.[69] Dispensing with polite conventions that had ruled face-to-face meetings—such as formal introductions and chaperones—users of the phones redrew spatial and social boundaries, blurring the lines between the public and domestic world, and male and female, spheres in the process. Telephone users' pronounced desire for connection and sociability, and for more informal modes of communication, says something about how privacy was being remade by rural and urban folk far outside Henry James's ken.[70]

Fascination with the potential these technologies held for penetrating others' secrets was evident in pulp thrillers about "the wire" published at the turn of the century. Novels like Arthur Stringer's *The Wire Tappers* (1906) and *Phantom Wires* (1907) were populated by villains and heroes able to intercept, cut, and redirect supposedly private communications.[71] The latter novel wove a sensational narrative around tapping the wire of a key character, "whereon instructions and information were secretly hurried about the city to his dozen and one fellow-operators." The hero of the novel "worked for an hour . . . before the right wire fell under his thumb. Then he listened intently, with a little start, for he knew he was reading an operator whose bluff, heavy staccato 'send' was as familiar to his long-practiced ear as a well-known face would be to his watching eyes."[72] The notion that a telegraph operator's "send" could be as recognizable as a "well-known face" hints at the novel ways that individuals were becoming known in a society linked by wires. Clearly, the kind of virtual spying that the telegraph and telephone permitted could enthrall as well as endanger their users. Social practices and popular culture alike suggest a certain amount of comfort with trespassing on others' privacy—and forfeiting some of one's own—in the era that would produce the first legal calls for a "right to be let alone."

New uses of the camera would place even more pressure on reigning norms of privacy and propriety. Photography had in its early days been slow and cumbersome, awkward equipment and long exposure times making it "virtually impossible . . . to capture an image of someone" without the subject's express permission. Samuel Morse, inventor of the telegraph, was reportedly surprised during a visit to the workshop of Louis Daguerre, inventor of the daguerreotype, to see no human figures in depictions of "even the busiest places in Paris." Daguerre explained that because of exposure times of fifteen to twenty minutes, individual people and even carriages on the street eluded capture.[73] But by 1884 George Eastman had developed the "snap" camera that dramatically reduced the amount of time necessary for exposure. Two years later, what was tellingly labeled the "detective" camera could take a picture "instantaneously," no longer depending on the cooperation of its subject. These would be followed by the true amateur device, the Kodak, advertised as a camera that required no expertise at all. By 1889, the taking of instantaneous photos was described as a common hobby and even a "craze."[74] With cheap, automatic cameras on offer to consumers, the phrase "Kodak fiends" entered the vernacular.[75]

These developments set the stage for virtual invasions of a new kind, whether from picture hunters hoping for candid shots of the unsuspecting or the urban mass press. The sudden ubiquity of photography and photographers in late nineteenth-century America, historian Jessica Lake argues, "radically altered the experience of seeing and being seen by others."[76] Amateur cameras were small and explicitly designed to be used surreptitiously—shaped as hip flasks, pocket watches, binoculars, and even revolvers. Advertisements for them banked on the "thrill of capturing the likeness of another person without their knowledge or consent."[77] Early skirmishes over covert photo taking themselves garnered plenty of publicity, with amateur photographers the object of irritation as well as serious protests. Public outcries quickly led to restrictions on the use of cameras not only in the White House but also on trains, ferries, and private property. The capturing of women on camera was of special concern to those already wary about changing norms of gendered propriety. In England, there were reports of the formation of a "Vigilance Association" in 1893 whose aim was the "thrashing of cads with cameras who go about in seaside places taking snapshots of ladies emerging from the deep."[78] By the turn of the century, "Kodaker" had become an insult, "an unflattering term used to describe the impertinent and annoying behavior of chronic picture takers."[79]

American newspapers, for their part, were already known for their impertinence. One critic of the 1870s lambasted "keyhole journalism" for

1.1. Kodak's Brownie camera, so simple to use that it could be "operated by any school boy or girl," was introduced at the price of one dollar in 1900.

carrying out "espionage as universal and active as any despot ever estab-lished."[80] Readers were scandalized, for instance, by published revelations about ex-President Grant on his deathbed in 1885, detailing "all his private, personal habits," up to and including "a minute description of the state of his teeth."[81] Such audacity would be compounded by the pairing of instan-taneous photography with a prurient press, possible once the halftone printing process was perfected. The first newspaper photograph was pub-lished in 1880, opening the floodgates for the mass circulation of images. By 1885, "illustrated journalism" had arrived in the form of 10-cent weeklies such as *Harper's* and *Scribner's* as well as "society news" pages in venues like New York's *Town Topics*, a self-proclaimed pioneer of society journalism.[82] The kernel of Henry James's consternation can be seen in the latter organ's boast, a mere six years later, that "nearly every Sunday paper in New York now devotes a full page to the movements and habits of society people."[83]

The new papers made exposure their mission, their primary target the exclusive parties and displays of wealth that had come to define the upper echelons of American urban society. These affairs inspired a brew of popular curiosity and hostility in a class-conscious culture—a voyeurism that the commercial press was only too happy to satisfy.[84] Gossip about the parties, marriages, honeymoons, and divorce trials of the urban elite flour-ished at the turn of the century, circulating in newly visible and durable fashion.[85] To cite just one example, a Newport, Rhode Island, beach that had been favored by social elites "had long been off-limits to reporters." In 1902, Joseph Pulitzer's *New York World*—its motto, "Spicy, Pithy, Pictoral"—was emboldened to print, for the first time, candid photos of beachgoers enjoying what had been theretofore "regarded as private space."[86] Glimpsing a market for pictures and news about members of so-ciety who had largely been shielded from public view, reporters pursued all manner of tactics to pursue a story. Libel proceedings against *Town Topics* in 1906 disclosed allegations of blackmail and character assassination—as well as evidence that a journalist on staff had "disguised himself variously as a telegraph operator, a tambourine player, and a mathematics professor in order to get inside information about society folk."[87]

Society folk were not the only ones to come in for close and embarrassing scrutiny. Inside the same broadsheets and magazines that circulated scan-dalous photographs and salacious gossip were new "human interest" stories featuring bizarre or tragic incidents in the lives of private citizens.[88] As the press sought out this untapped source of drama—thriving on tales of secret marriages, hidden crimes, and loose conduct (and with few scruples about the truth of its reports)—lives that at one point would have been lived in obscurity were placed on display. Offense over the tarring of one's reputation was not restricted to the elite. The striking uptick in libel suits in the last decades of the century by citizens from all walks of life speaks to the felt damage of "false, embarrassing, and unflattering depictions" in both print and image. As legal scholar Samantha Barbas argues, the anonymous settings of late nineteenth-century urban society and the growth of a mass-mediated culture were awakening Americans across the class spectrum to the importance of managing the personas they projected to the world.[89]

That project was made considerably more challenging by another set of commercial invaders: advertisers, easily the equal of journalists in circulating embarrassing depictions. In a context where photography was still new and questions of copyright favored the picture taker rather than the pictured, advertisers made brazen use of people's likenesses for profit. It meant that individuals could discover without warning their own image adorning a product or plastered on a public building. This was the essence of what Barbas has termed the "crisis of the circulating portrait." Particularly at a time when many viewed advertising for commercial goods as "disreputable and even immoral," the pairing of one's image with a product could be a deeply felt affront.[90] The intense media publicity attending President Grover Cleveland's wedding to his legal ward, Frances Folsom, only 21 years old, produced a flurry of public outrage in 1886. So did the unauthorized use of the new First Lady's image, which found its way into advertisements for products ranging from soap to pianos to cigarettes.[91] The actress Marion Manola, who had appeared "in tights" while performing on Broadway, went to court in 1890 to protest having a photograph (surreptitiously taken) of the same in circulation.[92]

Unwanted publicity—whether via print or photograph—was the product of new technologies. But it was also the sign of a changing culture, in which commercial interests might override class prerogatives. For elite commentators, the harm to polite standards by "newspaperization" (to use Henry James's term) was self-evident.[93] They chafed not so much at the fact of scrutiny as the fact that it was coming from those outside their social circle. For those used to controlling the terms of disclosure, the unfettered circulation of news stories and commercial photographs carried significant risks. The founding editor of *The Nation* and longtime editor of the New

York *Evening Post*, E. L. Godkin, spoke for many of his class when he called for a man's freedom to "draw the line between his life as an individual and his life as a citizen, or in other words, the power of deciding how much or how little the community shall see of him, or know of him."[94] Godkin, who judged reputation "the most valuable thing on earth," understood that familiar methods of establishing and managing one's public portrait were giving way to less controllable techniques by which a man might be identified or exposed.[95] His worry was the protection of one's good name in a culture where the rules regulating speech, disclosure, and discretion seemed to be unraveling.

And yet, even those most strenuously opposed to the new modes of exposure conceded that publicity was not always unwelcome. "To some people it causes exquisite pain to have their private life laid bare to the world," reflected Godkin. But others—whose "taste must be recognized as . . . depraved," he urged—"put themselves in the way of having their private life explored by the press."[96] Included in this group were certain members of high society, who deliberately courted publicity and burnished their reputations by opening the interiors of their homes to photo spreads for the new Sunday papers.[97] Godkin's code of honor and reputation was coming up hard against the desire for notoriety and the "frenzy of renown," a common theme of contemporary critics and novelists.[98]

Popular journalism, along with telegraph cables and telephone wires, made citizens' private affairs newly vulnerable. At the same time, the very fact that private life had become a subject of public exposure could encourage fuller disclosure.[99] A culture newly immersed in advertisements and other visual media was slowly but surely changing its understanding of what would be known and what could be displayed without shame. This swirl of practices—not simply the novel array of intrusions but also the new quest to see and be seen—did not just distress Henry James. It also generated the first modern American crisis around privacy.

Inventing the Right to Privacy

It was not a novelist but rather two lawyers, Samuel Warren and Louis Brandeis, who would be credited with sounding the alarm about privacy and the modern person. But the source was the same: the potent trinity of press, photography, and publicity in the late nineteenth century. In 1890, the two published a *Harvard Law Review* article on "The Right to Privacy" that went on to become a legal as well as a cultural sensation.[100]

Brandeis and Warren, law school classmates at Harvard in the 1870s (first and second in their class, respectively) and then partners at a Boston law firm, had collaborated most recently on two articles on the law of ponds.[101] Their decision to wade into the arena of privacy—prompted by the well-born Samuel Warren's irritating brushes with the Boston society papers—catapulted both the authors and the issue to prominence.[102] Intriguingly, it was a decision they made with publicity in mind, hoping to broadcast the name of their firm and to produce provocative copy for the journal, which Brandeis had helped establish.[103] They succeeded beyond their expectations. Their demand that the individual's "private personal affairs shall not be laid bare to the world," Dean Roscoe Pound of Harvard Law School later declared, "did nothing less than add a chapter to the law"—earning Warren and Brandeis pride of place as modern privacy's expounders up to the present day.[104] Their 1890 essay offered a compelling case for privacy as a defense against contemporary society's press on the individual, as well as a set of concepts and tools that some citizens immediately took up in state courts.

The career of Warren and Brandeis's essay has been nothing short of extraordinary, its mere twenty-eight pages spawning a vast legal and scholarly corpus. The subject of immediate interest and commentary, "The Right to Privacy" is an enduring presence in American jurisprudence, cited in "virtually every case utilized by the highest state courts as a vehicle for recognizing or refusing to recognize privacy rights" and relied on as recently as 2001 (by concurring and dissenting justices alike) in an important Supreme Court privacy case, *Kyllo v. United States*.[105] Scholars have examined Warren and Brandeis's arguments with great care, plumbing the genesis of their understanding of the "right to be let alone" (a phrase that was not theirs but Thomas Cooley's in his 1879 treatise on torts), the French and Roman law examples they drew on, and the aptness of their extrapolations from copyright law, intellectual property, and the protection against self-incrimination.[106] Still others have dissected the consequences of their 1890 formulation of a "right to privacy"—notably the four U.S. privacy torts that would develop over the course of the twentieth century—and its present relevance.[107] Even Warren and Brandeis's sharpest critics have been unable to escape the essay's lasting imprint.[108]

HARVARD
LAW REVIEW.

| VOL. IV. | DECEMBER 15, 1890. | NO. 5. |

THE RIGHT TO PRIVACY.

" It could be done only on principles of private justice, moral fitness,
and public convenience, which, when applied to a new subject, make
common law without a precedent ; much more when received and
approved by usage."

WILLES, J., in Millar *v*. Taylor, 4 Burr. 2303, 2312.

THAT the individual shall have full protection in person and
in property is a principle as old as the common law ; but
it has been found necessary from time to time to define anew the
exact nature and extent of such protection. Political, social, and
economic changes entail the recognition of new rights, and the
common law, in its eternal youth, grows to meet the demands of
society. Thus, in very early times, the law gave a remedy only
for physical interference with life and property, for trespasses *vi
et armis*. Then the "right to life" served only to protect the
subject from battery in its various forms; liberty meant freedom
from actual restraint ; and the right to property secured to the individual his lands and his cattle. Later, there came a recognition of
man's spiritual nature, of his feelings and his intellect. Gradually
the scope of these legal rights broadened ; and now the right to
life has come to mean the right to enjoy life,— the right to be let
alone ; the right to liberty secures the exercise of extensive civil
privileges ; and the term "property" has grown to comprise every
form of possession — intangible, as well as tangible.

Thus, with the recognition of the legal value of sensations, the
protection against actual bodily injury was extended to prohibit
mere attempts to do such injury ; that is, the putting another in

1.2. Samuel Warren and Louis Brandeis's essay on "The Right to Privacy" called
for legal recognition of "a right to one's personality."

The Boston lawyers, like Henry James and E. L. Godkin, built their case for privacy on the shoals of publicity. They cited the indignities of the "unauthorized circulation of portraits of private persons" and of newspapers that trafficked in gossip "as a trade," adding to the list the exploitation of "any other modern device for rewording or reproducing scenes or sounds." They pointed in particular to recent inventions, the "mechanical devices" that "threatened to make good the prediction that 'what is whispered in the closet shall be proclaimed from the house-tops.'" The precariousness of privacy in these new conditions, they argued, fully warranted "the next step which must be taken for the protection of the person."[109] Whereas other late nineteenth-century commentators on the problem (namely Godkin) could only muster remedies such as "the cudgel or the horsewhip," Warren and Brandeis spied a solution in tort law.[110] In seeking to justify a right to be free of unwanted publicity, a right that they argued was not new but rooted in the common law, the lawyers sought to protect the private person as well as the seemliness of public discourse.

Warren and Brandeis argued that new technologies of publicity—"instantaneous photographs" and a "prurient" newspaper enterprise—had "invaded the sacred precincts of private and domestic life," overstepping the "obvious bounds of propriety and of decency." Their figuring of such incursions as a spatial breach borrowed rhetorically from a physical, property-based understanding of privacy. Yet their essay signaled an important rethinking of privacy's reach. Warren and Brandeis pointed to modern conditions as triggering new privacy questions. They would also modernize the claim to privacy itself, suggesting that feelings and emotions might be just as important as property lines in judging whether an individual's personal realm was violated. While the lawyers sounded many of the same notes as their peers, they underscored the psychic as much as the reputational harms that flowed from publicizing one's private affairs. The printing of an unwanted photograph or story, they urged, could create "mental pain and distress, far greater than could be inflicted by mere bodily injury." They went further still in arguing for "the right not merely to prevent inaccurate portrayal of private life, but to prevent its being depicted at all."[111] Simply to be revealed—to be known when one wished not to be—ought itself count as an actionable harm.

Importantly, this harm resulted not simply from new methods of publicity, or even from the "intensity and complexity" of urban society, which had made "solitude and privacy" more "essential to the individual."[112] For

Warren and Brandeis, the damage stemmed from the very makeup of the modern person. The contemporary "personality," the lawyers maintained, was uniquely pained by exposure. E. L. Godkin had declared privacy "a distinctly modern product, one of the luxuries of civilization." It was "not only unsought for but unknown in primitive or barbarous societies"—even, he ventured, in those of "our Anglo-Saxon ancestors in England."[113] For Warren and Brandeis too, Americans' sensitivity to the airing of private matters was a historical development, a triumph of civilization's advance. In this sense, both the new-fangled invasions of privacy and the desire to escape them were marks of modernity. The collision between the highly refined sensibilities of contemporary citizens and the novel means of offending them was what required, even made "inevitable," a response by the law. Thus at the close of the nineteenth century, as perhaps they had not before, "thoughts, emotions, and sensations demanded legal recognition."[114]

Most famously, the Boston lawyers called for a shield around something they called the "inviolate personality," or "the right to one's personality."[115] In doing so they echoed the German sociologist Georg Simmel, who believed that "the personality value of the individual"—one's "spiritual private property"—suffered any time the "ideal sphere" around it was transgressed.[116] Simmel and the authors of "The Right to Privacy" alike turned to "personality" to capture an interior essence that both belonged to and defined the modern person.[117] Privacy in this light was not simply an aspect of individual liberty or property but a psychological, even spiritual matter.[118] A sensibility as much as a state, its violation did more than cheapen one's public currency: it assaulted one's very sense of personhood. While defamation law, the traditional resort for damage to reputation, responded only to one's external relations with the community, a right to privacy might encompass incursions on a person's "estimate of himself" and "his own feelings."[119] Warren and Brandeis's call for novel legal protections was thus a bid for extending privacy's scope as well as the law's.

Given the ways that privilege and property colored elite understandings of privacy in the late nineteenth century, it is worth asking what the "obvious bounds of propriety" meant to Warren and Brandeis, and for whose rights they advocated. Some have pointed to an egalitarian strain in the lawyers' thinking that was missing from most critiques of invasive journalism of their day.[120] In arguing for their new right, Warren and Brandeis asserted for example that it should "protect all persons, whatsoever their position or station, from having matters which they may properly prefer to keep private, made public against their will."[121] They did not wish to shield only the polite classes from the scrutiny of a rogue press. But it is also clear that the privacy of "The Right to Privacy" was specific to the gender, race, and social class of its authors. Privacy's appearance in the pages of the *Harvard Law Review*—the fact that it seemed to require deliberate enunciation—was a sign of privilege under siege.

Warren and Brandeis could not, for example, fully put aside Godkin's understanding of privacy as a bourgeois entitlement. Their article can be read as a brief for reestablishing proper social boundaries and regulating public morality. One scholar calls the real subject of Warren and Brandeis's concern a man "with a certain standing, habituated to controlling his environment and information about himself, and with an interest in continuing to do so."[122] Others have detected the conservative intent of the essay, even as they grant its radical approach to the law. A recent assessment characterizes Warren and Brandeis's call for privacy rights as part of "a broader legal strategy by late-nineteenth century elites to protect their reputations from the masses in the face of disruptive social and technological change."[123] The lawyers focused on prominent men like themselves, whose delicate sensibilities and public standing purportedly caused them to suffer most—both psychologically and practically—from privacy invasions.[124] This vision of privacy was patriarchal as well as privileged. Quoting approvingly Godkin's defense of "a man's house as his castle," the 1890 essay linked a man's reputation to the modesty and reserve of his wife and daughters, enlarging his privacy as it circumscribed theirs.[125] As two feminist legal scholars write, "The privacy tort was the brainchild of nineteenth-century men of privilege, and it shows."[126]

Privacy would have been imagined otherwise by those situated differently from the Boston lawyers. To establish the limits of their vision is not however to dethrone their social analysis or their essay's place in privacy jurisprudence. The two authored a ringing statement of the right to be let alone that resonated in 1890 as much as it does today. If they were, indisputably, speaking from a particular vantage point, they were not only speaking for themselves. Nor is it to deny what many later commentators have applauded: Warren and Brandeis's prescient articulation of the need for sanctuary from the invasiveness of modern society and their "acute insight into the ways new technologies can so disrupt social life and practices as to threaten moral and political values."[127]

Situating Warren and Brandeis in their place and time simply clarifies the multiple strains in American ideas about privacy that were churning around them. To identify new kinds of intrusion in "The Right to Privacy" was to reinforce an argument about particular spaces as private and needing protection. Yet it was also to glimpse a changing social landscape. An older sort of privacy that the lawyers prized, grounded in propriety and the male-headed household, was beginning to come apart—the victim not simply of new technologies and commercial impulses but also of the social practices and political demands of a more democratic culture. These developments were fraying the assumption that a wall of secrecy was universally desirable and in need of buttressing, even among their peers. Brandeis seemed to recognize this in a letter to his fiancée, Alice Goldmark, regarding the famous essay. He mused, "Our hope is to make people see that invasions of privacy are not necessarily borne—and then make them ashamed of the *pleasure* they take in subjecting themselves to such invasions."[128]

Indeed, by setting in motion a modern narrative of privacy in peril, he and Samuel Warren simplified the problem. Positioning an aggressive, prurient press against discreet and properly regulated individuals, they underestimated the force of citizens' desire to know others and also to be known as they wished. As the rapid emergence of the "Kodak fiend" and the eager readers of the illustrated weeklies implied, fear of intrusion was always only one side of the coin. A desire to transgress settled boundaries, in order both to discover and to disclose, was the other. The evident allure of new technologies and opportunities for self-display pointed to substantial disagreement with Warren and Brandeis's social vision in both the lower and upper echelons of American society. For all their essay's fame, then, the lawyers may have been poor guides to what was happening to privacy at the turn of the twentieth century. Trying to ward off threats to a set of values they held dear, Warren and Brandeis could not see that new conceptions of personal privacy were already at play in the social practices around them.

In contrast, the readers of wire thrillers, writers for the popular press, and listeners on party lines may have been finding their way to a modern understanding of the private person. This amounted not to a renunciation but a redrawing of the line between public and private—and a clue to the way self and sociability were being reorganized in a mass-mediated world. Godkin for instance in 1890 pronounced "social promiscuousness" along with "loss of seclusion" as a special kind of grievance for those of finer sensibilities.[129] A New Orleans sleeping car conductor in 1899 begged to differ. He claimed that "the average American doesn't want privacy"—and indeed that his patrons regarded "the privacy of a [rail] compartment as a positive infliction." Travelers instead, he declared, sought out the "promiscuous mingling of passengers."[130] We need not substitute the conductor's judgment for Brandeis and Warren's, or "promiscuous mingling" for the "inviolate personality." Rather, their juxtaposition helps us better perceive what was at stake in debates about privacy at the turn of the century than does the famous *Harvard Law Review* essay alone.

In the late nineteenth century, the "sacred precincts of private and domestic life" were not simply being invaded; they were also being rethought. New means of sharing and communicating information were altering the very contents of public and private life. Telephone wires and photojournalism were just two of the modern technologies prompting this change. But they did not cause the boundaries around the private person to collapse. Those boundaries were just becoming less material and less tethered to the bourgeois household—and they could still be ardently defended.

Such would become clear in the many attempts by litigants to make a reality of the "right to privacy" and in the ways privacy would be wielded in struggles over how citizens would and should be known in the years to come. Even if designed with men of reputation in mind, the new right clearly carried much broader appeal. From the outset, it was employed by a diverse cast of characters. In the decade after the two Boston lawyers published their essay, a right to privacy would be tested in a series of state court decisions, especially in New York. Not surprisingly, unwanted publicity cases were rare, its victims wary of drawing still more press. Instead, and quite conspicuously, most of the early trials centered on disputes over the rightful ownership of photographs. These were cases in which individuals sought control over their images and did not shrink from using the law to seek redress for emotional distress, embarrassment, and hurt feelings.[131] Something like the "inviolate personality"—rather than property or even propriety—would underpin these claims.

Even before Warren and Brandeis took up the issue of privacy, Congress had introduced legislation designed to bar women's images from being used in commerce without written consent—a direct consequence of the outrage visited on Frances Folsom, President Cleveland's bride. "A Bill to Protect Ladies," introduced in the House of Representatives in 1888, responded to the fact that women were much more often than men the subject of surreptitious photographs.[132] The bill did not refer to individual privacy, however, but to the offense caused by the circulation of "vulgar and unauthorized" images of "the wife, daughter, mother or sister of any citizen of the United States." As its language suggests, the bill was a paternalistic effort, rooted in understandings of domestic respectability and aimed at shoring up female modesty. Yet it was also an admission of the threat that commercial culture, and its new agents of penetration and publicity, posed to that vision.

Female litigants would mount an equal challenge to patriarchal privacy in the years to come. Embarrassed, even disgraced, by the use of their faces and bodies in advertisements and other commercial peddling, they would soon take up the tools of the law on their own behalf, employing the first modern uses of a "right to privacy" in the courts. At a time when women were the minority of litigants overall, historian Jessica Lake has found that they constituted the majority of privacy plaintiffs. They pioneered arguments about the dangers that publicity posed not to the bourgeois household but to individual personality. Their suits were certainly undergirded by gendered norms of modesty and decency, but women's protest against the unwanted use of their images struck a different note than did the "Bill to Protect Ladies." They staked their claims to privacy as individuals, decoupling that right from the family, household, or physical home. Female plaintiffs, Lake contends, thus helped divert the law of privacy from its focus on property to a more modern concern with personality.[133]

Such arguments did not immediately succeed, notably in the notorious 1902 case, *Roberson v. Rochester Folding Box Company*. Abigail Marie Roberson's 1900 claim was lodged against the Franklin Mills Flour company for "equitable relief and damages" to compensate for the unauthorized use of her image. More specifically she cited the making and then displaying—in stores, saloons, and other public venues—of 25,000 "lithographic prints, photographs, and likenesses" of herself without her knowledge or prior consent. (Indeed, she only learned of the campaign when she glimpsed her own face on a neighbor's bag of flour.) Roberson charged that the advertisements and their viewing by acquaintances caused her "great distress and suffering in both body and mind." A sympathetic lower court acknowledged that "the theory upon which this action is predicated is new." Still, it ruled in her favor, judging her "right of privacy" violated. The New York Court of Appeals, however, reversed the decision. Testifying to changing norms around publicity, it did so in part based on its determination that the portrait in question was not libelous (indeed it was "a very good one") and that some would have found the advertisement "agreeable"—even a "compliment to their beauty."[134]

Referring to the celebrated Warren and Brandeis article only to dismantle its arguments, the Chief Justice of the New York Court of Appeals found no precedent for "a right to be let alone," nor even any mention of such a right before 1890, when it appeared "in a clever article in the Harvard Law Review." The judge dismissed what he derided as the "so-called right to privacy" for its preposterous claim "that a man has the right to pass through this world, if he wills, without having his picture published, his business enterprises discussed, his successful experiments written up for the benefit of others, or his eccentricities commented upon either in handbills, circulars, catalogues, periodicals or newspapers."[135] In effect, the court dismissed out of hand the law's interest or ability to comprehend what it termed "psychological injuries"—although in so doing, it seemed to confirm the popular demand for such a remedy, positing the "vast amount of litigation . . . bordering on the absurd" that would follow from recognizing a right to privacy.[136]

Others, however, embraced Warren and Brandeis's notion of an inviolate personality, entitled to society's protection. Commentators pounced on the judge's unyielding heart toward the humiliated Abigail Roberson, furious about the wanton use of her features to advertise flour. A popular outcry against the decision would lead the New York legislature to pass the nation's first privacy tort statute the following year. It allowed individuals to sue for invasion of privacy where their "name, portrait, or picture" was used without consent "for purposes of trade."[137] Three years later, the Supreme Court of Georgia would be the first to recognize this species of privacy claim, in this instance a man's right not to have his photograph accompany an advertisement for life insurance.[138] In time, nearly every state would follow Georgia's example.[139]

The inviolate personality would thus have its day in court.[140] Roberson's suit, after all, was unrelated to literal trespass or invasion of private property. In litigants' claims to their own images and their attempt to halt others' use of them, we can chart a sea change in commonplace understandings of privacy. A version of Warren and Brandeis's right to privacy would be embraced, although it would not typically be in the service of shielding the polite classes from an impolite press.[141] A far more eclectic group of individuals sought instead to bar the unauthorized commercial use of their unique personalities in the form of a name, likeness, or photographed image. State laws and courts would in ensuing decades define a range of privacy harms, falling into four more or less distinct categories: intrusion on seclusion or solitude; public disclosure of private facts; publication placing a person in a false light; and appropriation or unauthorized use of one's name or likeness.[142] As these privacy torts evolved in the twentieth century, easily the most successful of them—and the one in best working order today—was the last, the so-called right of publicity, including the privilege of profiting from one's distinctive persona.[143] That a right to publicity is the most enduring legacy of Warren and Brandeis's 1890 article is ironic indeed.[144] But it testifies to the force with which ephemeral and distinctly nonpropertied matters of "personality" had moved into the legal as well as popular definition of privacy.

Techniques of Public Order

Photographers and journalists attracted the lion's share of attention in privacy controversies at the turn of the twentieth century because they encroached upon the well-defended lives and spaces of urban elites. The ability of upper- and middle-class citizens to define what counted as a violation of privacy would prove a durable pattern. But the press was not the only party seeking to know citizens or to provoke debates over how and to whom Americans ought to be known. Novel techniques of "publicity" were taking root in many other corners of U.S. society in these years. Some of the most significant of these arrived not in the service of scandal or entertainment but in the name of public order—and in the hands of those tasked with policing, governing, and otherwise deciphering urban crowds.

This form of knowing citizens was the work of public officials, private companies, and enforcers of the law. Together, they represented the stirrings of a modern surveillance society. Their techniques differed from those employed by the popular press, although they often relied on the same technologies that had prompted Warren and Brandeis to take up their pens. Instead of splashing private matters across the front pages of newspapers, these agents of exposure quietly collected and collated information, putting private facts to work for larger purposes. They did not, as a rule, target elites. And their labors would not result in anything as enduring as a new legal claim or a "right to one's own personality." Yet credit bureaus, census schedules, and public health campaigns, along with innovations in tracking criminals and other suspect citizens, sparked insistent questions about individual privacy. They kept open—and widened—the debate over the proper bounds of a knowing society.

The judge in the 1902 *Roberson* case had pointedly disputed the notion that "a man has the right to pass through this world, if he wills, without having his picture published." That same year, a Chicago editorialist suggested that the very category of "private citizen" was becoming obsolete in an ever more "organized" society. Once, he argued, there had been a meaningful distinction between a public man and a private one. The former rose "into the scope of the public eye by reason of his wealth or business or philanthropy or interest in politics." Such a figure was "in a sense public property," required on account of his power and prominence to "turn over his life to the public." Private citizens, by contrast, were properly "the unknown," their concerns the business of no one but themselves and their families. For this writer, it was ordinary Americans, not denizens of high society, who were the true claimants to privacy. The critical difference between a public and a private life was, however, dissolving—the "so-called private citizen" falling victim to a long list of inquisitors: the city health department, the board of education, the gas inspector, the life insurance agent, the loan officer, the detective sergeant, the telephone directory, and the marriage license clerk.[145] If less spectacularly than the popular press, each agency on this list played a part in making "public men" of all Americans.

As this writer implied, new modes of sharing and recording information at the turn of the century alerted citizens to the fact that the hidden recesses of their lives might not remain hidden. Public health measures, for one, seemed more uncomfortably probing to some at the turn of the century. Earlier reformers had often, without much comment, entered into the homes of the urban poor in search of the roots of contagious disease.[146] African American washerwomen in Atlanta and Baltimore and Chinese laundry workers in San Francisco, suspected of being vectors of tuberculosis and plague, had been especially prone to "sanitary surveillance."[147] Scholars have documented how intrusive such inspections were. Early tuberculosis case reports in Maryland included not only information about employment and earning power but also data on the size and habits of the family—whether members kissed each other on the mouth, shared utensils and napkins, or spat on the floor, for instance—and on sleeping arrangements and cleaning practices.[148]

Only as disease prevention became professionalized in the early twentieth century and as more Americans came under the gaze of public health officials, however, did the indignities of "disease surveillance" become an object of mainstream discussion. During the New York City polio epidemic of 1916, for instance, officials placarded the homes of the infected and also turned to the press to publicize the path of contagion, broadcasting a daily list of the names and addresses of those with the disease in the local papers.[149]

City health departments and boards of education were simultaneously bringing individual inspections and disease tracking into the schools. Even the youngest of citizens were now subject to what some deemed improper prying. If the American schoolboy "has had smallpox, diphtheria, or measles, the Board of Education wants to know it," charged one critic. As if this were not enough, officials would periodically appear at the student's school, "look at his tongue and in other ways pierce the veil of privacy to see whether he has been careless enough to contract croup or anything that may be dangerous to the pupil that sits next to him."[150] Considerable resistance to compulsory vaccination in the early twentieth century, as historian Michael Willrich has shown, exposed the rift between those who brought "the best scientific knowledge" to bear in the service of social welfare and the "right of a free people to take care of their own bodies and children according to their own medical beliefs and consciences."[151]

New methods of tallying the population inspired their own scattered protests. The invention of the Hollerith card puncher in 1889 made possible the astonishingly swift processing of census forms the next year—a task previously done by hand, by hundreds of clerks—and at a fraction of the cost. Automated counting made new kinds of cross-tabulation feasible, a development that dovetailed with new demands for statistical data from Congress, as well as business associations, reformers, and "university men," leading to calls for a permanent federal agency. The upshot, observes historian Margo Anderson, was that apportionment became almost incidental to the census, which was now a "full-fledged instrument to monitor the overall state of American society."[152]

As did the new public health measures, the expanded length and inquisitiveness of the census schedule came under fire. In particular, questions added to the 1890 census about matters related to health and finances—quickly dubbed the "disease and debts" questions—provoked a storm of criticism.[153] E. L. Godkin once again weighed in, this time to protest the propriety of a "stranger popping in from the street with a notebook" to probe one's history of contagious disease or levels of indebtedness. Godkin charged, "No man, and especially no woman, likes to tell a stranger about a secret disease or disability—that is, about one which is not visible—and about debts and liabilities."[154] The New York *Sun* likewise branded the questions "an outrageous invasion of the personal and private business of the citizen."[155] Some of these citizens protested with their silence, refusing to answer the questions or even reveal their names to census enumerators. Whereas fewer than a half-dozen "total refusals" had been recorded for previous censuses, in 1890 there were sixty arrests for noncompliance in New York City alone.[156] This particular scuffle between official information seekers and the public would be resolved by a less capacious census form in 1900. In the meantime, it revealed that the quest for better information about the population could fuel popular resentment.

Newfound capacities to know and to track citizens were, however, most telling—both in their practical use and their political logic—in the domain of law enforcement. When Warren and Brandeis made their case for a right to privacy in 1890, the state's grip on citizens' lives was light and its role in crime control minimal. Policing was relegated to localities and private detectives, with just a few federal enforcement units in existence to combat mail fraud, counterfeiting, and the like.[157]

This situation was changing rapidly at the turn of the century. The "mechanical devices" that the Boston lawyers had singled out for imperiling privacy, including instantaneous photography and the telephone lines, were partly to thank. Agents of the law had early on glimpsed the possibilities of photography for extending the eyes of the police, following early experiments in France. Already in 1858, the New York City Police Department had organized the nation's first "rogue's gallery," reasoning that by placing criminals' faces on file, police officers would be better equipped to apprehend them.[158] In police work, the camera—once "an artistic device for portraying and honoring individuals"—was transformed into "a powerful political technology with which to capture and control them."[159] In the later nineteenth century it became a routine tool for identifying criminals and establishing permanent records, giving new substance to a person's classification as a "known criminal." Wiretaps would likewise become a favorite instrument of urban police, and eventually federal law enforcement.

The period spanning "The Right to Privacy" and the 1920s witnessed the at first hesitant and then far more confident steps by the police and the federal government to keep tabs on those Americans judged a threat to the public order. "In the space of a few decades," summarizes historian Alfred McCoy, the United States went from being a "society with fragmentary records and local constables" to one with "centralized criminal files, wired cities, nascent intelligence services and systematic social indices."[160]

More systematic policing was the joint product of separate developments that fused in the first two decades of the new century: the rise of a national security apparatus to ward off external threats and the churn of disorder from anarchists and criminals within American society. Official U.S. surveillance capacities, honed during the Philippine-American War in the waning years of the nineteenth century, would find a home in the domestic Bureau of Investigation. The Bureau was founded in 1908 as an outfit for thwarting customs and postal fraud, but it would soon expand its portfolio. Rife with class conflict, the late nineteenth and early twentieth centuries witnessed a rash of violent attacks, bombings, and assassination attempts. These riveted local and federal agents' attention to the threat of radical and labor movements and the unchecked flow of immigrants entering the country. The Bureau in turn began to use the tools that had been employed to quash insurrection abroad to quell problems at home.[161]

In the 1910s, as conflict brewed overseas, the war in Europe and class warfare in the United States became "increasingly intertwined" in the eyes of those responsible for law enforcement and national security.[162] The fledgling Bureau of Investigation would remake itself into a domestic surveillance unit as fears of German spying grew, with the agency almost doubling in size during the war.[163] As scholars have well documented, wartime prejudices and fears of subversion during Woodrow Wilson's administration led to the extensive monitoring of radicals and other suspect citizens, which included the censorship of mail, the interception of international telephone and telegraph communications, immigrant roundups, and loyalty investigations.[164] Especially critical to the evolving shape of policing was the "wartime assault on enemy aliens," which as one historian notes, "laid the foundations of twentieth-century political surveillance."[165] It did so by enlisting, via the American Protective League, several hundred thousand volunteers to watch their neighbors and engage in mass raids.[166] This effort revealed the vigilance with which some citizens were willing to invade others' privacy in the name of patriotism and national security.

Collectively, they generated a million pages of surveillance reports in just eighteen months of war.[167]

World War I made clear the perils of being known to authorities. The federal government in sudden and unprecedented fashion reined in dissent and "seditious speech," such that more than a thousand men and women were imprisoned for the crime of "speaking out" under the Espionage Act of 1917.[168] Believing African Americans to be especially receptive to antiwar propaganda and a "weak link in the political, economic, and military cohesion required for total war"—ironically, precisely because of their unjust treatment in American society—the Wilson administration unleashed a "constant watch on the activities of black civilians and soldiers," including equal rights organizations and publications.[169] Even more intensive scrutiny was brought to bear on German Americans, non-naturalized aliens, and radicals.

The knowledge that resulted was often slapdash and inaccurate. Domestic surveillance reports on African American "subversives" revealed, in one historian's assessment, "just how little whites typically knew, or could be bothered to know, about their black fellow citizens."[170] But this did not mean the watching was inconsequential. Nor would the crackdown let up after the war, as race riots, labor strikes, communist plots, and bootlegging took center stage as the new forces of disorder. The Red Scare of 1919–1920 led to the deportation of hundreds of immigrant radicals. And as historian Lisa McGirr documents, the "war on alcohol" following the passage of the Volstead Act in 1919 "left a powerful imprint on the federal state, tilting it toward policing, surveillance, and punishment." Calls for law and order enabled the Bureau of Investigation to federalize its knowledge of criminals and pilot new surveillance strategies.[171] It would make ample use of the technologies of publicity to strengthen the capacities of the central state.

The war and its aftermath revealed the extent to which a knowing society had grown up in the early twentieth-century United States. Its victims would find champions in the new American Civil Liberties Union, which mounted an organized response to the draconian wartime constraints on speech and dissent.[172] But this did not amount to a defense of individual privacy or a right to personality—suggesting that privacy was not yet a plausible civil liberty equal to freedom of speech or association nor the most promising place to ground a claim for protection.

Early twentieth-century law enforcement exposed the unevenness with which citizens were coming to be known in a modern state. It also made clear that the kind of privacy imagined by Warren and Brandeis to be imperiled by publicity and the sort of privacy compromised by the demands of public order might have different trajectories. Elites lodged loud protests, provoked by the impudence of the society press. But the burden of new technologies of scrutiny fell much more heavily on those at the other end of the class spectrum. These invasions did not however stir the outrage of the privileged; indeed, they were rarely classed under the banner of privacy at all. Claims to a right to privacy may have been expanding in this era, but they still belonged first and foremost to the white, law-abiding middle and upper classes.

This disparity is underscored by the strong appeal of biometric techniques for both law enforcement agents and elite Americans in these same decades. Fingerprinting was yet another new technology of the 1890s, identifying the person not through a photograph or a news story but through a unique pattern on the tip of a finger. Dactyloscopy, as it was known in scientific circles, was the product of the search for "a better technology of criminal identification" during the last decades of the nineteenth century. Bertillonage—a set of precise bodily measurements taken by calipers and rulers to create an individual record, and which vied with fingerprinting for preeminence as a method of identification—was another.[173] First used systematically by the Argentine Central Police in 1891, then by colonial police in India in 1897, and by Scotland Yard beginning in 1902, fingerprinting was, as Simon Cole writes, a technique made for "modern, anonymous, socially mobile societies ... brimming with people who were strangers, both to one another and to the state." U.S. police departments became enthralled with the technique after viewing demonstrations at the 1904 St. Louis World's Fair. For them, fingerprinting held out the promise that they might be able to detect and thus control "the invisible danger hidden beneath the social fabric."[174]

Fingerprinting, Cole makes clear, was developed not with the respectable but with the suspect classes in mind: the natives of European colonies, recent immigrants, people of color, vagrants, degenerates, and prostitutes. It was a technique thought to be particularly well suited to the Americas, where vast immigration waves and native whites' equally vast suspicion of the foreign born mingled so powerfully. Cole argues that fingerprint identification was early on adopted by U.S. police departments and then the

Federal Bureau of Investigation for its ability to decipher the masses of "racially unfamiliar" and thus menacing streams of newcomers to America's cities whom the state might have an interest in knowing. Only later would its advocates and professional societies look toward an era when the fingerprint might serve as a key "civilian identifier" used "in all aspects of daily life and social interaction."[175]

Like the new journalism, then, fingerprinting was a modern instrument for monitoring individuals. But whereas the popular press had pursued some of society's most privileged citizens, this particular technology of publicity homed in on much less favored populations: anarchists, aliens, dissidents, union members, and potential criminals. These were people who had never been sheltered by social codes of reputation and honor or an implicit right to privacy. The difference this made was evident in the disputes over proposals for mandatory fingerprinting that unfolded in scattered cities in the 1910s and 1920s. "Universal registration societies" composed of affluent citizens and corporate leaders led the campaign.[176] Although it might seem counterintuitive, it was no coincidence that many who endorsed mandatory identification were drawn from the same ranks of the respectable who would have in Warren and Brandeis's day been most chagrined by unwanted publicity. The visibility promised by a fingerprint registry was not intended for them.

As it turned out, the ostensible objects of this campaign had no desire for this form of publicity either. Mandatory fingerprinting was greeted with strong denunciations and organized protests. Taxicab drivers and hotel employees, along with the young American Civil Liberties Union, were the strongest claimants to this version of a right to privacy. A 1920 cabbie strike, 300 people strong, in fact began as a protest against a Cleveland fingerprinting ordinance, complete with "antifingerprint picket lines." The struggles that broke out in several other U.S. cities would eventually derail the campaign.[177]

In the 1890s, privacy was a tool of the elite, brandished against less prominent citizens who pried into their affairs. In the 1920s, laborers invoked the right to be free of elite scrutiny. The inversion of class positions suggests privacy's growing rhetorical availability. By the second decade of the twentieth century, workers, and not simply "men of reputation," believed themselves possessed of a right to privacy, of domains where middle-class reformers had no right to intrude. The strikers had a hold on the concept, a certainty about what privacy meant, that paralleled the claims of 1890s elites. If theirs was not precisely the right to privacy that Warren and Brandeis envisioned, they still made a bid for something like personal inviolability. Fingerprinting could appear, in one angry letter writer's terms, as an "outrage upon the individual."[178]

The cabbies who refused to be tagged subscribed to an understanding of privacy detached from property. This was a form of privacy unyoked from status—rooted not in reputation but in personhood or "personality."[179] Underneath Warren and Brandeis's seminal 1890 essay and the fingerprint protest alike was this shifting conceptual ground. In this sense, the legal treatise signaled an important reworking of privacy's contours for those far beyond the social elite. A concept like the "inviolate personality" was not the Boston lawyers' alone. Its other users, whether litigants or laborers, were no less serious in their search for some accord between society's scrutiny and the person's need to be free of it. Women suing for the right to their photographs and taxi drivers who would not abide fingerprinting were thus, alongside the famous essayists, authors of the modern claim to privacy.

To travel from the concerns of Henry James and E. L. Godkin in the 1890s to those of striking "chauffeurs" in the 1920s is to glimpse the broad landscape of privacy debates that accompanied the growth of a knowing society, even as it throws into sharp relief the unequal attention they garnered. Calls for a right to privacy in the United States escalated alongside an aggressive press and commercial culture. But they did not end or even truly begin there, despite later claims that Warren and Brandeis had singlehandedly "invented" the right.[180] Turn-of-the-century Americans did not require legal exposition to persuade them that their privacy was endangered by new technologies of scrutiny or that they were entitled in some situations to be left alone. Even before Warren and Brandeis had framed the complaint, citizens had made scattered assertions of "private rights" in opposition to irksome forms of "publicity," ranging from compulsory vaccinations to census taking.[181] What enabled a right to privacy to gain traction in the last decade of the nineteenth century was not an unprecedented set of violations but that new right's primary subjects and spokesmen. The fact that new media and communications technologies had come to intrude even on the lives of powerful Americans, prompting them to call for the private citizen's inviolability, made the claim stick.

The modern right to privacy was first floated as a means of preserving an older form of propriety rooted in the domestic household and polite society. But its appearance, in the culture as much as the courts, signaled a fundamental transformation of the concept. Privacy's meanings became less stable and more splintered after Warren and Brandeis's "The Right to Privacy." Private homes and private men were not the fortresses they were once presumed to be. In a mass-mediated, "organized," information-hungry age, privacy would have to be found elsewhere. Conflicts over telephone lines and tattletale journalism, postcards and photographs, fingerprints and files, would over time shuttle new ideas about inviolability and rights, and more elastic boundaries around the person, into common culture.

Devotion to a right to privacy—that "distinctly modern product"—proved to be both fragile and fickle in the decades surrounding the turn of the century. The question of its contents as well as who it would cover closely tracked existing lines of privilege. While a few complaints and even lawsuits were lodged concerning the use of criminals' images for display in rogues' galleries, they did not rise to the level of public comment.[182] And elites who railed against a "shameless" and "impudent" press for reporting on their affairs fell silent when it came to fingerprinting immigrants or common laborers. The unbounded surveillance of suspect persons during World War I and the Red Scare—often by their own neighbors and fellow citizens—far outstripped the transgressions of turn-of-the-century journalists and photographers, even though it sparked no privacy crusade. Still, privileged citizens alongside less prominent ones were giving voice to a question that would define many public debates in modern America. In a society that relentlessly sought to know, what claim did citizens have to a private realm or even to their own persons? Or as Warren and Brandeis put the same question in reverse, at what point must "the dignity and convenience of the individual" bow to "the demands of the public welfare"?[183]

In this fashion, the "end of privacy," or at least the end of one sort of privacy, would be fertile terrain for thinking about the nature of citizenship in a modern public. The debate that began in the late nineteenth century echoed an old question about the proper boundary between self and society. But it gained urgency by pitting inviolate selves against the unique intrusions of a knowing society. That clash generated a call for rights. More importantly, it set in motion a new politics. Demands to be free of

2

Documents of Identity

Every law-abiding citizen today has his vest pockets crammed
with credentials. . . . Practically all of these items stress the fact
that I am me and nobody else; without them, I would officially
cease to exist.

—WEARE HOLBROOK,
"Unmistaken Identity," *Atlanta Constitution*, 1942

By the time the stock market crashed in 1929, Americans were familiar
with virtual invasions, whether from cameras, the press, or the newly ubiquitous telephone. "Tied together by a net-work of telephone wires," mused
one commentator, private homes were "in many ways different institutions
from the isolated places they were when Anglo-Saxon doctrine was forming
on a man's right to privacy and safety in his own residence."[1] Just a year
earlier, the telephone had been at issue in the most important privacy case
to reach the Supreme Court before the 1960s. The government's secret
wiretapping of private individuals' telephone communications, in this
instance to ensnare a multimillion dollar bootlegging ring, was deemed
constitutional. Justice Louis Brandeis—architect of the 1890 "right to
privacy" and now sitting on the court—issued an eloquent dissent. "Subtler and more far-reaching means of invading privacy," he warned, "have
become available to the government."[2]

Brandeis's shifting attention from the intrusions of the press to the invasions of the central state was indicative of the way U.S. privacy discussions
were trending in the early twentieth century. The decades marked by
the Great Depression and World War II in particular launched renewed
debates about the known citizen. This time it was not the brash media—the
photographers and journalists who had done so much to spur early calls
for a right to privacy—that were centrally at issue. Rather, public attention

fixed on the government, and particularly its new, or at least newly visible, methods of tracking citizens. In these years, novel methods of administering social welfare altered Americans' sense of when and to what end they could be legitimately known to their state.

Techniques for monitoring the U.S. population did not suddenly materialize in the 1930s. But they had been cordoned off in public consciousness, associated as they were with the marginal and the troublesome: the anarchists, aliens, and "Reds" who had been closely watched, if not jailed and deported, during World War I and its aftermath, as well as the criminal and diseased, who came under the tighter supervision of urban police forces and public health authorities in the same years. In the New Deal era it would become evident that the eyes of the government were no longer trained only on threats to the public order, or on those who had attracted the notice of the Bureau of Investigation. In a striking reversal, state programs in this era sought to track the affairs of relatively privileged citizens. Indeed, being known to the government would become increasingly constitutive of citizenship itself: a necessary exchange for steady employment, increased economic security, and free movement across borders.

Administrative tracking entered all citizens' lives in unfamiliar ways and to novel ends during the first three decades of the twentieth century.[3] Life without a paper trail would still be possible, but it was becoming rarer as state and local officials flexed their muscles and private agencies increasingly relied on identifying records. Whether through an application for a birth certificate, a driver's license, or a passport, a broad swath of the citizenry would be drawn into the swelling bureaucratic apparatus of U.S. society. By 1925 it was possible for a Chicago man to editorialize about "the terrible invasion of privacy" effected by the piling up of automobile licenses, mortgage and tax records, and marriage and death certificates, each an index to matters an individual might rather keep out of public view. Yet, making reference to the largest credit reporting agencies of the day, he recognized the dilemma. To "burn up all the Duns and Bradstreets, abolish all credit departments, destroy all directories and prohibit hotel registers, keep no more records" would allow Americans to have privacy—"but not much else."[4] As this writer suggested, the state was not the only author of the documentary impulse. Life insurance and credit agencies were just two of the powerful entities driving the creation of what we would now call "personally identifying information."[5] The public and private sectors would be co-conspirators in this "terrible invasion."

An administrative state and society preceded the New Deal.[6] Yet the decade of the 1930s was "the moment when bureaucratic structures and techniques first became dramatically visible in many ordinary people's lives."[7] The change was most obvious in the scope of the federal government, which ballooned during the Depression crisis and then again even more dramatically during World War II, when the scale of its activity came to dwarf "the New Deal programs that had seemed gargantuan only a few years earlier."[8] The state had been a locus for fears of centralized authority since the first days of the American republic.[9] But the state understood as bureaucracy, apart from the once-a-decade administration of the U.S. Census, was a product of this era.

As federal agencies loomed larger in Americans' lives, they became a focal point for reflecting on individual privacy. Citizens in a mediated age had become increasingly conscious of their public images. In an administered one, they increasingly understood that their personal details—their age, address, or employment history—once compiled, made them intelligible to the society's authorities. How much information about its own citizens ought a government possess? And what would it mean to be known by its offices and bureaucrats? The state's new tracking projects would prompt sharp questions from across the political spectrum. Yet we must not read backward from an anxious contemporary stance toward identity documents and assume that the government's access to "private" information was something that Americans only and always resisted. Allowing the state into one's personal affairs was a less troubling—and perhaps even a welcome—proposition in an era when new benefits flowed to visible citizens.

Visible Citizens

Questions about how thoroughly the state ought to know its own people became less theoretical with the passage of the Social Security Act of 1935, signed by Franklin D. Roosevelt in the midst of the worst economic crisis in U.S. history.[10] Intended to provide benefits for the elderly, dependent, and unemployed through a payroll tax, it pledged—in a word—"security" for millions of Americans.[11] Social Security was politically controversial when proposed and underwent significant modification and compromise before being enacted.[12] Yet the program it established garnered a great deal of popular support, a sign perhaps that citizens agreed with one of its leading assumptions about material existence in the twentieth century:

that "life is safer, but living less secure," as a 1937 Social Security pamphlet phrased it.[13]

A vast scholarly literature examines the impulses behind, the architects of, and the ideological assumptions built into Social Security and other institutions of the New Deal state. Not surprisingly, most of the debates about the implementation of Social Security have involved the particulars of the legislation and its impact: how the program was circumscribed by the model of private "earned" pensions, how it shifted the relationship between the state and the economy, how it determined benefits and for whom, and how effectively it shrank the rates of poverty among the elderly.[14]

Less considered have been the byproducts of the new bureaucracy, particularly the government's assigning of specific identifying numbers to private citizens. What did this intersection of numbering and state-building mean for Americans of this era? Clues can be found in the program's rollout, as viewed both by the agency officials most involved in communicating its workings to the public and by the citizens newly in Social Security's embrace. The nine-digit number we now take for granted was the product of intensive debate and discussion by policy makers, bringing to light the political realities and cultural sensitivities that accompanied the task of knowing citizens. Likewise, Americans' encounters with this new system of documentation reveal how their relationship to their own "private" information—the basic facts that described and placed them—was being transformed in a knowing society.

What was clear, through the efforts of both public and private agencies, was that modern Americans were becoming deeply enmeshed in webs of bureaucratic verification. A columnist for an Atlanta newspaper wryly testified in 1942 that "every law-abiding citizen today has his vest pockets . . . crammed with credentials," including "a draft registration card, a social security card, a driver's license, a hospitalization card, an insurance card, a gasoline ration book, a sugar ration book, a finger-print identification card, a shopper's credit card," and so on. "Practically all of these items stress the fact that I am me and nobody else; without them, I would officially cease to exist," he quipped. "Merely keeping them handy is a career in itself, and the fear of losing them is always in the back of my mind."[15]

For this commentator, Social Security cards were just one piece of a "thoroughly classified, documented, and cross-indexed" modern existence.[16] Yet these cards warrant special attention for the fashion in which the numbers imprinted on them bound personal data to social entitlements. The state enumeration of citizens, and the potential tracking it permitted, did not escape public notice. Quite apart from discussions of Social Security's substantive merits, this feature of its operation engendered strong criticism from a strange set of bedfellows: the Republican opposition, as well as African Americans, labor unions, working women, and religious groups. Yet in years of depression and war, apprehension about Social Security numbers and what they enabled the state to know competed with another view, in which the nine digits were broadcast—even cherished—as proof of membership in a newly generous polity. Social Security made the rewards of identification manifest, enlisting Americans in their own bureaucratic visibility.

During the New Deal, state monitoring would come wrapped in the semblance not of social order but of social benefit—indeed, social *security*. A landmark piece of legislation, still considered the most important social welfare program in the United States, the Social Security Act ushered in old-age and unemployment benefits for a large segment of the population. It also marked the U.S. government's first widespread use of personal information to identify and administer specific individuals, in the form of the Social Security number (SSN). The SSN was an essential mechanism of the ambitious new program, which as reformer and social scientist Sophonisba P. Breckinridge put it in 1935, "contemplates the participation in all of our lives of the federal, state, and local governments and puts, for the first time, a degree of validity into the expression 'American standard of life.'"[17]

"Standard" here referred to a minimum threshold for subsistence, but it implied a kind of standardization common to large-scale administrative projects. Unprecedented though it was in scope, Social Security was in step with a set of documentation practices well advanced by the early decades of the twentieth century.[18] Its planners drew from other nations' experiments with administering citizens' identities, particularly those of France, Britain, and Brazil. "Seeing like a state," in James C. Scott's influential formulation, hinged on making citizens "legible" and thereby amenable to the designs of officials and planners.[19] The expansion of "paper identities" was intertwined with a specific mode of governance able to register and recognize specific persons.[20]

For the whole arc of that story, we would need to turn back several centuries. The most ambitious projects of modern industrial societies—state-building, militarization, economic mobilization—have been accompanied, indeed made possible, by regimes of documentation and the associated work of quantification and mapping.[21] These were the tools that enabled polities to be governed over time and distance, even if those tools never worked as efficiently or unerringly as advertised.[22] State practices that allowed populations to be known ranged from the standardizing of surnames to the creation of vital statistics to the registration of aliens.[23] The project of affixing specific identities to particular bodies has been evocatively described as the "memory of the state."[24] As this enterprise grew, official paper documents could in some settings become truer than the word or even body of the person to whom they referred.[25]

Even before the nineteenth century the tasks of conscription and border control had led European states to develop identity documents. But into the twentieth century the American federal state did not "know" its citizens in this way, its data-collecting capacities lagging woefully behind its industrialized peers. The "Missing Soldiers Office" created by Clara Barton after the Civil War illustrated the problem, drawing 68,182 letters from family members and friends in pursuit of men who had disappeared in the course of battle. Writes historian Drew Faust, "hundreds of thousands of men—more than 40 percent of deceased Yankees and a far greater proportion of Confederates—perished without names," designated only as "unknown."[26] A half century later, the 1917 Selective Service Act revealed that modern war making would remain hampered by the nation's lax identification practices. Its requirement that all men ages 21 to 31 register for the draft begged the question: How would a man—or the authorities, for that matter—supply definitive proof of his age? In the end, plenty of men managed to evade both the eyes of the state and the burden of enlistment. This was especially true in rural areas and the South, which were only gradually joining the regime of "paper identities." During World War I, writes historian Michael Kazin, "three out of four southerners still lived on the land, and millions of them had neither a birth certificate, a bank account, nor a marriage license—and they had never paid either income or poll taxes." Black southerners and those living on Indian reservations were especially difficult to pin down for the purposes of conscription.[27]

The early twentieth century saw a number of attempts to remedy this situation by extending documentation practices to the population at large. Only some of them succeeded. Birth registration, for instance, was established as a nearly universal practice by the 1930s, although not without considerable effort on the part of labor and health reformers during the prior two decades.[28] Births had been recorded in a variety of ways up until this point, etched in family Bibles or on baptismal certificates, or captured on insurance policies. As birth certificates became standard proof of one's age and citizenship status, observes historian Shane Landrum, moments that had once been rites of passage—naming, schooling, employment, military service, and marriage—were also now "moments of governmentality" when individuals "built or confirmed an identity relationship to the state."[29] An individual's very existence was becoming a matter of public record.[30] A notice of the New York City Department of Health made this quite clear in 1930, as part of its push to increase the prompt reporting of births. It cited the "various hardships" that would befall those without proper documentation, since a birth certificate or its legal equivalent was required "to enter school, make a contract, hold office or marry; to obtain inheritances, insurance, compensation or pensions, and to obtain a passport."[31]

Even so, systematizing births—and thus, age—was a patchy process. During World War II, the citizenship requirement for working in defense industries uncovered the fact that a full one-third of Americans of working age had no proof of birth, with rural African Americans and southwestern Spanish speakers the most poorly documented.[32] Social Security, as an age-pegged entitlement program, would run up against the same problem. Old-age insurance benefits were to take effect the day a worker turned 65. And yet few reaching that age in the 1930s or 1940s could lay claim to official documentation. The agency had no other option but to accept alternative forms of proof: Bibles, baptism or census records, military discharge forms, and sometimes affidavits of witnesses. One poignant irony of the story of expanding economic citizenship came in the fact that for some African Americans, proof of age—and Social Security benefits—flowed only from the paperwork of enslavement: ownership records or court notices of sales.[33]

Unlike the system of certifying births that slowly but surely took hold across the first decades of the twentieth century, the universal fingerprinting campaigns of the Progressive era failed.[34] The technique's stubborn association with criminality was to blame. While early birth certificate holders were often white and middle class, those with their prints on record were much more likely to be poor, foreign, or nonwhite.[35] Fingerprinting's unsavory reputation complicated efforts, still afoot in the 1930s, to make the practice mandatory.[36] The California chapter of the American Legion, for one, was enthused about the possibility of a sure-fire method for identifying individuals and supported legislation to this end. Partisans were certain that "save for the fact that few finger prints, other than those of criminals, are taken now, there would be and could be no real feeling against the plan." Once the practice was regularized, it was thought, the stigma would simply fade away. (Indeed, in support, this writer noted that "not only the carrying of identification papers, but registration at a police office of every newcomer to any community, is required in various parts of Europe, and universally accepted without complaint."[37]) The Department of Justice was similarly confident that universal fingerprinting would come to pass.[38] But methods of documentation, it turned out, could be tainted by proxy if too closely identified with suspect populations.

Not surprisingly, fissures of class, race, and nationality run through the history of identity practices. In a nation in which the original "undocumented" were white middle- and upper-class citizens, to be known to the authorities was at the turn of the century a badge of deficiency. The introduction of passports, not used in the United States until World War I, challenged this understanding.[39] Border entry had before this typically been a matter not of documents, writes the scholar Craig Robertson, but of "bodies and personal appearances." On these grounds, immigration officials turned away Chinese laborers, as well as "idiots," "lunatics," convicts, prostitutes, polygamists, those suffering from contagious disease, and others likely to become "public charges"—each of these categories suffused by class and racial hostility.[40] Well-heeled citizens' resistance to the new passport requirements was in part opposition to the fact that state agencies were treating respectable Americans "as objects of inquiry," akin to criminals or the insane.[41] It was a rude shock that traditional ways of proving one's identity were suddenly no longer sufficient to ensure passage across national borders or reentry to the United States. Such individuals believed that their word or reputation, and not official papers, ought to certify their identity.

Likewise, "mass registration" existed in the United States before the 1930s—notably, in the case of German enemy aliens during World War I.[42] It was a different matter to extend such practices to upstanding citizens and patriots. Federal attempts to track that segment of the population would require a level of subtlety and persuasion—of careful consideration—that had not accompanied earlier efforts to identify anarchists, agitators, foreigners, strikers, and criminals. The privacy concerns and claims of these more privileged subjects would have to be reckoned with.

This history of documentation and all the associations it called up thus made the question of enlisting Americans in a "universal" program like Social Security both familiar and fraught. For citizens who had not yet felt the scrutiny of the state, legislation that asked Americans to "register" with the government appeared a radical departure. Social Security's success would therefore require more than a monumental effort of bureaucratic coordination. It would turn on an intellectual transformation. Identification techniques would have to be reimagined as a path to social benefits and not simply a means of social control. In a political culture pledged to individual freedom and autonomy, state monitoring would itself need to be normalized, a route to privilege rather than privation. Whereas criminals had once been the primary targets of the state's gaze, Social Security would by design bring under scrutiny the most normative of Americans: white, male, able-bodied workers. This pivot in whom the government would document helps explain why one of the most remarked-on features of Social Security in the mid-1930s was the number itself.

Given its exclusion of certain classes of workers—agricultural laborers and domestics, and thus African Americans most prominently—Social Security was not in 1936 a truly national system covering all citizens or residents. Initially, only those in commercial and industrial employment, roughly 60 percent of the paid workforce, were encompassed by the program.[43] Nevertheless, the legislation's reach was unparalleled. Importantly, Social Security also differed in kind from most prior state ventures that had gathered facts about the population as a whole. The U.S. Census Bureau and the collectors of vital statistics—although charged with aggregating reams of personal information—made no decisions pegged to *particular* individuals' data. In contrast, the Social Security system was designed to do just that: keep tabs on specific workers' contributions over their lifetimes, and even beyond, in order to pay out appropriate benefits. Its task, pronounced a pair of advisors to the Social Security Board, was "of a magnitude never before equaled in any Government or private undertaking, even including the United States Census, the World War draft, or the payment of the veterans' bonus."[44]

The new agency could however trade on earlier experiences of tallying the people, not only the periodic enumeration of the population, stretching back all the way to 1790, but also the introduction of the 1913 income tax and more episodic efforts such as military mobilization.[45] The U.S. government had faced the problem of registering some ten million World War I draftees in 1917—a task it undertook in a single twelve-hour day in June. Reports of the "vast" and "decentralized civilian machinery" that made the draft possible hinted at the new scope of information gathering that accompanied it.[46] The registration process involved a twelve-point questionnaire and a signed and stamped registration card that "the young man should carry with him always." An eight-page questionnaire "giving all details of his life" would be his next step after registering.[47]

Social Security presented a still larger and more complex undertaking. It was estimated in 1935 that 26 million workers would need to set up Social Security accounts, with 2.5 million new accounts added annually; 3.5 million employers would also be enrolled in the system.[48] The overarching problem for the brand new Social Security Board (SSB) was how, in very short order, to enlist those multitudes of workers and employers into the program, as well as those joining the workforce in subsequent years—and then to keep them in its sights for decades to come. Not only did millions of workers need to be enrolled so that taxes paid on their earnings could begin accumulating. But because benefits would be calculated based on each employee's "lifetime working record," a correct accounting was required so that years into the future each employee "would receive his due under the law."[49] Faced with this staggering proposition, the SSB called in consultants of various stripes, from private actuaries to state workers' compensation administrators to international experts in pensions and social insurance.[50] Those consultants agreed that a careful tracking system of those paying into the program, one that could link each Social Security contribution to just one person, would be essential. For the new program to work, its beneficiaries—masses of Americans who had not been under the state's gaze before—would need to be made precisely and continuously visible.

Numbering the People

But how to keep track? This was, in 1935, a loaded question. Two of the Social Security Board's technical advisors were emphatic that using the most familiar way to identify people—individual names—"would result in endless perplexities." Driving home the point, they projected that Title II of the Social Security Act—which covered only those workers who died or reached age 65 in the period between 1937 and 1942 (when the first monthly benefits were to be paid out)—would cover 294,000 Smiths, 227,000 Johnsons, and 165,000 Browns.[51] Other methods for keeping tabs—stamp books as were used in Britain, for example, or photographs (too burdensome for the worker and too difficult to keep up to date)—were discussed and discarded in turn.[52]

Some participants in this discussion were certain that there was an identification technique far better than names or anything else on offer: fingerprints. Fingerprinting had the alleged virtues of "permanency, positiveness, and simplicity" and was already in use by a number of federal agencies, including the War and Navy departments, the Veterans Administration, and even the Post Office (for Postal Savings depositors) and some maternity hospitals.[53] A superior method of identification, fingerprinting was, however, not a viable option. "Unfortunately, the method has for so long been associated with the tracing of criminals that there seemed little likelihood of the American people's accepting it as an aid in social security identification," lamented the same advisors to the SSB who had cautioned against using names.[54] Another key consultant to the Social Security Board, the French Pierre Tixier, came regretfully to the same conclusion. He acknowledged that "the use of finger prints," which had been employed in Brazil for similar purposes, "would doubtless be unpopular with American workers, who would oppose it because of the connotations attaching to it from police usage."[55] In a 1942 report, the SSB would confirm that fingerprinting had been "fully explored and carefully considered," but scuttled for these reasons.[56]

This is where unique account numbers came in. Tixier insisted that, for precision's sake, "numbered registration" of the insured was absolutely essential, since it would create an unambiguous match between a particular worker's earned wages and his account.[57] The decision to number may in fact have been a foregone conclusion. Yet Social Security's planners were deeply anxious about numbering—or, rather, were convinced that the American public would be. Although supporters and opponents of the New Deal agreed on little, here was a rare point of alignment. State identification numbers summoned the prospect of regimentation and dehumanization: of authoritarian governments that knew their citizens all too well. As one of Social Security's detractors, a director of the Chase National Bank of New York, put it, "our wage-earning citizens . . . may well resent a system of surveillance in which every individual among them is kept under the eye of the Federal Government." He declared, "Our people have been accustomed to privacy and freedom of movement."[58]

On this score, the SSB was quite sensitive. Regarding enrollment in the program, its chairman stressed "the importance of presenting it to the public in the right manner."[59] Keen sensitivity to the semantics at issue was evident in instructions from the Field Organization Committee, which counseled the staff to avoid "the implications of the word REGISTRA-TION" and instead "adhere closely to the word ENUMERATION" when setting up accounts. (Indeed, the committee urged that "steps be taken" to ensure that this terminology was not just "preferred" but required.) This was, it seems, an attempt to assimilate the new practice to the long-standing one of census taking. Additionally, the Board was urged to "do everything possible, particularly in memorandums, conferences, press releases, and public addresses, to carefully impress upon the public that the assignment of the number is made to the *account* and *not* to the person" so as to mini-mize the "charge of regimentation." It insisted in emphatic memos (and many capital letters) that "the number is directly related to the ACCOUNT and is not a means of 'mechanizing' or 'regimenting' the individual."[60]

Partisan politics soon proved that the SSB's anxieties were well founded. Republicans mounted plenty of criticisms of the new act, from its methods of financing to its federal management, not to mention the payroll tax itself, routinely described as a form of "theft." But Social Security's op-ponents also played up the dangers of state invasion into—and control of—citizens' private lives that would come from assigning them identifi-cation numbers. It was an issue tailor-made for partisan combat, and Re-publican operatives did not squander the opportunity. Posters and leaflets circulated by the Republican National Committee (RNC) prominently an-nounced that workers would not only be "forced to register" for a program of "mandatory pay cuts"; they would also be required to hand over to the state a stash of highly sensitive private information.[61]

This was the point of a colorful political stunt engineered by the pub-lisher William Randolph Hearst and RNC chairman, John D. M. Ham-ilton, on the eve of the 1936 presidential election. In what the SSB billed as a "forgery," the RNC circulated to newspapers a supposed "reproduc-tion" of the official Social Security enrollment form, which included ques-tions as to whether the worker had ever divorced; his church and union affiliations; his "general health," "physical defects," and property holdings; his reasons for leaving a former position; whether he was a naturalized cit-izen; and the like.[62] As one Hearst organ explained, "Your personal life will be laid bare," "your life will be an open book," and "you are to be regimented—catalogued—put on file." It added, for good measure, "This is what the Roosevelt Administration did not intend to have you know until AFTER the election." The same article imagined a dialogue between an ordinary worker and a lawyer, in which the former discovers in amazement, "Why, the government wants to know everything about me!" He then muses, "Supposing I got a new job. Would my new boss be able to get all these facts about me?" The lawyer replies, "When your employer assembles the records, he could read them if he wanted to, I suppose." The worker's further queries about the fate of these personal details were met with similarly unsettling answers.[63]

This campaign was, of course, meant to stir up fears of heavy-handed government intrusion—and to expose "prying into intimate secrets of the worker's life" and "the private lives of American working men and women" as the true intent of the New Deal legislation. Under the headline "Social Security Application Blank Bares Personal Record to Bureau Official," a purported facsimile of the form indicated, via ominous black arrows, the "regimented information required, together with space for number by which workers henceforth will be listed."[64] This was not the only misrepresentation of the account form in circulation. A trade magazine printed an illustration of a Social Security card application that revealed "a series of detailed questions of a very personal character, together with fingerprint reproductions." In very small type the caption noted, "Possible registration form."[65]

As the references to fingerprinting suggested, detailed questionnaires probing for personal information about a worker's health, history, family, and politics were only part of the problem. The threat of a national identification system was the other. As a Boston tabloid put it, "The New Deal's so-called Social Security program gives you a number . . . [and] a RECORD in the files at Washington. It will be as complete as any convict's or prisoner's."[66] In this view, visibility to the government automatically led to constrictions of personal freedom, making a prisoner of a private citizen. Indeed, "if the Roosevelt administration is returned to power, we shall see two groups of citizens in this nation," thundered the RNC chair Hamilton at a political rally in Boston: "those who are numbered and those who are not numbered." The former were the unlucky "27 million men and women who will be forced to report to a politically appointed clerk, every change of their residence, every change in their wages, every change of their employment." For at least some in the crowd of 20,000 at the Boston Garden who responded with "repeated waves of applause" to Hamilton's "vigorous blows at the administration," this was the road to despotism. For the RNC chair it was also the road to Europe, where "people carry police cards and are subject to police surveillance." Thus far, "American citizens have not been subject to these indignities and no administration ever has dared to suggest that they should be," he railed. "But just that kind of surveillance is a part of the Roosevelt administration."[67]

The politician was not specific in his reference, but knowledge of the Nazi registration laws requiring proof of ancestry and political loyalty, instituted in 1933, surely abetted the Republican case.[68] As Americans learned of developments afoot in Hitler's Germany, the association of Social Security with other techniques of state coercion presented a potential public relations quagmire.[69] In this light, the most inflammatory Republican charge of all was that citizens would soon be compelled to wear "dog-tags" proclaiming their state-issued Social Security number. Hamilton announced in his stump speech that the New Deal administration had already sought bids for the machines that would manufacture them, and he brandished a purported specimen of the new stainless steel dog tags, "similar to those worn in the World War."[70] The Republican National Committee made the dog tag a central exhibit in its opposition to Social Security, supplying to reporters a photograph of the offending item, pictured on a chain around a young man's neck. The Hearst papers ran with the story and photograph, the *New York American* declaring that the tag would be required "for the privilege of suffering a pay cut under the Social Security Act."[71] The *Boston American,* which also printed the photo, clinched its case against Social Security by quoting the sentiments of a bartender in East Boston: "In the army you were in for a good reason. . . . But with this thing, we're all drafted, and there's no war."[72] Dog tags "have been prepared and submitted to the social security board for its approval," warned the *Boston Herald.* "Will fingerprinting be next?"[73]

The Social Security Board was quick to respond to this organized effort to ratchet up fears of state omniscience.[74] Acting chairman Arthur Altmeyer called out the "authors of this canard," stating that there was not the "slightest particle of truth" in statements about the Social Security Board soliciting data about "items of an intimate personal nature." The Board had no need for such information, no intention of seeking it, and "no legal authority to do so."[75] A spokeswoman further charged the RNC with "deliberate falsehood" and a "hostile campaign to confuse, deceive and scare the people of this country by threats, coercion and by misleading statements," not only in the press but also on pay envelopes and posters tacked up in factories. She described information about marital status and union ties as "matters private in their nature and of no legitimate concern to the Federal Government," adding that "no such questions would be asked now or at any time in the future." Only a few simple questions, such as name, age, and address, would be required to apply for an account. Further, the Board emphatically did not "intend nor had it ever intended to issue identification disks to American workers."[76]

In fact, the SSB had contemplated issuing metal nameplates or "identification tokens" rather than a Social Security card made of paper. These would have resembled the metal cards that some department stores issued for keeping track of customer credit and that the Agricultural Adjustment Administration had adopted as recently as 1934 for identifying famers participating in an acreage reduction program.[77] The experts at the Bureau of Standards were in agreement that metal, whether in the form of a plate, token, or disc, was "the only product which will serve our purpose."[78] Moreover, several key Social Security officials were "inclined to discount the argument that the metal token smacked of regimentation or a fingerprint system," given that many workplaces already used similar metal discs for identification.[79]

Yet the Board's eventual decision to issue a paper card rather than risk the negative connotation of a metal token and its whiff of regimentation (despite the fact that the metal plates would have been more durable, error proof, and cost efficient in the long term), suggests that the RNC's critique hit its mark.[80] Looking back from 1941, the Board acknowledged that metal plates "had a connotation of 'dog tag' and might also appear more definitely as 'regimentation'" and that this was likely a factor in the decision to not to approve them.[81] Fifty years later, Senator Daniel Patrick Moynihan claimed that the agency "remained traumatized" by charges of regimentation all the way into the 1990s. He pinned the simple pasteboard design of the Social Security card—in his view, laughably easy to counterfeit—to that moment in 1935 when "opponents of Social Security, and of President Roosevelt, charged that the administration was creating an identity card, of the sort recently introduced in Nazi Germany."[82]

To counter charges of regimentation, the Board in 1936, and in its retellings of Social Security's origins, insisted, somewhat disingenuously, on the "entirely voluntary" nature of applying for an SSN.[83] Citizens were not registered by the state; they were merely assigned account numbers upon applying for them. Social Security's planners offered reassuring precedents for what evidently required careful justification. Account numbers, they urged, were "not a new departure," given that "similar methods of identifying records have been used by savings banks and insurance companies for more than a hundred years."[84] The state was simply borrowing time-honored methods from the private sector.[85] In fact, the Social Security account card was not unlike the department store credit cards many Americans had begun to use.[86] Moreover, the numbers on that card—it was stressed—were *not* for identification. The SSN identified only a particular record or wage account; the Social Security card in turn indicated the person whose record was identified by the number. Hence, the card itself "was not meant to identify the bearer."[87] This tortured logic may have baffled account holders, but its intent was crystal clear. The point was to dissolve the link between identification documents and state monitoring, to reassure Americans that the person was not a number and that being known to the state would not reduce him or her to one.

It is difficult to know for certain if the Social Security Board was correct in its estimation of the American public's deep resistance to being numbered. But, plainly, the agency's planners felt constrained by the public culture in which the new program was taking root. Each decision the SSB made was carefully weighed not just for its administrative implications but also for its political ones. Ongoing debates about how best to track Social Security's beneficiaries, vigilant attention to questions of public relations, and strenuous avoidance of fingerprinting or anything that resembled "registration" all point to a bureaucracy focused on exerting the lightest touch possible.[88]

After "months of careful study," the Social Security Board finally settled on the combination of an account number and individual signature on a simple paper card as its preferred method for enrolling workers. "This, it was decided, was the only procedure which would be adequate and yet satisfactory to a public which has always been fearful of anything that might suggest the loss of some personal freedom through formal records of identities."[89] The signature, we might guess, was yet another concession to public sensitivities: a mark of individuality in the worker's own hand that would accompany the now-familiar nine-digit chain. But it was the digits that would affix to their holder through thick and through thin. This was the number, the Social Security Board proclaimed, that would "in the normal course of events, serve [the worker] throughout his entire working life, and will be used in mailing him benefit checks until his death."[90] Its legal basis was written into Title VIII of the Social Security Act, which stated simply that "an identifying number will be assigned to each employer and to each employee."[91] With this final step, the SSN was born.

The Early Days of Tracking

The Social Security Board in 1936 thus found itself on the leading edge of debates over the modern "information state."[92] Even as the Board attempted to ease Americans' worries about being numbered, it grappled with its newfound ability to track them. Workers had their own hesitations about the numbering project. These were rooted in the collection and maintenance of what even the agency described as "considerable personal and confidential information."[93] As such, SSNs raised in early form the dilemmas of a society organized around stored data.

Alert to potential criticism, the Board had determined that the "minimum necessary" information was to be requested of the worker in order to set up a Social Security account. Only the individual's name, address, date and place of birth, sex, "color," parents' names, and name and address of employer were ultimately deemed "essential for either identification or the actuarial studies required of the Board."[94] Internal Social Security memos hint at "some discussion as to the advisability of determining the race" of the worker on the form. But the inclusion of a racial category—for "identification" as well as "actuarial need"—was not surprising in the 1930s, given the routine use of racial designations in job advertisements, as well as in insurance schemes and mortality tables.[95] Still, this was a considerably less capacious list than the Republican National Committee had manufactured in its campaign against Social Security during the 1936 election season. Stung by the charges, the Board was at pains to explain that the official application questions were "in sharp contrast with those which were forecast in the heat of the political campaign" and were designed only to identify the employee.[96] (The queries were also, it was noted, less confidential in nature than those asked by census takers.[97])

Nevertheless, the agency was aware that "a great many employees were naturally very anxious to know how the information on the employee's application was to be used." The Board reported receiving "numerous inquiries . . . as to the publicity to be given information furnished for the

2.1. Big data, circa 1936: Social Security was the heftiest venture of its kind, the agency describing itself as "the largest bookkeeping operation in the world."

administration of the program."[98] There was, first, skittishness on the part of particular populations about registering for an account number. A handful objected on the "ground of conscientious or religious scruples."[99] African American leaders, in more concerted fashion, protested the application form, incensed by its inclusion of a racial designation. "The element of color was inserted for one reason and for only one reason," charged an editorial in the *Pittsburgh Courier*: "to more easily discriminate against Negroes." The Social Security card would become as a consequence "just one more instrument for penalizing a minority group."[100] Another critic charged that the government had "no business" setting up "an official caste system." He predicted that the "check mark after the word 'Negro' will dog our lives for decades to come."[101] The National Association for the Advancement of Colored People vigorously but unsuccessfully challenged the SSB on this point, convinced that such information would "inevitably be used in various ways, both obvious and subtle, to practice discrimination based on race."[102] Being tagged bureaucratically by one's race, these writers understood, was to be made more visible and thus more vulnerable in a society still structured along caste lines.

A desire to keep aspects of identity private—whether one's age, marital status, religion, ethnicity, or employment history—was apparent in others' reactions to the prospect of being "registered" by Social Security. Workers had often kept these sorts of personal details carefully shielded from their bosses and managers, and so it is not surprising that giving up such information on official forms raised alarms. Yet this concern was not rooted in fears of a looming police state. It was soon clear that many Americans worried less about government prying than what employers might do with their newly divulged personal information.

The problem arose as soon as enrollment began. In order to obtain an SSN, workers were to fill out an application blank and return it to the Post Office—which was spearheading the initial enumeration effort—either directly or through their union or workplace. Almost immediately, the Board began handling questions about employer coercion. Numerous workers complained of having been instructed to return their forms via their employer or else be fired. As the SSB noted, women and Jews were especially reluctant to do so—the former "because they have falsified their age to their employers or because they are married women representing to be single in order to retain their positions"; the latter because "they are jews [sic] who have changed their names because the organization for which they work is anti-semitic."[103]

Here the Board simply acknowledged well-known facts. Religious minorities occupied a precarious place in American society in the 1930s. One 1934 study documented still-high levels of discrimination against Jews in employment and housing, and against Catholics in political and civic affairs.[104] Arthur Altmeyer, the second and long-serving chairman of the Social Security Board, later recalled an "ugly situation" that faced the Board itself, when it was criticized by the House Ways and Means Committee for appointing "too damned many New York Jews" (a complaint that made it all the way to FDR).[105] Divulging personal information about one's religion or ethnicity via a telling surname on an official form would have been especially worrisome for Americans already at risk for discrimination. Of particular concern was the chance that these details would make their way back to employers.

On their part, hundreds of working women reportedly called the Social Security Board to ask whether their bosses would be alerted to their age or marital status, information women often falsified in order to get or keep a job.[106] Married women workers, often blamed for taking jobs that were rightfully men's, were greeted with hostility during the Depression if they were not fired outright.[107] Registering one's date of birth was also quite nettlesome for female employees.[108] Employers favored young, single women because they were inexpensive to hire and judged least likely to quit to start a family. And so, on both counts, women workers were inclined to lie.

Given these circumstances, an anonymous letter to the *Chicago Daily Tribune*, signed by "The 'Fibbers,'" fretted over the dilemmas the government forms were causing. The writers asked whether Social Security applications must be handed over to employers or could be sent to the agency directly, and whether discrepancies between what was reported to Social Security and what had been furnished to the company would be discovered. They explained, "For instance, we have given our ages as 30, whereas we are really in the neighborhood of 38. If we put down 30, and when we really arrive at the age of 65, can we claim our pension if we show our birth certificates and explain then that had we given our correct ages we could have been out of a job, as nowadays work is for the young only?" What these writers worried about was not the lie but the eventual squaring of accounts. "Will the government check up with our employers as to our ages?" they wondered. "There are a number of us who are in a bad predicament; if we give our correct ages we may lose our jobs, and if we put down the ages which we have given to our employers we may have to wait a number of years before we really get our pension."[109]

Confirming the regularity of this particular sort of misrepresentation, a journalist observed that even if women had "lied about their age to their employes [*sic*], their sweethearts, or even their husbands . . . the truth is recorded on the oblong papers in the custody of the Social Security Board." Female workers, he joked, "may have deceived everybody else, but they came through truthfully for Uncle Sam."[110] It was no joking matter, of course, to vulnerable employees. Truth did indeed have consequences for Jewish and female workers, who faced serious penalties if the accurate and yet potentially damning information they reported to the government was uncovered by an employer. The peril of registration for them was not state overreach or even mismanagement, but the very honesty of their Social Security record.

Labor union members harbored a similar fear about the new SSN: that information about a worker's previous position, along with a clue to his union affiliation, might now be available to a prospective boss.[111] That is, an individual's employment history, once recorded and filed away, could come back to haunt him. Union members' distrust of bosses and managers had been well earned. The long history of using Pinkertons and labor spies for union busting made certain of that. Handing over one's details recalled other practices for prying into employees' political sympathies, long-standing by the 1930s.[112] Noting that the strongest "adverse criticism" of documentation came from "labor sources," the Social Security Board designed the enrollment process in such a way that workers would not have to share personal information with their employers.[113] Strikingly, the agency offered assistance in bypassing intrusive bosses. The SSB made it known that "cards need not be returned through the employer"; workers could instead mail or hand forms to the post office directly or via their labor union. The agency even suggested that incorrect information supplied to an employer might be corrected later, on a separate application form, so that the workplace and Social Security might have different "facts" on file about particular employees.[114]

When it came to their bosses, African American, Jewish, female, and unionized workers alike had no trouble grasping the dark side of legibility. This swirl of concerns about how Social Security data were to be used and accessed prompted the SSB to act. Official press releases, one the day before the first applications for SSNs were distributed, and another the following month, underlined the agency's assurances that workers' personal information would be carefully protected. The details on the application form, the Board declared, would only be retrievable by government employees connected to Social Security. In June 1937, the agency's first regulation—Regulation No. 1—formalized its pledge of confidentiality for information collected and maintained.[115] Even so, the new administrative system threatened to unravel tried-and-true practices by which workers both kept certain kinds of information private and kept their jobs.

The launch of Social Security made evident that they were right to worry. Many employers had fought the New Deal legislation. They were nevertheless tantalized by the new cache of information on their workers that the program promised to generate and sought to use it for their own purposes. It soon came to light, on the heels of the act's passage, that opportunistic companies were circulating their own official-looking forms demanding data from their employees—including the worker's nationality, years of residence in the United States, religious background, educational level, home ownership, number of dependents, relatives employed in the same plant, and political and trade union affiliations. In one early such example, from December 1935—nearly a year before the actual enumeration for Social Security began—the Ferris Tire and Rubber Company disseminated a questionnaire inquiring, among other details, about the worker's age and labor union membership, "for government purposes only."[116] A New Jersey firm created a spurious "Form C-53-A," titled "Social Security Record System: Employee History Record," intended to glean similar sorts of data. Another company produced a form titled "United States Federal Social Security Act—Compulsory Information from All Employes [sic]." Still another informed workers that personal information (of a sort never entertained by the New Deal agency) was required "to make you eligible for social security benefits."[117]

Clearly, some employers used the prospect of federal information gathering as a foot in the door for their own more probing inquiries. A Social Security spokeswoman put the number of incidents in which firms fished for data on their workers "under the pretext that such information was demanded by the Federal Government" in the hundreds.[118] The ruse was common enough to provoke an official rebuke. A press release in February 1937 firmly warned employers against the practice of distributing "unauthorized questionnaires which appeared to be required by the Social Security Board and which were intended to disclose employees' union affiliations, religion, or personal affairs."[119] That so many businesses masqueraded as the state in order to more closely surveil their employees inverts our expectations about whom Americans worried about most as invaders of their privacy in the 1930s. Contemporary debates—real or fabricated—centering on "state regimentation" sidestepped the extensive prying into citizens' affairs from the private sector. As far as many workers were concerned, the Republican National Committee had targeted the wrong culprit.

Certainly the government's new role as data collector raised some concerns, particularly the fact that it would, under the auspices of Social Security, possess files on millions of Americans, with more to be added every year. An anonymous query from "T. C." to the *Chicago Daily Tribune* in 1940—"Can the internal revenue bureau or some other government office get any information about my social security account?"—suggested as much.[120] Warnings about what the state might do with its knowledge about citizens had been a centerpiece of the Republican "dog tag" campaign. Yet what surfaces much more clearly in existing sources than worries about state tracking is both the reality of corporate surveillance and workers' recognition of such.[121] If it now seems remarkable how readily Americans entrusted sensitive personal information to the federal government, it is because private employers—not public agencies—were the chief source of their apprehension.

Who could gain access to the rich storehouse of information lodged in rows of double-decker file cabinets at Social Security's headquarters, the Candler Building in Baltimore, was one concern. Another centered on the nine-digit identifier itself and the possibility it presented for keeping tabs on specific individuals. Here once again labor unions were most vocal, arguing that this kind of tracking would naturally follow from the SSN. As the SSB knew from conferences with state administrators of unemployment insurance even before Social Security was launched, "a good deal of fear was evidenced . . . that the identification token given to the employee would be used for black-listing by the employer."[122] Once the program was up and running, unions fully expected that employers would use the new numbers to keep track of and punish "troublesome" workers. United Automobile Worker members, for instance, were given "reason to suspect that there was a certain black list which had been established, because of their participation in strike activities." This was because "when they went to get a job they discovered that their Social Security number had been listed."[123] As labor unions perceived, the state may have assigned the numbers, but many others would see the advantages of an identifiable citizenry.

Many indeed sought to make use of the SSN's convenience as a tracking mechanism. Even as Social Security pledged to protect the personal information in its charge, it was besieged by requests for its records. SSNs may not have been intended as a means of identification, but they were certainly treated that way, right from the beginning. Individuals tried to put the new numbers to work for a variety of purposes, often to hunt down acquaintances who had moved or disappeared without a trace. The Board reported that "immediately following the registration . . . a considerable volume of 'domestic relations' inquiries began to be received . . . pleas for help in locating missing husbands, wives, relatives, or friends."[124] Such pleas echoed those of universal fingerprinting advocates who argued for a national registry through which individuals could easily be identified. For those who had lost track of a family member or friend, the value of the state's newly systematic records was clear. Their queries reveal the "demand side" for better, more detailed information about individual citizens, which was never the government's alone. In April 1937, the *Washington Evening Star* confirmed that "Social Security Board offices all over the country are flooded each day with requests for confidential information contained in the cards filed away in Baltimore. Wives seeking their husbands, mothers looking for lost children, sons who strayed away, war veterans in search of former buddies, all these—and others—bombard the Social Security Board."[125] The Board refused such requests, although for a short while it adopted a policy of forwarding inquiries to the individual concerned, "where the public interest would be served by so doing."[126]

Direct appeals to the agency thereby foreclosed, citizens still made use of the SSN's potential for locating individual account holders. This was evident, for example, in newspaper notices like the one that appeared in connection with an employee of "Mad Cody Fleming Shows" of Columbus, California. It read, "Carnival Owners Attention: I want to know the location of JAMES HARRISON SHORT, Social Security Number 210–01–0443. He is a ride man, driving 1937 green Oldsmobile sedan. Information will be held strictly confidential."[127] SSNs featured regularly in the missing person sections of newspapers as well. A Georgia man hoped in January 1940 to track down his wife, "missing since last August," by broadcasting her SSN to the *Atlanta Constitution*'s readership.[128] A similar ad appeared in the *Baltimore Afro-American* the same year, seeking a Mr. and Mrs. Webb and disclosing, among other identifying details (the college he attended, her occupation and hobbies), the man's SSN.[129] The *Pittsburgh Courier*, which ran a regular column on missing persons, included a notice in 1950 seeking Nathaniel Edward Taylor, who had not been seen since 1945. Even before noting his hair color, height, or personal history, the advertisement's author—the man's mother—listed Taylor's Social Security number.[130] (A 1940 report of a robber revealed by carelessly leaving his Social Security card at the scene of the crime attests to other uses of the SSN not contemplated by its creators.[131])

These sporadic efforts, in which individuals grasped hopefully at a number that might put them on the trail of a physical person, were different in scale from the uses of the SSN envisioned by powerful interests, whether in public administration or private industry. Social Security did not at first permit any nonagency uses of the numbers assigned to those workers paying into and collecting benefits from its old-age and unemployment programs. Slowly but surely, however, it moved in this direction.[132] FDR furthered this process via a 1943 Executive Order encouraging the use of SSNs in federal agency record keeping. The order endorsed "a single, unduplicated numerical identification system of accounts" in the interest of "economic and orderly administration."[133] In the post–New Deal era, SSNs would evolve without much comment from a "single-use" identifier into one useful to a profusion of agencies in both the public and private sector.[134]

One of the chief tasks of the Social Security Board (and after 1946, the Social Security Administration) was contending with how to respond to a stream of requests for the numbers and the data they indexed beyond their original purpose. Social Security did not here play the part of an overstepping bureaucracy, interested in expanding its reach and power. Instead, its directors—committed to preserving trust in the agency's promises of confidentiality—fought hard to maintain the SSN as an identifier of retirement accounts alone. It was other parties who glimpsed in Social Security's trove of information a convenient way to better know or trail citizens, for purposes ranging from military duty to family support to law enforcement.

Thick internal files speak to the pressures on Social Security to allow others into its records. As early as March 1937, a New York City bank trying to locate a depositor and a Minneapolis immigration inspector working on a deportation case were knocking on the agency's doors.[135] So were police officers attempting to identify injured motorists and other accident victims.[136] The FBI, the Attorney General, the Veterans Administration, and the Comptroller General were right on their heels. The FBI's J. Edgar Hoover, for instance, requested a search of Social Security records in 1937 "to determine if a certain individual, under his true name or under any of his known aliases, is registered with the Board."[137] The Veterans Administration wished to scour the same records to establish "the death of a veteran who has disappeared and has been unheard of for a period of seven years."[138] In each of these early instances the SSB rebuffed the request to open up material in its files.[139] The Board in 1937 "object[ed] strenuously to making the Old-Age Benefits records available to the Department of

Justice or any other similar agency."[140] As a Washington reporter explained, "officials of the board believe the giving out of one single fact would destroy the effect of the entire set-up. . . . No power on earth can pry from the Social Security Board any information whatsoever about any one individual, man or woman, registered in the list of those entitled to unemployment and old-age benefits."[141]

Yet in 1943, when the Board sat down to establish a policy on releasing confidential information to other government agencies when it was requested "in connection with the prosecution of the war," the issue was trickier. One thorny case concerned whether the Department of Justice could examine Social Security's wage records to ascertain whether a Connecticut man was falsely claiming his father as a dependent in order to sit out the war. Those weighing the pros and cons fretted over the propriety of releasing the data from one individual's Social Security record (the father's) in order to investigate another's status (the son's) under the Selective Service Act. They were equally concerned that complying with the request would be tantamount to "divulg[ing] publicly the fact that the Social Security Board does make available data as to any worker's earning accounts under certain circumstances." Social Security regional representatives and field office managers were uniformly against disclosure. On the other hand, the Board recognized the merits of releasing data relevant to special wartime circumstances—well aware that, by refusing to divulge the information, Social Security could be "depicted as protecting . . . a potential draft evader." The agency finally relented, even as its directors recommended against the precedent.[142] Just a few weeks later, perhaps realizing the futility of fending off similar entreaties, the Board affirmed "a temporary and partial relaxation of standards" in order to assist the government "in prosecuting the war effort."[143]

The Board would get plenty of practice fielding such inquiries in the coming months and years. The requests illustrate the dearth of existing resources for locating specific persons in the United States in the early 1940s, given the fact of a large, mobile, and still lightly tracked population. They reveal as well the appetite that Social Security records had whetted in other corners of the federal government. As Arthur Altmeyer would later recall, "nearly every Attorney General, at the urging of the Federal Bureau of Investigation, requested access to this information."[144]

Many of the early requests for individual records had a direct connection to military matters. What if an SSN could help pinpoint a missing person, a draft evader, an army deserter, or a soldier presumed dead?[145] The number was often the best, and sometimes the only, way to know where an individual lived, if he was drawing a paycheck, or whether he was alive at all.[146] The Board made clear that its compliance with such queries would end with the cessation of hostilities.[147] But as the war years slid into the tense postwar era, as the Korean War erupted in 1950, and as a new national emergency was proclaimed, petitions for data related to national security only increased. The Board was called on to assess the costs and benefits of opening its files to outside interests, all of whom argued that their rationales were so compelling as to supersede promises of confidentiality. Should Social Security always turn over its records "in cases relating to the act of sabotage or espionage inimical to the national security"?[148] Ought the Attorney General be privy to "available information as to the identity and location of aliens in the United States"?[149] Or the FBI to the wage reports of Communist Party members?[150] What if Social Security information could help break up a ring smuggling Chinese into the United States or other organized criminal activity such as payroll fraud, racketeering, or extortion?[151] What if, as J. Edgar Hoover framed the question, the SSN could be put to the service of facing down the "unparalleled threat from international communism?"[152]

A set of other queries, which multiplied across the 1940s and 1950s, spoke instead to the peacetime value of data in Social Security's files. Requests flowed in for the purpose of tracking disability and vocational rehabilitation, child support, communicable diseases, Nazi war criminals, foreign birth or illegal alien status, and prison escapees.[153] What if SSN-linked information could be used to determine a violator of tax laws or even a fraudulent Social Security benefits claimant?[154] Could the agency reasonably divulge confidential information about an account holder's earnings, address, or disability to another party in the event of his or her insanity, amnesia, or death?[155] What about records that allowed law enforcement officers to track down deserting husbands or delinquent parents of children in receipt of assistance payments?[156]

The Board's answer was often a firm "no." But increasingly as the years passed, such queries were greeted with grudging compliance.[157] This was despite the agency's repeated acknowledgment that its pledge of confidentiality was at the very core of both its public reputation and administrative effectiveness. "A general relaxation of the policy," worried a 1954 memo, "might be considered as a breach of trust" with a "resultant loss of goodwill toward the program." "Relaxation" could engender resentment from account holders who considered their wage data to be their business, shared with the state only in order that they might draw benefits. Moreover, breaches of confidentiality, if made public, could imperil the records themselves, leading people to "apply for new numbers under fictitious names" and others to "give misleading information because of the possibility that correct information might some day be used against them."[158] In this way, any extension of the SSN's uses might sap its integrity. But the web of data that had been spun out of an initial thread—the decision to assign nine-digit identifying numbers to workers in 1936—was too valuable and alluring for other interested parties to resist.

Arguably, the stage was set for a backlash. Vast stores of sensitive data and the sharing of confidential files—not to mention a steady stream of reports of stolen numbers, an early form of identity theft—carried risks for Social Security account holders almost from the beginning.[159] Yet for the first three decades of the program's existence, save the flurry of questions sparked by the initial enumeration campaign, there would be little public discussion of those risks. Nor was much attention paid to the weaving of SSNs through the society's record-keeping organizations. Workers took great care to prevent employers from discovering private information. By contrast, one finds few references to account holders shielding their unique number from others' eyes.[160] Throughout the 1940s, for example, specific individuals' SSNs were routinely printed in the newspaper without raising any hackles.[161] Radio stations in the 1950s commonly employed listeners' SSNs to boost their ratings, announcing strings of numbers on the air and offering cash prizes to the matching holders. One enterprising man in Tulsa, Oklahoma, even formed a short-term business to listen for his clients' SSNs on the radio while they went about their day.[162] Other promotions used Social Security numbers to dole out door prizes, or invited employers to send in their employees' numbers as entries for drawings. Testifying to the regularity of this gimmick, Social Security officials considered the possibility of "legislation which would prohibit the use of social security account numbers for contests and other promotional purposes" in 1959.[163]

It is possible that a lack of concern over the proliferating uses of SSNs was the result of public ignorance, whether about the numbers' spread or the risks of visibility. But it seems equally likely to have stemmed from the high degree of trust in the state's administration of individuals' information. It spoke to a confidence that the state, unlike some employers, would in fact only use that information to a worker's own benefit. Added to this perhaps was the sense that a Social Security account was more a collaboration between citizen and state than an imposition from on high; as Arthur Altmeyer put it, the program depended on "the closest co-operation and understanding between Government officials charged with [its] administration and with the workers and employers of this country who are so vitally affected."[164] Either way, we are left with the curious case of a bureaucracy seemingly more agitated about the potential disclosure of its records than were the subjects of those records themselves.

Historian James Sparrow describes the 1940s as a rare era in the United States "in which the basic goals of the government were widely accepted as valid and necessary." He adds that, "unlike earlier periods of dramatic government expansion, the basic legitimacy of the federal government's efforts in World War II were not successfully challenged within the political mainstream."[165] Americans were willing to live with a more intrusive—a more knowing—government in large part because of the entitlements it brought. Social Security numbers, a kind of legibility with benefits, were a key early instance of this bargain struck between citizens and the state. In a period marked by economic crisis and war, the nation's claims over the citizenry kept privacy fears in check or at least out of the limelight, much as Franklin Roosevelt's wheelchair was kept out of view in press conferences and photographs. The state's new powers to know could both alarm and reassure. Many citizens in the 1930s and 1940s, it seems, were willing to take a chance on the latter.

Our SSNs, Ourselves

Even if Americans temperamentally resisted "regimentation," as so many assumed, Social Security's enumeration effort came off with remarkable speed and efficiency. On December 22, 1936, a mere twenty-eight days after the initial distribution of enrollment forms, the Post Office Department reported "the receipt of 22,129,617 completed applications of an expected total of 26,000,000 applicants."[166] Social Security trumpeted the "smooth registration" of all these millions of workers, which, it claimed, had wiped away the objections of those "who doubted its successful accomplishment."[167]

Americans' alacrity in filling out the government forms was impressive. But the nature of their compliance with the project of creating a visible citizenry is difficult to assess. Billed as a voluntary venture, albeit one with a round-the-clock public relations apparatus, applying for a Social Security number was a complex political act. It was motivated by a compound of interest, obedience, and coercion, this last clarified by a 1936 Treasury regulation making the SSN mandatory for all covered employees, meaning that a worker would not earn credit for paycheck contributions without it and that employers were responsible for registering the "delinquent employee."[168] Internal Revenue officials immediately began checking lists of taxpayers against income tax records "to limit efforts to escape taxation under the Security Act" and to reach "persons who have failed to register through ignorance."[169] Laggards were also brought to light. It was reported in the summer of 1937, for instance, that Mayor William B. Hartsfield of Atlanta, up to that point negligent in filing his Social Security application, had finally gotten on board. In this fashion, he "became a number just like all other common American citizens." The article that reported this detail also matter-of-factly published his number: 252–12–4939.[170] Before May 1937, when the question was settled by the Supreme Court, mentions of some employers and workers inscribing "under protest" on their registration cards in order "to note a belief that the act might be declared unconstitutional" suggest some citizens' attempt at resistance even while technically complying.[171]

There was also the important fact that having a number made one's working life easier. Works Progress Administration workers—not initially assigned SSNs because they were on the public payroll—reported by early 1937 being "handicapped in getting private employment for want of a Social Security account number," citing the hassle its absence caused for employers.[172] Others made the same complaint. As the *Washington Post* reported it, "The advantage of a social security number is already being felt in the employment field. If six men are lined up for a job and the first five do not have social security cards, the job probably will go to the last one."[173] A worker already in possession of an SSN saved the employer from the burden of paperwork; it was also proof that the man had already held down a job. The lack of a number could bring troubles in an "organized society." One critique of this state of affairs, embedded in a story about a jailed youth earnestly trying to "go straight," predicted that the boy's biggest problem would be landing a paid position, given his lack of documentation: "There's a little thing called a Social Security number that's going to pin him down."[174]

These concerns about numbering the population were practical: matters of paperwork and convenience. Others were more philosophical. Beginning in 1936, there were critics of the new bureaucratic apparatus and what it seemed to imply about the contracting realm of freedom in modern life. Aware of the SSB's carefully chosen language to refer to enumeration, *Time* magazine explained as the enrollment effort began that "each employe [*sic*] will be issued a numbered identification card. Not tags (they have no strings) nor discs (they are not round), these cards will bear a triple hyphenated number." Not so reassuringly, it added, "Lest workers feel they are being numbered like convicts, each number is called an 'Account Number.'"[175] Fears of regimentation were not a mere phantasm of the Republican National Committee. In one columnist's telling, "the only difference" between a Social Security account holder and "the boys at the federal prison is that he has to buy his own clothes and meals, pay rent and doctor bills."[176]

Such complaints were often coupled with nostalgic reflections about a bygone era when "you could get yourself a job, at least, without the necessity of registering with the government and being assigned a 'Social Security' number."[177] Referring to the draft in 1940, the *New York Times* mused that "we are a much more registered and classified people than we were in 1917. Most of us have a social security number."[178] Earlier that year, an editorialist judged the arrival of SSNs a sign that "maybe liberty is shrinking" in the United States. "When father was a boy, he needed neither union card nor social security number to get a job. And when he took his girl riding of a Sunday afternoon, he didn't have to hold a driver's license to navigate the horse and buggy."[179] In the same vein a commencement address at the University of Chicago implored graduates to seek "high adventure" rather than the security planned out for them by "Washington bureaucrats." Envisioning a world in which SSNs were embossed on college diplomas, the speaker made the number the proxy for enfeebling dependence on the state.[180]

Others, sometimes humorously and sometimes with more bite, wondered if the advent of state identification numbers meant that Americans had relinquished their individual, private selves. One 1936 cartoon pictured Uncle Sam asking a U.S. citizen, "What did you say your name is?" and the man offering up only his nine-digit number.[181] The Santa Fe *New Mexican*, which had supported the Republicans in the 1936 election, afterward made its political stance clear by identifying the editor and each of its reporters by SSN rather than name in their bylines.[182] In a 1943 letter to the *Chicago Daily Tribune,* a man reflected on Republicans' initial opposition to Social Security. Their charge that "your social security number would very soon become your identification and that your name would be of secondary importance" had in his view come to pass. "Today 75 per cent of an employee's employment papers must carry his or her social security number. . . . You will also find a space for it in Uncle Sam's income tax form. Who said it would never become your identification? It is unlike the dog tag only in that it not only goes with you but often precedes you in your travel. Call the sexton and have grave prepared for social security No._____."[183]

Yet, some had always hoped for just such a universal identifying mechanism. This was the other side of the debate about regimentation. Its advocates made their case less loudly than those locked in partisan battles over the scope of the state, but they were insistent about the benefits of an easily identified populace. Officials at the Census Bureau in 1936, for example, looked forward to the day that birth and death registrations would be merged with the files in the Social Security system. Others saw in the creation of the new federal agency a step toward the "ultimate acceptance of universal registration."[184] Proponents in Congress drafted a bill calling for universal fingerprinting in 1940, as well as a Citizens Identification Act in 1943.[185] In the immediate postwar years, there were renewed proposals for such a scheme. The Council on Vital Records and Vital Statistics proposed a "fixed identity number" that could link individual records, arguing that the wartime experience had revealed the "growing need for such a number-name for each individual in the United States." Not surprisingly, it turned to the Social Security Administration in hopes of creating such a system.[186] Some military advisors chimed in on the advantages of universal legibility. The assistant secretary of defense, for example, in 1955 proposed that all citizens "have their blood type tattooed on their bodies in anticipation of a military attack."[187]

Although none of these plans came to pass, the specter of a national identification system always accompanied the Social Security number, for good or for ill. A reader of the *Los Angeles Times,* for example, viewed the 1947 Vital Records plan for enumeration from birth as collapsing the "last flimsy barrier between our already overorganized life and outright regimentation."[188] For him, Social Security was a key culprit. Posing as an "old-fashioned individualist," he praised the fact that one could as yet evade Social Security's bookkeepers by remaining outside the program's bounds. After all, "anyone who feels strongly enough about it can divorce himself from it, one way or another," for example by refusing to work in one of the covered occupations. It was still theoretically possible to escape the eye of the state, despite the fact that "nearly everyone, as a potential Selective Service candidate, taxpayer, property owner . . . is on the nation's record books, identified as a resident of a certain State or a certain community." But the writer feared that such "secluded nooks and glades" were vanishing, along with the last vestiges of a "diaphanous bulwark of privacy." For the United States to issue every baby a number—an "innocent, disarming bit of systemization"—was a "bureaucrat's dream." It was to assume godlike powers. And it was, inevitably, to invite more intrusion. "What real true-blue bureaucrat" could possibly resist the temptation to observe, track, and judge a numbered populace?[189] For such observers, SSNs conjured up an overweening identification project, the slippery slope to an all-knowing state.

There were still other ways to look at these numbers, however: less as a grand organizing system or an existential threat than as a personal possession or a claim on national membership. To focus solely on the problems—or even the ambitions—that Social Security numbers summoned up for politicians and planners would be to miss the more mundane but also more surprising ways that they traveled through American culture. What is clear is that the new digits garnered plenty of publicity in their early years. Both their novelty and their instrumental value made them objects of considerable interest. On the eve of the election in 1936 that would decide Social Security's fate, a Colorado editorial reflected, "'What's your number?' may easily become the form of greeting among El Paso county residents after the election Tuesday, the same as it may become the greeting among 26,000,000 million [sic] Americans." Its author paused to underscore this still-unfamiliar fact: "In short, men and women will be numbered in the United States."[190] For many newly numbered citizens, as for this writer, the SSN was first and foremost a curiosity. It was a piece of information that was somehow theirs but also the government's, and which identified them to the Social Security Board but perhaps to others as well.

The SSN for this reason was not an incidental aspect of discussions of the new legislation. Many understood it as the entry point to material rewards—and less concrete but equally significant economic rights. The

SSN was best referred to not as an "account number" but as the "employee's benefit account number," advised Arthur Altmeyer, because this "brings home more forcibly the fact that the card is valuable to the employee in establishing his benefit rights."[191] The Social Security Board was eager to get the first checks in the hands of recipients in 1937 precisely because doing so would "help considerably in efforts to get all the Nation's workers catalogued by number and into the social security files."[192]

This message about the number's benefits came through especially strongly in the black press. There had been strong criticism of the Social Security Act for its exclusion of many African Americans and of the enrollment process for including a racial designation. Nevertheless, Social Security was described in some quarters as "the hope of the Negro in America" and the most critical of the government programs pertaining to African Americans, given its focus on the "economic security of the masses of this country."[193] Readers fortunate enough to be covered by the program were regularly reminded of their right to request a statement of wages reported to the government, what to do if they suspected any errors, and, most importantly, how to proceed if they had lost their number.[194] After the expansion of Social Security's scope in 1939, which extended new benefits of life insurance and "family protection," another cascade of news accounts underlined the number's significance to American workers and their dependents.[195]

The SSN from this angle was a nine-digit claim on equal personhood, especially for those long excluded from that category. It served as proof of one's membership in the national polity and enabled one to lay claims on the state. Given that not all workers were covered and most black workers were not, the SSN could be prized as a badge of a particularly coveted form of economic citizenship. The New York Amsterdam News counseled African American workers: "Do not lose your Social Security number. This number is important. It is important both to you and your government . . . and evidence of your rights under this law."[196] News outlets often focused on the number as the tangible sign of and means to social protection.[197] In this light, the SSN could appear less like an identifier useful to the state and more like an entitlement to be jealously guarded by the holder. Certainly, many working-class Americans saw it this way. In the words of a 1937 essay in American Labor World, "probably second in importance only to 'your daily bread,' in the lives of working men and women in New York State is the individual possession of a Social Security Account number."[198] Never simply a means of tracking citizens, the SSN—by re-mapping the population via exclusions and benefits—helped to produce a specific kind of national citizenship, one that carried substantive privileges. If "seeing like a state" could reduce and simplify, it could also shore up individual rights and dignity.

Working Americans were therefore urged to hold tight to their number and to remember it. Account holders seemed to take this responsibility se-riously. Scattered reports suggest that mastering the new system included committing the nine-digit number to memory, so that the bearer would be prepared when asked for it by an employer. This was a discipline that individuals may not have had cause to develop before 1936, except perhaps in the case of a telephone number, a military service number, or automo-bile license.[199] Reflecting a society in which both identity and benefits were increasingly fastened to numbers, various authorities offered tips for keeping them in order. In an article aimed at veterans, the author asked, "What is your serial or service number, ex-service folks? If you've been out of the service for as much as six months, I'll bet you had a tough time trying to remember that old number you knew so well." He urged ser-vicemen to make a record of it, along with "your disability claim number. . . . And, for luck, your Social Security number. All of these num-bers are likely to be needed one of these days. So record them."[200] As the North Carolina Employment Security Commission would note by 1941, "Everyone has certainly become familiar with the expression 'my Social Security number is.'"[201] Some Americans complained about being over-documented. But given the inconvenience and distress that came with being undocumented, memorization or careful recording of one's digits became a new task of citizenship and one undertaken without noticeable resentment.

Social Security numbers' arrival in popular culture provides another window onto the ways the new digits were woven into American life. The number cropped up as early as 1937 in a Nancy Drew mystery, *The Whis-pering Statue,* in which the young detective applies for a job at a rare book shop in order to do some sleuthing ("Nancy was fearful that [the shop owner] might ask her for a social security number or other type of identifi-cation but he said nothing about it and she bubbled eagerly, 'How soon may I start?'"[202]). Hollywood heroines paid it tribute: "Well, I still have my social security number," exclaimed one in 1939 when all else seemed lost. As one commentator observed, "The audience smiled in comprehension"—noting that "in all probability at least one-third of that movie audience" was also in possession of an SSN.[203] Adding glamour to the number were reports in 1939 that actress Bette Davis wore a gold link bracelet bearing hers and in 1940 that film star Lana Turner's "favorite wedding present from husband Artie Shaw is her social security number—in diamonds!"[204]

A thicker sense of what the new numbers were coming to mean can be glimpsed in the curious commercial bonanza that followed the passage of the Social Security Act. A host of businesses cropped up in the mid- to late 1930s to offer, for a small fee, protection or security for one's SSN. This was not security in the sense we might imagine it today: that is, blocking the number from public view. Rather, it was security in the form of preserving the account number for its holder, given that the official card was made of nothing more than paper, and liable to wear and tear.[205] The Republican leadership had whipped up partisan fervor in 1936 by predicting that the Social Security Act would result in state-mandated "dog tags." In the years to follow, such tags would become a reality—but not because the federal government had issued any. Instead, canny entrepreneurs responded to a ready private market for them.

"Is the Card bearing your Permanent Social Security Number torn, smeared, perhaps already Worn Out?—If Not, In Time It Will Be!," advertised one such outfit in 1937 in the AFL-CIO's journal, *American Federationist*. The solution was a nickel-silver badge that "would not rust or tarnish."[206] The *Chicago Defender* similarly offered to its African American readership a "lifetime" bronze plate, "lasting" as well as "beautiful and serviceable," engraved with the Social Security account holder's number.[207] As another *Defender* ad explained, "You know the importance of having your Social Security number handy at all times. You probably are aware that over 50,000 people each month lose trace of their Social Security card either as a result of wearing it out or losing it." Promoted as a form of protection and a gift to its patrons (who were billed only for the cost of shipping and handling), the bronze plate would "not wear out" but serve as an enduring record. Having one's name and SSN stamped "indelibly in the metal" was a kind of insurance for the account holder, who could now avoid being "embarrassed and perhaps hurt financially" by an inability to call up his or her number. The newspaper offered a further service should the etched plate be misplaced: it would keep the individual's SSN on "permanent file" with the engraver.[208]

FREE!   FREE!
A LIFETIME GIFT FOR YOU
Protection For Your SOCIAL SECURITY NUMBER

A BRONZE PLATE OF YOUR OWN

Engraved With
Your Name and
Social Security
Number

COMPLIMENTS OF THE
Chicago Defender
WORLD'S GREATEST WEEKLY
CHICAGO, ILLINOIS
SOCIAL SECURITY
AS REGISTERED WITH U. S. GOVERNMENT
№ *176~96-118*
NAME
Harley Nelson

It's Handy! Serviceable! Convenient!

This beautiful and serviceable SOCIAL SECURITY NUMBER and NAME PLATE illustrated above is convenient in size and made of lasting bronze metal. It can be carried in vest pocket or purse and cannot be misplaced very easily. It is no larger than the government regular card.

ALL YOU DO is clip the coupon appearing below—MAIL OR BRING to The Chicago Defender, with only 10c to cover postage and handling cost, and your plate will be mailed to you direct within the next few days. ADD 5c EXTRA if you wish a genuine leather carrying case.

HURRY! THE SUPPLY IS LIMITED!
MAIL OR BRING THIS COUPON NOW!

SOCIAL SECURITY PLATE
COUPON

THE CHICAGO DEFENDER,
3435 Indiana Avenue,
Chicago, Ill.

GENTLEMEN:
    Please find inclosed herewith 10c to cover cost of handling and mailing my permanent Social Security bronze plate. Please forward plate to:

PRINT YOUR NAME, ADDRESS AND NUMBER PLAINLY.

Name ....

Address ....

Social Security Number ....

Check If
Leather
Case Is
Desired ☐

ANOTHER DEFENDER SERVICE

2.2. Some Americans prized their new Social Security number enough to pay for its preservation in bronze; African Americans in particular treated the number as a badge of economic citizenship.

Commercial outfits sought to capitalize on the fact that the account cards, devised after much discussion by the early Social Security Board, were surprisingly flimsy, given their evident significance. The products for sale, by contrast, were invariably fashioned of more durable stuff than paper—"lasting bronze metal" complete with a leather carrying case, in one instance—with the spare nine digits embellished or otherwise digni-fied.[209] As such, these goods restored the proper weight and gravitas to a number that represented an individual's ticket to economic rights, whether unemployment insurance or a guaranteed retirement pension. Something as ephemeral as "security," especially future security, perhaps required this sort of palpable proof.

Social Security-themed tokens provided short-term benefits as well. A cottage industry dangled the allure of extra income from selling such items, playing to the demand for supplemental work during the Depres-sion. The Key Tag Specialty Company of New York City, for example, ad-vertised in 1937 "a complete business for twenty dollars" based on a "new social security number specialty."[210] The J. P. Routier Company of Roch-ester similarly offered in 1938 a "lightweight and attractive" chrome-plated identification tag that could be affixed to a key ring after being stamped with one's social security number, auto and operator license numbers, name, and address. The ad urged, "You should have one," but also that the company was seeking independent agents to peddle them.[211] Yet another company in 1939 trumpeted a "rare opportunity for clerks, factory, mill or office workers to earn extra money," namely a 50 percent commission selling "social-security life-time plates and cases." Simply order the neces-sary kits and accessories for making patriotic red, white, and blue metal plates emblazoned with a worker's name and Social Security number, and the seller could count on earning "$35 a Week or More at Home. . . . In Spare Time!" (with a "big profit on each sale"). Even during the Depres-sion, the pitch suggested, this was an item that "sells on sight to working people everywhere."[212] Ads selling a piece of such businesses—in Wichita Falls, Texas, in Lansing, Michigan, and in Baltimore, Maryland—testify to a going market in SSN keepsakes.[213] These outfits banked on the no-tion that, far from rejecting identification numbers, Americans would pay for the privilege of protecting them.

Browse the advertising pages of any number of newspapers or middle-brow journals from the later 1930s or early 1940s and such items appear. Products appearing in *Popular Mechanics* in August 1938 included one's

"Social Security account number engraved and enameled on [a] beautiful brass key ring tag" (the ad continued, "Send 25c coin with security number for sample").[214] The *Atlanta Constitution* ran an ad for one's "Social Security Record made permanent" on a solid bronze plate, guaranteeing that "Your name and Social Security number" could be "pressed into metal forever" for as little as nine cents.[215] In 1942, *The Billboard*—the "World's Foremost Amusement Weekly"—similarly advertised for $1.98 a high-quality black calfskin billfold, with one's name, "lodge emblem," army or navy insignia, and address, as well as one's Social Security number "Engraved in Gold ABSOLUTELY FREE!" (the ad mentions four pockets, "each protected by celluloid to prevent the soiling of your valuable membership and credit cards"). Sweetening the deal was a bonus gift: a "beautiful three-color life-time Identification Plate" that "carries your full name, address and social security or draft number exactly the way you want it." Pitched to consumers during wartime, alongside Hitler pincushions, "victory heat pads," and military banners, the SSN here took on additional connotations of patriotism and civic inclusion—a badge of national belonging to be proudly presented alongside one's service number.[216]

Commodification of the Social Security number was linked to the new problem Americans were faced with after 1936: how to remember one's digits. Inscribing one's SSN on a luggage tag or wallet (if not a frosted bronze plate) was arguably just a mechanism for recalling the number without having to depend on an easily misplaced card or one's own memory. Accounts of Americans recording their Social Security numbers on their dentures attest rather startlingly to this need. An Omaha man, "reporting in for his disabilities pension check" in 1950, simply removed his "upper plate, where he had had the number engraved."[217] A Minnesota man likewise had his SSN "imprinted on his lower denture . . . so he will always have it handy."[218] The difficulties that many Americans had experienced producing proof of age in connection with the World War I draft—or even in their application for a Social Security account—may explain why these individuals were so eager to have their SSN close at hand. In an age increasingly reliant on documentation, having immediate access to proof of one's identity or eligibility to work may have been a source of comfort if also a subtle marker of coercion.[219]

But other products and rhetorical uses of the SSN argue for more expansive meanings. What to make, for example, of women's fashion billed as the height of "Social Security Style"? A 1942 piece that ran in the *Los*

Angeles Times described a jersey shirtwaist dress, "suitable for the career woman," in exactly this way. It opened with this text: "Are you supporting yourself? Do you have locked in your purse a social security number? Do you spend your daytime hours in an office?" If so, "you're in the market for today's career woman dress . . . designed especially for the business woman."[220] As scholars of gender and the welfare state have documented, much New Deal legislation presumed a masculine labor force, with women as dependent or at best irregular workers.[221] In this light, possessing a Social Security number was a proxy for female economic independence. Already in 1937, women of means could purchase a "tiny gold wafer, to wear on your charm-bracelet," embossed with their Social Security number. This product was advertised as "a new species of identification-disk" that would mark the wearer as an "honest working-girl," as well as settle "all questions about where—and what—that number is."[222] If, fearing political fallout, the Social Security Board had shied away from issuing such disks, department stores would not. Merchandisers, employing a familiar rhetoric of self-fashioning to sell customers goods, clearly understood the SSN as a signifier with resonance for the modern working woman.

And what of "the latest in Rings," advertised in 1938 for $3.95? This was a sterling silver ring, engraved with the wearer's Social Security number and embedded with his or her birthstone. "The S. A. Meyer Company offers them first . . . on easy terms with weeks to pay." Perhaps such jewelry was intended to help people remember their numbers. It seems more likely, however, that "a really *personalized* ring for men and women," as the manufacturer put it, held a different appeal, identifying its wearer willingly and even proudly.[223] In ways difficult to perceive now, a number could individualize, signifying the uniqueness of its bearer. Rings and other items "personalized" by an SSN suggest that some Americans were taking intimate ownership of what in another guise was a bureaucratic tag.

Most striking of all, however, were those who sought a more permanent bond to their nine-digit number by inking it on their bodies. Scholars of tattoos note that they have "long been a way to mark one's membership in a group" and to "signal belonging."[224] Dorothea Lange's iconic 1939 photograph of an unemployed lumber worker in Oregon, a Social Security account number imprinted on his bicep, prompts a question: Could a tattoo express a vital stake in the welfare state, a claim on what were still only

2.3. Jewelry "personalized" with one's Social Security number suggests the ways Americans made the number their own.

future "earned benefits"—and perhaps the bureaucratic project of visible citizenship itself?[225]

Whether because they affirmed inclusion in a munificent nation or simply the pressing need to recall those nine digits, Social Security numbers appeared on American bodies in this era more often than we might expect. SSNs were in fact widely thought to be behind the uptick in business for tattoo parlors in the 1930s, the *New York Times* declaring that, in the wake of the Social Security Act, "entire new industries" in card frames but also tattooing had been created.[226] "Sailors, stevedores and sideshow freaks no longer have a corner on the tattoo market," announced the *Washington Post*: "social security numbers have changed all that."[227] An observer at the *Nation's Business* agreed that tattooing was experiencing "a boom," in part because it was "quite the fashion for the safe carrying of your Social Security number."[228] A practitioner confided on a radio show that he was getting "a lot of calls . . . from customers who want to have their serial numbers stenciled on their chests."[229] Confirming reports came from both coasts. Mildred Hull, a former burlesque dancer turned tattoo artist who set up shop in New York in the 1920s, found that although her business lagged during the Depression, it "picked up again in the late 30s thanks to FDR." She credited the president with supplying her "10 customers a day."[230] Two tattoo artists working in Portland, Oregon, in the early 1940s likewise reported that their business had "practically doubled since the issue of Social Security numbers."[231] Capitalizing on the trend, one proprietor advertised his wares with a simple, hand-lettered directive: "Don't Forget Your Number. Have it Tattooed on Now."[232]

Accounts that circulated in the second half of the 1930s and early 1940s clearly indicate that the practice of tattooing SSNs—if by no means common—was not unknown. *The Atlanta Constitution* reported in 1939, for instance, that a receptionist in a public employment office was startled to have a "neatly dressed" job seeker of about 30 years old begin to strip off his shirt when asked for his Social Security number. "Already reddening profusely, the startled Miss Bledsoe tried to head him off," but the man replied, "My social security number is tattooed on my back. I was afraid I'd lose it."[233] A "husky applicant for a job" in La Porte, Indiana, responded similarly to a request for his number at a state employment office, "peeling back his jacket and shirt, baring a number tattooed on his chest."[234] *Popular Science* reported on a New York man who, fearing he would misplace or forget "the number assigned to him by the Government," went ahead and "had the numerals tattooed on his forearm." As the writer noted, "Now, when he reaches the pension age of sixty-five, he can produce his number merely by rolling up his sleeve."[235] A similarly tattooed man, the chief engineer at a Memphis theater, wasn't "taking any chances on losing his social security number."[236] A like-minded Broadway showgirl was photographed in the process of having her number imprinted on her knee.[237]

Other, more mute, evidence comes from instances of individuals easily identified after their death because of an inked SSN: a Lake Worth, Florida, musician, for example, who fell or jumped to his death in the summer of 1943; and a Washington, DC, man, whose heavily tattooed body bore the name "Agnes" on his left arm and the number 579–09–3713 on his left leg.[238]

Treated as quirky rather than offensive, such reports of identification numbers printed on the body suggest a sensibility not yet shaped by images of concentration camp victims or other totalitarian visions.[239] They signal, instead, a society coming to terms with the need for, or at least the fact of, documented identities. And they reveal in some Americans a surprising willingness to be numbered and stamped, to be made visible to the administrative state. SSNs undoubtedly meant different things to different bearers of those digits. And surely many citizens thought little about them, if at all. As Social Security numbers became yet another new bureaucratic requirement in the 1930s and 1940s, they were likely most typically regarded as a necessary feature of modern life, the price of admission for a guaranteed check in retirement.[240] But when emblazoned on a chrome plate, a pocket token, a watch, a ring, or a bicep, the SSN signified something more: not merely an identity document but a positive identification with one's status as a known citizen.

The SSN, although just a number, could be much more than that. It could stand in for the Social Security program, the nation that had enacted it, or a particular individual's affinity with either. It is impossible to know how many Americans engraved or displayed their own numbers, but it is clear that numbering—and legibility to the government—could have its rewards. As a Census Bureau official noted in 1940, "Each step we take toward the goal of social and economic security for everyone makes more precious each individual's proof of his rights to such benefits."[241] For citizens of the twenty-first century, who often think first of the SSN as a risk to their privacy, to imagine a Social Security number as a "precious" proof of rights requires some rejiggering of assumptions. Looking back to the social and political circumstances of the 1930s and 1940s, we realize that the embrace of one's bureaucratic ID expressed an anxiety now difficult to summon up: the fear, in an age of increased social provision, of being *unidentifiable*. Being a known citizen in that era raised alarms about the tentacles of the state reaching more deeply into the personal affairs of the populace. But being an unknown one could provoke even greater concern.

Thus did a piece of data that Americans now treat as one of the most private facts about themselves start out as a visible and tangible part of public culture. The proud claiming of a Social Security number, a mechanism of the expanding welfare state, reveals how intelligibility to the government, and bureaucratic tracking itself, could be regarded as a beneficent technology of citizenship. In years of crisis and war, questions of individual privacy could perhaps take a back seat to the urgent projects of economic security and national solidarity. As they encountered a still more knowing state in the postwar era, however, citizens' assessment of the state of their personal data—and of the Social Security number itself—would shift. Only then would an item that many Americans had once literally burnished and broadcast become something they carefully concealed.

3

The Porous Psyche

Brain watching . . . has made your mind, inner thoughts, political opinions, frustrations (including the sexual), aspirations—what we commonly call *personality*—the raw material of a humming, seemingly insatiable American industry.

—MARTIN GROSS, *The Brain Watchers*, 1962

In 1958, with Joseph McCarthy's red-baiting a fresh memory, the political journalist and former Communist sympathizer Richard Rovere reflected on the state of his fellow citizens' privacy. In a wide-ranging essay for the *American Scholar*, Rovere called attention to wiretapping, bugging, and uses of state power that accompanied an age of heightened national security. But he also cataloged a surprisingly varied and seemingly more trivial set of intrusions to which Americans were subject: television cameras that tracked shoppers in grocery stores; on-the-job inquiries into employees' drinking habits; the prying of behavioral scientists but also of neighbors; the work of professional social workers as well as volunteer organizations; even the sights and sounds of passersby. Invoking Louis Brandeis, both his 1890 essay and his dissent in the 1928 wiretapping case, Rovere called the "right to be let alone" unique in that "it can be denied us by the powerless as well as by the powerful—by a teen-ager with a portable radio as well as by a servant of the law armed with a subpoena."

Rovere reflected that the latter, official kind of privacy violation might well be reined in by legislation or public policy. But the other sort was more nettlesome, tied as it was to "the growing size and complexity of our society" and involving rights of speech, press, and inquiry. Even if legal abuses—easy to conjure up in 1958—were curbed, it would leave "all those invasions that are the work not of the police power, but of other public authorities and of a multitude of private ones." What exactly was the nature of these "private" invasions? Rovere ticked off an illustrative list: "A newspaper reporter asks an impertinent personal question; the prospective employer of a friend wishes to know whether the friend has a happy sex life; a motivational researcher wishes to know what we have against Brand X deodorant; a magazine wishing to lure more advertisers asks us to fill out a questionnaire on our social, financial and intellectual status." Transgressions of the intimate realm, that is, were as much the work of the society and the citizenry as the state. Far from trivial, the persistent prying of a knowing society profoundly shaped the degree to which individuals could move through that society undisturbed and undisclosed. Rovere concluded, "My privacy can be invaded by a ringing telephone as well as by a tapped one. It can be invaded by an insistent community that seeks to shame me into getting up off my haunches to do something for the P.T.A. or town improvement or the American Civil Liberties Union." The right to be let alone, he declared, "is a right I may cherish and from time to time invoke, but it is not a right favored by the conditions of the life I lead."[1] That the ACLU, the leading defender of civil liberties in the United States, appeared on this list indicates just how all-encompassing the invasions of citizens' solitude could appear by the late 1950s.

Rovere's meditations capture a paradox of the early Cold War era. Potential threats to citizens' privacy from the national security state, in construction since the turn of the century and fortified by military conflicts around the globe, were real and well known. The tools of espionage and surveillance that Woodrow Wilson had seized during World War I were now state of the art, a "sub rosa matrix that honeycombed U.S. society with active informers, secretive civilian organizations, and government counterintelligence agencies."[2] A new kind of twilight conflict with the Soviet Union, coming immediately on the heels of World War II, meant that the nation remained, seemingly permanently, poised for war.[3] The "culture of secrecy" that developed on both sides of the superpower divide altered the relationship of the U.S. government to its own people.[4] Although the state kept more secrets in this era than in the past—cloaking a range of national security actions, including the atomic weapons program—it increasingly distrusted them in its citizens.[5] As had been the case in Wilson's day, vigilance in protecting a "free society" was turned inward as well as outward. By the 1950s, the House Un-American Activities Committee hearings, federal and state loyalty programs, the Smith and McCarran Internal Security Acts, the tapping of citizens' phones, and extensive FBI dossier keeping were ample evidence of a government empowered to conduct domestic surveillance.[6] Authorities' attempt to root out subversives affected the personal and professional lives of suspected Communists, but also of progressives, labor union members, sexual minorities, and civil rights activists, along with their families and associates.[7]

Arguably, the perils posed to individual privacy by the U.S. state and its agencies ought to have overshadowed all others. Yet the focus of much public commentary was elsewhere. A vocal segment of the population turned its attention instead to the subtle pressures on the person flowing from modern social organization and, indeed, the surrounding culture itself: "policemen" to be sure, but also "prying acquaintances, sociological field workers, and psychoanalysts."[8] For these observers, the imagined threat to citizens' sovereignty and solitude was neither the Cold War enemy nor the domestic state forged in its image. It was, rather, dominant American values and modes of living. And it brought into focus a host of daily trespasses by private citizens—whether marketers, teachers, employers, or neighbors. Together, they comprised, in critic Myron Brenton's memorable phrase, "Big Brother in his civilian clothes."[9]

Why, in an age of alarming infringements on civil liberties, should so many have worried about matters as mundane as a ringing telephone, an "impertinent" question on a job application, or an "insistent community"? Certainly, government surveillance, if more visible than it had been in earlier decades, was simultaneously more difficult to challenge in the cautious political climate of the 1950s. Too, most citizens did not consider themselves to be direct targets of national security measures and, as a consequence, worried little about their implications. More critical than either of these factors, however, was what was experienced as a sea change in the prospects for personal autonomy in the decades following World War II. Citizens' entanglement with the institutions, gatekeepers, and norms of their society seemed indicative of a peculiarly modern form of unfreedom—a coercion that flowed as much from the encouraging tones of experts as the explicit control of official authorities.

Across the decade of the 1950s and into the first half of the 1960s in the United States, we can track a blossoming concern with the vanishing boundary between the self and the social world. It was a concern at once abstract and palpable, hard to pin down yet clearly felt. Social critics may have spied it first, but other Americans identified it in their own fashion. Whereas public discussions about privacy had up to that point focused on those prying into citizens' *affairs*, in the 1950s they fastened on probes into the personal *interior*: the mind, emotions, thoughts, and psyche. This was not the late nineteenth-century concern about damage to reputation or even to "personality." Nor was it a concern about the state administering the outer traces of individual identity, as in earlier twentieth-century controversies over fingerprinting and numbering. The puzzle of postwar privacy, as well as Cold War-era individualism, was that the person herself seemed porous, her perimeter unfixed, her very being improperly inhabited by the larger society. This was a new stage in Americans' thinking about the known citizen, and it would make something akin to psychological privacy both an urgent problem and an elusive goal.

Incursions into the Interior

Threats to the "inviolate personality" had of course been the catalyst for modern privacy claims. The actions of intrusive journalists, advertisers, and photographers in the late nineteenth century were not, however, imagined actually to infiltrate that personality or to be capable of invading one's psyche. Brandeis would later speculate that "advances in psychic and related sciences may bring means of exploring unexpressed beliefs, thoughts and emotions."[10] But this was not a live fear for Americans until the mid-twentieth century, when suddenly, it seemed, a host of parties sought to know citizens more thoroughly, inside and out, both for their own benefit and the good of the society. Loyalty boards—the infamous House Un-American Activities Committee (HUAC) and its state-level analogues—were the most prominent of these, their probes into citizens' associations, beliefs, and histories attracting wide publicity. But the same impulse stimulated the growth of psychoanalysis, aptitude and personality testing, and motivational research in the postwar period. These practices did not simply attempt to render individuals intelligible; they attempted to get inside people's heads. Citizens too sought a deeper knowledge of their psychological interiors in this era. But the prospect of one's "inviolate personality" being tested, dissected, and revealed by an outside party could be unnerving. As such, the postwar person faced invasions right at the core of the self.

The incursions of a yet-more-knowing society accumulated in disparate precincts of American life during the late 1940s and 1950s. Only at the close of this period would they add up to a clear consensus of privacy imperiled. Complicating and perhaps delaying this analysis was the fact that citizens had themselves invited the intruders in. Postwar practices in business management and residential building, in selling goods and schooling children, hinged on more intense scrutiny of citizens' values, beliefs, and behaviors. Yet—typically framed as benefiting consumers or employers or parents—they were installed without much public notice or protest. Likewise, middle-class Americans by the 1950s avidly pursued self-knowledge through therapy sessions and advice columns. Only gradually did they come to worry about the use of such material in others' hands, grasping that psychological inquiry could be a route both for discovering the self and for infringing on it. One critic posed this as the chief dilemma of the "modern man," a figure who allegedly thrilled to scientific "probes into the mind," yet also resented them in the name of "his own little-remaining privacy."[11]

A quickening sensibility around psychological privacy has been difficult to recognize due to the strong Cold War frame that dominates characterizations of the era. The postwar United States has been portrayed as indelibly imprinted by the gloomy geopolitics of the day, suffused by atomic fear and anticommunist hysteria.[12] Its political culture has, perhaps too easily, been depicted as a hothouse of conformity, generated on the one hand by the Soviet threat and on the other by the strictures of the homegrown security state. Backyard fallout shelters and civilian defense measures, anti-fluoridation campaigns and renewed investments in the nuclear family, have all been treated as displacements of the superpower struggle.[13] This has not left much room for the political and even philosophical questions that citizens posed, more insistently as the years passed, about the nature of their "interior" privacy.

Certainly, the terms of the Cold War surfaced regularly in postwar public life. The geopolitical struggle animated partisan logics, nurturing postwar conservatism and centrist liberalism. Yet historians have perhaps overstated the centrality of totalitarianism, the Soviet enemy, and even Communist subversion to public consciousness. Contemporary sociologist Samuel Stouffer instead emphasized how remote these issues were to the lives of most Americans. "The internal Communist threat," he explained, "is not directly felt as personal. It is something one reads about and talks about and even sometimes gets angry about." But he dismissed as "nonsense" the "picture of the average American as a person with the jitters, trembling lest he find a Red under the bed." Stouffer's detailed examination of a national cross-section of respondents, conducted at the height of the

Red Scare in 1954, could not contain its surprise at how little Americans took Cold War concerns as their own "in spite of all the headlines and radio and television stimuli." Published the following year, his *Communism, Conformity, and Civil Liberties* found that, unlike elite opinion leaders, the fraction of ordinary citizens voicing distress about the Communist threat was, "even by the most generous interpretation of occasionally ambiguous responses, *less than 1%!*"[14]

Even if Stouffer seriously underestimated or missed Americans' unarticulated fears about Communism, it is fair to say that the issues that preoccupied postwar foreign policy elites, pundits, and politicians were not uppermost on the minds of most citizens. Still, the Cold War helped give words to citizens' quite personal disquiet about their own society and the place of the private person in it. In official understandings, after all, the United States and the Soviet bloc were not simply enemies but polar opposites, with one of the primary points of contrast the value placed on privacy. Unlike Soviet citizens, Americans were known to honor the private sphere. This was the foundation of their rights as liberal-democratic subjects and a domain where the government, theoretically anyway, did not reach. The sovereignty of the private home and the belief that the individual citizen stood apart from, and before, the state were founding orthodoxies. Communists, by contrast, were thought to sacrifice their personal lives and their "most private selves" to "party discipline, including their decisions about love and marriage, childbearing and child rearing."[15] Already infiltrated by the state, Soviet citizens possessed no separate, inner, private realm to speak of.[16]

Yet, by the mid-1950s, a certain isomorphism between the contemporary United States and USSR informed many discussions of American society, with life in the Soviet Union regularly invoked as a mirror to developments at home. The effect sometimes was to sharpen the contrast. At other times a surprising commonality between "us" and the enemy gestured to parallel forces at work in the two societies.[17] Some operated at the level of the state—and pointed directly to the links between a knowing society and an authoritarian one. From the vantage point of those charged with the nation's security, the risks inherent in A-bombs and subversive activity explained the need to know, test, and vet people as thoroughly as possible. But the inquisitorial procedures of the House Un-American Activities Committee, the use of political informants, the state controls over information and the press, and the policing of dissent, all in the name of staunching the Communist threat, led some to ask: Was the United States approximating its totalitarian foe in the effort to contain it? As the Republican senator John Bricker put it, "I cannot believe that the road to freedom is one which requires us to adopt the methods of our potential enemies."[18] Similar sorts of blurring could be found in the daily "conditions of life," to borrow Rovere's phrase: the felt lack of privacy from one's fellow countrymen on both sides of the Iron Curtain, as well as the discomfitingly similar techniques of the Communist "brainwasher" and the Madison Avenue "persuader." As such, heavily freighted geopolitical categories helped to pinpoint unease with developments reshaping postwar America.

A knowing society provoked this unease even as it ministered to it. The proceedings of loyalty boards ran roughshod over some citizens' liberties in order to reassure others that they were safe and secure. The powerful norms of middle-class suburban and corporate life offered guidance and belonging to those willing to live by them, but punished non-conformists. The interventions of experts in the applied human sciences were welcomed by some and considered harmful meddling by others. All of these developments raised questions about the proper boundary between the private citizen and the surrounding culture. Together, they undercut prized assumptions about the space for freely chosen action in American life. Soviet citizens, in thrall to ideology or state socialism, were thought to have forfeited this space, whether willingly or unwillingly. Americans appeared to be trading it away unthinkingly, ceding precious dimensions of their private existence for the sake of individual comfort and security—or, put more generously, economic and social progress.

Underlying this concern about the collapsing border between self and society was the intimate entwining of psychological discourse and public culture at mid-century, what one scholar calls a "watershed in the history of the exposure of Americans to psychological practice."[19] Psychologists had been recruited into the war effort in large numbers, and their confident advance out of the clinic continued during the Cold War. The rising star of the behavioral sciences was apparent in the military funding for studies of hypnosis and interpersonal influence, as well as the techniques of counterinsurgency and psy-ops.[20] But psychology's applications extended far beyond statecraft. With the passage of the National Mental Health Act of 1946 and individual therapy reaching new heights of popularity in the mid-1950s, its explanatory capacity was expanding dramatically.[21] Therapeutic language coursed through public culture, even giving a name to the era. The "Age of Anxiety" was both the title that W. H. Auden gave to a book-length poem published in 1947 and a phrase that the historian Arthur Schlesinger used to title the first chapter of his defense of New Deal-style liberalism in an age of communism and fascism, *The Vital Center* (1949).[22] Psychological frameworks were energetically applied to problems ranging from the persistence of racism to the roots of McCarthyism. Behavioral scientists' embrace of psychoanalysis and the unconscious "as a tool for deciphering political behavior" meant that Communist Party membership could itself be figured as a mental disorder, as were garden-variety forms of political dissent.[23]

A host of professionals wielding expertise in human behavior and motivation were the tangible sign of this new order: psychotherapists and psychologists, but also marketers, advertisers, motivational researchers, corporate managers, personnel officers, school counselors, and personality testers. Formally trained in psychological science or not, they borrowed liberally from its insights. So did their clients and consumers. Despite its reliance on intimate intrusions, psychological expertise was not an unwelcome intruder in the postwar United States. On the contrary, middle-class Americans in the 1950s sought out psychological self-knowledge in great numbers, divulging their anxieties and their secrets to marriage counselors and psychotherapists. Those undergoing new techniques of family therapy allowed experts into their most private relationships, some even via one-way mirrors or filmed observation.[24] Major newspapers discovered that advice columns with titles like "The Worry Clinic" and "Let's Explore Your Mind" were indispensable to circulation, propelling a small industry of 10- to 15-cent self-help pamphlets.[25] Citizens conversed in a newfound psychological key, influenced by popular Freudian thought that treated self-disclosure as an important pathway to self-knowledge.[26]

Even this, perhaps, understates the extent to which psychological practices had permeated American culture by mid-century. *Life* magazine could proclaim in a new series of 1957 that U.S. citizens lived—willingly, it seemed—in "the Age of Psychology," the "science of human behavior" having thoroughly revolutionized daily life. As its first installment had it, psychological insights now informed the magazine advertisements and road signs people saw, the advice on family and marital relations they imbibed, the decisions corporations made, the evaluations school counselors issued, and even the news stories journalists chose to broadcast.

Although psychologists had once been interested primarily in building their apparatus of facts and theories, the *Life* essay claimed, the majority now attempted to apply their knowledge "to help people live happier and more efficient lives." Fully half of the 16,000 members of the American Psychological Association, the author noted, had moved out of teaching and into other realms: "as personnel men and efficiency experts for industry; as vocational counselors in colleges, the Veterans Administration and the U.S. Employment Service; as designers of tests for the Army; as counselors on children's problems in public and private schools; as pollsters of public opinion."[27]

This burgeoning corps of professionals was widely seen as a response to the "stresses placed upon the individual in an industrialized, urban environment."[28] The conjunction of expansive psychological expertise and national security imperatives in the postwar decades would however reinvigorate and politicize public debates about the known citizen. Mentally and emotionally secure individuals, some argued, were the building blocks of a democratic society, and therefore of central interest to the state.[29] Private selves might properly be public concerns. But heightened devotion to the psychological self also led to efforts to identify the conditions supporting its healthy development. As historian Jamie Cohen-Cole has shown, expert prescriptions about the importance of tolerance, autonomy, and creativity came to constitute the ideal citizen and modal American in this period.[30] This raised the stakes on the matter of psychological freedom. State or societal forces that impinged on that freedom—including attempts to know or sway the inner person—could come in for fierce condemnation as undemocratic, even totalitarian, in these years. Official propaganda and subtle social norms could both be reimagined as trespassing on an invisible yet essential personal boundary.

As citizens took up questions of internal freedom and psychic privacy, they turned their attention to an unlikely set of Cold War invaders: those modern experts who had aided and abetted the growth of a knowing society. The new status of the psychological sciences in American life, many recognized, could both reinforce and undermine individuality. What implicated its experts in debates over the boundaries of privacy was their capacious sense of what was knowable about the person, as well as what might be done with that knowledge. Whether in the pursuit of science, schooling, or sales, professionals in diverse fields claimed new efficacy in locating inner truths. Insofar as those truths called for interventions—and they generally did—expert knowledge about human motivation and be-havior embedded itself in far-flung corners of postwar society. Citizens who actively contemplated their communities, their workplaces, their schools, and even their leisure time noticed the novel ways that scientific techniques and professional authority were being brought to bear on daily life. As they did, they discovered fresh dangers in old practices: the selling of products but also the assessment of schoolchildren and the conduct of social research. By the 1960s, "psychological surveillance" or "psycholog-ical espionage" was a live category, encompassing activities as disparate as market research, personality tests, lie detectors, opinion polling, sublim-inal suggestion, truth drugs, polygraphs, and "brain signal reading," as well as "telemetry" and "mind control." Others placed psychiatric evaluations and psychoanalysis itself in this category.[31]

The culture of experts and American society itself seemed to press more heavily on the person in the postwar years, at once knowing more and demanding more of the individual. Citizens' qualms about this state of affairs—and in some cases, their resistance to it—accelerated between the close of World War II and the dawn of the 1960s. They occasionally lodged their complaints in a Cold War syntax, through charges of a creeping American-style totalitarianism. But more frequently, they articulated the dilemmas of their social order, both its norms and its knowingness, in the language of privacy. The new premium placed on psychological knowl-edge by society and citizen alike was at the root of this debate. It explains why a personality test could be as worrisome as communist intrigue, the vigilance of neighbors as unsettling as that of the national security state. Public concern about interiors breached—domestic spaces but also in-dividual minds or psyches—was pervasive by the later 1950s. To grasp its contours requires a tour of the postwar middle-class world: the suburban home, the consumer marketplace, the public school, and the white-collar workplace.

Through the Picture Window

The outrages committed under the watch of legitimate governments during World War II virtually ensured that the private sphere would become a dominant concern of modern publics. George Orwell's novel *Nineteen Eighty-Four*, published in 1949, supplied the imagery: Big Brother, the all-seeing eye of a totalitarian state, bent on obliterating the spaces for individual freedom and conscience.[32] Where to seek cover from an overweening state and society? The place that many looked to first in the postwar era was that old redoubt, the single-family home.

In the postwar years, Hannah Arendt, the German emigré author of *The Origins of Totalitarianism*, located freedom in exactly this form. "The four walls of one's private property," she wrote, "offer the only reliable hiding place from the common public world, not only from everything that goes on in it but also from its very publicity, from being seen and being heard."[33] That Arendt, a formidable theorist not just of authoritarianism but also of the social invasion of the self, could valorize private property in this fashion perhaps bore the marks of her new homeland. But it was a sensibility that stretched across the industrialized democracies, a response to Hitler's and Mussolini's depredations, as well as the physical dislocations of world war. In West Germany alone, two million homes were destroyed, three million homes were damaged, and three million people made homeless, making "the urgent pursuit of privacy . . . inseparable from the dream of having a home of one's own." Survivors described the Nazi period as a world without privacy—indeed "without walls"—and where "police and militia were seemingly everywhere." The "withdrawal into privacy" afterward, writes historian Paul Betts, was a conscious effort to "reimpose a strict line between self and society."[34] Even those who had not suffered at the hands of dictatorship placed new emphasis on the spaces within modern society that provided shelter from the state. British public housing reformers in these years, for example, underscored citizens' "space rights, including the right to a plot of land."[35]

Americans did not suffer the same deprivations as did other combatants in World War II. Yet they too were "homeward bound" in the postwar years, infusing home ownership with new meaning after years of Depression hardship and wartime constraint.[36] The war had been sold to Americans in part as a battle to protect private interests, most especially the private family.[37] During the early 1940s, advertisers and builders enticed citizens with detailed visions of plans for the modern family home that would be within their grasp once the fighting was over.[38] The importance of a walled-off domestic sphere to American understandings of privacy went much deeper and further than this, however—all the way back to the nation's founding myths. A scholar notes that "one of the most significant though underappreciated points of stability in privacy discourse" in the United States "has been the projection of privacy onto the home."[39] The dynamics of the Cold War era would both nourish and heighten this tendency. Following Arendt into the domestic sanctuary, we can begin to appreciate the ideological significance of the postwar home, as well as emerging fissures in its foundation.

Americans lived in many different kinds of homes at mid-century. But for commentators, the focal point for assessing the quality of private life in these years was a very specific configuration: white, middle-class, owner-occupied suburbia.[40] A number of New Deal programs had already "institutionalized the suburban vision" before the war, ranging from the Home Owners Loan Corporation to greenbelt towns, where families with working wives were explicitly barred. The Federal Housing Administration, as one scholar summarizes, favored new construction over rehabilitation, the periphery over the central city, and segregation over integration, as did the Veterans Administration's housing plan for returning servicemen.[41] With the return of prosperity, new American suburbs were developed rapidly in the postwar decades, a product of pent-up wartime demand, federal housing policy, the new interstate highway system, and the baby boom.[42] This was no neutral demographic fact, but rather an orchestrated reorganization of the population along lines of race, class, and sexuality. The new communities promised security in the white middle class, and thus ethnic and economic assimilation, for some. Others, African Americans and other nonwhites but also unmarried and homosexual Americans, were carefully filtered out.[43] The flight to the suburbs was thus a private act full of political resonances, with important consequences for racial and gender politics.

Later critics would often equate suburbanization with retrograde motion, a cultural protest against the progress of desegregation and the entrance of women into the workforce.[44] Even more prominently, ever since Lewis Mumford penned in 1934 his description of American suburbia as the "collective effort to live a private life," analysts have associated these communities with a particular ethos, a "preference for the private over the public."[45] For mid-century sociologists as well as the historians who followed their lead, the postwar suburban explosion was proof positive of the embrace of private life by an expanding middle class. White Americans who could manage it seemingly flocked to the new communities to escape crowded urban domiciles and blue-collar and working-class urban neighborhoods—these spaces' intensive multigenerational bonds along with their brew of racial and ethnic tensions.[46] After the war, the economic boom and easy credit allowed them to put their money where their values were: that is, in residential, familial privacy.

Contemporary evidence lends some support to this analysis, if not in such clear-cut terms. The enormous market of potential home buyers beginning in the mid-1940s led developers to survey, and hew more closely to, consumer preferences than they had before the war. This effort allows us to glimpse what builders thought American home buyers wanted. One such study undertaken in 1949–1950 explained that builders were "coming to believe they must have some fundamental knowledge of the particular requirements and desires of people who are to be expected to buy their houses."[47] It found that the inadequacy of the buyer's current housing, growth in family size, and job relocation were the main triggers for suburban house hunting, with the financial benefits of owning over renting playing a role too. Nine percent of those surveyed, however, did express a desire for "independence or privacy." The study also revealed that Americans voted with their feet (or moving vans, at any rate) in prioritizing "good neighborhoods." Although this formulation obscured more than it clarified, for many buyers "it was prerequisite that the new home must be 'away from the center of town,'" indicating perhaps a wish for a measure of solitude or quiet. Most revealing, three out of ten, having already bought, declared themselves dissatisfied with the size of their lot, wishing it were wider so as to offer "more elbow room" from their next-door neighbors.[48] Some Americans, at least, craved physical and perhaps also social distance from others.

Buyers may have offered up a range of motives for relocating to suburbia. But postwar planners and policy makers argued in one voice for the virtues of private life as enclosed in the single-family dwelling. As the longtime editor of the magazine *House Beautiful*, Elizabeth Gordon, avowed in 1953, "The modern American house—the good modern house . . . provides privacy for the family from the community, and privacy for individuals of the family from each other." There was a politics to this notion of domesticity that diverged from the ideals of the Victorian household and its "aggregate," patriarchal privacy. A postwar house with sufficient privacy was believed to promote "democratic living" by fostering the individuality of each of the family's members: not just that of the man of the house but of his wife and children too.[49] Individual bedrooms for teenagers would, for instance, first become normative for middle-class families

in the 1950s. Spaces for retreat within the home were the fruit of prosperity and smaller family sizes following a brief uptick after the war. That
a measure of physical but also psychic privacy was critical to one's emotional health—and perhaps even the health of American liberal democracy—was also the growing consensus of child development experts.[50]

State and private-sector policies conspired to shore up this message, and
not only through the stream of federal monies subsidizing white suburbanites' mortgages. "Bedroom privacy" in particular was written into public
housing codes starting in the 1930s and then literally built into the new
suburbs. Endorsed by psychological experts as well as middle-class reformers dismayed by the sexual mores on display in crowded urban streets
and apartments, the private adult bedroom and, increasingly, the private
bathroom, became standard in postwar Levittowns.[51] Architects sought
to ensure privacy within the house, placing stairs and hallways such that
intimate quarters were not in easy reach of the home's more public
areas: outsiders were thereby channeled away from areas reserved for
"sleeping," "excreting," and "love making." In a major departure from
prewar dwellings, even low-budget homes usually came with a second
lavatory or half-bathroom for guests.[52] Builders too, through careful attention to window placement and materials that muffled sound, sought
to ensure privacy between adjacent "family units." Privacy, "one of the
most widely discussed aspects of postwar residential architecture," became an advertisement for and asset of suburban life, a saleable feature
and part of a property's price tag.[53]

Paradoxically, another part of that price tag was intrusion onto one's private affairs. Achieving the carefully structured homogeneity of postwar
suburbia required digging deeply into the lives of potential residents. In
perhaps only this respect, the new communities mirrored the other track
of residential construction underwritten by the state in this period: the
urban housing projects increasingly filled by low-income African American residents. The 1937 federal housing program that established those
projects was both means- and morals-based. With public housing reserved
for only the most deserving and respectable, eligibility came through intensive examination of personal character and habits. Applicants "underwent rigorous and lengthy interviews" in order that the program could
know whom to weed out, namely the unsteady, the unemployed, and those
not properly schooled in middle-class aspirations. Writes historian Rhonda
Williams, "Personal worthiness and good housekeeping—in addition to

low incomes, substandard housing, and traditional family forms—were indispensable attributes for securing residency."[54] In parallel fashion, developers, builders, lenders, and realtors with a stake in property values found
common cause in populating the suburbs with those considered to be the
most desirable, reliable residents: white married couples with children (or
those planning on having children, and thus requiring extra bedrooms).
To that end, potential homeowners were carefully scrutinized for telltale
signs of non-normative sexuality, less-than-harmonious marriages, job
trouble, and other "unstable family conditions," each of which signaled
potential foreclosure or financial risk.[55]

Even for those who made it past that gauntlet, the assurance of individual and familial privacy could falter. A truly secluded life in the new
communities was elusive and registered as such—perhaps precisely because
so much had been promised. The very design features meant to encourage
livability, comfort, and informality, notably the big picture windows or
"window walls" of suburban ranch houses, almost immediately raised privacy concerns.[56] The brainstorm of a glass manufacturer, picture windows
debuted in American homes in the early 1930s and gained cachet over the
next decade for both their aesthetic and market value (a "view" being a
new item added to appraisal forms in the 1940s real-estate market). Standardized in postwar construction, these windows, however, quickly evoked
complaints about living in a goldfish bowl. If residents could easily peer
out, after all, neighbors could just as easily peer in. The market responded
in its way, one company advertising its blinds as "windows that peeping
Toms can't see through."[57] And home magazines obsessed over fences,
trellises, and screens that would artfully block neighbors' views. An entire
issue of House Beautiful in 1960 focused on "Landscaping and Privacy,"
the editor demanding (the answer obvious): "Is Privacy Your Right or a
Stolen Pleasure?"[58] Builders seem to have paid heed. Over time, suburban
construction was modified so that "fewer and smaller windows appeared
on the street façade," coincident with peepholes and intercom systems that
allowed those inside to screen those at the home's exterior.[59]

Even walls and landscaping did not promise impermeability, however.
Adding to the portrait of the not-so-private suburban home was Americans'
heightened awareness of the ways that invisible technologies could invade
the domestic sphere. Beginning in the 1940s, a host of popular television
programs about spies and other federal agents entered suburban homes,
captivating viewers with new-fangled gadgets.[60] Americans would soon

realize that domestic espionage was not just the stuff of entertaining diversions. While surveillance itself—either the desire or the practice—was not new, mid-century commentators became alarmed by "the marriage of advanced scientific technology" to "classic surveillance methods."[61] A national discussion of electronic spying was in full flower by the mid-1950s, with extensive press coverage of its breakthroughs in penetrating private spaces.

Some of these capacities, notably wiretapping, were quite old, having lurked in the background of American life since the late nineteenth century.[62] But in the 1950s, the open secret that various parties—the police, the FBI, and, increasingly, private detectives—were listening in on some citizens' rather less open secrets gained fresh attention. By one account, seventy-eight magazine articles on electronic eavesdropping or the use of concealed microphones were published between 1930 and 1955.[63] Several experts who convened at mid-decade to consider the state of the law noted "considerable public awareness about wiretapping"—including the belief that the practice was rampant, its practitioners "wildly tapping every phone within their reach." They also cited rumors of fantastic new technologies, including "a super-sonic ray which can be beamed at a wall or window to retrieve voice–sound vibrations" from within a building.[64] This last was a reference to wartime technologies that were being repurposed by domestic "snoopers," who were learning how to break and enter virtually, without leaving a trace.

Surveillance did not need to be high tech to cause consternation. The sudden uptick in the use of private investigators in this era was of special concern. Whether hired by suspicious spouses, employers, or credit and insurance companies, these investigators relied on the fact that neighbors were often the guardians of each other's secrets. Suburbia was a treasure trove of information for those with a financial stake in personal "character" and habits, knowledge of which permitted finer discrimination among clients.[65] And so agents roamed residential neighborhoods in search of peers who would talk. For example, a routine insurance report on a California man, after characterizing his family life and neighborhood, noted that the applicant "is known to drink wine and other intoxicants moderately, but has never been known to drink to excess. He has not been seen driving while under the influence of intoxicants. He is well regarded by his neighbors and there is no criticism of his habits and morals."[66] Personal details of this sort had long been coveted by creditors and insurers.[67] But reliance

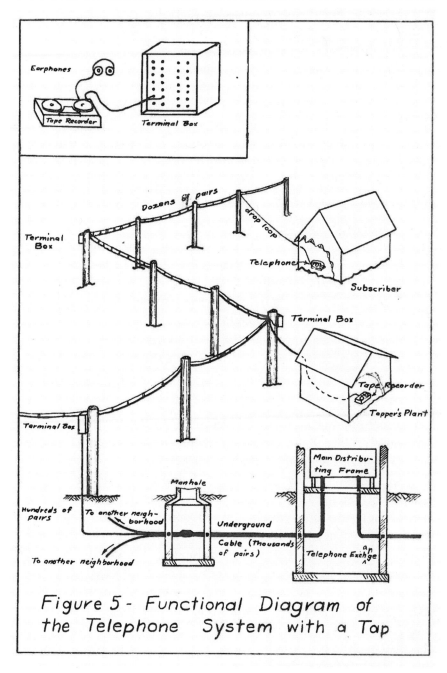

Figure 5 - Functional Diagram of the Telephone System with a Tap

3.1. Americans at mid-century were becoming aware of both the prevalence of wiretapping and the porousness of their homes.

on neighbors as "informants" was newly troublesome, simultaneously under-mining suburbia's promise of familial and individual privacy and con-juring up the tactics of a police state. As one critic mused, "Imagine all the varieties of hell that would be raised if a government agency relied on the blanket use of neighbors to obtain information."[68] Yet the practice was perfectly legal, and the private outfits employing it seemed to have no trouble securing cooperation with their inquiries.

Still more banal practices, from telephone calls to direct-mail adver-tising, infiltrated the postwar home. It was no coincidence that the soci-ologist Edward Shils, in a meditation on the elusiveness of contemporary privacy, plucked many of his examples from the domestic realm:

> A religious zealot insinuates himself across the threshold of a dwelling and then refuses to leave. The telephoning solicitor of a commercial custom or the telephone interviewer, who, having got the subscriber to "answer" the ringing telephone, presses his listener to take some form of action or to answer certain ques-tions, approximates a coercive entry into a private space. The clutter of postal advertising that falls through one's letter slot is clearly a coercive, if minor, intrusion. The noise of one's neigh-bor's television set that comes in through one's walls or windows is coercive, even if not so intended by the neighbor.[69]

The affront to privacy caused by advertisements, surveyors, or televisions may sound trifling. But it was a persistent complaint. Technologies that had once dazzled the homeowner, like the telephone, were by the 1950s as often regarded as irritations or intrusions. "It goes without saying that no in-vention, not even the doorbell or the mailbox, is as effective as the telephone in penetrating the inner recesses of our homes," charged critic Myron Brenton. Writing in an age before answering machines or call screening, he viewed the phone as an agent of special disruption: "The salesman who rings the doorbell may be ignored; the advertising circular that comes through the mails may be tossed unopened into the wastebasket; but it takes an iron constitution and a will made of unearthly stuff to disregard the persistent ringing of the telephone."[70] The fact that the telephone and the doorstep alike had become platforms for salesmen and opinion pollsters—a means, that is, for the external world to perforate domestic tranquility—was espe-cially decried. One market researcher pinned increasing "public confusion, annoyance, and distrust of field interviewers" to the fact that sellers posing as "legitimate" market surveyors had overtaken the field.[71] But it was not clear that Americans made such fine distinctions: they simply disliked un-invited encounters in their homes.

Nor was Shils's mention of noise an isolated complaint. The sensory in-trusions of strangers and neighbors was one facet of the problem, but so was the clatter *within* houses, captive to new-fangled household appliances like blenders, garbage disposals, vacuum cleaners, air conditioning units, and clothes dryers—prompting one writer to call the kitchen "the noise center of the modern home."[72] Other sounds of modern life, from highway traffic to jet planes and supersonic booms, could "penetrate houses and become the unsuspected cause of such ills as dizziness and fatigue."[73] Experts increasingly remarked on the "difficult to show" and yet signifi-cant "subjective effects of noise on individual and societal mental well-being."[74]

Betty Friedan, author of *The Feminine Mystique*, would soon critique the suburban residence from another angle: for its erosions of privacy within the family. This was particularly a problem for middle-class mar-ried women, who lived more fully within the home than either their spouses or children, who regularly departed for the office and for school. As critic August Heckscher put it, in the new suburbs, "women never quite withdraw into these homes, and yet never entirely emerge from them."[75] Designers had structured kitchens and the new "family rooms," including their typical placement overlooking a back yard, to facilitate mothers' watch over their children. Women could thus "run the house without ever leaving the kitchen."[76] In Friedan's analysis, however, the "open plan" de-sign of the suburban home, which did away with walls and doors, enabled the surveillance of women as well. Never truly alone in this "private" space, she "could forget her own identity in these noisy open-plan houses."[77] No mere design flaw, the open plan exposed the regulating functions even of supposedly secluded space, the way the promise of privacy could be thwarted by other social imperatives. The home, actually or symbolically, could not offer shelter from the press of modern society for the simple reason that it was part of it, as anxieties about the status of one's appliances and keeping up with one's neighbors would soon reveal.

In the 1950s, there were many signs that the private home was not the sanctuary it was held out to be. And yet postwar suburbia without a doubt offered more opportunities for retreat and more cordoned-off spaces than did prewar housing. Siblings, boarders, and stray aunts and cousins were no longer bunked in with others as they were in tenement neighborhoods. Live-in servants were not privy to family secrets as they were in urban bourgeois dwellings in the nineteenth century. Broader yards meant that neighbors did not accost each other right on the doorstep. The historian John Demos, prompted to reflect on contemporaries' cries of declining privacy by his study of colonial American family life, protested. He declared, "We in our homes of the mid-twentieth century have more privacy, more actual living space per capita, than any previous generation in history."[78] It was also true, though, that despite the fact that "most postwar Americans lived more privately than ever before," as another scholar puts it, "evidence indicates that they worried far more about it."[79]

Why did they worry so much? Americans had written about efforts to secure domestic privacy and had also moved to suburbs since the early nineteenth century.[80] It was only in the Cold War era that this quest was transformed from a practical struggle into a sign of a culture in trouble. Some Americans may have sought out suburbia as a haven for the development of private life and personality, but sociologists, novelists, and cultural critics did not believe that they had found it. Indeed, these commentators suspected that suburbanites did not truly want privacy, or know what to do with it—itself a sign of how thoroughly their private selves had been compromised.

Such observers found in the new suburban communities something like a natural experiment. The swiftness of their development, their sudden mixing of unfamiliar residents, and the emerging patterns of a new style of living all cried out for investigation. One of social scientists' first discoveries was that if American suburbia was a product of postwar citizens' aspirations to privacy, it also exposed the ambivalence of that project. Like the picture windows that permitted a view both out of and into the suburban home, citizens claimed to value their privacy even as they exhibited themselves, and their houses, in new ways. Indeed, the picture window became a fixation of cultural critics, who saw it a vehicle for putting the family and its increasingly conspicuous consumption on display. One novelist berated it as a "vast and empty eye" staring at its identical counterpart across the street.[81] For another critic, "the picture window, serving in the typical housing development more as a means for having others look in than for letting the owner look out," stood "as a perfect symbol of the confusion of realms."[82] The place that was supposed to serve as a refuge from society—"the only reliable hiding place from the common public world," in Arendt's words—turned out to be infiltrated by it through and through. This was not simply the consequence of new technologies, investigative practices, or design choices. It was a product of residents' own desires to showcase their status through consumer goods and gadgets and chase after the approval of their peers.[83]

The social relations that took place in suburban living rooms and across backyard fences became a cottage industry for postwar social scientists. Most famously, sociologist William H. Whyte's 1956 study of the community of Park Forest analyzed the micropolitics of "the social ethic": the vigilance with which suburbanites watched their neighbors and the creeping totalitarianism—to return to Arendt's territory—of the peer group. As Whyte saw it, suburbanites were never actually alone. Even when physically solitary, they were always shadowed by the community and its coercive social expectations. "Fact one" about suburban privacy was that there wasn't much, wrote Whyte. "In Park Forest not even the apartment is a redoubt; people don't bother to knock and they come and go furiously. The lack of privacy, furthermore, is retroactive." Whyte illustrated this with the poignant words of one of his informants: "'They ask you all sorts of questions about what you were doing' . . . 'Who was it that stopped in last night? Who were those people from Chicago last week? You're never alone, even when you think you are.'"[84]

The observer of these patterns could not himself escape the prying eyes of neighbors. Whyte noted that "one of the occupational hazards of interviewing is the causing of talk, and I am afraid my presence seriously embarrassed some housewives in several suburbs." As the sociologist ruefully recounted, "In one of the instances I later learned about, a husband arrived home to be greeted by a phone call. 'You don't know who I am,' a woman's voice announced, 'but there's something you ought to know. A man stopped by your house this afternoon and was with your wife *three* hours.'" Whyte concluded that "even the most outgoing" found the neighborly life of suburbia exhausting and sought occasional respite through a complex set of social codes. "To gain privacy, one has to *do* something," he explained. One man Whyte interviewed disclosed for instance that "he moves his chair to the front rather than the court side of his apartment to show he doesn't want to be disturbed." But the sociologist noted that "there is an important corollary of such efforts at privacy—*people feel a little guilty about making them.*" As Whyte judged it, rather than being prized by suburbanites, privacy itself had become "clandestine" and thus suspect.[85] The surprise of his study wasn't that there was less opportunity for privacy in the postwar suburbs than its residents had experienced before, but that they resisted so strenuously the privacy their new environment offered.

Community norms had typically been understood as a force for good, undergirding social order and ensuring cultural continuity. But in 1950, David Riesman's sociological study, *The Lonely Crowd*—which claimed that modern Americans had become "other-directed," having lost their internal nineteenth-century compass—led the bestseller list.[86] Sloan Wilson's bestselling 1955 novel, *The Man in the Gray Flannel Suit*, which dramatized a white-collar father and husband's existential concerns about whether to be true to himself or the corporation, was made into a well-regarded Hollywood film the next year.[87] Social norms—or, more pejoratively, social conformities—were becoming a fraught topic. For Riesman the central problem facing postwar citizens was *"other people"* and the subtle force of their judgments.[88] A host of other analysts saw in suburbia the encapsulation of a deeply invasive culture, its demands all but suffocating postwar selves.[89] Songwriter Malvina Reynolds could later count on public familiarity with the image of conformist suburbia in her hit, "Little Boxes," recorded by Pete Seeger in 1963, which derided the "ticky tacky houses all in a row." Picture windows and nosy neighbors, in this critique, were not trivial. They stood in for insidious social forces that subtly entered the person, adjusting and adapting him to reigning norms. What was worse was that the residents of suburbia did not chafe at such invasions, but seemed to welcome them.

Appropriately enough in the "Age of Psychology," some therapists would connect the dots between the new mode of suburban living and dilemmas of mental health. Psychotherapist Sidney Jourard, author of *The Transparent Self* (1964), was one of them. Individual psychological and spiritual well-being, he wrote, required "private places," inviolable by others except by express invitation. Yet such refuges—where "a person can simply be rather than be respectable," a critical distinction in the watchful neighborhoods of suburbia—were in short supply. Jourard argued that "in present-day America, architecture and living arrangements are such as to make it extremely difficult for people to find inviolate privacy either for solitude or for unobserved time spent in the company of another person." Like Betty Freidan, he singled out houses built on the open plan, where "inhabitants are seldom out of sight or earshot of one another." Escaping the observation of others thus became a "desperate, futile, and costly quest," making

3.2. The vigilance with which suburbanites watched each other was the subject of social criticism as well as humor by the mid-1950s.

a "prison or a dormitory out of one's daily living arrangement." Jourard was especially concerned about the way public pressures forced individuals into social scripts, confining the individual to "his usual roles." These were not the conclusions of a mainstream practitioner, as was suggested by Jourard's admiration for the Beats, the poets and writers who colorfully cast off society's restrictions in the mid-1950s. Yet his prescription for "public mental health"—"socially acceptable check-out places to which people could go whenever they found their daily existence dispiriting"—was perhaps the logical conclusion of anxious postwar debates over Americans' privacy, seemingly thoroughly defeated by neighbors and norms.[90]

Suburban walls had seemed a solution to the predicament of privacy in modern American society. But more and more observers were coming to the conclusion that the private home only shielded the real problem: its inhabitants. It would be the consensus of commentators that it was not the interiors of homes, but the interiors of individuals, that posed the most profound challenge to the postwar ideal of domestic privacy. It was not the physical structures of American society but rather its psychological structures that were to blame for a status-driven, conformist population with too little regard for privacy. This meant that even if access to solitude and se-clusion was in some literal sense expanding for those in the middle and aspiring middle classes, postwar Americans could easily be convinced that it was shrinking.

Mediated Minds

Criticisms of suburbanites' inability to enjoy or respect privacy suggested that something more fundamental even than the failings of the home or the community was at stake. Perhaps the postwar person was to blame, lacking some essential capacity for integrity or boundedness. This was an analysis that took hold in the literature on suburbia, but resonated far be-yond it. The susceptibility of individual psyches to outside influence is an unmistakable theme of the era's popular culture, from George Orwell's dystopian novel of 1949 to the science fiction film *The Invasion of the Body Snatchers* (1956), in which aliens took over the bodies of individual humans by assimilating their personalities. Real-life scenarios issuing from the world of media and marketing appeared to echo these plots rather too closely. Although anxiety about propaganda had a longer lineage in American culture, it moved to the very center of privacy debates at mid-century.[91] Postwar experts' application of ever-more subtle techniques of probing and persuasion impinged on what some feared were the only re-maining oases of seclusion in modern society: individuals' innermost thoughts and beliefs.

The fragility of the human psyche—and more pointedly, the American psyche—in the face of social pressures found sensational focus in the de-bate over brainwashing in the 1950s.[92] Indeed, brainwashing (and its filmic representation in 1962's *The Manchurian Candidate*) has stood as a kind of perfect Cold War fantasy, coupling as it did the enemy's duplicity and Americans' worrisome lack of control over their own inner resources.[93] The term first appeared publicly in 1950, three months into the Korean War, launched by a journalist and undercover CIA agent, Edward Hunter, who hoped to alert U.S. citizens to the Chinese Communists' program of "thought reform."[94] The POW scandal during the Korean War—in which not only numerous U.S. soldiers made damning confessions but also twenty-one American servicemen refused repatriation—brought brain-washing squarely into public view. The scandal, which triggered a con-gressional investigation in 1958, kicked up a firestorm over the mettle of American troops and the nature of their betrayal: Were they willing collaborators or subject to forces beyond their control?[95] Although the POW issue would fade, brainwashing's presence in public life lingered. Traveling under the names of coercive persuasion and "menticide"—brainwashing's "pretentious twin"—the concept circulated far beyond its origins, becoming a touchstone for fears about vulnerable American interiors.[96]

As most behavioral researchers then recognized, brainwashing was less Communist plot than species of science fiction (a fiction that the CIA, nevertheless, did its best to make operational).[97] Like its fictional counterparts, it never referred only or primarily to external threats. Instead, brainwashing's peculiar durability in postwar culture came from the ways it reflected back on American consumer society and its own forms of "programming": propaganda and persuasion in the form of advertising and public relations. Brainwashing became believable in some sense only because it lined up with more routine practices taking hold in the general society.[98] Indeed, the questions that brainwashing provoked made room for a sustained critique of American capitalist enterprise in an age usually noted for its free-market orthodoxy and political quietism.[99]

That brainwashing was useful shorthand for debating "thought control" within American society is bolstered by the large gap between popular and scientific views of the phenomenon. Nearly all military scientists, behavioral researchers, and communications theorists downplayed the novelty and efficacy of techniques going by that name. They lamented the term's capture by journalists and supposed victims, debunking "an all-powerful, irresistible, unfathomable, magical method of achieving total control over the human mind."[100] Yet, the concept exerted a stubborn hold. The term was only occasionally used precisely, one critic observed: that is, to refer to Chinese Communist practices. More often it was deployed as a "diffuse term of abuse to refer to any persuasive attempt one dislikes."[101] There were plenty of such attempts to choose from at mid-century: the fields of public relations and political consulting, the work of market researchers and advertisers, and the calculated allure of popular entertainments. Many, for example, took it for granted that "information management—a polite term for media manipulation—was inevitable in all modern political regimes," the United States and the USSR alike.[102] All societies, that is, employed the best instruments on hand to convince and compel.

Social scientists tended to have a more skeptical view of the powers of suggestion than did popular commentators. Behavioral scientists were well aware of the barriers to mass-media manipulation and other popularly hyped propaganda techniques. The limits of persuasion and the notion of the individual as a selective rather than passive receiver of messages were hallmarks of mid-century communications theory.[103] Still, as had cinema and radio before the war, TV in particular attracted a good many social scientists interested in its social effects.[104] An earlier generation of scholars had inquired into how new entertainments remade the "use of leisure."[105] But the fundamentally psychological tilt of postwar scholarship opened up the possibility of media's deeper and longer-lasting mark on its audiences. A 1949 study found for example that, "particularly to children, television is not something intruding upon already established patterns, but is an accepted fact in their lives, present virtually from the beginning." Researchers speculated that TV was "adding a completely new dimension to the experience of these children," and turned to the question of "how the medium is changing the habits, attitudes, and values of individuals and family groups."[106] Even if television was thought to bring families together in suburban living rooms, who could know the limits of its sway over suggestible viewers?

Public uptake of theories of mass persuasion meant that what Americans chose to do in their "free" time could appear considerably less free in the postwar years than it had previously. This was especially apparent in worries over the influence of the new television sets, ubiquitous by 1950. The central place that TV occupied in suburban living rooms triggered fears of uninvited ideas and images beaming themselves into Americans' homes and minds.[107] The rock 'n roll music entering teenagers' bedrooms through transistor radios prompted similar questions from parents.[108] So did graphic reading delivering sex and violence to youth. Public debates over comic books, ignited by the writings of psychologist Fredric Wertham, made evident the complex privacy concerns raised by mass culture.[109] Media, unbidden, could infiltrate the mind and personality of the susceptible consumer. And in some cases, the very privacy allotted to postwar middle-class youth, now often housed in their own separate bedrooms, facilitated the incursion.

Even more obviously, new techniques of marketing and advertising appeared to trouble the boundaries between private and public, the inner person and external social forces. How exactly, some citizens wondered, did advertisements work on individual consumers? And what could—and should—experts know about purchasers and audiences in order to sell? Modern market research practices, especially researchers' boasts about burrowing into consumers' minds with the help of psychological insights, provided plenty for fodder for such questioning at the height of the affluent society.[110]

Most important was the self-consciously scientific approach of what was called "motivation research" or MR. It was often attributed to Ernest Dichter, an Austrian Jew who emigrated to the United States in 1938 as a refugee from fascism and who founded the Institute for Motivational Research eight years later.[111] As a 1960 tract explained, motivational research was simply psychological, psychiatric, sociological, and anthropological knowledge applied to the consumer in order to glean "what induces people to react favorably or unfavorably to various products and sales appeals." The field was gripped by the question not of "what" but of "why"—particularly, the author noted, "in those instances where the consumer himself may not know or may be unwilling to give an accurate answer."[112] The problem, as marketers saw it, was that asking people about their opinions or habits often yielded misleading results, producing "rationalization or evasion." This was not a sign of dishonesty; rather, it was because individuals did not know their own minds, and it was "in an attempt to surmount this obstacle that more subtle research techniques have been tried."[113] The insight was a hallmark of popular Freudian thought, which had become mainstream in U.S. culture by the 1950s.[114] MR represented marketers' embrace of Freud, an attempt to get around the problem of consumers' lack of awareness of their true motivations.[115]

A 1948 study of "motivational analysis" could still deal in direct—or what would later be termed "surface"—questions to the respondent, such as whether the beer purchaser enjoyed a hoppy flavor.[116] Across the next decade, however, captured by the promise of psychoanalysis along with the rest of American society, marketers turned to a new quarry: the consumer's unconscious. If people's choices flowed from "influences at work below the level of the conscious mind," it followed that those influences would be discovered only by delving down to that level.[117] Practitioners were not shy about borrowing from clinical psychiatry and its focus on "biologically and socially unacceptable motivational considerations such as sex, toilet-training and nursing," not to mention "selfishness, greed, envy, prestige, sadism, love of violence" and other hidden impulses. Moreover, the new-fangled marketer aimed to diagnose such motives "without the consumer being aware that this is being done."[118] Projective techniques such as sentence-completion exercises, word association problems, Rorschach inkblots, and assessments like the Thematic Apperception Test—in which subjects were offered standardized images of people in ambiguous scenes to write stories about—especially fascinated mid-century marketing professionals. The Rorschach, for example, was considered a kind of "X ray" of the psyche that was highly useful because "only those well versed in the technical literature and in Freudian symbolism could convincingly fake responses."[119] The "depth interview," although never well defined, was still another calling card of the modern marketer.[120]

All of these techniques sought to know purchasers at a more fundamental level than their own conscious reflections allowed: indeed, better than the purchasers could know themselves. By giving consumers a "chance to *project their views*" onto a standard series of images, it was believed that they would "reveal some hidden motivations that influence their buying behavior." Likewise, sentence-completion and rapid association tasks told the researcher "a little more about the emotional values and tensions" of respondents, exposing not the directly accessible parts of their thinking but what noted market researcher Lawrence Lockley called the "side lights" of the mind. The "penetrative and exploratory capacities" of such psychological techniques made them the preferred route for "prying information out of the unconscious minds of respondents."[121]

By the mid-1950s, it was clear to those in the field that a new and shiny, psychologically inflected version of motivational research was making both "a great splash in the market research world" and a large dent in corporate budgets.[122] Although debates persisted about MR's worth, there is no doubt that it transformed the business of sales. By one account, it was the primary technique applied "to the problems of selling insurance, to the riddle of brand preference for bread, to consumer attitudes toward broadloom carpeting." Preferences about coffee, canned soup, household cleaners, automobiles, men's shoes, and soft drinks were all probed via these methods, as were the mysteries of why some people traveled by air and others turned to photography as a hobby.[123] MR's vogue in fact gave rise to warnings that psychological techniques were being employed indiscriminately, improperly, and by those with "inadequate training" to peer inside people's heads.[124]

It is not difficult to understand why those concerned about the borders of the American psyche would look askance at such practices. Some chafed against the newly intimate relationship between sellers and buyers. They objected not only to the highly personal questions that market researchers asked but also the psychological material they became privy to thereby. Others responded angrily to marketers' boasts that they knew things even about those they had never probed, reading into specific purchases a psychological significance. A columnist for the *Atlanta Constitution* charged in 1958, for instance, that it was "high time for someone to protest further invasion of the private lives of millions of Americans" by that "newcomer to Madison avenue," the MR expert. His complaint was not about psychological investigation in its appropriate context. The professional psychologist, he noted, was "devoted to helping individuals unmask their conflicts and frustrations in the privacy of a mental health clinic." But the motivation researcher sought "to unclothe all of our most personal and deeply-hidden desires" for his own gain. What consumers selected—from the color of toilet paper to the model of car—telegraphed their inner secrets to experts, the "psychological urges underneath their buying."[125] One's personality and even one's "innermost feelings" were thereby improperly exposed to others, "rolling stark naked down the street for one and all to see."[126]

In other words, while clinical psychologists gained the consent and trust of the humans they "worked" on, motivational researchers gazed, knew, and revealed without permission. They sounded a person's depths less for the insight than the profits it would bring. Coopted by the capitalist market, therapeutic tools could thus be used to sway rather than heal. By the very act of examining someone's insides, an expert could know—as well as act on and perhaps fundamentally alter—that person. This could be a desirable prospect for an individual seeking change. But what if that desire originated on the outside, from the expert looking in? Motivational researchers in this way compromised the self-knowledge that therapy offered, turning an age of psychology into an age of psychological exploitation.

Critiques of such methods of selling gained a wide audience in the later 1950s. The warm reception of Vance Packard's *The Hidden Persuaders*—by ordinary readers if not marketing professionals—was indicative of heightened concern about the integrity of the inner self.[127] Packard's 1957 book, which lambasted the "black arts" of publicity and advertising, spent a full eighteen weeks on the bestseller list.[128] Its dust jacket proclaimed, "This book is your eye opener, your guide to the Age of Manipulation," and in its pages readers were invited to see themselves as pawns in marketers' psychological games. They were by turns intrigued and offended by the techniques Packard so ruthlessly exposed. But many recognized the ubiquity of attempts to "get inside" their heads, including one Kentucky housewife infuriated by the MR experts who "with dollar signs instead of hearts," assumed they could hoodwink shoppers through their shadowy techniques in the supermarket.[129] This protest was not simply about being revealed and thus embarrassed or exposed, not simply a denunciation of "publicity" in the nineteenth-century sense. It was also a concern about being changed by being known—perhaps without even being aware of the forces at work on one's interior.

A practice that Packard decried, subliminal advertising, inspired fierce public controversy on precisely these grounds. Psychologist and market researcher James Vicary's 1957 experiment to stimulate the consumption of popcorn and soda might have gone unnoticed. But his announcement that he had successfully done so by repeatedly inserting the words "Eat Popcorn" and "Drink Coca-Cola" into a movie in 1/3,000-second installments—"long enough for the subconscious to pick up, but too short for the viewer to be aware of it"—unleashed a major media blitz. As it turned out, Vicary's impressive results (he claimed an 18.1 percent increase in Coke sales and a stunning 57.8 percent increase in popcorn sales) were fraudulent. Under the glare of publicity, it became evident that he had perhaps not even conducted such an experiment, as the manager of the movie theater in question claimed. At any rate, no one, including Vicary, could replicate the results, and the man who had caused the furor would later downgrade his finding to a "gimmick" with too little data behind it to be meaningful.[130] Meanwhile, however, public outrage about "invisible" advertisements and their attack on moviegoers' minds triggered congressional hearings.[131] The media frenzy sent Vicary into disrepute and then nearly into hiding: the psychologist cancelled all public appearances and even got an unlisted phone number.[132]

Much like other dramatic accounts of mass persuasion during the Cold War era, subliminal advertising's suggestive powers would be readily cut down to size. But the vociferous reaction to Vicary says much about growing public sensitivity to the ways experts—and a mass-mediated culture—seemed to know and act on individual minds. The person's buried thoughts and motives, some worried, were being made transparent precisely in order to be controlled. In this understanding, a known psyche could never be fully autonomous. The consequence of selves becoming visible was that they became not just less private, but less stable. Or perhaps there was no real inner self at all, an emerging view of social psychologists and sociologists in this era.[133] Either way, an anxiety about the plasticity of American interiors pervaded the entire realm of social thought on "conformity," whether it stemmed from suburban norms or advertising maxims.[134]

Frustration with such "omnipresent intrusions on our privacy" could even prod some commentators into sympathy with the Russians. A columnist for the *Los Angeles Times* defended the Soviet premier Nikita Khrushchev's complaints about the U.S. radio channel, Voice of America, and "the meddling efforts of western diplomats to incite unrest and rebellion in the Soviet zone of influence" in just these terms. Musing that "somehow this is one of the extremely human things" the Soviet leader had articulated, the journalist argued that "people everywhere were fed up with" such meddling. Americans, he added, could hardly complain about Russian propaganda "when we perpetrate the same nuisances ourselves." In his estimation, what was wrong with both societies (with a nod to the unfolding struggle over integration in Little Rock, as well as reported interference in labor union elections) was the impulse toward "intervention" as against "the right to personal, regional and national privacy."[135] Characterizing U.S. psychological propaganda as an improper invasion of the Soviet enemy's sovereignty, rather than a critical tool for winning hearts and minds in the Cold War, this writer's analysis is difficult to parse without an appreciation for the burgeoning debate over psychological privacy and the known citizen at home.

The Surveilled Student Psyche

If the neighborhood and the world of goods both looked more invasive of Americans' interiors in the 1950s than they had before, so too did the very training ground of youth: the public school. This was because the institutions tasked with imparting knowledge also sought—in the name of improving teaching, as well as managing the social relations of the classroom—to better know their charges. Psychology's march into the schools across earlier decades had paved the way.

"Do you have fewer friends than other children? Should you mind your folks even when they are wrong? Do you wish you could live in some other home? Do you feel that no one at home loves you?" These were the queries that infuriated a parent enough to dash off a letter to the *Los Angeles Times* in 1957. The questions were drawn from the California Test of Personality, an instrument sanctioned by the state department of education and administered to children in kindergarten through third grade "without the knowledge or consent of the parents." Against the belief of school psychologists that the school had the right "to obtain as much information as possible" from students to further the learning process, this writer viewed such questions as a clear trespass against the "privacy of the home."[136] As like-minded critics saw it, prying into students' psyches encroached on the home in two distinct ways. First, in assessing, analyzing, and guiding the character of the child, it treaded on parents' traditional domain. Second, personality tests revealed information that otherwise would not have been disclosed: individual interests and capabilities, perhaps, but also large caches of information about a student's domestic and internal life. It did not go unnoticed that the personal affairs of adults—the schoolchild's parents, most prominently—could be caught in the same net. As such, the school joined the home and marketplace as a site for debating postwar privacy.

Testing had come under fire before. During World War I, a controversy raged over intelligence testing in the Army and what it revealed about the average mental state of enlisted men, with an array of commentators disparaging the test's utility and validity.[137] The debate had a different flavor in the post–World War II era. It would focus less on a particular instrument and more on the expansive place and power of testing—and especially psychological testing—in American society. The scale of such testing was indeed vast. In 1960 alone, according to the *New York Times*, approximately 130,000,000 psychological tests were administered to U.S. students. This was above and beyond intelligence and aptitude tests, amounting to an average of nearly three tests per student from first grade to graduate school.[138] A series of popular magazines took up the question in the late 1950s, asking if testing was "overdone" or overrated, perhaps even counterproductive. Was it possible that testing primarily served the function of pigeonholing? What sorts of valuable characteristics and traits did the tests not test?[139] A leading exposé in 1962 described a veritable "tyranny of testing."[140] The question of the test taker's privacy arrived late to that discussion, but it did arrive. Could such instruments, some wondered, probe too far into students' lives?

Two years after that angry letter in the *Los Angeles Times*, the Houston Independent School District, one of the largest in the nation, summarily ordered that the answer sheets to a series of socio-psychometric tests be burned. Although the instruments in question had been approved by school officials—and diligently filled out by 5,000 ninth graders—parents' complaints to trustees concerning the "content and purpose of the tests" sealed their fate in ashes. Journalists aired some of the offending items, which once again made clear the prominence of popular Freudianism in American culture: "I enjoy soaking in the bathtub"; "Sometimes I tell dirty jokes when I would rather not"; "Dad always seems too busy to pal around with me." It did not seem to matter that some of the questions had been adapted from the Texas Cooperative Youth Study of 1956—a survey, puzzled a psychologist, that had been administered "without parental objection" just a few years earlier.[141] Concluding that "the public relations of psychometricians is in a sad state," she recommended that in the future testing "be preceded by a public 'warm up.'" Psychologists could not assume that "their ethic is shared by the people they study," she lamented. Where the "student of behavior" understood his actions to be serving science and the community, his misguided subject saw only "intrusion on my privacy."[142]

Bonfires did not sweep the United States in the wake of this instance of test burning. But nor was the Houston school board's action an oddity. A year or so later, a similar debate flared in semi-rural Columbia County, New York, over a community psychological research program that had been in place since 1955. The specific study focused on aggression in third-grade children, involving classroom "games and tests" with a team of psychologists, as well as parental interviews. Despite carefully laying the groundwork with teachers and local leaders (a strategy that included information meetings, consultations, speaking engagements, and news items, as well as cocktail parties), a campaign was launched against the research by the local American Legion. Irate parents in response demanded a meeting with school authorities and the researchers, ultimately engaging a lawyer "to see what action could be taken to prevent this study from going any further." Although resistance came primarily from a few vocal parents (themselves suspected of being proxies for organized interests), the decision was made to suspend testing until an investigation could take place; parents could also request to have their own children's records destroyed.[143]

These and other incidents revealed a percolating anger over intrusive psychological testing in schools, and perhaps expert knowledge more generally. Much of the initial resistance came from right-wing opponents of mental health measures.[144] Controversies over school psychological instruments were often spearheaded by suburban women just beginning to flex their organizational muscles in a grassroots conservative movement.[145] Psychology was "a suspect science" in their view because it seemed to undermine family, Christianity, individualism, and patriotism. It also had been invoked to consign those same conservatives to the paranoid fringe of American society. In the 1950s, the "mental health establishment" would become a favorite punching bag for the Far Right, encompassing "research psychologists, therapists, psychiatrists, community mental health workers, guidance counselors, government bureaucrats, and anyone else who advocated a progressive interventionist vision for psychological expertise in society," often on behalf of minorities or disadvantaged groups.[146] In these protests, privacy was often a screen for other, more pressing ideological agendas. Schools in this period were swept into a number of key partisan conflicts: over the legitimacy of mandatory education, local control over school systems, the prerogatives of parents vis-à-vis educators, and, the most contentious of all, desegregation. Those arrayed against "Communist influence" and liberal threats to family values discovered "privacy" to be a valuable rhetorical resource in these fights.

Researchers in the Columbia County case, although aware of this constituency, did not, however, consider conservatives their central problem. Most parents did not believe that "members of the research were partaking in a communist plot to implant alien, subversive ideas in the minds of innocent children," they reported. On the other hand, "many thought that we were indeed invading their privacy," sure that experts were there "to tell them how to raise their children." Others who objected to the aggression study did not seem to trust the researchers' promise of anonymity and confidentiality. Another set, reflected one of the psychologists involved, simply "thought we were prying into what is none of our business." The fact that the same upstate New York community had recently been subjected to other scrutiny—a study conducted by the American Cancer Society on personal health habits, and a family life study probing the causes of juvenile delinquency—may have cemented this point of view.[147]

Such protests began as partisan affairs, the work of local anticommunist campaigns. But they went mainstream by the 1960s, as critiques of expert culture jumped political lines. Whereas earlier liberals had placed great faith in social scientific as well as military experts, a more radical position on the dangers of bureaucratized knowledge was gaining ground.[148] As the psychologist and concerned onlooker Michael Amrine explained, psychological testing and mental health services initially had been a lightning rod for "the extreme right wing of American politics." But soon enough these had become matters of concern "to the other side of the political spectrum, not to mention those in the middle of the road." By the time he wrote, in 1966, Amrine lamented that "tests and testers are . . . attacked by the right and the left, from outside psychology and from inside."[149] In 1964 conservative spokesman Russell Kirk was protesting in the conservative *National Review* that psychological tests "may force children to incriminate themselves, cast aspersions upon their parents, and expose their sensibilities to any snoop."[150] Nearly identical sentiments were voiced that same year by liberal critic Myron Brenton. He castigated such tests as "designed to lay bare each student's psyche and expose the most secret parts of his personality": the child's worries, fears, family relations, dating habits, feelings about sex, and the like. As did those on the Right, he objected in part to the school's takeover of "highly personal matters" that were "once considered the exclusive province of parents."[151]

Critiques sometimes led to action. One instance was the halting in 1963 of a questionnaire "inflicted upon the incoming freshmen" at a community college in Montgomery County, Maryland, that surveyed students' attitudes, ambitions, and family backgrounds. It was condemned on the grounds of invading students' and parents' privacy.[152] Monroe Freedman, a liberal law professor at nearby Georgetown, cheered the decision. He argued that the manner in which students and their families "live their private lives, and think their private thoughts, is none of the business of the Educational Testing Service." He added, "There is a point at which the inviolability of the candidate's personality is more precious than the completeness of the testers' dossiers."[153] The critic Jacques Barzun also registered the change in attitudes toward testing. In the 1940s, he claimed, "testing by check-mark was established everywhere in American life," and it was "manifestly useless to raise even a question about the value and effect of these tests." By the early 1960s, however, the tide had turned, and it was "the testers who are on the defensive."[154]

Dale Tillery, an educational researcher, could corroborate this change. He described "fatiguing and fascinating encounters with students, parents, administrators, teachers, trustees, press, radio, television and political groups" that had resulted from his involvement in a large longitudinal youth study (90,000 subjects) called Project SCOPE, funded by the College Examination Board. Although the researchers had been prepared for some public resistance, "the extent of the concern for the protection of the

individual student and his home was far greater than had been anticipated." Tillery was surprised that some of the most vigorous pushback to
the study came from politically liberal teachers, who raised concerns about
what was going to be done with students' private information "very much
like those from groups that were clearly associated with the extreme right."
Whereas liberals seemed to think the study was "connected to the C.I.A.,"
conservatives were convinced it was "connected with the Kremlin," he
wryly observed. In his telling, the research team had expended "disproportionate energy" simply to get schools to agree to take part in the study;
later, "irrational or destructive" protests and "face-to-face confrontation"—
some of it sparked by inaccurate media coverage—had required substantial
resources and time to manage. Given these standoffs, Tillery pondered
how best to "bring others into the research enterprise with us."[155] Some on
the other side of the issue proposed more radical remedies, including a test
takers' Bill of Rights.[156]

One commentator, trying to sum up the state of American privacy in
1958, reflected that "one hardly needs to emphasize the inquisitorial spirit
that has characterized the past decade. A man's beliefs and convictions,
even the degree of his enthusiasm or doubt, have been matters for public
inquiry. More than that, the opinions of his parents—or his own distant
and perhaps indiscreet youth—have seemed fit subjects for the authorities
to investigate."[157] The writer referred to McCarthyism, HUAC, and the FBI.
But the "inquisitorial spirit" of psychological testing was raising similar
hackles in less obviously political sites: the classroom, as we have seen, but
also the corporation.

Brain Watchers at Work

From the vantage point of 1964, the critic Myron Brenton mused, "There
was a time—right up to the approaches of World War II—when a person
applying for a job in an office or a factory was usually asked to fill out just
four items of a personal nature on the employment application form." One's
name, address, emergency contact, and after the mid-1930s, one's Social
Security number, were all that was required. Brenton's point with this minimalist list was that times had changed. "These days the job applicant may
face 'in-depth' employment application forms, private detectives, lie de-
tector tests, psychological tests, maybe even a direct interview with the company psychologist, before the hiring decision is made." In the postwar era,
multi-page applications detailing one's "life history in miniature" were in-

creasingly the rule.[158] As another critic protested, where once hiring had depended on resumes and interviews, it was now "abdicated" to the "new working Sovereign—the tester."[159] But this was not the end of the matter. As men in white-collar occupations especially came to understand, personality tests were a permanent presence in the workplace, used not simply to screen new hires but also to evaluate employees on the job, gauge their readiness for promotion, and probe their management prowess. This battery of evaluations would, in time, generate a sustained debate about psychological secrets and to whom—the expert who pried them loose, the employer who paid for them, or the employee who housed them—they rightly belonged.

From one angle, the advent of personality testing at the office was surprising. Suburban housewives, feminized mass-market consumers, and school-age minors all seemed more likely candidates for this kind of psychological monitoring than were white middle-class men. But from another angle, the white-collar workplace was an especially hospitable environment for the promises dangled by psychological knowledge. As the field of human relations gradually became the domain of psychologists, it increasingly focused on matters of personality and character, motivation and morale. These in turn became the ruling concerns of personnel specialists in American corporations.[160] Experts' ability to detect the unsavory motivations and personality flaws that simmered under an otherwise pleasant façade could save a corporation from any number of bad investments. Indeed, one 1959 study found that "personality and temperament" headed the list of factors employers considered when hiring. Wrote one legal expert, "In many instances, 'personality' has become more important as an employment criterion than other qualifications"—astonishingly, this included even the "ability to perform the required task."[161] The emphasis was related to the premium on teamwork and "getting along" in the postwar corporation. William Whyte, who wrote the book on the matter, explained that whereas the old boss wanted your sweat, "the new man wants your soul."[162] And in fact, even the boss's soul attracted the gaze of psychological experts, as the robust market for executive-specific evaluations attested.

The personality test had been pioneered in World War I, but its future was assured during World War II.[163] The war was a boon for psychological testing, with some 9 million servicemen sitting for the Army General Classification Test.[164] As exemplified by the Armed Services Vocational

Aptitude Battery, which became the most widely used such test in U.S. schools, the translation of psychological instruments from the military to the civilian sphere was relatively seamless. What distinguished these tests from their predecessors, which had most often been self-reports, was their "actuarial interpretation" based on specific statistical correlations and the trained eye of an expert.[165] Although exact numbers are difficult to come by, there is no doubt that personality testing on the job—as in the schools—expanded precipitously in the postwar years. The American Management Association estimated that the proportion of companies employing selection tests of any sort increased from 57 percent in 1947 to 75 percent in 1953. Personality tests' ascent was still more dramatic. A *Fortune* survey recorded a jump in corporations using them from 33 to 60 percent between 1952 and 1954.[166] One critic suggested that psychological testing, born of the elevation of "personality" in American life as well as the managerial revolution, affected some 50 million Americans by the time he wrote in 1962.[167] Charles Alex's *How to Beat Personality Tests* of 1966, which revealed the tests' secrets in the hope that individuals might better be able to conquer them, suggested the popular currency of these measurements in American life.[168]

Personality testing was a big business. As Martin Gross's contemporary exposé brought home, it was also an unregulated one, with a wide array of instruments and practitioners jostling for preeminence in the postwar period. The 125-question "Personality Inventory," for example, inquired straightforwardly about emotional stability, sex life, work attitudes, health matters, and religious values. The Activity Vector Analysis was an eighty-one-adjective word game. Other tests resembled those favored by motivational researchers, complete with "inkblots, free-association techniques, uncaptioned cartoons, and nude drawings," which as Gross wryly observed had originally been designed to detect "paranoids and schizophrenics." Like marketers, most personality testers aimed squarely at the subconscious. They did so not to divine purchasing motivations, however, but in hopes of finding the "company man"—or screening out deviants or slackers. In service to this goal, testers sometimes plied their trade brazenly. According to Gross, "wife-testing" was on the increase in some corporations. This was a practice whereby a man's spouse was subjected to scrutiny, whether formally or surreptitiously, in order to shed light on the prospective hire. There were even reports of "undercover" psychologists who posed as an employee from another city in order to share a hotel suite with a prospect and "keep watch" for a few days.[169]

The most popular instrument, and the one that would garner the most public attention, was the Minnesota Multiphasic Personality Inventory or MMPI. The MMPI had its origins in 1940 as a diagnostic test for identifying and sorting mental disorders. But its claim to reveal a spectrum of normal personality types—its 566 questions a divining rod for neuroses of all sorts—was evident to many parties, making its leap from the clinic to the corporation surprisingly swift. By one account, demand for the MMPI was so heavy by 1946 that its publisher couldn't keep up with orders. Its uses steadily expanded to "spheres far beyond the mental ward: business suites, army barracks, courtrooms, high schools, doctors' offices." In the early 1960s it was administered "at least as often to normal people as to psychiatric patients, used to screen job applicants, offer vocational advice, settle custody disputes, and determine legal status."[170]

The MMPI's attractiveness to human relations specialists—and its threat to employees—lay in its deep and wide-ranging excavation of the individual psyche. Employers in an earlier day regularly pried into workers' politics and union membership, a key fear raised by the issuing of Social Security cards. But the MMPI contained questions that were once considered well beyond the bounds of legitimate corporate concern. These were a mix of medical, sexual, political, social, and psychological items designed, in a contemporary opponent's view, to "cut through the work record and references painstaking built up over the years" so as to reveal the otherwise invisible inner man.[171] The MMPI offered access to matters that employees were determined to hide but that employers were keen to know. Its inventory was used to screen for "neurotics" but also to ferret out hypochondriacs and alcoholics—those who would, through their character or habits, hinder a company's productivity. It could also bring to light hidden "sexual deviates," especially those indicating "homosexual tendencies." An alarming score on the masculinity-femininity scale was more damning than a revealed tendency for absenteeism or, indeed, almost anything else.[172]

Like other such instruments, the MMPI promised to disclose things of which the worker might not be aware and, indeed, would not learn. As with motivational research, it turned on its head the kind of self-knowledge that emerged through therapy. The psychological profile it churned out was the property of the corporation; its subject was rarely privy either to its insights or to its uses. The test taker, moreover, could never be sure what the tester was after or how his own answers might betray him. As a *Washington Post* article explained, only a small fraction of the items on a personality inventory dealt with sensitive topics of sex and religion. The great majority, it reported, were more along the lines of "I drink an unusually large amount of water every day," or "It takes a lot of argument to convince some people of the truth."[173] But this was not particularly reassuring. What became clearer as the contemporary debate unfolded was in some ways more unsettling than brash questions about intimate matters. It was the testers' admission that they often did not actually care about the test takers' religious or moral beliefs despite asking about them. These were merely "surface questions," designed to get at deeper matters.[174] Like sex, religion was simply "one of these areas of life in which feeling is strongly expressed and the real 'I' comes out." Their significance deliberately masked, the test items were a device for finding out something more buried, perhaps deliberately, about the subject's "mode of behaving and performing."[175] And so the test taker could know that his responses had consequences—just not how they were consequential. Powerful parties, experts and employers, could shed new light on the worker's insides, but left the employee himself in the dark.

If suburbia's picture windows had raised the question of improper peeping, the one-way mirror of the corporate personality test was even more disturbing. And so, even as the furor over brainwashing ebbed in the late 1950s, reservations about what the muckraker Martin Gross skewered as "brain watching" were on the rise. Critiques issued from a number of quarters. Some, like William H. Whyte, saw personality tests as operating hand in hand with suburbia's subtly coercive norms, the corporation and the community neatly conspiring against the individual. "Loaded with debatable assumptions and questions of values," he charged, personality tests produced "a set of yardsticks that reward the conformist, the pedestrian, the unimaginative."[176] In his analysis, personality tests not only crossed the line in terms of employees' privacy and led to new forms of gatekeeping by self-appointed experts. They also imperceptibly but exquisitely insinuated their norms—and the culture's—into the test taker. What the tests measured best was how thoroughly the employee was *already* pervaded by the corporation.[177] In a move similar to suburbia's critics, Gross for his part lambasted not just the tester's invasiveness but also the testee's willingness to submit. This tendency itself was a product, he thought, of a too-knowing culture—of frequent exposure to motivational research, opinion polling, school guidance counselors, and credit checks. Corporations' access to employees' "psychological innards" was facilitated by the fact that the average worker was "almost aggressively voluble about himself without too much prodding from the tester."[178]

But the vital question was whether individuals ought to have to submit to probes of their feelings, emotions, and values as a condition of employment.[179] As Whyte framed it, "Is the individual's innermost self any business of the organization's?"[180] Criticism along these lines would come even from within psychology's ranks.[181] As one of the leading authorities on psychological testing, Lee Cronbach, explained, "Any test is an invasion of privacy for the subject who does not wish to reveal himself to the psychologist." If this was true of intelligence and subject-area testing, personality testing led to even deeper feelings of violation. "Every man has two personalities," observed Cronbach: "the role he plays in his social interactions and his 'true self.'" The personality test sought to align the two by searching out attitudes and beliefs that the individual typically kept hidden. Whether a test attempted to assess reactions to authority, the love of a mother for a child, or the strength of "sexual needs," it sought information "on areas which the subject has every reason to regard as private, in normal social intercourse." The person being tested was normally "willing to admit the psychologist into these private areas only if he sees the relevance of the questions to the attainment of his goals," noted Cronbach.[182] Corporate personality tests, of course, were attuned to the goals not of the test taker but of the test giver. Unlike the voluntary disclosures made by a person seeking a psychologist's assistance, "institutional testing tries to determine the truth about the individual, whether he wants that truth known or not."[183]

Novelists and sociologists captured the unease with these instruments emerging by the mid-1950s. Tom Rath, the hero of 1955's *The Man in the Gray Flannel Suit*, revealed his strength of character by refusing to disclose his personal history during an interview for a position with a public relations firm.[184] William Whyte offered sly guidance to the tested in an appendix to *The Organization Man* (1956) titled "How to Cheat on Personality Tests." His key piece of advice was to fake "normality." "When in doubt," he counseled, "repeat to yourself: I loved my father and my mother, but my father a little bit more. I like things pretty much the way they are. I never worry much about anything. I don't care for books or music much. I love my wife and children. I don't let them get in the way of company work."[185]

Although it is difficult to track down firsthand accounts of the tested, contemporary research supported Cronbach's notion that individuals were generally reluctant to disclose information about their "personality," as opposed to their interests and behavior, and indeed sometimes considered this a harm.[186] In a rare study devoted to objections to their own procedures—triggered by the controversy over testing—a pair of psychologists in 1965 set out to examine which questions on the MMPI truly bothered respondents. One group of subjects was asked to omit all items they considered objectionable "under any circumstances," another to strike those questions offensive specifically in a job context. Among other things, the study revealed a weary familiarity with the test. One subject refused to participate when he learned that the "task involved taking the MMPI"; several others reportedly complained, "Oh, no, not again."[187] The study found wide variability in responses, but four areas stood out as objectionable: "Sex," "Religion and Religious Beliefs," "Family Relationships," and "Bladder and Bowel Function." Another catchall area concerned mental processes that the subject "does not, should not, or cannot reveal to others." Finally, questions about political attitudes and what were classified as "confession-type" items also surfaced as problematic. In the end, the researchers identified a total of 76 "Objectionable Items" out of a total of 566.[188] Perhaps not surprisingly, the psychologists concluded that the offensive questions ought not to be deleted, citing the "selective loss of important behavioral information." Instead they called for "better administration" so as to preempt the subject's "predictable reaction"—evidently, a negative one—"after he has completed the inventory."[189]

Psychologists' certainty that the MMPI was "a sensitive matter," but one that could be finessed by better prepping subjects, underestimated the resentment building against personality testing. In the court of popular opinion, observers did not generally debate the precise content of "objectionable items" or what questions were appropriate for which contexts. Instead, personality tests—known through press reports, critical exposés, or people's own experience submitting to them—were distrusted and even feared for their intrusiveness, their influence, or both. More problematically for those in the personality business, similar reservations about what would be dubbed "The 'I Love My Mother' Tests" would begin to emanate from employment lawyers as well as Congress, where politicians aired scandalous questionnaire items for their colleagues—questions, conservative Congressman John Ashbrook of Ohio maintained, referring to school psychological exams, that "literally undress young people."[190] Stripped of their proprietary secrecy and expert rationale, test items could spark political outrage.

As items from diagnostic tests were leaked by politicians and the press, they became targets of public mockery. The range and incongruity of the topics could indeed be truly bizarre: "I believe in the second coming of Christ," "I am seldom troubled by constipation," "I very much like hunting," even, "Someone has control over my mind."[191] Their familiarity in capsule form is perhaps the best evidence for their prominence in postwar culture. Humor columnist Art Buchwald, for instance, published a satiric questionnaire of true-false statements that, he implied, would not look amiss in the MMPI. Among them: "Spinach makes me feel alone"; "I am never startled by a fish"; "Frantic screams make me nervous"; "As a child I was deprived of licorice"; "When I look down from a high spot, I want to spit"; "My eyes are always cold."[192] Such derision mixed easily with foreboding about such instruments' power to invade citizens' inner lives and mete out society's rewards. As such, personality testing became a key target of animus even in a culture awash in psychological knowledge—and the topic of congressional hearings by the mid-1960s.[193]

The MMPI and its kin raised specific fears about the diagnostic instruments taking root in postwar institutions: both the unaccountable authority they carried and the impact of their judgments. They also roused more general misgivings about the invasive social world in which midcentury Americans found themselves. Experts and neighbors, corporate norms and mass media, seemed not only to coexist with or surround the postwar citizen: they threatened to infiltrate and saturate her. The troubling prospect of invasions into the individual interior helps explain why the promised privacy of the suburban home could not properly reinforce the division between public and private in modern America. The real barriers that needed fortifying against intruders were those within the person herself.

By the time the 1960s rolled around, a veritable explosion of public discussion centered on the shrinking sphere of personal privacy in American life.[194] In 1964, Myron Brenton—author of the best-selling *The Privacy Invaders*—observed that "during the past 20 years less than half-a-dozen popular magazine articles dealt at all with the meaning of privacy in our lives and tragedy of its loss to modern man."[195] This, however, had changed almost overnight. A rash of exposés in the 1960s, including Brenton's, warned of privacy's imminent eclipse: *Privacy: The Right to Be Let Alone* (1962), *The Naked Society* (1964), *The FBI Nobody Knows* (1964), *The Intruders* (1966), *Privacy and Freedom* (1967), and, what would be a winning formulation, *The Death of Privacy* (1969).[196]

For Brenton, growing intrusions in the marketplace, at work, and in the community—ranging from direct mail advertising to life insurance inspections, "in depth" employment application forms to corporate spying—added up to a "prying, digging, peering and poking" Goldfish Age.[197] Vance Packard, author of *The Hidden Persuaders*, reinforced this vision of U.S. society in another bestseller of 1964. Each chapter of his *The Naked Society*, including "How to Strip a Job-Seeker Naked," "The Hidden Eyes of Business," "The Very Public Lives of Public Servants," and "Are We Conditioning Students to Police State Tactics?" added to Packard's dire portrait of "mounting surveillance" on all fronts.[198] Popular journalists were among the first to sound the alarm, but politicians, academics, and activists—an emerging corps of privacy specialists—were not far behind. Together, they publicized an ever-growing list of surveillance impulses, psychological invasions, and technological breakthroughs in piercing previously impenetrable privacies.

Whether old like wiretapping or frighteningly new like subliminal advertising, the techniques of invasion appeared to be escalating in citizens' daily lives. The threat came not from one particular direction but from every corner of American society.[199] The government and the military, corporations and workplaces, universities and hospitals, media and marketers were each and every one "intruders." To Senator Edward Long of Missouri, author of his own tract about incursions into citizens' private lives in the 1960s, this amounted to an "undeclared war on privacy."[200] The regions of private life susceptible to prying appeared boundless, with some of the most threatening incursions being invisible and imperceptible. This would prompt a lawyer, reflecting on personality testing, to describe "the type of searches made by colonial patriots" as "in many respects, preferable to those of the present day which seem to search the private actions, habits, and innermost thoughts of our citizens.[201]

The most important questions raised by peer surveillance in suburbia, by marketers' tools of persuasion and projection, and by psychological testing at school and work were, at root, the same. Who needed to know psychological secrets, what techniques could be employed to discover them, and what effects might this kind of probing have on the "inner person"? When was a personal habit or tendency a public concern, leaking into one's social duties and roles, and when was it in fact "private" and no one else's business? How transparent ought the citizen be to the society—and even to him- or herself? And what leverage did individuals possess against unwanted personal or psychological disclosure? As brainwashing's persistent presence in postwar culture suggested, the intimate, private sphere—even the domain of the mind—had come to appear worrisomely porous. The American citizen, as much as the Soviet one, was fully interpenetrated by the social world. In contrast to the unproblematic distinction that late nineteenth-century privacy advocates had drawn between one's public image or reputation and the private self, postwar observers began to wonder if anything remained beyond the reach of society. What personality, indeed, could be inviolate in an age of knowing neighbors, psychological probes, and expert vision?

The considerable gulf between the vulnerable person found in postwar discussions and the autonomous liberal actor idealized in U.S. civil society would demand a resolution. Indeed, if a realm of privacy appeared more difficult to achieve in the Cold War era, it also seemed ever more imperative for citizens to hold onto. The mid-1960s would witness the first concerted effort to stake out its boundaries. A constitutional right to privacy would be defined against the backdrop of a new psychologically inflected understanding of how the postwar person might be known—and being known, might be altered. Individual rights talk in the 1960s has often been lauded as the language of an empowered citizenry. But it was also rooted in Americans' worries about the weakness of their interiors in the face of a highly socialized, organized existence.

4

A Right to Be Let Alone

The right to be let alone is indeed the beginning of all freedom.

—WILLIAM O. DOUGLAS,
Public Utilities Commission v. Pollak, 1952

In 1948, the Universal Declaration of Human Rights put into words an international commitment to individual privacy, forged in from the cauldron of war.[1] Shepherded through the United Nations by Eleanor Roosevelt, the Declaration was a legacy of Nuremberg, meant to set down "a jurisprudential underpinning for political or philosophical assertions of the dignity of the individual irrespective of local, domestic laws."[2] Its Article 12 stated forthrightly, "No one shall be subject to arbitrary interference with his privacy, family, home or correspondence, nor to attacks upon his honour and reputation. Everyone has the right to the protection of the law against such interference or attacks."[3] In the corridors of the UN, "privacy" was not a deeply considered or contentious item. Although its drafters, in multiple sessions, parsed nearly every word and provision in the Declaration, they were silent on both "privacy" and the "private." Apart from a few semantic scuffles, Article 12 itself was barely discussed, seemingly unproblematic for delegates from around the globe.[4] Privacy was taken to be part of an assumed bundle of protections concerning people, their dwellings, and their papers that had been articulated in a line of distinguished documents, from the French Declaration of Human Rights (1789, 1793) and the United States Bill of Rights (1791) to the Atlantic Charter (1941) and Bogota Declaration (1948).[5]

In practice, however, privacy would not so easily make the passage from paper ideal to tangible entitlement. The Declaration, nonbinding on member states, proved to have little traction in the postwar United States. Becoming entangled with Cold War ideological battles—and to some, synonymous with "Soviet-led subversion"—human rights quickly receded as a resource for substantive discussions about the status of individual dignity and autonomy vis-à-vis the state or other agents of modern society.[6] Public concern about the dwindling spaces for privacy in a knowing society escalated during the early Cold War era, but it did not yield official remedies. This was true even though rights to privacy had gained ground in tort law since the late nineteenth century, with many state statutes on the books, and even despite the fact that rights language was finding its way into discussions of full employment as well as movements for racial justice.[7]

It was nearly two decades after the Declaration of 1948 that privacy was pronounced a full-fledged individual right by the U.S. Supreme Court. A beneficiary of the sweeping rights talk of the 1960s, privacy suddenly acquired at mid-decade a constitutional pedigree and a civil libertarian inflection.[8] The timing can only be explained by reference to the modern civil rights movement. The "rights revolution" was brought into being by the black freedom struggle in both the North and South, and it defined the era, leading to the passage of the Civil Rights Act of 1964 and Voting Rights Act of 1965. Due process was revolutionized in these years too.

Galvanized by social movements, new rights were championed and secured in the courts—most spectacularly during the years of the liberal Warren Court, bookended by the landmark desegregation ruling of *Brown v. Board of Education* in 1954 and the *Tinker v. Des Moines Independent Community School District* decision safeguarding students' free speech rights in 1969. Rulings on criminal procedure, the rights of the indigent, and the protection of racial and religious minorities led the way. The rights to counsel, to "remain silent" during interrogation, to a fair trial, to refuse self-incrimination, to protest, to travel, to religious and associational freedom, and to marry across the color line were all elaborated in these years.[9] Moving still faster and further than judicial statements, a restless popular rights consciousness was everywhere evident in the broader society. Even President Lyndon Johnson traded on it, sometimes implying in his lofty promise of a Great Society that not just civil rights but also social rights to a "richer quality of life and decent standard of living" were waiting in the wings.[10]

In this climate, it was not surprising that the mounting privacy concerns of earlier decades would intersect with the language of rights. "Rights" in fact already, if informally, colored how postwar citizens made their claims to a measure of freedom from intrusion or scrutiny. But it was the 1965

Supreme Court case, *Griswold v. Connecticut*, overruling a ban on married couples' use of contraceptives, that would finally supply privacy its constitutional bona fides. This dramatic moment in privacy's history is the one that most Americans recognize and most U.S. historians register. The "right to privacy" has been treated as one of a bundle of recognitions burnishing the dignity and freedom of the individual in the 1960s—an example of what sociologist Peter Clecak has termed the "democratization of personhood" in the latter half of the twentieth century, born of "enhanced cultural options, rising economic resources and rewards, strengthened legal guarantees, and augmented personal and political rights."[11] Once *Griswold* is followed to its jurisprudential conclusion, 1973's *Roe v. Wade*, privacy tends once again to disappear from sight, however. The birth control case becomes the origin point for a story about reproductive rights—and fights—in the later twentieth century, its divisive legacy bewailed by legal scholars and political commentators alike.[12]

But *Griswold v. Connecticut* was not yet this in 1965, when in ringing terms, Justice William O. Douglas affirmed "a right of privacy," which he dignified as being "older than the Bill of Rights—older than our political parties, older than our school system."[13] The ruling is properly remembered as a milestone in establishing a new right. But it must also be understood as an intervention in a wide-ranging dialogue already underway, carrying the potential to generate new privacy claims and to sidestep others. In giving *Griswold* its due, we should not err in making it the whole story of privacy in the 1960s. The junction of privacy and rights in that decade—and the fashioning of a "right to privacy" from the peculiar material of a birth control case—was only one development, albeit a significant one, shaping privacy's career in U.S. public culture.

Griswold may be familiar, but its consequences for debates about the fate of privacy in American life are surprisingly unknown. What visions of privacy would the ruling bolster, and which would it shunt aside? How would the rights of the marital bedroom translate to other spheres: the workplace, the police station, the classroom, the welfare office, the laboratory? Were rights even the best vessel for securing individual privacy? And how would they speak to the quandary of the known citizen, which had reached such a high pitch by the mid-1960s? These were the questions that Americans immersed in contemporary privacy debates would ask. Like the ruling itself, the answers they found were not at all straightforward.

Constitutionalizing Privacy

Griswold v. Connecticut, the case that would announce the modern constitutional right to privacy, had its roots in a different sexual era and an old law. It stemmed from Warren and Brandeis's day, when the forces of "Comstockery"—named for the zealous morals crusader, Anthony Comstock—were at work criminalizing contraception and abortion, as well as sexual expression of all kinds. Connecticut's birth control statute of 1879, crafted by none other than the showman P. T. Barnum, was part of the wave of anti-obscenity reforms that rolled through state legislatures in the late nineteenth century.[14] As part of this broader societal campaign to rein in vice, Connecticut enacted the most restrictive anti-contraception statute in the nation. It barred not just the display and dissemination of contraceptives but also their use, as well as the issuing of related medical advice.[15]

By 1961, the first time a challenge to the Connecticut law wound its way to the Supreme Court, assumptions and practices around birth control had changed.[16] The birth control pill had just been approved by the Food and Drug Administration the prior spring, and longer-term developments had decisively altered the landscape: the federal judiciary had ruled in 1936 that the Comstock law could not be used to prevent transporting contraceptives for medical uses, a major movement in support of birth control had gained steam, and middle-class women, at any rate, had for a generation managed to secure relatively easy access to contraceptives.[17] "Contraception," writes legal scholar Lawrence Friedman, "was on its way to becoming a non-issue."[18] Indeed, a quiet sexual revolution, not entirely visible until later in the decade, was already afoot.[19] Alongside all of this were organized efforts by the American Law Institute, a body charged with monitoring and modernizing legal codes, to decriminalize certain consensual sexual practices.[20] Connecticut's harshly restrictive statute seemed, to most observers, a relic: there had been almost no prosecutions under the law, and there was little support for it even in the ranks of the Catholic Church.[21]

The Court nevertheless dismissed a 1961 challenge in *Poe v. Ullman* on technical grounds of standing, also citing the statute's lack of enforcement.[22] But the case would return, bearing the name of Estelle Griswold, executive director of the Planned Parenthood League of Connecticut, and supported by the American Civil Liberties Union (ACLU) and the national birth control movement. In the wake of *Poe*, hoping to press the question, Griswold and Lee Buxton—chair of Yale Medical School's Department of Obstetrics and Gynecology—opened a clinic offering contraceptive counseling for married women. The two carefully arranged to be arrested under the 1879 law. When the Connecticut Supreme Court upheld both the arrest and the statute, the Supreme Court finally agreed to weigh in on its merits.[23]

The Court's long-awaited ruling in 1965 identified a constitutional "right to privacy" for the first time in American history. Yet that stark summary fails to capture *Griswold's* full significance. As legal commentators then and since have noted, the Court's language in declaring that right was ambiguous and its reasoning difficult to parse. Although seven of nine justices agreed to strike down the Connecticut statute, they could not agree as to why. Was this a case with clear precedents grounded in the right to association or speech? Could contraceptive use be encompassed by the "ordered liberty" guaranteed by the Fourteenth Amendment? Or had a right to privacy that included birth control existed all along, hidden in the seams of the Bill of Rights? Immediately after the ruling was handed down, a legal scholar remarked that "the extraordinary thing about this case is not its result, but rather the divergencies in the theories of the Justices who wrote the opinions to explain it."[24] Casting broadly for a rationale that would allow the Connecticut law to be invalidated, the *Griswold* ruling constituted, in a more recent observer's words, "one of the most idiosyncratic opinions in the two centuries of Supreme Court history."[25]

There had been intimations—in a patchwork of the Court's prior majority and dissenting opinions—that a constitutional right of privacy might exist. Some stretched as far back as the 1886 *Boyd v. United States* decision, which concerned the use of a man's private papers as evidence against him. It boldly rejected "all governmental invasions of the sanctity of a man's home and the privacies of life."[26] An even earlier claim to bodily privacy, revolving around who could be present when a woman delivered a child, was made in the Michigan state courts in 1881.[27] Certainly the Fourth Amendment's prohibitions on search and seizure had carved out a place for privacy with respect to one's "person, papers and home," a protection closely associated with property rights.[28] But Justice Louis Brandeis's eloquent dissent in *Olmstead v. U.S.* (1928), the federal wiretapping case, was more typically the point of departure for jurists. In it, Brandeis balked at the Court's refusal to establish a right of privacy from the state, invoking "the right to be let alone" as the "most comprehensive of rights and the right most valued by civilized men."[29]

Other resources for the Court in the 1960s came from far-flung precedents involving family decision making, the right of association, and freedom of conscience. Two cases in the 1920s, *Meyer v. Nebraska* and *Pierce v. Society of Sisters*, suggested that there were limits to state interference in parental decisions related to child-rearing and education.[30] In the 1940s the Court struck down laws stipulating the forced sterilization of criminals (*Skinner v. Oklahoma*, 1942) and schoolchildren's obligatory salutes to the flag (*West Virginia State Board of Education v. Barnette*, 1943), both of which gave support to the notion of a private sphere that the state could not touch.[31] Justice Douglas, author of the *Griswold* opinion, would be on the leading edge of these arguments, his personal and somewhat idiosyncratic commitment to privacy evident in a series of dissents in the early 1950s concerning incriminating testimony and free expression.[32]

A set of later rulings, most prominently *NAACP v. Alabama* (1958)— which barred a state from gaining access to a private organization's membership lists—shored up political privacy and the privacy of association.[33] And 1961's *Mapp v. Ohio*, decided at precisely the same moment as *Poe v. Ullman*, made the federal exclusionary rule binding on the states, citing the privacy of the home as a barrier to the use of illegally procured evidence not just in federal but also in state criminal prosecutions. *Mapp* clearly stated that "the right to privacy embodied in the Fourth Amendment is enforceable against the States."[34] Although it spoke to developments outside constitutional law, it is worth noting too that by 1960, tort law, which had gradually answered Warren and Brandeis's 1890 call, recognized four distinct sorts of privacy invasion in the civil courts: intrusion on a person's solitude, public disclosure of embarrassing private facts, false publicity, and false appropriation of one's name or likeness.[35]

That birth control, however, could be construed as a matter of privacy was not foreordained. Like abortion, contraception up until this point was understood to be in the domain of either public morals regulation or public health and medical authority. Regulated by state law, "contraceptive devices" were not particularly "private" in the sense that they were available only through transactions with doctors and clinics. Indeed, *Griswold* concerned Connecticut's regulation of a Planned Parenthood clinic, and not (directly, anyway) people using contraception in a private bedroom. If it now seems self-evident that birth control belongs to the private sphere, this was not the case in 1965: *Griswold* was more the cause than the consequence of this understanding. If it also seems obvious that the "right to privacy" would lead to a chain of rulings specifying reproductive rights and, eventually, sexual liberty, this was even less clear. It took decades of labor, beginning in the 1920s, for the American Civil Liberties Union to successfully frame birth control as a personal right.[36] For the ACLU, as was true for its position on obscenity and nudism, the issue centered from the outset on rights to free speech and expression. The organization, influenced by birth control advocates like Margaret Sanger, would only very gradually shift from defending the dissemination of information about contraception to defending its use. The case for sex as a civil liberty was, even by 1965, tentative and partial. The ACLU and its allies in pressing the Connecticut case, for example, did not dare to introduce the subject of abortion into the mix.[37]

The fact that *Griswold* originated in arrests for contraceptive counseling at a public clinic made the privacy argument still more difficult to locate. Yet that argument had been introduced in *Poe v. Ullman* by lawyers for Planned Parenthood and the ACLU, citing not the clinic but the privacy of "sacred relations between a man and his wife" and the right to be "let alone in the bedroom" as the true site of the law's violation.[38] Estelle Griswold herself proclaimed that "we merely desire freedom in this most intimate of all our practices."[39] Under her canny leadership, Connecticut's Planned Parenthood chapter was happy to forward the analysis. Already in 1955—right on the heels of Senator Joseph McCarthy's fall from grace—it was soliciting support for overturning the birth control statute by invoking the imagery of a police state. One of its publications pictured police officers "hiding beneath beds, pad and pencil ready to record any activity that might take place on the mattress above." The caption read, "A policeman in every home is the only way to enforce this law."[40] The ACLU, engaged at this time in questions raised by *Mapp v. Ohio* concerning the possession of obscene material in the privacy of one's home, was beginning to connect the dots, its lawyers uniquely poised to apply a privacy claim across a broad spectrum of concerns, from search and seizure to contraception.[41] Although the Court would not overturn the Connecticut statute in 1961, there were four promising dissents. Justice Harlan's was particularly auspicious for its strong hints regarding the plausibility of a constitutional right to "marital privacy."[42]

Spring   SPECIAL LEGISLATIVE EDITION   1955

A POLICEMAN IN EVERY HOME IS THE ONLY WAY TO
ENFORCE THIS LAW.... passed in 1879

Section 8568: "Any person who shall *use* any drug, medicinal article or instrument for the purpose of preventing conception, shall be fined not less than fifty dollars or imprisoned not less than sixty days nor more than one year or be both fined and imprisoned."

Section 8875: "Any person who shall assist, abet, *counsel*, cause, hire or command another to commit any offense may be prosecuted and punished as if he were the principal offender." (This means it is a criminal offense for a doctor to prescribe a contraceptive to a married woman, even if her life is endangered by pregnancy.)

REPEAL....AMEND....or ENFORCE?

BILLS NOW BEFORE THE LEGISLATURE

HB 1177 — To Repeal Section 8568 of the General Statutes.

HB 1182 — The provisions of Sections 8568 and 8875 of the General Statutes shall not be construed to prevent (a) any physician duly licensed to practice in accordance with Section 4634 of the General Statutes from prescribing any method or means for the temporary prevention of pregnancy in a married woman, when, in the opinion of such physician, pregnancy would endanger the life or seriously impair the health of such married woman; or (b) a married person from using the method or means so prescribed, or (c) duly licensed pharmacists and druggists from filling said prescription.

OPEN HEARING
before the
Public Health and Safety Committee

Date: **WED., APRIL 20**

Hour: **1:30 P.M.**

Place: State Capitol
House of Representatives

! COME TO THIS HEARING !

AN IMPRESSIVE SHOW OF SUPPORT
FOR THESE BILLS IS VITAL

MEN and WOMEN of CONNECTICUT

Show Your Determination To Be Heard!!

46 States have liberal Maternal Health Laws....Why Can't We?

4.1. Advocates of legal contraception portrayed a "policeman under the bed" as the only way that bans on birth control could be enforced.

Despite these efforts, privacy would be neither the first nor the leading rationale for most of the key players in the 1965 ruling. Justice William O. Douglas, who wrote for the majority in *Griswold*, had initially been inclined toward the right of association and "peripheral rights" of the First Amendment, referencing several key rulings that protected the National Association for the Advancement for Colored People from state harassment.[43] It was only later drafts of his opinion that turned critically on what he referred to as "penumbras" and "emanations" of the Third, Fourth, and Fifth Amendments—their combined protections from the quartering of soldiers, arbitrary search and seizure, and self-incrimination amounting to a "right to privacy."[44] A few of Douglas's colleagues were willing to go along; Justice Brennan, in particular, had urged Douglas to make the privacy argument. But others struggled to find a more compelling logic for overturning a law that only recently would have been thought to fall squarely within the state's legitimate police powers.[45] Justice Harlan, as he had in his *Poe v. Ullman* dissent, relied on the notion of fundamental liberties protected by the Fourteenth Amendment's due process guarantee. Justice Goldberg, who joined Douglas's opinion, wound up authoring a long concurrence invoking the Ninth Amendment and matters "left to the people." This startling innovation—the Ninth Amendment had received almost no attention in the whole history of the Court's jurisprudence—suggests the stretching and strain that the case entailed for jurists committed to finding a principled privacy in the Constitution.[46]

Some justices, try as they might, had trouble discerning privacy in the case at all. Chief Justice Earl Warren harbored a strong sense that a right was implicated somehow, voicing the view in conference that "basic rights are involved here—we are dealing with a most confidential association, the most intimate in our life." But he was "bothered" that he couldn't find the proper grounds on which to invalidate the law.[47] Warren's clerk, calling Douglas's reasoning "dangerous," urged the Chief Justice to join a concurrence written by his colleague Byron White, who believed the law should be tossed out, but on grounds of equal protection rather than privacy. Indeed, many of the Court's law clerks scorned what they thought was a weak opinion, one recalling years later that "no one who read it liked it."[48] Douglas's mystical language of penumbras and emanations flowing from the Bill of Rights came in for particular ridicule.

Tellingly, even the lead counsel's brief for Estelle Griswold did not privilege privacy above other concerns. Thomas Emerson afterward described the "unusual variety of possible doctrinal solutions" the case allowed.[49] The fact that it "did not readily fit into any existing legal pigeonhole" meant that any direction the Court took to overrule it would be entering "uncharted waters." Emerson did himself characterize the statute as an invasion of privacy. He believed that even though the Court had not "spelled out" its boundaries, "plainly the right extends to unwarranted government invasion of (1) the sanctity of the home, and (2) the intimacies of the sexual relationship in marriage."[50] But the privacy argument shared space in his brief with arguably more powerful and popular reasons for supporting access to contraception—including population control and the rights of physicians to advise their patients.[51] He cited other reasons beyond "privacy" for overturning Connecticut's law as well, including the challenges of its enforcement and its discriminatory impact on poor women.[52]

Nor did the other attorneys arguing the merits of Griswold's case consider the privacy logic uppermost, perhaps judging those waters simply too uncharted. Their briefs suggested that the key issue at stake was either due process (whether the contraception ban aligned with a legitimate legislative purpose) or the First Amendment (whether it violated the free speech rights of the clinic directors).[53] Other rationales were contemplated too. A bold argument about contraception as central to women's equal citizenship rights, which had appeared in *Trubek v. Ullman*, one of the dismissed cases en route to *Griswold*, was feasible, if unlikely to succeed given the gendered assumptions of the time.[54] Much more seriously entertained were questions of equal protection centered on economic class, namely the differential imposition the birth control law posed for low-income women. As public clinics' main clientele, they were more directly affected by Connecticut's ban than were middle-class women, who could afford private physicians or obtain contraception by traveling out of state. Planned Parenthood's brief in the case tarred the statute as "grossly discriminatory," and a couple of the justices (Warren and White) favored this reasoning.[55]

And then there were the dissenters, Justices Hugo Black and Potter Stewart. Both disparaged the Connecticut law, Stewart branding it as "uncommonly silly." But neither believed in the existence of a right that could bar a state legislature from regulating as it saw fit in the domain of health and morality—let alone by recourse to a constitutional "right to privacy." As one commentator put it, the dissenters rejected "all of the proposed privacy theories as constitutional nonsense," and Douglas's opinion in particular for crafting "a fanciful new constitutional right out of thin air."

Justice Black called the right of privacy that *Griswold* carved from the Bill of Rights utterly "vague and standardless."[56] As for privacy itself, it was a "broad, abstract and ambiguous concept," its meanings too easily expanded or contracted to be useful material for the law. "I like my privacy as well as the next one," he asserted in the course of his twenty-page dissent, "but I am nevertheless compelled to admit that government has a right to invade it unless prohibited by some specific constitutional provision."[57]

Black's adjectives—broad, abstract, and ambiguous—aptly characterize the terms in which 1960s-era citizens discussed privacy, annexing the word to physical, virtual, and even psychological intrusions. Heightened sensitivity around privacy was evident in protests against prying into personal life via the home, the workplace, the school, or the marketplace, and it was almost certainly at play in the Court's ruling. Yet, at least in the ways Americans envisioned it at the time, it was a difficult concept to tether to a right.[58] If, as a contemporary legal scholar noted, privacy was "one of the warmest words in the literature of political and legal philosophy," it was also the case that there were few concepts "more vague or less amenable to definition and structured treatment." Indeed, "under this emotional term march a whole congeries of interests, some closely interrelated, some almost wholly unrelated and even inconsistent."[59] There was little disagreement that Connecticut's law was bad. But there was even more consensus that the Court had disposed of it improperly by invoking privacy. More than three dozen legal critiques of *Griswold* were issued in the next several years, many expressing disquiet over its "nebulous language" and "curious, puzzling mixture of reasoning" even as they endorsed its outcome.[60]

The Accidental Right

How was it that a constitutional right to privacy was not just pronounced in 1965, but wrested from this particular case? Justice Douglas's personal tilt toward privacy arguments notwithstanding, there were larger forces at work than either personality or precedent. Although impossible to prove, it seems undeniable that the Court was responding to more than an antiquated birth control law. The intensifying privacy debates of the past decade surely played into Justice Warren's sense that "basic rights" were at stake in the birth control case, even if the substance of such rights was hazy and difficult to discern in the Court's prior rulings.[61] Particularly evocative given the geopolitical climate was Justice Douglas's language of police patrolling domestic space—searching "the sacred precincts of marital bedrooms for telltale signs of the use of contraceptives"—which he suggested was the logical ending point of the Connecticut statute's enforcement.[62] Although the case concerned a public clinic, not a private bedroom, Douglas asked his readers to imagine this insupportable violation of intimacy.

At its crux was the married couple. The justice treated the marriage bed as a timeless, "pre-constitutional," privileged space.[63] The assumption of inviolate privacy in the marital bedchamber was in fact not age-old but relatively recent, and given new force by the ideology and architecture of postwar suburbia. It would anchor Douglas's fabrication, as one critic described it, of a "modern morality play, with much judicial finger-shaking at fictional police invading a fictional bedchamber of a fictional couple in search of evidence of the use of contraceptives."[64] In some sense the ruling was less an endorsement of individual privacy rights than a bolstering of protections for marriage and the family, aligning the United States with more modern constitutions and the Universal Declaration of Human Rights.[65] The family had been central to the American social order long before the Cold War. But marriage carried enormous political freight in the mid-twentieth-century United States. The family it produced was sign and substance of citizens' freedoms, the proof of their birthright to liberty and privacy. What the U.S. Supreme Court did in *Griswold*, writes historian Nancy Cott, was "set these linkages into constitutional interpretation," knitting together "the protection of marital intimacy with the political principles of American democracy."[66] All of these interpretations help fit *Griswold* into a Cold War and anti-totalitarian frame, making it a key symbolic statement of American commitment to a private sphere free from state interference.

Still, given the welter of privacy concerns in the postwar United States, the binding of marital sexuality and reproduction to the constitutional right to privacy should strike us as odd, even accidental. Marital intimacy of the sort that Douglas invoked and made vulnerable in *Griswold* had played almost no part in postwar debates over the state of Americans' privacy. Heterosexual unions, shadowed as they were by the increasing visibility of homosexuality in American life, were publicly affirmed and celebrated in the Cold War era.[67] Unlike residential, school, work, and even market relationships—all of which were newly shot through with privacy questions—the marital bond was not particularly troubled by intruders, unless one counted the family therapists to whom couples voluntarily flocked in the 1950s.[68] Indeed, earlier attempts to overturn the Connecticut statute had foundered on the fact that the law's challengers "had failed to demonstrate any real risk of prosecution."[69] All of this points to the largely symbolic nature of the ruling's language, at least as far as direct intimate regulation was concerned. *Griswold* had important immediate results: it decriminalized and widened access to contraception for working-class people who depended on public clinics. It would also become in time the foundation for consequential reproductive rights rulings. But in an era staked to the promise of "bedroom privacy," no matter what Justice Douglas implied, it did not respond to or remedy a *literal* concern about the state patrolling the intimacies of married couples.

This stood in stark contrast to the sex lives of other citizens. Married couples may not have had to worry, but plenty of other Americans who desired sexual privacy in this era were denied it. *Griswold*, in extending some citizens' rights, underscored widespread societal misgivings as to how others would make use of such privacy if only they had it. Single women, gay people, and those who violated dominant sexual norms—by marrying across the color line in many states, for example—were subject to very public regulation and policing.[70] Female sexuality was rarely viewed as a private matter. Unmarried women had long been targets of family and community strictures, and eventually public and institutional ones, around reproduction.[71] This was especially true for poor, working-class, and nonwhite women whose sexual decision making attracted far more public concern than that of affluent white women and who could marshal fewer resources in the project of sheltering their sexual lives from others.[72]

Douglas's dramatic scenario of police patrolling bedrooms was, for example, not at all fictional in the case of female welfare recipients. The modern welfare regime in the United States doled out invasive scrutiny alongside benefits, bringing new levels of surveillance into the homes of poor people, and especially of poor women.[73] Most egregiously, what were known as "man in the house" rules allowed public assistance to be stripped away if female recipients were found "consorting with men." Investigators routinely appeared in their homes in the middle of the night in search of "substitute fathers"—evidence that a woman might be receiving undocumented financial support and making her potentially liable for criminal charges.[74] The intimate lives of homosexual men and women were even more zealously policed, in raids of public restrooms and episodes of public shaming. Any privacy that gay people were able to eke out was judged not as a "positive public good," historian Marc Stein points out, but instead as a "secret evil."[75] With intimate privacy a privilege reserved for those respecting the boundaries of normative sexuality, homosexual men and women's struggles registered only faintly in the well-publicized debates over privacy intrusions at mid-century.

Nor, emphatically, was these citizens' privacy at issue in *Griswold*. What the ruling clarified instead was that were different allowances of privacy for different kinds of citizens in American society. Class and sexuality, along with race, helped determine whose privacy mattered in the dominant political culture, all the way up to the Supreme Court. Thus did a "right to privacy" that looked universal, indeed constitutional, in fact serve only some. As Stein shows, the "liberal" Warren Court was in fact deeply conservative in matters sexual, going out of its way to emphasize that its rulings did not protect sexual intimacy outside of heterosexual marriage.[76] Goldberg's and White's concurring opinions stated explicitly that the holding "in no way interferes with a State's proper regulation of sexual promiscuity or misconduct"; Harlan employed similar language.[77] The Court, it is clear, sought to protect not sexual privacy writ large, but marital, heterosexual, and reproductive privacy up until and well beyond its controversial ruling of 1973, *Roe v. Wade*.[78] The Catholic Church, the ACLU, and Planned Parenthood in 1965 did not challenge this emphasis, deliberately ignoring contemporary proposals calling for the decriminalization of consensual adult sex.

Moreover, the conclusions that Americans were beginning to draw about the state of personal privacy at mid-century—focused on intrusions from modern institutions that seemed to know them too well—were rooted in a range of experiences that differed from those at a birth control clinic. The probing questions of employers and psychologists, the invasiveness of neighbors and the media, the existence of private detectives and wiretaps, and the investigations of credit bureaus and insurance agents were likely all seen as more offensive to privacy than bans on married people's contraceptive use, particularly since so many middle-class men and women found their way around those restrictions. Citizens could not so easily evade the sense that the space for solitude and secrets in American society was shrinking. Had public opinion rather than the nine justices of the Supreme Court been in the driver's seat it is entirely possible that the "right to privacy" would have arrived with a very different tenor.

Viewed as an episode in the history of privacy—rather than the history of reproductive freedom or women's rights—*Griswold v. Connecticut* thus offers a paradox. The Court's historic ruling raising privacy to the status of a constitutional right resolved an issue that almost no one at the time associated closely with privacy. Undoing a morals regulation that affected fewer Americans by the year, it addressed neither the actual harms of policing intimate life nor the deeply contested issues around individual privacy that by 1965 begged for attention. Still, *Griswold* and its fictional policeman partook in some ways from the privacy discourse that preceded and surrounded it. The ruling's line in the sand, definitively cordoning off the normative domestic sanctuary from the state, was a clear statement that there were tangible places and situations where privacy continued to reign in modern society, where individuals' lives would be sealed off from an insistently knowing society. Some citizens, at least, could be certain that the government would not interfere with sexual decisions or practices within the private home. That is, the ruling sketched the boundary between public and private in a way that seemed easy to defend and straightforward to regulate. More even than the assurance that marital intimacy would remain intact, the promise that there remained "zones of privacy" for retreat and repose in American society, places that the state did not reach and could not know, may have been *Griswold's* true public import in 1965.

What seems clear is that the meeting of birth control advocates and the Warren Court on the terrain of a "right to privacy" was an odd turn in privacy's history and—perhaps, given the range and bulk of issues collecting under its name—an understandable narrowing of its scope. Time would alter its accidental quality, knitting together privacy rights with decisions about sexual-reproductive matters such that the conjunction no longer seemed strange. In the years after 1965, the Court would continue to rely on *Griswold* and its language of privacy in cases having to do with contraception, abortion, and eventually sexuality.[79] This was true of 1972's *Eisenstadt v. Baird,* which struck down laws banning contraception for the unmarried, making privacy, in one scholar's words, "a more portable, individual right."[80] The Court here announced that "if the right to privacy means anything, it is the right of the individual, married or single, to be free from unwarranted governmental intrusion into matters so fundamentally affecting a person as the decision whether to bear or beget a child."[81] This tilt toward individual autonomy in decision making and to reproductive rights would be even clearer in the following year's *Roe v. Wade*, which proclaimed that the "right to privacy . . . is broad enough to encompass a woman's decision whether or not to terminate her pregnancy."[82]

These rulings crystallized *Griswold*'s place in the history of reproductive freedom, situating the right to privacy squarely in that tradition and also facilitating its branching off in the direction of what has been termed "decisional autonomy" rather than intrusion per se.[83] In this way, the Court made a new right-to-privacy idiom more available even as it limited its purview. The Court's rhetorical power to shape public understandings can be potent. Public commentary on *Roe*, for example, quickly adopted its language and lead, cementing the view that abortion, once considered a public health matter or issue of medical privacy, turned fundamentally on individual women's autonomy and "choice."[84] Much of the criticism of the Court's privacy rulings from *Griswold* onward has centered on the impoverishment of discourses of reproductive freedom, the way abortion in particular became locked to "privacy" and "choice" rather than gender or economic equality, becoming entangled in a bitter, single-issue politics. That disappointment has led to a near-consensus among legal scholars that the Court's bold foray into privacy was both a grave and a consequential error.[85]

Fewer have asked what happened to privacy because of the way *Griswold* and reproductive rights jurisprudence interrupted a public debate in progress about "the right to be let alone"—as well as the desire, in many circumstances, to remain unknown. Strikingly, *Griswold* and nearly all the Supreme Court cases that came on its heels crafted the constitutional right to privacy within the context of sexual intimacy and family life.[86] Abortion came to be obviously, if contentiously, a matter of "privacy." The intrusions of community life, advertising and marketing, school and employment testing—all those issues that raised the pitch of privacy discussions in the decade before *Griswold*—did not. The Supreme Court may in 1965 have responded to a broad social unease with the state of Americans' privacy. But in doing so, at least in the realm of jurisprudence, it helped to hijack those meanings.

Griswold's Little-Known Progeny

In the immediate "afterglow" of *Griswold*, however, the brand-new right to privacy looked expansive.[87] Popular observers were none too surprised that the Court had located it. That such a right existed seemed intuitively correct, the law catching up to what citizens already sensed. And even if *Griswold* referred only to marital privacy and only with regard to contraception, commentators spied a more inclusive and capacious right in the offing. The *Nation*, for example, noted a "clear suggestion that the majority will recognize other forms of a general right to privacy." *Time* magazine anticipated much more discussion to come: "Lawyers can now spend years happily fighting over just what else the new right of privacy covers."[88] For many, *Griswold* seemed to indicate that clear lines could be drawn between the public and private spheres of modern life, that protections of privacy from all manner of intrusions were forthcoming, and that the Court was ready to lend its considerable authority to that project.

The fact, if not the text, of the ruling buoyed such expansiveness. Today understood as the progenitor of reproductive rights, *Griswold* in its own time appeared applicable to an array of quite different scenarios, observers easily imagining its implications for a whole complex of institutions that, in seeking to probe Americans' personal lives, had done so much to rouse privacy debates since World War II. The birth control case thus could easily be assimilated into well-developed debates over the known citizen. The state's potential access to confidential counseling central to the doctor-patient relationship, but also the intimate conversations between spouses regarding family planning, linked *Griswold* to privacy discussions that had come before it. Many journalists, commentators, and professional associations predicted that the ruling was just the first step in a broader recalibration of privacy in American society and that a comprehensive right "to be left alone" was imminent. Sexual conduct outside marriage was one candidate for new protections. But so was a citizen's ability to be free of wiretapping and eavesdropping, compelled disclosures through lie detectors, and employment testing, for example. Even the home lives of the poor looked less open to interference post-*Griswold*. Most of the potential rights to privacy that the ruling would inspire outstripped the protections that the Court was prepared to offer. But their plausibility in the later 1960s should not be underestimated.

A handful of legal observers viewed *Griswold* less as a milestone than a decision grooved by other fundamental rights, simply another step along "a worn and familiar path."[89] But most were certain major change was at hand. One expert contributing to a *Michigan Law Review* panel on *Gris-*

4.2. Estelle Griswold (left) celebrating the Supreme Court ruling announcing a constitutional right to privacy in the case that bore her name.

wold contrasted the "slow and gradual" evolution of privacy rights in tort law following Warren and Brandeis's famous 1890 essay to privacy's precipitous and startling constitutional appearance in 1965. Disconnected from search and seizure or self-incrimination rulings that it might have built on, the jurisprudential link was forged "only by use of the term 'right of privacy' to apply to both type of rights."[90] *Griswold*, in this analysis, was a break with and decisive step beyond the haphazard mentions of privacy in the Court's earlier rulings. Another on the panel believed the Court's language would provide the "constitutional underpinnings" for "situations which do not fit established categories neatly but still seem to rest on values thought to be vital and which, for lack of a better term, are called privacy."[91] There was no doubt, predicted another, that "many forces in our society will press hard toward fuller realization of its great potential."[92] For a last expert, the ruling was nothing short of "the birth of a new facet of constitutional meaning." *Griswold* was "the nearest articulation to date (although it is none too clear at that) of the constitutional foundations of a yearning for 'privacy.'" This was true even if the ruling remained longer on yearning than on substance.[93]

What impressed these commentators was not that privacy talk was in the air. As one noted, "It takes a special form of foolhardiness to raise one's voice against the right of privacy at this particular moment in its history."[94] The novelty was the Court's engagement with it. Before *Griswold*, it had seemed that privacy was everywhere in U.S. public culture *but* the law. Harkening back to Warren and Brandeis, the Duke legal scholar Clark C. Havighurst mused that three quarters of a century later, "privacy still remains primarily a nonlegal concept," and an "awkward" one at that. "The law," he claimed, "has never absorbed the privacy concept comfortably or made it altogether its own." As he saw it, it was popular exposés and the mass press that had elevated privacy as a social value in order to express a "congeries of public fears and annoyances." Treating law as a latecomer to the party, Havighurst believed, however, that its moment of reckoning had arrived, given privacy's new status as "a rallying point for those concerned about the encroachments of mass society on the individual."[95]

On the heels of *Griswold*, it appeared that lawyers and legal scholars would be forced to take heed. A sense of coming legal recognition, even revolution, pervaded one 1966 symposium on the "right to privacy." To the philosopher Glenn Negley, it was remarkable that "after centuries of failure to recognize privacy . . . we suddenly find ourselves concerned with the right of privacy as one of the most critical problems of contemporary political and legal analysis."[96] Why now? William M. Beaney, a Princeton political scientist, argued that to understand privacy's mid-1960s moment it was necessary to look less at legal precedents than at the society at large, at the human relationships undergoing "radical transformation as the result of new ways of carrying on governmental and private organizational activities." He reflected on the difference from Warren and Brandeis's day, when it was the privacy of "public men" that was most at issue. In 1966, "certain forms of visual and auditory surveillance," as well as opinion surveys, behavioral research, and computerized data gathering, were "rapidly destroying the privacy of the obscure 'common man.'"[97]

In this, Beaney echoed legal scholar Robert Dixon Jr., who in his own reflections on *Griswold* moved seamlessly from the marital bedroom to the "evolution of democratic socialism and the security state, in which the forces of organization threaten to crowd out privacy." Elaborating in a footnote, Dixon referred precisely to the issues that had preoccupied writers on privacy in the past decade revolving around the known citizen: the "growing corporate and government practice of psychiatric evaluation and psychological testing of employees" and related issues of permissible "range and depth of probing."[98] Thomas Emerson, the prevailing attorney in *Griswold*, similarly gestured to larger fish to fry. At stake was the protection of the private realm, "which belongs to the individual" and loomed ever larger as "modern society has developed." For Emerson, "all the forces of a technological age—industrialization, urbanization, and organization— operate to narrow the area of privacy and facilitate intrusions into it." Sounding the same symbolic notes as Justice Douglas, he argued that preserving a private sphere in this context marked "the difference between a democratic and a totalitarian society."[99]

None of these commentators, in their sweeping invocations of mass society and transformed social relationships, dwelled on anything so concrete or narrow as a state ban on contraceptives. The substance of *Griswold* was almost beside the point. Rather, they took the ruling to be speaking to a specifically modern set of pressures on the person. As such they offer compelling evidence that many believed the Court to be responding to a profound social and political—perhaps even structural—shift in American society. At issue, in Havighurst's estimation, was the "preference of individuals to live their lives and maintain their personalities and affairs free from undue intrusion by, or exposure to, the outside world." Some threats to this "personality" flowed from the state. But many did not. Beaney fingered contemporary intruders such as "business, labor organizations, universities, and other private entities" that "affect our daily lives more immediately and in many cases more substantially than do governmental agencies."[100] For Negley, the culprit was simply modern "organization," which he characterized as "the complex of corporate pressures that prescribe the possibilities of action for every man."[101]

In the mid-1960s, legal observers were certain that harms to privacy, however defined, stemmed from the very workings of the contemporary social order. On these grounds, some critiqued the Court's attempt to confine "zones of privacy" to particular spaces or physical entities; that is, the home or the bedroom. Beaney believed that *privacy*—suggesting "aloofness and withdrawal from everyday life," and thus a practical impossibility—was in fact the wrong word for the set of problems it sought to address. Following Warren and Brandeis, he preferred the rights of "personality" (had the term not, alas, already been captured by the psychologists) or perhaps the "dignity of the individual" as a counterweight to the troubles that plagued the modern person.[102] Yet another contributor to the

1966 symposium, Cornell law professor Milton R. Konvitz, likewise objected to the "right to privacy" phrasing for its association with what was "withdrawn from public view—like the marital bedroom" and its implications of darkness and secrecy. He was partial to Thomas Cooley's phrase, "the right to be let alone," or what he simply called "breathing space." Sounding a distinctly 1960s-era note, Konvitz urged that humans' need for such space was something that applied no matter where the individual happened to be. It was "a sphere of space that has not been dedicated to public use or control. It is a kind of space that a man may carry with him, into his bedroom or into the street. Even when public, it is part of the inner man."[103] For the Chicago sociologist Edward Shils, the essential thing was the "capacity for 'keeping to one's self,' to be unobserved, to withhold information about states of mind and actions, i.e., the capacity to retain possession of these emanations of the self."[104]

These philosophical ruminations about breathing room for the "inner man"—particularly the concern with mental or interior spaces and psychological freedom—were clear outgrowths of the multilayered discussions about privacy in the postwar era. And they were nurtured by the widely available language of totalitarianism that circulated in mid-century America. The Supreme Court's decision to pronounce on privacy seemed to open the door to remedies for harms less tangible than a policeman under the bed. Curbs on personality testing, eavesdropping, forced confessions, and perhaps even ubiquitous marketing, such observers speculated, might be where the Court would head next. Their aspirations for the new right went far beyond the Court's declarations about "zones of privacy" and protected statuses such as marital intimacy. Would *Griswold* be the opening wedge to a serious reworking of the relationship between the individual and the social order—a sign that the pressures of contemporary life might be met in law? A flurry of hopeful new privacy claims would test the question.

Legal scholars were not the only ones who assumed that *Griswold* was a stepping-stone to more expansive privacy protections. This was clear in popular commentaries about the likely effect of the decision on contraception bans and certain reproductive decisions even if—as is also clear—few initially made the link to abortion rights.[105] The War on Poverty just launched, advocates for the poor imagined that public health clinics and social welfare programs would now be free to engage in contraceptive counseling, for example.[106] Commentators predicted that, even construed narrowly, the decision would have implications for other birth control regulations on the books, as well as compulsory sterilization laws.[107] Others simply dismissed or ignored the Court's carefully tailored language of "marital privacy," assuming that a more capacious right to sexual privacy had already been elaborated or soon would be. Indeed, the press as often as not misrepresented the right to privacy that the justices had actually established. As Marc Stein has found, popular accounts portrayed *Griswold*, along with the reproductive rights cases that would follow, "as more sexually libertarian and egalitarian than the texts of the decisions stated or implied."[108] Many outlets in 1965 reported, inaccurately, that laws banning contraception were now unconstitutional or that all forms of birth control were constitutionally protected. Even when the decision was rightly cast narrowly, as one that protected married couples' use of contraception, reports often implied that broader change was inevitable. The meager public attention to *Eisenstadt v. Baird*, the 1972 case that extended *Griswold's* protections to unmarried people, may have stemmed from the fact that many Americans assumed all contraception bans had already been overturned.[109]

More intriguing were expectations about the impact of the 1965 ruling that had nothing to do with marriage, family, or reproduction. A host of commentators, scholarly and popular, immediately perceived *Griswold's* relevance to far-flung domains. Again, this is surprising only if we see the ruling as mostly about reproductive rights. But for contemporaries, the pressing questions having to do with privacy were elsewhere, and *Griswold* was simply a tool for answering them. Sounding much like a latter-day Samuel Warren or Louis Brandeis, one commentator, for example, hoped "the right of privacy is not to be limited narrowly to the facts of Griswold, but is meant to foretell broad protection for the dignity of man and the inviolability of his rights of personality." If so, it might bolster citizens' rights vis-à-vis legislative investigation, travel, loyalty oaths, and religious freedom.[110] Others added intrusive police tactics and lie detectors to the list. Some ventured further, wondering a bit fancifully what *Griswold* portended for those seeking "a greater degree of freedom from unsolicited phone calls from pollsters and salesmen."[111] One legal analyst, looking at concurrent trends in Fourth Amendment law, boldly laid out privacy's future without even mentioning sexual or reproductive rights; he observed that "the right to be left alone by medical experimenters" and even the right to be free of radio programs on public transportation seemed to be "assuming constitutional proportions."[112] The new right to privacy was enticingly elastic, able even perhaps "to form a protective shield for the individual against an increasingly intrusive world."[113]

Most commonly mentioned in all this flurry of speculation, however, was *Griswold*'s significance for wiretapping and electronic eavesdropping. Wiretapping, deemed constitutional in 1928 in the *Olmstead* case, had long troubled citizens and legal scholars alike. The Federal Communications Act of 1934 had already outlawed information procured by wiretaps in federal courts, but not the wiretaps themselves, and evidence gleaned from them was still allowable in state courts.[114] The birth control case provided critical ammunition for extending the ban. When the *Duke Law Journal* applauded the fact that the Court in *Griswold* had "seized a propitious opportunity" for dealing with other "problematic areas in which an interest in privacy may be paramount," it put wiretapping and eavesdropping at the head of the line.[115] Estelle Griswold's lawyer, Thomas Emerson, argued too that electronic eavesdropping was an "obvious area" in which the right to privacy "is sure to be pressed and may well be successful." He reasoned that "the scientific possibilities are so fantastic and the invasion of privacy so devastating that it is hard to believe a civilized society will not feel compelled to throw up some protection to individuals."[116] Justice Earl Warren, the man whose name was stamped on the Warren Court, himself had stated in 1963 his belief that "the fantastic advances in the field of electronic communication" now constituted a "great[] danger to the privacy of the individual."[117]

What was sometimes called "conversational privacy" seemed to some a natural corollary of the way that the right to privacy was conceived in *Griswold*. The *New York Times* explained that even though "the connection between birth control and wiretapping may not seem obvious to the naked eye," legal experts believed the 1965 ruling likely to lead to bans on wiretapping and other forms of virtual eavesdropping. The link was, of course "the right of privacy, which was given a constitutional home of its own for the first time in the Connecticut case." *Griswold* appeared promising for this purpose because the new right seemed to "override" the "technical distinction of a physical intrusion" that the Court had required to find an invasion of privacy, via the Fourth Amendment, in the *Olmstead* decision.[118] In that case, because telephone wires extended outside the residence in question, listening in did not violate any physical boundary and so was not judged an invasion. Justice Taft argued in his ruling that the language of the Fourth Amendment was limited to "material things": a person, his house, his papers, or his personal effects. Since an individual's spoken words were not "material," he or she had no privacy interest in them as they traveled over the phone lines. Despite its references to a specific place, the marital bedroom, *Griswold* gestured to a broader realm of discussion and conversational intimacy—among physicians and patients, but perhaps others as well—that was constitutionally protected.[119] As one commentator put it, "If there is a right to marital privacy in the home, why should there not be as well a right of privacy in the home or place of business against the unwelcome intrusion of uninvited participants in conversations intended to be private?"[120] For those inclined to this interpretation, it was a foregone conclusion that the Court would be required to "knock out all forms of eavesdropping."[121]

An answer would soon come in the 1967 Supreme Court ruling of *Katz v. United States*. The case centered on the admissibility of evidence obtained by the FBI's bugging of a public phone booth on Sunset Boulevard in Los Angeles, where a man named Charlie Katz habitually placed illegal interstate bets.[122] Although Katz was engaged in a criminal practice in a public locale, his conviction was overturned. In the process, the Court advanced a new interpretation of the Fourth Amendment's protection against "unreasonable searches and seizures." Henceforth the Constitution would protect Americans not simply from physical trespasses—the "material things" that had been the sticking point in *Olmstead*—but from trespasses against their "reasonable expectations of privacy." The ruling's most famous line decoupled privacy rights from property rights, declaring forcefully that the Fourth Amendment "protects people, not places."[123] By making the person and his or her expectations—and not that person's physical surroundings—the subject of privacy, the ruling indirectly answered some contemporary critiques of *Griswold*'s limited language of protected "zones."

The more mobile (and subjective) understanding of individual privacy advanced in *Katz* responded to new technologies like "detectaphones" and "spike mikes" that could glean private conversations without physically breaching private space.[124] *Life* magazine's cover story in 1966, for instance, introduced the reader to tiny bugging devices that might "wind up in the olive of a nearby martini, in the mouthpiece of his telephone, in a knob on his car's dashboard, in the handle of his briefcase, even in a cavity in the tooth of an intimate associate."[125] Journalistic fascination with transmitters small enough to fit in a cigarette pack, and particularly the ubiquitous martini olive (with a "built-in sending device and a toothpick antenna"), was evident in the widespread coverage of increasingly available and affordable spy gadgets.[126] *Life* gave a human face to these techniques—a glimpse into "a world suddenly turned into a peephole and listening post"—in its profile of a day in the life of "master eavesdropper" Bernard B. Spindel. A family man with seven children and a "svelte wife," Spindel was "an accomplished barbecue chef, a horse fancier, builder of floating electric Christmas trees," who incidentally had been indicted or arrested 204 times for surreptitiously recording strangers' conversations.[127] *Life*'s interest was in exposing a figure in the shadows, a man who knew something about everyone. But the reporter couldn't conceal his own voyeuristic interest in Spindel's futuristic gadgets and considerable expertise.

Alan Westin, who authored a landmark book, *Privacy and Freedom*, the same year that *Katz* was handed down, offered a more sober accounting of the ways miniature listening, transmitting, and recording devices along with tiny cameras and telephoto lenses were "dissolving the walls" that Americans had once naïvely trusted to shield them from prying eyes and ears.[128] He provided a partial but daunting catalog of technological hazards under the header "New Tools for Invading Privacy": florescent powders or dyes, miniature transmitters, "radio pills," two-way mirrors, "electric eyes," "hidden television-eye monitoring," closed-circuit television, infrared film, telephoto-lens cameras, sniperscope viewers, third-party eavesdropping, micro-miniature tape recorders, electrically conductive paint, remote-control tone devices, "spike" and parabolic microphones, ultrasonic generators, powerful binoculars, safe-cracking listening devices, telephone or teletype taps, television signal measurement, and "needle-thin flashlights" for reading sealed mail.[129] Privacy, imagined as a physical retreat from others' eyes and ears, would be much harder to secure in this new technological context. In a sense, though, *Katz* was an answer, if long in coming, to the virtual invasions that accompanied the arrival of the telephone and telegraph. That physical trespass was not an essential component of a privacy invasion had seemed obvious to many Americans nearly a century before *Katz* was decided.

And yet the resolution of that long-simmering question, along with Charlie Katz's win, came with a price. Although many observers had confidently expected that the Supreme Court would make all forms of wiretapping illegal, the holding permitted the practice—"so long as it proceeded pursuant to a judicial warrant." What was most controversial

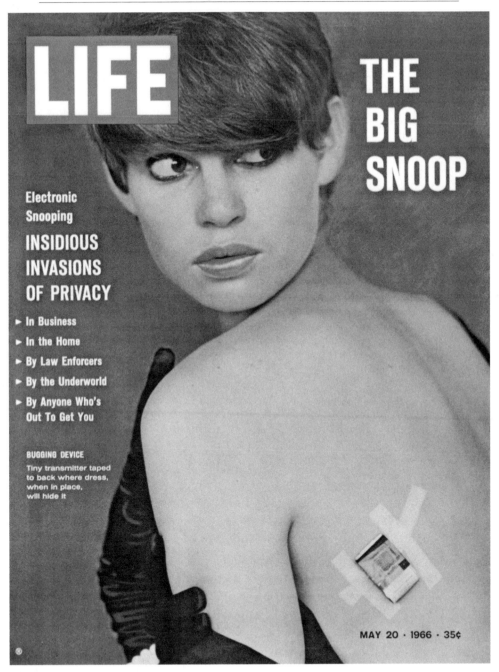

4.3. Concerns about wiretapping and electronic eavesdropping were at a high pitch in American society by the mid-1960s.

and surprising about *Katz* in 1967 was not its modernizing of privacy rights or its grappling with virtual intrusions, maintains one legal scholar. It was that electronic eavesdropping was ruled "constitutionally permissible."[130] In *Katz*, new privacy claims came up against the interests of law enforcement in employing a highly useful technology for uncovering criminal activity. Weighing the two interests—the right not to have one's private conversations known and the duty of the police to apprehend known criminals—the Court offered the warrant requirement as a middle ground.

As it turned out, *Katz*'s compromise would be more telling for the future than *Griswold*'s deceptively solid language of "zones of privacy." Already in 1967, the window of possibility opened by that 1965 ruling was closing. In the 1970s, privacy's jurisprudential fortunes would take a turn for the worse as the backlash around *Roe v. Wade* intensified and a less expansive understanding of individual rights took hold. The right to privacy would be considerably less appealing to the more conservative Burger and Rehnquist Courts than it had been to Earl Warren's. It would be subordinated, along with other of the Warren Court's key rulings, to rising calls for "law and order" in American public culture. The new Supreme Court Justice, William H. Rehnquist, the man who would "be instrumental in defining the scope of constitutional privacy for the next quarter century," mused in 1973 that when "the balance is struck in favor of 'privacy' some other societal value will suffer." Law enforcement was his key example.[131] As political scientist Naomi Murakawa has argued, conservatives and liberals alike would subscribe to the tenets of this platform in the Nixon years, whereby "the implicitly white right to safety was paramount, not to be threatened by special 'minority' or 'criminal' rights."[132]

Citizens would learn in the years to come that privacy questions raised by national security or policing, along with an array of others bearing on society's ability to know and to track individual citizens, could pose even thornier challenges than did those related to morals regulation. In 1967, however, *Katz* may have looked like a blip rather than a portent. Privacy advocates had the wind in their sails, and they boldly pressed the question of rights.

Privacy Democratized

The *Griswold* ruling not only allowed Americans to imagine more robust applications of the "right to be let alone." Arriving when it did in the mid-

1960s, the heyday of civil rights energies and the New Left, it also raised questions about whom that right served. Before the 1960s, cultural commentators often treated privacy as a middle- and upper-class entitlement, and a concern of little interest to minorities and the poor.[133] This explains, if only in part, the cloistered nature of earlier Cold War privacy debates, trained resolutely on issues that most affected the white, suburban middle class.

But this limited view—along with its elitist assumptions about a greater desire for privacy among the privileged—would temporarily be revised and even reversed in the later 1960s. The poor, some would come to argue, might be even more in need of privacy than the comfortable. Activists and advocates pressed for protections that would secure the dignity of all citizens, especially those who had rarely been the imagined holders of rights. And for a brief time, the privacy claims of special classes of citizens, including criminals, prisoners, juvenile delinquents, vagrants, and the poor, gained traction. Professionals and policy makers would be pushed to reevaluate a whole set of practices that had governed the lives of those on society's margins. On closer inspection, many of those practices now looked like improper invasions of privacy. As privacy earned a new status in American society—no longer simply a privilege or a preference or a sensibility but a constitutional right—it seemed that new kinds of people might lay claim to it.

One commentator, writing immediately post-*Griswold*, understood the Warren Court's concern for extending equal protection to "disadvantaged individuals and minorities" as a critical step "toward protecting the privacy of ever-larger numbers of people." Although aware that privacy had often been viewed as the province of "higher status individuals," he glimpsed in the 1960s the possibility of its extension to all citizens, including criminal suspects, religious and racial minorities, and welfare clients.[134] He was correct that class- and race-based limits to privacy were beginning to crumble alongside substantive efforts to combat discrimination and inequality in American society. Social movements were the engine, but the Warren Court played a critical role, striking down key instances of unequal treatment and enlarging through its rulings the "rights of belonging" in American society.[135] Similarly, the Court's decisions in this era—on vagrancy, for example—took steps toward "dismantling the criminal law as a method of social control."[136] A new pluralism, bolstered by law, was evident in the flourishing of privacy claims in multiple spheres. It spoke both to the cross-cutting appeal of privacy as an answer to social problems and to the way the very demand for privacy was being democratized.

The Warren Court's creation of new protections for criminal suspects is the best-known instance of this expanded arena for individual sovereignty. In a brief span of years, the Court codified the right to counsel and appeal; the rules for excluding wrongfully obtained evidence; and protections against self-incrimination, warrantless searches, forced confessions, and other forms of police coercion.[137] Some of these rulings were more closely linked to individual privacy than others. But the overall pattern helped give shape to a 1960s-era revisioning of who ought to have access to privacy and in what circumstances.

So did the political rhetoric of the era's social activism. The civil rights movement's exposure of many forms of social exploitation and its insistence on human dignity were crucial. The New Left's suspicion of authorities, its profession of faith in ordinary citizens' judgments, and its quest for personal freedom and authenticity bolstered the presumption of an individual's claim on privacy vis-à-vis institutional or professional prerogatives.[138] Even as it challenged society's division between public and private, the women's movement strengthened this particular sort of claim to sovereignty over one's person and self. This was especially clear in activists' challenges to medical paternalism and the male physicians who exerted so much control over women's bodies—extending even to the knowledge they possessed of their own physical beings. The landmark publication of the Boston Women's Medical Collective, *Our Bodies, Ourselves*, hit notes of self-possession, even self-authentication, that would resonate powerfully by the early 1970s. A book emphatically "by and for women," the manual reminded readers that "it's your body" and not anyone else's.[139] By invoking privacy, citizens wrested some control from authorities and gained leverage in their interactions with powerful institutions in American society. Nourished by the courts and social movements alike, privacy was becoming part of a popular lexicon of rights—even for those citizens who had been able to claim precious little of it in the past: soldiers and patients, juvenile delinquents as well as welfare recipients.

Remarkably, even the military, long a social world bound by its own rules, became a site for probing privacy's boundaries in this era. Writing in the *Military Law Review* in 1964, a lieutenant colonel surveyed debates on the extent to which soldiers were entitled to a sphere apart from state scrutiny. He concluded that "an Army career today demands some sacrifice, but not total submission to authority." This writer made the case that the complex of rights, privileges, and immunities that enlisted men enjoyed were really "manifestations of a single, more fundamental right, one which should be called 'the soldier's right to a private life.'" He also suggested that although the Constitution had not been much of a resource for soldiers up to the mid-1960s, times were changing. The privacy rights of soldiers, like those of civilians, might get a hearing in the courts.[140] That promise would not bear out, at least in the way the lieutenant colonel hoped: a 1975 ruling of the U.S. Court of Appeals, referencing *Katz*, stated plainly that "the 'expectation of privacy' is different in the military than it is in civilian life" and that "the soldier cannot reasonably expect the Army barracks to be a sanctuary like his civilian home."[141] Yet the very belief that the military might be remade to protect soldiers' private lives—inspired by the broad critique of totalitarianism that underwrote *Griswold* as well as the spirit of the New Left—was a powerful testament to the expansiveness of privacy talk in this era.

Hospitals and the medical arena also witnessed new thinking about privacy in the late 1960s and early 1970s, ranging from the ruminations of medical ethicists to the decision making of nurses at the moment of care. It is as if medical workers saw their profession with new eyes, their familiar workaday routines gaining a different aspect in the intense focus on privacy of the day. The eminent Christian ethicist Paul Ramsey, in his lectures on "the patient as person," asked how best to "show respect for, protect, preserve, and honor the life of fellow man."[142] One answer was to treat the patient first as a human being; another was to accept limits to the search for knowledge about him. Others wrote of the need for medical staff to root each and every decision in the "basic concern for each individual's right to his private cloak of personal dignity."[143] A nurse, Dorothy Smith, granted that "experiencing some intrusion upon one's privacy is a necessary part of patienthood." It was a status that compelled physical exposure, as well as personal disclosure of private matters. Medical care, as she saw it, was a human interaction in which "one of the persons lacks his usual ability to 'cover his nakedness' and to protect himself from loss of personal privacy." The obligation of the nurse therefore was to protect the privacy of the person who couldn't do so himself, to help the patient, in other words, "re-clothe" himself. Smith called on medical personnel to "reinforce the patient's personhood regardless of the physical or emotional exposure that makes him particularly vulnerable."[144] Writing in 1969, her reflections owed something to *Griswold* but also to *Katz*: the notion that the individual was entitled to a "reasonable expectation of privacy," no matter the setting.

In fundamental ways, this charge rewrote the rules of medical care. The nurse, Dorothy Smith explained, must help patients not only protect their privacy but also "deal with that loss of privacy which is inevitable in the situation." It behooved her to protect her patients' modesty, to shield them from embarrassment, to refrain from inquiring needlessly into their affairs, and to help them learn what sort of sharing of information was necessary—all the while carrying the burden of their confidences. Smith offered instructions on "Arranging for Privacy," spelling out small details (moving a chair close, wheeling a patient to a quiet hallway, drawing a curtain, closing doors to the nurses' station) that would help create a private enclave—indeed a zone of privacy—around the patient. Smith further argued that such principles ought to guide the blueprints for new hospital wards, which "we should appraise . . . not only with an eye to efficiency and safety but also to patients' privacy."[145] By 1973, such concerns had made their way into the Patient Bill of Rights, adopted by the American Hospital Association. Beyond stating that all patients had a right to privacy, it encouraged respect for the patient's body, stipulating that it be shielded "from the view of others."[146] The patient, like the accused, was to be treated as a rights-holder, deserving of authorities' respect and restraint.

The newest note in all of this, however, was the sudden concern for the privacy and self-respect of welfare recipients. In the long history of public relief in the United States, it is fair to say that the question had scarcely been contemplated. In the 1960s, however, legal scholars, poverty experts, and, most importantly, a welfare rights movement propelled largely by African American women were emboldened to raise it. Old assumptions about the link between privilege and privacy were coming under fire. One sign was a searching exploration of "privacy, poverty, and the Constitution" in 1966 by Albert Bendich, a lawyer and professor at U.C. Berkeley. He offered up the maxim that "poverty and privacy are intimately and inversely related," arguing that the "willingness to intrude upon and manage the lives of others" evident in the welfare system stemmed from a belief that those on public assistance were "less than full citizens and persons, even if not quite criminals." This made them "fair game for treatment [we] would consider unconstitutional if applied to persons of means." As he saw it, the vital task was to demolish what he pointedly called "the right to *invade* privacy which such attitudes nurture."[147]

As Bendich's analysis suggests, the question about the privacy rights of the poor brought critical attention to more than just criminal procedure and policing. It also generated a reappraisal of the administrative state and the social welfare guarantees of the New Deal and now Great Society—and particularly the behavioral strictures that accompanied their benefi-cence. Social Security's public assistance provisions could look different through a right-to-privacy lens. A lifeline of benefits to poor people might also result in damaging incursions on their dignity. One legal scholar in *Griswold*'s aftermath wondered, for instance, about "the reach of the inquisitorial power of the state in the case-worker-client relationship" common to programs like Aid to Dependent Children. That power of case-worker over client, he thought, raised "serious questions precisely in the area of privacy now constitutionally zoned by the Supreme Court." Would that right to privacy now "extend to such matters as frequency of sexual intercourse, ethical outlook, savings habits, drinking habits"—all of which were regularly noted and monitored by caseworkers? He probed the issue further: "What may be made a matter of record, and what guarantees of confidentiality are legally mandated? How far (apart from birth control) may the 'planning' in family planning be carried?"[148]

If privacy was a constitutional right, to what degree could or should it be restricted for those most directly in the government's sights? The state's close tabs on those drawing public assistance was typically justified by the need to guard against benefits fraud and abuse. This was a concern, importantly, only about certain kinds of "welfare," even within the same federal agency: Social Security's Aid to Dependent Children rather than Old Age Benefits. The discussion that crystallized around welfare recipients' dignity and rights after *Griswold* thus reveals how privacy talk could challenge the harms of class and potentially enlarge poor people's citizenship claims.[149]

The two-tiered welfare state that separated "entitlements" from "wel-fare," it seemed, had birthed a two-tiered privacy regime as well. Some citizens—suburban homeowners with private bedrooms, those who paid into and drew out of Social Security's retirement fund—were accorded a constitutional shield around their privacy. Less fortunate Americans, those on public assistance or living in public housing, had no such protection from the gaze of the state. The Yale legal scholar Charles Reich would develop the point in a series of essays exploring the constitutional implications of the modern welfare regime.[150] Observing that the law had barely taken note of public assistance administration and the rights of beneficiaries, he argued that welfare recipients "have been subjected to many forms of procedure and control not imposed on other citizens." The poor, he intoned, "are all too easily regulated."[151] Reich indeed believed that the most challenging constitutional issues raised by welfare programs were related to questions of "personal liberty and privacy." Both were regularly transgressed by inquiries, all in the name of efficient management, into recipients' personal and family affairs—"the sort of things that are, to the average person, nobody else's business, certainly not government's." As Reich saw it, "the evils of any public welfare system" consisted in subjecting large numbers of people to just this sort of "bureaucratic discretion." Encouraged by *Griswold*, he sought to bring such issues under the banner of constitutional rights.[152]

One immediate target was the despised practice of "midnight raids" to check up on welfare recipients' living arrangements. Looking to precedents regarding the sanctity of the private dwelling as well as justifications for entry, Reich judged it obvious that such raids violated the Fourth Amendment.[153] The only reason they transpired was that "persons on public assistance are in no position to enforce a constitutional right of privacy."[154] Social Security and public assistance had become an essential infrastructure for contemporary society, argued Reich. The question was whether they had to come bundled with "official condescension and prying." "Must the price of state support," he demanded, "be the erosion of self-respect, and individual rights against government?"[155]

The welfare rights movement of the late 1960s, energized by civil rights successes and the rights-friendly rhetoric of the Warren Court as well as the organizing prowess of women on public assistance, answered in the negative.[156] The very fact that the government subsidized low-income housing and other social benefits was an entering wedge for activists' claim as citizens to a right to decent living conditions. Perhaps paradoxically, the fact that the "previously private sphere of home had become public and political space," writes historian Rhonda Williams, motivated welfare rights advocates to demand more autonomy from and less scrutiny by the agents of the government.[157]

The movement would even win some contests in this arena. In *King v. Smith* of 1968, the Supreme Court took up the claim of an African American welfare recipient from Alabama, Mrs. Sylvester Smith, whose Aid to Dependent Children benefits had been abruptly cut off. The rationale for that decision—as Smith's caseworker informed her—were reports indicating occasional visits of a boyfriend. That fact in turn had been discovered through a note in Smith's case dossier and confirmed via the questioning of a "third party." In Alabama by the mid-1960s, in what was commonly understood as a bid to trim welfare rolls, any sexual liaison with a man was enough to trigger the state's "substitute father" regulation. The law presumed that a woman in Smith's situation was receiving male support for her children and was thus not eligible for aid—even if the man neither lived with her nor paid her bills.[158] Caseworkers complied with these rules, even interviewing children in some cases about their mother's sexual practices. This was as about as close as one could get to a policeman in the bedroom, that evocative figure used by both Planned Parenthood and Justice Douglas in arguing for a constitutional right to privacy. In the words of Alabama's Commissioner of Pensions and Security, a mother could choose "to give up her pleasure or to act like a woman ought to act like and continue to receive aid."[159]

The ignominies did not end there. As the *New York Times Magazine* detailed the situation in a profile, for Mrs. Smith to regain the public aid that she had lost, she was required to notify the state of Alabama that "she had broken with the phantom father"; moreover, her statement needed the corroboration of two references, such as a law enforcement official or a minister. As the incredulous reporter explained, "With Mrs. Smith's permission, an investigator would have gone to her favorite policeman or grocer to inquire whether she was still enjoying sexual relations with Williams [the man in question] and, if so, where and how often." What eventually landed Smith's case before the Supreme Court was the fact that she did not grant her caseworker any such permission. "I told her it was none of her business," was how Smith was quoted by the *Times*. More than this, she was indignant "at the idea that the welfare people could punish her family, which she had kept together for years by main determination and hard work, because they didn't like her private doings." Smith argued that she was entitled both to public assistance and to some protection from the state welfare department's investigation of her sex life.[160]

King v. Smith would be a signal victory for the welfare rights movement. Although not on privacy grounds, the Supreme Court sided with Smith, stating that recipients of aid under the Social Security Act "had the same right to make choices about their intimate affairs as did other citizens."[161] Withholding federal dollars from those on public assistance "because of race, sexual activity or other activities irrelevant to their need" was ruled unconstitutional.[162] Even if the Court made no constitutional claim for privacy, *King v. Smith* was still an important widening of protections for sexual privacy in practice.[163] And yet the stubborn link between welfare administration and intimate intrusion persisted. One of the key accomplishments of activists was the winning of a right to fair hearings, which prevented the denial of benefits without evidence or argument. But the hearings could themselves be highly invasive of beneficiaries' personal lives, often centering on the judgments of caseworkers about "the client's honesty, sexual practices, parenting skills, housekeeping abilities, and effectiveness as a money manager."[164] Welfare rights could in this way quite easily collide with privacy rights.

The overlap of the War on Poverty and a set of novel privacy claims created sharp dilemmas, as advocates for those under the closest watch of state agencies keenly perceived. Needy citizens, after all, were some of the best-known citizens to the state. To truly shield their private lives from officials would collapse the entire apparatus supporting welfare provision in the United States. Experts in administrative law and juvenile justice, Joel Handler and Margaret Rosenheim, took it as a given that privacy had "different boundaries depending on one's status in the society." The poor and dependent, unable "to interpose the customary screens around their private activities and to keep themselves shielded from the prying eyes of others," were less likely to be secure in a "private personality" than were other citizens. The condition was only partly financial. It also stemmed from "a peculiar vulnerability of the needy and dependent to official or quasi-official inquiry and surveillance."[165] Governmental programs had an undeniable interest in efficiency and making sure their goals were met, the scholars acknowledged. In an age of expanding welfare but also urgent privacy claims, this created intractable quandaries.[166]

The stand-out social policy for thinking through this tug-of-war was public assistance. To a much greater degree than income taxes and retirement benefits, each of which entailed some monitoring of the middle class, welfare payments hinged on individual visibility, or as Handler and Rosenheim put it, "the unique personal circumstances of the recipients."[167]

Whereas benefits programs aimed at the comfortable typically took "one's word at face value," that was very much the exception in means-tested assistance. Public relief required "an intimate knowledge" of the recipient's "appetites and needs" and demanded "exposure of the applicants' lives and affairs to those who administer it." It also, inevitably, degraded those assisted by opening them "to a kind of scrutiny and control from which the rest of us are ordinarily exempt."[168]

In fact, this sort of scrutiny was intensifying in the 1960s, even as privacy claims were being raised loudly throughout the society. The War on Poverty's penchant for treatment, counseling, training, and rehabilitation programs meant that state agencies were tasked with probing even more deeply into the lives of the poor than previously. Juvenile justice was one setting where this was evident, with family life and personal conduct matter-of-fact subjects for official observation and concern. Given the focus on attitudinal changes—"a youth cannot be 'helped' unless he has recognized his guilt and is willing to be rehabilitated"—such programs justified "the penetration of government into the mind itself," authorizing officials "to roam at will" in the lives of juveniles and their families. This was an alarming version of the "brain watching" that had been lambasted in the context of psychological testing. But, even for juveniles' advocates, such prying appeared unavoidable. Handler and Rosenheim's stark conclusion was that "programs to prevent delinquency, dependency, and neglect can be expanded, but, however labeled, they will be expansions of official regulation of private lives." Indeed, it was in the most "humanitarian, progressive" programs of social welfare that the most trying issues around privacy were beginning to surface.[169]

The ruling in *Griswold v. Connecticut*, alongside the many varieties of privacy talk that proliferated in the 1960s, could be empowering, equipping patients and soldiers as well as criminal defendants and welfare recipients with some recourse against the forces that impinged on their intimate lives and private affairs. But the expanding scope of privacy claims also generated thickets of complications. The social programs associated with the War on Poverty—promising dignity and autonomy to those who had typically been relegated to the margins of U.S. society— were a case in point. New entitlements, even new rights, often came bundled with a level of administrative invasiveness that perhaps would have rankled at any time, and even more so in an age keenly attuned to privacy.[170] More generally, policy making on social problems, including those addressing racial discrimination and invidious distinctions, often rested on the "investigation of characteristics thought to be private."[171] Knowledge of individuals' intimate affairs was sometimes essential, it seemed, in the name of those same people's rights. Americans of the 1930s, at an earlier moment in the history of the welfare state, had faced the prospect of surrendering some of their personal information to the state in exchange for social insurance. In an age steeped in privacy talk, whether Americans would tolerate a much more intensive species of prying in exchange for the benefits of fuller citizenship was an open question.

In 1890, Samuel Warren and Louis Brandeis had described privacy as "the right to be let alone." By 1965, the phrase resounded with both citizens and courts. Newfound respect for citizens' privacy was announced in the highest court in the land, and privacy law would be remade in the cascade of rulings that began with *Griswold v. Connecticut.* If, one commentator mused, the Boston lawyers could have imagined that contraception— something rarely discussed in polite society in their time—would be the vessel for privacy as a constitutional right, they may well have been scandalized.[172] The framing of this right, tethered to "notions of privacy surrounding the marriage relationship," meant that a narrowed version of sexual privacy and autonomy would be privileged in future jurisprudence. It also departed markedly from the kinds of privacy citizens had worried over most intently in the decades leading up to 1965.

Nevertheless, the Connecticut birth control case played a key role in shaping legal and popular understandings of privacy in the 1960s. By the end of the decade, through the work of activists, lawyers, and professionals, it had helped to generate a capacious imagining of the entitlement to be free of society's scrutiny. Criminal defendants and hospital patients, welfare recipients and enlisted men, all staked claims to privacy in these years. Not all or even most of them achieved constitutional status, of course. Yet the Court's effort to supply borders and tangible contents to privacy backfired. A certain boundlessness infected the way that citizens talked about their right to be let alone in these years, as if the Court's attempt to define the claim only made its contours blurrier. One of the conundrums of the 1960s was how expansive the new right appeared to be even as the possibility of identifying clear zones of privacy seemed to recede. As more and more citizens gained a purchase on privacy, conflicts over its meaning escalated. Open to all comers, "privacy" would become vexingly compromised by competing interests. Universalist—and even constitutional—claims about "a right to privacy" masked this more specific truth.

Some would begin to argue that a right that could be called on to solve debates over contraception as well as electronic eavesdropping, abortion well as social welfare administration, was overburdened from the outset. There were those who pinpointed rights themselves as the problem. Legal scholar Mary Ann Glendon, for example, has criticized the right to privacy as exemplifying the "isolated character of the rights-bearer" in the United States. The distinctive feature of the American rights dialect, she writes, is "its extraordinary homage to independence and self-sufficiency, based on an image of the rights-bearer as a self-determining, unencumbered, individual, a being connected to others only by choice."[173] This fiction, that society is peopled by autonomous individuals who wield rights against others, was perhaps incapable of resolving a problem as socially complex as privacy. Others contended that privacy rights, which seemed mostly to address liberty from the state, were ill suited for situations in which the government was called on to help. Privacy in this sense could cut against demands for equal treatment: by ensuring that the state would stay out of "private" questions, the law could leave existing power dynamics in place. A final question revolved around when and for what reasons citizens' privacy affirmatively *ought* to be curbed. As public officials called attention to the costs of the welfare state or the crime rate or the deterioration of the family in the decades to come, the pendulum would begin to swing away from the expansive aspirations for privacy that the Court's 1965 ruling had kindled.[174]

Griswold dangled the possibility that privacy rights were the answer to the dilemmas raised by a knowing society. Other hallmarks of its era, however—the fight for racial justice, the growth of the administrative state, and the increased ambition of social and political interventions—called into question the Court's containment of privacy to particular places and particular people. Indeed, the hopes raised by the recognition of a "right to privacy" revealed the shaky ground on which it rested: that there was a discernible line between private and public at all. If "people, not places" were to be the locus of privacy rights, what happened when those people chose to exercise their privacy in public places? If the advance of personal autonomy depended on retreating from moral regulation, what of the new conflicts triggered by unwanted intrusions from liberated people and bodies? And, perhaps most significant, if to police, manage, or research effectively was to know those who were to be punished, administered, or studied, what would determine the proper balance between privacy rights and socially valuable information about citizens? Neither *Griswold*'s "zones of privacy" nor the rulings that followed it could resolve the case's most generative questions.

5

Codes of Confidentiality and Consent

We are close enough to 1984 . . . without the science of human
behavior being enlisted in this last onslaught on man's privacy.

—EDWARD SAGARIN, Review of *Tearoom Trade*, 1970

In the late 1950s, prominent University of Chicago sociologist Edward
Shils suggested that "the deepening of intellectual curiosity about the
motives and the very tissue of social life," apparent across the behavioral
sciences, defined modern scholarship. Inquiry of this sort was only possible because of the "diminution of inhibitions on intrusiveness into other
persons' affairs." Others seconded his analysis about the invasiveness of
much social research, one psychologist remarking that "practices which
not long ago seemed questionable tend now to be almost fashionable."[1]
Summarizing the techniques that enabled such knowledge—deception,
manipulation, collusion, and false rapport, among them—Shils fretted
over their consequences. What would this brave new world mean for
human dignity, the "autonomy of individual judgment and action," and
personal privacy?[2] A few years later, Shils's colleague at Chicago, psychologist John M. Shlien, was scrutinizing newly developed psychological instruments being used to penetrate the secrets of human behavior. Were
they as rational as they seemed? More importantly, were they humane?
And what of the power they bestowed on a small circle of practitioners?
Shlien wondered: Was the applied psychologist the "baby brother" who
would "grow into the menacing Big Brother of 1984"?[3] The scholars
voiced an ambivalence that would grow stronger in researchers' ranks as
well as the wider society in the years to come.[4]

That Big Brother was looming over the research enterprise was a sign of
the new wariness attached to a knowing society. It was also a sign of the
expansive understanding of the individual rights-holder taking hold in

American public culture. Privacy claims were making headway in court-rooms and social movements, and even in the unlikely realms of welfare administration and juvenile justice. They would soon be percolating in psychological laboratories, sociological experiments, and anthropological fieldwork too, where the transactions between researchers and their subjects were drawing new attention. Contests over scholars' "right to know" in the second half of the 1960s were an early indication of the way privacy concerns were altering the scholarly landscape. By the mid-1970s, the deferential terms used to describe human subjects—"the research participant" and "the patient as person"—telegraphed the shift. Although not as clear-cut as a judicial ruling, public and even scholarly sensibilities about the proper relationship between the observer and the observed were undergoing significant revision. So were assumptions about the place and priority of social knowledge in American life.

The enormous expansion of universities and of state- and foundation-supported scientific and behavioral research in the postwar period laid the groundwork for privacy's entrance into the scholarly domain.[5] In that arena, the fledgling right of privacy confronted another right: that of investigators to conduct research. While medical researchers attracted attention first, social researchers would also face important challenges to their expertise, including assertions about the autonomy, dignity, and privacy of the people who served as their research material. This was true even as the behavioral sciences in the 1960s attracted unprecedented federal funding and prestige, with academic social scientists' work often shaping government policies and agency recommendations, blurring the line between state and nonstate actors.[6]

A boon to researchers in most ways, this new public visibility presented novel problems. The fact, one practitioner noted, that social research suddenly "seems to matter—to society and to the subject" alike, invited scrutiny, including queries regarding the kind of knowledge about citizens that it was appropriate and perhaps even legal to pursue.[7] Some social researchers, Shils and Shlein among them, joined in on the questioning. In what circumstances, they asked, did the quest for knowledge reap not social gain but its opposite: individual or collective harm? And who would be charged with making that determination? A privacy-conscious public after the mid-1960s would in this way unsettle those professions most devoted to "the right to know."

Social Inquiry as Surveillance

Precisely as the Supreme Court was framing *Griswold v. Connecticut* and a right to privacy linked to the marital bedroom, a doctoral student in sociology was preparing to undertake a parallel if strikingly different inquiry into privacy, sex, and space. The fate of his study illuminates the complex forces reshaping privacy discourse in the later 1960s: the transformations wrought by contagious rights talk, the new solicitude for citizens' dignity, and the widening tolerance for difference in American society. Together, these developments—even without the help of laws or the Court—were working to expand the scope of what privacy claims were thought capable of covering and of whom privacy was imagined to protect. *Griswold*'s limited right to privacy served equally as a barrier and an inspiration to push beyond it. As more and more citizens claimed privacy rights as their own, the attempt to contain that right to particular people or places, whether normative majorities or the domestic sanctuary, would begin to founder.

Laud Humphreys was an Episcopal minister and civil rights activist who over the course of a decade had counseled numerous homosexual men in his parishes in Oklahoma, Colorado, and Kansas.[8] A married but closeted gay man, he was fascinated by his contacts with the gay community. It was likely these experiences that drew him to graduate study in urban sociology, ethnography in particular, and to Washington University in St. Louis, where he began his studies in 1965.[9] As a student, Humphreys was "gripped" by the work of leading "symbolic interactionists" like Howard Becker, Erving Goffman, and Harold Garfinkel who used the technique of the participant-observer to decipher the rules of social behavior.[10] Goffman had employed these methods to understand the experience of mental patients in psychiatric hospitals and to probe topics like impression management and stigma in everyday human exchanges.[11] But, apart from an aborted attempt in the 1930s—where the researcher in question found "striking up relationships with these people" too distasteful—no one had yet extended such detailed study to homosexual behavior.[12] Humphreys would find Washington University a supportive place for such an investigation. Its sociology department proudly emphasized "a new and radical tradition" in which there were "no taboo topics or forbidden strategies."[13] Students there, he later recalled, "were expected to be original, imaginative, and controversial."[14] The new doctoral student would not disappoint.

The budding sociologist's first impulse was to decamp to "the most so-cially visible gathering places for the group he was interested in," namely the city's established gay bars and coffee houses. But Humphreys would be prodded by his advisor, Lee Rainwater—intrigued by research on ho-mosexual hustling but also depictions of gay culture in novels—to go where no ethnographer had gone before: into the "tearooms," or public restrooms, where those in the know went to engage in surreptitious gay male sex.[15] These men, "consumers" but not full participants in the "gay world," were in Rainwater's words "the invisible men of the literature on homosexuality."[16] That is, they were precisely those most heavily invested in sheltering their sexual behavior from view, whether from police officers or their own fami-lies and peers. Well aware of this, the police in this era used the tactic of publicizing offenders' names in the newspaper or, alternatively, keeping offenders "on file," rather than arresting them, as a strategy of deterrence. "Discovering and divulging secrets," one scholar writes, "was the very es-sence of the policing of homosexuality."[17] Humphreys was cognizant of the steep sociological—if not always the ethical—challenge such a project posed. But he was thrilled by it too. After some preliminary reconnais-sance in gay gathering spots, the former minister embarked on his field-work in the spring of 1966. The research would form the basis of his 1968 dissertation and then his 1970 book, *Tearoom Trade: Impersonal Sex in Public Places.*[18]

Humphreys's dissertation, completed a year before Stonewall and the eruption of the gay liberation movement, grew out of a well-established sociological tradition focused on deviance.[19] Pioneered by the likes of Howard Becker and William Foote Whyte, it treated the rules by which gang members or drug users or criminals operated no differently from those of "normal," law-abiding social actors.[20] Rainwater, engaged at the time in a study of "ghetto living" in the infamous Pruitt-Igoe Housing Project in St. Louis, adopted this stance as well.[21] For Humphreys and those advising him, only an unflinching view could get at the truths of the tearoom and, by extension, the sexual behavior of a "deviant" group. It re-quired a close, even intimate, familiarity with the subjects of investigation. One of his friends recalled that Humphreys believed other sociologists "erred by using only questionnaire data." To understand a phenomenon like public sex, "Laud felt it was essential to collect direct observational data."[22] And this he would do, first locating active tearooms with the as-sistance of gay contacts and then "passing as a deviant actor to gain access to the setting."[23] Humphreys later described taking on the trusted position of lookout or "watchqueen"—a kind of sentinel who enabled sex to transpire by manning the restroom window and signaling if others approached. "Fortunately, the very fear and suspicion of tearoom participants," he cheerfully noted in his write-up of his methods, had produced "a mechanism that makes such observation possible."[24]

Humphreys would come to know the role well. Over the course of two years, the sociologist directly observed sexual encounters in a series of restrooms located in public parks, singled out for their proximity to major commuting routes. This was a highly intrusive, if secreted, variety of ethnography: in all, Humphreys made a total of fifty "systematic observations" (recorded in detail on a standardized form, after the fact) of fifty-three acts of fellatio. These in turn allowed him to dissect the complex, coordinated, and overwhelmingly silent actions of strangers who managed through shared social cues to engage one another in brief, anonymous, but consensual sex.[25] In his role as voyeur, Humphreys guarded the temporary privacy of participants in sex acts even as he thwarted the intended visual protections built into the New Deal-era restrooms that served as his research sites: the windows with "opaque glass . . . covered with heavy screens" and the exterior privacy walls.[26] It was a vantage point that permitted him to document the subtle "micro-management of time and space" in the tearooms, the nonverbal system of communication its users employed, the functional fluidity of "insertors" and "insertees," and the close correlation between age and sexual role.[27]

This was only the initial stage of Humphreys's research, however. The next step was, depending on one's point of view, either ingenious or alarming. Because he sought to know more about the men he watched than was possible from the actual encounters, and because he was certain he could not inquire directly, thereby revealing his true identity as sociologist, Humphreys devised a second phase of the study.[28] Here again he followed Rainwater's suggestion and fashioned a sample of the tearoom participants—he estimated about 10 percent—by "tracing the license plates of the autos they drive to the parks."[29] This sleuthing relied on both public records and semi-public information accessible to those who knew how to ask for it. Humphreys noted the "friendly policemen" who helped him obtain the men's names and addresses from license registers (ostensibly for a market research study) without asking too many questions; metropolitan directories furnished additional marital and occupational details.[30] Then,

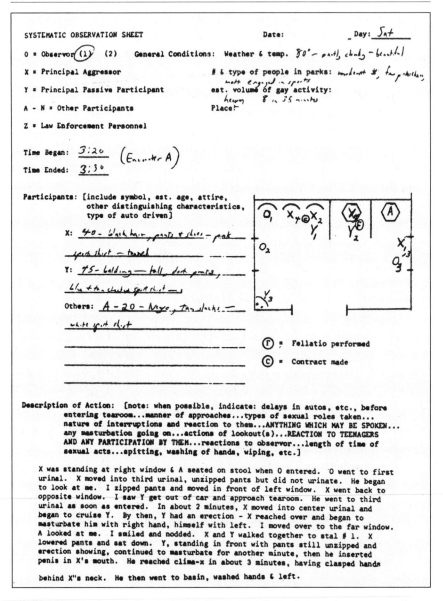

5.1. Laud Humphreys observed and diagrammed men's sexual encounters in public restrooms for his study *Tearoom Trade* (1970), taking note of the "manner of approach," "types of sexual role taken," and "length of time of sexual acts."

a year later, driving a different car and adopting an altered appearance and style of dress, the sociologist went on to interview these same men about their health, habits, employment, social attitudes, and family life. The pretext was a men's "social health survey" conducted by a research center that serendipitously had enlisted Humphreys's assistance. After gaining permission from the study's director, the sociologist simply folded his sample into it. Humphreys was thus free to talk at length with men whom he had first identified in the tearooms in their own homes, watching them "prepare barbecues, have their evening drinks, and converse with their families."[31]

Being privy to these men's secrets—and sure that they were unable to glean his—the sociologist was thus able to place his subjects' private histories in dialogue with their public personas. What he discovered was that many in his sample were conservative, outwardly "straight" men, whether middle or working class. The majority (54 percent) were married and living with their wives, and many were churchgoers, active in the community. Only a small minority had contact with a "homosexual subculture."[32]

Humphreys came to pointed conclusions about their political views. Noting how few self-described liberals showed up in his sample of tearoom goers, he pinned their often vocal conservatism to the "illegal roles these men play in the hidden moments of their lives."[33] The sociologist characterized his subjects as overweening adherents to the dominant norms of the mid-century United States: "Motivated largely by his own awareness of the discreditable nature of his secret behavior, the covert deviant develops a presentation of self that is respectable to a fault. His whole lifestyle becomes an incarnation of what is proper and orthodox. In manners and taste, religion and art, he strives to compensate for an otherwise low resistance to the shock of exposure." The study proposed private sexual deviance as the flip side to perfectly performed public respectability, complete with a tidier home and better-kept yard than the neighbors. Humphreys dubbed this complex "the breastplate of righteousness."[34] A peerless public persona was the cloak in which a non-normative private life could be hidden. It was a kind of privacy that social science, in the form of Laud Humphreys, had a strong interest in uncovering.

The study was revealing in other ways. Humphreys's dissertation cracked open a window onto a much broader range of claims to and practices around sexual privacy in the 1960s than mainstream commentary countenanced.[35] As Humphreys observed, all kinds of sex—"at this stage in the development of American culture, at least"—seemed to require a measure of seclusion. But "when . . . the form of sexual engagement is prohibited privacy decreases risk and is even more valued." The sociologist thus recognized that sexual privacy was most vital for those who were not legally entitled to it. His research pointed to the ways privacy could be found, even manufactured for a few minutes, in public settings such as parks and restrooms. Having no protected bedroom to repair to, the men who frequented the tearooms became expert readers of the "ecological factors" promising reprieve from intruders, whether vice patrols or picnickers wandering by. The silence of the tearoom was insurance that participants' names and identities would remain secret. As Humphries explained, "At first, I presumed that speech was avoided for fear of incrimination." But he became convinced that silence was "much more than mere defense against exposure to a hostile world." It was, rather, "a normative response to the demand for privacy without involvement" and a means of ensuring that "this interaction [would] be as unrevealing as possible."[36] For most men, silence was the best guarantor that they could return to their public lives without disturbance, preserving their families, their careers, and perhaps even their self-conceptions.[37]

Tearoom Trade reveals as perhaps does no other source the inverse of *Griswold*'s heterosexual, marital, bedroom rights. It documented the quest of a diverse array of men—working class and middle class, black and white—for illicit sex, and the carefully choreographed if transient "zones of privacy" in which they found it. The entire tearoom arrangement, designed to ward off identification, embarrassment, or arrest, testified to users' urgent desire to protect their privacy. Like others who lived dangerously in public spaces—African Americans under Jim Crow, for example—gay men created enclaves where they might evade the watchfulness of a hostile society.[38] In their own way, they took up *Katz*'s reformulation of privacy as protecting "persons, not places," the tearoom fostering a reasonable expectation of privacy for those inducted into its hidden codes. Although its version of sexual privacy was wildly different from the one the justices of the Supreme Court imagined, the tearoom was interlocked with the rights they endorsed. Protecting normative sexuality and policing non-normative sexuality went hand in hand, the juridical privileging of "sanctified" marital bedrooms and illicit encounters in public restrooms two sides of the same coin.

Unlike the claim to privacy that married couples possessed thanks to *Griswold*, the one that tearoom users asserted was unauthorized by any court. And it was precarious. They had to worry about legal charges as well as physical beatings, entrapment through decoys as well as discovery by acquaintances. Indeed, "the solid, well-regarded family man suddenly disgraced by an arrest in a men's room or a public park was a familiar story, replayed again and again throughout the 1960s."[39] It was a story that met with more unease as the decade unfolded, however. The destruction of seemingly "normal" married men's lives—one of the most notorious cases being President Johnson's own aide, Walter Jenkins—accounted for some of the distaste.[40] Intolerance of homosexual "vice" remained the rule in that decade, but homophile advocates were slowly making a dent in mainstream public attitudes toward "respectable" gay men and women, and morals regulation of all kinds was loosening.

Importantly, judges and legal scholars were also backing away from sodomy laws. This was not simply for philosophical reasons (the fact that those laws punished a victimless crime), but because of their consequences for law enforcement.[41] As a contemporary study explained, "Because homosexual crimes usually involve the consent of their participants . . . surreptitious enforcement techniques must be employed to enforce the laws." These involved the use of "plainclothes police decoys and clandestine observations," as well as "routine patrol, harassment, and revocation of licenses of business establishments catering to the homosexual trade."[42] The liberalization of the Court and the power of totalitarian imagery, argues legal scholar David Sklansky, placed these practices—and restroom surveillance—in a new light. "Homosexual policing," with its covert spying on sexual activity, looked more and more unsavory across the decade of the 1960s, tempting law officers into bribery and extortion but also deepening existing concerns about the role of the police in a free society.[43] A 1965 House Special Subcommittee on Invasion of Privacy went so far as to investigate postal surveillance, wiretapping, and peepholes in restrooms as instances of "police state techniques."[44] And although restroom surveillance was never mentioned in 1967's *Katz v. United States*, Sklansky speculates that it was a subtext for that ruling's extension of privacy protections to "people and not places" and thus to semi-public spaces like phone booths, and perhaps even tearooms.[45]

For his part, Humphreys wrote sympathetically about his subjects' dilemmas around sexual gratification and its fulfillment. He was personally untroubled by gay sex or even sex in public—which, as the sociologist pointed out, was noncoercive and nearly always invisible to the "straight" users of the restrooms for their standard purpose. Rather, a perceptive reviewer explained, "The police and the moral enforcers are the true evil-doers in this setup."[46] Humphreys himself was arrested merely for hanging around a restroom on one occasion and subjected to attack by a group of young "toughs" while serving as watchqueen on another.[47] His ethnography could lead one to see that the harsh policing of gay sex had not so much halted illegal activity as generated behaviors and codes aimed at securing room for privacy in the interstices of public space. One of Humphreys's most appreciative reviewers observed that the study raised "profound questions as to what is private." If "in private" was simply equivalent to "consent," he reasoned, then "the games people play in tearooms may be no less private than those played at cocktail parties."[48]

These glimpses into sexual privacy as practiced in public would not be the chief contribution that readers and critics drew from *Tearoom Trade*, however. The study instead gained its significance, even notoriety, from a quite different set of questions it raised about privacy. These concerned the rights of Humphreys's subjects and the associated responsibilities of the researcher. Despite precedents in what was sometimes called "underdog sociology," *Tearoom Trade*'s methods pushed hard at scholarly and ethical boundaries.[49] Humphreys, after all, did not only observe and record criminal activity; he actively facilitated it.[50] Still more problematic, many came to believe that he had violated his (unwitting) subjects' dignity as well as their privacy. The study's revelations about illicit sex, silent communication, and the incongruity between public and private personas would nearly be lost in the debate over the legitimate bounds of social inquiry that ensued.

Tearoom Trade thus furnishes a remarkable index of swiftly changing sensibilities around sexuality but also privacy and social inquiry. A daring but unproblematic research venture in 1966, it would by the time of publication in 1970 provoke a scholarly tempest. This was not because of its object of investigation—a detailed and sometimes graphic depiction of men's illegal sex in public facilities. It was because its author was thought to have improperly infringed on those men's privacy.[51] As one critic of Humphreys succinctly explained, "my objections are not to the topic but to the tactics."[52] That is, even though the activity studied by Humphreys offended dominant norms, was legally punishable, and officially shunned, the outcry about it concerned the *researcher*'s behavior. A growing unease with police surveillance of men's restrooms attached, it would seem, to sympathetic sociologists too. By disguising his intentions and taking down license plate numbers, Humphreys, it was argued by academics and journalists alike, had exposed the men he studied to damage and danger.[53] He had, perhaps, even encroached on their rights. Much like welfare recipients and medical patients, the subjects of social research were coming to look vulnerable to the knowers in American society and in need of some protection from them.

The Ethics of Knowing

Unfortunately for the minister-turned-sociologist, *Tearoom Trade* appeared at a pivotal moment in national discussions about research ethics. Long-simmering worries about medical and social scientific uses of the person finally rose to the level of public scrutiny just as Humphreys was completing his study. For researchers, "privacy"—understood as a constellation of legal and ethical claims about the dignity of the person—would be no minor concern. The issue was first aired in connection with medical research, but it soon migrated to the social and behavioral sciences. By the middle of the 1970s, federal regulations for research had been put in place, including a National Commission for the Protection of Human Subjects, representing "a new stage in the balance of authority between researcher and subject."[54] The requirement of "informed consent" and institutional review boards became standard, and the field of bioethics would capture the attention of many philosophers, lawyers, and social scientists.[55]

There was a longer lineage to such concerns, most notably in the immediate aftermath of World War II and revelations of Nazi human experimentation, and most urgently in the biomedical domain. The resulting Nuremberg Code of 1947, which laid out ethical requirements for medical research, had little impact on U.S. laws or practices, however, with American physicians unable or unwilling to draw parallels between foreign atrocities and their own investigations.[56] But by the 1960s, converging developments—the new prominence of federally funded research, the civil rights movement's critiques of exploitation and authority, and, not least, a fresh series of research scandals at home and abroad—were bringing renewed attention to the rights of human subjects. All of this meant that the "legal atmosphere . . . was becoming less sympathetic to the claimed needs of researchers."[57]

Several major statements on medical ethics were crafted by mid-decade, including the U.S. Food and Drug Administration's Drug Amendments of 1962 and the World Medical Association's Declaration of Helsinki in 1964. Harvard anesthesiologist Henry K. Beecher's 1966 exposé of twenty-two scandalous medical experiments—on "mentally defective" children, the elderly, charity patients, alcoholics, and the terminally ill, all of them undertaken by respectable researchers—was an additional call to action.[58] That same year, a new federal policy required that researchers who received federal monies and who studied human beings would henceforth need to obtain prior approval from a review committee.[59] Federal human subjects regulations formalizing these guidelines, hammered out by committees of social scientists as well as medical researchers, would eventually be established in 1974. That year's National Research Act was a reaction to especially shocking revelations in 1972 about the Tuskegee Syphilis Study, in which hundreds of African American men, without their knowledge, went untreated for decades for a disease that had an effective cure.[60]

Although research regulations had been sparked by medical experimentation, the discussion afoot in biomedical circles would not be foreign to social scientists, particularly psychologists. The American Psychological Association was already by the early 1960s embroiled in discussions over ethical standards regarding human subjects and studies of "mental functioning": the effects of sensory deprivation and the like.[61] The very public debate over personality testing had culminated in congressional hearings on privacy invasions in 1965. Negative publicity around motivational research and subliminal suggestion did not help. As one lawyer's analysis of the possible implications of psychological research had it, "Legally, it is difficult to regard psychological experimentation as other than an intentional invasion of the subject's interest in peace of mind."[62] The new vogue of deception as a methodology in this same era brought research ethics to the fore of public consciousness, making it a topic that professional psychologists could no longer avoid.[63]

A number of controversial studies added fuel to the fire. Psychologist Stanley Milgram's 1963 obedience-to-authority experiments, meant to mimic ordinary people's compliance with Nazi rule, were the best known.[64] By allowing subjects to believe that they were administering painful electric shocks to unseen confederates, Milgram put the technique of deception to dramatic purpose. He drew vocal critics in the process.[65] In response to his detractors, Milgram argued that "the participant, rather than the external critic, must be the ultimate source of judgment." The psychologist defended both his careful "dehoax" of participants in the experiment and the reassurance he dispensed regarding their behavior. He also noted the

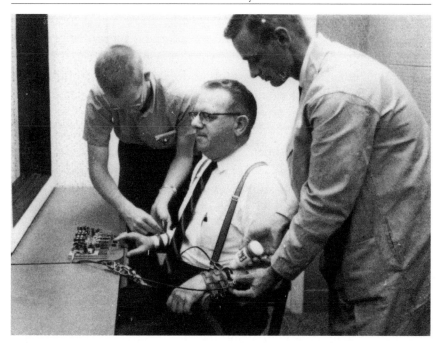

5.2a. Stanley Milgram's controversial obedience-to-authority experiment was a touchstone for debates over research ethics; here, the "victim" is strapped into a chair in order to be "shocked" by a research subject.

positive feelings toward the study obtained in follow-up questionnaires, some of which he quoted in an appendix to his later book—particularly subjects' sense that they "learned something of importance about themselves" by taking part.[66] And yet the experiment would trouble many for its willful infliction of intense psychological distress on unwitting subjects. While it would not attract a great deal of public interest until 1974, when the study was published in book form, Milgram was a common reference point for social scientists worried about the ethics and politics of their craft.[67] Philip Zimbardo's Stanford Prison Experiment of 1971, which transformed college student "guards" into psychological tormenters of their "prisoner" peers so effectively that it had to be terminated early, functioned in much the same way.[68]

It was not obvious that concerns about deception, consent, and coercion in the research enterprise had anything to do with privacy. Early criticisms of human experimentation, whether biomedical or social scientific, had turned instead on physical and mental harm. As the 1960s advanced, however, questions of research ethics were more and more interpreted as bearing on the dignity and self-determination of the research subject. Given new public sensitivities, as well as developments in constitutional law—the decisional autonomy invoked in reproductive rights cases in particular—these aspects of the person were increasingly tethered to a "right to privacy."

Stanley Milgram's experiment, for example, raised quite novel concerns about psychological damage, including the harm of people's exposure "to unsavory aspects of their own natures." Might individuals have a right to be shielded from this kind of "involuntary self-knowledge"?[69] Concerns about privacy arose briefly even in foreign area research, most prominently in the controversy over Project Camelot, a government-funded counterinsurgency program brought to light in 1965. Did people in South America and Southeast Asia have a right to be left alone by scholars, especially since the findings from their research might be used against them?[70] The ethical problem posed by government conscription of social scientific experts was an old one in the history of anthropology, central to a famous article by Franz Boas written during World War I on scholars as spies.[71] But the focus on the research subject and the state of that subject's privacy and dignity was new. In the wake of Milgram and Camelot, professional organizations—the American Anthropological Association, the American Sociological Association, and the American Psychological Association, among them—got to work on framing internal ethics codes.[72]

At the root of this professional second-guessing was a new understanding of the individual research subject as fragile, potentially exploitable, and in need of safeguards vis-à-vis the scholar.[73] The head of the Russell Sage Foundation, Orville Brim, mused on the problem facing the human sciences in 1967. Conflicts between science and the community were age-old, he noted, citing Galileo, but there seemed to be something new at stake in the debates of the 1960s. The content of the science was rarely at issue. Instead the standoffs were between "the methods used by behavioral science to reach knowledge," on the one hand, and "larger community values," on the other.[74] Consternation over the manipulation of human subjects was raising difficult questions about the proper limits of scholarly inquiry. "It's very difficult to conclude that society does not want some of the knowledge which it is possible for us to produce, if the cost involves giving up of values of personal dignity and privacy," Brim reflected. Yet, he concluded, "The majority of the people in society do not want to pay that price."[75]

In the 1960s, discussions of the research subject's vulnerability almost inevitably opened up the question of rights: both the right to informed consent and the right not to be harmed. In the second half of the decade a set of commissions and panels explicitly addressed the tension between social inquiry and privacy or, as one commentator characterized it, "scientific knowledge" and individual "self-determination."[76] An influential report coauthored by Brim and Oscar Ruebhausen on privacy in behavioral research posited an inevitable opposition between scientific research and "the right . . . of private personality." They argued, much as Warren and Brandeis had in the late nineteenth century, that legal, propertied definitions of trespass were inadequate to address researchers' violations of privacy, which constituted a special sort of injury to the person. They acknowledged that "the claim to privacy will always be embattled" since "its collision with the community's need to know is classic and continuous." But the authors also understood contemporary behavioral science to be under particular pressure on this score.[77]

The report was a sign of the times, critics of behavioral and social science evincing the same concern for vulnerable populations as had critics of welfare policy and its invasions of recipients' homes and private lives. For the first time, investigators themselves placed the privacy of research subjects squarely in their sights. The result was to cast the researcher in a new light. In seeking to understand the ingredients of human obedience in 1963, Stanley Milgram had also exposed the power relations of the laboratory: the way that the men in white coats could, if they wished, exert unchecked dominance over those they studied. The psychologist or sociologist or anthropologist could suddenly look like an authority figure, if not an outright authoritarian. Ruebhausen and Brim pointed to this power dynamic by citing "examples of 'forced' submission to privacy probes." Although these were most obvious with regard to prison research, which was still prevalent in the United States in the 1960s, such probes were not confined to that area. They could be found in "our hospitals, our schools, our social welfare programs, our research institutes, and our institutions for the disturbed, handicapped, or retarded."[78] Ruebhausen and Brim in these comments singled out groups thought to be particularly defenseless: prisoners and mental patients, hospital patients and youth. But their larger report made clear that these populations stood in for *all* subjects and the

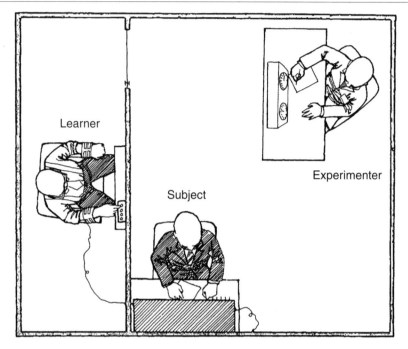

5.2b. The experimenter's improper and unchecked authority over the research subject was a criticism leveled at social investigators by the later 1960s.

hazards to their "privacy"—by now a shorthand for individual dignity and self-determination—that could come from participating in social research.

If nearly any human activity was now open to the "threat of illicit invasion of privacy," a different sort of harm threatened the social scientific enterprise. Ruebhausen and Brim feared the "recoil and revulsion" of a public newly attentive to invasive research techniques, whether "direct observation, one-way mirrors, concealed cameras, personality and ability tests, or psycho-active drugs." If scientists themselves did not exercise discretion and self-control, their report cautioned, "the community will inevitably feel compelled to act for itself," turning to privacy-protective legislation. "It requires no Cassandra," they wrote for example, to predict lawsuits and regulation "if those who administer [psychological] tests in schools—even for the most legitimate of scientific purposes—do not show a sensitive appreciation for both individual and group claims to a private personality."[79] The social scientists were keenly attuned to their own subjects' awareness of privacy threats, whether from wiretapping, lie detectors, or personality tests in employment. In recent years, they wrote, there had been a "severe erosion" of the right of the individual "to decide for himself how much he will share with others his thoughts, his feelings, and the facts of his personal life." As a consequence, "Our society has become more and more sensitive to the need to avoid such damage."[80] The critical problem for social scientists was finding a better balance between what Ruebhausen and Brim characterized as "excessive privacy" on the one hand and "indecent exposure in behavioral research" on the other.[81] If, as this language implied, the "private personality" subjected to researchers' scrutiny was as defenseless as a naked body, social scientists were clearly also newly vulnerable to the public's disapprobation.

Such commissions and reports posed a trade-off: a "gain in knowledge" ranged against a "cost in privacy."[82] Scientific curiosity and social insights but also academic careers and professional reputations all rested in some sense on what Edward Shils had described as "intrusiveness into other persons' affairs." In such matters, *Griswold's* right to privacy, or at least its designation of a specific zone of privacy, offered little help. The conflict between the right to research and the right to decide if one wanted to take part in research, and on what terms, required something else: a balancing act, a case-by-case weighing of the importance of individual dignity against the importance of social knowledge. Along with ethics codes and research standards, this sort of judgment was becoming a professional obligation for social scientists by the end of the 1960s.

The subject's willingness to participate, of course, might offer a way out, mitigating the privacy invasion. Calls for a more robust regime of consent in these years aimed to reinstall an autonomous actor in the position of research subject. Yet this was a solution that was in its own way a problem. Many social scientists in the postwar era did not in fact typically assume that people were fully independent beings, who acted free of social pressures. Relying on informed consent as the moral basis for research thus led to certain internal contradictions.[83] Rattling off the inducements attached to participation in research—scientific prestige, monetary compensation, the regard of peers or employers, extra credit in a college course—Ruebhausen and Brim made clear that the "distinction between consent and concealed coercion may be difficult to establish."[84] Moreover, unlike in the physician-patient relationship often invoked as its parallel, in social scientific studies the rationale for granting consent was not obvious. The research subject in a psychological experiment, for instance, "had little to gain from the relationship."[85] The benefit, it often appeared, was the expert's alone.[86]

But there was a more urgent practical issue. In much social and psychological research, again unlike the medical scenario, informing the subject fully about the experiment about to take place stood to invalidate its results. Consent—a fix that relied on the individual's ability to decide whether to revoke his or her own privacy—was, as many commentators recognized, no fix at all. "Taken literally," it would require that behavioral researchers "refuse to engage in the probing of personality, attitudes, opinions, beliefs, or behavior without the fully informed consent, freely given, of the individual person being examined," wrote Ruebhausen and Brim. In a footnote, they worried: "How many people . . . could be expected to participate willingly in a test to devise a standard of homosexual tendencies? Or to measure intra-family hostility?"[87] Interest in such sensitive issues, and the desire to better understand the true motives behind human behavior, had underwritten the increasing use of deception in the postwar behavioral sciences.[88] It was now unclear whether the field could get along without it. Yet, the very methods that had led to many social scientific advances and to their broad purchase in American society seemed to be in doubt.

Nevertheless, Ruebhausen and Brim's report like most others shied away from recommending legislation or regulation—or explicitly recognizing the rights of human subjects—as the answer to the dilemma. The solution could only be professional discretion and self-policing through research standards and ethics codes. Responsibility rested with the expert to set the "conditions that give fullest protection to individual human dignity."[89] Thus, hand-wringing about subjects' privacy and researchers' duties worked both to acknowledge the growing rights claims in American society and to check them. Preferring the language of professional ethics to constitutional rights, social investigators in diverse fields found their way through new terrain, fully aware that the ground was shifting under their feet.

Navigating Subjects' Rights

In the years after *Griswold*, experts in every field dependent on human subjects elaborated strategies to preempt the challenge that new privacy sensibilities posed to their work. An academic psychologist, for example, proposed a systematic method for assessing trade-offs between the value of a specific research project and the "price extracted from human subjects"— an "ethical payoff matrix" that would facilitate better decision making.[90] The authors of a 1966 book on "unobtrusive measures," a handbook for what they billed as "nonreactive" social science research, argued for new techniques that would foster "the privacy of the individual, his freedom from manipulation, the protection of the aura of trust on which the society depends, and by no means least in importance, the good reputation of social science." Perhaps, they speculated, practitioners could protect privacy by extracting information from people without "ever identifying individual actors or in any way manipulating them." Seeking a less intrusive path to socially useful knowledge, they outlined a program of archival methods and "trace" measures. The amount of wear on tile flooring at a museum could be used to reveal the popularity of specific exhibits, for example; tracking the radio-dial settings on cars brought in for service could help monitor listening habits with no impact on the listener. Such methods might permit "ethically scrupulous social scientists to do their work effectively and to sleep better at night."[91] In each instance researchers evinced a new sensitivity around privacy intrusions and heightened care for the subject of research.[92]

A few—although only a few—would conclude that safeguarding subjects' privacy outweighed the priorities of their own research. One study in this period found that scholars had been "forced" to think much harder about the confidentiality of their data, but that there was no "widespread tendency to inquire into the value of research and weigh it against the intrusions into the subjects' lives." Yet there were some who treated new privacy claims quite seriously. A handful of social scientists took up the question of how to avoid submitting their subjects to indignities when examining sensitive topics, whether poverty, employment, or health. The medical sociologist and civil rights activist, Edward H. Peeples Jr., for example, had in a study of poverty and nutrition compiled a good deal of evidence on poor Americans' consumption of dog food. Peeples, however, discouraged calls for further research through a national survey. This practice was a "mark of failure and shame in our society," he argued, and "to submit thousands of persons to the lengthy, deeply probing and tiresome interviews necessary to confirm whether or not they eat pet food is intolerable." He added, "Those who deny the reality of poverty, hunger and malnutrition in America have always had an insatiable appetite for 'hard data' from those of us who have witnessed or experienced these misfortunes first hand." Rather than spend money on follow-up studies, Peebles suggested putting those funds toward finding better solutions for the poor. Some information, the sociologist contended, "is not worth the cost, both in terms of privacy invasion and dollars."[93]

By the late 1960s a chorus of professionals in applied research began to wonder more self-interestedly about how all this talk of subjects' privacy and right to refuse their inquiries might play out. The research community writ large depended on access to Americans' private behavior and thoughts: their hidden habits, desires, and attitudes. Their image and livelihood at stake, marketers, motivational researchers, testers, pollsters, and census takers had legitimate concerns about the way privacy discussions were trending. The congressional hearings on privacy invasion in 1965 loomed especially large for those in the testing business, one legal expert forecasting that "a successful constitutional attack on psychological testing" was "a real possibility in the near future."[94] Personality testers, even those who dismissed their critics as "adherents of victorian [sic] conventions," began advising that specialists employ these tests with much greater restraint. This was evident in one psychologist's sober cost-benefit analysis: "It seems unlikely that a system-wide survey of junior high school students, made without parental consent for it, will produce scientific data of sufficient importance to offset the public uproar and damage to the reputation of psychology and education that may result."[95]

Testers of all stripes were chastened. Wrote an educational researcher, noting that schools and communities were now resisting cooperation with research projects, "It seems safe to say that purported invasion of privacy in research and testing has become a persistent and sometimes urgent public concern."[96] The U.S. Office of Education publicized that it was "on the alert" for and prepared to delete objectionable questionnaire items in a broad array of data-gathering instruments funded by federal monies: personality questionnaires, intelligence and achievement tests, vocational interest inventories, curriculum surveys, and so on. Particularly suspect were items that were highly personal, "self-demeaning," "excessively 'psychiatric,'" or likely to have "an adverse psychological effect," as well as those that requested confidential or personal information about someone other than the respondent.[97] A spokesman for that office, keen to ensure that social science "not become identified in the public mind with 'snooping' and 'prying,'" presented the Bureau of Research as "an honest broker between the scientist who presses for scientific freedom, and the public which, generally speaking, places considerably greater emphasis on the value of personal privacy."[98]

New attention to privacy and research subjects' rights rippled out beyond the testing arena. Even opinion pollsters found themselves part of the conversation. In 1966, a past president of the American Association for Public Opinion Research wrote at length on the topic. Robert O. Carlson viewed the future of his field "with some alarm." He predicted that those in survey research would not "escape the searching eye of critics and the general public with respect to the issue of privacy." Carlson frankly acknowledged that it was in the very nature of public opinion research to "invade the privacy of our respondents," but it was a necessary trade-off between the rights of the person and the "needs of our society for better scientific information on human behavior." Carlson's concern was that the tide seemed to be turning against the researcher. As he saw it, the "research fraternity" needed to act to polish its image or else risk public disfavor and even regulation.[99]

Carlson's admonitions to his colleagues spoke not only to the high pitch of privacy concerns but also to their intersection with attention to the rights of the most disadvantaged in American society. This was evident in his discussion of authority and consent, issues which were surfacing just as surely in polling as in psychological experiments. Surveyors might believe that individuals freely consented to their questions, he remarked. But critics might easily ask whether the poor, the uneducated, or the intimidated were aware of their right not to answer—and whether they were "equally prepared psychologically to exercise this right." And what about the fact that researchers often reported findings by age, sex, race, or socioeconomic status and that "subgroups in our samples . . . might be identified and damaged by such revelations"? Indeed, Carlson professed surprise that pollsters had not already felt pressure from groups organized to protect minority rights, when "in theory, it can be argued that any subgroup that can be identified by data in a survey report has had its privacy invaded."[100] How, Carlson asked, should surveyors respond to critiques of this "real-life power situation"?

Carlson worried, finally, about pollsters' potential association in the public mind with "professional snoopers and private CIA agents." The link was not entirely misplaced, given that surveyors often made queries about the actions or attitudes of a respondent's family, neighbors, or fellow workers. Moreover, Carlson explained, the interviewer, having gained access to a respondent, "is free to move from his relatively innocuous initial questions into subject areas of a highly personal nature . . . having to do with the political, religious, economic, and moral beliefs and practices of the respondent." Acknowledging widespread dismay over the use of electronic spying devices, Carlson wondered whether his fellow pollsters would be attacked for "psychologically bugging the minds of our respondents and causing them to reveal information about themselves that they otherwise would not."[101] Carlson's invocation of bugging, his awareness of the power relation inherent in questioning, his invocation of minority rights, and his sense of incipient public refusal show how strongly researchers were coming to believe that they would need to alter their practices to meet new sensibilities.

Marketers were similarly attuned to the threat. In their view of things, claims to individual privacy represented less a precious personal possession than a "constraint" or even a harm to business. The newly enunciated but still shadowy right in *Griswold* was of special concern. In an effort to identify risks to their profession, two writers in the *Journal of Marketing* scoured contemporary privacy law for answers. Having done so, they labeled not the constitutional right but the tort of intrusion "the gravest future threat for the unhampered execution of marketing research." Noting that courts had defined wrongful intrusion as having physical, visual, and auditory components, as in a series of "Peeping Tom" and eavesdropping cases, they anticipated that the step to the psychological was not far off. Indeed, they admitted, "If the courts are willing to recognize intrusion on the physical level, they should be even more disposed to entertain intrusion actions at the psychological level where the right to solitude appears to be more fundamental."[102]

The implications of privacy rights for market researchers appeared ominous, as this damning admission about incursions into the psyche revealed. Motivational research had by this time taken firm root in industry, and it depended on both deception and intrusion. The "disguised-projective questioning technique," for example, was "designed specifically to gain access to the respondent's psychological level," one marketer noted in 1969.[103] As another put it, "Must we really explain, when we ask the respondent to agree or disagree with the statement, 'Prison is too good for sex criminals; they should be publicly whipped or worse,' that it is really the authoritarianism of his personality we are investigating, and not public opinion on crime and punishment?" Where, he wondered, should the practitioner "draw the line between deception and discreet silence"?[104] The fact that expert techniques relied on dissembling meant that issues of consent were, once again, tricky. The respondent in such studies only agreed to reply to "surface level" questions—not the actual, more meaningful queries lurking underneath. Were he fully informed, "it is unlikely that he would willingly consent to have his psyche plumbed by an interviewer." Courts, certainly, would not consider an individual's agreement to answer such questions as equivalent to consent. Calling legal scrutiny "a safe prediction" and legislation "a threat," these analysts put their colleagues on alert.[105]

By the late 1960s, bills before Congress proposing limits not only on the kinds of queries the decennial census could include but also on the requirement to answer them underlined the real and present danger to those who relied on respondents for data. What was new about these proposals was that strictures regarding confidentiality no longer seemed enough. To curb privacy invasions, it seemed, the questions (and questioners) themselves needed disciplining. Republican congressman Jackson Betts of Ohio, arguing that the Census Bureau's "probing of people's affairs is certainly unwanted and unnecessary," tagged its questions as invading citizens' privacy and serving no public purpose. His supporters suggested that "titillating questions" (such as whether households shared a shower) were out of bounds, constituting "invasion of privacy" as well as "harassment." Notable champions of individual privacy in Congress, such as Democrat Cornelius Gallagher of New Jersey, opposed such efforts to curb the census, testifying to how far the discussion about questioning citizens had moved by the end of the decade. Conscious of "the lease of power such information will give to the government to invade the private lives of its citizens," Gallagher nevertheless worried that reining in official data-gathering would imperil the "government's need to know."[106]

The need to know was precisely what was at issue. But what talk of ethics, privacy, and consent made evident is that the knowers were no longer solely in charge of defining the stakes. The fact that researchers in a wide array of fields aired their concerns about their subjects' privacy so freely and frankly after the mid-1960s—often, of course, in connection with the difficulties the claim posed for them—suggests that those who promised to make social problems intelligible through their expertise had become a problem themselves. The recasting of a whole range of professionals as "invaders" expressed well the rising consciousness around privacy rights. Regulated by ethics codes and a smattering of federal guidelines, professional researchers' prerogatives would not in this era be dismantled as effectively as Connecticut's birth control law.[107] But the new solicitude for individual privacy and dignity would reshape the field of social inquiry, both the sorts of questions that could asked and the ways research subjects—soon to be rechristened "research participants"—would be treated.

A Right to Research?

For Laud Humphreys, the trouble began when he tried to file his dissertation in 1968. His study on the tearooms would be strenuously opposed by a senior faculty member at Washington University, Alvin Gouldner, on the grounds of ethical violations. Gouldner, who referred derisively to Humphreys as a "peeping parson," had attacked other sociologists of deviance in print for what he considered to be the immorality of their methods, and the tearoom research was no different.[108] By Lee Rainwater's account, the research also troubled the university administration, a concern that became more weighty when it was discovered that Humphreys "had not filed the very new human subjects review papers," a federal requirement tied to his pre-doctoral grant from the National Institute of Mental Health (NIMH).[109] These guidelines had been hastily put into place in 1966 in the wake of Henry Beecher's exposé and were more honored in the breach than in the observance.[110] But Humphreys, a student known for his activism and his multiple confrontations with Gouldner—with whom he had come to physical blows over research methods, a scuffle that made its way into the pages of the *New York Times*—may have come in for special scrutiny.[111] Those who disliked him, or his subject matter, now could hide behind methodological concerns.

After his PhD defense, Humphreys received notice from the chancellor that in his dissertation research "he had failed to follow university regulations and federal law in the protection of human subjects and may also have violated the criminal law of the state of Missouri." Humphreys scrambled to make sure his records documenting illegal activity in the tearooms were safe from subpoena. Meanwhile, he was advised of the possibility of his degree being revoked and that he "would be well advised to refrain from, or at least postpone, the use of the title 'Doctor.'" The university went on to attempt to bar and then delay the study's publication.[112] As all of this was unfolding, the NIMH—responding to a request from the chancellor—sent in a team to investigate the sociology department before releasing a $1.2 million grant to Lee Rainwater. The department had already attracted the notice of the higher administration for its radicalism. Its vocal leftist contingent included one of Humphreys's advisors, Irving L. Horowitz, who wrote extensively about the profession and its role in society, including its military and intelligence links. But the request for an external investigation was at least in part rooted in uneasiness with the tearoom research. The NIMH team's final assessment that "nowadays sodomists are rarely if ever prosecuted for this felony, and lookouts or 'watchqueens' probably never," persuaded the chancellor to allow the grant to proceed. But he did so "only on the condition that Laud would not be employed at the university." With the assistance of the vice provost and the sociology department secretary, who took the fall for failing to submit the human subjects paperwork, the charges against Humphreys were dropped, and he received his degrees in sociology and criminology.[113]

The controversy did not end with the resolution of matters at the university. As Humphreys soon learned, whatever legal risks he had incurred in conducting his research, the professional ones would be greater. The sociologist secured a teaching position at Southern Illinois University and then the State University of New York at Albany. His book on "impersonal sex in public places" won the prestigious C. Wright Mills Prize from the Society for the Study of Social Problems in 1970.[114] But Humphreys—caught between older conventions of professional responsibility, which relied almost completely on the researcher's discretion, and a new attention to subjects' rights—would be dogged by questions about his study's involuntary conscription of tearoom habitués. He would say as much, in response to a critic, a decade later. By then teaching at Pitzer College in California, Humphreys explained that when he launched his tearoom investigation in the mid-1960s, "the sociologist had no Code of Ethics mentioning the need for 'informed consent.'" He continued, "The issue was never raised in my graduate studies, and I had never thought about that as a matter of concern."[115]

Humphreys was aware of the delicacy of his brand of research all along, of course. Just as he embarked on his ethnographic work, in fact, his advisor was publishing on research ethics. With a colleague, David Pittman, Lee Rainwater coauthored a key article on the ethical dilemmas of studying a "politically sensitive and deviant community," in this case, the African American residents of St. Louis's Pruitt-Igoe public housing project. Today we might expect the ethical dilemmas to center on harms to members of that community. But what was centrally at stake for the sociologists then were the rights and autonomy of *researchers,* not their subjects—even if those rights included scholars' efforts to protect the privacy of those same subjects.[116] Rainwater and Pittman defended their right to know against city officials' desire for their data. Pressured for access to their results by interested agencies (the Housing Authority as well as the Police Narcotics Squad), the sociologists voiced "a concern with our rights," seeking to "legitimate those rights in the eyes of other institutions and the public." Focused on protecting informants' identities and their research materials from subpoenas, the two pointed to "a very sticky situation" that would result "if others are not willing to recognize our right to behave ethically (for example, by preserving confidential relations with our informants)."[117] Strikingly, the sociologists in this meditation on research ethics in a "politically sensitive community" did not take up any other rights—notably, those of their poor, African American subjects—that might have been in question.

Rainwater and Pittman, however, did raise a number of other ethical issues bearing on privacy, among them the damage to a group's reputation that might result from social scientific inquiries and the misuse of research findings. They pondered, "If one describes in full and honest detail behavior which the public will define as immoral, degraded, deviant, and criminal, will not the effect be to damage the very people we hope our study will eventually help?"[118] They fretted over the fact that studies of ghetto life had been fodder for anti-integrationists, for example. They also referenced the way the findings of Rainwater's own study on working-class women's use of contraception—commissioned by the Planned Parenthood Federation of America in the late-1950s, pre-*Griswold*—had been distorted by those opposed to family planning services in public health and welfare agencies.[119] Unmentioned but hovering in the background was Daniel Patrick Moynihan's 1965 *The Negro Family: The Case for National Action,* also known as the "Moynihan Report." Written under the auspices of the U.S. Department of Labor, the report claimed to have discovered a "tangle of pathology" in black urban America that, as much as joblessness, mired African Americans in poverty. Praised by some for its counterintuitive findings and denounced by others for cultural bias and "blaming the victim," controversy over the study was still boiling at the time Rainwater and Pittman drafted their reflections on research ethics.[120]

Questions of academic freedom, racism, and who could presume to speak and write about African American life directly involved Rainwater, both as a friend and defender of Moynihan and as a white sociologist studying the ghetto.[121] The notion that whole communities might be tarred or deprived of their dignity by the findings of social research was a brand-new kind of privacy harm. Kenneth Clark, the African American psychologist whose research on children's racial attitudes had helped determine the *Brown v. Board of Education* ruling and was also a major influence on *The Negro Family*, would come in for just this kind of criticism for his study of Harlem, *Dark Ghetto*, of 1965. By the later 1960s, Clark's depiction of New York's black community, which "so exaggerated Harlem's problems and ignored its rich cultural life that it reinforced negative racial stereotypes," looked to some like sociological racism. White sociologists, until the 1960s the primary academic claimants to expertise on people of color and the poor, would also suddenly confront the question of their authority to represent or speak for subjects unlike themselves. The very ownership of social knowledge was becoming a political question. Clark would, for instance, in 1970 criticize Rainwater's own study of the black ghetto for its "normative pornography type description of the Negro poor and his predicament."[122] These were glimmers of the way a new stage of civil rights action, centering on the politics of self-definition and cultural rights, would confront social science as usual. Rainwater could acknowledge this critique, but he could not get on board with it. Despite his qualms about the political uses of research, the sociologist believed that "the moral obligation of scholars was to tell the truth, regardless how uncomfortable or embarrassing that might prove for African American leaders or lower-class African Americans."[123]

Rainwater's scholarship and allegiances thus placed him right at the center of controversies over researchers' power vis-à-vis their subjects, achieved not just through their ability to probe but also to publish and thereby define social problems. He was, it would appear in hindsight, out of step with the times and the new concern for subjects of research. He and Pittman were unwavering on the point that any rights and responsibilities related to social research were lodged primarily with the scholar. For example, confidentiality was less an informant's due than a tool or "*inducement*," as they put it, to elicit cooperation.[124] And sometimes, as the sociologists made clear, confidentiality ought *not* be extended. Arguing that "we should re-think our automatic assumption that we offer to maintain the privacy of our informants," they proclaimed that such a decision depended first and foremost on the "needs and goals of a particular research." The scholar's control over such matters, wrote the sociologists, "makes explicit our claim to *a right* to study social behavior in certain situations." Declared Rainwater and Pittman, "Obviously we do not claim the right to study all kinds of behavior in non-confidential ways and to make public our findings, but we do and should study certain kinds of behavior in this way."[125]

Humphreys's sensibilities, although gentler, were very much in line with his advisor's. For him, the chief ethical question in the tearoom study was the relatively straightforward one of safeguarding his subjects' confidentiality so that they could not be identified by outsiders. That settled, he had free rein to design a study that would advance his scholarly aims. The decision to conduct his research covertly, he implied, was in this sense not truly a choice: that method being the best means to his end, it was also necessarily subordinate to it. "I had to become a participant-observer of furtive, felonious acts," he stressed.[126] As his defenders pointed out during the controversy over *Tearoom Trade*, Humphreys did take extraordinary precautions to protect his subjects. He did not record names or other identifying information on his questionnaires and kept the master list in a safe-deposit box a thousand miles away. He also transcribed all the interviews himself, eventually destroying them completely, spending "some weeks early in the summer of 1968 burning tapes, deleting passages from transcripts, and feeding material into a shredder."[127] It is worth noting, however, that Humphreys took this last precaution only once his work attracted negative scrutiny from the university administration, which troubled some of his cooperating respondents enough to ask for reassurances that they would not be exposed.

Yet in his write-up of methods the sociologist barely paused over the use of deception to observe men in the midst of illicit sex, his discovery of their names and addresses by tracking license plates, or his further reliance on disguise and deceit when he arrived a year later on their doorsteps.[128] In the brief, even breezy, ethical reflections contained in the final chapter of his 1970 book, Humphreys mused, "Is it unethical to use data that someone has gathered for other purposes, one of which is unknown to the respondent?" He did not dwell long on the question, raising neither the issue of deception nor informed consent. Answering his own query, he judged the practice "quite ethical" so long as appropriate security procedures were followed. Remarking that the same strategy was "frequently employed by anyone using such data banks as the records of the Bureau of the Census," he felt little need to say more.[129] Only after his study came under fire did Humphreys publicly contemplate the risks his subjects faced—along with the fact that they had never agreed to undertake them.[130]

As the reviews of *Tearoom Trade* make apparent, Humphreys's colleagues and readers were quicker to see the dangers. Most were willing to grant that valuable social scientific knowledge had been turned up in the tearooms. But the five years since the sociologist had plotted his fieldwork had made a difference. In the early 1970s few scholarly commentators were able to resist inserting discourses about professional ethics and research subjects' privacy alongside their praise. A British colleague, for example, applauded the intrepid nature of the research, in which Humphreys "managed not only to observe deviant sexuality without disturbing the situation but also to interview the participants at a later date." By these means, the sociologist had produced "some of the first information we have on the concealed and hidden homosexuals that researchers have long been aware of but whom they have found impossible to trace." Yet these plaudits came with a caveat. "The whole book," noted this writer, "raises the thorny problem of ethics in social research. To what extent can the snooping methods of a concealed and undisclosed Humphreys into the private sex lives of men be justified ethically?"[131]

Similarly, although a clear admirer of Humphreys and his study, a fellow sociologist was wary of his means. He called the study unique in its "concatenation of misrepresentation and disguises," which he argued "must surely hold the world record for field research." On balance, he reckoned that "the dangers to respondents, to the researcher, and to the precious sense of respect for the privacy of others seem too great for the returns."[132] Social scientists, urged another writer, "assume a great responsibility"—likely too great—"when they deny respondents the rights of voluntary participation."[133] He believed that "those whom we hope to help by our efforts" ought "not be put in such jeopardy except with their explicit consent."[134] An anthropologist, although he didn't sit in judgment himself, pointed out, "There are many social scientists who will consider Humphreys's use of the guise of the gay guy to gain admittance to the tearooms as a violation of professional ethics."[135] After observing that "few sociological books in recent years have received the attacks and accolades that *Tearoom Trade* has," another scholar confirmed this, pinning its "notoriety" in the media and the profession alike to "its controversial research ethics rather than its subject matter or findings."[136]

In raising matters of consent, disclosure, rights, privacy, and ethics, these scholars bore the marks of a new and circumspect relationship to their subjects. Whereas Rainwater and Pittman had earlier invoked the rights of the researcher, many of their colleagues were attending to the rights of the researched—indeed, setting the two in opposition. Defenseless, even "powerless"—their privacy and dignity in the balance— subjects of social investigation were now in need of protection. Writing of the second stage of the tearoom study, the home visits, a sociologist charged that Humphreys "took no personal risk by being there, but his presence did pose a potential threat to the men and their families." There was no way, for instance, to know if any of the men were distressed in the moment, and "there has been no follow-up inquiry to alert us to any anxiety that they may have suffered as a result of the coverage that the research has received in the mass media."[137] The researcher's right to know was confronting the research subject's right not to be known, except under conditions where consent had been both sought and obtained.

Yet another of Humphreys's critics, an ethicist, pondered the longer-range damage that invasive social research could inflict. Not only had Humphreys "taken advantage" of a vulnerable population but he had also likely left the men with lingering anxiety about the fact that "*someone knows*."[138] Invoking resonant biomedical scandals—Nazi medical experimentation as well as the recent exposé of the injection of live cancer cells into healthy patients at Brooklyn's Jewish Chronic Disease Hospital—he wondered "how far the social scientist can intrude into the inner reaches of the self without jeopardizing freedom."[139] He concluded, "Whatever the current state of legal definitions of privacy, Humphreys intruded much too far into the lives of the men he observed and studied." Indeed, he lamented, "From now on tearoom participants must be on the alert not only for blackmailers and policemen, but for sociologists in voyeur's clothing."[140] Even if the law did not prevent the scholar from undertaking this research, the reviewer suggested, Humphreys's own ethical compass should have.

Some reviewers went further in questioning the sociologist's motives, suggesting that Humphreys had deliberately sacrificed his subjects' humanity, privacy, and freedom of choice for his own professional advancement. A criminologist, airing his "tremendous sense of uneasiness" while reading the ethnography, accused Humphreys of a lack of compassion toward his subjects, deriding him as a "first-rate sociological pornographer" and his work as the equivalent of "ghetto tourism."[141] Still more damning was the assessment of Edward Sagarin, a sociologist and criminologist who had also built his career on studying homosexual behavior. "Granting without question the careful guarding of the confidentiality of the information," he began, "I must nonetheless look with great dismay on men who, in their capacity as sociologists (or psychologists, or any other) delve into the most private and secret and fear-inciting aspects of people's lives, without their knowledge or consent, and not for the purpose of aiding the object of their study, but of adding to knowledge and aiding themselves."[142]

Such reviews called into question the researcher's judgment. They also explicitly weighed his scholarly prerogatives against the lingering damage of fragile lives exposed. Like Moynihan's report on the black family, Humphreys's gaze in the tearooms made subjects vulnerable—not just at the moment of observation but also in the lasting impression it left. As several critics noted, the study made the tearooms more legible to law enforcement and thus potentially more dangerous for users, imperiling his subjects and others like them in the future. "We are close enough to 1984 . . . what with totalitarian regimes and democratic ones where personal and human rights are under constant threat," charged Sagarin, in a dramatic flourish, "without the science of human behavior being enlisted in this last onslaught on man's privacy."[143]

Sagarin would not be the only reader to enlist such imagery in his attack. Nor was he the only one to suggest that Humphreys's brand of social research transgressed more than professional codes of conduct—indeed, that it might violate fundamental human rights. The ethicist who had summoned up Nazi experiments in his review of *Tearoom Trade* raised the specter of a totalitarian society where "one must constantly look over his shoulder or check under his bed to be sure that he is not being observed or heard." At this point in history, he warned, "We must be concerned not only about the impact of the single intrusion, but also with the cumulative effects of thousands of acts of prying on the quality of human life."[144] Here the social scientist joined the fictional policeman in the bedroom and the FBI wiretapper as a threat to the enclaves of human privacy and dignity that still remained in U.S. society.

Reactions to *Tearoom Trade*, it is clear, were never only reactions to that study. They were steeped in a host of other concerns about the state of privacy in 1960s and 1970s America, which were mostly far removed from the realm of scholarly research. A reviewer invoked in one breath Humphreys's ethnographic work and "the FBI, salesmen posing as survey researchers, and credit checkers entering suburban homes under various guises" in the next.[145] Writing in 1973, another would link the study to "recent disclosures of widespread military surveillance of civilians, the ever-growing use of phone tapping, and the burgeoning data banks on millions of American citizens."[146] It is impossible to read their commentaries, littered with similar references, as concerned with tearooms alone. This last writer made the point explicit: social scientists, he wrote, "should be scrupulously careful about contributing to the fast-growing reservoir of suspicion and distrust that plagues the United States in the closing decades of the twentieth century."[147] Those who criticized Humphreys's study asked of the tearoom users, but perhaps also of themselves, what secrets were theirs to keep. The risks to the ethnographer's subjects were more proof of the risks that all people faced in a prying society—and their protection from the researcher one more defense against it. In this imagined bridge linking "deviants" to putatively normative others, privacy rights of an unofficial sort widened.

The debate about *Tearoom Trade* would spill out of these academic confines, most visibly in the pages of the *Washington Post*, where columnist Nicholas von Hoffman had gotten wind of the forthcoming book.[148] Von Hoffman placed Humphreys's study in unsavory company—with the "credit checkers," "counter-espionage men," "dope sleuths," and "divorce detectives" who were "peeping into what we thought were our most private and secret lives." The sociologist was simply another creature intent on invading others' privacy, but perhaps one more odious in his self-serving bromides about advancing human knowledge. No matter how much care Humphreys had taken with his subjects' secrets, wrote von Hoffman, "it remains true that he collected information that could be used for blackmail, extortion, and the worst kind of mischief without the knowledge of the people involved." This last phrase was crucial. "Most of the people Humphreys observed and took notes on had no idea what he was doing or that they, in disguised form, would be showing up in print at some time in the future," railed the journalist. Von Hoffman knew that Humphreys's project would be justified on the grounds of producing "needed, reliable information about a difficult and painful social problem." But the police, the Justice Department, and J. Edgar Hoover professed worthy motives for gathering information too, he charged—at the cost of "invading some people's privacy." He concluded, "My newspaper could probably learn a lot of things that the public has a right and need to know if its reporters were to use disguises and the gimmickry of modern, transistorized, domestic espionage, but there is a policy against it. No information is valuable enough to obtain by nipping away at personal liberty, and this is true no matter who's doing the gnawing."[149]

Such an argument may not have been surprising coming from a journalist and outsider to the field. What would be astonishing, over the course of the next decade, is how many social scientists would publicly come to similar conclusions.[150] The Yale sociologist Kai Erikson had already in the spring of 1967 written a critical essay on the practice of "disguised observation." The technique had been used to study people in Alcoholics Anonymous groups, millennial cults, army barracks, and mental wards without those people ever knowing about their status as research subjects. But Erikson urged that the "practice of using masks in social research compromises both the people who wear them and the people for whom they are worn." Calling disguised research "an ugly invasion of privacy," Erikson asserted that it carried injuries for the people being researched, whose trust and intimacy were compromised in potentially consequential, long-term ways. It also took a toll on sociology's professional reputation, something he feared at a time when the discipline was attracting larger audiences and more public respect, as well as grant money and tenure lines. Erikson compared the ethics of disguised observation to undisclosed medical experimentation, asking whether "we have the right to inflict pain at all when we are aware of these risks and the subjects of study are not." Writing at a moment when the rules of research were regulated almost exclusively by the individual researcher, Erikson contended that it was unethical for a researcher to misrepresent either his research or himself "for the purpose of entering a private domain."[151]

Humphreys's own decision to append a set of essays on ethics to the revised 1975 edition of *Tearoom Trade* testified to the way the field was trending.[152] Questions of ethics constituted an enormous growth area for social scientists in the decade spanning the mid-1960s and mid-1970s, as a lengthy "selective" bibliography of works assembled by a 1978 task force on ethics in social research reveals.[153] The conveners of the task force, Robert Bower and Priscilla de Gasparis, registered a "rapidly increasing concern about the protection of the rights and welfare of human subjects." At pains to specify the nature of the social scientific harm, they observed that if biomedical research tended to "place the welfare of human subjects at risk, social research tends to threaten the rights of its subjects."[154] Bower and de Gasparis singled out six possible risks in social research: coercion, deception, invasion of privacy, breach of confidentiality, stress, and what they called (with the Moynihan Report in mind) collective, group, or social risks—the potential damage that issued from identification of intergroup comparisons and invidious distinctions. The harms ran the gamut from "anxiety, shock, horror, fear" or "psychological injury" to "loss of self-esteem" and "generation of self-doubt."[155] But the feature that most distinguished social research, they contended, was its special capacity to invade privacy.[156] Although an infrequent concern in biomedical research in the 1970s, invasions of privacy were "among the major risks to which subjects of social research may be exposed."[157] The very topics social researchers inquired into, the chance that confided intimacies would not remain confidential, and the use of deception to gain information were all cause for concern.[158]

Tearoom Trade could not have been far from the minds of task force members as they grappled with setting principled guidelines for social research. It was, after all, a textbook case of the ways a researcher might "actively entrap the subject into the expression of attitudes, or confessions of sins, or displays of behavior that he would otherwise withhold."[159] And it potentially imperiled the privacy not just of its actual research subjects but of *all* tearoom users by exposing their practices and secrets, creating collective risks. Yet the report acknowledged two quandaries. First, there was the categorical puzzle, given that there were "no real guides to what people or most people consider to be private." Second there was the tug of the researcher's *desire* to know, if not his or her right to know. "Among the most important things to study" in order to better grasp human relations, noted Bower and de Gasparis, "are precisely those aspects of attitudes, actions, and interpersonal behavior that are most 'private.'" In their joint appreciation of and consternation about Humphreys's methods, the authors laid bare the problem of privacy and social research by the 1970s.

Social scientists still claimed the value of scientific inquiry and the pursuit of knowledge in its own right. But, intoned Bower and de Gasparis, "in some prestigious circles the argument appears to be losing some of its force."[160]

For their part, Laud Humphreys's mentors resolutely defended the primacy of "the right to know," as well as his particular study's "principled humanness" and "courage to learn the truth."[161] They pinned criticism of *Tearoom Trade* to a reaction against social inquiry itself, particularly the growing public role of sociology in defining and addressing problems. They accused Humphreys's detractors of resisting self-knowledge. And they warned of the coming of "a tame sociology" that would replace the robust progress of the discipline in recent years should such critiques succeed. They argued that "what we have here is not a conflict between nasty snoopers and the right to privacy, but a conflict between two goods: the right to privacy and the right to know." Privacy, they ventured, might simply need to be sacrificed on the altar of socially useful research. "The really tough moral problem," they concluded, "is that the idea of an inviolable right of privacy may move counter to the belief that society is obligated to secure the other rights and welfare of its citizenry."[162] In their view, social knowledge about citizens sometimes necessarily ought to prevail over those same citizens' liberties.

Not surprisingly, Humphreys agreed that "the pursuit of truth, the creation of countervailing knowledge, the demystification of shadowy areas of human experience" were all worth the possible risks to research subjects' privacy.[163] Prior to his foray into the tearooms, he stressed, the only "systematic observers" of sex in public restrooms had been law enforcement agents. He lamented that the references in a lone study of arrests in Los Angeles County for "felonious homosexual offenses" from 1962 to 1964 (and of which a stunning 56 percent, 274 of 493, occurred in public restrooms) constituted "nearly all the literature on this subject."[164] The sociologist did not remark on the striking similarities between his tactics and those of the police for gathering knowledge about the tearooms. That, perhaps, would have been too risky an admission of their shared investment in social surveillance. But he justified his study by noting that law enforcement agents ought not be the sole source of information about public sex. Deviance would be known in one way or another, he implied. Properly trained scholars would put that knowledge to better and more humane uses than would agents of the law. Noting that vice squads had employed closed-circuit TV, one-way mirrors, and decoys to catch tearoom users in the act, he opined, "To my mind *these* are the people who're the dangerous observers."[165]

Laud Humphreys, if grudgingly, eventually came around partway to the position of his critics. In line with new regulations on human subjects, he advised his own students to obtain the consent of all research participants before interviewing them. He stated too that were he to begin the tearoom study all over again he would spend an additional year cultivating willing respondents rather than observing them unawares, no matter what information would be lost. Yet he and some of his social scientific colleagues continued to decry the costs of public ignorance about the realities of social life, and to champion the need for risk-taking researchers to reveal them.[166] Still vigorously defending his methods at the end of the 1970s, the sociologist argued that "not one of my 100 respondents has ever reported suffering harm as a result of my research" and indeed that many, even the "deceived" ones, "have expressed appreciation for the ways they have benefited from the study."[167] Humphreys was also busy protesting, along with colleagues who had formed a "committee of concern," the updated human subjects regulations being proposed by the Department of Health, Education and Welfare. Interference of federal authorities in research, in the form of prior review, was "improper and unconstitutional"—a form of "censorship"—the committee declared. Scholarship should "in a free society" be guided not by government oversight but by "private and professional decisions."[168] The researcher's right to know may have been tamed, but it was still a prerogative worth fighting for, even in a new age of privacy.

What in the end did distinguish the vice patrol from the ethnographer, the Peeping Tom from the "peeping parson"? Ought those in the business of social knowledge have special leeway to uncover others' secrets? Scholars would divide on the question of whether they themselves ought to be counted as "dangerous observers," some believing that the risks to research subjects had been overblown and others deeply troubled by ethical quandaries about deception and consent. Today's regime of Institutional Review Boards and federal regulations reflects the current shape of that debate. As one recent commentator writes, that system is sustained by "the suspicion . . . that researchers might try to get away with something unethical if not monitored—and the strong sense that because researchers have to be monitored, they must be untrustworthy."[169] Scholars in Laud Humphreys's day as well as our own have chafed at such rules. And yet, in the 1970s, some spied in public discussions "considerably more exquisite ethical sensitivities" about research participants' dignity and privacy than those contained in federal guidelines.[170]

The clearest outcome of the fracas over *Tearoom Trade* was not the new regulations for research, but rather the emerging sensibility they imperfectly sought to capture: that the individual's privacy and dignity had to serve as a kind of baseline against the pursuit of new knowledge. In the 1975 "Retrospect" to his book, Humphreys wrote, "It should be evident to the reader that an author who devotes twenty percent of a monograph to exposition of his research methods and their ethical implications anticipates that some controversy will be raised about them." He swore that "in 1969, however, I did not foresee the degree of both positive and negative reaction this study would inspire or that interest in its ethical implications would continue well into the following decade."[171]

The sociologist indeed both fell victim to and helped inspire a new ethical complex around social inquiry. An example of pioneering ethnography in the late 1960s, by 1979 Humphreys's study could be characterized in the pages of the journal *Science*, alongside Stanley Milgram's and Philip Zimbardo's experiments, as "a classic in the fast-growing field of ethics in social science research, where it is commonly cited as a crass violation of subjects' rights." In the author's crisp summary, Humphreys had "deceived his subjects, failed to get anything remotely resembling informed consent from them, lied to the Bureau of Motor Vehicles, and risked doing grave damage to the psyches and reputations of his subjects." She explained that, no matter how protective of the subjects' confidentiality, "such a project is regarded as indefensible in the ethical climate of the late 1970's."[172]

Decades later, this is how the study is most often remembered, sociology textbooks referencing Humphreys's work under headings such as "Ethical Issues in Sociological Research" and "Invasion of Privacy."[173] When *Tearoom Trade* was resurrected by the *New York Times* in 2007 to comment on the bathroom arrest of a Republican senator, Idaho's Larry Craig, its usefulness as social ethnography was noted, but so was its status as "a primary example of unethical research."[174] Laud Humphreys's present-day admirers find themselves caught on the horns of the same dilemma. His biographers recognize that research like that in *Tearoom Trade*, in part responsible for the rise of Institutional Review Boards, could never be conducted today.

They worry over such regulations' impact on the stock of social knowledge. At the same time, they admit that Humphreys's research "contributed to the constantly shrinking private space in the modern world."[175]

That contracting space more and more occupied Americans who reflected in the 1970s on the fate of privacy in a knowing society. The questions were now more complex than simply whether citizens would be known and by whom. Americans would ask what *kind* of privacy citizens could reasonably achieve in the modern United States. And they would wonder, along with the tearoom study's critics, who would police the knowers. Increasingly, these concerns would fix not on the individual research subject or researcher but on the masses of identifying information quietly accumulating in the society's data banks.

6

The Record Prison

Although we feel unknown, ignored
As unrecorded blanks,
Take heart! Our vital selves are stored
In giant data banks . . .

—FELICIA LAMPORT, "Deprivacy," *Look* magazine, 1970

Protests—against the denial of civil rights and free speech, as well as the escalation of the war in Vietnam—punctuated the U.S. political landscape from the mid-1960s onward, as college campuses and draft boards became staging grounds for increasingly radical dissent from official policies, domestic and foreign. They would be countered, as would later be revealed, by extensive FBI, as well as CIA and NSA, monitoring: by infiltration, informants, wiretaps, mail opening, and illegal searches.[1] This covert apparatus of domestic surveillance would ensure that demonstrators and marchers would become especially well-known citizens in these years.

Hiding amidst the more prominent protests of this era was one focused precisely on the state's effort to gather intelligence on its own people, if not in the way we typically imagine it. Its target was the National Data Center, a 1965 proposal to pool statistical information held by the Census Bureau, the Internal Revenue Service, the Bureau of Labor Statistics, the Social Security Administration, the Federal Reserve Board, and a dozen or so other federal agencies.[2] Against the backdrop of the Free Speech Movement convulsing Berkeley's campus and the collective burning of draft cards, a bureaucratic plan to merge records may seem an unlikely subject for controversy. Yet it sparked a sharply hostile public reaction, evoking charges of Big Brother-style surveillance and defenses of citizens' right to move through society unrecorded. The pushback against the proposed center revealed a transformation in Americans' stance toward their information and powerful authorities alike. In the past, citizens had by and large accepted state tracking for the material benefits it delivered, surrendering identifying details to government agencies like the Social Security Administration with little thought. But in the mid-1960s the political winds were shifting, the computer age was dawning, and privacy concerns were gathering. It meant that state access to citizens' data could appear much more menacing.

First recommended by the Social Science Research Council (SSRC) and endorsed by the Bureau of Budget, the proposal for a national data center was the outgrowth of a three-year study concluding that the decentralized nature of the government's statistical information thwarted its effective use.[3] Housing these data in a single location struck advocates as eminently rational. Coordination among federal agencies had become onerous, their inability to easily share information creating reporting burdens for individuals and institutions. Moreover, valuable data were lost in the shuffle, making them difficult to unearth and apply to contemporary social problems. "Issues have multiplied faster than our present ability adequately to evaluate them," urged an official at the Bureau of Budget. A good number of these weighed on his mind: the rate of population increase; the relation between education and economic growth; the interplay among prices, productivity, and wages; the causes of unemployment; and the tracking of disease.[4] Each was an area in which coordinated data—and the boon of modern, computerized record keeping—could be pressed into service. As the SSRC noted, other nations had already created centralized statistical institutions.[5] Why not the United States?

None of these planners seem to have anticipated any sort of public outcry. After all, no pieces of information would be included in the center that had not already been collected by agencies of the federal government. But the bureaucrats were behind the curve, caught off guard as members of Congress, journalists, scholars, and citizens pilloried the initiative, variously calling it a "monster," an "octopus," and a "great, expensive electronic garbage pail"—not to mention a dangerous violator of Americans' "secret lives."[6] Proponents had been confident that composite data were necessary for a well-ordered society, their benefits self-evident.[7] The center's opponents, in a version of Laud Humphreys's tearoom dilemma writ large, instead emphasized the dire risks to citizens of becoming overly legible to authorities. The public outcry foiled the creation of a national data center in 1965, as well as successive iterations floated in 1967 and 1970.[8]

Coming as it did before revelations of widespread domestic surveillance of "subversives," the campaign against the National Data Center signaled rising public awareness of the power of collated—and, especially, computerized—files. To some, the proposal for a national warehouse of citizens' data looked like concrete proof of the government's ambitions toward omniscience. Even those not inclined to sympathize with 1960s-era protesters would inch closer to their analysis of the state-as-surveillor, adept at penetrating its people's secrets even as it sheltered its own. Neither the security of personal data nor the trustworthiness of its keepers could any longer be assumed. Not just radicals but citizens at large, that is, were coming to fear being known by the record keepers.

Data as Dilemma

If the prime motivation for turn-of-the-century privacy claims had been shielding individuals from too much publicity, the key problem in the late 1960s and early 1970s was the invisibility of the watchers. In the years surrounding the National Data Center controversy, citizens mobilized around what they had known, in low-grade fashion, since at least the 1930s: that many agencies, public and private, were not just collecting information about them but were also capable of monitoring their habits and histories in increasingly sophisticated fashion. Most Americans up until this point paid scant attention to the information about them steadily mounting in the society's files. In the mid-1960s, quite suddenly, the existence of silent record-keeping systems on private citizens—from credit bureaus to school dossiers—burst into political debate.

Mounting distrust of society's gatekeepers and credentialing systems propelled the critique. "Every major area in which large-scale organizations made controlling decisions about people" came in for fresh scrutiny in the 1960s, noted two contemporary scholars, leading by the 1970s to "demands that information about the exercise of lawful political dissent, cultural nonconformity, and homosexual preferences should no longer be used to bar otherwise qualified individuals from basic opportunities and rights."[9] The Vietnam War—in particular, the multiple conflicting and ultimately fraudulent accounts of its progress—helped to erode public confidence in officialdom. The Freedom of Information Act had already been enacted in 1966, born of a struggle over citizen access to government records on military activities; the compromise was the right to obtain information, but only "after the fact."[10] As Americans learned of covert U.S. actions at home and abroad in the Nixon years—CIA coups, a secret war in Laos, assassination programs—their trust in authorities plummeted further, prompting urgent calls for public oversight.[11] Distrust would adhere even to the mundane data-gathering operations of agencies like the Internal Revenue Service and Census Bureau.

Hidden monitoring devices, vast warehouses of private information, and menacing bureaucracies loop through the cultural and political texts of the period. Films like *The Parallax View* (1974), *The Conversation* (1974), and *Three Days of the Condor* (1975) took the perspective of lone men—an investigative reporter, a CIA employee, and even a surveillance expert—trapped in the labyrinthine plots of shadowy but powerful organizations.[12] Citizens found themselves ensnared in less dramatic but no less worrisome conspiracies against their ability to act undetected: closed-circuit television, magnetic stripe technology, and endless paper trails.[13] In the popular media they began to encounter a trickle of reportage about the widening of surveillance practices and even a coming "surveillance society." Federal and state agencies were only part of the picture. Powerful private institutions that amassed, stored, and processed personal information formed the other part. Law enforcement and the Selective Service but also mortgage programs, financial institutions, and the insurance and credit industries all came in for newfound questioning in these years.

It was in this context, dense with foreboding about new authorities, new lines of power, and new kinds of domination, that the Supreme Court would elaborate—in a register that could already seem outmoded—an individual civil and bodily right to privacy. In the very years that French theorist Michel Foucault's writings on classification and distributed discipline were starting to be translated and read in the United States, a homegrown analysis of social surveillance was crystallizing. This analysis called attention to the ways citizens were captured or hemmed in by the many social institutions that "knew" them, whether through a rap sheet, a school dossier, or a credit report. Even if the term itself would have been unfamiliar to many, Foucault's description of "panopticism"—a system of control that worked because individuals never knew when they were being watched—shared much with discussions about an emerging surveillance society in the United States. Foucault had borrowed the concept from English philosopher Jeremy Bentham, who had designed a building along these lines in the late eighteenth century as a means of better inculcating discipline in prison inmates. Bentham's panopticon would in time become one of the leading metaphors for thinking about modern surveillance. In the 1960s and 1970s, however, Americans who contemplated such questions talked of another sort of institutionalized discipline, the "record prison."[14]

It was not bodies but files that would dominate these new privacy discussions. Public law scholar Alan Westin's influential book *Privacy and Freedom* (1967), which called attention to "data surveillance," was the opening salvo in a long and tangled reckoning with the place of records in American life.[15] Westin wrote at length about both physical and psychological surveillance, the latter referring to lie detectors, personality tests, and market research, all of which had sown privacy fears in the prior decade. Yet it was data surveillance that proved to have the most staying power in the swirling debates of the day. Even Westin's definition of privacy in 1967 was oriented to what we now call "information privacy." For all his book's attention to the sweep of privacy violations in that era, one can detect a subtle privileging of data as the real threat in Westin's focus on "the claim of individuals, groups, or institutions to determine for themselves when, how, and to what extent information about them is communicated to others."[16]

Talk of surveillance had, prior to the 1960s, typically referred to the act of spying, whether physical or virtual. But it was tilting decisively toward data and the less individualized and intentional—but more continuous— means through which citizens were being watched in American society. Writing just a couple years after Westin, a sociologist called for sustained attention to the record systems firmly lodged in Americans' lives. Because "the making, keeping, and reading of records" profoundly affected both individuals and the larger society, he urged, they presented a problem of major significance.[17] Research subjects' rights, as we have seen, were coming into focus in this era. Citizens who turned their attention to the place and power of records in everyday life were beginning to grasp that social and medical research was only the tip of the iceberg. Everyone was now a subject of data, captured ever more minutely by recording techniques that had without a great deal of notice taken hold in U.S. society. Some of the technologies in question were long-standing: paper filing systems, for example. It took the computer, however—still novel to most Americans in the 1960s—to ignite the debate. A new and wary focus on records, along with intense speculation about the implications of the new machines, would combine to push other privacy discussions to the background.

Not nearly as exotic as the bugged martini olives that appeared in spy thrillers and on screen, personal information preserved in files was surfacing as a pressing concern and one with a broad reach. The dizzying array of privacy threats, seemingly issuing from everywhere in the mid-1960s, would thus assume a more defined shape by 1970. In the coming decade, the privacy-invading technology that would surpass all others in Americans' imaginations was the data bank. A steady drumbeat of congressional hearings, scientific commissions, print and broadcast exposés, scholarly studies, science fiction accounts, and social protests would conspire to make record systems, especially computerized ones, the new face of privacy fears.[18] Around the globe too, privacy was coming increasingly to mean "data protection," an issue that attracted political attention in many Western nations. Legislative solutions to the problem of secret and unaccountable record systems would be proposed. And, in a kind of scholarly analogue to contemporary science fiction accounts, a series of sober studies attempted to grasp the implications of a world run by automated managers.[19]

Vance Packard's and Myron Brenton's exposés on the scale of information banks in 1964 had already unnerved readers. As a writer for *Life* magazine put it that same year, "Most Americans who have served in the armed forces, taken out mortgages or insurance, made large purchases on credit or worked in defense industries know that, somewhere, dossiers on them are maintained. But few people have any notion of the extent of this dossier-keeping or of the number of facts (and gossip and lies) on file . . . on virtually every adult U.S. citizen."[20] A 1966 survey estimated that the government's stores of knowledge alone comprised "more than 3 billion records on individuals, including 27.2 billion names, 2.3 billion addresses, 264 million criminal histories, 280 million mental health records, 916 million profiles on alcoholism and drug addiction, and 1.2 billion financial records."[21] Recognition of this state of affairs—in academia, in policy circles, and in the public at large—would swiftly take hold in the years to come.

The very term "dossier," not to mention a "giant dossier bank," as the *New York Times* characterized one of the proposals for centralizing federal record keeping, had already acquired a bad reputation.[22] Linked to those with a criminal record or who had engaged in subversive political activities during the McCarthy years, the word "dossier" conjured up a suspect citizen who had through his own activities earned the attention of authorities. Merely having a dossier implied having something to hide; indeed, possessing "a record" was one feature distinguishing the bad citizen, or the noncitizen, from the good. For this reason, keeping tabs on law-abiding Americans, no matter that it was a routine practice of credit card companies and the IRS alike, could generate considerable unease. The headline of one negative report on the National Data Center, "There's a Dossier on You," tapped into just this sense of disquiet.[23]

But if every American now had a record, what did this imply about the society they inhabited? And what would "data surveillance" mean in practice for putatively free citizens? The easy reach many commentators made for George Orwell's *Nineteen Eighty-Four*—or occasionally, Russian dissident Aleksandr Solzhenitsyn's *Cancer Ward*, which was eloquent on the matter of how individual threads of information could, if dense enough, strangle individual freedom—suggested one answer.[24] Even the Congressional Committee on Government Operations speculated that a national bank of citizens' information would instill "a suffocating sense of surveillance," which was "not an atmosphere in which freedom can long survive."[25] Files on ordinary Americans were not at all new in the 1960s, but awareness of them was, and they would become a node of public debate, even outrage.

Dossiers and records were the point of entry for these discussions, but they were soon joined by the specter of the "data bank."[26] The notion of a data bank (or, sometimes, "memory bank") was linked to the computer in most imaginings, even if it was not indebted to the new machines.[27] Political scientist Harold Lasswell had felt it necessary to enclose the term in quotation marks in 1960, but these would fall away as data banks gained more currency in American life, attracting the keen suspicion of privacy watchers.[28] Acknowledging in 1970 that the word was commonly used to describe "*any* . . . aggregation of like data," two British scholars used it as shorthand for "computer files of personal information, integrated and fully cross-referenced," while the *New Scientist and Science Journal* defined a "data bank" in 1971 as a "generalized collection of data not linked to one set of . . . questions."[29] Others noted confusion over the term, but couldn't mistake its pejorative ring.[30] What is clear is that the worry preceded any settled meaning of the word, as awareness of the kind and volume of personal information filed away by corporations and especially the federal government increased.

The extent of such records was only one issue. The record keepers' lack of accountability to those they documented—indeed, the widespread ignorance of these records' very existence—was even more disturbing. As a more vigilant public and press scrutinized the U.S. government in the Nixon years, the worry grew. The British coauthors of *The Data Bank Society* publicized the "vast collection" of personal and business facts that their government housed in its archives, but looked even more warily at what had been "achieved by the FBI and the State police forces of America" as their records were computerized.[31] Bombshell revelations in the early 1970s about U.S. Army spying on domestic political activity along with COINTELPRO, a series of covert, illegal FBI surveillance operations trained on dissidents ranging from Martin Luther King Jr. and the Black Panther Party to antiwar activists and feminists, opened all government data gathering to suspicion.[32] Legal scholar and privacy advocate Arthur R. Miller reported in 1971 that "rarely does a week go by without some new information system being uncovered." He pointed to recent revelations about

> the existence of the Department of Housing and Urban Development's Adverse Information File, the National Science Foundation's data bank on scientists, the Customs Bureau's computerized data bank on "suspects," the Civil Service Commission's "investigative" and "security" files, the Secret Service's dossiers on "undesirables," the National Migrant Workers Children Data Bank, the National Driver Registration Service, and the surveillance activities of the United States Army.[33]

Miller viewed these heretofore clandestine record systems as deeply troubling in their implications for democratic transparency and civil liberties. Unlike the public face of political surveillance in the 1950s in the form of the House Un-American Activities Committee—which operated on the principle of "trial by publicity"—these were records that almost no citizens were aware of. Yet they relentlessly shaped Americans' fates and fortunes through a perhaps even more ominous use of state power.[34]

Again, this power was not the state's alone, and only some of the dossiers that would inspire protests in this period were those of the government. Few distinguished between state and commercial uses of citizens' information in their misgivings about the mounting and often- inaccessible piles of data inside file cabinets and mainframe computers. More important than an agency's public or private status was the fact that it collected and housed information about millions of citizens, using it to make any number of consequential decisions about them. Indeed, the credit, banking, and insurance industries were leading candidates in discussions about the harm that could come from being monitored too closely or, even more crucially, inaccurately. Many consumers' first brush with the potency of their files came when they were denied insurance or had difficulty applying for a job or a loan.[35]

Given these experiences, it is not surprising that the first piece of privacy legislation to make it out of Congress targeted consumer credit. Regulation came on the heels of reports about outfits like the Credit Data Corporation, which enabled subscribers to procure credit checks on individuals in a mere ninety seconds.[36] Unsavory practices later revealed in a suit by the Federal Trade Commission against the Retail Credit Company included the deliberate misrepresentation of its agents in seeking information, as well as false or fabricated material in consumer files, born of the expectation that agents would supply "a prescribed amount of adverse information."[37] Trafficking in a mountain of detail about individuals' "character" and habits, with few checks on the fidelity of the reporting, these agencies were rightly understood as unaccountable gatekeepers. The Fair Credit Reporting Act (FCRA) of 1970 entitled a consumer who had been denied credit on the basis of information from a reporting agency to be advised of this fact and also informed of the source of the report—although it did not go so far as to permit access to the record itself.[38] Nor, noted one commentary, "is he or she even advised that the record exists until it has been used for an unfavorable decision."[39] Still, the only law of the era to rein in private sector data practices, it testified to widespread concern about privately operated, inaccessible records on American consumers.[40]

If what Alan Westin had termed "data surveillance" largely operated in the shadows before the mid-1960s, it earned a place in the sun in the early 1970s. Even before Watergate, millions tuned into special television reports with titles like CBS's "Under Surveillance" and ABC's "Assault on Privacy." In these productions, the spotlight was trained equally on the government and the private sector. The CBS program investigated both credit bureaus and policing in its program on surveillance practices in Philadelphia, chosen "not because it is . . . special, but because we believe it is typical." Among other items, it revealed that the city's police surveillance unit alone had compiled files on approximately 18,000 individuals and 600 local organizations.[41] ABC's broadcast detailed "the many ways in which vast volumes of information are being gathered on millions of Americans," also focusing on law enforcement and consumer credit reporting. "The net effect is the compilation of a staggering amount of data—accurate, inaccurate, properly used, sometimes abused—on virtually all adult Americans."[42] This last line was the real shock the program meant to administer to its viewers. It was common knowledge that criminals and other suspect groups might be "under surveillance." Now, ABC made clear, all citizens had come to share this fate.

One sign of a new consciousness about files was the emerging consumer audience for privacy protection, specifically understood as data protection. *Privacy Journal*, "An Independent Monthly on Privacy in a Computer Age," which launched in the fall of 1974, was designed to help citizens navigate a whole range of threats to the security of their personal information.[43] It brimmed with cautionary tales from around the country: a New Jersey high school girl subjected to FBI criminal investigation after writing to the Socialist Workers Party to gather information for a class project, for example. And it reported on small victories over privacy invaders: an action against the Postal Service, in which mail was addressed "First Class U.S. Mail: May Be Opened for Inspection by CIA, FBI, IRS, NSC, FDA & EPA"; and a Providence, Rhode Island, mother's physical removal of her eleven-year-old son's offending middle school file from the school premises, announcing, "These records are about my child and they are not staying in this building any longer."[44] The publication plumbed topics ranging from "your psychiatrist and the insurance company" to unauthorized police record checks.[45]

Privacy Journal educated consumers about the new black-and-white markings beginning to appear on canned and packaged products, also known as the Uniform Product Code: "the key to a computerized retail system which may radically alter American shopping habits" and carrying the potential for "receptacles of individual financial information or personal purchase patterns."[46] It told of "a closed-circuit system of 109 covert TV cameras . . . activated in the U.S. Capitol complex to monitor the comings and goings of visitors."[47] It alerted readers to the presence of a black magnetic stripe on the back of their new credit cards, which eventually "may be electronically coded with unfavorable information . . . as the waitress slips away with [a customer's] credit card for a few seconds when he pays his luncheon check."[48] It laid out a "snooper's walking tour" of downtown Los Angeles, whereby an enterprising individual could get ahold of a troublingly detailed collection of public records on just about anyone.[49] And it offered a layperson's guide to the coming electronic funds transfer system—already projecting a future "cashless society"—that "will replace money, check and credit card transactions" with a direct link to a bank computer, such that the transaction could "be indefinitely retained in the terminal." As one expert warned of the last innovation, such a system would know "where an individual is in real time, as well as what he is buying, every time he makes a financial transaction."[50]

The journal reported on a dizzying set of practices: fraudulent IDs, wiretaps (which had increased precipitously after Watergate, the journal claimed), "junk phone calls," exchanges of information between government and commercial data banks (the sharing of motor vehicle records with auto insurance companies, for example), new fingerprint reader technologies, spectrographic analysis or personally identifying "voice prints," anonymous yet traceable questionnaire responses (via invisible ink or code numbers), "activated two-way systems" like cable TV, polygraph tests, exploitative experimentation on prisoners and Veterans Administration patients, and the invasions of "Big Mother" (the Bell System telephone company).[51] But the weight of its concern was on data banks of one kind or another: the FBI's National Crime Information Center, the Michigan Youth Services Information System, a proposed centralized Parent Locator Service to track absent fathers, an "Individual Recipient Basic Data File" requirement for public assistance clients, federal mailing lists, drug program records, medical and psychiatric files, arrest records, airline travel reservation systems, drivers' license banks, television subscriber lists, computerized credit files, magnetic tape lists of bad checks, and even religious organizations' troves of membership information.[52]

To a reader of the *Privacy Journal*, the quest to keep one's personal information safe from corporations, the government, and one's fellow citizens must have seemed impossibly daunting. A crop of advisors stepped up to help. The General Binding Corporation advertised "your own privacy machine": a paper shredder.[53] Social critic Vance Packard's advice for evading the "all-seeing eye" of modern society was still simpler: "Don't tell it to the computer."[54] A new genre of self-help manuals offering guidance on how to ward off public and private agencies thirsty for private data, with titles such as *Privacy: How to Protect What's Left of It*, began to appear.[55] Citizens were becoming protective even of information that had once been unproblematically public, such as telephone listings.[56] By the end of the 1970s, the Committee on National Statistics would confirm the change that had taken place in American sensibilities. "Privacy and confidentiality have been receiving increasing attention from the public," it reported. The cause was the "growing concentration of individual data records."[57]

The New Face of Privacy Fears

The National Data Center proposals could be understood, in one observer's view, as a "lightning rod for the vague feelings of discontent generated by the computer revolution."[58] In political action and legislative proposals, survey responses and TV specials, public concerns about privacy were beginning to focus not just on the single file but on its linkage to others in vast, unseen repositories. Computing would play a transformative role in shaping this new consciousness.

Utopianism had greeted computers, as with new technologies more generally, in the postwar United States, but their presence stirred up more ambivalence as the machines took root in society.[59] Estimates vary, but there were just a handful of computers in the government's employ in the early 1950s; by 1971, according to a federal inventory of automatic data-processing equipment, there were 5,961 (with approximately 7,000 in use nationwide).[60] Jerry Rosenberg, author of the 1969 book *The Death of Privacy*, reported with some alarm that in that year there were "at least 5,000 people about the capital who do nothing but sell, coordinate and maintain computers for the government, and more than 75,000 people who operate them."[61] The increasing prevalence of computing was shadowed by an anxious public debate about the machines. Arthur Miller could by 1971 chronicle the frequent "scapegoating" of the computer in popular culture: errors in billing and accounts blamed on the machine rather than the operator, naked protesters at IBM with signs proclaiming "Computers are Obscene," and the establishment of the quixotic International Society for the Abolition of Data Processing Machines.[62]

Still, expectations that a computerized world would usher in tremendous benefits were alive and well. The faith that computer systems would help government run better, deliver public services more effectively, and engineer new solutions to social problems animated discussions of expanding electronic networks. The municipal government of New Haven, Connecticut, for example, paired with the IBM corporation in the later 1960s to create a prototype for the computerized city. The vision, spelled out in a popular magazine, was compelling. Say a fire alarm rang out. A computer at the firehouse would instantly get to work compiling "an entire information file about the burning building even while the firemen are sliding down the pole: What sort of a store is on the first floor? Any paint or varnish stored there? Sprinkler system? Skylights? Apartments upstairs? Any invalids or children? Then the computer automatically notifies the electric company to shut off power and the police to block the street." Likewise, a Detroit agency charged with evaluating antipoverty programs was proud to have "computerized the most intimate problems of 46,000 poor people" in that city. This was done "not to keep a dossier on them," stated its director, but to ascertain with much finer precision than ever before how well their needs were met by social services.[63]

These promises of efficiency and coordination, of rapid access to and ability to act on critical knowledge about citizens, were, however, increasingly understood to come with darker implications for individual privacy. Observers found both promise and peril in the merging of data that computerization permitted. The National Data Center's planners, to their chagrin, had neglected privacy entirely in their early proposals, one later admitting this to have been a "gigantic oversight."[64] A task force, headed by the economist and former deputy National Security Advisor Carl Kaysen, scrambled to clarify the proposed center's interest in aggregates rather than individuals—general economic, social, and demographic data, rather than personnel records or "rap sheets." The Center, they hastened to explain, was conceived as a statistical system, not an intelligence center.[65] This distinction may have eluded privacy watchers in the mid-1960s, some of whom were inclined to believe that the former could easily shade into the latter.[66]

Other advocates of computerization would not make the same mistake. Even in their starry-eyed projections, they acknowledged the tension between technological marvels and individual privacy. Detroit's antipoverty administrator, well aware of the temptation that a stash of data on poor urbanites might hold, reflected in 1968 that a federal law to protect outsiders from getting into his files might be necessary. The city controller in San Jose, California, charged with maintaining newly computerized material—of welfare files, schoolchildren's grades, and hospital clinic records—hoped to "make it a felony for anyone to misuse the computer" and was working on plans to issue metal identity cards, switched out monthly, to city employees who would have access to the computer terminals. In an age of heightened suspicion of authorities of all kinds, the trade-offs between the benefits and the risks of electronically accessible records were becoming obvious. Casting an anxious eye on the "rapid computerization of credit-company files," one observer understood that, as convenient as this trend was for department stores and consumers, it was also leading to a national network "with ready information on nearly every family." Others raised questions about plans afoot for regional medical data banks, spinning out hypothetical scenarios. A Chicago man suffering a heart attack in New York might, through the push of a button, have his medical chart, including electrocardiograms, transferred to a physician on site. "Such information might well save his life," pondered a reporter for *Look* magazine. But that same information, "if extracted from the computer by an unscrupulous person, might also destroy him."[67]

Able to save or destroy, the new machines assumed godlike powers, appearing in such accounts as vital actors in modern society. A young adult book of 1964, *The Story of Computers*, captured the tone: "Although you may never have seen a computer . . . your life is almost certainly going to be affected by these mechanical wizards. In other words, they think about you even if you don't think about them."[68] Similar analyses appeared in serious reading for adults. As computing spread in American society, a reporter for the *Wall Street Journal* reflected, "Individuals tend to feel molded to fit the computer's needs rather than the other way around."[69] The personalization of the computer mirrored the depersonalization of individual identity now confined in databases and bureaucratic categories. The boundary between science fiction and lived social experience nearly dissolved at this point. As Arthur Miller testified in Senate hearings, referring to the popular film of 1968, "There are many, many millions of people in the country who went to see '2001: A Space Odyssey,' and they have a feeling that computers are creative, that they are domineering, that they can think for themselves."[70]

Computers were at once material, mundane things and cultural apparitions with elusive, almost mystical powers. Such visions predated the data bank era. By the mid-1950s, "thinking machines" were often represented as an incipient threat to individual autonomy and freedom.[71] A host of novels, poems, essays, short stories, and films in the 1960s provided a rich canvas for such fears. Eugene Burdick's novel of 1964, *The 480*, envisioned computer simulations replacing the political deliberations of the U.S. public. Theodore Tyler's "outrageous novel of an unlikely hero who took on the world's biggest, smartest computer," *The Man Whose Name Wouldn't Fit* (1968), followed the exploits of a hero driven to sabotage of the Randolf Datatronic 8080 because his name was too long for a standardized punch card form to handle. Films ranging from *2001: A Space Odyssey* (1968) to *Colossus: The Forbin Project* (1970) imagined epic battles between sentient machines and the humans who, theoretically anyway, were their masters.[72] Rhetorical attacks on computers in 1964 during Berkeley's Free Speech Movement compared dehumanized and standardized students to newly valued IBM cards, begging the university not to "destroy, spindle and mutilate" its own.[73] A later wave of campus protests sometimes pivoted into actual battles. Data centers on university campuses that held big mainframe machines were the target of thirteen direct protest actions between 1968 and 1972.[74]

Increasingly, however, animus toward computers shifted away from the physical machines and toward the unseen and yet formidable data they housed. The discovery that discrete pieces of information could be merged in what amounted to an electronic biography roused both popular and scholarly trepidations. *Look* magazine posed the question dramatically: "The Computer Data Bank: Will it Kill Your Freedom?" Its cover article in June 1968 announced that "the private lives of 200 million Americans are now being stored in the computer's memory." The magazine likened computers to file cabinets—just ones equipped with "phenomenal memories" and "instant recall." While intimate personal information had "always been available to a persistent investigator with enough time and money to sift the paper trail we leave behind," computerization meant it was now easily accessed by "any snooper . . . without even leaving his office chair."[75] In 1970, a behavioral scientist and computer scientist declared that 1984 had arrived early: a whole host of organizations now had "the technical power" to implement Orwell's "chilling vision of a society under surveillance and control." Computers, those seemingly "innocuous boxes," had "voracious appetites, and can digest, churn around, and regurgitate information at prodigiously high speeds." They warned of a new form of domination: rule by "computerocracy," which harbored the "potential destruction of freedom in our society."[76]

LOOK

50 CENTS · JUNE 25, 1968

ROSEMARY'S BABY
From best seller to movie chiller

COMPUTER DATA BANKS
Do they know too much about you?

ETHEL'S KENNEDYS
How she manages them

6.1a. In scholarly analyses and popular magazines alike, the computer data bank was the new face of privacy fears.

LOOK ■ JUNE 25, 1968 Volume 32, No. 13

THE COMPUTER DATA BANK:

DID YOUR SISTER have an illegitimate baby when she was 15? Did you fail math in junior high? Are you divorced or living in a common-law relationship? Do you pay your bills promptly? Are you willing to talk to salesmen? Have you been treated for a venereal disease? Are you visiting a psychiatrist? Were you ever arrested? Have you taken an airplane trip in the past 90 days; with whom; and in which hotels did you stay?

The answers to these intimate questions and hundreds more like them have always been available to a persistent investigator with enough time and money to sift the paper trail we leave behind in file cabinets around the country. But now, for the first time, in this age of computers, it is becoming possible for any snooper to get such information quickly and cheaply, without leaving his office chair.

Since the early 1950's, tens of thousands of computers have gone into service in America. Some keep track of payrolls and others mail out bills or help an architect design a skyscraper. Increasingly, hundreds of computers serve as data banks: electronic file cabinets with phenomenal memories and instant recall. Such banks can be located a great distance from their users—with information often fed into them from thousands of miles away or retrieved from thousands of miles away. There is nothing to keep a network of computers from being tied together by telephone lines that will link all their memories.

"Everybody is commencing to use such data centers," warns Rep. Cornelius E. Gallagher (Dem., N.J.), whose Special Subcommittee on Invasion of Privacy has been worrying about this for the past two years.

"Computer data banks are at the same stage of development as the early railroads and the first telephone companies, which took a number of years to link themselves together in a nationwide network. Welfare departments, credit bureaus, hospitals, police departments and dozens of other institutions are putting their files into hundreds of relatively small data centers. No matter what you call them, they're still data centers, and they can be linked."

What bothers Representative Gallagher and Sen.
continued

WILL IT KILL YOUR FREEDOM?

All around the U.S., computer centers may be talking too much about everybody and everything

BY JACK STAR LOOK SENIOR EDITOR

PHOTOGRAPH BY
PHILLIP HARRINGTON

6.1b. Reporting on the capacity of computers to link files, *Look* magazine asked, "Will It Kill Your Freedom?"

There were arguments moving in the other direction, although they were usually made by the keepers of data. Scientist and science fiction author Isaac Asimov was one who speculated about the beneficence, rather than the dangers, of a national computer bank. Society's quest to know citizens intimately, indeed much more thoroughly than was currently technologically feasible, struck him as a positive development. In 1973, Asimov welcomed the thought that each person might come to be "represented by a completely personal and individual symbol" legible to the computer—permitting as this would, perfectly tailored and "personal" social experiences. Indeed, having a "code that is yours and only yours," imagined the writer, might beget a whole new form of individualism. Basing his discussion on the targeted mailing lists then beginning to make an appearance, Asimov reasoned, "What [the consumer] receives will be so likely to be of interest to him and to be slanted to his particular needs that, even if he does not buy, he will feel that someone has gone to the trouble of knowing what he might want."[77] Indeed, it was perhaps only in a thoroughly computerized world that a person *could* be fully individualized. Until that day, "his wants and needs are unknown to anyone but himself and his immediate associates," making him a "faceless nothing."[78] The known citizen, in his futuristic scenario, was a well-cared-for citizen.

Where Asimov contemplated choice and personalization as the fruits of the computer's gaze, more of his fellow citizens spied control and dehumanization. Surveys just beginning to track American attitudes toward computing suggested that the science fiction writer's vision would not have been comforting to his readers. One, sponsored by the American Federation of Information Processing Societies and *Time* magazine in 1971, reported that 53 percent of respondents believed that "computerized information files might be used to destroy individual freedoms" and 58 percent that "computers will in the future be used to keep people under surveillance."[79] It was a significantly gloomier forecast than Asimov's for the computer age.

Trapped by Traces

The United States had been, for all intents and purposes, what scholars termed a "records-based social system" since at least the 1950s.[80] Indeed, Americans even in the 1920s and 1930s regularly grumbled about the new bureaucratic credentials they needed to gain access to basic opportunities and rights, all of these backed up by paper records. What was novel in the mid-1960s was not so much the existence of data systems as the heightened awareness of their power. Publicity about technological advances in record keeping was partly responsible. Modern "machine to machine" reporting via magnetic tape may only have made manual practices faster and cheaper, but it raised hackles nonetheless. That federal agencies—the Federal Trade Commission and the IRS, for example—were communicating in this fashion was roundly denounced as "shocking" and "unconscionable" in 1964.[81]

Cooperation among powerful gatekeepers became even more suspect in the 1970s. An ABC News investigative documentary on government records, which aired under the provocative title "The Paper Prison," made clear why. This hard-hitting 1974 report examined, among other things, a three-number code known as a Separation Program Number, or SPN, that appeared on veterans' discharge forms. ABC's correspondent, Frank Reynolds, informed viewers that since 1967 alone, upward of 200,000 veterans who had been honorably discharged were nonetheless carrying on their record—unbeknownst to them—a damning SPN number. The digits alerted those schooled in the code that the bearer was a "shirker," a "latent homosexual," or a "marginal producer"; harbored an "apathetic attitude"; or evinced "substandard personal behavior," or any one of approximately five hundred other such classifications.

As ABC reported, despite the fact that the SPN lists were marked "For Official Use Only," major corporations—among them Firestone, the Chrysler Corporation, Standard Oil of California, Republic Steel, Boeing, McDonnell-Douglas, and Honeywell—had managed to obtain them in order to "screen prospective employees." Even men who had earned combat awards were vulnerable to this form of blacklisting. An ex-Marine interviewed on the program noted that his "chestful of ribbons" and promotion to sergeant had not helped him evade an ambiguous but worrisome "early separation" code. Other veterans wondered if an SPN had cost them a job or was the price they paid for civil rights agitation or entirely legal political activity, such as circulating a petition to end the Vietnam War. Asked on air whether the Army used these numbers to "punish a man," a colonel insisted that this was not at all the intent, although he was willing to allow that "it may be the effect."[82] In this slippage from intent to effect lay the whole conundrum of data sharing.

Soldiers had often tattooed their draft numbers on their bodies, a mark of their dedication to the service. A black mark on their record at discharge, although they might not be aware of its presence, was similarly indelible. Exposés like ABC's disproved the popular notion that a record was a kind of rap sheet, trailing behind only those who had earned society's distrust. Veterans willing to make the ultimate sacrifice for their country were just as likely to have a record as a common criminal. Moreover, that record could be dangerously misleading. As the publicity for "The Paper Prison" explained, "Government records can contain highly personal facts about you—as supplied by your neighbors, your teachers, your employers. Many of the facts may be wrong—but they're on your record."[83] This characterization of an ever-expanding and inescapable information net was becoming conventional wisdom. A reviewer of the ABC program described as "frightening" the "unfair, immoral, and punitive use of the billions of pieces of information filed on ordinary Americans by government agencies across the nation."[84] What made it frightening was not just the volume of the data: it was the manifold possibilities of error, and—worst of all—its easy availability to those with an interest in knowing.

Computerization and record keeping proved an especially combustible combination, and their coupling could cause unremarkable features of modern life to take on a sinister aspect. This was the case for a much more familiar set of digits than the SPN: the Social Security number. In the mid-twentieth century, SSNs had—in a way never intended or anticipated—become the next best thing to a national identification number.[85] Decades after their début, they would erupt as a political issue, prompting the creation of a federal task force in 1970 and multiple congressional hearings in the early part of the decade.[86] This timing stemmed from the numbers' crucial role in newly networked filing systems. As even Social Security's commissioner would concede, the agency's records constituted "one of the world's largest concentrations of personal data"—identifying information on 256 million people and their earning histories, as well as family, financial, and sometimes medical data—"all of it indexed according to SSN, and much of it instantly retrievable from computer records."[87]

More ominous still was the fact that millions, even billions, of pieces of information were connected to other pieces through the simple fact of sharing, somewhere, the identical string of nine digits. By the late 1960s, it was common knowledge that "our Social Security number has become the key in the registering of . . . billions of transactions."[88] The American Medical Association strongly protested, in light of this fact, a uniform discharge form proposed by the Department of Health, Education, and

Welfare in 1976 requiring an SSN from every patient. "In this age of great concern over the right to privacy," charged the AMA, "we are shocked that a federal department would now formally propose to establish a mechanism by which most physicians and every hospitalized Medicare, Medicaid, and Title V recipient could be classified, identified, matched, compared, reviewed and computerized with the impersonal ease of electronic machines."[89] Some would even call for repeal of FDR's Executive Order 9397 of 1943 authorizing the SSN for federal record keeping.[90]

Many more Americans in the 1970s were prepared to see the menace rather than the promise in what had become a de facto national identity number: few, if any, contemplated a Social Security tattoo. Beginning in the mid-1930s, the SSN had been required of employees in the majority of the nation's workplaces and had even been prized by some as a badge of economic rights. But observers in the 1970s insisted that something had happened to that proud, independent citizen as the society's record-keeping systems churned and grew. If some citizens had once claimed a stake in New Deal security through their SSNs, those same numbers, now ubiquitous, seemed to impinge on the citizenry's psychic "life space," as one philosopher had it.[91] In further Senate hearings in 1974 on the computerization of personal data—this time focused on financial, medical, educational, and census records—California congressman Barry Goldwater Jr. averred that "the average citizen" had come to view the SSN as both "dehumanizing and threatening."[92] Palpable in such comments was the sense that power was shifting in American society in favor of the institutions that controlled individuals' data—and thus also their daily lives and opportunities—and away from individual citizens themselves.

The diminished status of the individual in a sea of computerized records preoccupied many of the early writers on data banks. In their analyses, the data bank had gained the upper hand. Sociologist Michael Baker, for instance, noted that the "ownership and control" of what he called "record identities" were "firmly in the hands of organizations." The individuals in such systems were objects, not citizens with rights, and had few tools with which to protect their "record privacy." The key dilemma was the tremendous mismatch between the capacity of the record system and of the citizen to keep track of data. Given what it would take for a person "to genuinely *take charge* of records about himself," the sociologist reasoned, "it does not seem likely that we can expect self-protective vigilance from more than a few dedicated citizens." The problem did not admit of an easy solution. As Baker cautioned, "We have to beware of establishing remedies which turn out to be fictional because they require daily acts of minor heroism on the part if [sic] the individual, as he challenges clerk, manager and officials on record-keeping matters and works to grasp the significance for his interests of each record-related choice he is given." On these grounds, Baker believed that solutions to the records problem would not and, indeed, could not come from empowered citizens. They would "have to be accomplished primarily for, not by, the individual—a paternalism which, while perhaps not welcome, does reflect the individual's position in this society and his existential relationship to everyday record-keeping processes."[93]

If few matched Baker's resignation concerning the individual actor's impotence in a records-based society, others echoed his primary theme. Arthur R. Miller posited that "many people have come to feel that their success or failure in life ultimately may turn on what other people put in their file." The passage of time, he mused, was no barrier to a computer data bank. Its memory was permanent, "absent an electronic eraser and a compassionate soul willing to use it."[94] Miller was particularly concerned with the way that the record could harden, or imprison, one's personal history.[95] He offered an unsettling hypothetical example:

> Consider the potential effect of a computer entry: "arrested, criminal trespass; sentenced, six months." Without more data how will the user know that our computerized man was demonstrating for desegregation in the South in the 1950's or equal employment opportunities in the North in the 1960's and was convicted under a statute that was overturned on appeal as an unconstitutional restraint on free speech?[96]

The computer, Miller feared, had become the "unforgetting and unforgiving watchdog of society's information managers."[97]

Miller's invocation of a "computerized man"—stripped of his privacy but also his individuality and social context—suggested the way that critics were grasping the changed relationship between human and machine in the age of the data bank.[98] Individuals were portrayed in such accounts as the mute subjects of record-keeping organizations. By contrast, the files were replete with vitality and power. People could be drowned out or swallowed up—incapacitated—by their own preserved traces. Arrest records, which often lingered even when a charge was dropped (and, even if

successfully expunged, could still leave a worrisome reference to the expunged record), were just one especially vexing example.[99] As a credit industry insider confessed in 1973 hearings on amending the Fair Credit
Reporting Act, "Every time I wrote a new application, I knew I was opening
up the customer's most intimate personal secrets and locking them in to a
computerized system that could not distinguish right from wrong, truth
from lie, and could never forget."[100] With a computer readout more enduring and authoritative than a person's word, how could an individual
ever escape the prison cell of his own record?

The very mindfulness of their files that Americans now carried around
with them was itself a dilemma. Given that many of citizens' interactions
and transactions were now transcribed somewhere, wrote a sociologist, "individuals have become oriented very early in life to making or maintaining
'a good record,' or sometimes to avoid if possible making any record at all
(as is clearly the point with police records)."[101] Senator Edward Long likewise warned, "Because of this diligent accumulation of facts about each of
us, it is difficult to speak or act today without wondering if the words or
actions will reappear 'on the record.'"[102] Yale Law professor and sociologist Stanton Wheeler feared a "dossier consciousness" taking hold in the
population: "Will people develop an increasingly bifurcated personality,
one part oriented to their private lives, a second part oriented to matters of
record?" He ventured that "we will become increasingly concerned, not
with what we are, but with what the record makes us out to be."[103] Arthur
Miller regarded this attentiveness to one's "record image in the eyes of
those who may have access to it in the future" as a new and subtle means
of social control. It was the "real evil of the record prison."[104]

In this light, collections of data were not just intrusive or irritating features of living in the modern age; rather they *did* things to people and
maybe even changed the nature of personhood. Data banks had a way of
ricocheting back on the person, inviting questions about what a "subject
of data" really was. "As the public becomes increasingly aware of the information orientation of modern life," wrote Miller, "it is understandable
that people may begin to doubt whether they have any meaningful existence or identity apart from their profile stored in the electronic cata-
combs of a 'master' computer."[105] So thoroughly known by their society
and its agencies, individuals risked losing a deeper sense of who they
were. The problem was not just how little Americans knew about their
own files but also how utterly unrecognizable one's own bureaucratic

identity could be—not to mention the observable fact that, in many settings, a credit history or medical file spoke more convincingly than the physical person it represented. To echo Miller, was a person even provable *as* someone outside his or her computer dossier?

The influential 1973 Report of the Committee on Records, Computers, and the Rights of Citizens to the Secretary of Health, Education, and Welfare—the culmination of years of hearings on a national data center and on the problem of the Social Security number—itself blurred the file and the person in its bleak references to citizens as "data subjects." It framed the conflict of human versus machine rather poignantly, calling the "struggle of individual versus computer" a "fixed feature of modern life." The problem was not Americans' alone. Rather, the report named the "loss of individuality, loss of control over information, the possibility of linking data banks to create dossiers, rigid decision making by powerful, centralized bureaucracies" as the common lot of industrialized populations. The power of pooled files, which made it possible "to bring a lifetime of information to bear on any decision about a given individual," was made abundantly evident in its pages.[106] The utopian vision of Isaac Asimov aside, these ever-more detailed caches of personal information seemed to dehumanize rather than individualize—and somehow to prevent a citizen from truly being known.

James Rule, an early theorist of the "surveillance society," would elaborate on this grim picture. Systems of criminal records, vehicle and drivers' licensing, health insurance, and consumer credit, he argued, were not simply pale, inert reflections of real individuals and their histories. Instead, they constituted a "paper world," parallel but not identical to the real social world, that at times "stirs with life of its own, and comes to shape and dominate men's experiences." Rule cautioned that personal data on private citizens might well be the future basis for controlling them. With Britain and the United States as his examples—although he was certain the same developments were afoot in all industrial societies—Rule envisioned an Orwellian order based on systematic "personal documentation."[107] The gathering public consensus, built from a steady accumulation of commentary about but also experience with bureaucratic potency, seemed to agree with him.

In fact, Rule's careful study of five existing bureaucratic systems of "mass surveillance" in the United States and United Kingdom demonstrated both the potential and the limits of social control via documentation—

**RECORDS,
COMPUTERS,
AND THE RIGHTS
OF CITIZENS**

6.2. A 1973 federal report called the problem of computerized records a "fixed feature of modern life."

whether gauged in terms of specific systems' size, centralization, speed of information flow and decision making, or "point of contact" with their clienteles.[108] In other words, what Rule termed surveillance capacity varied considerably. "Unlike Orwell's world," he observed, "modern societies provide many opportunities for those who wish to avoid the attention of the authorities simply to drop out of sight." While conceding that "available signs are disquieting," he acknowledged that the increasing reach of bureaucratic processes did not inevitably lead to diminished privacy or totalitarian control. He even allowed for the possibility that "the same social changes which make mass surveillance feasible and necessary may also release men from other forms of surveillance."[109]

There were other, similarly measured, positions that were staked out in the roiling data bank debate of the early 1970s. The most comprehensive of these was a report commissioned by the National Academy of Sciences and published in 1972. Coauthored by Alan Westin, the best-known privacy expert of the day, and the organizational sociologist Michael Baker, *Databanks in a Free Society* set out to temper public disquiet about electronic records with empirical evidence. As Orville Brim Jr.—president of the Russell Sage Foundation and coauthor of an important report on privacy and social research—explained in his foreword, "We have our doomsday prophets crying out about national data centers, our widely shared anecdotes about credit-card society and tattooed Social Security numbers, and plenty of wild and misinformed testimony at congressional hearings." The report was an attempt to weigh in on and correct confused thinking, with the express goal of separating hypothetical future uses of computerized records from present practices.[110]

The study summarized in the report was an ambitious ethnographic canvass of fifty-five "computerizing organizations," ranging from the Social Security Administration and the National Crime Information Center, to the Bank of America and Mutual of Omaha, to the Massachusetts Institute for Technology and the Church of the Latter-Day Saints. Its aim was to assess computing's impact on practices of record keeping and confidentiality. Specifically interested in what transpired when "people records" were automated, Westin and Baker debunked many popular fears about computer data banks. The authors found the increase in transactions "in the organizational world" to have preceded rather than followed computerization.[111] More strikingly, apart from increased efficiency in record keeping, they discovered no radical departures from the ways organizations had employed personal information in the precomputer era. Instead Westin and Baker documented gradual and partial computerization; the coexistence of manual and automated files; continuity in the contents, scope, and sensitivity of information entered into records; and data-sharing practices that resembled those of the manual era. The scholars in fact documented a marked *retreat* from centralized data bank projects—the effort "not merely to do the old things faster, but to do new things with information"—because of technical, conceptual, financial, and organizational constraints.[112]

Indeed, Westin and Baker found in their site visits in 1970 and 1971 that "there were no central computer databanks of the kind which had raised civil-liberties alarms." They were surprised to discover a number of organizations that were collecting *less* personal information than they had in the past, this the result of new legislation and social norms around the reporting of race, religion, nationality, sex, ethnic background, and marital status. The authors explained, for instance, that changes in entitlement to welfare aid meant that questions about identification and need were retained in automated systems, but that "historical reconstructions of the individual's personal life" (such as marriages and job history) had been eliminated.[113] Moreover they found no evidence to support widespread worries about machines replacing human judgment. Overall, they argued, "The first 15 years of automation have simply not as yet altered relationships between people, data, and organizations in the ways projected by those who first looked with anxious eyes at the relation of computers to civil liberties." Computer use, they pronounced, "has not created the revolutionary new powers of data surveillance" many had predicted.[114]

What had changed decisively was Americans' awareness of their own records. Individuals in an earlier day knew in a "dim way" that their "transactions generated a long trail of files," wrote the researchers, but they "didn't devote much thought or attention to them."[115] That era had passed. Data banks were on everyone's minds now, and popular convictions about a "dossier society" coming into being would be difficult to shake. Although for Westin and Baker it was little more than an afterthought, the arrival of a new public consciousness about the data traces lingering behind and beyond every citizen may have been their most significant conclusion of all.

Rights in an Age of Surveillance

James Rule completed his book on the theory and practice of surveillance just as the scandals that would embroil the Nixon administration broke. For him, as he noted dryly in the preface, "the Watergate affair hardly comes as a surprise."[116] One suspects that no one who had closely monitored the privacy landscape over the prior decade could have been shocked by revelations of spying in the corridors of executive power: the theft of Daniel Ellsberg's psychiatric records following the release of the Pentagon Papers, the bugging of the Democratic National Committee offices, the prying into citizens' tax returns for political purposes, the administration's resort to shadowing and sabotage. For those observers, Watergate—far from being an eye-opening moment—was a corroborating event, cementing rather than creating an analysis of the United States as a surveillance society.

If the scandal was not a revelation, it still had reverberations. Watergate brought into focus the reach and extent of surveillance practices at the highest levels of government, intensifying the spotlight on state secrets. But the glare extended to the more mundane surveillance of filing cabinets and data banks too. One of the casualties was the dispassionate, nuanced stance on record systems represented by *Databanks in a Free Society.* In the scandal's wake, almost no one could be found to defend the new data banks, not even those ostensibly in charge of them. President Gerald Ford voiced the threat posed by computerized government records in vivid, nightmarish terms. In a speech at Stanford Law School, he declared, "We must protect every individual from excessive and unnecessary intrusions by a 'Big Brother' bureaucracy," portraying the vulnerable citizen as a "faceless set of digits in a monstrous network of computers."[117] His predecessor, Richard Nixon—the man partly responsible for stirring up such fears—employed equally dystopian imagery. In a radio address during the Watergate hearings, he warned, "Until the day comes when science finds a way of installing a conscience in every computer, we must develop human, personal safeguards that prevent computers from becoming huge, mechanical, impersonal robots that deprive us of our essential liberties." The president went on to say, "It is becoming much easier for record-keeping systems to affect people than for people to affect record-keeping systems." With seemingly no sense of irony, Nixon called for open access to government records, claiming that "at no time in the past has our Government known so much about so many of its individual citizens."[118]

Indeed, politicians were discovering that privacy was, as Francis Sargent, the governor of Massachusetts, put it, "good politics." In 1973, he refused to allow his state's crime records to be entered into the FBI's computerized data bank system, believing it "poorly secured and loosely controlled." Far from being controversial, he reported, the move had been deeply popular with voters. "There turned out to be an untapped, large constituency out there—people concerned over their diminishing personal freedom and uneasy about a rapidly developing technology controlling their daily lives and environment." Sargent garnered praise not just from his own constituents but also from citizens nationwide—and from every corner of the political map. On what other issue, he asked, "could a governor attack the

FBI and be roundly applauded for it by both the New Bedford American Legion Post and the Newton Americans for Democratic Action?"[119]

Confirmation of illegal government surveillance ushered in a new vigilance to citizens' efforts to protect their secrets from the routine, relentless machinery of bureaucracy.[120] Watergate also gave privacy advocates leverage to press for legal remedies. Given that few politicians "wanted to appear friendly to government surveillance over private persons," the wheels of congressional action began turning more quickly.[121] The result was the passage of the Family Educational Rights and Privacy Act (FERPA), the amended Freedom of Information Act, and the Privacy Act of 1974.[122] The last of these was most significant, and its appeal defied partisan lines, as its House co-sponsors, conservative Republican Barry Goldwater Jr. of southern California and liberal Democrat Ed Koch of New York City, attested.[123] Groundbreaking legislation, it was heavily influenced by the "fair information practices" established by the federal report on *Records, Computers and the Rights of Citizens* the previous year. In one fell swoop, the Privacy Act disallowed secret data-gathering systems, prevented information collected for one use to be used for another, and enabled individuals to know of and to correct material in their records.[124]

With the Privacy Act, the United States joined a host of nations grappling with information privacy in the 1970s.[125] The first data-protection law was enacted at the opening of the decade in the Land of Hesse, Germany. Legislation quickly followed in Sweden (1973), the United States (1974), Germany (1977), and France (1978), with Portugal and Spain embedding individual data privacy protections in their respective constitutions in 1976 and 1978.[126] Although the substance of legal regulations would diverge, with European law offering stronger individual protections, this was a moment of broad transnational reckoning with computerized records.[127] International conferences and policy borrowings testified to the novelty, and the intractability, of the problem. In an unusual step for the inward-looking Congress, the U.S. Senate Committee on Government Operations in 1975 went so far as to commission a study of information privacy in peer nations, hoping to draw on the "wealth of European experience" with "preserving individual liberty from undue data surveillance."[128]

Recognition of the stubborn permanence of files, as well as the perniciousness of errors once deposited in a data bank, intensified after Watergate. As a report from the Freedom of Information Center commented, "Blacklists, 'secret files,' falsified records and other abridgements of individual freedom have been hot news items the past several years." Recent political events had made Americans "concerned with more than just 'personal privacy': they also want to verify the accuracy of whatever records have been accumulated on them."[129] The Family Educational Rights and Privacy Act, also known as the Buckley Amendment, exemplified this impulse. The legislation was signed into law—adopted by voice vote on the Senate floor, with no hearings—only twelve days after Nixon's resignation.[130] Both the quick assent to the legislation and its slowly unfolding implications make it an illuminating case study of attempts to protect privacy in the computer age.

The public discussions that led to FERPA unfolded on the terrain of the schoolyard, but were a microcosm of the larger debate, disclosing fears of secret gatekeepers, arbitrary categorizations, and bureaucratic errors that, unchecked, could become a permanent liability. The aim was to pry open school records to inspection by students and parents. At issue was not so much whether a pupil would be documented in a variety of ways by school authorities—this was by now expected and assumed—but whether that student's record would be documented accurately and fairly, how long it would be maintained, who else would have access to it, and how the subject of that record would go about finding out what it contained. Tellingly, advocates placed their emphasis less on curtailing record keeping than on securing access to files. Keeping sensitive or confidential information out of students' dossiers to begin with perhaps seemed implausible by the time the legislation was taking shape in 1973 and 1974.

FERPA was powered by "ideological and committed parents," coordinated by the National Committee for Citizens in Education (NCCE), based in Columbia, Maryland, and the Children's Defense Fund.[131] For these activists, the problem of records hit very close to home; indeed it built on worries over the privacy of the home that personality testing had raised across the prior decades. Activists—an "odd alliance of conservatives and civil-rights liberals," as one journalist described them—were united around a very particular anxiety.[132] This was the possibility of their children being "locked into a records prison" via questionable and potentially damaging information in public school files.[133] By the 1970s, parents were alert to the ways files intersected with the life chances of their children. Discrimination and stigmatization, whether on account of race, character, behavior, or "mental disability," could be the lasting product of materials in one's record. As a committee of African American teachers and counselors in San Francisco rather succinctly put it, "Black students' folders tend to be at least half an inch thicker than those of white children . . . which tells you something about the child even before you open the folder."[134]

Like the Fair Credit Reporting Act, FERPA marked a sharp departure from privacy fears centered on publicity or invasion: the broadcasting of personal details in the media or intrusions into one's private space. It was the closed nature and cloaked use of school records, not their public airing, that posed the threat. That their contents could be leaked to others but were sealed to the data subject—who might never learn of that fact—was the crux of the injury. The NCCE would both trade on and fuel "growing national concern over abuse of student records."[135] *Time* magazine's report on those abuses, meant to scandalize readers, noted that, among other travesties, the phrase "'homosexual tendencies' . . . was allegedly inserted in the files of one nine-year-old after he hugged a classmate."[136] A similar story in circulation told of a schoolboy who returned "unzipped" from a trip to the bathroom, only to have "the observation put in his file that he had 'exhibitionist' tendencies."[137] Such anecdotes captured the essence of the matter, revealing as well the lingering shame that could be produced by charges of non-normative sexuality even in a more liberated age.

The problem was both the authority and durability of school records. "Every United States public school system creates a file on each of its students that starts the day the child enters kindergarten and continues until the day he leaves school and graduates," intoned one commentator. "The test scores, personality profile and other data that are compiled when a person is six years old can, and usually do, remain 'on file' somewhere for the rest of his life." The upshot was that "a hastily concluded judgment by an annoyed, impatient third grade teacher could become a lifelong albatross around the neck of an innocent individual."[138] Wrote activist Diane Divoky in an influential article for *Parade Magazine*,

> You, the parent, probably can't see most of these records, or control what goes into them, much less challenge any untrue or embarrassing information they might contain. But a lot of other people—the school officers, welfare and health department workers, Selective Service board representatives, and just about any policeman who walks into the school and flashes a badge— have carte blanche to these dossiers on your child. And to top it off, parents are never told who's been spying on their children.[139]

Aggravating the problem, once again, were technologies such as magnetic tape, optical scanners, and computerized storage that worked together so smoothly and conclusively to lodge comments in a student's file. Divoky's protest encompassed "hard" and "soft" data alike: grades, IQ scores, and medical records as well as teacher anecdotes, notes on parent interviews, and disciplinary reports that were "routinely filed away in school offices or stored in computer data banks."[140] The student record had a place, Divoky argued elsewhere, but "like Frankenstein's monster, it now has the potential to destroy those it was created to protect." And its liability for misuse by authorities was ever present, transforming the "unwary kindergarten teacher" into a "government intelligence agent."[141] Even the National Education Association, a strong voice in favor of more comprehensive record keeping in the 1920s, had come out in favor of a code of student rights, which placed the interest of the student ahead of "all other purposes to which records might be put."[142]

These concerns responded in part to the accelerating use of psychological assessments in the postwar era.[143] Swelling school files were part of the quest for what Divoky termed "a picture of the 'whole child,' his family, and his psychological, social and academic development."[144] Another analyst explained that the need for a student right to records was especially acute given that "the educational system compels the student to reveal his abilities and personality to school authorities."[145] As they had been for journalists like Vance Packard and Myron Brenton, who had written exposés of school testing a decade before, psychological measures were a particular bone of contention, one court finding such testing "highly personal and probative of the family relationship."[146] There was a difference, however. The earlier debate about psychological instruments in the schools had focused on the privacy invasion at the moment of its occurrence. The record itself was now squarely the concern.[147] Temporally distant from the event in question, it was no less of—and in an age of permanent computer "memory banks," perhaps more of—a privacy violation.

Indeed, seeking to build its membership rolls, the National Committee for Citizens in Education identified the records issue as one that would mobilize public passion. It planned in 1973 to focus on invasions of privacy "at a higher noise and scare level" than previously.[148] A test mailing invited parents into the issue by alerting them to the extensive records on nearly every child in the country. The message was simple. School files were stuffed with questionable material and yet were wide open—in more than half of the nation's school districts—to a host of parties: the FBI, the CIA, juvenile courts, and prospective employers. The NCCE experimented with a "distinctly attention getting envelope" to get out the word. "Do you know what's in your child's school record? It might surprise you . . . ," it tantalized. A string of handwritten phrases—"unnaturally interested in girls," "history of bedwetting," "too challenging," "strangely introspective," "peculiar political ideas," "alcoholic mother"—dotted its face.[149] The NCCE summoned parents and citizens, heretofore "virtually powerless," to join the battle against "entrenched bureaucracy." "How would you like to know everything that's known about you?" inquired another of its mass mailings. The organization employed creative tactics, in one case inciting citizens to take action by testing for themselves record keepers' willingness to part with information. Request "a simple bit of data about yourself" from your own school, the NCCE urged, providing a fill-in-the-blank postcard. "When your request is denied or modified write to us and we will send you the necessary information to push right back."[150]

The NCCE aimed to serve as a training ground and catalyst for grass-roots action. Sympathizing with "how difficult it is to muster the courage, confidence and energy necessary to pursue issues with public officials," it armed interested citizens with strategies for gaining access to their sons' and daughters' records and for challenging school policies. The organization's field manual included a "plan of action": templates for letters of inquiry, suggestions for talking to principals and superintendents ("be pleasant," "do not be cowed," "kee[p] a diary"), tips for organizing town meetings, legal advice as to parents' rights over their children's education, and contact information for key officials in each state.[151]

As this effort took off, the NCCE became a clearinghouse for tales of students and parents wronged by records, with thousands of letters flowing in from all over the country. Many of these detailed the ways that "children and families are being harmed or intimidated" by the information keepers.[152] A parent who had sought unsuccessfully to see a child's record to discover why he had been placed in a "slower" class, asked, "Do I have any legal rights to demand to see these records and tests instead of just hearing personal opinion?" Learning of "character reports" maintained on her three schoolchildren, another wanted to know, "Is it possible that the very people and organization we entrust almost 75% of their young lives to is one more major threat"? One parent, even as she moved her family to a new school district, feared on her daughter's behalf the lasting "repercussions of a file that is fictional rather than factual." Still another wrote of "threatening the school and administration" in order to view a child's record and then finding out that the girl "had been branded as emotional and of a low potential by her first grade teacher." A high school senior and honor roll student who described himself as unjustly saddled with "a history of trouble-making" discovered that he had been turned down for a job because of his school record. "I feel like a criminal," he wrote, "and am being discriminated against because of the quick impressions that teachers write about in student's [sic] records." A man who had come across Divoky's article in *Parade* wanted advice on how to dig up his school file from many years past in the belief that it was continuing to hamper his employment prospects. He wrote: "I am male—37 and *it's very hard to find work.*" Still others confided their shock at finding commentary about themselves or their home lives through a glimpse of an open file on a counselor's or psychologist's desk. "What else has been written about my husband, me and my son . . . ?" asked one woman, and "what has been said about my girls in these juicy school records?"[153]

With FERPA's passage, these questioners would get some answers—and the slow burn over invasions of privacy at school, kindled in the late 1950s, finally received an official response. A provision that would have required parental consent before any psychological test or behavioral inquiry could be conducted did not survive in the final legislation. But the long list of materials that parents would now have a right to review told its own story about the trove of data schools housed: "identifying data, academic work completed, level of achievement (grades, standardized achievement test scores), attendance data, scores on standardized intelligence, aptitude, and psychological tests, interest inventory results, health data, family background information, teacher or counselor ratings and observations, and verified reports of serious or recurrent behavior patterns."[154] Just ten days or so after FERPA became law, a man sought the release of filed material on his son indicating "aggressive homosexual behavior" that had allegedly caused him to be denied a place at Vassar College. "Under the law," he asserted, "the contents of any information in your possession about my son must be revealed to me upon request."[155] A mother from Levittown, New York, a few months later emerged victorious in her quest for her son's school records. "They were so damaging, you wouldn't believe," she wrote to the director of the NCCE. "*Teachers stated that I was crazy* and my child was anything but good." The superintendent and principal agreed to transfer her son to another school—and perhaps more critically, "not to send his records along."[156]

The law was celebrated by the NCCE and others as a civil liberties victory and a lever for the rights of individuals—some eight million college and university students, and the parents of more than 45 million school-age children—against "insensitive and overreaching institutions."[157] Schools had been put on notice, and citizens would now have some means of redress against previously unaccountable institutions and records systems. One of the NCCE's leaders was optimistic that FERPA might "put a stop to the dossier mentality" in the schools.[158] A spokesman from the Children's Defense Fund chimed in: "If there are bonfires all over the place, we're delighted."[159] More profoundly, the act's supporters hoped it would stand "as a bulwark against the encroachments of a Big Brother society."[160] The NCCE remained vigilant, establishing a monitoring operation on the legislation's effectiveness the very day FERPA became law, enlisting other organizations' assistance as watchdogs and setting up a hotline "to give parents a chance to report their experiences in getting student information from schools."[161] It proposed that the new rights should be printed clearly on report cards, just like the consumer notifications that now appeared on credit card bills and cigarette packs.[162]

After FERPA's passage, some schools did destroy information in student files. The assistant superintendent of the Kentucky Department of Education, for example, instructed school districts to "purge cumulative record files of unsubstantiated or irrelevant miscellanea and unsubstantiated teacher opinions which might tend to categorize pupils," just as the law's backers would have hoped.[163] A school district in Columbia, South Carolina, urged its school commissioners to pay heed, predicting "numerous law suits if extreme caution is not used in the handling of student records."[164] The chair of the Providence, Rhode Island school committee posted public notices that parents would hereby have full access to student records.[165] The head of the Association of Elementary School Principals acknowledged that student files had become "dumping places" for "hasty teacher comments" and advised the organization's 28,000 members to expunge such material accordingly.[166] There were stories of other schools ordering "all unverified comments or opinions" to be removed from files or completely obliterated. (Tellingly, the superintendent in this case also asked school personnel to ensure that "no potentially defamatory references to parents are included in records inasmuch as, of course, parents will now have the right to inspect such records.")[167] In the lead-up to the law taking effect, the NCCE reported being "buried with requests" for information from state-level officials responsible for drafting bylaws and procedures.[168]

FERPA did not exactly amount to a turning of the tables, however. Other reports revealed significant or even "gross, gross" noncooperation with the legislation—which had no real penalties for violation or mechanisms for policing compliance—as well as instances of unauthorized transfer of student information to the juvenile justice system and the Immigration and Naturalization Service.[169] Representatives of higher education had lobbied hard to exempt colleges and universities from the legislation. Although they did not succeed, they found loopholes. Referring to new rules about access to college recommendation letters, the most controversial provision of the law, one of President Ford's advisors noted that the standard response by institutions was coercion: "students are strongly pressured to sign waivers."[170] The University of Virginia's dean of admissions, for example, sent a letter to all incoming students noting that "the act's purposes are best achieved when fewer records are kept and used"; the university proposed destroying all letters of recommendation, statements by teachers and counselors, and other confidential material—unless the student was willing to sign away his or her access rights.[171] Some schools, it was reported, had begun prohibiting teachers from writing letters at all.[172] The Ford advisor further noted that FERPA did not extend to individuals whose college applications were rejected, even though "this group is perhaps the most in need of Buckley Amendment rights."[173] And one commentator observed that "the law's first impact on college campuses" was in fact to increase data collection, as some schools "immediately began keeping files of students' written requests to see their records, instead of promptly granting access as required by law."[174]

At the primary and secondary school level there were also "numerous complaints" about the implementation of FERPA protections. One sore spot was the excessive copying fees that some school districts were planning to charge to those wanting access to their records "by including in the costs staff time, electricity, overhead and other items which have a clearly delaying, harassing character to them." The forty-five-day response period for record requests was also deeply frustrating, especially in cases involving special education placement or suspension hearings. And there were worries about records being destroyed, ironically enough, following requests for access. Given that "most parents and students" found school personnel intimidating "or can easily be made to feel that way," FERPA's policies required too much of the record seeker, concluded the NCCE. The procedure for gaining access to one's files "leads too easily to marathons of endurance, demanding persistence and extraordinary conviction."[175] The balance of power between data subjects and their gatekeepers may have shifted, but how much?[176]

A similar story unfolded regarding the implementation of the Privacy Act of 1974, described by one of its co-sponsors, Senator Edmund S. Muskie, as the first major U.S. legislation "aimed at the protection of personal privacy" and by *U.S. News and World Report* as a "new weapon to fight the growing trend of government to pry into people's private affairs."[177] The act aimed to resolve the conflict between civil liberties and official records. But if federal legislation was in some sense a victory for privacy rights, it was a profoundly equivocal one. Designed to empower citizens vis-à-vis the record keepers, the law would wind up stoking fears that the United States had become a full-fledged surveillance society in which individuals were outmatched from the outset.[178] In earlier periods, those whose privacy had been infringed sought to hold specific individuals or entities liable: a photographer, or an employer, or a police officer. The Supreme Court itself had imagined a tangible body and a zone of privacy for the autonomous individual. Americans in the 1970s contended instead with a virtual body, a body of data, caught up in dossiers and files. In an era of computer databases and anonymous agencies—what Hannah Arendt had chillingly called the "rule of Nobody" in her analysis of the evils of bureaucracy—it was increasingly difficult to identify those who invaded a person's privacy, much less curb them.[179]

Earlier in the decade, Arthur R. Miller had speculated that "the seeds of a computerized dossier society may have already been sown by the steady proliferation of data banks," such that "only the extremities of a vast, subterranean information structure may be visible."[180] The Privacy Act supplied conclusive proof. That there was no stopping the flow of data was the clear implication of a stream of commentaries in the national press following its enactment. The law's requirement that federal agencies publicly disclose their records systems exposed the real problem: nobody, not even the bureaucracies themselves, knew what they held in their files. As the *Washington Post* explained, "Some agencies were maintaining secret files and concealing some abusive practices from Congress and the public." The larger difficulty, however, was that "the government's data demands had grown so fast, and had been answered in so many uncoordinated ways, that not even the agencies themselves had a firm grasp of all their information practices." Even once the inventories were mostly compiled—by the fall of 1975, "over 8,000 records systems . . . summarized in fat volumes of the Federal Register totaling 3,100 pages and more"—they were so various and unruly as to be incomprehensible. The *Post* made the point with a ludicrous laundry list of its own: "There are listings for the sensitive files of the Defense Investigative Service; for records of the participants in National Security Council meetings . . . ; for HEW's roster of licensed dental hygienists; for the Agriculture Department's list of people interested in forestry news, and for the Export-Import Bank's roster of employees who want parking spaces."[181]

The Privacy Act tackled the problem of personal records not through redacting or reducing the amount of information that the government stored, but through transparency, in the form of still more data. But this information itself fueled public apprehensions. The Privacy Act had taken effect "after six months of preparation by federal agencies notable mainly for having produced the largest volume of federal paperwork since the Republic was founded," summarized one watchdog organization.[182] The *Los Angeles Times* reported that "what has been revealed . . . is that the government keeps track of its citizens on a scale that not even the most paranoiac critic of government snooping would ever have suspected." This article concluded, "There is apparently no detail about American citizens that does not interest some bureaucrat."[183]

As did others, this reporter recounted a bewildering array of records maintained by the federal government: lists of New Jersey driving examiners, "behavior performances" of Kentucky tollbooth operators, and hearing tests taken by Cincinnati firemen. Some of these data appeared harmless, but other records had a more sinister cast: "Why does the Department of Transportation need dossiers on everyone who ever had his driver's license suspended or revoked? Why does HEW keep a file on children with birth defects?"[184] Press coverage lent substance to Miller's earlier portrayal of government information collecting as "an unrelenting flow of data that is generated and consumed by some diabolical Sorcerer's Apprentice."[185] Even as officials swore that the "biggest fallacy" in the Privacy Act was the assumption that federal agencies were adept at pinpointing particular individuals and that "nothing could be further from the truth . . . [than] that the government keeps orderly files from which information is easily retrieved," the torrent of data lent itself to scenarios of total surveillance.[186]

This same outpouring of information about the mere existence of federal data systems (as opposed to their contents) prompted other suspicions, some critics wondering whether its sheer volume "could be so formidable that it will discourage public interest in testing the Privacy Act." One congressman complained that a number of agencies, in a "typical manifestation of bureaucratic behavior," were "carrying the reporting requirements to an extreme," thereby making it more difficult for citizens to unearth the information that they were now legally entitled to access.[187] In fact, in the first six months under the Privacy Act, the Department of Justice reported receiving "over 30,000 requests for access, a number far in excess of what anyone had anticipated," which "transformed this into a major area of departmental operations." The same was true for the Freedom of Information Act (FOIA), amended that same year: the level of requests would lead officials to complain of individuals "abusing" the new disclosure laws and even, in a few cases, of harassment. The office that administered FERPA had, eighteen months after the law's effective date, received less attention, but still more than 10,000 requests for information.[188] The Fair Credit Reporting Act, passed in 1970 to similar ends, saw much more regular use. One credit agency found that requests for access "jumped from 2000 to 200,000 yearly when FCRA passed"; another had such requests jump from an insignificant number to 200 per day in 1974. Associated Credit Bureaus reported in 1972 that its member bureaus conducted "1.7 million interviews with customers wishing to know the content of their files, 1.3 million of these prompted by a denial of credit," to the tune of $3.4 million annually.[189]

Such numbers indicate that some citizens were not shy about exercising their new rights and that they were able to circumvent significant obstacles in order to gain access to their files. Individuals who made use of the Privacy Act could view and possibly even correct some of their personal information that had been secreted away in government agencies. Just a decade earlier, this kind of admittance to official records would have been unimaginable. Likewise, one scholar noted that, until the passage of FCRA, "individuals had virtually no relationship with the commercial organizations which compiled credit, pre-employment and pre-insurance reports on them. Individuals were quite literally the objects of a report and little more."[190]

In this sense, legislation in the 1970s would not just lay down fair information practices. For better or worse, it would also endorse individuals' growing claim to possession of their virtual selves, those bits of biography distributed across the society's expanding data systems. Personal records, scattered across space and time, became legal entitlements, a kind of property. In theory, anyway, citizens might be the owners, or co-owners, of their files. Changing conditions of organizational life—faster computers, larger bureaucracies, expanding data banks—thus did not straightforwardly erode citizens' privacy, although it may have appeared that way at the time. These same conditions generated novel claims and claimants for the protection of personal information, ultimately producing new rights for the "data subjects" and increasingly well-known citizens of the Watergate era.

As with FERPA, an initial review of the implementation of the Privacy Act did not suggest particularly dramatic changes: some agencies had destroyed duplicate or useless files; seventeen had removed SSNs from existing records "when deemed appropriate." On the other hand, the act had vividly revealed the extent of the U.S. records infrastructure. There were at least 6,723 federal government data banks, with an average of "18 files for each man, woman and child in the U.S." and containing information on 3.8 billion "identifiable persons," reported one source.[191] A hopeful advocate ventured that the "law's restrictions could prove so costly and troublesome that the government might decide, on its own, to dismantle some data banks, unplug some computers and throw out some files."[192] But his was a lone voice against a chorus certain that the clock could not be turned back on a "record-based social system"—and that patient, persistent bureaucracy would win out in the end. Too much was to be gained through knowing citizens, most Americans suspected, to toss out the files. Policy makers also pointed out the weakness of the new laws in preventing the disclosure of personal data, laced as they were with exceptions for "legitimate business needs" in the case of FCRA or "routine use" in the case of the Privacy Act.[193] In all the commentary about the new legislation, few doubted that sensitive records on citizens, lodged in only partially penetrable systems, would continue to proliferate.[194]

Nor did the Privacy Act, which applied only to the agencies of the federal government, address the private sector. It thus was silent about the problem Myron Brenton had memorably described as "Big Brother in civilian clothes": the extent of data collection by private employers, banks, insurance companies, telecommunications outfits, and marketing firms, all of which had helped create the crisis around personal data and the "record prison."[195] Although its authors hoped the Privacy Act would be "only a beginning," paving the way for "an expanded law protecting the privacy of all of us, in every aspect of our daily lives," such would not come to pass.[196] A federal Privacy Protection Study Commission took up the question of extending the Privacy Act to private entities, only to shelve it.[197] Indeed, the political will to clamp down on the record keepers seemed to ebb as Watergate receded in the headlines.[198] The commission itself would close up shop in 1977 with none of its recommendations realized—but not before concluding that the Privacy Act "had not resulted in the general benefits to the public that either its legislative history or the prevailing opinion as to its accomplishments would lead one to expect."[199]

Despite all the protest kicked up about the quantity of personal records in state and corporate hands by the mid-1970s, then, there seemed to be no easy way to reverse these developments—or to restore privacy to some imagined status quo ante. Under the Privacy Act, as with FCRA and FERPA, one could know of and even correct one's information in a file. But one could not escape being filed in the first place. That the assertion of broader privacy rights could be so quickly followed by retraction of practical control was a sign that legal regulations around information privacy would not, and perhaps could not, alter the basic terms of U.S. society, fully entwined as it was with computerized data banks. Indeed, the 1974 Privacy Act in certain respects worked more to facilitate than to staunch or even slow the flow of data into record systems. Privacy policy in its aftermath veered away from regulating the type, amount, and control of personal information stored in files and toward norms of fairness, accuracy, and security.[200] This was the new, if uneasy, pact that would be achieved in the 1970s between citizens and those who would know them through their records.[201]

The final report of the Church Committee, convened in 1975 to investigate intelligence abuses of the FBI, CIA, NSA, and IRS, was damning. "Too many people have been spied upon by too many Government agencies and too much information has been illegally collected," it declared. Another of the report's findings—that the government had "swept in vast amounts of information about the personal lives, views, and associations of American citizens"—would not have surprised those coming to see themselves as data subjects in the 1970s.[202]

Newfound attention to the risks of computerized records in that era coexisted with and confounded more corporeal and physical understandings of privacy that accompanied Supreme Court rulings beginning with *Griswold v. Connecticut.* Even as the Supreme Court moved to protect Americans' physical "zones of privacy," other trends were alerting citizens to the vulnerability of their virtual bodies: the stash of personal information steadily accumulating in the society's data banks. But the individual who could be frisked by police, was involved in intimate marital relations, or could carry a child or terminate a pregnancy was a different matter to regulate than the body of records that accompanied citizens through society. The Court's expanding protections of "decisional autonomy" in the reproductive rights cases were likewise difficult to apply to the data subject, who did not make a conscious choice to house personal information in record-keeping systems in the same way that a woman might decide to have an abortion. Americans typically did not choose but rather discovered themselves to be enmeshed in a network of files through a lifetime of interactions with the public and private institutions of U.S. society.

Dawning recognition of the problem appeared in the Court itself, in the 1977 ruling *Whalen v. Roe.* At issue was whether New York State, in the interest of monitoring drug abuse, could require the disclosure of the names and addresses of patients who were prescribed certain medications.[203] The Court ruled that it could; however, it deliberately left open the question of the relationship between individual privacy and the society's increasing reliance on networked records. Justice John Paul Stevens noted, "We are not unaware of the threat to privacy implicit in the accumulation of vast amounts of personal information in computerized data banks or other massive government files."[204] Forty years later, those remain almost the Court's last words on the ways advancing technologies of data collection, storage, and transmission might impinge on the privacy and security of citizens' digital lives.[205]

Information preserved in files presented a thorny problem. Immaterial and invisible, it was nevertheless socially valuable, as well as personally consequential. Distributed across many sites, it could not be cordoned off physically like a bedroom or overseen like a research laboratory. Slippery and difficult to contain, it could at the same time be remarkably intractable. If built up sufficiently, as critics of the "record prison" warned, it could entrap a person. Citizens' concerns about burgeoning data banks triggered novel claims for the safeguarding of personal information, as well as landmark legislation. But the evident limits of those protections also cast doubt on the federal regulations associated with the privacy jurisprudence of this era—not to mention the very notion of the autonomous citizen they were meant to safeguard. Bureaucratic and technological developments alike suggested that the conditions that had informed American notions about personal privacy no longer obtained. Thus, in an era when both Congress and the Supreme Court intervened in new fashion to protect citizens' private affairs, privacy could seem ever more vulnerable.

The naming of the United States as a "surveillance society" was a product of this conundrum, one of the first appearances of the term coming in a 1970 opinion piece in the *Los Angeles Times* by Arthur R. Miller.[206] The coinage connoted something beyond government watchfulness and control. Like other concepts of the day—"record prison," "dossier personality," "information power"—it pointed to a type of social organization that had the collection and scrutiny of personal data as its basic feature and a citizenry fundamentally shaped by new capacities to observe, record, and track.[207] Legal experts and social theorists but also muckraking journalists, science fiction writers, grassroots activists, policy makers, and others newly worried about their Social Security numbers all sensed its arrival.[208] This was a vision of society and a vision of power that called into question the civil liberties and individual rights remedies of the recent past.[209] If privacy was going to survive, it would need to be rethought.

7

The Ethic of Transparency

These days, if you want to know a secret, you just turn on the television.

—MARION WINIK, "The Neighbor, d. 1978," 2007

In striking fashion, both the "record prison" and the state's watchful eye on the citizenry became objects of public contention in the 1970s. In response, many Americans sought to better shield themselves from the agencies that tracked their affairs. They did so in part by turning the tables on the watchers. New legislation promising citizens access to record-keeping systems and the formation of oversight committees intended to put some brakes on the clandestine activities of the government were course corrections.[1] Each targeted the level of privacy claimed by central authorities in American society. And each offered "transparency" as a solution to the political problem of cloaked power, whether in the form of state secrets, military cover-ups, or the routine whirring of the bureaucracy. If a person could be exposed through the traces he or she had left in the society's files, perhaps the same logic could be applied to the record keepers. Although transparency did not necessarily translate into effective law—as FERPA and the Privacy Act attested—its ethos shaped many aspects of American political culture in the post-Watergate years, "a presumption of disclosure" replacing "the presumption of secrecy."[2] Openness and access were seized as tools for balancing the scales between powerful authorities in American life and ordinary citizens, between the knowers and the known.

A new insistence on transparency, evident in public talk and social movements, coexisted uneasily with heightened concerns about citizens' visibility to gatekeepers of all kinds. Americans of means redoubled their efforts to secure their private affairs in these years, often by inviting technologies of surveillance and counter-surveillance into their daily lives. A booming market in do-it-yourself spying was only the most obvious way that surveillance was domesticated in the post-Watergate years. In the 1970s, CCTV cameras had been trained on city streets in the name of public safety. By the 1980s these tactics came home, as property owners borrowed from new theories of urban policing, design, and management.[3] Gated communities, caller-ID, video surveillance, and other home-monitoring devices arose, fittingly enough, out of privacy concerns—and from the sense that citizens were on their own in facing them. Security systems first used by the military and then by industry moved into the consumer realm as part of the "larger political culture's story of ubiquitous threats and individual solutions."[4]

Historians have pegged the steep investment in private communities, or "gated utopias," and enclosed shopping malls in the 1980s to Reagan-era truisms about the failures of government as compared to private enterprise and to associated disinvestments from public streets, services, and schools. In that decade, white middle-class Americans "increasingly deserted parks for private health clubs, abandoned town squares for shopping malls, enrolled their children in private schools, and moved into gated communities governed by neighborhood associations and policed by private security patrols."[5] Fears of crime, and often of black neighborhoods, quickened the trend. But the "privatization of everyday life" can also be understood as a consumer-driven quest for more control over personal and domestic privacy. Americans with the ability to do so privatized their very claims to privacy in that decade, relying less on the law, regulatory agencies, or courts and more on individualistic strategies to protect themselves from trespasses onto their private space and affairs. To a certain extent, as had been true of the mass migration to the suburbs after World War II, privacy could be purchased. In the 1980s and 1990s this would take the form of private communities, complete with their own services and zoning requirements as well as gates, guards, and entry codes. The fastest growing residential designation in the United States, such communities, nearly as racially homogeneous as their 1950s counterparts, would by the mid-1990s house 28 million Americans.[6]

Even as upper- and middle-class homeowners patrolled their own property lines, however, they made prurient excursions into others' affairs. Practices seemingly hostile to individual privacy—surveillance, voyeurism, and the extracting of confessions—would to a surprising extent in the 1970s and 1980s migrate from authorities to the citizenry itself. New modes of capture and surveillance, from investigative reportage to documentary filmmaking, became firmly rooted in American society from the 1970s onward. So did demands for increasingly full disclosure in the name of the public's "right to know."[7] Tracking and exposure would no longer be the privilege of state authorities or powerful corporations alone. These tools, it became clear, could be wielded by voters, directors, journalists, audiences, and activists too. As a consequence, the hidden moments not only of public figures but also of private citizens became more accessible.[8] Political speeches and social protests were conducted in a new key, with personal matters right at the fore. In the newspaper and on TV, audiences peered into the intimate secrets of ordinary people, made interesting through exposure, as experimental media formats ushered cameras into formerly private spaces. Surveillance was becoming a spectator sport.

The consumer market helped to prod this new culture into being, but so did the media and the courts. A press that went far beyond the invasiveness of Warren and Brandeis's day led the way. Newly aggressive investigative reporters competed with avant-garde filmmakers to pry open the hidden facets of public persons. Domains of life that had once been largely off-limits, most notably domestic and intimate relations, were subjected to searching scrutiny. An ethic of transparency could in this way shade into intrusion. If journalists pushed the envelope of what could be asked and printed, courts struck down restrictive speech and dress codes as violations of free expression. The same Warren Court that had affirmed a right to privacy dismantled obscenity laws.[9] One irony of the "right to privacy" was that it enabled "images, messages, and behaviors once considered private" to "saturate public culture."[10]

Although for different ends, social movements also pushed for a more open and transparent, and thus, many believed, a more authentic and liberatory politics. Feminists and gay activists insistently questioned the rationale for keeping personal matters out of public view. We might think of them as cultural whistleblowers who hoped to banish certain kinds of secrecy from politics and social life. Ordinary citizens may have been tracked more thoroughly by social agencies in the 1970s. But those in the public eye were also held to account for their private lives as never before. Politicians as well as homosexual and reclusive celebrities were among those affected by a new standard of personal disclosure linked to the citizenry's right to know.

Many things, then, in the name of transparency, lost their privateness in the 1970s. As the covert acts of powerful authorities came under suspicion, so too did concealment of all kinds. The shedding of secrets may have begun as a tactic to make American politics and public life more accountable. But as openness became an instrument for social justice as well as entertainment, the impulse transformed private life too, unsealing adoption records, the intimate details of marriages, and other matters that had in the past been carefully sheltered from public knowledge.[11] By the end of the era it was unclear if there was any agreement as to what ought to be honored as a secret, whether medical procedures, family dysfunction, or sexual identity. Indeed, some asked, should anything remain private if exposing it could be considered a social or political good? Surveillance would sneak into American culture, beguiling even those who had meant to evade it.

Shedding Secrets

There had been rules about what belonged in the political sphere and what did not: matters that properly should be kept quiet versus those that needed to see the light of day. In the 1970s, these conventions began to break down. Scandals as well as social movements subjected the traditional buffer between public and private life to interrogation. How much did an individual's private affairs—his finances, his family, his infidelities—bear on his fitness for office? What could or should be revealed in political venues? Ought voters judge public figures by the secrets they kept or by those they spilled? Questions like these unsettled the established line between public affairs and private talk and wound up redrawing it.

The New Left's search for authentic personhood as against the formulas and codes of Cold War society was one form of a more "personal" politics, as was Black Power activists' targeting of cultural identity as a dimension of social power, encapsulated in the phrase "black is beautiful."[12] In their claim to a new politics, activists of all stripes reworked the boundary between private and public, discovering the links between individual subjectivity and social domination. But it was feminists who most radically politicized private life, spying in mundane family, reproductive, and sexual relations the inexorable workings of male power and hierarchy. That standard bearer of women's liberation, "the personal is political," depended on the airing of "private" sentiments and experiences as the precondition for a truly transformative politics. Understanding women's oppression as shared and systematic, whether through consciousness raising or other means, was a crucial step in toppling sexual inequality.[13] To protect certain matters—abortion, rape, and sexual abuse—from public view came itself to be seen as an unjust act of power.[14]

An explicit politics tying transparency to the exposure of injustice was one impetus for the distrust of secrets in public life.[15] Already in the 1960s civil rights and New Left activists challenged a "politics of civility" that privileged deference and politeness over racial and military obscenities thrown into stark relief by bloody battles in Selma as well as Vietnam.[16] The sexual revolution underwrote the linkage between sexual liberation and political freedom, an equation that, as one historian notes, "had rumbled and murmured among 'free lovers' and bohemians for at least a century."[17] But letting it "all hang out," in that evocative phrase of the era, spoke to a still broader cultural transformation, as citizens of all political stripes began to cast off earlier strictures on behavior and discourse. In their language, their dress, and their attitudes toward authority, many Americans adopted a more casual and less decorous style of social interaction. This was true in private spaces—bedrooms and living rooms—but also in public arenas, where "ties were loosened or disappeared entirely, top buttons came undone, hair was allowed to hang down to shoulders, mustaches drooped, sideburns crept, chest hairs peeked and first names began to replace formal modes of address." A new attention to "identity, life-style, and the appropriate means of self-regulation" began with the counterculture, but it made notable inroads elsewhere in a process sociologist Sam Binkley refers to as a "loosening" of middle-class culture.[18] This new benchmark of authenticity and transparency in personal relationships loosened secrets too.[19]

Whatever the precise combination of forces, it is clear that there was by the mid-1970s a new legitimacy to, and even a demand for, public disclosure of matters formerly deemed private. The shift was perhaps clearest in the realm of national politics. Abigail McCarthy, former wife of the 1968 Democratic presidential hopeful Eugene McCarthy, tracked the changing standard neatly. Writing of her very first speech as a candidate's wife in 1948 in St. Paul, Minnesota, itself a novelty (in her opinion, the "speaking wife" was a political "gimmick"), McCarthy recounted her decision to omit an anecdote about how she had met her husband. She recalled, "Gene always had a horror of revealing anything personal in public and even at that time refused to use the pronoun 'I' in his speeches."[20] But the grammar of politics would change across the next decade, and by the 1960s it entailed exposure and publicity, not just for the candidate but for his family as well. McCarthy later told the story of her slow, sometimes agonizing coming to terms with the demands of publicity and disclosure. It was during a campaign stop for her husband in Indiana, McCarthy recounted, that "I finally carried out my resolution to overcome self-consciousness and laid aside any reluctance to be photographed or to face television." Soon enough, she was taking all interviews that came her way, "one local Indiana station after another." She appeared on television's *Today Show* with Dick Cavett, traveled for a week with *Life* magazine, and spent three solid days with reporter Haynes Johnson so that he could write a profile of her, the candidate's wife.[21]

"I found that it was not such a horrible experience after all," wrote McCarthy. Still, she struggled with being "constantly under the observation of the women's press corps" and wrote, as the 1968 Democratic convention loomed, of "fortifying myself for this final glare of publicity for Gene and me and for the children." Ailing with gallstones, McCarthy was particularly troubled by advice from the campaign in the wake of Robert Kennedy's assassination that she discuss her illness publicly. Ironically, her advisors considered this an unimpeachable explanation for her desire to stay out of the spotlight and to refrain from commenting on the tragedy, something she chose for herself out of "a sense of decent restraint." But McCarthy balked, recalling "press reports of previous hospital stays" as "unattractively anatomical," including a headline that read simply, "ABIGAIL'S GALL BLADDER." She protested what she called "an undue interest in my insides"; as she recalled, "I argued that it was very bad taste to discuss the mechanics of my various illnesses." Observing that such "medical frankness had been started by President Eisenhower," McCarthy simply stated, "I did not feel the same obligation."[22] Resisting political pressure to reveal what she considered to be intimate information, she kept her own counsel.

By 1972, however, McCarthy was moved to tell the story of her personal history and marriage. In her memoir of that year, *Private Faces/Public Places*, she wrote of a life "defined by others—by wifehood and motherhood," with "no individual achievement to measure."[23] Abigail McCarthy's book reflected on the pains of publicity and took the form of a personal narrative, although it was not what we have come to expect of such a work. Her recounting of the end of her marriage, for example, comes at its conclusion, in a just a few stark sentences. Gene McCarthy, she writes, "left our home in August of 1969." Her explanation: "He had long since come to the conclusion that the concept of life-long fidelity and shared life come what may . . . was no longer valid. And many people today do find this—or any permanent commitment—an impossible ideal."[24] This terse and rather abstract statement, which admitted nothing of her own anger or anguish, was as personal as McCarthy would get about the dissolution of her long marriage. Like McCarthy's illnesses, her husband's affair (with a journalist, it turned out) and desertion were not in her view appropriate material for public consumption.[25] And so, despite promising to probe the private effects of publicity, her book's contents, like its title—taken from a W. H. Auden poem—reinforced the sturdy border between one's public persona, on the one hand, and one's intimate life, on the other.

The line between proper and improper disclosure that Abigail McCarthy walked in 1968 and even 1972 would shift significantly by the mid-1970s, propelled by fast-moving developments. One of these was Watergate. With its origins in the illegal machinations of the executive branch and the extensive cover-up that sought to hide it, the scandal led to urgent calls for public accountability.[26] Desperate to restore trust in government, Congress passed a flurry of post-Watergate reform measures even beyond FERPA and the Privacy Act of 1974, including legislation making campaign contributions public for the first time in American history.[27] Many politicians also took the unprecedented step of voluntarily disclosing their tax returns. By early May 1974, sixty members of Congress had already released their private financial data to the public, with more planning to follow their lead.[28] Noted one such member of Congress, who acknowledged this practice as an invasion of his and his colleagues' privacy, "Under the circumstances we face today I think we must take that extra step . . . to win back the confidence of the people in this country." He went on to say that "as distasteful as it is personally to me—and it frankly is—I think it is the price we have to pay."[29]

Sociologist Michael Schudson has observed that Congress in the 1960s was "shielded from the public," not only by its own traditions and procedures but also by a "complacent and compliant journalism and the absence of watchdog public interest groups."[30] These norms were changing already by the late 1960s, a response to civil rights agitation, frustration with entrenched rules by newly elected legislators, and democratizing efforts within Congress itself—by Eugene McCarthy, among others. As public disclosure came to be associated with good government, "sunshine" reforms led to the public recording of votes, the disclosure of campaign contributions, the right to judicial records, new ethics codes, and the airing of congressional procedures to those beyond the corridors of the government, including by television and radio broadcast.[31] Watergate simply, but crucially, exerted additional pressure. Openness and transparency were becoming the watchwords of politics.

This sort of accountability was on the rise in many corners of American society: in movements for "truth in packaging" and "unit pricing," as well as "truth in lending" and environmental impact statements.[32] It came with a high level of intrusion into public figures' affairs. As late as 1972 there was surprisingly little vetting of a political candidate's biography, finances, friendships, or medical history. Only after Thomas Eagleton was named as the candidate for vice president on the Democratic ticket that year, and through an anonymous tip, for example, did his hospitalizations for depression and electroshock treatment became public knowledge. The party's presidential nominee, George McGovern, reluctantly confirmed this report with the psychiatrists in question, and Eagleton was swiftly removed from the ticket.[33] The "Eagleton affair" marked the end of an era. The lesson was that private life was now fair game in politics and that secrets could end a career in public office. Openness could engender its opposite: tremendous caution and careful scriptedness of candidates and campaigns. In a world of transparency, a politician could not afford a misstep or checkered personal history.[34] The scrutiny of Republican Gerald Ford during his confirmation hearings for vice president just a few years later, following Spiro Agnew's resignation, showed that the lesson had been learned: the vetting drew on the work of 350 special agents from 33 FBI field offices, who interviewed 1,000 witnesses and compiled 1,700 pages of reports. Americans, one scholar notes, "knew more about Ford than they had ever known about any president or vice president."[35]

On assuming the presidency after Nixon's resignation, Ford declared, "In all my public and private acts as your president, I expect to follow my instincts of openness and candor."[36] And yet it was the new president's wife, Betty Ford, who was more responsible for ushering in new levels of frankness to national politics. She began her career as a political wife finding "all those interviews . . . terrifying."[37] As First Lady, however, she embraced all that Abigail McCarthy had found distasteful. Often considered the most "outspoken" woman to occupy that role since Eleanor Roosevelt,

Betty Ford ventured strong opinions, lobbying on behalf of abortion rights and the Equal Rights Amendment.[38] But the new transparency in politics was exemplified by Ford's public handling of her personal life, especially her hospitalization for breast cancer and her resulting mastectomy in September 1974.[39] Normally, this was a matter that would have been kept quiet, by the patient and her staff alike. The diagnosis and treatment of cancer—and especially breast cancer—were still spoken of in hushed tones, if at all.[40] As recently as the 1950s, the *New York Times,* for instance, would not publish either the word "breast" or "cancer."[41] In her press secretary's words, however, the First Lady and the White House vowed to be "extraordinarily candid and complete in reporting on her operation and its aftermath."[42]

That decision was undoubtedly motivated by Betty Ford's interest in publicizing the disease and its diagnosis to counter the shame many women associated with it. But it was also a political calculation, meant to draw a contrast between the Ford administration and its predecessor. Nixon's stonewalling press office was the obvious point of reference.[43] As a *New York Times* editorialist perceived, "In a curious way, the publicity given to the breast surgery of Betty Ford and Margaretta Rockefeller [the vice president's wife, who was also diagnosed with breast cancer soon after] seems to be related to the Watergate-induced need to tell the truth and nothing but the truth, instantly and preferably on color TV."[44] The First Lady herself pinned such openness to the political climate. "Rather than continue this traditional silence about breast cancer, we felt we had to be very public," Ford told an interviewer. She assured him that "there would be no cover-up in the Ford administration." The confluence of political reckoning and Ford's temperamental frankness led in one scholar's estimation to "the most candid remarks that a first lady had ever made in public about her health."[45]

Speaking openly about the disfigurement and scars from her operation and the effect of losing a breast was a dramatic departure for someone in Betty Ford's role. Its reverberations were immediate, measurable in the uptick not just in mammograms but also in more forthright public discussions about women's health.[46] Many commentators praised Ford for bringing new attention to a disease that had received so little. Public support came in the form of 5,000 calls to the White House switchboard and in letters to the editor, such as one woman's praise of Ford for her bravery in talking about "a disease a lot of people would like to hide, like leprosy."

7.1. Betty Ford, here shown post-surgery with Gerald Ford, garnered both praise and criticism for her openness about medical matters.

Given that "most don't want to read or hear about [breast cancer], let alone have it on the front page headlines," she judged that the First Lady had performed a valuable public service.[47]

As this writer suggested, the extensive publicity attending the First Lady's mastectomy was not uniformly applauded. The press came in for a beating for offering too much detail, too relentlessly, and so too did readers for their "voyeurism" in following it all.[48] Critics raised questions about medical privacy (one noted that the press was reporting on Ford's post-op condition before the anesthesia had even worn off), about the exploitation of illness for political gain, and about the patient's right to dignity. Ever since Betty Ford's surgery, wrote one, "the world has been immersed in clinical detail about her case. . . . People say that since it's the First Lady, we have the right to know, but do we? What about her right to privacy?"[49] *Boston Globe* columnist Ellen Goodman opined that "one of the worst things about being a public person—by marriage and not by choice—must be having a private problem. When the removal of your breast becomes a media event, you've had the ultimate invasion of privacy."[50] Similarly, a reader of the *Hartford Courant* expressed disgust at "the sick invasion of privacy foisted on people in the public eye." The "reporting on Mrs. Ford's operation is the last straw," this writer fumed. "Why couldn't the press have the decency, the good manners, and the sensitivity to report this as a straight news item, without sensationalism, lurid details, and gloomy prognostications?"[51]

For writers in this vein, the intrusion of personal details into reportage was not just irrelevant to public affairs but a corruption of them. "What price news?" asked a writer for the *Atlanta Constitution*, the lament triggered by Betty Ford's appearances on Barbara Walters's talk show and the cover of *McCall's* magazine. Tagging such coverage "exploitation," he moaned, "Aren't things bad enough to have to drag a humiliated Betty Ford before an already cancerous economy. Is there no shame?"[52] To assume that shame was involved in speaking openly about one's health, and breast cancer specifically, however, could no longer be counted on. Reactions to Betty Ford's outspokenness reveal the way codes about public speech were rapidly being retooled, the joint product of a bolder, even brazen, press and the elevation of transparency and authenticity as social values.

Betty Ford's breaches of propriety went beyond the medical domain. The First Lady shocked many Americans with her plain talk about all manner of issues, including a glib reference to sleeping with the president "as often as possible."[53] The high-water mark, however, was her spilling of family secrets in a *60 Minutes* television interview with journalist Morley Safer in 1975. On air, when asked, she speculated about her four children's possible marijuana use, as well as her unmarried daughter's likeliness to conduct a sexual affair.[54] (As the *New York Times* reported it, "Mrs. Ford suggested that in general, premarital relations with the right partner might lower the divorce rate."[55] The CBS press release simply explained: "This is an unusual interview with an unusual woman."[56]) Afterward, Ford admitted that she had been thrown by the question about how she would react to her daughter having an affair. To that or any other question, she might have demurred. Instead, wrote a handler, she answered in a manner "unheard of in a First Lady."[57] Ford once again linked her remarks to her political surrounds—to the principles of "an open administration" and the values of "openness and candor."[58] Her on-camera admissions triggered plenty of hate mail blaming the First Lady for tarnishing the reputation of the White House and the presidency.[59] But Betty Ford was also deeply popular, her poll numbers the highest of any First Lady in history (and higher than her husband's).[60] Like her willingness to talk personally about her cancer and recovery, the First Lady's refreshingly "modern" remarks about family life gained her many admirers.

Betty Ford's frequent departures from decorum were as important to the evolving culture of disclosure in the United States as lawmakers' post-Nixon political quest for transparency. Her direct talk on delicate matters dovetailed with a more aggressive journalistic ethos that had been building in the era of civil rights and Vietnam, severing the cozy mid-century relationship between the press and the politicians it reported on.[61] Journalists beginning in the 1960s instead set themselves up as the exposers of back-stage politics and the enforcers of public accountability. As Michael Schudson explains, as the press took on this role, the government and other powerful institutions became "eager for media attention and approval," adapting to "a world in which journalists had a more formidable presence than ever before."[62] Watergate would cement the profession's new emphasis on ferreting out secrets in the name of exposing abuses of authority.[63] But that impulse was not so easily contained. One media scholar observes, "it would be very difficult to maintain a sharp distinction between secrets bearing on the exercise of power and secrets concerning the conduct of private life." Indeed, investigative journalism "would easily shade into a kind of prurient reporting in which hidden aspects of the exercise of power would be mixed together with hidden aspects of the lives of the powerful."[64]

60 Minutes, a "surprise hit," was a case in point. Its very premise was built on parting the curtain separating the public figure from the ordinary citizen: "here one got the story behind the story and experienced a feeling of intimacy with America's most famous people."[65] Betty Ford's biographer notes that her invitation to appear on a television newsmagazine show "was, in and of itself news."[66] No other First Lady had been asked to do so, the closest parallel perhaps being Jackie Kennedy's televised 1962 tour of the White House for CBS News, a carefully scripted production. And the queries of Morley Safer, who had gained acclaim for his tough reportage of U.S. Marines' "search and destroy" missions in Vietnam, probed further than many thought appropriate. Conventions around observing a polite distance were going by the wayside. Ford was asked, for example, whether she believed her husband had even been unfaithful, if she had ever visited a psychiatrist, and how she would characterize her relationship with her children. Her press secretary, Sheila Weidenfeld, demanded, "Would anyone have dared ask Mamie Eisenhower about subjects like that?" Weidenfeld worried about the effects of her boss's use of "shock words" like divorce, abortion, and marijuana on national TV, but then thought again, saying, "I suppose these are shock times."[67]

The publishing industry, at any rate was not shocked: it thrived on Betty Ford's revelations and ardently pursued more. Taking a page from her mother, Susan Ford accepted an invitation to write a regular column, "White House Diary," for *Seventeen* magazine, which among other topics dealt with male chauvinism and her own embattled privacy.[68] Soon enough, Betty Ford's press secretary was telling her own tales about the administration in a memoir of 1979, *First Lady's Lady*—"one of the first of what would be a long line of kiss-and-tell books written by White House employees."[69] This brand of "news" fell into the category of entertainment or even gossip, but investigative journalists were pouring more and more of their energies into uncovering intimate revelations about other public figures, especially those in government.[70] In 1976, for example, the *Washington Post*, celebrated for piecing together the Watergate scandal, produced another exposé, this time the story of Ohio congressman Wayne Hayes, who had employed his mistress as his secretary. Hayes's impropriety was newsworthy in part because it was an abuse of public trust but also because it violated new feminist norms of appropriate behavior. The sexual affairs of other politicians, from Franklin Roosevelt in the 1930s to John F. Kennedy in the 1960s, had not been the stuff of news, even when well known to reporters. But by the mid-1970s, historian Edward Berkowitz writes, the *Washington Post* "saw such a story as fair game and, even more, as a story of vital news importance that should run on page one."[71] Once the old taboos were broken, political and sexual scandals became increasingly valuable quarry for investigative reporters.

Clearly, the norms of political decorum were shifting. Figures in the public eye—and not only politicians' wives—felt compelled to issue more intimate and revealing details in public statements. Not just tax returns but also personal foibles and indiscretions moved into the spotlight. Just after he was nominated as the Democratic candidate for president in 1976, Jimmy Carter, for example, owned up in a *Playboy Magazine* interview to committing "adultery in his heart many times." If Carter went too far, the *New York Times* calling his admission "unusually candid for a Presidential aspirant" and many evangelicals whom he had courted withdrawing their support for his candidacy, his comments were calibrated to meet a new political standard.[72]

The Domestication of Surveillance

In the 1970s, "secrets were simply more secret," writes author and professional blogger Marion Winik, who has herself crafted a career out of highly personal stories. "Back then, there were only three [television] channels and none of them had shows where people who were not professional actors wept and threw chairs at one another."[73] But in fact secrets were already becoming much less secret in that decade. A key force was TV itself, which beginning in the early 1970s challenged all sorts of proprieties about what could and could not be done in public view and earshot. *All in the Family,* Norman Lear's hit show for CBS that premiered in 1971, gleefully broke old barriers, showing childbirth and mentioning menopause on the air. In preparation, the network "arranged for extra operators to take complaints from offended viewers." Few, however, came in, and the show led in the ratings for five years.[74] Curse words and flushing toilets, previously banned in television programming, soon followed.

The year before the Privacy Act was signed into law by President Ford— and attracting far more attention, it must be said—another groundbreaking television program appeared in the nation's living rooms. *An American Family,* which first aired on January 11, 1973, was a new breed of on-screen entity: a documentary series that chronicled seven months in the life of a real family, the Louds of Santa Barbara, California.[75] The Public Broadcasting Service (PBS) ran the series for twelve weeks, immersing upward of ten million viewers every Thursday night, at 9:00 pm Eastern Standard Time, in the domestic turmoil of Bill and Pat Loud and their five teen-aged children: Lance, Kevin, Grant, Delilah, and Michele. As the episodes unfolded, the audience was privy to Delilah's romantic explorations, Grant and his father's squabbles about ambition and work, and Pat's visit to her aging mother, as well as to glimpses of family breakfasts, dance recitals, and summer jobs. More serious matters were aired too, as emblematic of the forces transforming American families in the 1970s as they were unprecedented as TV content. Millions watched as the oldest son, Lance, made clear to his mother, in scenes shot at the Chelsea Hotel in New York, that he was gay.[76] And viewers remained riveted as they followed, hour by hour, the dramatic arc of the series: the collapse of Pat and Bill's twenty-year marriage.

Unlike Betty Ford and Jimmy Carter, the Louds were not public figures. Until the camera arrived in their living room, their personal affairs were obscure, well and truly their own. But what the Louds represented—the white middle-class American family—was as ripe for unveiling in the 1970s as were politicians' sex lives, as Ford herself was soon to discover on *60 Minutes*. The domestic sphere, and the middle-class home specifically, had been figured as the bulwark of American private life in the postwar era, perhaps privacy's last best hope. Filmmakers in the early 1960s who had hoped to document the "home side" of Kennedy's presidency were rebuffed by Jackie Kennedy, who declared, "Nobody is going to move into the White House with me."[77] Suburban architects and the Supreme Court itself in *Griswold v. Connecticut* had affirmed that the private spaces of family life, especially the heterosexual, marital bedroom, were off-limits to intruders. The camera's invasion of the Louds' domestic intimacies—puncturing its outward placidity to discover the raging emotional conflicts of the contemporary suburban family—suggested a more penetrating view on the matter. Like the franker revelations of public figures, the dissection of middle-class family life signaled a more skeptical stance toward the surfaces and sanctities of American life. As such, the PBS series collaborated in a broader collapse of personal secrets, seemingly announcing the end of a certain species of privacy.

Funded by the Corporation for Public Broadcasting and the Ford Foundation to the tune of $1.2 million and culled from 261 days of shooting and 300 hours of footage, the 12-hour program that comprised *An American Family* is now widely acknowledged to be the progenitor of reality television.[78] Its producer, Craig Gilbert, had cut his teeth on documentaries about public affairs—wartime events in *The March of Time* and *Victory at Sea*—and public figures such as artist Pablo Picasso and Irish writer Christy Brown. But in the later 1960s the documentary was being put to new ends: both the "private exposure of public events and figures" and "the public display of private, even secret, lives."[79] Filmmakers were "turning increasingly to more private subject matter in autobiographical forms," and Gilbert turned with them.[80] At an opportune moment he pitched the idea of recording the life of an ordinary middle-class family to National Educational Television, PBS's predecessor. He was surprised but gratified to get the green light.[81]

Even in an age of experimental "direct cinema," Gilbert's creation was unique. PBS publicists crowed, "There has never been anything on television—or anywhere else—to prepare you for 'An American Family.'" For all the hyperbole, they captured a truth. The show's unscripted content, its unsparing exposure of intimate relationships, and, perhaps most of all, its ordinary subjects willing to conduct their affairs before the camera heralded a new form. The series "announced the breakdown of fixed distinctions between public and private, reality and spectacle, serial narrative and nonfiction, documentary and fiction, film and television."[82] These features made *An American Family* "the most hotly debated documentary ever broadcast on American television." Not coincidentally, the series also drew the largest audience for public TV of the 1970s.[83] Anthropologist Margaret Mead (who had been Gilbert's subject in an earlier documentary) praised the series as "a new kind of art form . . . as new and as significant as the invention of drama or the novel—a new way in which people can learn to look at life."[84] Media scholars would later judge *An American Family* one of the most influential and innovative television shows of the decade.[85]

Unable to forecast a future of televised reality contests, video diaries, and personal webcams, however, most critics reacted to *An American Family* with a mix of bemusement and outright hostility. The series was unsettling in both its form and content. Many acknowledged the powerful, if disturbing, picture of the nuclear family that the series projected.[86] If this was a profile of the American family, rather than simply "an" American family, critics intoned, that institution was in trouble.[87] Many found fault with the affluent Louds themselves, whose on-camera image was unflattering: shallow, uncultured, materialistic, uninterested in public affairs, and disconnected from one another. Unpersuaded by the documentary's "realness," other detractors blasted the truth of a depiction that could only be captured by an ever-present film crew. Surely, they argued, those additional members of the household distorted the family portrait.[88] But the greatest number of reviewers leveled their critique at the series' very premise. What was it, exactly, that the producer and filmmakers had hoped to reveal? Howsoever did the Louds agree to it? And why did Americans so avidly watch it?

Novel as it was, *An American Family* was shaped both by avant-garde filmmaking—the dream that the camera could erase "the divide between public and private"—and network news reportage that was by the 1970s carrying gritty images from the Vietnam War into American homes.[89] Filmmakers and journalists alike pressed forward into foreign social and moral territory, casting aside old tropes and verities. They counted on a less deferential audience, one more inured to shock and less satisfied with generic or political conventions. One scholar pegs 1969 as the year that prime-time television programming began to shift, adopting "a more abrasive style and more open confrontation with contemporary social issues," as compared with the harmonious family dramas of the 1950s and 1960s.[90] The same year that the PBS series aired, viewing audiences were treated to a new level of sexual explicitness and moral ambiguity in films like *The Godfather, Deep Throat,* and *Last Tango in Paris,* as well as in books like Erica Jong's *Fear of Flying.*[91] Equally scandalous real-life productions were waiting in the wings. The Watergate hearings, billed by one commentator "the greatest miniseries ever," would play out on television screens that summer—competing, in fact, with the rebroadcast of *An American Family.*[92]

Turning an unvarnished gaze on the domestic realm, an arena long prized as a sanctuary from public life, had disorienting results. *An American Family* revealed in the first instance a dissolving marriage. But it also exposed a set of intertwined issues that were coming to a head in the 1970s: changing social values, evident in the way the series undid traditional images of parenting, gender roles, and sexuality; the tug of media, especially television, on citizens' lives; and, of course, the moving line of what Americans considered to be private.[93]

For the Louds themselves, the meanings of *An American Family* came in two waves. The first, and easier, stage was the filming itself. It was guided by a set of ground rules negotiated by the family and filmmakers. The Louds would allow microphones, cameras, and a film crew (led by a young married couple, Alan and Susan Raymond) into their lives. They would make available, in addition, home movies, family photos, and other memorabilia. Access to their private affairs extended even to their telephone line. Midway through the shooting—even as debates over wiretapping raged in the broader society and Richard Nixon installed recording devices in the Oval Office—the Louds permitted the filmmakers to tap their phones so as to better record both ends of family members' conversations.[94] On the other hand, the camera was not to go behind closed doors. Gilbert explained, assuming a level of compartmentalization that may not have been possible, that the Louds could "transact interactions they didn't want recorded before or after the camera crew's arrival and departure."[95] The family on occasion exercised veto power over the filming of particular events—Pat's informing of her children (although not her husband) that she would seek a divorce, for instance.[96] Some things, if not many, were simply "too private for the series."[97] Although she went along with the filming of them, even Susan Raymond apparently "balked at capturing several of the series' rawest moments," including a pivotal scene of an argument between Pat and Bill Loud at a restaurant.[98] The Louds were permitted to review and raise concerns about the footage before it aired, a stipulation rare for that time.[99] Otherwise, they were "to live their lives as if there were no camera present."[100] That injunction perhaps indicated how much an older distinction between public and private matters had already faded.

Ignoring ever-present surveillance presented a challenge. At times, as Pat described it, the knowledge of being watched weighed heavily: "That camera was fixed in my brain like a tumor. It took months until I wasn't aware of it every minute." She referred to the camera as "another parent, an eleven-million-people parent" that she didn't want to let down. At other moments, the presence of the filmmakers seemed to offer Pat solace or at least distract her from her family's woes.[101] The Louds became quite close to the young film crew, especially Susan and Alan Raymond. The filmmakers, on the scene day in and day out, found themselves involved in aspects of the children's lives—Grant's breakup with his girlfriend, for instance—to which their parents were not privy.[102] And while she avowed that the series postponed rather than caused her split from Bill, Pat also suggested that the crew's presence emboldened her to seek a divorce, a move she had contemplated for several years.[103] Their arrival in her household meant that she "had an unprecedented amount of support"; her family simply "expanded" to include "everybody . . . who dropped in and dropped out, and we were one big functioning unit." This new family ensemble "took the edge off" her plan to separate from Bill.[104] Yet it was also true, Pat acknowledged, that playing to the camera had its own logic: "We were living a story that had to be told, and the story was building to a climax."[105]

The end of that story, along with the daily scrutiny of outsiders, brought its own difficulties. The family, it turns out, had become used to being watched. On December 31, 1971, a full seven months after the crew arrived, "the series was suddenly over," Pat wrote, "and they all packed up their cameras, their lights, their sound equipment, their problems, concerns, and what had been for me, their magic, and they left." Regular life paled in comparison. "We were done, back to a life that seemed appallingly ordinary, waiting for what was going to happen next." Pat described the time that elapsed while the editors worked on the film as a "state of suspension." For a whole year, "it didn't matter to anyone what we said or did, because nobody was filming us anymore."[106] Private life without an audience felt different—lonelier and drained of significance.

The second stage, the broadcast of *An American Family* from January through March 1973, would bring the bright lights back. Whatever reservations Pat Loud had harbored during the filming, she declared herself "simply astounded, enormously pleased and very proud" of the finished series, praising the filmmakers for handling her family's affairs honestly and with "as much kindness as possible."[107] But the critical response to *An American Family* was not as the Louds had envisioned, whether Bill's belief that they would come across as a West Coast version of the Kennedys or Pat's half-conscious hope that "if Bill didn't love me, a lot of the viewers out there would."[108] Whereas the family had experienced the filming as an "intimate affair," the same could not be said for the glare of publicity that followed.[109] Pat Loud described her shock and sense of betrayal at their portrayal in the advance publicity from PBS and the raft of reviews that followed, claiming "horrid psychic damage." She lamented, "We've lost dignity, been humiliated, and our honor is in question."[110] Only then did the consequence of letting the camera in become clear. The Loud family would be "embattled and condemned in the center of a mass-media paroxysm of interest, comment, zings, arrows and judgment."[111]

Critics roundly decried the way the Louds conducted their affairs. Almost invariably, they fastened that judgment to the family's decision to expose their private lives to anyone who would watch. Explanations for such untoward behavior ranged from simple vanity to a more troubling cause: a vacuum in the Louds' family life that publicity promised to fill. Irving Horowitz, the same sociologist who had so stoutly defended *Tearoom Trade*, told *Time* magazine that the Louds revealed "a tendency towards exhibitionism," and that the "very act of being filmed for public television" made them atypical of America's families.[112] But a lurking worry was that the Louds' desire to enact their private woes in the public spotlight made them all too representative. Perhaps the constant presence of observers and recording equipment in the lives of the Louds did not constitute an invasion at all. Quoting the show's producer, a writer for the *New York Times* speculated that the family allowed the film crew in because its members had lost the ability to communicate with one another. They hoped "the presence of the camera—an objective third party—might help 'fill in the empty spaces.'"[113]

Unlike the subjects of sociological and behavioral research, who by the early 1970s were characterized as vulnerable and even in need of rights, the subjects of the PBS documentary were regularly censured for their participation in this particular social experiment. The Louds' seeming hunger for attention set them apart from the unwitting performers in Laud Humphreys's study or Stanley Milgram's laboratory. Only a few observers even made the comparison. Allen Grimshaw, a sociologist concerned with researchers' use of sound and image recording, referred to the Loud family as an exemplary case of "severe individual distress" caused by being captured on film. He quoted Pat Loud's post-broadcast statement that she was frightened and confused, finding herself "shrinking in defense, not only from critics and detractors, but from friends, sympathizers and, finally, myself." Grimshaw linked the Louds' exposure to increasing media intrusiveness in society writ large: public officials being caught on camera in bad behavior, Jackie Onassis and her children being harassed by paparazzi, and distraught families in the face of tragedies being queried by reporters: "how do you feel?"[114]

Likewise, a writer on documentary film, Calvin Pryluck, noted that, although the medium had "shown us aspects of our world that in other times would have been obscured from view," the gain in social knowledge could be a loss for those it documented. Documentary film, he argued, was "filled with pitfalls for the people involved." Inevitably, this brought him to what he called "actuality filming" and the Louds. "The criticism—deserved or not—directed to the Loud family following their appearance as *An American Family*," he wrote a full three years after the broadcast, "is too well-known to bear repeating."[115] Pryluck wondered about the damage that had come to the Louds in its aftermath. Like many supporters of research subjects' rights, he considered the securing of documentary subjects' consent inadequate, nothing more than a fiction useful to the filmmaker.[116] It was a violation of a "fundamental human right," he claimed, to force subjects "to disclose feelings they might prefer to keep hidden." This is what made "coerced public revelations of private moments . . . so clearly objectionable.[117]

Pryluck's was a rare intervention, however. And his key assumptions seemed wobbly: objectionable, after all, to whom? Even the Louds—with some wavering only from Pat—allowed that, given a choice, they would do it all over again. Lance, despite his substantial critiques of the final form of the documentary, vowed that he would agree to the filming again "in a minute."[118] Most critics would thus view the problem of "public revelation" as not one of improper suasion, but its opposite: a baleful willingness to disclose. To some, the PBS production suggested that hitherto private feelings and actions were losing their privateness, or worse, becoming the very currency of American public life. If coercion played a part in bringing secrets out into the open, it functioned in much subtler fashion than did the standard inducements of social scientists. And if overly eager subjects required protection, it was not from the prying camera or filmmaker. What they needed protection from was themselves.

The Loud family was one concern. But so was their audience. This was because *An American Family* was wildly and, to some critics, inexplicably, popular: one night's episode, for instance, reportedly drew more than 70 percent of Boston's entire viewing audience.[119] The *Chicago Tribune* quipped that the documentary "made the trials of the Louds a shade better known than those of Job."[120] And the fact that acclaimed essayist and human rights activist Elie Wiesel refused to watch the show alongside other dinner-party guests was considered newsworthy.[121] Fan letters, cartoons—references to the Louds appeared in Gary Trudeau's "Doonesbury," as well as *The New Yorker*—and extensive media coverage cemented the series' place in popular culture. The Louds, it seemed, had exposed not only themselves but also a voyeuristic streak in the population at large. The series raised troubling questions about the lure of televised "reality" and the disrobing of private life. What *did* the Louds' readiness to be filmed in the intimate, daily rounds of their household mean? And what *was* signified by millions of viewers' commitment to tuning in, twelve weeks running?

For Pat Loud, the most interesting questions sparked by the series were not about her family at all, but about the watchers. She wondered, "What nerve have we touched? . . . What is it that has switched on the audience"?[122] The Hollywood-esque attractiveness of the Louds was part of the answer. More than one critic commented on Pat's striking resemblance to Jackie Onassis.[123] But something else seemed to be at work behind the "unusually intense level of interest in the Louds."[124] Although the family was largely condemned as shallow and detached when the show aired, critics conceded that the Louds' experiences and troubles resonated with middle-class viewers.[125] Few of them doubted Americans' tendency to identify with the Louds or their capacity to enter into intimate dramas enacted by strangers. Commentators implied as much of the documentary's producer. An "angry man," Craig Gilbert was, one speculated, upset at the failure of his own marriage and hoping for illumination and therapy by

7.2. Advertisements for the premiere of *An American Family* promised that there had "never been anything on television" like it.

wielding a camera.[126] In the Louds, he hoped to find answers: to the decline of the American family in the 1970s but also to the end of his own. The intentness with which viewers followed the Louds spoke to the power of domestic secrets unleashed.

The family of *An American Family*—shot through with infidelity, homosexuality, adolescent angst, profanity, and alcohol—may have offered some relief from impossible domestic ideals in the 1970s. Viewers' identification was strongest with Pat, who referred to "boxes and boxes of letters, some two thousands of them, most of which tell me how brave and honest I am" that arrived from fans. These missives empathized with, encouraged, and even thanked the family's matriarch for her candor about her domestic struggles and divorce. Unlike the critics who branded the Louds "untraditional"—who were "scared," Pat suggested, by a family seemingly "too loose, too scattered"—the television audience of 1973 seemed to find itself reflected in the documentary's frank, conflict-filled depiction of domestic life.[127] Even as a reviewer asked whether television was "the right form for this content," she admitted that she was, "quite frankly, surprised at how interested I became in [the Louds]" and unprepared for how difficult it was to find "critical distance" from the residents of 35 Wooddale Lane.[128] Novelist Anne Roiphe likewise claimed to feel "despair and fascination" while watching the Louds' lives unfold, which, she admitted, "could only have been caused by vibrations ricocheting down through my own experiences." The Louds, she wrote, were "enough like me and mine to create havoc in my head."[129]

Throughout 1973, commentators bewailed the Louds' willingness to subject themselves to publicity. But they also noted viewers' readiness to affirm them for it. The popular response to *An American Family*, like voters' embrace of Betty Ford, points to broad changes in sensibility around the sharing of "private" material. Peering into others' households from the comfort of one's own living room was an old impulse, stretching from the Puritans to the 1950s picture window. What was new was the public rather than surreptitious nature of the surveillance. As such, the "looser" family that played out on the nation's TV screens helped erode one of the key private planks of American public life.

Living out Loud

Even critics who conceded that the PBS documentary was helping Americans make sense of cultural and familial change were skeptical about the medium. Could true self-awareness really come from watching strangers air their dirty laundry on national TV? "*An American Family* was hailed as a great breakthrough in the use of the camera in the service of knowledge," wrote Abigail McCarthy, who was tapped to review the documentary for the *Atlantic Monthly* the spring of its broadcast. Comparing the PBS series to photographer Edward Steichen's panoramic, globe-spanning images in the "Family of Man" exhibit (1955), where the family was taken to be a "paradigm of unity," McCarthy saw in the Louds only "disintegration and purposelessness." She believed that the viewer was "diminished and drained" by the watching—not elevated, as with Steichen's images, but instead "humiliated." The former wife of a presidential candidate, McCarthy knew something about the fine line between private life and public exposure.[130] Her reticence about her own failed marriage in her 1972 memoir may account for the mix of fascination and dismay with which she greeted the Louds' separation before the eyes of millions the following year.

McCarthy was aware that many reviewers belittled the Louds for putting themselves in the sights of a film crew, but she thought this reaction wrong-headed, betraying "ignorance of the unique hold of the medium on people today." In public life, she averred, "one learns quickly that everyone wants to be on television." Surely thinking of her husband's presidential campaign, she mused, "Let a television crew appear to follow a campaigner and a crowd gathers almost at once, pushing each other, pressing close so that they, too, will be on screen. Appear on a talk show and you take on new reality, even for close friends." McCarthy went on to offer other examples, including that of the wife of a released prisoner of war who had permitted her husband's very first phone call—unbeknownst to him—to be recorded by a television crew. McCarthy stated as fact that "there are very few private people left." Given this and other signs of television looming larger than life in contemporary culture, she asked, "Can we condemn the Louds?"[131]

Pat Loud, in her autobiography of 1974, echoed McCarthy's sentiments (which she had devoured, along with any number of reviews and essays on the PBS series). In the chapter titled "Why We Did It," she asked, with a hint of sarcasm, "Doesn't everybody want to be on television?" Referring to her initial understanding of the terms of her family's participation in the documentary, she continued, "Wouldn't *anybody* have done it, thinking it was going to be for *one* hour on educational television? Or even not thinking?"[132] In another venue, Pat framed the question as others had: "Why did we let the cameras in, and once in, why did we let them roll on, over our lives, apart and together, soaking up things that many people wouldn't tell their lovers or tax accountants?"[133] But Pat didn't actually think this decision required explanation, even if it had entailed "serv[ing] up great slices of ourselves—irretrievable slices."[134] The thrall of a mediated life was all too clear.

Indeed, many were coming to the conclusion that what mattered to citizens was life on the public stage, one's image only as it played out in full view. One media analyst explained, "The Louds were not disturbed by the nationwide publication of facts that are usually considered embarrassing (divorce, homosexuality). They were upset, rather, by the gracelessness and lack of style they exhibited on the screen." The family's reaction to the broadcast of their lives made evident that "it was not their privacy but their performance that had been abused." Closely following their reviews and energetically disputing their portrayal, the Louds were first and foremost interested in managing their public personas. "In other words, they have conducted themselves as show business people," was his scathing conclusion.[135]

The problem of *An American Family*, in this view, was not that it had swept unsuspecting people into a world they didn't understand, altering their private lives through the glare of publicity. It was that the Louds had in some way anticipated the performance. Pat commented that, when the family was approached about the series, "Bill, of course, was dying to do it." (She later relayed that her husband "adored being filmed—he basked in it. He was the only one who ever *asked* to be filmed.") She added, "The kids, of course, were desperate to do it" too.[136] In that repeated "of course" was the supposition that her audience would have felt the same. To the extent that Pat was correct, charges of the Louds' exceptionalism were undermined. Craig Gilbert had told the *New York Times* that part of the selection process for the series entailed locating a family that "would put up with a major invasion of privacy." But in fact, none of the several dozen prospective families he interviewed was unwilling to take part.[137] Was it possible that their ready embrace of the camera's surveillance was the one feature that actually made the Louds—living on the West Coast; upper-middle-class owners of a swimming pool, four cars, and a horse; and who traveled widely—representative of American families?

The PBS series in this fashion raised questions that pressed far beyond the flaws of one particular family or the documentary form. It laid bare a shift, some critics sensed, in how Americans were imagining themselves. Central to this transformation were the mass media. The more closely one looked at the Louds, the more shaped by its codes and products they appeared to be. Wanting the family to be instantly recognizable from domestic dramas and TV commercials, the producer's experiment in realism had from the beginning relied on fictional and televised models. For this reason it was apparently crucial to Craig Gilbert, despite all the transformations that were rewriting gender roles in the 1970s, that Pat be a housewife.[138] The title sequence for the finished series, framing each family member separately but simultaneously on screen, even bore a strong resemblance to those of contemporary hits like *The Brady Bunch* and *The Partridge Family.*[139]

But Gilbert had not in any simple sense invaded the home with a mass-mediated sensibility. That sensibility—it was clear—had already moved in. The Louds, regularly portrayed on TV watching TV, were fully fluent in media references and keenly aware of the power of publicity. Pat referred to the powerful grip that cinema had on her as a young woman.[140] Lance easily analogized happenings in his home to the soap opera *As the World Turns.*[141] One critic noted that the Louds thought it would be "fun" to be on TV: "They know they are attractive, and no fewer than three of the five children hope to be performers"—rock stars or even makers of documentary films.[142] For the Louds, the in-home camera was less an intruder than a potential ticket to stardom.[143]

The interpenetration of the family and the medium went still deeper, apparent in the way the Louds borrowed the very terms of the filmmakers to relate their experiences. Pat, for example, named the episode in which she revealed to her brother and sister-in-law her aim to separate from Bill (a conversation she was initially averse to having filmed) "her best scene."[144] She also referred to herself and her eldest son as the "stars" of the show.[145] Kevin Loud complained on the *Dick Cavett Show* that he had only been given the opportunity to play "walk-on laugh parts."[146] Pat even implied that she and Bill were "luckier than most people" in being able to do "our big number"—by which she meant their splitting up—"on nationwide TV." Others' marital spats, by contrast, were small-bore affairs, consisting of "tiny ineffectual little knocks within the privacy of their houses."[147]

Something about the fact that those "knocks" were registered only by the parties directly involved diminished them.

Comments like these could only heighten long-standing concerns about the force of mass media in Americans' lives, and especially television's improper inroads into sturdy families and selves. One critic observed that Pat Loud "talks as though she believed until recently that she was a producer of the film," a member of the cast rather than the subject of the filming, with creative control over the product. This was, he thought, because "she was, after all, the producer of the live show on which it was based."[148] If *An American Family* had invaded the family's intimate home life, such critics suggested, the door had already been propped open by a thoroughly mass-mediated existence. Under such conditions, could the camera capture the private Louds? Had the family indeed ever lived a truly "private" existence?

The TV set and American family life had first intersected in the suburban living rooms of the postwar era, when it became clear that the new and overwhelmingly popular medium would largely be devoted to domestic drama.[149] A form of entertainment "whose imagery has always been fundamentally familial," television both beamed out an invigorated domestic ideal and reorganized the households in which it came to play so prominent a part.[150] Already by the late 1940s, researchers had observed that the "electronic hearth" was profoundly shaping family members' behaviors.[151] The enormous success of *An American Family* sparked a new debate over television's infiltration into not just homes but also psyches and imaginations. The documentary would serve as a platform for gauging the reach of the medium into U.S. citizens' very subjectivities. By the 1970s, one scholar reported, television had become "more common to us than any race, creed, or political affiliation, electromagnetically living in 98.5 percent of American homes." Watched, in average, an excess of six hours a day, television was "a constant resident in the American home" and "intimately ingrained in family life." Characterizing the TV set as an "electronic invader," this writer also personified it, unnervingly, as an increasingly compelling "friend" to the watcher. "Because it poses no physical threat as would an undesirable stranger, TV has all the time it wants to say and do whatever it wants." He speculated that "its relationship role will become ever more critical for many."[152]

The blurred line between television-as-intruder and television-as-entertainer had been there all along, and it spoke to an ambivalence about being exposed on screen. *Candid Camera*, a program designed to "catch unsuspecting people in the act of being themselves," first arrived on TV in 1948 and became a syndicated hit by 1960.[153] Its creator, Allan Funt, used secret recordings to entertain, making ordinary people "candid stars." He dreamed in 1952 of photographing "the way a man spends his entire working day—every public minute of it," so as to capture "a sunrise-to-sunset documentary of the life of an average man."[154] Funt intended his camera to provoke awareness of the craftedness of self-image, the contrast between what people "feel about themselves on the inside and what they see of themselves on the outside."[155] This is not far from what Craig Gilbert desired for his PBS series. In both cases, the idea was to make the "private" person less so: more accessible, tangible, and transparent to viewers and perhaps even to him- or herself. This ambition distinguished *Candid Camera* from its nineteenth-century counterpart, "instantaneous photography." To capture individual personality on TV, candidly, was to reveal the real person, not the actor. The show's popularity, though, arguably inspired greater self-consciousness about behavior in public, one's every move potentially recorded for a viewing audience.[156]

Sociologists like Erving Goffman and historians like Daniel Boorstin had tagged American society as a peculiarly dramaturgical or spectatorial one already by mid-century, the consequence of living in an "image society."[157] *An American Family* supplied compelling evidence for that analysis. Early tidings of a new sort of media constellation could be found in the widespread interest occasioned by the Louds' reactions to their own broadcasting: the criticisms that individual members of the family lobbed at *An American Family* as it aired, ranging from what they saw as sensationalistic press releases to the accumulated misrepresentations wrought by editing.[158] A critic at the *New York Times* complained that, at this point, "the content of 'An American Family' slowly began sinking into a mindless ooze about the making of 'An American Family.'"[159] Media outlets, capitalizing on the series' popularity, were happy to provide a platform. (The Louds, one reporter snidely observed, have been "highly available to the media.")[160] The entire family's appearance on ABC's *Dick Cavett Show* in the middle of the program's run was a kind of turning point.[161] As it turned out, the documentary (or docudrama, as some labeled it) was just the opening act in the creation of celebrities from the stuff of ordinary lives, media "personalities" who became such simply by virtue of having the camera trained on them.

Even after the cameras had ceased rolling and the broadcast had come to its conclusion, it seemed, the Louds couldn't stop performing—and the audience couldn't stop watching. A second national broadcast in the summer of 1973, along with a spin-off of transcripts and fuzzy images from the series packaged as a Warner paperback, suggested that the family, in allowing their personal lives to be exposed, had claimed more than an ephemeral place in public consciousness.[162] The Louds may have been disabused of their status as "co-producers" of the series. But it was becoming obvious that they would command the cameras after the fact.

On the *Cavett* show, Craig Gilbert was given a few minutes of airtime at the program's outset, but then was "gently eased out of the picture." After that, the *Times* reported, "the show belonged to the Louds."[163] This was literally, but also metaphorically, the case. When, after the show's taping, security guards offered to escort the Louds through the crowd of autograph seekers, Bill reportedly said "Hell no" and "marched out to meet his fans." And "teen-aged girls stood in line to kiss Grant and Kevin, the rock musicians."[164] For the *Washington Post*, the family's talk-show appearance cemented that the Louds had been lifted "to celebrity status."[165] Rumors swirled that Delilah and Grant had been invited to appear on *The Dating Game*, itself a new genre of televised reality, that Lance was writing his own account of the show for *Newsweek*, and that Bill had received an offer to host a game show.[166] As Pat noted, with not a little pride, Dick Cavett "got the highest ratings for that show he had ever gotten."[167] The *New York Times* viewed this same fact as tragedy. Rather than the series being remembered for the important questions it had raised about "values, institutions, and consumerism," its success would be marked by the Louds having "almost doubled" Cavett's ratings. The way was cleared for the "massive publicity-entertainment mills" to "devour the Louds."[168]

Indeed, the family made a tour of the talk-show circuit—appearing on the shows of Mike Douglas, Jack Paar, Dinah Shore, and Phil Donahue, as Pat recalled—and had additional stints on radio, the BBC, and Dutch TV.[169] The Louds would grace the cover of *Newsweek*'s issue on the state of the family, trivial details about its members would be dissected in print, and the real-life drama of their disputes with the filmmakers would make headlines.[170] "If there is a superstar in the Loud family, Pat is it," proclaimed one writer, citing a host of magazines profiling the "real" Mrs. Loud's interests and routines.[171] A single issue of the *Ladies' Home Journal* in 1973 included not one but two articles about the new celebrity: "Pat Loud Talks about Love, Marriage, Divorce—and Herself" and "A Beautiful Week for Pat Loud." Lance Loud would find another sort of fame as television's "first openly gay TV personality."[172] He became a bit player in Andy Warhol's factory, writing for the artist's magazine *Interview*—even penning a few installments of its "Invasion of Privacy" column—and headed a punk rock band called the Mumps.[173] Although Lance's minutes of fame stretched longer than Warhol would have predicted, they derived first and foremost from his having appeared in the televised documentary.[174] His was a persona brought into being by the technology of publicity itself. The Louds, one critic proclaimed, had "achieved stardom of a kind only possible in America."[175]

What one newspaper billed as "The Loud Phenomenon" is common enough in the twenty-first century. The Louds' peculiar celebrity, one critic wrote in 2002, was the "first instance of the hall-of-mirrors effect that has become so achingly familiar in the age of O. J. and Monica . . . in which folks who've been on TV programs about themselves then turn up on other TV shows and write books to defend or explain themselves, after which the whole process repeats till exhaustion."[176] But in the mid-1970s, this sort of publicity feeding on itself struck contemporary commentators as novel. One reviewer remarked that writing about the Louds was like "reviewing a novel in which the characters spin on after the last page, popping up in the *Daily News* or on the *Dick Cavett Show* to demonstrate new attitudes, new characterizations and new hairstyles."[177] Another critic mused that "a delightful only-in-America scenario presents itself: will the Louds eventually appear on TV to promote the book they'll write about having been on TV?"[178] In fact, they would.[179] Yet another accused the Louds of turning their private lives into "spectacle."[180]

Commentators' befuddlement about this state of affairs begged larger questions. How was it that people could become celebrities merely by baring their private lives on TV? What did it suggest about the hold of the medium and its faux reality, seemingly more compelling than the real thing? And what did it reveal about the status of privacy in American society? Queried about the experience of having her adolescence tracked by a film crew, Delilah Loud ticked off her grievances. But did she expect to "fade into obscurity" after the series' end? She replied, "I hope not. I really hope not. I enjoy talking to people of the media." Citing interviews with magazines like *Vogue* and the opportunity to meet celebrities, she continued, "I've really enjoyed the experience and I hope I can go on into it."[181] In her embrace of publicity with full awareness of the cost to her secrets, Delilah looked like the harbinger of a new culture.

Outing Privacy

In 1973, Lance Loud looked like something new under the sun too, jarring viewers' sensibilities with his unconventional style of dress and behavior, even appearing in one scene wearing his sister's makeup.[182] As a television presence, Lance was novel enough that commentators had trouble finding the right words to describe him, some opting for the code of "lifestyle" and others awkwardly referring to him as "living in a homosexual scene."[183] His family's tolerance further baffled some. In an essay for the *New York Times Magazine*, novelist Anne Roiphe, whose *Up the Sandbox!* (1970) was a feminist sensation, condemned Lance's "flamboyant, leechlike, homosexuality."[184] Roiphe wrote that Pat, visiting her son in New York, was "confronted, brutally and without preparation, with the transvestite, perverse world of hustlers, drug addicts, pushers, etc., and watched her son prance through a society that can be barely comprehensible to a 45-year-old woman from Santa Barbara."[185] She was astonished by the fact that Pat, although critical of her son for traveling to Washington, DC, to protest the suppression of the Pentagon Papers, "expressed no open horror at Lance's homosexual friends or ways."[186] Another writer for the *Times* opined that Pat's unflinching visit to Lance could be judged admirable had it stood for acceptance. "But it doesn't." In twelve installments, "not once do they utter the word 'homosexual.'" The Louds, she wrote, "simply refuse to acknowledge the reality. In the end the silence is shattering."[187]

Roiphe's aversion and the Louds' silence alike would be targets of the gay liberation movement that sprang, newly confident, from the Stonewall protests ignited by the routine policing of a New York gay bar in 1969. Shouting "out of the closets and into the streets!" activists gave voice to a new phase of the quest for civil rights, one built on "the potency, magnetism, and promise of gay self-disclosure."[188] This milestone in the modern history of gay activism would be followed by others, including the removal in 1973 of homosexuality as a disorder in and of itself (although the disorder would remain in other forms) from psychiatry's bible, the *Diagnostic and Statistical Manual*.[189] But Lance played a role too, one critic later noting that "American television came out of the closet through *An American Family*," and another singling out Lance's appearance as "one of the defining images of the Gay Decade."[190] Judging by his fan mail—letters thanking him "for being a voice of outrage in a bland fucking normal middle-class world"—Lance meant something different to gay youth than to the *Times*'s critics.[191] He stood for "being yourself," a new catchphrase of the era, and also for a changed assessment among gay Americans about the perils of keeping one's sexual identity hidden.

The 1970s cracked open the vexed relationship between privacy and what Laud Humphreys and his dissertation committee would have called the "gay world." Feminists had laid the critical groundwork, challenging dominant assumptions about privacy's beneficence as a public value. In consciousness-raising groups and manifestos, they disrobed privacy's politics, arguing that male prerogatives were maintained by sealing off the "private" sphere of family and home—and thus domestic violence, child abuse, and marital rape—from state intervention. As feminist theorist Catharine MacKinnon would summarize, for women, "a right to privacy looks like an injury got up as a gift."[192]

Privacy would take on a new aspect for gay liberationists as well. Secrecy and discretion had long appeared the best protection for American men and women living outside the bounds of normative sexuality, who—if found out—risked their jobs, their families, and their physical security. The need for sanctuary from a hostile society would give rise by mid-century to the metaphor of the closet, an outward performance of heterosexuality that masked the truth within.[193] Correspondingly, the organized homophile movement of the 1950s, in the form of the Mattachine Society, had explicitly counseled a quiet respectability as the best path to securing civil rights.[194]

But the call by gay liberation activists in the 1970s for public rights, including the right to freedom of sexual expression, challenged these counsels of discretion.[195] Gay organizations began to argue that, to the extent that homosexual behavior was tolerated only because it was contained behind closed doors—that is, "private"—it was rendered shameful to its participants and negated by the larger society.[196] To *choose* privacy was one thing, but to be coerced into it was quite another. Privacy and liberation, that is, seemed to be at loggerheads. As such arguments took hold, the closet would be figured more as prison than protector, preventing homosexual men and women from living free and authentic lives. "Coming out" was a disavowal of stigma. But it was equally a repudiation of a particular kind of privacy. And so, as historian Robert Self writes, even as gay men and lesbians demanded "the right not to have their lives policed, the right to be left alone," many recognized that to obtain true privacy as gay men and lesbians, they had to make their sexuality public.[197]

Countering critiques of his invasion of tearoom users' privacy in the early 1970s, Laud Humphreys had demanded whether it was better for social researchers "not to know." More swiftly than the sociologist could have anticipated, visibility would become the watchword of gay liberation.[198] Humphreys's own career exemplified the shift. Four years after filing his dissertation and just two years after his first book appeared, he published *Out of the Closets: The Sociology of Homosexual Liberation* (1972). From into the tearooms to out of the closets, from a stance of secrecy and shame to one of liberation and pride, the sociologist's scholarship pivoted with the times. His personal life did too. In a dramatic public confrontation with a fellow scholar of homosexuality at a session of the American Sociological Association in 1974, Humphreys "came out" for the first time as a gay man, his stunned wife sitting next to him in the audience.[199] The sociologist had made a career of concealment, disguising the reason for his presence in the tearooms, his study's objectives, and his own appearance to the men he interviewed. His last and perhaps most successful deception—his public persona as a heterosexual man who "passed" as gay in the name of social inquiry—was thus uncovered. Or, rather, it was voluntarily abandoned.

Even as he watched men having sex in the tearooms and defended his decision to invade others' privacy in the ensuing years, Humphreys had always carefully sheltered his own private self from public view. By 1974 that project was over, and not just for Humphreys. The following year, *Time* magazine devoted its cover to a photograph of Air Force sergeant Leonard Matlovich, who had, after boldly coming out to his superiors and with full knowledge of the consequences, been discharged from the military. The headline read simply, "I Am a Homosexual." The magazine referred to recent "jolting" public announcements of homosexuality "by a variety of people who could be anybody's neighbors—a Maryland teacher, a Texas minister, a Minnesota state senator, an Ohio professor, an Air Force sergeant."[200]

Time recounted what was in fact for many a gradual and agonizing decision to unseal sexual secrets. In an article titled "Gays on the March," it quoted an anonymous oil company executive: "Other minorities have everything to gain by demanding their rights," he pondered, but "we have everything to lose."[201] It also offered the story of Dr. Howard Brown, a former New York City health commissioner, who had been urged by gay activists to reveal his homosexuality. "At one point before he did so, all Brown could think of was 'What will my secretary say?'" As *Time* had it, what ultimately compelled the doctor to come out was his belief that doing so would advance collective rights.[202] It would "help free the generation that comes after us from the dreadful agony of secrecy, the constant need to hide."[203] Others, of course, sought to preserve the secret of their sexuality from the straight world. The same year that *Time* placed homosexuality on its cover, an ex-marine, Oliver Sipple, thwarted an assassination attempt on President Gerald Ford. He also launched an invasion of privacy suit against the *San Francisco Chronicle,* which had implied in its coverage of his heroics—based on the former marine's frequenting of the city's gay bars and community events—that Sipple was homosexual. Sipple had been "out" to friends, but closeted to his family in Detroit. In the aftermath of the assassination attempt, reporters besieged him, his mother disowned him, and he began a decline into alcoholism and early death.[204]

Assumptions about the benefits of sexual secrecy and the harms of disclosure were not lightly shed. But they were undergoing rapid revision. The changing reputation across the 1980s and 1990s of Laud Humphreys—billed in the 1970s as a violator of "deviant" men's privacy—is instructive. Although his professional star dimmed after *Tearoom Trade,* the sociologist continued on the faculty at Pitzer College, becoming an expert on violence against gays in the 1980s and, eventually, a part-time psychotherapist in Los Angeles. His work on gay liberation, criticized for its "tendentiousness and partisanship," was less celebrated than had been his first book.[205] A small corps of scholars of homosexuality acknowledged, however, that Humphreys had helped make research on the "growing gay movement," not to mention "sexuality in general," legitimate. If in the decades to come *Tearoom Trade* was still invoked by sociology textbooks primarily as an object lesson in unethical research, the nascent field of queer studies would come to recognize it as a pioneering work. In 1991, a group of scholars commented that the "research and the risks" that Humphreys had undertaken "opened the way to almost all sociological research on gay topics that followed."[206] Many would come to agree that the "importance of *Tearoom Trade* to the early years of gay studies" was clear, its conclusions revisited, confirmed, and warmly praised.[207]

Indeed, *Tearoom Trade* found in the 1990s a much more comfortable landing, as scholars once again took up the question of sex in public places. For the young field of gay and lesbian studies, the 1970 study's flaws were outstripped by its daring efforts to "look" and understand. Humphreys appeared prescient in his questions as to what was truly private about sex and truly public about public space, which were really questions about the ongoing state regulation of sexuality.[208] Moreover, the privacy protections in the form of ethics codes, institutional review boards, and federal regulations that would now halt a study like Humphreys's were greeted with new skepticism from scholars of homosexuality. For many, especially in the age of AIDS, the need for social knowledge about gay practices outweighed the need for stringent research regulations. Some stressed the "limitations of such constraints" and devised "alternative proposals for ethical compliance." Introducing a collection of essays on public sex that paid elaborate homage to Humphreys, the anthropologist William Leap argued that "discussions of ethics, while certainly important, should not become impediments to effective inquiry." This extended to *not* waiting to obtain "informed consent agreements from all participants" when investigating men participating in public sex, if doing so "would irreparably disrupt the situated intimacy which we are attempting to describe."[209]

As visibility became central to gay politics, invasions of privacy could appear less urgent than the work of recognition and representation. Indeed, many were beginning to question the privileging of privacy rights, the path that had been carved by *Griswold* and *Roe*.[210] In some activists' hands, "privacy" was being conceived as a barrier to progress rather than a coveted entitlement. If the state had the power to enforce normative sexuality and determine whose private behavior was protected from interference and whose was not, as in *Griswold*, did a "right to privacy" signal freedom—or oppression?[211]

Gay men and lesbians had desired sexual privacy as much as anyone in postwar America. But by the 1980s, they had had enough of it. Or perhaps privacy was simply shape-shifting, coming to rest on a new foundation. If so, it was first evident in the changing tactics of gay activists. One sociologist observes that the distinctive feature of the social movements of the later 1960s and 1970s was the way the "issue of civil rights was tangled with the issue of cultural rights . . . the right of persons to a measure of social space and a degree of social tolerance, even acceptance, of differences."[212] Like feminists and black power activists, gay liberationists contended that full citizenship hinged not simply on being admitted to but also being *seen* in the public sphere.[213] Eventually (and often pejoratively) labeled "identity politics," this kind of agitation took seriously how, when, and where gay—or black, Latino, or female—Americans appeared in policy decisions as well as news coverage, the professions as well as popular culture. One gay activist noted in 1982, for instance, that "it is primarily our *public* existence, and not our right to privacy, which is under assault."[214] Trumpeting the values of community, collective identity, and publicity, some liberationists came even to believe that "limiting the goals of the gay movement to the right to privacy" amounted to "sexual counterrevolution."[215]

Two developments on the national stage in the mid-1980s propelled the strategy of disclosure to the forefront of gay activism. One was a case that came before the Supreme Court in 1986, *Bowers v. Hardwick*, which concerned the right of the state of Georgia to regulate sodomy. In what looked like a stark reversal of trends in privacy jurisprudence since *Griswold*, the Court ruled that the right to privacy did not extend to homosexuals because their sexual behavior had "no connection" to "family, marriage or procreation."[216] Privacy rights were not faring well on the Right by the 1980s.[217] Even despite this, the outcome in *Bowers* might have been predicted, following as it did the heteronormative and procreative logic of *Griswold*. It would not finally be reversed until 2003 in *Lawrence v. Texas*. Yet, as historian Marc Stein has shown, popular readings of the Court's privacy jurisprudence were significantly more progressive than the Court intended.[218] This made *Bowers* a crushing blow for gay activists.

When the Court flatly declared that privacy rights did not apply to homosexual Americans, those rights began to look like just another form of discrimination. As had been revealed already in the 1960s in the context of "midnight raids" and public restroom patrols, a right to privacy that looked universal on its face served in reality to prop up dominant sexual norms. As one commentator put it, "All the senses of sexual privacy that are relevant to gays—the status of not being spied on, the integrity of the body, the importance of personally affecting values, and the need for sanctuary" were violated by the Court in *Bowers*.[219] Literary scholar Deborah Nelson observes that the ruling posed "excruciating questions about self-representation, identity, public discourse, and political action." In her analysis, the solution to the crisis was found "not in a reconceptualization of privacy but in the formation of queer publics." This was because sexual autonomy could only come in a "transformed public space."[220] It was more proof that, paradoxical as it might seem, public visibility was the key to sexual privacy and thus full citizenship.

If *Bowers* was an important factor in demoting privacy rights among gay activists, the AIDS crisis was crucial. Acquired immunodeficiency syndrome, which first appeared in the early 1980s tagged as a "gay disease" and sometimes as the "Gay Plague," was virtually—and many concluded, scandalously—ignored by Ronald Reagan's conservative administration.[221] As it became clear that the speed with which the epidemic traveled and the number of lives it claimed would not be joined by a proportionate federal response, activists mobilized to make AIDS awareness unavoidable. As in the case of breast cancer—with advocates adopting the slogan "Don't Die of Embarrassment"—publicity became central to the attack on foot-dragging around the epidemic.[222] It meant that HIV infection was treated simultaneously as one of the most private of facts about oneself and a status desperately in need of visibility.

A series of organizations in the 1980s and 1990s—the Gay and Lesbian Alliance against Defamation (GLAAD) in 1985, the AIDS Coalition to Unleash Power (ACT UP) in 1987, and Queer Nation in 1990, among others—placed the gay and lesbian presence in the U.S. public sphere at the top of their agendas.[223] "Die-ins," "kiss-ins," and "Queer Nights Out" in public venues were just a few of the collective tactics activists employed in an effort to remake public culture as well as attract attention—political, scientific, and medical—to the crisis.[224] The demand for cultural representation did not banish privacy as a political goal: privacy and gay rights activists fought to keep HIV-infected people's names out of public health registries for fear of "coercive, even draconian control measures" that might further stigmatize.[225] But slogans like "We Are Everywhere" and "We're here! We're queer! Get used to it!" would reshape privacy's meaning for gay politics. Stated the director of the American Association of Physicians for Human Rights in 1991, "I believe we are in the long run fighting less for the right to privacy than for the right not to have to be private."[226]

ACT UP's slogan, "Silence=Death," telegraphed the stunning inversion of the mid-century homophile stance.[227] The equation suggested that "language, discourse, public manifestations, and the production of identity are necessary weapons of defense in a contemporary strategy of gay survival."[228] This was, after all, an era when AIDS victims' families attempted to hide the diagnosis even after death, and obituaries did not name the disease, "famous bachelors preferr[ing] to die of other causes."[229] The silence and discretion that had once offered protection were now judged fatal to individuals, as well as to the larger gay cause. Hiding one's sexual identity had in some corners of the gay liberation movement become "a kind of violence in itself."[230]

In this new context, disclosure and exposure were seized on as critical political tools. AIDS "taught two lessons," writes communications scholar Larry Gross. "First, a disease that strikes gay people (and people of color, and drug users, and poor people) will not receive adequate attention. Second, people will begin to pay attention when famous and important people are involved—even if they are revealed to be gay."[231] The second of these lessons, concerning publicity, carried implications beyond the epidemic. Gay Americans had in increasing numbers since the 1970s voluntarily called attention to their presence in the society by coming out of the closet. By the 1990s, propelled by the AIDS crisis, as well as by setbacks in gay civil rights, a small group of activists saw the "next logical step" as forcing others' hands, particularly those of prominent politicians and celebrities unwilling to publicly acknowledge their homosexuality.[232]

"Outing," the term first coined by *Time* magazine, was intended as a "condemnation of passing" and a demand for "public affirmations of gay identity."[233] The man who took credit as "outing's pioneer" in the early 1990s, the activist and journalist Michelangelo Signorile, argued that "truthful discussion of the lives of homosexual public figures" was crucial to the project of emboldening "gay people who stay in the closet out of fear and shame."[234] The lesbian and gay weekly newsmagazine, *OutWeek*, led the way by reporting the story of Malcolm Forbes's many homosexual liaisons soon after the publishing magnate's death in 1990.[235] A rush of similar "open secrets" were committed to print. Gossip columnist Liz Smith, actress Jodie Foster, Assistant Secretary of Defense Peter Williams, and a string of congressional Republicans became targets of the campaign.[236] These and other "outings" of closeted politicians and celebrities pressed the point that gay Americans could be found in all walks of life.

To its detractors, including the writer of a *New York Post* article under the headline "Magazine Drags Gays out of the Closet," outing was an outrageous and unethical invasion of privacy—a kind of sexual McCarthyism.[237] Although Signorile acknowledged the practice to be divisive, he insisted on treating a secretive, fearful recourse to privacy as a form of harm. "May the individual privacy of sexual orientation be infringed upon when the exercise of privacy in this area clearly damages a larger group?" he asked.[238] Far from invading gay citizens' privacy, he and others argued, outing was critical to advancing their dignity and civil rights.

Outing attacked the urge to "speak in codes and treat homosexuality as some scandalous secret, the name of which we can't invoke."[239] The debate it sparked raised the question of whether sexual identity (unlike sexual behavior, as its advocates were at pains to explain) was or should be considered "private information" when the seemingly analogous categories of race and ethnicity were not.

Never a mainstream practice, outing created deep fissures within the gay community.[240] The controversy nevertheless revealed how much assumptions about sexual privacy had shifted since mid-century. The "power of exposure" had typically been a weapon wielded *against* homosexuals. It deprived World War II veterans charged with homosexuality of GI benefits, and it drove gay men and women out of government service in the McCarthy era, most obviously.[241] But it also worked to police their conduct in every other sphere. As Signorile put it, "For years the media had no problem reporting the names of closeted gay private citizens who had been arrested in dubious public-restroom sting operations or wrongly accused of child molestation." These were private rather than public figures who were "wrenched from the closet for all the wrong reasons" and found their lives destroyed. The personal damage that came of exposure had made Laud Humphreys vigilant in protecting the names of men he observed in the tearooms. Now that same act could empower gay activists. None other than Lance Loud, writing for the gay news magazine *The Advocate*, would report on Queer Nation's plans to disrupt Hollywood's Academy Awards ceremony in 1992. Protesting the industry's simultaneous marginalization and demonization of gay people in its products, activists threatened to "out" sixty movie stars. The tables had been turned on exposure. "Revealing who is homosexual," crowed Signorile, "would now advance the lesbian and gay movement."[242]

Advocates of outing named their real target as a homophobic media that, although in all other respects by the 1990s fed on gossip about famous people's private affairs, maintained a "conspiracy of silence and deception about the real lives of lesbian and gay celebrities." "Somehow," wrote Signorile, "to publicize heterosexual liaisons was right—it was considered 'reportage'—while to cover homosexuality was to invade people's privacy."[243] That the highly intrusive media were complicit in this secret keeping exemplified the second-class status of sexual minorities. As in other political arenas, publicly exposing collective secrets was intended to unmask hypocrisy, in this case the "tacit agreement by which gay private lives were granted an exemption from the public's 'right to know.'"[244] If reporters were willing to write about the sex lives of straight public figures—"from Gary Hart and Donald Trump to Liz Taylor and Warren Beatty"—they were duty bound to write about the sex lives of homosexual ones too. To act otherwise furthered the stigmatization of gay people. In essence, outing's advocates demanded equal opportunity for privacy invasions. Only in an age in which publicity had gained such esteem, secrets had incurred so much suspicion, and cultural visibility had moved to the center of gay politics could such an argument stand.

A robust critique of surveillance took root in 1970s America. But secrets and hidden lives—of public figures, of families, and of sexual identity—also came under increasing scrutiny as the century wore on. Calls for the vetting of politicians' private lives and the announcing of one's authentic sexual self alike spoke to this new cultural mode. The government would be held to a new standard of transparency, but so too would its citizens. In the process, the variable functioning of privacy in American life and its associations with power came to light. "How can being gay be private when being *straight* isn't?" demanded Signorile.[245] No longer could privacy—or privacy rights—be an unquestioned social good, assumed to play a benign role in all citizens' lives and prospects. As with so many other goods in U.S. society, this one was inequitably distributed and unevenly claimed. The politics of privacy had been outed.

If a culture of exposure had arrived in the United States by the century's close, there seemed no better proof than the Bill Clinton-Monica Lewinsky scandal of the late 1990s, during which a sitting president was impeached on the grounds of lying about an improper sexual relationship with a 24-year-old intern in the White House.[246] It was a long way from Jimmy Carter's *Playboy* interview. But the spectacle played out as the logical culmination of a society that mandated the public vetting of private affairs, in both meanings of the phrase. The scandal was propelled by now-familiar set pieces: a highly invasive media complex; the outing of (hetero)sexual secrets; and the extraction of embarrassing personal details, this time from the most powerful man in the nation.[247]

The road had been paved earlier in the decade, on the same 60 *Minutes* program that had gotten Betty Ford into hot water in 1975. On that program, presidential candidate Clinton, then governor of Arkansas, along with his wife, Hillary Rodham Clinton, discussed allegations of his adultery before a television audience.[248] Clinton, in 1992, admitted to "causing pain in my marriage." But he also lodged a protest: "I think most Americans who are watching this tonight, they'll know what we're saying, they'll get it, and they'll feel that we have been more than candid. And I think what the press has to decide is, are we going to engage in a game of gotcha?"[249] Hillary Clinton added, "There isn't a person watching this who would feel comfortable sitting on this couch detailing everything that ever went on in their life or their marriage. And I think it's real dangerous in this country if we don't have some zone of privacy for everybody."[250] That same season, charged sexual claims would enter even into the business of the Supreme Court, roiling the nomination proceedings for Clarence Thomas, who was accused of sexual harassment by a former employee, Anita Hill.

Six years later, new Clinton allegations surfaced, from Lewinsky and others, leading not only to a sexual harassment suit but also impeachment hearings. The spectacle, not surprisingly, attracted unremitting attention. By one account, nearly 50 percent of the news stories aired on major networks in the early months of 1998 concerned Clinton and some aspect of the Lewinsky scandal.[251] Journalist Jim Lehrer would pronounce the trial that ensued that May "tabloid Nirvana."[252] Attracting almost as much coverage was the inquiry provoked by the scandal, the infamously extensive Starr Report, meticulously compiled by independent investigator Kenneth W. Starr. Left-leaning critics did not mince words in describing the report. Investigative journalist Renata Adler billed it "an utterly preposterous document," "a voluminous work of demented pornography," and "prurient gossip raised, for the first time, to the level of constitutional crisis."[253] Joan Didion in the *New York Review of Books* wrote in disbelief about an "attempt to take down the government" that was "based in its entirety on ten occasions of back-seat intimacy as detailed by an eager but unstable participant who appears to have memorialized the events on her hard drive."[254] Citizens may have been inured to the swirl of intimate matters in the public sphere, but not to this use of them.

If one could see past the thicket of salacious details, the key questions raised by the scandal turned on the meaning of "public" affairs, "private" behavior, and the proper relation between them. Conservatives like William Bennett berated President Clinton for the "seamless web of deceit" connecting his "private and public life," positing this link as the rationale for removing him from office. In doing so, they revealed their embrace of a thoroughly personalized politics. Liberals took aim instead at the conditions of Clinton's exposure, citing society's failure to clearly demarcate the difference between public and private issues.[255] The president may have crossed a line, they argued, but so had his inquisitors. Yet these positions were flexible, as Clarence Thomas's Supreme Court confirmation earlier in the decade—and the role reversal of partisan critics—had made painfully obvious.[256] What mattered was that private life had become a newly volatile, and seemingly permanent, ingredient in national politics.

Critical commentary about the Starr Report was not unlike that concerning the tell-all memoirs and talk shows that had become fixtures of late twentieth-century popular culture. *U.S. News and World Report* called the Starr Report "breathtaking" in its revelations, which included graphic accounts of blow jobs, masturbation, and phone sex; the *New York Times* noted that there was "no end" to the detail; the *Wall Street Journal* charged Starr with "stepping over the line" by including material that was "gratuitous and embarrassing to the president"; and *USA Today* simply asked of the investigator, "Have you no decency, sir?"[257] Others implied voyeurism in the report's "own limitless preoccupation with sexual material" and the press's doggedness in reporting it.[258] Noting that the FBI in the 1960s had secretly recorded and circulated the sexual transgressions of Martin Luther King Jr. in an attempt to discredit him, Renata Adler pointed out that public officials and the media in that instance had refused to circulate those reports. The difference in the 1990s with respect to such materials was that "the press welcomes, broadcasts, and dwells upon them; the House rushes to publish them, with the congressional imprimatur."[259] This was transparency—"the right to know"—with a vengeance.

The president himself was subject to conflicting interpretations. Some applauded his effort to preserve some privacy for himself and his office by admitting to inappropriate behavior while also calling the investigation—and especially the level of disclosure it sought—unseemly. "Even presidents have a private life" he maintained. "It is time to stop the pursuit of personal destruction and the prying into private lives and get on with our national life."[260] Pointing to his high poll numbers throughout the episode, supporters asserted that Clinton's claim to privacy resonated with citizens: that most Americans saw his affair as a private matter, not a public one.[261] Even as the media called for fuller confession and contrition, writes one scholar, "the public in general gave the impression that it had heard enough and wanted no more."[262] Others, however, found the president not forthcoming enough, his legalistic arguments unsatisfying to a populace accustomed to more lavish tales of sin and redemption.[263]

In the 1970s and beyond, a host of old proprieties slipped away as private material, not least sexual and familial relations, moved out into the open. Citizens worried about control over their personal financial, medical, and identifying data. They sought to limit their legibility to authorities. But they simultaneously released the floodgates on what could and even should be revealed in public life. Transparency's newfound cultural and commercial value—evident in second-wave feminism as well as documentary filmmaking, lawmakers' financial disclosures as well as gay liberationists' tactics—ushered legitimate forms of surveillance into election campaigns, popular entertainment, and social movements. The undoing of secrets would become the very substance of politics and self-making alike. In an era of new privacy rights, it turned out, many things would become less private, and more citizens would be watching.

8

Stories of One's Self

> Who knew that there were so many people with so many
> necessary things to say about themselves?
>
> —BROCK CLARKE, *An Arsonist's Guide to Writers' Homes*
> *in New England*, 2007

On the cusp of the twentieth century, Samuel Warren and Louis Brandeis
had hoped to rein in an aggressive media so as to sequester personal matters
and images from general view, except in that limited band of cases that
concerned "public men." This was the only way, they argued, to protect
the "inviolate personality" from newly intrusive forces in American society.
Many in the decades that followed made similar claims for the necessity
of privacy and of privacy rights in a democratic society. These claims
accompanied anxious discussions of identification systems and psychological testing, reproductive decision making and welfare administration,
electronic eavesdropping and computerized dossiers.

At the century's end, however, a reversal appeared to be at hand. Something that commentators began to call "confessional culture" seemed to
impel the very public airing of highly personal stories and what in another
day would have been tightly concealed secrets.[1] Unlike the forced disclosures of gay public figures or the calculated comments of politicians, these
were voluntary utterances, willingly offered up. They did not carry an obvious public message or political intent. These confessions, instead, spoke
to the heightened value of personal expression of all kinds. Americans, it
seems, were actively seeking out new venues for self-revelation. As they did,
shame in disclosing private matters seemed to tilt decisively toward shame
in concealing who one really was.

The rise of a much-decried "confessional culture" appears at first glance
like a fundamental discontinuity from the rights-oriented privacy talk of

the 1960s, with its emphasis on protecting citizens from the gaze of others. How was it that some individuals had come to relish the prospect of making their own lives, not to mention the lives of others, an open book? To a remarkable degree, privacy discussions by the 1990s concerned not just the intrusions of authorities into private life but also the extrusion of private matters into public places. The flip side of the relentless exposure of prominent figures—President Bill Clinton's sexual escapades the most sensational example—was ordinary citizens' own quest for publicity: their voluntary divulgences of matters ranging from child abuse to drug addiction in confessional talk shows, tell-all memoirs, and reality television. What if we have met the privacy invaders, some critics implored, and they are us?

So it was that at the end of the twentieth century, journalists, corporations, and state authorities were joined by yet another set of actors seeming to imperil Americans' privacy: willing exhibitionists, happy to dispense with the concept altogether as they foisted intimate details of their personal lives on strangers. Their unceasing urge to divulge provoked philosophers and social critics to issue dramatic pronouncements: that privacy was dead or dying or that "the destruction of privacy is the great collective project of our time."[2] The recent arrival of self-broadcasting genres such as blogging and social networking has only cemented the analysis. Some legal scholars would even pivot from devising ways to curb privacy intrusions to calling for laws that would restrain citizens from giving their privacy away. Arguing that privacy is both "so important and so neglected in contemporary life," Anita Allen for example envisioned "a rescue mission that includes enacting paternalistic privacy laws for the benefit of uneager beneficiaries." The state of public culture was such that there was perhaps a need and a place for "coercing privacy."[3]

What commentators often neglected to take into account was the broader context in which late twentieth-century Americans were moved to "confess," as well as the way new modes of disclosure grew out of a longer dialogue about privacy in the United States. Americans gleaned important lessons from this history, both the failure of political rights to protect individuals from exposure and the inevitability of classification by opaque bureaucratic operations. Especially critical was the simultaneous establishment of privacy rights and the recognition of their inadequacy in solving the problem of privacy in a "surveillance society."[4] Depending on how you looked at it, the democratic citizen was either being extended or dissolved by the technologically advanced, mass-mediated, and data-hungry world he or she inhabited. In a society that knew so much, where might "zones of privacy" or autonomy be found? The search for an answer pushed ideas about personal privacy in surprising directions. Whereas privacy had once been conceived as a retreat from public view, in some domains it was being rethought as a matter of very public self-definition.

Making Oneself Known

The confessional genre, whether in its religious or secular guise, was hardly new in the 1990s. Both St. Augustine at the turn of the fifth century and Jean-Jacques Rousseau in the eighteenth century penned what they called "Confessions." Confessional speech has long served in Western culture as a way for individuals to establish their "inner truth."[5] But when surveying that time-honored tradition in 2000, literary scholar Peter Brooks suggested that this method of laying the self bare "to know oneself and to make oneself known" had gotten seriously out of hand. "In a contemporary culture that celebrates the therapeutic value of getting it all out in public," he lamented, "confession has become nearly banal." Citing television talk shows in particular, full of "people speaking confessionally about their own lives in ways unthinkable to earlier generations," Brooks condemned "a generalized transparency, in which each of us is fully open to all others without dissimulation." That impulse was tyrannical, "a policing of the very privacy that selfhood requires."[6]

Brooks was not the only critic to bewail the way a discipline that had been part of Roman Catholic practice for centuries—a "secret transaction carried out in the closed space of the curtained and grilled confessional box" set apart from the "usual confines and censorships" of daily life—had become so very undisciplined.[7] A host of observers concluded in the 1990s that confession had come to define American public life. Volubility about one's faults and shames, to anyone who would listen, had become standard practice. Whether celebrated or lamented, the trend was clear: in all kinds of venues, people sought the sympathy (or attention) of others for acts that they had previously kept quiet. That American culture had gone "confessional" was so obvious that books on the topic did not even feel the need to prove the point.[8] Examples were not hard to come by. Televised talk shows, pioneered by Phil Donahue in 1967, took on a more spectacular form in the decades that followed, with guests spilling ever more painful and provocative stories.[9] Jerry Falwell's Moral Majority in the same period energized evangelical Christians to merge their political and religious activities, making narratives of weakness and salvation a regular feature of national politics.[10] Meanwhile, twelve-step groups such as Alcoholics Anonymous ushered personal testimonies into Americans' public vocabulary.[11]

The biggest domestic political story of the 1990s for many confirmed the trend. The Clinton impeachment was proof positive of a society bent on exposing secrets. But for some observers the imbroglio was less significant for how ruthlessly the scandal was investigated than for the manner in which the president and his accuser told their stories. In an age when public apologies for national sins had become commonplace, Bill Clinton and Monica Lewinsky alike seemed rather too ready to talk in a register of recovery and redemption.[12] The careful parsing of the president's multiple "confessions" by rhetoricians and reporters showed how finely tuned such public acts had become.[13] Some viewed the president, like the nation he led, as a product of a confessional culture pure and simple. "In Bill Clinton's America," wrote one scholar, "the intersection of Protestant practice, therapeutic technique, and talk-show ethos was complete."[14] Clinton "combined legal evasion with the repentant fervor of the sinner," argued another, while also "displaying signs that he wished to be treated as a recovering addict." Had the president "not been under the shadow of the perjury charge," this writer mused, "one suspects he would happily have appeared on a talk show to tell all, to seek consolation in the community of fellow-sinners."[15]

For critics, this kind of self-exposure was harmful in two distinct ways. First, unseemly disclosure of personal matters affronted individual sensibilities as well as public decency. One person's voluntary expression, that is, could be another's violation. Similar defenses of propriety and "community standards" had accompanied debates over privacy for at least a century. The question of the "unwilling audience" and a claim on something like a collective right to privacy had surfaced in outcries in the 1960s over sexually explicit materials sent through the mail, for example.[16] "Crossing a border to impose upon the person," privacy scholars would note, could be as much an infringement of privacy as was deliberate prying into one's affairs. Telephone and mail solicitations, neon signs, public nudity, loud music, or the sharing of inappropriate information were perhaps not first-order privacy intrusions.[17] But to be assaulted by others' excessive revelations—to be "constantly exposed to other people's life stories . . . their breakups, the health of their portfolios, their psychotherapeutic progress, their arguments with their bosses or boyfriends or parents," as one critic described American society in the age of the cell phone—could impinge on one's sense of solitude and peace of mind as surely as could a breach of one's personal space.[18]

The second and perhaps greater problem was what some going back to the 1960s called "self-invasions of privacy."[19] Individuals who revealed themselves too readily were thought to do themselves damage by failing to recognize the important distinction between personal and public life. In this analysis, the outflow of personal stories in the 1990s signified a character problem: a troubling borderlessness between intimate thoughts and deeds, on the one hand, and their recounting, on the other. To some, Americans' very capacity for inwardness and introspection—what Peter Brooks described as the "privacy that selfhood requires"—appeared in jeopardy.[20] Worry about citizens' willingness to cede their privacy was thus the uneasy companion to concern about intrusions by powerful authorities. Bewailing the confessional impulse in American life, some commentators wondered if citizens had ever cared about privacy to begin with.

Observers had in fact periodically fretted over Americans' tendency to disclose more than they ought, as well as to seek to know more than they should. That had been one response to the arrival of postcards in the 1870s, and their apparent lack of concern with who might have access to private communications. In more sustained form, the complaint accompanied the rise of tabloid journalism. Samuel Warren and Louis Brandeis spied dangers to privacy not merely in the intrusions of photographers and reporters but also in a coarsened and trivialized public sphere awash in citizens' peccadilloes and foibles. Believing that readers' "demand" for gossip was stimulated by the press, they sought to staunch its effects on public morality. Warren and Brandeis in 1890 targeted the media, but they sensed the lure of self-disclosure for the discloser and the audience alike.

The same recognition underlay the success of *True Story Magazine*, a publication created by physical culture enthusiast Bernarr Macfadden in 1919 that circulated the "authentic secrets" of ordinary Americans. A cornerstone of the emerging "confession industry," it was soon plagued by imitators.[21] Debates over how much revelation was too much—whether of one's body, biography, emotions, or secrets—were provoked not just by the press and publishers but also by new styles of public comportment at urban dance halls and other mass amusement sites of the early twentieth century, by the social uses of the telephone in the 1920s, by the vogue of psychoanalysis in the 1940s, by the emergence of confessional poetry in the Cold War era, and by the counterculture's embrace of more casual modes of self-expression in the 1970s.[22] Each of these developments in its turn seemed to threaten established conventions of propriety, violating the border between public and private affairs. The premium on personal disclosure in the twentieth century thus had deep roots. Why then, did American culture suddenly appear to "go confessional" only in its final decades?

A number of trends, some long in the making, conspired to make private matters newly prominent in public forums in the 1980s and 1990s. They were the work of both the political Left and Right and both religious and secular culture. The growing presence of evangelical Protestantism in the postwar United States was one important source. Whereas the modern Catholic tradition of confessing one's sins was an expressly private act, public testaments of conversion and religious revivals had been integral aspects of Protestant practice in America from the beginning.[23] In the twentieth century the confessional form, wherein individuals stood before a congregation to voice their transgressions, would gain a wider audience.

Radio ministry starting in the 1920s and its televised counterpart by the 1950s transmitted the practice of confession into American hearts and homes, and preachers with an extensive national following like Oral Roberts and Billy Graham popularized it. Graham's televised "crusades" to bring sinners redemption were major cultural events, with regular programming often canceled to cover them—drawing audiences rivaling those for other media spectacles such as Queen Elizabeth's coronation. After 1960, when federal restrictions on religious programming changed, "confession-oriented programming became the most visible, the most aggressive, the most familiar of all religious broadcasts." The practice of public testifying, Susan Wise Bauer notes, "moved from church to airwaves, and then, sideways, from sacred airwaves to secular programming."[24] During the 1980s, a surge of televangelists, led by figures like the husband-and-wife team of Jim and Tammy Faye Bakker, prodded guests "to reveal more and more about their private lives, their sins and shortcomings" in order to engage and hold their broad television audiences as much as to convert them.[25]

Secular confessions can be traced to the strength and spread of a therapeutic approach to personal problems that had expanded from its postwar purchase to infiltrate every cranny of U.S. culture. A new vocabulary of the self moved into political discourse in the second half of the twentieth century, such that mental fitness, authentic emotion, and self-interrogation all came to matter in public life.[26] Contemporary commentators pointed to the grip of Freudian theory, which held that discovering—and talking about—the hidden truths of one's personal history, especially of one's childhood, held the key to emotional well-being and psychic health.[27] The rapid growth in those seeking counseling in the postwar United States, therapists' emphasis on the hard work of self-knowledge, and radio's and television's amenability to the therapeutic mode all played a part in building a psychological society. What seemed most distinctive in its later twentieth-century manifestation was the way therapy seemed to flow outward, such that highly personal narratives of suffering and healing infused public culture.[28]

In the later 1970s, the most remarked-on instance of this impulse to "open up" was the emergence of group therapy and "human potential" or encounter groups, in which individuals loosened their inhibitions as part of their quest for personal transformation.[29] Openness and directness were the currency of this movement, which encouraged people to find self-acceptance by sharing their deepest struggles within a safe circle of others.[30] To doubters, the point was to "invite people to collaborate in their own exposure—and frequently their humiliation as well."[31] Much like television viewers' attachment to the Louds, a critic argued in the *Wall Street Journal*, such practices made evident that "the inner self is no longer sacrosanct and that the intimate lives of strangers constitute meaningful emotional experiences for those to whom they are revealed." Reporting from California's Esalen Institute, where people came "precisely for the purpose of making public their private selves, of disclosing to total strangers their covert fantasies, their angers, their delights," she believed that "this exercise in total undress" revealed that privacy had "become a negative value, the unmistakable opponent of the 'openness' that is here equated with the realization of human potential."[32]

As the 1970s gave way to the 1980s, the most popular site for such confessions, however, was surely the televised talk shows that were taking over the airwaves. TV hosts like Phil Donahue acted in the guise of counselors extracting secrets from television guests so as to banish those secrets' power over their holders. Beginning in 1986, the Chicago-based Oprah Winfrey fused the links among confessional discourse, television, and sales as did no other media personality, such that the televised talk show became identified first and foremost as a "vehicle of personal transformation."[33] Guests on the *Oprah Winfrey Show*, speculates one scholar, appeared on the program precisely "because of their belief in the curative potential of TV talk, in the form of public confession."[34] The host herself, who described the show as "a ministry," would eventually brand its distinctive blend of uplift, self-help, "inner revolution," and consumerism as "Change Your Life TV."[35]

The social movements of the 1960s and 1970s, themselves inflected by the psychological currents of the age, were yet another factor propelling personal stories into public fora.[36] The reorientation of politics around identity categories and toward questions of damage and status, theorists have speculated, shifted the way publics in postindustrial democracies operated.[37] In the new "life politics" of late modernity, truth-telling in the form of personal narratives was a means of critiquing what many saw as the crippling falsehoods of American society.[38] Confessing was understood as an act not solely of individual redemption but also of social politics and protest, most notably in feminist consciousness-raising groups. For this reason, privacy claims had—in both the women's and gay liberation movement—been subject to considerable suspicion. In some arenas, the claim looked like a cover for exploitation, rendering some voices and subjects unknowable.

By the 1990s, the longer-term consequences of these developments were becoming evident. The quest for authenticity in relationships and the post-1960s critique of authority were still palpable forces in American life, but they now often appeared decoupled from an explicit collective politics. For example, the once politically motivated "coming-out moment" for gay Americans served by the 1980s and 1990s a largely subjective purpose linked to "feelings of self-worth and self-fulfillment," notes historian Heather Murray. As one advisor on the practice urged in 1990, coming out was "the first step in liberating yourself to be a whole, complete, and powerful adult—the authority figure in your own life."[39] Emotional satisfaction and closure, forms of personal rather than social transformation, were the new rewards of revelation. Although some gay Americans, reflecting on their pre-Stonewall days, missed the sense of belonging to a hidden subculture, more and more seemed to feel the tug of confession, disclosing their true identities to friends and family members to foster genuine bonds.[40] As gay citizens made the transition from "secret to known, even formalized, selves," writes Murray, gay expressive culture became marked by autobiographical accountings and explanations. The personal was, above all, to be "named and talked about."[41]

Yet only the fact that personal disclosures still carried a political charge, and still held the power to disrupt, can fully explain what made "confession" both so resonant and so reviled in the late twentieth century. The ownership of one's story and the desire to tell it were often trivialized. But the amount of attention such narratives captured in American political culture suggests that the impulse to reveal oneself in talk, on television, in print, or online was not in fact trivial. When critics denounced a topsy-turvy world in which the most private of matters received the most public of vettings or argued that some of the most important privacy invasions of the age were self-inflicted, they implied a deficiency in both public culture and private life. What they responded to was nothing so simple as an urge to share. Confessional culture, 1990s style, had many taproots: the media forms and celebrity culture that made self-publicity so alluring, the critique of secrets that was transforming political culture, and the incitements to authenticity and redemption emanating in equal measure from the couch and congregation. But it found ground as well in Americans' sense that they lived, inescapably, in a society that knew too much about them already.

Bearing and Baring All

In 1974, the cameras having decamped, the controversy over *An American Family* subsiding, and the Louds moving on to life beyond the show, the family's matriarch published her autobiography. *Pat Loud: A Woman's Story* relied "entirely on the notoriety of the television show, and Pat Loud's subsequent celebrity, as its raison d'être."[42] The book is indeed only conceivable in the wake of the broadcast, Pat's story notable because her privacy had already been breached, her life already exposed. In its pages she mused wryly about the effects of that publicity: "Most people become famous for a reason. They develop a vaccine, or cross the ocean on a raft, or star in a movie, or embezzle a lot of money or . . . or . . . or. But we, the Louds, Pat, Bill, and our five kids, managed to get famous without doing a thing except giving our permission for PBS to follow us around with a camera for a while—to lend our lives for seven months to the making of *An American Family.* And it seems that if you're on TV, you're famous, and free game in a weird way, no matter what you're on TV *for.*"[43]

Pat Loud, along with the rest of her brood, had of course been roundly criticized for their part in exposing themselves. Relying on a set of psychological experts, *Time* magazine suggested that the Louds were "symptomatic of a cultural 'compulsion to confess'" and that parading their troubles in the mass media was just another species of therapy.[44] Likewise, a writer for the *New York Times* opined that the Louds were just like other, lesser-known people trying to "solve personal problems in public," flocking, for instance, to encounter groups in an attempt to fix what ailed them.[45] As Pat surely knew, her decision to surrender still more of her secrets in print would draw similar censure. But it was 1974, and she had already allowed her family to come apart on public television before millions. So, "since we're letting it all hang out" as she put it, Pat detailed—often with winning humor—her upbringing, her marriage in 1950, her love for her children but also her loneliness in being a housewife, her discovery of her husband's infidelity ("in '66 the whole thing blew up"), the course of Bill's affairs (and her own, offered without much elaboration, but the mere fact of them a bold admission), her resulting depression and sessions with a psychiatrist, her visits to lawyers to initiate divorce proceedings and then to halt them, and her postdivorce dating life.[46] In doing so, the woman who inadvertently became one of television's first reality stars placed herself on the leading edge of yet another cultural phenomenon.

Pat Loud's autobiography, even if it now seems rather chaste, is a recognizable contribution to a new breed of memoir—or, at least, a new emphasis within memoir writing on offering up one's most closely held secrets.[47] In the pages of *Pat Loud*, we can glimpse the lineaments of a genre that would overtake the publishing market in the final decade of the twentieth century.[48] Confessional memoirs—termed "redemption memoirs" by one critic, and "traumatic memoirs" by another—were crafted from the author's intimate pains and triumphs.[49] Culturally, they were of a piece with other forms of popular revelation, the talk show as well as the "coming out" moment. These highly personal narratives chronicled distress, damage, and abuse (sometimes self-inflicted) and typically also how such hardships were overcome.

The ascent of the confessional memoir told a bigger story too, shining a light on the peculiar status of privacy at the century's end. It arrived, after all, in a period when many citizens took for granted that they lived under the watchful eye of both state and society. Not just instant celebrities like Pat Loud but also ordinary Americans in the 1970s came to understand their lives as recorded for the benefit of strangers. Any number of agencies, known and unknown, gathered and housed pieces of their history in databases and files—whether to advance them credit and insurance, record educational achievement, or track health and retirement benefits. It cannot be a coincidence that some individuals began displaying their own lives very publicly in these same years. Meant not to pin down identity but to illuminate it, the confessional memoir was nevertheless bound up with these trends. Memoirists exposed themselves, but on their own terms. They put revelation in the service not of regulation but of self-realization.

The personal narratives that would soon fill publishing houses and bookstores stood apart from older forms of self-narration like diary keeping, usually meant for the author alone rather than an audience of strangers. They also differed from standard autobiography. Autobiographical writing is, one scholar writes, "always a gesture toward publicity, displaying before an impersonal public an individual's interpretation of experience."[50] Indeed, public figures, from the early American statesman and inventor Benjamin Franklin to the African American intellectual and leader of Tuskegee, Booker T. Washington, and from the blind teacher Helen Keller to the immigrant novelist Mary Antin, had in the past shared their histories in order to inspire and instruct. From the early nineteenth century on, publishing one's life story was a familiar genre for lesser-known narrators too, whose personal experiences generated curiosity and sometimes a profit in a thriving print culture; beggars, criminals, captives, soldiers, and fugitives all peddled their stories.[51] The slave narrative became a genre unto itself in the same era. There the telling of a life served larger political ends, mobilizing abolitionist sympathies and often—reversing the autobiographical tradition of famous men—propelling a hitherto unknown writer onto a public platform.[52]

Whether authored by little- or well-known Americans, these works stressed public actions and events and the biographical incidents, character traits, or personal aspirations that shaped them. They did not typically hinge on divulging intimate secrets. On the contrary, most steered clear of the author's "private" life. Frederick Douglass included only cursory discussions of his childhood in slavery before he set out into the public world. And even in a careful reading of *Up from Slavery* (1901), one could miss that Booker T. Washington was married three times and fathered three children. Late twentieth-century memoirs, by contrast, made such matters—and far more sensitive ones—their soul and substance. In the process, the very definition of what constituted a memoir shifted. The term, notes critic Ben Yagoda, had once been reserved for reminiscences about notable persons, with the author merely a character and observer. The new-style memoir was instead "resolutely focused on the self."[53]

In hers, Pat Loud recorded for public consumption aspects of her biography—love and sex, depression and counseling—to which not even her viewing audience had been privy. Once again, reviewers were not particularly kind. To some, Pat's life story appeared flimsy and potted, modeled on well-worn commercial formulas. The *Washington Post* called it "a composite of those flashy best-sellers the public buys in carload lots and the more cultivated reviewers regularly denounce as libels on American life."[54] Others spied more profound cultural developments at work. Robert Kirsch of the *Los Angeles Times*, although he judged Pat intelligent and articulate, read the autobiography as the product of an age in which "self-exposure" was the rage, with Americans confusing "the two-dimensional illusion for the three-dimensional reality." Putting her book in the company of contemporary phenomena such as nude streaking and theatrical politics, he described Pat as angry and hurt by her experience before the camera, yet "strangely elated by the instant celebrity." It was a hallmark of the times, Kirsch believed, that "seeing ourselves exposed is a way of establishing our identities."[55]

Pat Loud's memoir may indeed have been an act of identity making. She did not, however, frame her memoir in those terms. Pat made clear instead that a central reason for writing the book was to correct "the impressions the television camera left."[56] No longer the object of a film and at the mercy of a director's gaze, Pat leveraged celebrity in order to exercise some control over the story of her life. She also needed the money. Her divorce final and short on funds, Pat explained that she had broken her vow of "purity of motive" regarding the television series and was determined to capitalize in any way possible on her newfound—but she recognized, temporary—notoriety. "We are all unabashedly trying to get anything we can from the instant fame brought us by the series," Pat admitted. The family had even auctioned off "a weekend with the Louds" for the local public TV channel ("a nice-sounding couple who got us for $210 is coming to stay," she remarked).[57] The memoir was surely part of that campaign.[58]

Already, however, there were "fewer and fewer talk shows. It won't be long before they're saying, Pat who?"[59] This was less a lament—as her critics would have it—than a pragmatic reckoning about how much more she might eke out of her fame. In fact, as time passed, Pat became the most reticent of all the Louds regarding *An American Family*.[60] In 1982, she declined to talk about the series to a reporter, saying, "I just don't want any of that."[61] Even as she unburdened her sex life in the 1974 autobiography, Pat fantasized about regaining her privacy. Its final chapter charts her moving away from a town that knew too much about her to New York City, where "nobody knows anybody else" and "you have privacy, you can get lost in the crowds."[62] Pat Loud claimed, anyway, to want an "all private" existence, where *"nobody knows what we're doing."*[63] Her desire for privacy, and specifically for a place where she could be unknown, challenges easy assumptions about the inducements and aftereffects of a publicized life.

For all that, there was something undeniably transformative for Pat Loud in choosing to open up her own life and that of her family in the early 1970s. This much is evident in her brief musings on women's liberation in her memoir and even in its subtitle. Hers was, after all, "a woman's story," and the press coverage of the book focused on its most au courant aspects: "single motherhood, divorce, sexual liberation, and the women's movement."[64] Underwriting the late twentieth-century memoir was the legacy of feminism and its insight that personal harms were profoundly enmeshed in power relations—requiring painful excavation and publicity to exorcise. Although Pat claimed she felt "too old" to be part of the women's liberation movement, she grasped the affinities between her life and the cause. Sending tentative feelers out to the revolution in gender roles, she understood that letting loose her marital woes, treating them as neither shameful nor secret, entailed seeing them as something more than mere individual injury or failure. In this way, her autobiography—no matter the harsh reviews—partook of a broader turn to personal narrative as a route to analyzing one's own social formation. If this meant dispensing with old strictures regarding talking about personal matters, so be it.

In the 1970s, even Betty Ford didn't say all that was on her mind or reveal everything about herself. In a memoir published in 1978, *The Times of My Life*, she discussed topics ranging from her physical attraction to her husband to problems with her prosthetic breast.[65] The cultural proscriptions on talking about bodily, sexual, and medical matters were clearly loosening. But Ford made no reference to a facet of her biography that was for her still more private as well as shameful—her addiction to painkillers and alcohol—even though suspicions had been raised on this score during her time in the White House.[66] Only years later would she append a chapter dealing with her substance abuse. It was not until 1987, and the writing of a second memoir, titled *Betty: A Glad Awakening*, that she would tell this story in full.[67] In the meantime, the former First Lady had founded a treatment facility, the Betty Ford Center, and become the most visible spokesperson in the nation on the problems of substance abuse and addiction.[68] Reflecting on the evolving shape of her autobiography, she explained, "The first book was on the outside—about people, places, and things. This book came very much from the inside."[69]

In this decade-long journey from relating her "outer" story to resolving to tell her "inner" one, Ford traced a path that others would follow. By the late 1980s, others too were beginning to divulge the darkest, most painful details of their lives in print. The most thorough scholar of the memoir, Ben Yagoda, finds that up until the late 1960s, nearly all works in that category presented their subjects in a positive light. While a handful of personal narratives on mental illness and addiction did appear in the early postwar decades, they were almost always fictionalized or written under pseudonyms.[70] Sylvia Plath's novel *The Bell Jar* of 1963, published under the name of Victoria Lucas, was a case in point.

However, "like many other things . . . autobiography broke loose in the middle and late 1960s." A trickle of wrenching firsthand accounts, named and narrated as such, began to appear. African American memoirists were among the first to offer their searing personal histories to the reading public.[71] Dick Gregory and Malcolm X, Anne Moody and Maya Angelou, all mined the "trauma of their pasts" in order to bear witness to the harms of the American racial order.[72] Holocaust memoirists followed suit, offering testimony about and finding a reading audience for lives marked by tragedy and sometimes transcendence.[73] The floodgates then opened to a stream of memoirs by "minor celebrities" in the mid- to late 1970s. These typically focused less on social or political traumas than domestic ones.[74] The best known, Christina Crawford's *Mommie Dearest* (1978), offered a no-holds-barred portrait of the actress Joan Crawford from the perspective of her estranged daughter in the same year that Betty Ford published *The Times of My Life*.

Mining the damaging dramas of personal and family life would become the memoir's métier. Across the next decade or so, the genre would take on its distinctive contemporary shape. By the 1990s, the ranks of memoirists had increased far beyond the "minor celebrities" of the 1970s. And prior levels of frankness would be surpassed, with books pouring out on childhood abuse, mental illness, family dysfunction, sex addiction, physical disfigurement, grief, alcoholism, drug abuse, and incest.[75] Critics turned to William Styron's 1990 "unexpected best seller" and memoir of depression, *Darkness Visible*, as one origin point for what they labeled the "memoir boom."[76] In it, Styron, a successful author, divulged the self-loathing, anxiety, confusion, and dread that took hold of him suddenly at age 60. He explained his decision to write about his crippling depression as a desire to overcome public ignorance of the illness. "My need to communicate," he reflected, "overrode the risks of self-exposure."[77] While it is impossible to catalog all the other motives that led memoirists to dissect their own lives for the reading public, a quest for fame, visibility, and more book contracts surely played a large role, as critics suspected. But a therapeutic quest for "closure," an interest in unmasking power in family and sexual relationships, and—less noticed at the time—a desire to renarrate an already-told life were also recurring themes.

Changes in the commercial publishing industry were part of the explanation for the warm reception of such narratives. With television coverage one of the best ways to boost sales, the promotion of books was increasingly keyed to talk shows—themselves a leading factor in fostering a culture of self-revelation by placing "ordinary people and their problems in the spotlight."[78] Media scholar Joshua Gamson writes that the promotion of "the guest-who-is-expert-in-her-own-life" was "indebted to a talk show ideology and format in which emotional experience is the most respected reality" and in which "getting people to talk revealingly and personally" was the primary draw for the audience.[79] Indeed, the publishing industry rule-of-thumb was that the best way for a book to get noticed was through the hook of "a dramatic or unusual personal story." As one editor instructed *Vanity Fair* readers as to why memoir trumped fiction in the marketplace, "You can send the 'I' out on tour."[80] Early TV hosts like Phil Donahue, Sally Jessy Raphael, and Montel Williams, as surely as Oprah Winfrey's book club, were behind the flurry of memoirs by the 1990s. The commodification and salability of personal suffering—the evident financial, rather than simply psychological, rewards of unburdening—also account for some of the sharp criticism directed at the genre.

But a hunger for realness and authenticity in print drove the memoir boom as well. The new confessional narratives were much like documentaries in their piercing of facades and their search for raw truths.[81] They built on the new esteem for personal transparency. The cofounder of Random House estimated that when he entered the publishing business in the 1920s, fiction had outsold nonfiction by four to one. By the late twentieth century, he observed, "that ratio is absolutely reversed."[82] In 2000 a scholar supplied more evidence for the appeal of the real. "Although it is unclear whether the market has led or followed," she observed, "market demand currently encourages marketing practices such as subtitling an author's first book 'a memoir' when in previous years it might have been classified as fiction."[83] What was abundantly obvious was that many were finding their voices by confessing. "The triumph of memoir is now established fact," pronounced a critic in 1996, with even academics getting into the act by using personal pronouns in their scholarly writing and penning "*moi* criticism."[84] Americans had clearly, and volubly, plunged into "the Age of Memoir."[85] The 1990s would be both known and scorned as "the decade of revelation."[86]

In this era, writes Ben Yagoda, there was "none of the coyness or veiling strategies" that had marked earlier memoirists' treatment of their most private moments. Instead, "authors faced the camera straight on and told the truth—the more unsettling, shocking, or horrifying the truth, it sometimes seemed, the better."[87] Kathryn Harrison, author of *The Kiss*, a 1997 memoir about her four-year-long sexual relationship with her own father, perhaps pushed the form the furthest.[88] A writer for Amazon.com, noting that Americans now lived in a world awash in "ordinary citizens selling their personal traumas," nevertheless struggled to summon up a list of topics as shocking as the one Harrison had written about: "Mothers Who Sleep with Their Daughters' Boyfriends; Men Who Wear Their Girlfriends' Clothes; People Whose Families Have Been Murdered before Their Eyes." Clearly the culture had reached the point where "no subject is too salacious or too shameful for public consumption."[89] Responding to Harrison's memoir, *Entertainment Weekly* asked, "Just because a writer can speak the unspeakable, does that mean that she should?" This same writer reflected on how jolting the book's contents had been for reviewers, *The Washington Post* blasting *The Kiss* as "slimy, repellent, meretricious, cynical," and a critic for the *Wall Street Journal* resorting to a phrase of her grandmother's, urging the author to "hush up."[90]

Harrison responded to readers' and critics' revulsion with some surprise: "I expected some people to be angry with me," she wrote, "but I imagined their anger would be directed toward what I had done, not toward the choice to write about it." Borrowing a metaphor from the gay liberation movement, she acknowledged the fact that "I'm held up as one of the writers who have changed the complexion of memoir as a form—that my example has helped open the collective closet" and that "a lot of skeletons have been dragged out into the light." That act was welcomed by some readers but shunned by others. Of her harshest critics, Harrison later wrote, "I accepted their vehemence, because they mirrored my private responses to my history with my father. It frightened me and it made me angry. It disgusted me. It still does. It's supposed to. It's taboo."[91] But what Harrison's and other memoirs suggested was that the age of taboos was over, that there was nothing one could not broach in print.

This overstates the case, of course. There were limits to disclosure, even in an age of relentless confession. Women's persistent silence surrounding their own abortions, although a constitutionally protected right, was a case in point. Whether the decision to keep one's abortion "private" was an exercise of privacy was, however, not so clear. As legal scholar Carol Sanger argues, that choice had more to do with secrecy, which was motivated not by the "right or preference to keep something to one's self" but by "fear of the consequences of revelation."[92] Some topics, even in the 1990s, still carried enough stigma to keep them largely out of public conversation. And certainly, most Americans did not make it a practice to reveal their greatest shames to utter strangers. Yet it was still striking that what Victorians would have considered to be their deepest, darkest secrets were now the common currency not just of psychotherapy but also of politics and popular culture.

E. L. Godkin had sworn in response to the inquisitive census of 1890 that "no man, and especially no woman, likes to tell a stranger about a secret disease or disability."[93] Memoirists a century later were proving him wrong in spades. Writers like Harrison told strangers about far more than disease or disability. They played brilliantly to a public eager to peel away the layers of a person and to enter into another's inner life, perhaps especially if something scandalous was involved. And they benefited handsomely—in fame, dollars, book contracts, a place on the talk show circuit—from the bargain they made to dispense with some of their secrets. Detractors railed against the trend, art critic William Grimes protesting, "Is there not something to be said for the unexamined life?"[94] Invariably, they pegged it to the waning fortunes of privacy in American society. Blaming the recovery movement, a therapeutic culture, a "strong interest in victimhood," and, most worrisome of all, a shrinking "concern for privacy," commentators lamented that "what used to be private is becoming increasingly public."[95] Pronounced the *New York Times Magazine*, "We live in a time when the very notion of privacy, of a zone beyond the reach of public probing, has become an alien concept."[96] Many words were spilled in the attempt to understand why so many Americans were so freely baring their intimate lives. After all, these were typically not citizens who had been pressed to disclose their affairs by others—who had attracted the glare of the media, who were driven by political necessity, or who had been outed. Rather, they exposed themselves willingly and, critics suggested, indiscriminately.

Why was privacy, one of the most charismatic concepts of the postwar era, being disavowed with such abandon? In the debate over the tell-all memoir, few registered the ways that releasing personal details out into the stream of public culture could be a response to a sense of privacy already violated or diminished. Whether one was going to be known might be out of one's hands. For some confessional writers, however, telling one's story was perhaps the best means of controlling the *way* in which one would be known. Disclosure could be less about giving information away than about reining it back in—and publicness a path for reclaiming private life or at least one's own version of it. Confessional memoirists thus discarded privacy as traditionally understood even as they sometimes embraced the airing of one's life as its best protection. Was writing *The Kiss* a supremely exhibitionist act or the only way to banish private shame? It was not always possible to sort out whether a given memoir was an assertion of privacy or a rejection of it, a yearning to be surveilled or a flight from it. What does seem clear is that the confessional mode represented yet another episode in the story of how Americans have both fought to enlarge privacy and invade it—often at the very same time.

Correcting the Record, Controlling the Narrative

One of the most notable of the new crop of memoirs was, like William Styron's, a work on mental illness. Written by Susanna Kaysen about her eighteen-month psychiatric confinement at McLean Hospital for borderline personality disorder when a teenager in the late 1960s, *Girl, Interrupted* (1993) was a runaway bestseller.[97] It was also acknowledged by many critics to have "helped spark the memoir craze."[98] In its pages, using spare but eloquent prose, Kaysen offered an account of the daily rounds of mental illness. Of the young women on her ward, she observed, "In a strange way we were free. We'd reached the end of the line. We had nothing more to lose. Our privacy, our liberty, our dignity. All of this was gone and we were stripped down to the bare bones of our selves."[99] It was an apt description of the new memoir form too.

Compared regularly to Sylvia Plath's *The Bell Jar*—also set at McLean and trained on psychiatry and female adolescence—*Girl, Interrupted* was, however, a product of its own time. Plath had written under a pseudonym, careful to distance this difficult story from her public self. "The difference of three decades," noted one critic, "is that Susanna Kaysen leads off her book with a facsimile of the first page of her own case record folder at McLean Hospital."[100] Indeed, the very first things the reader learns about Kaysen are plucked directly from her confidential medical file: her name, her parents' names and address, her date of birth, and her diagnosis of "borderline personality." Rather than cloak such details, Kaysen fixed on them, interspersing her narrative with the administrative paperwork that recorded her experience of psychiatric confinement.[101]

In this respect, *Girl, Interrupted* bears some resemblance to *The File: A Personal History* (1997), another memoir of this era, by English journalist Timothy Garton Ash. Ash had conducted research in Berlin in the late 1970s and would later learn that he had been closely scrutinized by the East German secret police during his time there. The memoir was his attempt to reconstruct this two-decades-old history in dialogue with the Stasi's newly opened files. Ash compared the "subjective, allusive, emotional, self-description" of his own diary entries from that period with the "cold outward eye" of the Stasi's observation reports.[102] If less overtly, Kaysen's was also an account of studying others' surveillance of herself—nurses, doctors, psychiatrists, and orderlies—and placing their interpretations alongside her own to unsettle the reader's sense of whom to trust. Did the doctor who committed her to McLean while knowing so little about her do so after only twenty minutes (her recollection) or three hours (his documented account)? Should one rely on the *Diagnostic and Statistical Manual*'s characterization of "Borderline Personality Disorder," on which Kaysen spends a chapter, or the less technical and more engaging chapter that follows it, called "My Diagnosis," for one's understanding of the author?[103]

As such, Kaysen posed in stark terms the question of the known citizen and its consequences. Just how well did the doctor, the hospital staff, and

8.1. Emblematic of the new frankness of memoirs in the 1990s, Susanna Kaysen reprinted documents related to her psychiatric confinement at McLean Hospital.

the broader society that committed Kaysen to a psychiatric hospital know her? On what grounds, indeed, was authoritative knowledge of a person built? And what kind of power and responsibility came with the knowing? Kaysen's response was to offer a more intimate version of her history. Coming on the heels of the period in which Americans first contended with the "record prison," the shape of her memoir is noteworthy. Although it goes unmentioned in *Girl, Interrupted*, the author's father was the economist Carl Kaysen, who had headed the federal task force on the storage of government statistics during the National Data Center controversy of the mid-1960s. The Kaysen Report addressed public concerns about the warehousing of citizens' data, ultimately backing the proposal.[104] In 1993, Susanna Kaysen resurrected her own warehoused data in order to tell a story that was a quarter-century old. She did so, at least in part, to challenge the file.

Girl, Interrupted is littered with reproductions of documents from Kaysen's medical dossier. Her case record folder, admission form, medication and treatment chart, nurses' reports, progress notes, and discharge form—not to mention interoffice memoranda about her and letters from her doctor offering assessments that she is ready to rejoin the outside world—tell their own spare story. Their inclusion invites questions about others' categorizations and about the ways Kaysen herself was classified and filed: she titles one of her chapters "Stigmatography." Kaysen's closing words are a meditation on a Vermeer painting that haunts her, titled "Girl Interrupted at Her Music." She writes, "Interrupted at her music: as my life had been, interrupted in the music of being seventeen, as her life had been, snatched and fixed on canvas: one moment made to stand still and to stand for all the other moments, whatever they would be or might have been. What life can recover from that?"[105] Implying that she had been "fixed"—not by an artist, but by the judgments in her medical file—and never fully seen, Kaysen in her memoir refocused the reader on the life beneath the paperwork.[106] Disclosing the details of her institutionalization could be read less as a casting off of privacy than a reclaiming of those "snatched" months.

Indeed, Kaysen vigilantly sought to preserve her privacy after her memoir came out. As *Time* magazine reported, the fact that the memoirist wrote so openly about her struggles with mental illness made her a "cult figure," bringing her many letters, fans, and invitations to take part in public debates about, for example, antidepressants like Prozac.[107] It was not, Kaysen claimed, a welcome publicity. Rather, many readers, drawn in by the transparency of the author's prose, assumed a familiarity that made her uneasy. Kaysen objected to such overtures, saying, "I don't believe I have any obligation to let people into my private life." *Time* probed the seeming paradox: "as Kaysen becomes famous for writing a confessional book, it is her reticence that is most striking."[108]

In an interview years later, in response to a second memoir concerned largely with her sex life, Kaysen again attempted to draw a line between herself and the person who appeared in the pages of her books. That distinction confounded readers and critics alike. Kaysen wanted to have it both ways, they implied. The interviewer, insistent, asked, "Why did you withhold information about your family in *Girl, Interrupted* and why are you now unwilling to answer the natural follow-up questions about your current sexual functioning?" Kaysen replied, "People assume that if you're willing to say something about personal matters, you must say everything. You're a bad sport if you don't participate in total self-revelation." Although she included documents from a confidential file in her first memoir in part to signal her account's transparent truth, and although she divulged highly personal details, psychological as well as physical, with an arresting directness in the second, Kaysen rebuffed those who believed they were entitled to know her. These firsthand accounts were just as crafted and artificial as a novel, Kaysen asserted, not "a CAT scan of my emotional life."[109] Full disclosure had never been her interest or her point.

As many memoirists were coming to discover, however, their fans often demanded a more intimate relationship. Noting that "many readers feel they know me after they read one of my books," author Cheryl Strayed explained her need to set boundaries with audiences who took for granted that her "entire life is up for discussion."[110] People seemed to believe that "a memoirist has simply opened a vein and bled on the page," writer Ayelet Waldman protested. "The reader thinks they know all of you . . . but you don't owe your reader everything, every story of your life, every element of you. You owe your reader only what you want to reveal."[111] Critics of the memoir boom notwithstanding, these writers spoke to readers' desire for more particulars, not fewer. And, whether sincere or savvy about their reasons for withholding personal details from their fans, these authors also indicated that there were limits to what even a confessional writer would reveal. For her part, frustrated by her fans' persistence in wanting an unmediated view and personal access, Kaysen would later claim to have given up on the memoir as a genre.[112] Each of these public protestations about privacy from memoirists came on the heels of highly revealing accounts of their personal lives. The pattern underscored privacy's ambiguous allure—do we want it or don't we?—and perhaps even its commercial value. Would readers, one wonders, have been as interested in memoirists if they had truly revealed all, leaving nothing to the imagination, or to fill the pages of the next book?

Kaysen's second memoir would test the boundaries of public discourse. It would also probe the limits of privacy law. Was there any protection for the lives a memoirist dragged into the spotlight along with her own? This was one of the thorny issues raised by Kaysen's 2001 book, *The Camera My Mother Gave Me*, which was centrally concerned with ongoing, seemingly incurable vaginal pain and its effects on her sexual and emotional life. Critics classed it as "autopathography," a term coined to describe the raft of new autobiographical work homing in on individual illness, both physical and mental.[113] Like Kaysen's first memoir, the book stood out for its brutal honesty and transgressive subject matter. Less favorably reviewed, however—*Publishers' Weekly* billed it a "thin, disappointing chronicle of what happened when 'something went wrong' with her vagina"—some dismissed it, in a telling phrase of the period, as "TMI": too much information.[114] BookPage, for example, noted that Kaysen was "being criticized for taking autobiography to a new level of exposure with her personal confessions."[115]

It was the nature rather than the amount of that information that would trigger a legal challenge against Kaysen by her then-boyfriend. At the core of the lawsuit was the author's characterization of him as aggressively sexual, unsympathetic to her pain, and, in one episode that she recounted, physically coercive. The dramatic arc of the memoir would come in her soul searching as to whether his actions constituted sexual violence. Although the boyfriend was unnamed in the text and some identifying details had been changed (his occupation, his home town), it would have been obvious to any of their acquaintances—he charged—precisely to whom she referred. Under one of the torts that had grown out of Brandeis and Warren's call for a right to privacy, he sued for the "public disclosure of private facts."

Memoirs of this era were regularly portrayed as navel-gazing or unseemly. Kaysen's, however, led to questions about the impact of intimate revelations on others within the memoirist's circle—and, more distantly, about the consequences of true confessions in the public sphere. To what kind of privacy was a character in the life of a writer entitled? And what had happened to the right to protect one's reputation, one's "inviolate personality"? In *Bonome v. Kaysen* of 2004, the Massachusetts court agreed that the boyfriend (now publicly identified, as he had not been in the book, as Joseph Bonome) had a right to privacy and even a right to control the dissemination of private information about himself. Yet the court acknowledged that "it is often difficult, if not impossible, to separate one's intimate and personal experiences from the people with whom those experiences are shared."[116] The court went on to emphasize the public's legitimate interest in Kaysen's memoir, particularly its examination of how "a person's physical difficulties would affect her relationship with her boyfriend, including highly intimate aspects of it."[117] Most importantly, however, Kaysen's right to "publicity" and "to disclose her own intimate affairs" was protected by the First Amendment. The court concluded that "Kaysen's own personal story—insofar as it relates to matters of legitimate public concern—is hers to contribute to public discourse."[118] As one legal analyst described it, any other ruling would unfairly restrict an individual's "ability to describe his or her own life."[119]

In 2004, the law, like the media and the culture at large, seemed to line up on the side of self-publicity rather than privacy.[120] It was an illuminating commentary on the dramatic changes in public discourse since Warren and Brandeis's time. As legal scholars have demonstrated, the "right to privacy" that the Boston lawyers envisioned in 1890 was treated increasingly in the twentieth century by courts as a frail claim against First Amendment rights. The privacy torts their essay triggered largely failed to shelter individuals from unwanted publicity, amounting to "a jurisprudential dead end."[121] The evolution of free speech jurisprudence, shifting notions of decency, and increasing deference to the press as to what counted as "newsworthy" had all made claims of emotional damage of the sort Warren and Brandeis laid out very difficult to sustain.[122] As the most recent edition of the *Handbook of the Law of Torts* summarizes, "The law is not for the protection of the hypersensitive, and all of us must, to some extent, lead lives exposed to the public gaze."[123]

Exemplifying the strong U.S. tilt toward freedom of speech (including commercial speech), press, and expression as compared to Europe, *Bonome v. Kaysen* revealed "a road not taken in American privacy law—that of a right to personality."[124] It pointed to the failure of Warren and Brandeis's concept of an "inviolate personality" to gain any real traction in U.S. society and law.[125] Or perhaps it revealed a legal as well as cultural preference for the confessing rather than the reticent personality. For some, the prioritizing of individual self-expression over the texture of public discourse was the wrong turn that privacy law had taken as far back as the late nineteenth century, its effects on American life painfully apparent in the no-holds-barred quality of public talk at end of the twentieth.[126] At the very least it implied that the conflict between the freedom of speech and the right to one's "personality"—the right to express oneself and the right to be known in a particular way—had no easy resolution.

The issues in the Kaysen-Bonome dispute were unusual in being adjudicated by courts. Similar standoffs had been fought in the pages of literary magazines, newspapers, and the court of public opinion, leading to a searching debate in the 1990s over the consequences of unrestrained self-expression. Biographers, autobiographers, and even historians would be implicated in controversies over improper disclosure.[127] These were pitched struggles for "control over the story of a life" by subjects, authors, and estates, each with their own position on which contents of a life ought to be shared and which sealed.[128] Although the privacy of famous figures, living and dead—and how specific revelations would affect their reputation—was often the primary consideration, broader cultural sensibilities about the boundaries of propriety entered the discussion too.

One of these disputes surfaced right at the beginning of the decade. Fittingly, it concerned the "confessional" poet Anne Sexton, known for writing about matters "many people thought should be kept entirely private" in the early 1960s, including mental illness, abortion, and addiction.[129] Her life was the material for Diane Wood Middlebrook's *Anne Sexton: A Biography*, published in 1991.[130] There was in this case no unwilling subject, no "unconfessional confessionalist," as Susanna Kaysen had been tagged for her stubborn refusal to elaborate on what appeared between the covers of her memoirs. Sexton, who committed suicide in 1974, had left exhaustive files and clear permission for a biographer to use them. Her daughter Linda, executor of her will, was happy to hand over those materials to Middlebrook, whom she had selected as her mother's biographer. But the volume stirred up a storm nonetheless for making use of more than 300 hours of tape-recorded psychotherapy sessions between Sexton and her psychiatrists. The controversy rested on the special status of medical records, even those of the dead. These sorts of documents were holdouts in a tell-all age. Linda Sexton had, however, consented to their use, declaring, "My mother had no sense of privacy, and I don't believe it's my place to construct one on her behalf." The Sexton estate had moreover agreed to the arrangement and even planned for the tapes' deposit in a research archive. Even so, the American Psychiatric Association filed a formal ethics complaint against the psychiatrist who had consented to publication. Only several years after the biography was issued would he be exonerated.[131] All along the way, Middlebrook and Linda Sexton affirmed that the poet herself had intended that the psychotherapy sessions be part of her life's record.

Whose life was it anyway? Critic Janet Malcolm dissected the dilemma of who owned an individual's story in her 1994 book *The Silent Woman*, a meditation on the ways multiple biographers had impinged on the lives of the poets Ted Hughes and Sylvia Plath (Sexton's contemporaries and the subjects of a later biography by Middlebrook).[132] Hughes, who kept his own counsel about his famous, estranged wife after her suicide at age 30, had been lacerated by various Plath chroniclers in what Malcolm called "punishment by biography." In a voluble world, Hughes's reticence, as he well understood, was itself suspect. Thus, Malcolm wrote, it was "Hughes's bitter fate to be perpetually struggling with Plath over the ownership of his life, trying to wrest it back from her."[133]

Casting the biographer as a "professional burglar," Malcolm set out to expose the voyeurism at the genre's core, which she likened to reading someone else's mail. But she also made clear that such prurient curiosity was abetted by the machinery of a knowing society. Hughes had at one point, in frustration, written, "I hope each of us owns the facts of her or his own life." Malcolm strongly, if regretfully, dissented. "Of course," she wrote, "as everyone knows who has ever heard a piece of gossip, we do not 'own' the facts of our lives at all. This ownership passes out of our hands at birth, at the moment we are first observed." In her view, "The organs of publicity that have proliferated in our time" were just an instance of "society's fundamental and incorrigible nosiness." Indeed, claimed Malcolm, "Our business is everybody's business, should anybody wish to make it so. The concept of privacy is a sort of screen to hide the fact that almost none is possible in a social universe."[134]

Malcolm furthered her point by recounting the tale of Sylvia Plath's first biographer, who published an account of the poet's life in 1976 without the benefit of any access to her family and friends, archival materials, or published letters and journals.[135] How could this be? "Facts as such are relatively easy to come by in a society whose growing complexity has spawned a growing network of official institutions," Malcolm explained. Schools, libraries, newspapers, government offices—all "were there for the plundering, as every credit house and FBI investigator well knows." This made it relatively easy for the would-be biographer to "construct a reasonable collage from the bits and pieces resurrected from these bureaucratic mausoleums." Malcolm went on to observe that this first biography of the poet bore a "striking resemblance" to the many later ones, despite their reliance on a more intimate trove of materials, including Plath's own published letters and journals. "The traces we leave of ourselves are evidently so deep that every investigator will stumble upon them," she mused. "If the door to one room of secrets is closed, others are open and beckoning."[136] The record prison, it turned out, was a goldmine for the diligent biographer. As Susanna Kaysen had discovered too in dredging up her adolescent medical file, a documented life was easy to find.

The biographer's ability to ferret out facts even about subjects who defied being known was most impressive in the case of novelist J. D. Salinger, the famous—and famously reclusive—author of *The Catcher in the Rye* (1956). Plagued by fans, photographers, the press, and those who wished to tell his life story, Salinger attempted to deter them all by retreating to his home in Cornish, New Hampshire, and steadfastly refusing public engagement. Salinger, who was said to have "elevated privacy to an art form," would nevertheless be the subject of four separate book-length exposés in the late 1980s and 1990s, with two more following shortly after his death in 2010.[137] His resistance to confession was in fact part of what made him so captivating to biographers and the reading public both.

One of the more persistent intruders was British writer Ian Hamilton, who embarked on a biography of Salinger in the 1980s. The angle Hamilton took, however, was a postmodern one: the challenge of a quarry who didn't want to be caught, a subject who resisted the biographer's entreaties. As such, Hamilton aimed to make himself rather than Salinger the central character in the book. But the premise did not pan out. Janet Malcolm recounts, "As Hamilton pursued his researches into Salinger's childhood and youth, his own role as comically thwarted biographer was pulled out from under him." Indeed, "far from being thwarted, he was amassing a great deal of information about his subject." Salinger, though he had been in seclusion for more than twenty-five years, "had lived in the world until the mid-sixties, and had left the usual traces."[138] These included many private letters that had wound up in archives. Eventually the biographer and his subject would come to a head over these documents in a court of law. Salinger sued for the rights to his unpublished correspondence and won, barring Hamilton from using the letters.[139] The biographer's ill-starred project delayed, he would finally publish a much diluted and quite different version of his book in 1988.[140]

Salinger was the victor in that particular case, although ironies abounded: he had to publicly testify and also file his private letters at the Library of Congress.[141] But knottier issues surfaced when his intimates— an ex-lover and his own daughter—sought to write about him as part of their own life stories. Joyce Maynard, a woman who had been romantically involved with the much-older Salinger when she was a teenager, and Margaret (Peggy) Salinger, now a middle-aged woman with a family of her own, wrote not as biographers, but as memoirists. For both writers, the author's privacy was a cloak for ugly secrets, whether Salinger's exploitative relationships with young women or his emotional abandonment of his family. Each described a need to tell her own story, in which Salinger just happened to play a pivotal role. These were "autobiographies of women whose lives were damaged by him," writes a literary scholar, and which "narrate the harm that Salinger's obsession with privacy caused for the women who participated in his private life."[142] Maynard, for example, recounted an episode in which Salinger turned on her for purportedly allowing his phone number to fall into the hands of a *Time* magazine reporter, telling her that the book she was writing "could be the end of us."[143] Peggy Salinger related that before taking an overdose of pills as an adult, which she knew would send her to the emergency room, she verified that the hospital would not be able to identify her as Salinger's daughter.[144] Both memoirists made the point that striving to keep something private could be as harmful as disclosing something secret.

In terms of content, these memoirs were hardly unusual fare in the 1990s. But their authors faced severe criticism for raiding Salinger's carefully curated solitude.[145] Maynard's *At Home in the World* (1998) came in for special rebuke, especially in connection with the author's decision to sell Salinger's letters.[146] As a writer for the *New York Times Magazine* summarized, "For years, Maynard refused to discuss this affair. In doing so now, she is violating the privacy of a figure who is revered in a very personal way by a great many people, both for his writing and for his decision to retreat into the silence that Maynard is breaking. She will be—indeed she already has been—called shameless and mercenary. Maynard knows this, of course."[147] Indeed, "knowing this" was part of her shame. Her lack of consideration for J. D. Salinger's reputation, but also for her own in violating his, was a key feature of the criticism that rained down in the wake of her memoir. Maynard was a well-known figure even before the Salinger controversy, a standard-bearer for what some saw as excessively self-regarding and intimate essays. The same *New York Times Magazine* article displayed this animus, taking the writer to task by introducing readers to her fans—those Maynard referred to as her "website community"—who, it was reported, followed her every move on her highly personal web log, one calling Maynard "the literary equivalent of 'The Truman Show' or Princess Diana."[148] Such details, a kind of 1990s shorthand for overexposure, cemented the case of the memoirist as exhibitionist.[149]

The controversy over Salinger's "outing" laid bare what had been barely hidden to begin with: the gendered nature of the memoir boom. Many of the path-breaking contributions to the genre had been authored by men, including Frank McCourt, who wrote about his impoverished childhood in Ireland in *Angela's Ashes* (1986); Tobias Wolff, who recounted his life with a hostile stepfather in *This Boy's Life* (1989); and Dave Peltzer, who narrated a harrowing story of childhood physical and emotional abuse in *A Child Called "It"* (1995).[150] Despite acclaim for these works, the highly personal nature, domestic settings, and emotion-laden thrust of most of the era's memoirs ensured that the genre was readily feminized.

Women confessors—memoirists like Pat Loud, Susanna Kaysen, and Joyce Maynard, but also public disclosers of others' sins in the 1990s, like Anita Hill and Monica Lewinsky—were often the vessels for the new explicitness about matters sexual and traumatic in public life.[151] They were also routinely blamed for debasing both the private and public sphere and scorned for their lavish regard for their own small lives. For Joyce Maynard and Peggy Salinger, the implicit, and sometimes explicit, comparison was to the larger-than-life man they dishonored. While for instance Jonathan Yardley of the *Washington Post* called Hamilton's biography of J. D. Salinger "decidedly unauthorized," he branded Maynard's and Peggy Salinger's memoirs "self-serving."[152] The latter was "an unattractive and unwelcome book . . . almost indescribably self-indulgent, and it invades the author's father's cherished privacy to the point of disloyalty and exploitation." It was, he summarized, "a blow beneath the belt."[153] Maynard came in for even more stinging reviews.[154] Yardley wrote of her memoir that "you may . . . find yourself struggling to comprehend self-infatuation so vast and reckless that the victim cannot imagine a detail of her life so minute or trivial as to be of no interest to everyone else on this planet." A former Yale classmate of Maynard's wrote that she suffered from "a delusion torn from the Oliver Sacks casebook: The Woman Who Mistook Herself for Someone Interesting."[155]

Against this account of the disrobing of a "private man" in the service of self-promotion, however, was another story concerning feminism's transformation of the meaning of the private and, along with it, the power of intimate revelation. Peggy Salinger described her "sacrilegious" decision to break the silence about her father and "generations of moldy secrets, both real and imagined," as akin to allowing "some light and fresh air" into her life.[156] "I have come to believe that my greatest protection comes in self-disclosure," was how Joyce Maynard defended her own decision, characterizing it as a holding-to-account of a powerful man, as well as an act of self-liberation. As she put it, "It's shame, not exposure, that I can't endure."[157] Another woman in Salinger's life, Jean Miller, applauded Maynard's work: "She was very courageous in breaking the code that we all had, not verbally but emotionally, signed onto: don't talk."[158]

In tune with other memoirists, especially those who sought to publicize exploitation—whether by parents, partners, or priests—Maynard defended "a woman's right to her own story" because, she said, "the most powerful tool most of us possess is our own voice."[159] Maynard, moreover, understood the attacks and trivialization she faced in doing so as a matter of gender politics. "One day I hope some feminist scholar will examine the way in which a woman's recounting of her history is so often ridiculed as self-absorbed and fundamentally unimportant," she charged. "One need not look far for examples of male writers who have written freely and with no small measure of self-absorption about the territory of personal experience, who are praised for their courage and searing honesty."[160] Maynard herself countered her detractors with "letter after letter" from readers who found solace in her story, given their own experiences of family alcoholism, exploitative relationships, and unrealistic standards. Among those letters, she noted, in a gesture to sisterhood, were those "I received from two other women who had also engaged in correspondences with J. D. Salinger eerily like my own." Maynard's reflections turned the tables on those who viewed privacy as "sacred" and her own spilling of secrets as "a profound betrayal of trust." Although "the pursuit of privacy has been portrayed by many as evidence of purity of character," she contended, it was just as often a shield for behavior that was much more fundamentally "inappropriate and invasive" than was her own.[161] Privacy, so often figured as a social good, was here billed as a conspirator against the weak and vulnerable. Confession might offer a surer path to possession of one's story or one's life.

It was no accident that famous men who shunned publicity became culture heroes in these same years—Salinger, of course, but also the novelists Don DeLillo and Thomas Pynchon. Unlike the Pat Louds and Joyce Maynards who seemed to thrive on the attention that came from public fixation on their stories, these men did not spill their secrets and seemingly required no such confirmation from an audience. In a tell-all culture, many admired them for bucking the trend. DeLillo in fact made this a running theme of his work. His *Great Jones Street*, as early as 1973, revolved around a rock star "who tries to step out of his legend"; the hero, one scholar notes, earns the admiration of "a cultish group" for whom privacy becomes "a revolutionary wish."[162] Inspired by a photograph of J. D. Salinger that appeared in the *New York Post* in 1988, DeLillo placed a reclusive writer at the center of his novel *Mao II* (1991).[163] As the novelist grasped, obsessive interest attaching to the recluse made those who opted out of publicity the most fascinating of public figures. Jonathan Yardley remarked in the *Washington Post* in 2004 that he had "largely forgotten" about *Catcher in the Rye* (which he judged overrated) since its publication a half-century earlier. But he could not say the same for Salinger, "whose celebrated reclusiveness has had the effect of keeping him in the public eye."[164]

Yardley contrasted Salinger's thin publishing output with the outpouring of writing about him. "Whether calculated or not," mused Yardley, "his reclusiveness has created an aura that heightens, rather than diminishes, the mystique" of his literary production.[165] As the question of calculation here suggests, even Salinger, the most private of writers, was shaped fundamentally by a culture of disclosure. This was not simply because others relentlessly sought to expose him, although that they certainly did. The most recent Salinger biography to date—a compilation of ephemera, photographs, and remembrances about the author—pledges that it finally answers the mysteries of the man's life: why he stopped publishing, why he disappeared, and what he wrote during those reclusive years. It also promises, via nine years of research on five continents and more than 200 interviews by which the authors "disclose, track, and connect" the pieces of Salinger's life, to "place the reader on increasingly intimate terms with an author who had been adamantly inaccessible for more than half a century."[166] One conclusion of all this digging echoes a uniquely damning revelation in Maynard's memoir: that Salinger obsessively followed his own press. "Far from being a recluse," these chroniclers observe, Salinger "was constantly in conversation with the world in order to reinforce its notion of his reclusion."[167] The author "ferociously monitored every blip on the radar screen and cared hugely about his reputation," refusing to speak to reporters only until "the press had forgotten about him for too long." What appeared important to Salinger, in an environment in which it was impossible truly to withdraw from the world—a truth his biographers inadvertently demonstrate—was that "he controlled the communication, the narrative."[168] Despite the apparent gulf between them, Salinger and his former lover Maynard may have shared this particular definition of privacy.

Controlling the narrative may have been the most that citizens could hope for by the end of the twentieth century, given that their lives were co-owned by so many others. Much as the Louds had aspired to be their own producers, memoirists seized the opportunity to shape and edit their lives for a broader audience. As a media scholar put it, "Representation in the mediated 'reality' of our mass culture is in itself power."[169] Sociologist Joshua Gamson has made a similar case for the rise of "trash" talk shows in the 1990s and their particular appeal for those of nonconforming sexualities: "While you might get a few minutes on national news every once in a while, or a spot on a sitcom looking normal as can be, almost everywhere else . . . you are either unwelcome, written by somebody else, or heavily edited." On the other hand, "on television talk shows, you are more than welcome. You are begged and coached and asked to tell, tell, tell." Gamson sees what are, in one light, exploitative spectacles as subversive vehicles for "moving private stuff into a public spotlight, arousing all sorts of questions about what the public sphere can, does, and should look like."[170] The airing of intimate matters, in this view, might nurture a more hospitable public culture for privacy, understood as personal self-determination.

Easily caricatured and dismissed, the confessional memoir of the 1990s—still alive and well today—was not simply an exercise in narcissism nor an evacuation of privacy.[171] Some memoirists wrote to puncture others' secrets or to unburden their own, carrying on the legacy of feminism and other social movements that had transformed the rules of public discourse beginning in the late 1960s. Others sought to take the reins of their own narrative. Pat Loud and Susanna Kaysen each wrote not only in order to add to but also to counter the information about them already out there in the world, whether in the form of a television camera or the quieter but still weighty judgment of a medical file. In their memoirs, we recognize a desire to be truly seen. We can also glimpse the effects of the multiple forms of surveillance that had taken root in American culture by the time they wrote, continuous media coverage as well as the running bureaucratic record. That those who attracted the most condemnation for their revelations were women spoke to the fact that, by the 1980s and 1990s, it was no longer just "public men" who were engaged in tending their public reputations or personas. Citizens of all stripes had a vested interest in the ways they broadcast their lives to the larger society, as well as new tools to put to the task. Battles over the memoir, pitting private citizens against one another, gave vivid testament to the fragmenting of an official consensus about privacy in the latter half of the twentieth century, an era in which the boundaries of propriety had been exposed as having a politics all their own.[172]

At the century's end, the combination of new vehicles for telling all, the imperatives of authenticity, and every individual's steadily accumulating record meant that achieving some semblance of privacy—or control over one's narrative—could entail talking rather than hiding, divulging rather than seeking solitude. That doing so could place one in a community of disclosing others meant that the confessional turn was never as solipsistic as critics imagined, just as a mania for privacy could prove narcissistic and public facing.[173] What the talk shows, the memoir boom, and a thoroughly personalized public sphere indicated was that the old terms for thinking about privacy, laid down in the nineteenth century, were being sloughed off for new ones.

Publicists of Their Own Lives

The memoir boom showed no sign of retreat in the twenty-first century.[174] Between 2004 and 2008 alone, sales of those books categorized as Personal Memoirs, Childhood Memoirs, and Parental Memoirs increased more than 400 percent.[175] Memoir, a critic argues, had become "not only the way stories are told, but the way arguments are put forth, products and properties marketed, ideas floated, acts justified, reputations constructed or salvaged."[176] The proliferation of memoir-writing guides and websites (such as one "dedicated to delivering the message that Everyone has a story to tell and telling those stories!") and the spate of false or faked memoirs in recent years are indicative of the memoir's pride of place in American popular culture.[177] Those who write and teach about memoirs are often rueful regarding the genre's status: one dedicates her book to "those who read memoirs and those who write memoirs," as well as "those who wish we wouldn't."[178] But they do not doubt its relevance or staying power. As one of them puts it, "Memoir is, for better and often for worse, the genre of our times."[179]

Debate over the implications of the tell-all mode continues apace. Looking askance at the phenomenon in 2010, one writer believed that it fed off a "dramatic confusion . . . between private and public life."[180] Defenders of the genre instead described writing about oneself as the most authentic sort of examination available to contemporary citizens. David Shields, an essayist—and a biographer of J. D. Salinger—had started out as a fiction writer. But he found himself increasingly "bored by out-and-out fabrication, by himself and others; bored by invented plots and invented characters." Compared to exploring one's own life, "everything else seems like so much gimmickry."[181] He hoped these narratives "(autobiography, confession, memoir, embarrassment, *whatever*) can perhaps produce something that is . . . 'truer,' more 'real.'"[182] A teacher of memoir criticizes the critics who treat memoir writing as "nothing more than a New Age Excrescence, a latest fad, the apotheosis of a self-as-victim movement sponsored in equal parts by therapists, confession gurus, and scandalmongers eager to cash in on the bottomless societal appetite for self-exposing disclosure."[183] He argues instead that at its best the memoir responds to the Socratic injunction to "Know thyself." Faithful self-knowledge is its true product, a "necessary wisdom" that cannot be found in any other way. The pressure on individuals to make sense of personal experience "is as intense as it has ever been," he writes, and the need for exemplars that light the way "if anything, growing."[184]

This argument over what truly motivated contemporary confessions— was it self-discovery or was it self-exploitation?—raged on even as disclosures on the page were joined by those online.[185] Structural changes in the very nature of communications at the turn of the twenty-first century, heralded by the arrival of "Web 2.0," both tapped into the confessional impulse and renewed debate about it. The social media platforms of the early 2000s were perhaps as significant as the telegraph cables and phone lines of Warren and Brandeis's day. And they resulted from a similar partnership of technology and commerce. Affinities between the new memoirists and the "new media" would be immediately apparent. Social networking, video sharing, blogging, and microblogging (that is, status updates and tweets) did not simply permit their users to "create and share their own content."[186] They practically incited them to do so, calling on users to offer a steady stream of opinions, stories, reviews, likes, and dislikes, preferably eliciting others' interest in the process. To be "invisible" on social media—meaning "to post content without others noting it in some way"—was to have fundamentally botched the project.[187]

As technology scholar danah boyd makes clear, what was novel about this networked mode was precisely its encouragement to share and spread information. Personal communications, as a consequence, were more visible and accessible than ever before. Wiretapping and "listening in" had been products of a society that presumed most exchanges of information to be privileged or at least hard to get at. In stunning fashion, new media platforms inverted this "private-by-default, public-through-effort formula." This was evident in social media companies' public ethos of "sharing," underwritten by their interest in the profits to be made from consumers' data. It was also part of their hidden architecture, which ensured that privacy settings were difficult to manipulate.[188] The new code—technical and cultural both—supported publicity rather than privacy.

If new confessionals upended traditional autobiography and even traditional memoir writing, the web log (or blog) reinvented and recharged the diary for the Internet age. New formats for circulating one's story proliferated, spurred on by the ease of projecting one's life into cyberspace and the lure of winning untold readers and fans. Whatever one's stance on this "global autobiography project," there was no gainsaying its appeal.[189] By 2006 there were 27.2 million web logs in existence, with the number of new blogs doubling every five months or 75,000 new blogs being created a day.[190] Five years later, a Nielsen survey put the number of blogs around the world at 181 million, with three of the ten largest social networking sites—Blogger, WordPress, and Tumblr—housed in the United States.[191] This "unprecedented movement of modern autobiographical speakers" was explained as the confluence of digital diarists' "relaxed view of personal privacy, the desire to share their stories publicly, and the technological access to reach a widespread audience."[192] Others characterized the trend less charitably: "Kids today. They have no sense of shame. They have no sense of privacy. They are show-offs, fame whores, pornographic little loons who post their diaries, their phone numbers, their stupid poetry—for God's sake, their dirty photos!—online."[193]

The pivot to "kids today" was not incidental to the discussion. While the memoir was often the province of the middle-aged or older—a medium for those who had lived enough of a life to reflect on at length—web-based formats were initially the territory of the young. Fear and fascination about new modes of self-broadcasting centered on adolescents who appeared to have no understanding of, or placed no value on, personal privacy. A *New Yorker* cartoon from 2010 pictured a mother sitting in her attic thumbing through an old diary; her daughter asks: "What was the point of writing a blog that nobody else could read?"[194]

Some saw teens as harbingers of networked sociability, their inner selves firmly beamed outward toward a host of friends and followers. Others portrayed them as the society's true realists, the "only ones for whom it seems to have sunk in that the idea of a truly private life is already an illusion" in a world of not just known but surveilled citizens.[195] The most popular refrain by far, however, was that the young pioneers of social media were on a mission to do away with personal privacy. This was true even as scholars dismantled the assumption that teenagers were any more interested in baring themselves to the world than was anyone else.[196] In this analysis, social media was simply the latest stage for struggles over "private space and personal expression" that adolescents had waged before in their diaries and suburban bedrooms.[197] Indeed, it was yet another site where teenagers sought to evade the most irritating privacy intruders of all: their parents, who often insisted on monitoring teens' social media use. Privacy, concluded one study, was something that youth "are actively and continuously trying to achieve in spite of structural or social barriers that make it difficult to do so."[198]

The publicness of social media presented opportunities for young and old alike: the ability to keep track of a wide range of acquaintances, and its converse, a much-expanded potential audience for one's own daily life. It for the same reasons introduced new privacy problems. As two scholars of surveillance would summarize the state of things, particularly in light of the rise of powerful data aggregators, "If you figure that your life is so disorganized, private, and fragmented that no biographer would or could keep track of it, think again."[199] Managing what about oneself

*"What was the point of writing a blog
that nobody else could read?"*

8.2. Blogs and other social media provoked much consternation about changing privacy norms in the early twenty-first century.

should and should not be made available to others suddenly became fraught with complexity. Social media users in response devised creative strategies to control the flow of their data. One of the most interesting of these, as documented in an ethnography of teenagers conducted by danah boyd, was sharing information in order to maintain one's privacy. "In a world in which posting updates is common, purposeful, and performative," she writes, "sharing often allows teens to control a social situation more than simply opting out. It also guarantees that others can't define the social situation." By emphasizing, excluding, or rewriting aspects of their personal lives on platforms premised on "unlimited sharing," boyd contends, these users have both sought out and been able to achieve meaningful privacy online—even and perhaps especially when they appeared to be telling all.[200] Teens thus navigated the unfamiliar technological platforms on which social life now played out with the tools at their disposal. Much like confessional memoirists, they deliberately projected narratives about themselves that might shelter private life or at least their preferred telling of it. They spilled secrets, but they also worked to shape their stories.

Social media users' ability to regulate how and to whom they are known, however, was hardly as simple as that. The same technology that facilitated connection and sociability carried unprecedented possibilities for surveillance, as well as the prospect of forced visibility. Norms around privacy were, as always, a complex amalgam of individual choices and societal coercion. The ability of giant technology corporations to set the terms for online "sharing" was a case in point. The deliberate weakening of Facebook's privacy policies from 2005 to 2009, argue two scholars, "betrays that this medium isn't simply adapting to new conceptions of privacy as embodied by younger people—it is actively shaping those conceptions and slowly pushing users toward acceptance of further exposure and less control."[201] The notion that users of these platforms in any real sense consented to trade away some of their privacy for access has been called a fiction (or worse). As the same scholars pointedly ask, "To what extent are we truly willing participants when a nearly universal architecture of communication . . . dominates our social world and becomes necessary for keeping a job, attending school, or having a life? Can you really opt out? Can you really even *imagine* opting out?"[202] A journalist likewise observes, "In a culture where people judge each other as much by their digital footprints as by their real-life personalities, it's an act of faith to opt out of sharing your data."[203]

Yet the fact that so many opted in was the easier target and more potent fascination for commentators. This included one cybercritic who dismissed blogging as confessional culture's end of the line, where "narcissism and voyeurism join together in a closed circuit and the lines between inner and outer life dissolve entirely."[204] Blogs were not the half of it. Reality television, webcams, and smartphones were each roundly criticized for violating the categories of inner and outer, public and private, watcher and watched.[205] That sense of transgression had defined the memoir boom too. By the turn of the twenty-first century its technologies of talk had escaped its generic confines to become the very texture of modern public life, animating what one critic described as "the inexhaustible eagerness of people to tell their life stories."[206]

Once again, *An American Family* pointed the way. The series was regularly returned to as ground zero, seeming to foreshadow the nonstop exhibitionism of reality TV and a larger culture of self-display.[207] One twenty-first-century critic described the voluntary self-exposure of the Louds in 1973 as "quaint" measured against later developments (he noted programs like *Fear Factor* that competed for ratings by heaping abuse on participants) that would make it "grotesquely obvious that many Americans will do anything to be on television."[208] The PBS documentary was also the acknowledged template for *The Real World*, a trail-blazing program that gathered a set of young adults, strangers to one another, in a residence in a new city and then let the cameras roll. It would, however, dispense with the sort of negotiations that had enabled the Louds some control over what would stay off the camera. The show debuted on MTV in 1992 and went on to become the longest-running reality program on television; at this writing it is in its thirty-third season.[209]

No longer were commentators surprised, as they had been in 1973, by Americans' desire to play out their private moments before strangers. According to one 2000 source, *The Real World* received upward of 35,000 applications to appear on the show each year. Competitors such as *Survivor* and *Big Brother* joined the field even as individuals discovered that they could bypass them all by setting up shop as their own documentarians. The Internet by the late 1990s teemed with web cameras broadcasting "live feeds from their offices and boudoirs." By the turn of the new century, a quarter-million webcam sites were registered, with more coming online every day.[210] Once again, as had been the case a century before, the camera was critical to the shifting relationship between private life and public persona—and right at the center of debates over what was becoming of privacy in modern America.

The Louds were not just precursors to this brave new world of self-display, but active participants in it. Ten years after the original PBS series aired, Susan and Alan Raymond made another documentary about the family. Titled *An American Family Revisited* (1983), it focused largely on how publicity had entered and then altered their private lives.[211] Afterward, the filmmakers vowed never again to intrude on the family. But in 2001, reversing the usual positions of documentarian and subject, Lance Loud invited the Raymonds, who had remained friends, to start up their cameras. His request: that they film "one final chapter." The occasion was Lance's imminent death from complications of hepatitis C and HIV.[212] According to the *Los Angeles Times*, Lance viewed this as his last shot at the screen and a chance to repair his family's image—to prove to the American viewing public that the Louds were, in the words of Susan Raymond, a "strong family" and not a "disjointed, fractured" one. Tellingly, the newspaper reported, "He wanted to do it on camera . . . even though it was television that had also deeply wounded the family in the first place."[213] It would be difficult to find a stronger testament than this to the idea that publicity makes people real, to the profound transformations that reality TV had effected in citizens' consciousness, and to the confessional impulse itself. Lance Loud's private life had been uniquely entangled with his televised self since age 19. Even as it ended, his sense that its message required a large, anonymous audience persisted.

Lance's desire to have his last days broadcast may not be particularly shocking in an age when blogging, sexting, and twenty-four-hour camera surveillance have become normal. But it should be emphasized, as had been the case for his mother's memoir (and also of a later biography she wrote of her son), that Lance was not intent on disclosure for its own sake. He had particular ends in mind. Most of all, he wanted to correct the record: to be known publicly as he knew himself.[214] He told the Raymonds that the film was "for the naysayers that claimed 'American Family' revealed us to be vacant, unloving, uncaring morons of the materialistic '70s." And he vowed that "this image will be proven wrong when Mom and Dad remarry." The Raymonds agreed to the project. *Lance Loud! A Death in An American Family*, which PBS promoted as the "final episode" of the famous series, aired in January 2003, portraying Lance's physical decline, as well as his attempt to "sort things out about his life."[215] Uncannily, as if scripted beyond the grave, soon after the broadcast Pat and Bill Loud were reported to have reunited. In this they granted "one of their oldest son's last wishes," the *Los Angeles Times* observed. The film ended, "as Lance wanted, with a written epilogue stating that his parents, Pat and Bill, are now living together again."[216]

Lance's biography, the newspaper reflected, was a "cautionary tale of the aftermath of a life profoundly affected at a young age by instant celebrity brought on by intense media exposure."[217] In its analysis, the blurring of private and public matters had undone him. The *New York Times* echoed the sentiment in its obituary, reflecting that "overnight celebrity created special problems for Lance, as a young gay man in Manhattan." The filmmakers concurred. Among the themes of the new film, said Alan Raymond, was the "price of media celebrity." Lance, he observed, "carried the burden of being the first openly gay person on American television, frozen at age 19, forced to forever carry that wacky gay guy persona into his mature adult life"—a sentiment reminiscent of Susanna Kaysen's reflections on her own interrupted life.[218] Lance Loud was, in other words, never able to return to a purely private life or to distinguish it from his public one. He was a known citizen all the way to his core, and this was a form of tragedy.

The makers of the series appeared scarred by the experience too. The *Los Angeles Times* reported that the Raymonds found it a "mixed honor" to be credited with reality TV, of the sort that flourished in the new century, judging shows like *The Real World*, in a word, "terrible."[219] A retrospective on Craig Gilbert in the *New Yorker* in 2010—in response to yet another retread of the documentary, this time a fictionalized version of the making of *An American Family* for Home Box Office—also found the director uneasy with what he had wrought. Prolific up until that point, Gilbert never made another film after the 1973 series, and "he has spent the years since then trying to avoid the notoriety that came with his creation."[220] The article noted lasting animosity between the director and his crew, with Susan Raymond charging that "Craig destroyed that family." The *New Yorker* suggested that battles over ownership were instead the cause: "the Raymonds are still bitter that they weren't given proper credit for effectively creating reality TV." Gilbert, for his part, "seems crushed by the knowledge that he did."[221]

Lance himself took a less anxious and ultimately more generous view of the phenomenon. Twenty-five years after his screen debut, he was asked to comment on "the genre of exhibiting somebody's life" and whether "we've been exposed to too much of it." He joked that the greatest contribution in his case was to supply a trivia question for the game show *Jeopardy*. Nevertheless, he thought *An American Family* had been worth doing: "It gave people solace. As for the invasion of privacy, we don't have that much privacy in the first place, and offering other people comfort is a good way to spend it."[222] Acknowledging the already existing limits to personal privacy at the turn of the twenty-first century, as well as the pleasures of disclosure, Lance's reflections might get us closer than did his interpreters' to understanding what a confessional culture offered to those who inhabited it.

In the three decades spanning the two PBS documentaries, private life—to a degree that would have astonished Americans of earlier generations—would be played out in public. A couple's failing marriage and divorce, a woman's struggle with psychological and sexual disorders, a daughter's emotional suffering at the hands of her father, and a dying man's final days became publicly visible and consumable in print, on screen, and online. Some proponents of the searing new standard of disclosure praised these developments for their honesty, arguing that they exposed exploitation and healed pain, enabling their audiences to form more empathetic imaginations.[223] A greater number billed these same trends as voyeuristic and damaging, a sign of Americans' emptiness—but also their misapprehension of the proper place of privacy in their emotional and psychic lives. Parties on both sides of this argument might have agreed that an era of privacy, as it had once been understood, was ending.

Was Lance's last performance an act of control, a successful bid to take charge of his public image and vindicate a vision of his childhood? Or had TV, as he memorably charged on another occasion, "swallowed" his family? Was the documentary, and the whole apparatus of reality TV and self-broadcasting that it gave rise to, simply another sort of record prison? Or the only way to escape it? Were the new modes of public introspection in the late twentieth century, from confessional memoirs to talk shows and blogs, always and only a repudiation of privacy? Or were they a sign that a new relationship between the private person and the technologies of publicity was under construction?

If nothing else, the full-throated embrace of publicity at the turn of the twenty-first century—unimaginable to those who first called for a right to privacy a century before—made evident the ways past debates were impinging on the present. At least some portion of the impulse to disclose and become visible, to stage one's public story by plumbing its private dimensions, was a response to what had come before. The urge to talk so palpable in our own age of social media was already there in the confessional turn of the 1990s. And underneath that confessional turn was both the expansion of the documentary record on all citizens and the failures of legal rights and regulations to enforce secure boundaries around the person. "This confessional age," as one journalist put it, "in which memoirs and personal revelations tumble out in unprecedented abundance," was in this light a long-germinating response to the dilemmas posed by a knowing society.[224] Even if we conclude that the new mode of self-exposure exacted a price, we should not ignore the fact that it came with its own strategies for personal autonomy and control.

Americans did not simply start giving their privacy away or in any straightforward way change their minds about its importance in the late twentieth century. From a certain angle, privacy was valued more than ever in this era. So was the right to tell one's own story. Critics who assumed that the confessional turn meant a weakening of America's moral fiber or that citizens had become inexcusably self-consumed missed the complex of developments that made personal revelation so potent. They could not grasp the way that confession might turn the surveillance society inside out. Early in the twenty-first century, a commentator declared that "our physical bodies are being shadowed by an increasingly comprehensive 'data body,'" a body of data, moreover, that "does not just follow but precedes the individual being measured and classified."[225] In such circumstances, continuous visibility on one's own terms, whether through a memoir, a spot on reality television, or a status update, begins to look like a tactic—if not an unproblematic one—for defending a privately claimed identity.

The impulse to tell one's story that reached such a pitch in the 1990s and is with us still charted a shift in social imaginings of privacy. In an era of dossiers and databases, tabloids and transparency, privacy no longer was to be found in cordoned-off places—indeed, such spaces no longer seemed to exist—but rather in the act of controlling one's information and image, those pieces of external representation that more and more seemed to constitute one's inner self. Shape the narrative; mobilize the facts and details of yourself; get out ahead of your critics; be your own image maker, editor, and producer; live out loud: this seemed to be the emerging practice of privacy at the turn of the twenty-first century. Both a symptom of and a solution to an all-knowing society, the trend suggests that the age of confession may be just beginning.

Conclusion

By some lights, the conclusion to a book tracking the history of privacy in modern America should be brief: an epitaph for something that was always going, even as it arrived, and is now definitively gone. By the early twenty-first century, privacy was finished, many said. Or at least, its historical arc was by that point clear, more than a century of efforts to carve out a sphere for individual solitude and sovereignty from the insistent demands of modern social organization at an end. Experts in a wide range of fields, including technology, business, law, media, and behavioral science, subscribed to this view. Privacy was quaint, outmoded, or dead, the victim of a relentlessly knowing society's practices of governing, selling, reporting, and discovering—coupled with the citizenry's willingness to go along. Yet, the very statement, laced with regret, betrayed a strong allegiance to a realm where the person might be free of scrutiny. To decry privacy's end, as had been true in the late nineteenth century, was an investment in the concept. And not everyone was convinced that privacy's clock had run out.[1]

The early decades of the twenty-first century arrived with their own distinctive brand of privacy talk. Instead of instantaneous photography or brainwatching or the record prison, the conversation teemed with clouds, mosaics, and algorithms. Rather than eavesdropping or diary snooping, Americans worried about geolocation tracking and Facebook account tampering. If the particulars were new, the themes were familiar: Who should know us and how?—along with its corollary: What might be altered by others' possession of that knowledge?

The questions are as fundamental today as they were in 1890 when Samuel Warren and Louis Brandeis penned their famous article. Indeed, in the age of big data, when many parties traffic in "personally identifying information" and all are alert to its value, the problem of the known citizen has moved to the center of public consciousness as never before.[2] Commentators warn that we are nearing the tipping point to a completely "transparent" or "post-privacy" society; others, that we have already tipped.[3] CEOs and political leaders openly question the feasibility of personal privacy, and scholars and technologists ponder whether there is any return from a world where citizens are already known so well.[4] Privacy, at least in this form, is palpably present in American public life.

The explanations proffered for the current privacy crisis often center on the poor choices made by individual users of social media and their array of connected devices—as if the only choice for citizens facing a "fishbowl life" is that between "excessive caution or foolhardy fearlessness."[5] Conducting one's life on the web has been billed as a kind of hoodwinking: the great "privacy give-away" or the "offer you cannot refuse."[6] Others name the culprit as corporations' rapacious profit-seeking drive to know us, or the state's urge to make citizens legible in order both to punish and protect. The question of whether Americans' valuations of privacy were changing or were being forced to change under technological, governmental, and corporate pressure, however, was difficult to unravel. A recognition of privacy as a fundamentally subjective concept was built into the Supreme Court's language in *Katz v. United States* specifying a standard of "reasonable expectation." With inexpensive aerial drones available for purchase and copious information about just about anyone available in a quick Google search, would those expectations need to shift, and if so, how much?[7]

Those with a vested interest in unlimited information sharing, notably the new social media behemoths, declared that Americans' choice to conduct their lives online was proof positive that privacy norms were relaxing, that citizens cared less than they once did about releasing personal details out into the world.[8] They, along with retailers and marketers, also worked to adjust those norms, "teaching people what they have to give up in order to get along in the twenty-first century." The most important of these lessons, one scholar suspected, involved "opening spigots to their personal information."[9] Less interested parties found plenty of anxiety lurking in

Americans' attitudes toward the security of their "private" information, not to mention their status as the raw material awaiting commodification in an emerging "political economy of informational capitalism."[10] According to a 2014 study, citizens were well aware of their lack of control over commercial and governmental uses of personal data—with Social Security numbers considered the single most sensitive item.[11] Law and technology scholars turned to the distinctly unscholarly word "creepy" to capture instances of the mismatch between older norms around privacy and newfound capacities to scour through others' lives with the click of a button. Practices labeled "creepy"—ambient social apps, personalized analytics, and data-driven marketing—noted two scholars, "rarely breach any of the recognized principles of privacy and data protection law. They include activity that is not exactly harmful, does not circumvent privacy settings, and does not technically exceed the purposes for which data were collected."[12] And yet such practices jostled against respect for individual privacy, as well as the civility that depended on not knowing everything you could about another.[13]

The picture is complicated by the fact that Americans' desire for privacy today is seemingly matched only by their quest for self-disclosure. Dave Eggers's dystopian novel of 2013 slyly probed the dilemma through the workings of a powerful Internet corporation, "The Circle," and its quest to render people fully transparent to themselves and others. Its slogans, an homage to Orwellian double-speak, are embraced by the novel's heroine, a tech worker. "Secrets are lies," "sharing is caring," and "privacy is theft," she earnestly proclaims. In protest, another character is finally driven to scrawl (on paper) a list of "The Rights of Humans in a Digital Age," including the following: "We must all have the right to anonymity"; "Not every human activity can be measured"; "The ceaseless pursuit of data to quantify the value of any endeavor is catastrophic to true understanding"; "The barrier between public and private must remain unbreachable"; and finally, "We must all have the right to disappear."[14] But, the reader had to ask, how could vanishing be the goal, when Americans devoted so much time to publicizing their daily lives in the form of photos and videos, blogs and tweets?

Since the 1990s, commentators had in large numbers worried about Americans trading away privacy of their own accord, their desire for recognition or attention besting the right to be let alone. In the Age of Confession 2.0, these new norms of disclosure encountered social networking. Those seeking to know citizens in finer detail benefited immensely from people's desire for platforms by which to share their personal histories, habits, preferences, and movements. The humor magazine *The Onion* skewered the impulse, outing the social media leader Facebook as a brilliant CIA operation: a mother lode for government spies, offering up caches of free data on every U.S. citizen, voluntarily divulged and conveniently uploaded for viewing.[15] One technology scholar provides a snapshot of this ever-growing data bank. During every minute of 2012, she writes, "204,166,667 emails were sent, over 2,000,0000 queries were received by Google, 684,478 pieces of content were shared on Facebook, 200,000 tweets were sent, 3,125 new photos were added to Flickr, 2,083 check-ins occurred on Foursquare, 270,000 words were written on Blogger, and 571 websites were created."[16]

Right now, the collision (or collusion?) between the outflow of personal information and the technological capacity to capture, analyze, and harness it looks like the defining feature of the twenty-first-century privacy landscape. The struggle for control over how one would be known—what of oneself would be revealed and what should be concealed—was an old dilemma. But individuals' ability to exercise some determination over their own public-private boundaries seemed to be receding in this new context. People were being made "borderless," speculated a sociologist, turned "inside out," a product both of the "piercing abilities of the new surveillance" and the increasingly valuable returns from knowledge.[17] Former U.S. government contractor Edward Snowden's exposés of sweeping National Security Agency surveillance on American citizens in the summer of 2013 illuminated the scope of the problem. A vast apparatus of electronic surveillance came to light, including the NSA's immense database of mobile phone location data, its ability to crack the encryption methods used by individuals and organizations to protect their email and e-commerce communications, its ability to install malicious software ("malware") in millions of computers around the world, its collection of telephone content and metadata from every call made in target countries, and its collaboration with major tech companies such as Apple, Google, and Microsoft to evade privacy controls.[18]

Spectacular as Snowden's leaks were, they came on the heels of other revelations. There was the federal government's post-9/11 Total Information Awareness program, which pledged to "collect it all," "process it all," "exploit it all," "partner it all," "sniff it all," and, finally, "know it all."[19]

There were CCTV cameras watching every corner of America's cities; by 2009, an estimated 30 million of them were recording 4 billion hours of footage a week.[20] There was the monitoring of users' photographs and posts by the company Facebook, described in 2007 already as "one of America's largest electronic surveillance systems," tracking "roughly 9 million Americans, broadcasting their photographs and personal information on the Internet"—that number skyrocketing to 800 million users worldwide just a half-decade later.[21] There were 8.3 million victims of identity theft in 2005 alone.[22] There were reports of massive data breaches and widely publicized search tracking by giant corporations like Google and Amazon.[23] There was dawning awareness of the tremendous power over individuals' futures and fortunes exercised by data aggregators such as Acxiom, ChoicePoint, Experian, and Equifax—billed as the "little-known overlords of the surveillance society" by two scholars—as well as the black market for sensitive information such as credit card and Social Security numbers on the "darknet."[24]

If self-broadcasting ever seemed like a way out of the record prison, a means for asserting control over one's own image and information, that hope dimmed considerably in the new century. Current privacy debates in the United States are shadowed by the knowledge that social media, the Internet of Things, wearable technologies, cloud computing, spyware, phone record metadata, radio frequency identification (RFID) systems, drones, electronic monitoring software, biometric readers, and predictive algorithms—key words of our time—intersect fatefully with the twin imperatives of corporate profit and national security.[25] Most citizens are aware that they can be tracked by their "electronic footprint" as well as their DNA, by phrases in their email correspondence as well as purchases on their credit cards, by their Social Security number as well as their GPS coordinates. But few can discern precisely when or how they are known or to what end. The phrases coined to capture the traces we leave behind in a networked age—"digital dossier," "data exhaust," "data shadows"—highlight their inadvertent nature.[26]

As in the nineteenth century, when wiretapping and fingerprinting were new, technological advances today furnish the most visible platform for privacy fears. Innovations that were the stuff of science fiction for past Americans—facial recognition programs and remote desktop viewing, a cashless society and fully personalized advertising—have a not-at-all-fictional potency in the present.[27] More than any one particular invention or device, it is the arrival of "big data" that has crystallized today's debate. The term refers both to the "exponential increase and availability of data" in an age when large volumes of information stream rapidly from electronic transactions, social media, audio and video files, sensors, and "smart metering" and to the capacity of powerful computers to sort and dissect it.[28] Not just the amount but the kind of information collected has changed. New data mining technologies, writes sociologist Gary Marx, hold "the potential to reveal and analyze the unseen, unknown, forgotten, withheld, and unconnected," able to "surface bits of reality that were previously hidden, or did not contain informational clues."[29] Once scattered and undecipherable, data on individual purchases, searches, and communications can now be accessed and digested, conferring on state and commercial actors potent powers of divination and prediction.[30]

The prospect of being known in this fashion, we will not be surprised, carries promise as well as peril for individual citizens. Big data's value for epidemiologists as well as marketers is that they might see social life freshly in the patterns derived from vast stores of medical, financial, genetic, and location information.[31] That same clarity and precision, employed differently, can do real harm to specific people.[32] As one reporter pointed out by way of example, subjects participating in a genomic study might "help advance science" only to "find themselves unable to obtain life insurance."[33] The specter of an information net so vast, and yet nimble enough to pinpoint an individual person, threatens to undo common conceptions of privacy defined as control over one's accessibility to others.[34] In an era of algorithmic knowledge, this sort of privacy, many fear, will be ever scarcer.

Already, being watched feels different in the twenty-first century.[35] A recent study found that the nation's top fifty websites installed an average of sixty-four pieces of tracking technology, allowing them invisibly to "scan in real time" users' "access location information, income, shopping interests, and health concerns."[36] Through their browsing, their buying, and their posts, individuals are profiled: pegged with psychological or medical ailments, identified as sexually assaulted, characterized as impulse buyers, or allotted "pregnancy prediction scores." Indeed, one of the viral stories of 2012 concerned a corporation (Target) that "knew" a woman was pregnant ahead of her intimates based only on its compilation of her online search patterns.[37] Recommendation software and canny computer algorithms, able to select for you what you had not even realized that you wanted, have posed the question of the known citizen anew.

Drones, Fitbits, and smart refrigerators alike make clear that who or what was capable of "knowing" individual citizens is itself shifting. Mundane objects of everyday life have become monitoring instruments and often reporting instruments as well—mobile phones, of course, but also cars, credit cards, televisions, household appliances, thermostats, wristwatches, and eyeglasses. One report found that 20 percent of U.S. residents owned a wearable device in 2014, not including smartphones.[38] These devices are prized by sellers and marketers because their close proximity to the body means that people are less likely to be without them, "the intimate, always-connected nature of the wearable device" facilitating "continuous tracking across time and space."[39] Surveillance scholars John Gilliom and Torin Monahan point out that Americans would never agree to a government program requiring that they carry a device providing live-streamed data on their physical location, communications, and personal interactions, archiving it all in data banks—and permitting, when deemed necessary, the monitoring of specific conversations and messages. Yet this is precisely what the nearly universal use of cell phones—now owned by upward of 90 percent of Americans—allows. Like credit cards, mobile phones are a surveillance technology "gladly, even fervently, adopted" by consumers, who more and more are "enmeshed in surveillant relationships just by moving through the world, even without an explicit gaze from above."[40]

Privacy sensibilities and rights have themselves created incentives for unobtrusive forms of surveillance—an echo of debates that opened up in the 1960s about how the "right to research" might coexist with the rights of the research subject. Today, those who wish to know "gather what is voluntarily radiated, unwittingly left behind, or silently and effortlessly made available by breaking borders that traditionally protected information."[41] Full-body scanners at airports caused a public ruckus when introduced at airports in 2010, Gilliom and Monahan suggest, mostly because they were so obvious at a time when so much tracking is inconspicuous and easily missed.[42] The fact that nonhuman observers are doing much of the watching paradoxically accounts for the surprisingly intimate, integrated feel of today's privacy invasions. As a recent study of "beacon surveillance" trained on retail shoppers has it, it is as if "the aisles have eyes."[43] Individuals abet their own observation, if often unwittingly. Even minor actions they take—a click or a keystroke—put them at risk of revealing themselves to an expanding and unknowable number of parties. The reason they go ahead, of course, is that these actions also bring all kinds of social goods, ranging from tailored recommendations to breaking news.[44]

The fact that personal information divulged for social connection or entertainment could as easily be put to use for commercial or political surveillance significantly eroded the distinction between different kinds of authorities in U.S. society: agents of the state and big business in particular.[45] The collaboration between the National Security Agency, law enforcement, large corporations, and data aggregators in the wake of the September 11, 2001, terrorist attack exposed the wide-open information channel between the public and private sector.[46] It was true that from the 1960s onward, Americans had often not distinguished between state and commercial data banks. And stretching back into the nineteenth century, the U.S. government had worked in tandem with private companies in matters of policing and national security—to intercept telegrams, for example. But these once fairly distinct realms seemed to be blurring further, even merging.[47] The implication was that autonomous decision making would be less and less available to the twenty-first-century data subject.

Today's particular information constellation, where profit, security, and self-definition mingle indiscriminately, is often hailed as unparalleled. But we gain more clarity by placing its development in a longer history of knowing citizens. A sense that Americans are known too well by government and corporate entities alike is not unprecedented. It was a discovery of the 1890s and then again of the 1930s and the 1960s. What gives the current moment its special urgency is a uniquely combustible combination: a deluge of volunteered or solicited personal information, on the one hand, and the increasingly sophisticated capacities of other parties for linking, sharing, and acting on it, on the other.

The problem of secret knowledge about citizens—of not knowing who knows you—was a fear sparked in the 1970s by silent record-keeping systems and hidden gatekeepers. The arrival of big data has given it a new and uneasy shape in the twenty-first century. Today's analog is the algorithm: the set of rules, often generated by machine learning, whereby individuals are systematically ranked and rated by a host of commercial, financial, and government agencies. Citizens' fates are being shaped by proprietary formulas that they could not decipher even if they had access to them.[48] The coupling of "increasingly enigmatic technologies" and their own carefully protected opacity means that "corporate actors have unprecedented knowledge of the minutiae of our daily lives," writes legal scholar

Frank Pasquale, "while we know little to nothing about how they use this knowledge to influence the important decisions that we—and they— make." This fundamental asymmetry between the knowers and the known makes the contemporary world less a "peaceable kingdom of private walled gardens," he argues, than "a one-way mirror."[49]

In response, legal scholars and technologists have turned their attention to algorithmic discrimination, including predictive harms. Some have proposed a novel sort of privacy right for the twenty-first century—a "right to quantitative privacy"—buttressed by codes of "big data ethics" and "fair reputation reporting."[50] The newfound volume and value of raw personal data, suggests one computer scientist, will require a whole new bundle of individual entitlements, including rights to access one's own data, to inspect data companies, and to amend, blur, experiment with, or port one's own data to other holders. Only then might "digital citizens" regain some semblance of autonomy and take charge of their own information in a "post-privacy economy."[51] In these renewed calls for access and transparency as a check on powerful institutions that control citizens' data, a legacy of the data bank debate of decades past, we spy the persistent appeal of civil liberties solutions. And yet, the entangled nature of data and disclosure with new technologies of divination places both the efficacy of transparency and the hope for personal autonomy in serious doubt.

The Quantified Self movement—also referred to as lifelogging, personal informatics, and personal analytics—is emblematic. Founded by two former editors of *Wired* magazine in 2007, it brought together enthusiasts around the project of harnessing "self-knowledge through numbers." Whether to track and optimize personal health, fitness, emotional well-being, or productivity, lifelogging is intended as a form of self-supervision, offering legibility and insight to the person who chooses it.[52] As an industry was built on the promise of "technologically assisted self-regulation," however, new notes of control have crept in.[53] Apps and devices are now available to help consumers stop smoking, track their fertility, curb their appetite, get more exercise or sleep, and monitor their blood pressure, stress, and hydration levels—indeed, to know themselves better. But the potential for others to extract information from this rich trove of detail about a consumer's pulse, REM sleep, skin temperature, and mood is ever clearer.[54]

Although billed as a voluntary and self-motivated practice, self-tracking has thus presented opportunities for others to follow along. In some contexts, explains sociologist Deborah Lupton, this kind of monitoring is "being encouraged, or even enforced on people."[55] Insurance companies, workplaces, and schools—sites that have always had plenty of incentives to know individuals better—have all grasped at the new devices and the information they provide, whether to track students' physical movements or employees' adherence to corporate wellness policies. In other contexts, the data streaming from tracking devices are monitored silently by the developers of software they use, third-party purchasers, data-mining companies, or government agencies.[56] As these practices take hold, the "quantified self" can become an extremely well-known citizen. As Lupton sees it, self-trackers through their own devices may come to resemble the involuntarily monitored: those under probation, on parole, or serving at-home sentences.[57]

Indeed, some wondered if the main thrust of new tracking and surveillance practices, imbued with a participatory ethos and full of advertised rewards for the user—convenience, efficiency, health, and happiness—was softening the very edges of what was once named and recognized as a privacy invasion.[58] Was the real goal cultivating pro-surveillance dispositions in the population at large? And was it working? Lupton observes that practices "once considered coercive and imposed forms of state surveillance, such as biometric facial recognition for security purposes, are now routinely used in social media sites such as Facebook for the purposes of tagging others in images."[59] Others point to the fact that fingerprints, once bitterly resisted as a technique for tracking criminals, now regularly open a phone or laptop. Indeed, a host of technologies, not just facial recognition but also retina scanning, voice spectrometry, and DNA typing, have migrated from criminal justice into the society at large in recent decades, serving as convenient forms of identification or security.[60]

Finally, in a variant of worries that first bloomed in the postwar era about society infiltrating individual psyches via brainwashing and subliminal advertisements, commentators worried in the early twenty-first century about the influence that came with new commercial tools for shaping and "nudging" users' behaviors.[61] It was not just that an array of companies sought to burrow into the "lives and psyches" of their current and prospective customers in order to better tailor their pitches. It was not even that such firms further "sought to draw psychological and behavioral lessons from the enormous amounts of data" they collected on a daily basis.[62] It was that, as in the 1950s, these external agents seemed to be getting inside people in new ways. Was feeding people information as a means of persuasion also, perhaps, a form of domination? Did an app that cued a user to resist her urge to smoke or consume calories or that encouraged a man idle at his desk to stand up harbor less beneficent possibilities of social control going forward? Theorists of "libertarian paternalism" preached the benefits of behavioral coaxing, enthusiastic about the possibility of channeling consumers' decisions through a properly designed "choice architecture." As they did, the security and integrity of Americans' mental states came back into view. Visibility, choice, consent, freedom, autonomy: these were the stakes once again in the early twenty-first century as citizens reckoned with their knowing society.

Privacy's philosophers of the present, contemporary counterparts of Louis Brandeis and Samuel Warren, have attempted to grasp the implications of this dizzying array of new practices, whether stemming from corporations, official agencies, or citizens' own desires. Some, noting the extensive, continuous, and distributed nature of watching people, speak of "liquid surveillance."[63] Others, focused on the way that law enforcement increasingly operates outside the bounds of "individualized suspicion," sweeping up massive crowds through drone surveillance or NSA metadata, write of "panvasive surveillence."[64] Indeed, a whole new scholarly field, "surveillance studies," came into its own at the turn of the twenty-first century, complete with a professional society and journal. Scholars devoted themselves to apprehending the web of watchers employed at company headquarters, airports, tollbooths, borders, traffic intersections, and schools—as well as in individual minds and homes as it became second nature to monitor oneself.[65] The notion of a "surveillant assemblage" that works by "abstracting human bodies from their territorial settings, and separating them into a series of discrete flows," is so far one of the field's most influential formulations.[66]

Many grappled with the interlocking nature of the parties who made it their project to know individual citizens so thoroughly. As one commentator had it, no piece of information was irrelevant or insignificant to the new surveillors, who pursued "every little desire, every preference, every want, and all the complexity of the self, social relations, political beliefs and ambitions, psychological well-being," such that their probes extended "into every crevice and every dimension of everyday living of every single one of us in our individuality."[67] It was difficult to characterize what was propelling this surveillance complex: was it the state, the private sector, or was it citizens themselves? "Knots of statelike power" is how this last writer describes it, "where economy, society, and private life melt into a giant data market for everyone to trade, mine, analyze, and target."[68] Others have traced the emergence of a "networked self" in an age of ubiquitous connectivity, a successor to the data subject or "dossier personality" of the last century.[69]

Updating earlier worries about being imprisoned by a photograph or a file, new critics have asked whether a digital-age citizen has a right to be forgotten.[70] The progress of that right in the European Union—in the form of requirements that search engines edit or delete offending information—has led to much speculation (and envy) in the United States as to what might be done about what one scholar calls "the threat of digital memory."[71] The fear of intimate, embarrassing, or shameful images and facts making their way to a broader public is of course as old as gossip. The modern framing of a "right to privacy" in the late nineteenth century derived much of its urgency from the way new media and technologies threatened reputation. The rapid spread of information today and its easy accessibility have raised the stakes, in the form of cyberbullying and "revenge porn" but also lost jobs and school disciplinary proceedings.[72] "In a connected world," as one scholar puts it, "a life can be ruined in a matter of minutes."[73] Extensive lawsuits waged to get one's life back in the form of a damaging photograph, video, or story both recall the past—Abigail Roberson's suit at the turn of the twentieth century against the flour company that borrowed her image—and remind us that contemporary Americans, no matter what critics say, are only sometimes "voluntarily" giving their privacy away.[74]

In the face of individuals' rush to divulge personal information and authorities' ability to make sense of it, the descriptive power of Jeremy Bentham's panopticon or George Orwell's Big Brother—for decades, the go-to metaphors for surveillance—suddenly seemed inadequate. Twenty-first-century conditions could not be likened to "a prisonlike panopticon where trapped people follow the rules because they're afraid someone is watching," mused two scholars. To begin with, the watchers were far more multifarious and more anonymous—indeed, unknown—than earlier theorists of surveillance imagined. Moreover, citing the hundreds of millions of users of Facebook and other social media sites, some suspected that Americans' larger fear was in fact that "no one is watching."[75]

As for Orwell, some alleged that he had misdiagnosed the future by not accounting for individual desire: the entertainment and pleasure that came from being enmeshed in a data set far deeper and richer than anyone in the postwar decades could have dreamed up. Moreover, he had underestimated citizens' embrace of the convenience and comfort of being known. The author of *Nineteen Eighty-Four* in this analysis did not anticipate how modern supervision would be made palatable to its subjects, allowing "softer, more manipulative, engineered, connected and embedded" forms of suasion to enter into daily life. Focused on authoritarian states in 1949, Orwell had also neglected the threats to personal autonomy from the private sector.[76] Helping to make the point, a reality television show titled *Big Brother* was an international hit of the late 1990s. Contestants on the program were confined to a house in which they were subject to an omnipresent authority figure known to them only as "Big Brother" and willingly had their every action recorded by cameras and microphones.[77] The Loud family had subjected their domestic life to television cameras in the early 1970s, but the nod here to totalitarianism as theater—and the embrace of total surveillance by producers and participants alike—was a new twist. In fact, *Big Brother* had been conceived as "a social and psychological experiment" to study the ways individuals coped with surveillance. But when it appeared that participants coped rather too well, this ambition was sidelined in the interest of pure entertainment.[78]

The unanticipated meeting of confession and surveillance in the last decade has led to some of the most robust arguments over and defenses of personal privacy since the 1970s. But in all the contemporary handwringing over lost privacy, remedies seem harder to come by. This too is an important feature of the present moment. The Internet age, like the computer age it followed, "would bring something of a privacy storm," writes one observer; but "no legal hurdles, in principle or practice, were put in place to slow these changes down."[79] In fact, the Federal Trade Commission, the Federal Communications Commission, Congress, and the White House continued to churn out proposals for protecting Americans' privacy. In the decades since the Privacy Act of 1974, several key pieces of federal legislation responded to specific issues. The Video Privacy Protection Act of 1988 was a direct counter to reporters hunting through Supreme Court nominee Robert Bork's video rental record. The Driver's Privacy Protection Act of 1994, which ended the kind of reverse searching that Laud Humphreys had used to identify tearoom users, was a response to abortion clinic tracking.[80] The Health Insurance Portability and Accountability Act of 1996 registered growing concerns about the privacy of medical records as they took electronic form. The Children's Online Privacy Protection Act of 1998, a reckoning with commercial data mining in the case of the most vulnerable citizens, made it illegal to gather personal information on or track children under the age of 13 without parental permission. Too, watchdog agencies like the Electronic Frontier Foundation, the Electronic Privacy Information Center, the Privacy Rights Clearinghouse, and the American Civil Liberties Union continue to advocate for individual civil liberties as insistently as digital technologies threaten to override them.

And yet few seem to turn with great expectation to the state or regulatory agencies to curb the tide, perhaps thinking it naïve, given past history, that a transformative court ruling or legislative act could alter our present course.[81] The central state's own changing aspect—long in the making—from relatively beneficent bureaucracy to menacing invader has something to do with this. Another part of the explanation is that the answers of the past appear outmoded, too flimsy to staunch the algorithmic power of commercial and state knowers. Privacy policies that in theory allow people to "opt out" have come in for particular disdain as a "failed disclosure regime," revolving around "the fiction that consumers can and will bargain for privacy, or 'opt out' of deals or jobs they deem too privacy invasive." The terms of service that customers sign off on, argues Frank Pasquale, are less "privacy policies" than "contracts surrendering your rights to the owner of the service."[82] What this means functionally is that citizens of the surveillance society are on their own. "If you believe that your privacy is being protected by laws and user agreements," write John Gilliom and Torin Monahan, "think again." Rapid technological advances and their implementation by corporations, law enforcement, and the military seem to empty privacy rights of their substance. Given the choice of "scrutinizing user agreements and privacy policies, writing our congressional representative, or learning how to use anonymizing software," they acknowledge, "we'd both pick the software. Hands down."[83]

A final piece of the predicament, once again, is that citizens seem so readily to succumb to the allure of being known. Some contend that with surveillance becoming a comprehensive, and even welcome, mode of social organization, the concept of privacy has outlasted its usefulness—"too limiting and dated" a notion to speak to the present.[84] As Andreas Weigend, former chief scientist at Amazon and founder of the Social Data Lab, puts the same sentiment, "Privacy is a concept that was only rather recently enabled by technology, and the concept may not be up to the task of protecting us in the age of social data." He counsels Americans to cast aside their fears of a knowing society and instead embrace the "value we get from sharing data about ourselves," its manifold "opportunities for discovery and optimization." Weigend looks forward to the day that social data "help us make some of the biggest decisions in life, including who we pick as a romantic partner, where and how we work, what medications we take, and how and what we study." It is time to give up on the illusion of privacy: "We shouldn't be fighting for privacy simply because it was a pretty good response to people's problems a hundred years ago."[85]

And yet: new tactics that have appeared on the horizon, outside the scope of legislatures and courts, suggest that many have not yet given up on fighting for privacy. A revised self-help literature, for example, emerged in the new century, offering a set of tools for navigating an all-too-knowing society. Not simply exposés of the parties infringing on Americans' privacy, these were guides for doing an end-run around them. While some counseled using paper shredders and paying only in cash, others turned to freelance sites, new encryption devices, proxy servers, secure hardware and software, and even secure chat programs and messaging systems. The Electronic Frontier Foundation maintains an advice website offering "Surveillance Self-Defense," and some schools have begun to teach "cyberhygiene"; businesses in droves hire "privacy professionals" to manage the escalating threats to their customers' data.[86] Popular privacy manuals have also proliferated, with titles such as *You're at Risk: A Complete Guide for You and Your Family to Stay Safe Online; The Smart Girl's Guide to Privacy; Life under Surveillance: A Field Guide*; and *Hack-Proof Your Life Now! How to Protect (or Destroy) Your Reputation Online*. New experts on how to move through American society undercover, in books such as *How to Disappear, The Incognito Toolkit*, and *The Art of Invisibility*, preach a gospel of hiding. "Do not, as long as you live, ever again allow your real name to be coupled with your home address," is step one, according to the author of *How to Be Invisible: Protect Your Home, Your Children, Your Assets, and Your Life*, currently in its third edition.[87]

As separate surveillance systems are joined, leading to the "progressive 'disappearance of disappearance,'" the state of being unknown or unrecognized seems to be rising in value.[88] The most promising contemporary avenue for achieving something like an "inviolate" state or space, it seems, may come not in the form of restraining those who seek to know but in carefully designed practices for hiding one's tracks. Guarding one's passwords and personal data, being savvy about how and where one goes online, and opting out of data-sharing platforms are today's words to the wise. Technologies like blind signatures, anonymous remailers, and encryption software promise that one might reclaim one's life by re-anonymizing it.[89] Rooted in private and individual solutions rather than state regulation, this kind of counsel is the dominant advice that privacy-conscious citizens encounter today despite the looming threat presented by sophisticated re-identification techniques.

Other solutions to the knowingness of American society come in evading the electronic gaze, via dark routes on Google Maps, for example, or apps that locate CCTV cameras and reroute the walker so as to avoid them.[90] A New York theater company in that spirit leads tours of surveillance systems in the city.[91] A 2016 book, *Obfuscation: A User's Guide for Privacy and Protest*, by well-respected scholars, offers a more confrontational approach.[92] The book announces that the time has come to "fight today's digital surveillance," and its authors urge "the deliberate use of ambiguous, confusing, or misleading information" to interfere with data collection projects. Evasion, noncompliance, refusal, and even sabotage are the weapons with which "average users" not able to opt out or otherwise exert control over data about themselves might yet defend themselves. Still others have called for "obscurity by design," enabling individuals to hide data that are technically public through techniques such as reduced search visibility, access controls, pseudonymous profiles, and the blurring of observed information.[93]

Spying opportunities in an emerging market, a large and increasingly profitable privacy industry seeks to fill the breach, peddling spyware, privacy-enhancing or anonymizing technologies (PETs), certified services for identity protection, online reputation management, and digital "vaults" complete with insurance for valuable data. Consumer demand for techno-precautions is large and growing. It is a development that may challenge information sharing between corporations and the state, and has already led to standoffs. In "a step opposed by intelligence officials," major corporations like Apple and Google beginning in 2014 and 2015 offered consumer encryption of data as a new privacy feature for operating systems.[94] The flip side of such products are market-based solutions that might enable savvier practices of evaluating the "return on data" one gets by giving up one's personal details.[95] Those exploring this option have proposed a "privacy-preserving marketplace" that could compensate people according to the level of risk they take in disclosing personal information.[96] Others in this vein floated a system of micro-payments for the use of one's data, a sign that propertied notions of privacy are still alive and well in a virtual age.[97] It is as yet unclear how far citizens will privatize their efforts to secure privacy or place their trust either in technology or the market, the very sites where modern privacy alarms were first sounded.

Most significantly, the double-edged nature of digital surveillance has introduced new prospects for holding authorities to account—and potentially far more powerful species of transparency than existed previously. "Ever since the advent of print, political rulers have found it impossible to control completely the new kind of visibility made possible by the media and to shape it entirely to their liking," writes a cultural theorist. "Now, with the rise of the Internet and other digital technologies, it is more difficult than ever."[98] Some launched projects of reverse surveillance with the aim of making the government—and government data—more accessible to citizens. Websites such as GovTrack.us, for example, aimed to empower civil society through the "continuous public surveillance of government."[99] Combatted by investigative reporters, congressional inquiries, and a few lone whistleblowers in the 1970s, the government's secrets would in the new century be countered by "doxing." This term referred to the practice of using public or private records against the powerful in society or to outing an anonymous person's or group's identity, a favored tactic of the hacker collective, Anonymous.[100] Its advocates believed that the open and connecting architecture of the Internet might serve as a "buffer against the control efforts of the more powerful and can also be turned against them."[101]

It was in the conduct of national security that the novel challenges of keeping secrets in a digital world became dramatically evident to the knowers as well as the known. WikiLeaks, an organization that burst onto the scene in 2009, led by Australian activist Julian Assange, took as its mission the release of classified documents—video footage, military files, and diplomatic logs—to expose shadowy government policies.[102] The ambition of the organization's "philosophy of transparence" was to "allow citizens to become the surveillors of the state and see directly into every crevasse and closet of the central watchtower, while rendering the public opaque and anonymous; to invert the line of sight." Assange himself called for a "worldwide movement of mass leaking."[103] As the co-director of Harvard's Transparency Policy Project, Mary Graham, has observed, old ways of resolving media-state conflicts over publicity could no longer hold "in a world where insiders can self-publish top-secret information on the Internet with no filters and no advance notice, and can operate beyond U.S. borders—and beyond U.S. laws." She referred to the army's Bradley/Chelsea Manning, who in 2010 copied more than 250,000 State Department cables, airstrike videos, and soldiers' reports from Iraq and Afghanistan and turned them over to WikiLeaks.[104]

Possibilities for a new privacy politics were built into the very infrastructure of a surveillance society. The variety of inexpensive technologies that equipped ordinary citizens with the ability to do their own watching and recording seemed especially promising in this regard. The term "sousveillance" was coined to describe the ways in which individuals could turn observation techniques back on authorities. Some called for the deliberate use of such powers to forge a "coveillant" society, where the ability to watch might be symmetrical. Might citizens have a "right to record," for example?[105] The use of mobile phones and body cams by the Black Lives Matter movement to document police brutality toward African Americans showed that the relationship between observer and observed could be reversed, at least temporarily.[106] Doxing and sousveillance alike took advantage of the double edge of a knowing society, and they suggested the new kinds of activism it inspired. As the gay advocates of "outing" in the 1990s understood, to know and to reveal could be potent tools for social change. The hierarchy between police officer and policed, watcher and watched, powerful and powerless might be disrupted through the targeted use of a knowing society's tools: publicity, identification, documentation, transparency recording, and outing.

These instruments of exposure carried another kind of power: the potential to bring visibility to the persistently unequal experiences of and entitlements to privacy in the contemporary United States. Scholars of race and racism in particular argued that "there is no such thing as a private sphere for people of Color except that which they manage to create and protect in an otherwise hostile environment," and indeed that the monitoring of African Americans from slavery forward had provided the template for a modern surveillance society.[107] Activists' work to publicize the policing of specific bodies in the second decade of the twenty-first century—whether immigrant female, non-white, or transgender—helped to cast new light on the uneven slant of American privacy policies and debates. In particular, it highlighted the disproportionate attention given to the privacy violations affecting better-off, normative, and usually white citizens.[108] If the trend line in the twentieth century had seemed to point away from physical violations of privacy and toward "informational" ones, it betrayed that pundits and politicians had prioritized some Americans' privacy at the expense of others.[109] Activists protesting the carceral state, "bathroom bills," and tightening restrictions on reproductive rights made clear that digital or data rights—whether the right to transparency or the right to disappear—would not be enough to create meaningful privacy for all citizens.[110]

Anonymity and inaccessibility, arguably less rich and humane concepts than "privacy," have taken center stage in American debates about a knowing society in the early decades of the twenty-first century. But is anonymity— or obscurity or ambiguity or blurriness—the same as privacy? It is worth asking whether autonomy in a digital age is or should be equivalent to whatever is left after the data miners are through. This minimalist understanding of what has often been judged a fundamental human value and social good tells us something of the chastened aspirations of today's known citizens.

We will do well to remember that this debate has been with us a long time now. Indeed, one of the reasons it is so difficult to imagine a resolution to today's privacy dilemmas is that the invasions many citizens rail against have become foundational to the workings of U.S. society. The unfettered media that outraged Samuel Warren and Louis Brandeis, along with Henry James; the identification infrastructure wrought by criminal policing and state benefit programs alike; the disciplines, experts, and corporations invested in demystifying human behavior; the continuously aggregating bureaucratic data banks for improved governance and selling; and, not least, the voluminous information voluntarily divulged in the public sphere together form the warp and the woof of contemporary social existence. As American society became more knowing across the last century and a half, the gain often seemed self-evident. Reporting the news, protecting national security, tracking public health and social welfare, understanding human psychology, improving commercial efficiency, fostering political transparency and accountability, and announcing individual truths all appeared compelling, even necessary, rationales for infringing on the "inviolate personality." Americans may not have set out to create the kind of political culture that they now inhabit—or wished for the kind of privacy now on offer—but neither have these developments been unintentional.

This book has traced Americans' reluctance but also their desire to be known across a century and more—a history not of a tangible thing but of a tense and ongoing debate. Even a knowing society remains full of uncertainties. One of these is the future of the known citizen. Not one of the privacy issues that Americans wrestled with in the past is settled or solved. Attempts to protect free expression but to rein in overly zealous media; to reap the rewards but not the risks of identification systems; to devise politically feasible laws honoring sexual privacy and reproductive rights; to discover new insights about human behavior and psyches while respecting those same humans' dignity; to deploy data in ways that enrich rather than damage individual lives; and to balance national security with civil liberties are still with us. What privacy can and will mean going forward will depend on how these debates are waged.

The story of the known citizen is not over. Nor—even in an age of social media, big data, and NSA spying—is privacy.[111] The corners of life presumed to be off-limits or beyond scrutiny are, we might guess, simply once again under reconstruction. The controversies that such changes spark alert us to moments of possibility embedded within a shifting social order. Can a known citizen be happy? Is a known citizen free? The fact that we are still asking Auden's questions, composed just as today's knowing society was coming into view, tells us that privacy is not yet a concept or a claim that we can do without.

Notes

Introduction

1. W. H. Auden, "The Unknown Citizen," in *Another Time* (London: Faber and Faber, 1940), 96–97; the poem was composed in 1939 and first published in *The New Yorker*, January 6, 1940, p. 19. See Edward Mendelson, ed., *W. H. Auden: Collected Poems* (London: Faber and Faber, 1976), 201.

2. Anita L. Allen and Erin Mack, for example, write of nineteenth-century women having "too much of the wrong kind of privacy." "How Privacy Got Its Gender," *Northern Illinois University Law Review* 10 (Spring 1990): 441–478. Recent writings on the power of recognition from the state have called attention to the detrimental effects of social invisibility for the disenfranchised. See Simon Szreter and Keith Breckenridge, eds., *Registration and Recognition: Documenting the Person in World History* (Oxford: Oxford University Press, 2012).

3. For a discussion of citizenship's legal and conceptual underpinnings in the United States and the distinction between "formal citizenship status" and "full and equal" membership in the nation, see Barbara Young Welke, "Law, Personhood, and Citizenship in the Long Nineteenth Century: The Borders of Belonging," in *The Cambridge History of Law in America*, vol. 2, ed. Michael Grossberg and Christopher Tomlins (New York: Cambridge University Press, 2008), quote on p. 363.

4. Historians, for instance, have noted the ways that the ability to participate in consumer markets became critical to citizenship in the post–World War II United States; see Lizabeth Cohen, *A Consumers' Republic: The Politics of Mass Consumption in Postwar America* (New York: Knopf, 2003). Other modes of citizenship, including social citizenship, biosociality, biological citizenship, and therapeutic citizenship, have been fleshed out as well. See for example

T. H. Marshall, *Citizenship and Social Class, and Other Essays* (Cambridge: Cambridge University Press, 1950); Paul Rabinow, "Artificiality and Enlightenment: From Sociobiology to Biosociality," in *Essays on the Anthropology of Reason* (Princeton, NJ: Princeton University Press, 1996), 91–111; Adriana Petryna, *Life Exposed: Biological Citizens after Chernobyl* (Princeton, NJ: Princeton University Press, 2002); and Nikolas Rose, *The Politics of Life Itself: Biomedicine, Power, and Subjectivity in the Twenty-First Century* (Princeton, NJ: Princeton University Press, 2006).

5. These are just three titles among a very long list from the last two decades: Julia Angwin, *Dragnet Nation: A Quest for Privacy, Security, and Freedom in a World of Relentless Surveillance* (New York: Times Books, 2014); David Brin, *The Transparent Society: Will Technology Force Us to Choose between Privacy and Freedom?* (Reading, MA: Addison-Wesley, 1998); and Robert O'Harrow Jr., *No Place to Hide* (New York: Free Press, 2005).

6. Richard F. Hixson, *Privacy in a Public Society: Human Rights in Conflict* (New York: Oxford University Press, 1987), xv; Amitai Etzioni, *The Limits of Privacy* (New York: Basic Books, 1999), 3–4.

7. See Colin J. Bennett and Charles D. Raab, *The Governance of Privacy: Policy Instruments in Global Perspective*, 2nd rev. ed. (Cambridge, MA: MIT Press, 2006).

8. An early book-length version of this argument appeared almost a half-century ago: Jerry M. Rosenberg's *The Death of Privacy* (New York: Random House, 1969). Recent statements have come from the likes of Sun Microsystems' CEO Scott McNealy, *New York Times* columnist Thomas Friedman, and Facebook founder Mark Zuckerberg. Polly Sprenger, "Sun on Privacy: Get Over It," *Wired* (January 26, 1999); Thomas Friedman, "Four Words Going Bye-Bye," *New York Times*, May 21, 2014, p. A29; Bobbie Johnson, "Privacy No Longer a Social Norm, Says Facebook Founder," *The Guardian*, January 10, 2010.

9. There are notable exceptions. See especially Rochelle Gurstein, *The Repeal of Reticence: A History of America's Cultural and Legal Struggles over Free Speech, Obscenity, Sexual Liberation, and Modern Art* (New York: Hill and Wang, 1996), and Deborah Nelson, *Pursuing Privacy in Cold War America* (New York: Columbia University Press, 2002). The nineteenth century has fared better, especially in the hands of literary scholars. See, for example, Milette Shamir, *Inexpressible Privacy: The Interior Life of Antebellum American Literature* (Philadelphia: University of Pennsylvania Press, 2006); Stacey Margolis, *The Public Life of Privacy in Nineteenth-Century American Literature* (Durham, NC: Duke University Press, 2009); and Katherine Adams, *Owning Up: Privacy, Property, and Belonging in U.S. Women's Life Writing* (New York: Oxford University Press, 2009). Other important recent works are David Vincent, *Privacy: A Short History* (Boston: Polity Books, 2016), and for the

British context, Deborah Cohen, *Family Secrets: Living with Shame from the Victorians to the Present Day* (London: Viking, 2013).

10. This literature is vast. For starting points, see Robert Post, "The Social Foundations of Privacy: Community and Self in the Common Law Tort," *California Law Review* 77: 5 (1989): 957–1010; Jeb Rubenfeld, "The Right of Privacy," *Harvard Law Review* 102: 4 (1989): 737–807; David J. Garrow, *Liberty and Sexuality: The Right to Privacy and the Making of* Roe v. Wade (New York: Macmillan, 1994); John W. Johnson, Griswold v. Connecticut: *Birth Control and the Constitutional Right of Privacy* (Lawrence: University Press of Kansas, 2005); Lawrence M. Friedman, *Guarding Life's Dark Secrets: Legal and Social Controls over Reputation, Propriety, and Privacy* (Stanford, CA: Stanford Press, 2007); and Neil M. Richards and Daniel J. Solove, "Prosser's Privacy Law: A Mixed Legacy," *California Law Review* 98 (2010): 1887–1924.

11. For exemplary recent works, see Samantha Barbas, *Laws of Image: Privacy and Publicity in America* (Stanford, CA: Stanford Law Books, 2015); Leigh Ann Wheeler, *How Sex Became a Civil Liberty* (New York: Oxford University Press, 2013); and Alfred W. McEvoy, *Policing America's Empire: The United States, the Philippines, and the Rise of the Surveillance State* (Madison: University of Wisconsin Press, 2009). There is also a well-developed literature on "private life." See the multivolume *A History of Private Life* (Cambridge, MA: Harvard University Press); most relevant to this discussion is volume 5, *Riddles of Identity in Modern Times*, ed. Antoine Prost and Gérard Vincent (1991). Patricia Meyer Spacks notes, however, that privacy has little to do with the traditional distinction between public and private spheres and that the term "privacy" "has received much less historicized attention." *Privacy: Concealing the Eighteenth-Century Self* (Chicago: University of Chicago Press, 2003), 4.

12. See, for example, the dueling plots of Christian Parenti, *The Soft Cage: Surveillance in America from Slavery to the War on Terror* (New York: Basic Books, 2003) and Garrow, *Liberty and Sexuality*.

13. As anthropologist Susan Gal writes, "public and private do not simply describe the social world in any direct way; they are rather tools for arguments about and in that world." "A Semiotics of the Public / Private Distinction," *differences: A Journal of Feminist Cultural Studies* 13: 1 (2002): 79.

14. Lawrence Tribe, *American Constitutional Law*, 2nd ed. (Mineola, NY: West Academic Publishing, 1988), 1302.

15. Christena Nippert-Eng, *Islands of Privacy* (Chicago: University of Chicago Press, 2010), 6.

16. In the influential terms laid out by David Hollinger, public discourses around privacy seem both to intersect with and inform the more precise discourses of specialized academic and legal communities. David A. Hollinger, "Historians and the Discourse of Intellectuals," in *In the American Province: Studies in the*

History and Historiography of Ideas (Bloomington: Indiana University Press, 1985), 130–151.

17. For a compelling recent statement of this argument, see Khiara M. Bridges, *The Poverty of Privacy Rights* (Stanford, CA: Stanford Law Books, 2017).

18. Simone Browne suggests for this reason that the "conditions of blackness" might "help social theorists understand our contemporary conditions of surveillance." *Dark Matters: On the Surveillance of Blackness* (Durham, NC: Duke University Press, 2015), 8.

19. One classic statement is by Edward Shils, "Privacy: Its Constitution and Its Vicissitudes," *Law and Contemporary Problems* 31 (1966): 301, 291, although Shils noted privacy's broader appeal to the "upper sections of the working classes" by the later nineteenth century. Alan Westin referred to the first calls for a "right to privacy" in the United States as "a protest by spokesmen for patrician values" against those of mass society in his *Privacy and Freedom* (New York: Atheneum, 1967), 348. See also Barry Schwartz, "The Social Psychology of Privacy," *American Journal of Sociology* 70 (May 1968): 743.

20. E. L. Godkin, "The Right to Privacy," *The Nation*, December 25, 1890, p. 497.

21. A number of other works by Auden in this period also carry themes of national or official culture's oppositional relationship to the individual, including his "School Children" and "Dover." As one authority writes, "Almost all critics have overlooked the depth and thoroughness of Auden's critique of that most modern marker of personal identity, nationality." Stan Smith, ed., *The Cambridge Companion to W. H. Auden* (New York: Cambridge University Press, 2004), 44.

22. Westin, *Privacy and Freedom*, 7.

23. Daniel Solove, *Understanding Privacy* (Cambridge, MA: Harvard University Press, 2008), 1.

24. Gary T. Marx, *Windows into the Soul: Surveillance and Society in an Age of High Technology* (Chicago: University of Chicago Press, 2016), 27.

25. Legal scholars, feminist theorists, and philosophers have made valiant efforts to pin down the term, something I will not attempt to do here. Key works include Westin, *Privacy and Freedom*; Ruth Gavison, "Privacy and the Limits of Law," *Yale Law Journal* 89 (1980): 421–428; Ferdinand Schoeman, ed., *Philosophical Dimensions of Privacy: An Anthology* (Cambridge: Cambridge University Press, 1984); Hixson, *Privacy in a Public Society*; Joan B. Landes, ed., *Feminism, the Public, and the Private* (New York: Oxford University Press, 1998); Etzioni, *The Limits of Privacy*; and Anita L. Allen, *Why Privacy Isn't Everything: Feminist Reflections on Personal Accountability* (Lanham, MD: Rowman & Littlefield, 2003). Leading treatments in the past decade include Solove, *Understanding Privacy*; Helen Nissenbaum, *Privacy in Context: Technology, Policy, and the Integrity of Social Life* (Stanford, CA: Stanford Law

Books, 2010); and Julie Cohen, "What Privacy Is For," *Harvard Law Review* (2013): 1904–1933. Another set of scholars has explored the politics of privacy—whether it is at base a liberatory or coercive social value—something I do not take up here except as it affects public debates in the past.

26. Historians have carefully unearthed the growing apparatus of the American surveillance state from the late nineteenth century onward, including covert intelligence networks and domestic espionage. Most Americans at the time lived blissfully unaware of this surveillance net, however.

27. One should not overdraw the distinction. Scholars have convincingly portrayed the work of governance in the twentieth century as a public-private partnership, with the duties of the state partnered with, taken over by, or outsourced to private or voluntary organizations. See Brian Balogh, *The Associational State: American Governance in the Twentieth Century* (Philadelphia: University of Pennsylvania Press, 2015), and Gary Gerstle, *Liberty and Coercion: The Paradox of American Government from the Founding to the Present* (Princeton, NJ: Princeton University Press, 2015).

1. Technologies of Publicity

1. Henry James, *The Complete Notebooks of Henry James,* ed. Leon Edel and Lyall H. Powers (New York: Oxford University Press, 1987), 40; quoted in Rochelle Gurstein, *The Repeal of Reticence: A History of America's Cultural and Legal Struggles over Free Speech, Obscenity, Sexual Liberation, and Modern Art* (New York: Hill and Wang, 1996), 35. See James's *The Reverberator* of 1888. The novel, which was originally serialized in *Macmillan's* magazine that year, concerns the publication of scandalous information about a Parisian family printed in an American newspaper.

2. Frederick S. Lane, *American Privacy: The 400-Year History of Our Most Contested Right* (Boston: Beacon Press, 2009), 30–31; Stanley Reiser, "Technology and the Senses in Twentieth Century Medicine," in *Medicine and the Five Senses,* ed. W. F. Bynum and Roy Porter (New York: Cambridge University Press, 1993), 265.

3. Robert H. Wiebe, *The Search for Order, 1877–1920* (New York, 1967), xiii, 2–3.

4. See James Vernon, *Distant Strangers: How Britain Became Modern* (Berkeley: University of California Press, 2014), 18–50. Sociologist Steven L. Nock argues that life among strangers "produced greater and more pervasive privacy," but that "social mechanisms of *surveillance* have been elaborated or developed" in response in order to manage the problems of reputation and trust. In effect, "a society of strangers is one of immense personal privacy. Surveillance is the cost of that privacy." *The Costs of Privacy: Surveillance and Reputation in America* (Hawthorne, NY: Aldine De Gruyter, 1993), 1; emphasis in original.

5. One scholar characterizes this era as one when "issues of 'privacy' and 'publicity' became something of a public crisis." See Stacy Margolis, "The Public Life: The Discourse of Privacy in the Age of Celebrity," *Arizona Quarterly* 51:2 (Summer 1995): 81–101; quote on p. 84.

6. The controversy stirred up by Anne Royall, "America's first nationally recognized gossip columnist," is just one example. Royall was a critic who from 1826 on "pried shamelessly into the lives of others" in order to skewer contemporary politics and personalities. See Nancy Isenberg, "The Infamous Anne Royall: Jacksonian Gossip, Scribbler, and Scold," in *When Private Talk Goes Public: Gossip in American History*, ed. Kathleen A. Feeley and Jennifer Frost (New York: Palgrave Macmillan, 2014), 79–100; quote on p. 89.

7. David Flaherty, *Privacy in Colonial New England* (Charlottesville: University Press of Virginia, 1972), 245.

8. Jonathan L. Hafetz, "'A Man's Home Is His Castle?' Reflections on the Home, the Family, and Privacy during the Late Nineteenth and Early Twentieth Centuries," *William & Mary Journal of Women and the Law* 8 (2001): 175–242.

9. See Flaherty, *Privacy in Colonial New England*; Edmund S. Morgan, *The Puritan Family: Religion and Domestic Relations in Seventeenth-Century New England*, rev. ed. (New York: Harper & Row, 1966); and Laurel Thatcher Ulrich, *Good Wives: Image and Reality in the Lives of Women in Northern New England, 1650–1750* (New York: Knopf, 1982).

10. John Demos, *A Little Commonwealth: Family Life in Plymouth Colony* (New York: Oxford University Press, 1970), 186, 152, 46–47. Demos emphasizes the scrutiny of Puritan households by the larger community, precisely because of the many important social functions the family played. "When a given family failed in some area, or experienced serious conflict among its individual members, the authorities might decide to intervene. The 'harmony' of husband and wife, the subordination of children to parents—even such internal matters as these came, in theory, under official scrutiny," 184.

11. Flaherty, *Privacy in Colonial New England*, 245. Flaherty establishes that colonists saw privacy as "part of their traditional English heritage" and that a "right of privacy existed . . . that was both traditional and customary," 242, 248.

12. See the discussion of existing protections of communications; "the sanctity of the mails"; the home; and client-attorney, patient-doctor, and penitent-priest confidentiality in Comment, "The Right to Privacy in Nineteenth Century America," *Harvard Law Review* 94: 8 (1981): 1892–1910.

13. Simone Browne, *Dark Matters: On the Surveillance of Blackness* (Durham, NC: Duke University Press, 2015). See also Sally E. Hadden, *Slave Patrols: Law and Violence in Virginia and the Carolinas* (Cambridge, MA: Harvard University Press, 2001).

14. John W. Johnson, Griswold v. Connecticut: *Birth Control and the Constitutional Right of Privacy* (Lawrence: University Press of Kansas, 2005), 57.

15. See Stephanie McCurry, *Masters of Small Worlds: Yeoman Households, Gender Relations, and the Political Culture of the Antebellum South Carolina Low Country* (New York: Oxford University Press, 1995).

16. David J. Seipp, "The Right to Privacy in American History" (Cambridge, MA: Harvard University, Program on Information Resources Policy, 1978), 5.

17. See Dorothy J. Glancy, "The Invention of the Right to Privacy," *Arizona Law Review* 21: 1 (1979): 1–39. She writes that "up until Warren and Brandeis published *The Right to Privacy,* most of the legal discussion had focused on the individual's right to privacy as a limitation on governmental interferences with individual freedom"; this began to change at midcentury, 29. Philippa Strum has argued in fact that there were few opportunities to invade privacy and no real need to articulate a right to such before the later nineteenth century. *Privacy: The Debate in the United States since 1945* (New York: Harcourt Brace, 1998).

18. Lane, *American Privacy,* 32–33; Seipp, "The Right to Privacy in American History," 15.

19. "To live an entirely private life," wrote Hannah Arendt, capturing this older sense of privacy, "means above all to be deprived of things essential to a truly human life: to be deprived of the reality that comes from being seen and heard by others." *The Human Condition,* 2nd ed. (Chicago: University of Chicago Press, 2013 [1958]), 58.

20. Michael A. Weinstein explains that "privacy, like alienation, loneliness, ostracism, and isolation, is a condition of being-apart-from-others. However, alienation is suffered, loneliness is dreaded, ostracism and isolation are borne with resignation or pain, while privacy is sought after." "The Uses of Privacy in the Good Life," in *Privacy and Personality,* ed. J. Roland Pennock and John W. Chapman (New Brunswick, NJ: Aldine / Transaction, 1971), 88. Solitude and isolation were considered sinful in classical thought because they were linked to self-love, privation, and man's ability to close in on himself. David Rosen and Aaron Santesso note that it was only "with considerable ambivalence that, over the eighteenth century, the connotations of being alone slowly shifted from the negative to the positive." "Inviolate Personality and the Literary Roots of the Right to Privacy," *Law and Literature* 23: 1 (2011): 1–25; quote on p. 11.

21. Patricia Meyer Spacks charts the emergence of these connotations of privacy in eighteenth-century novels in *Privacy: Concealing the Eighteenth-Century Self* (Chicago: University of Chicago Press, 2003), 228.

22. The literature on domesticity and separate spheres is extensive. Key early works are Barbara Welter, "The Cult of True Womanhood," *American Quarterly* 18

(1966): 151–174; Nancy Cott, *The Bonds of Womanhood: "Woman's Sphere" in New England, 1780–1835* (New Haven, CT: Yale University Press, 1977); and Mary P. Ryan, *The Cradle of the Middle Class: The Family in Oneida County, New York, 1790–1865* (Cambridge: Cambridge University Press, 1981).

23. Jeannie Suk, *At Home in the Law: How the Domestic Violence Revolution Is Transforming Privacy* (New Haven, CT: Yale University Press, 2009), 1–2.

24. Michael McKeon provides a comprehensive history of the public-private division as it solidified in England across the seventeenth and eighteenth centuries in *The Secret History of Domesticity: Public, Private, and the Division of Knowledge* (Baltimore: Johns Hopkins University Press, 2005). For the nineteenth century, see Inga Bryden and Janet Floyd, eds., *Domestic Space: Reading the Nineteenth-Century Interior* (New York: Manchester University Press, 1999).

25. John L. Locke, *Eavesdropping: An Intimate History* (New York: Oxford, 2010), 25.

26. Milette Shamir, *Inexpressible Privacy: The Interior Life of Antebellum American Literature* (Philadelphia: University of Pennsylvania Press, 2006), 4; S. J. Kleinberg, "Gendered Space: Housing, Privacy and Domesticity in the Nineteenth-Century United States," in Bryden and Floyd, eds., *Domestic Space*, 142–161.

27. John F. Kasson, *Rudeness and Civility: Manners in Nineteenth-Century Urban America* (New York: Hill and Wang, 1990).

28. Jane H. Hunter, "Inscribing the Self in the Heart of the Family: Diaries and Girlhood in Late-Victorian America" *American Quarterly* 44: 1(1992): 51–81.

29. Edward Shils, "Privacy: Its Constitution and Vicissitudes," *Law and Contemporary Problems* 31 (1966): 281–306. See also Martin Hewitt, "District Visiting and the Constitution of Domestic Space in the Mid-Nineteenth Century," in Bryden and Floyd, eds., *Domestic Space*, 121–141. Lawrence M. Friedman agrees that the notion that "home is the haven, the island of immunity, the place of private life" only became well established for "the average person" in the nineteenth century. *Private Lives: Families, Individuals, and the Law* (Cambridge, MA: Harvard University Press, 2004), 9.

30. Justine S. Murison, "'Nudity and Other Sensitive States': Counterprivacy in Herman Melville's Fiction," *American Literature* 89: 4 (2017): 699.

31. On the Beecher-Tilton scandal, see Richard Wightman Fox, *Trials of Intimacy: Love and Loss in the Beecher-Tilton Scandal* (Chicago: University of Chicago Press, 1999); and Debby Applegate, *The Most Famous Man in America: The Biography of Henry Ward Beecher* (New York: Doubleday, 2006). For the way Beecher's case would inform and constrain the later "right to privacy," see Susan E. Gallagher, "Privacy and Conformity: Rethinking 'The Right Most Valued by Civilized Men,'" *Touro Law Review* 33: 1 (2017): 159–175.

32. Henry Ward Beecher, as quoted in *Life Thoughts from Pulpits and from Poets*, selected by Alfred I. Holmes (Brooklyn, NY: A. I. Holmes, 1871), 218–219.

33. Deborah Cohen, *Family Secrets: Living with Shame from the Victorians to the Present Day* (New York: Viking, 2013). Cohen argues, in the British context, that "private" family life always entailed the external management of reputation. She argues further that the efforts of Victorian and Edwardian families to shield the indiscretions of their members from outsiders laid the groundwork for privacy rights of the later twentieth century: "the right to tell without cost," 268. See also Brian Connolly, *Domestic Intimacies: Incest and the Liberal Subject in Nineteenth-Century America* (Philadelphia: University of Pennsylvania Press, 2014); and Lawrence Friedman, *Guarding Life's Dark Secrets: Legal and Social Controls over Reputation, Propriety, and Privacy* (Stanford, CA: Stanford University Press, 2007). For debates over the propriety of publicizing domestic affairs in the political arena in the earlier nineteenth century, see Norma Basch, "Marriage, Morals, and Politics in the Election of 1828," *Journal of American History* 80: 3 (December 1993): 890–918.

34. Gallagher, "Privacy and Conformity," 168, 171–172.

35. Ruth H. Bloch, "The American Revolution, Wife Beating, and the Emergent Value of Privacy," *Early American Studies: An Interdisciplinary Journal* 5: 2 (2007): 223–251. A legal landmark was the 1824 case of *Bradley v. State*, "in which the value of familial privacy was joined to the (unfounded) premise that husbands possess an age-old right to physically chastise disobedient wives." See also Linda K. Kerber, *No Constitutional Right to Be Ladies: Women and the Obligations of Citizenship* (New York: Hill and Wang, 1998); and Reva B. Siegel, "The Rule of Love: Wife Beating as Prerogative and Privacy," *Yale Law Journal* 105 (1996): 2117–2207.

36. Quoted in Gurstein, *The Repeal of Reticence*, 29. Others made a similar case, including Crystal Eastman and later Virginia Woolf. See *Crystal Eastman on Women and Revolution*, ed. Blanche Wiesen Cook (New York: Oxford University Press); and Woolf, *A Room of One's Own* (London: Leonard and Virginia Woolf at the Hogarth Press, 1929).

37. Anita L. Allen and Erin Mack, "How Privacy Got Its Gender," *Northern Illinois University Law Review* 10 (Spring 1990): 441–478.

38. Quoted in Reva B. Siegel "She the People: The Nineteenth Amendment, Sex Equality, Federalism, and the Family," *Harvard Law Review* 115: 4 (2002): 947–1008; quote on p. 1001. As Siegel notes, the senator portrayed "the federal government enfranchising women in the form of a man meddling in another's marital business." See also Rebecca Ann Rix, "Gender and Reconstitution: The Individual and Family Basis of Republican Government Contested, 1868–1925" (PhD diss., Yale University, 2008).

39. *Boyd. v. United States*, 116 U.S. 616, 630 (1886).

40. Gurstein, *The Repeal of Reticence*, 17–18.

41. To cite just one example, some residents of Society Hill in Philadelphia in the late nineteenth century used "house mirrors" to monitor what was going on up and down the block; Locke, *Eavesdropping*, 27.

42. Shils, "Privacy: Its Constitution and Vicissitudes," 293–294. As he described it, this was "a new sector of the profession of journalism that regarded the penetration of the private sphere as its main occupational task."

43. David E. Shi, *Facing Facts: Realism in American Thought and Culture, 1850–1920* (New York: Oxford University Press, 1995).

44. Indeed, the eminence accorded to Samuel Warren and Louis Brandeis's "The Right to Privacy," published in the *Harvard Law Review* in 1890, has led scholars to overlook how peripheral its concerns were for Brandeis. Neil Richards contends that Brandeis's "subsequent public career shows a devotion not to the right of privacy, but to identifying and developing an alternative value he called 'the duty of publicity.'" "The Puzzle of Brandeis, Privacy, and Speech," 1300. See also Kenneth Kersch, *Constructing Civil Liberties: Discontinuities in the Development of American Constitutional Law* (New York: Cambridge University Press, 2004), 56. On the "duty of publicity," see Melvyn Urofsky, *Louis D. Brandeis: A Life* (New York: Pantheon Books, 2009), 98.

45. Martin Bulmer, Kevin Bales, and Kathryn Kish Sklar, eds., *The Social Survey in Historical Perspective, 1880–1940* (New York: Cambridge University Press, 1991); Ellen F. Fitzpatrick, *Endless Crusade: Women Social Scientists and Progressive Reform* (New York: Oxford University Press, 1990); Cecelia Tichi, *Exposés and Excess: Muckraking in America 1900–2000* (Philadelphia: University of Pennsylvania Press, 2004); Steve Weinberg, *Taking on the Trust: The Epic Battle of Ida Tarbell and John D. Rockefeller* (New York: W. W. Norton, 2008); Michael Schudson, *Discovering the News: A Social History of American Newspapers* (New York: Basic Books, 1978).

46. Gurstein, *Repeal of Reticence*, 32–33, 38. See also Helen Lefkowitz Horowitz, *Rereading Sex: Battles over Sexual Knowledge and Suppression in Nineteenth-Century America* (New York: Alfred A. Knopf, 2002).

47. David Seipp addresses in detail the political concerns about monopoly over the news, as well as campaigns for government ownership of the telegraph network, known as the "postal telegraphy" movement, in "The Right to Privacy in American History," 59–65; quotation on p. 56.

48. The Associated Press, writes Menahem Blondheim, was likely the first "private-sector monopoly to operate on a national scale in the United States." *News over the Wires: The Telegraph and the Flow of Public Information in America, 1844–1897* (Cambridge, MA: Harvard University Press, 1994), 7.

49. Richard White emphasizes the battles over the mass circulation and control of networked financial information and the possibilities it introduced for

corruption, as "quotidian faults—lying, deception, and dishonesty—played out largely on paper and along telegraph lines, but on a national and international scale." See his "Information, Markets, and Corruption: Transcontinental Railroads in the Gilded Age," *Journal of American History* 90: 1 (2003): 21, and more generally, *Railroaded: The Transcontinentals and the Making of Modern America* (New York: Norton, 2011).

50. Gallagher, "Privacy and Conformity," 171.

51. Seipp, "The Right to Privacy in American History," 104.

52. Alfred W. McCoy summarizes this burst of technological innovation in *Policing America's Empire: The United States, the Philippines, and the Rise of the Surveillance State* (Madison: University of Wisconsin Press, 2009), 21–23.

53. Quoted in Seipp, "The Right to Privacy in American History," 13.

54. Horowitz, *Rereading Sex*, 358–403; Donna Dennis, *Licentious Gotham: Erotic Publishing and Its Prosecution in Nineteenth-Century New York* (Cambridge, MA: Harvard University Press, 2009), 238–304.

55. See, for example, *New York Times*, July 10, 1872, p. 4; "Postal Cards and Privacy," *New York Times*, June 17, 1875, p. 4.

56. Quoted in Lane, *American Privacy*, 30–31.

57. See Simone Müller, *Wiring the World: The Social and Cultural Creation of Global Telegraph Networks* (New York: Columbia University Press, 2016).

58. David Hochfelder, *The Telegraph in America, 1832–1920* (Baltimore: Johns Hopkins University Press, 2013), 83.

59. Seipp, "The Right to Privacy in American History," 105.

60. Glancy, "The Invention of the Right to Privacy," 7.

61. Wiretapping had already been criminalized in some states by 1890 or was prohibited via "laws against interference with telegraph company property." In addition, "disclosure by employees, including operators and those with access to messages retained in office files, was prohibited by company rules and by statute in nearly every state." See Comment, "The Right to Privacy in Nineteenth Century America," 1901.

62. Tom Standage, *The Victorian Internet: The Remarkable Story of the Telegraph and the Nineteenth Century's On-Line Pioneers* (New York: Walker and Company, 1998).

63. Extensive congressional searches of telegraph messages during Reconstruction, sometimes with the cooperation of telegraph companies—related to questions of official misconduct and voting fraud during the 1876 election controversy—prompted "the first important appeal for legal recognition of a right to privacy" in the late nineteenth century, according to Seipp; "The Right to Privacy in American History," 30. He notes that issuing subpoenas for telegraph transmissions rather than direct wiretapping was the chief practice and concern, 105.

64. Seipp, "The Right to Privacy in American History," 107–108.

65. As the operator became less visible and party lines disappeared, expectations of privacy increased; Seipp, "The Right to Privacy in American History," 108.

66. Quoted in Claude S. Fischer, *America Calling: A Social History of the Telephone to 1940* (Berkeley: University of California Press, 1992), 71.

67. Quoted in Lane, *American Privacy*, 78.

68. Seipp, "The Right to Privacy in American History," 106–107.

69. Fischer, *America Calling*, 75–84; on rural women's use of the telephone, see 226–227.

70. Carolyn Marvin, *When Old Technologies Were New: Thinking about Electric Communication in the Late Nineteenth Century* (New York: Oxford University Press, 1988), 67–108; Claude S. Fischer, "'Touch Someone': The Telephone Industry Discovers Sociability," *Technology and Culture* 29: 1 (January 1988): 32–61; Fischer, *America Calling*, chs. 3, 8. Fischer notes that telephone companies even tried to "script appropriate conversation," including a failed campaign to suppress the greeting "hello" as a vulgarity, 70–71.

71. Robert MacDougall, "The Wire Devils: Pulp Thrillers, the Telephone, and Action at a Distance in the Wiring of a Nation," *American Quarterly* 58: 3 (2006): 715–741. For more on the fears and fascination raised by the "wire" see Linda Simon, *Dark Light: Electricity and Anxiety from the Telegraph to the X-Ray* (Orlando: Harcourt, 2004).

72. Arthur Stringer, *Phantom Wires* (Boston: Little, Brown, 1907), 221–222. See also *The Wire Tappers* (Boston: Little, Brown, 1906). The national telephone and telegraph networks set off both utopian and dystopian representations, complete with metaphors of the octopus, spider, and hydra; MacDougall, "The Wire Devils."

73. Lane, *American Privacy*, 22.

74. Jessica Lake, *The Face That Launched a Thousand Lawsuits: The American Women Who Forged a Right to Privacy* (New Haven, CT: Yale University Press, 2016), 27–28, 30. For a comprehensive cultural history of American photography, see Miles Orvell, *American Photography* (New York: Oxford University Press, 2003).

75. Robert Mensel, "Kodakers Lying in Wait: Amateur Photography and the Right of Privacy in New York, 1885–1915," *American Quarterly* 43 (March 1991): 24–45.

76. Lake, *The Face That Launched a Thousand Lawsuits*, 13.

77. Lake, *The Face That Launched a Thousand Lawsuits*, 30, 33.

78. Ronald R. Thomas, "Making Darkness Visible: Capturing the Criminal and Observing the Law in Victorian Photography and Detective Fiction," in *Victorian Literature and the Victorian Visual Imagination*, ed. Carol T. Christ and John O. Jordan (Berkeley: University of California Press, 1995), 147.

79. Lake, *The Face That Launched a Thousand Lawsuits*, 33.
80. Frank Luther Mott, *American Journalism: A History, 1690–1960* (New York: Macmillan, 1962), 444; Frederick Lane, *American Privacy*, 22; F. B. Sanborn of the *Springfield Republican* as quoted in Seipp, "The Right to Privacy in American History," 67.
81. See Minot J. Savage, "A Profane View of the Sanctum," *North American Review* 141 (August 1885): 145; C. B. Pallen, "Newspaperism," *Lippincott's* 38 (November 1886): 475. Both are quoted in Seipp, "The Right to Privacy in American History," 68.
82. John Gilmer Speed, "The Right of Privacy," *North American Review* 163 (July 1896): 73. Frank Luther Mott, *History of American Magazines*, vol. 4: 1885–1905 (Cambridge, MA: Belknap Press of Harvard University Press, 1958–1968), 1–14, 751–755.
83. Maureen E. Montgomery, *Displaying Women: Spectacles of Leisure in Edith Wharton's New York* (New York: Routledge, 1998), 143.
84. Sven Beckert, *The Monied Metropolis: New York City and the Consolidation of the American Bourgeoisie, 1850–1896* (New York: Cambridge University Press, 2001). Beckert has traced the consolidation of a monied elite by the 1890s, rooted in New York, which both saw itself as a class apart and was perceived as such by others, engendering deep class hostilities.
85. E. L. Godkin would charge for this reason that gossip had been altered by "the advent of the newspapers, or rather of a particular class of newspapers," converting curiosity into "an effectual demand" and gossip "a marketable commodity." Godkin, "The Rights of the Citizen: To His Own Reputation," *Scribner's Magazine* (July 1890): 66.
86. Lane, *American Privacy*, 48; Montgomery, *Displaying Women*, 147; *New York World*, Sunday Magazine section, August 10, 1902, pp. 6–7.
87. Montgomery, *Displaying Women*, 146.
88. Don R. Pember, *Privacy and the Press* (Seattle: University of Washington Press, 1972); Schudson, *Discovering the News*, 91–105.
89. Samantha Barbas, *Laws of Image: Privacy and Publicity in America* (Stanford, CA: Stanford University Press, 2015), 9. See also Neal Gabler's discussion of the new visual culture of the nineteenth century in *Life, the Movie: How Entertainment Conquered Reality* (New York: Alfred A. Knopf, 1998).
90. Barbas, *Laws of Image*, 45–62; quote on p. 46.
91. Lake, *The Face That Launched a Thousand Lawsuits*, 45–46.
92. "Will Not Be Photographed in Tights," *Chicago Tribune*, June 30, 1890, p. 6.
93. Glancy, "The Invention of the Right to Privacy," 8. See also Brook Thomas, "The Construction of Privacy in and around the Bostonians," *American Literature* 64 (December 1992): 719–747.

94. Godkin, "The Rights of the Citizen," 65.
95. Godkin, "The Rights of the Citizen," 58. As Dorothy Glancy notes, the fact that criminal libel and the law of defamation had fallen out of use as a defense against true but damaging information being printed made way for the new right of privacy; "The Invention of the Right to Privacy," 12–16.
96. Godkin, "The Rights of the Citizen," 65–67.
97. Montgomery, *Displaying Women*, 147.
98. See especially Edith Wharton's *House of Mirth* (1905). Leo Braudy, *The Frenzy of Renown: Fame and Its History* (New York: Oxford University Press, 1986).
99. Loren Glass writes that private life in fact "achieved its significance through public exposure in the new metropolitan dailies and mass-market magazines." *Authors Inc.: Literary Celebrity in the United States, 1880–1980* (New York: New York University Press, 2004), 11. See also Neal Gabler, *Winchell: Gossip, Power, and the Culture of Celebrity* (New York: Knopf, 1994); and Margolis, "The Public Life," 81–101.
100. Samuel D. Warren and Louis D. Brandeis, "The Right to Privacy," *Harvard Law Review* 4 (1890): 193–220. Fred Shapiro, "The Most-Cited Law Review Articles," *California Law Review* 73 (1985): 1540; James H. Barron, "Warren and Brandeis, 'The Right to Privacy,' 4 *Harvard Law Review* 193 (1890): Demystifying a Landmark Citation," *Suffolk Law Review* 13 (1979). Also see Linda Greenhouse, "Milestone Anniversary for the Right to Privacy," *New York Times*, December 26, 1990, p. 22. Dorothy Glancy notes, more precisely, that Warren and Brandeis did not invent the "right to privacy," but rather a legal theory that allowed other developments to be subsumed under that principle; "The Invention of the Right to Privacy," 3. A few critics have argued that Warren and Brandeis and later commentators all exaggerated the novelty of the claim and that in fact laws concerning the home, communications, and personal information in the form of public records added up to "ample and explicit protection of privacy in its own right" already by 1890. Warren and Brandeis took up one of the least protected areas: restraint of press. See Comment, "The Right to Privacy in Nineteenth Century America," 1894.
101. The two were law partners from 1879 to 1889, when Warren left to manage the family business; Glancy, "The Invention of the Right to Privacy," 5.
102. The origin of Brandeis and Warren's article has been the stuff of legal legend. One oft-told story—that the essay was provoked by the press coverage of Warren's daughter's wedding (impossible, as she was six years old at the time)—has been debunked by Amy Gajda in "What if Samuel D. Warren Hadn't Married a Senator's Daughter?: Uncovering the Press Coverage That Led to 'The Right to Privacy,'" *Michigan State Law Review* 35 (2008): 35–60. Others have judged the lawyers' characterization of the 1890s Boston press as inaccurate; see Pember, *Privacy and the Press*, 33–42.

103. Glancy, "The Invention of the Right to Privacy," 6.
104. Roscoe Pound, "Interests of Personality," *Harvard Law Review* 28 (1915): 343. The article is routinely described as the most influential legal essay in American history; Strum, *Privacy: The Debate in the United States since 1945*, 3. Benjamin Bratman argues that the article itself "gave birth" to a right to privacy in the United States. "Brandeis and Warren's 'The Right to Privacy' and the Birth of the Right to Privacy," *Tennessee Law Review* 69 (2002): 623–651. Indeed, the essay's prominence has overshadowed other genealogies of the right to privacy in the United States. Caroline Danielson, for example, has argued for the importance of an 1881 Michigan case (and a similar claim in Vermont the year before) that revolved around bodily privacy during childbirth, rather than the "inviolable personality." "The Gender of Privacy and the Embodied Self: Examining the Origins of the Right to Privacy in U.S. Law," *Feminist Studies* 25: 2 (Summer 1999): 311–344. See also Jessica Lake's account of *DeMay v. Roberts* in *The Face That Launched a Thousand Lawsuits*, 89–116.
105. See, for example, "The Right to Be Let Alone," *Atlantic Monthly* 67 (1891): 428–429; and "The Defense of Privacy," *The Spectator* 66 (February 7, 1891): 200. Allen and Mack, "How Privacy Got Its Gender," 457, n. 84; *Kyllo v. United States*, 533 U.S. 27 (2001).
106. Thomas M. Cooley, *A Treatise on the Law of Torts, or the Wrongs Which Arise Independent of Contract*, 2nd ed. (Chicago: Callaghan & Co., 1888) declared that the "right to one's person may be said to be a right of complete immunity" and that privacy was the right "to be let alone." See "Symposium: The Right to Privacy One Hundred Years Later," *Case Western Reserve Law Review* 41 (1990–1991).
107. These are the torts of: intrusion on seclusion, disclosure of private facts, false light, and appropriation of name or likeness. William L. Prosser, "Privacy," *California Law Review* 48: 3 (1960): 383–423. See, for example, Samantha Barbas, "The Death of the Public Disclosure Tort: A Historical Perspective," *Yale Journal of Law & the Humanities* 22 (2010): 171–215. Recently, a number of critics have suggested that Warren and Brandeis's conception has become irrelevant in the "information age." For a review, see Neil M. Richards and Daniel J. Solove, "Prosser's Privacy Law: A Mixed Legacy," *California Law Review* 98 (2010): 1887–1924.
108. Key critics are Harry Kalven Jr., "Privacy in Tort Law—Were Warren and Brandeis Wrong?" *Law and Contemporary Problems* 31: 2 (1966): 326–341; and Diane L. Zimmerman, "Requiem for a Heavyweight: A Farewell to Warren and Brandeis's Privacy Tort," *Cornell Law Review* 68 (1982–83): 291–367.
109. Warren and Brandeis, "The Right to Privacy," 196–197.
110. Godkin, "The Rights of the Citizen," 61.
111. Warren and Brandeis, "The Right to Privacy," 195–196, 207, 219.

112. Warren and Brandeis, "The Right to Privacy," 196.

113. Godkin, "The Rights of the Citizen," 67.

114. Warren and Brandeis, "The Right to Privacy," 196.

115. Warren and Brandeis, "The Right to Privacy," 205, 207.

116. Quoted in Gurstein, *Repeal of Reticence*, 37. Georg Simmel, "The Sociology of Secrecy," trans. Albion W. Small, *American Journal of Sociology* 11: 4 (1906): 454.

117. Many fields in addition to law contributed to naming and describing "personality," including psychology, philosophy, advertising, and literature. See David M. Lubin, "Modern Psychological Selfhood in the Art of Thomas Eakins," in *Inventing the Psychological: Toward a Cultural History of Emotional Life in America*, ed. Joel Pfister and Nancy Schnog (New Haven, CT: Yale University Press, 1997), 133–166. By the 1920s, "personality" had gained a more superficial, surface meaning. Warren I. Susman, "'Personality' and the Making of Twentieth-Century Culture," in *Culture as History: The Transformation of American Society in the Twentieth Century* (New York: Pantheon, 1984), 271–285.

118. Glancy, "The Invention of the Right to Privacy." Glancy observes that concerns about interior or psychological privacy were long-standing, discernible for example in James Fenimore Cooper's, Emily Dickinson's, and David Henry Thoreau's writings as well. Others have traced Warren and Brandeis's conception of an "inviolate personality" to older literary and poetic conceptions of the individual as "self-generated" and requiring solitude for authentic self-realization, as in Wordsworth. Rosen and Santesso argue that legal scholars, in neglecting that tradition, have consistently misread "The Right to Privacy." "Inviolate Personality and the Literary Roots of the Right to Privacy."

119. Warren and Brandeis, "The Right to Privacy," 197.

120. Dorothy Glancy, "The Invention of the Right to Privacy."

121. Warren and Brandeis, "The Right to Privacy," 215–216.

122. Mary Ann Glendon, *Rights Talk: The Impoverishment of Political Discourse* (New York: Free Press, 1991), 50. See her discussion of early claims to a right to privacy starting on p. 50 and her discussion of the "rights of personality," 61–63.

123. Richards and Solove, "Prosser's Privacy Law," 1892. Another scholar characterizes the article's impetus as "the 'problem' of access by the lower classes of society to information about the upper classes." Randall Bezanson, "The 'Right to Privacy' Revisited: Privacy, News, and Social Change, 1890–1990," *California Law Review* 80: 5 (1992): 1133–1175.

124. Harry Kalven would write of Warren and Brandeis's essay in the 1960s, "There is a curious nineteenth century quaintness about the grievance, an air of injured gentility. . . . One may perhaps wonder if the tort is not an anachronism, a nineteenth century response to the mass press which is hardly in

keeping with the more robust tastes or mores of today." "Privacy in Tort Law," 329. On late nineteenth-century elite norms of privacy, see Friedman, *Guarding Life's Dark Secrets*, and Deborah Cohen, *Family Secrets*.

125. Godkin, "The Rights of the Citizen," 65.

126. Allen and Mack, "How Privacy Got Its Gender," 441.

127. Helen Nissenbaum, *Privacy in Context: Technology, Policy, and the Integrity of Social Life* (Stanford, CA: Stanford Law Books, 2010), 19.

128. Brandeis as quoted in Philippa Strum, ed., *Brandeis on Democracy* (Lawrence: University Press of Kansas, 1995), 197; my emphasis.

129. Godkin, "The Rights of the Citizen," 65.

130. "Travelers Dislike Privacy," *Chicago Daily Tribune*, August 13, 1899, p. 39.

131. Barbas, *Laws of Image*, 4.

132. Lake, *The Face That Launched a Thousand Lawsuits*, 5, 46.

133. Lake, *The Face That Launched a Thousand Lawsuits*, 44, 12, 227. Lake thus argues that "in its infancy, 'a right to privacy' was forged and shaped" largely by "women who brought actions protesting the use or circulation of unidentified images of their faces or bodies by others," 4, 75. She argues that these concerns preceded Warren and Brandeis's "right to privacy" and have been overshadowed by it.

134. *Roberson v. Rochester Folding Box Co.*, 64 N.E. 442 (N.Y. 1902). For a useful summary and analysis of the case and its fallout, see Gurstein, *The Repeal of Reticence*, 155–160.

135. Jamal Greene notes that almost all references to the "so-called right to privacy" in state courts occurred in the context of unwanted publicity or commercial exploitation. "The So-Called Right to Privacy," *UC Davis Law Review* 43 (2010): 715–747.

136. *Roberson v. Rochester Folding Box Co.*

137. "'Right of Privacy' Denied: State Court of Appeals Reverses Decision Awarding Defendant Damages for Use of Her Likeness," *New York Times*, July 2, 1902, p. 6.

138. The case was *Pavesich v. New England Life Insurance Company*. Georgia's court located the right to privacy in natural law and as part of individual liberty rather than as a protection from voyeurism, which Lake links to the fact that the case centered on a male plaintiff. *The Face That Launched a Thousand Lawsuits*, 72–74.

139. Alan F. Westin, *Privacy and Freedom* (New York: Atheneum, 1967), 346.

140. The Supreme Court of 1891 also acknowledged a minimal right to "inviolability of the person" by ruling that railroad companies could not force a physical examination on injured persons; *Union Pacific Railway v. Botsford*, 141 U.S. 250 (1891).

141. Scholars have detailed the failure of Warren and Brandeis's concept of an "inviolate personality" to gain traction in U.S. society and law. That vision of

individual dignity, buoyed by public and legal deference to it, has been much more at home in Europe in the form of a "right of personality." See Robert Post, "The Social Foundations of Privacy: Community and Self in the Common Law Tort," *California Law Review* 77: 5 (1989): 957–1010; James Q. Whitman, "The Two Western Cultures of Privacy: Dignity versus Liberty," *Yale Law Journal* 113 (2004): 1151–1221; Paul Schwartz and Karl-Nikolaus Peifer, "Prosser's *Privacy* and the German Right of Personality: Are Four Privacy Torts Better than One Unitary Concept?" *California Law Review* 98 (2010): 1925–1988; and Spiros Simitis, "Privacy—An Endless Debate?" *California Law Review* 98 (2010): 1989–2005. For a defense of the "inviolate personality" concept, see Edward J. Bloustein, "Privacy as an Aspect of Human Dignity: An Answer to Dean Prosser," *New York Law Review* 39 (1964): 962–1007.

142. Prosser, "Privacy," 383–423.

143. The "right to publicity" was confirmed in a 2nd Circuit ruling from 1953, *Haelan Laboratories, Inc. v. Topps Chewing Gum, Inc.*, but was referenced as early as 1905 in *Pavesich v. New England Life Insurance Company.*

144. Richards, "The Puzzle of Brandeis, Privacy, and Speech," 1343; Samantha Barbas, "Saving Privacy from History," *DePaul Law Review* 61 (2012): 1022.

145. "No Such Thing as Private Citizen: Privacy Is Unknown, for Tab Is Kept on Him from Cradle to Grave," *Chicago Daily Tribune*, July 27, 1902, p. 39.

146. Judith Walzer Leavitt, *Typhoid Mary: Captive to the Public's Health* (Boston: Beacon Press, 1996); Howard Markel, *Quarantine! East European Jewish Immigrants and the New York City Epidemics of 1892* (Baltimore: Johns Hopkins University Press, 1999).

147. See Amy L. Fairchild, Ronald Bayer, and James Colgrove with Daniel Wolfe, *Searching Eyes: Privacy, the State, and Disease Surveillance in America* (Berkeley: University of California Press, 2007), 46. See also Tera W. Hunter, *To 'joy My Freedom: Southern Black Women's Lives and Labors after the Civil War* (Cambridge, MA: Harvard University Press, 1997), 189–193; Nayan Shah, *Contagious Divides: Epidemics and Race in San Francisco's Chinatown* (Berkeley: University of California Press, 2001); Amy L. Fairchild, *Science at the Borders: Immigrant Medical Inspection and the Shaping of the Modern Industrial Labor Force* (Baltimore: Johns Hopkins University Press, 2003); Emily K. Abel, *Tuberculosis and the Politics of Exclusion: A History of Public Health and Migration to Los Angeles* (New Brunswick: Rutgers University Press, 2007); Samuel Kelton Roberts Jr., *Infectious Fear: Politics, Disease, and the Health Effects of Segregation* (Chapel Hill: University of North Carolina Press, 2009); and Guenter B. Risse, *Plague, Fear, and Politics in San Francisco's Chinatown* (Baltimore: Johns Hopkins University Press, 2012).

148. Fairchild et al., *Searching Eyes*, 49.

149. Fairchild et al., *Searching Eyes*, 10. Other forms of reporting were also required: physicians were urged to report public-health-related information, with some cities in the early twentieth century (such as Boston) investigating or prosecuting those who failed to report tuberculosis cases for example, 48.

150. "No Such Thing as Private Citizen," p. 39.

151. Michael Willrich, *Pox: An American History* (New York: Penguin, 2011), 14.

152. Margo J. Anderson, *The American Census: A Social History*, 2nd ed. (New Haven, CT: Yale University Press, 2015), 109, 88–89. She notes that the new machinery "prompted the statisticians to attempt much more complex cross tabulations of the information on the schedules," 107.

153. Fairchild et al., *Searching Eyes*, 7. Question 22, for instance, asked "whether suffering from acute or chronic disease and length of time afflicted," and Question 23 inquired as to "whether defective in mind, sight, hearing, or speech, or whether crippled, maimed, or deformed, with name of defect." Seipp, "The Right to Privacy in American History," 44.

154. E. L. Godkin, "The Census Questions," *The Nation* 50 (June 5, 1890): 445.

155. "The Census—A Questionable Feature," *Los Angeles Times*, June 2, 1890, p. 4.

156. Seipp, "The Right to Privacy in American History," 49–50. Some newspapers urged that citizens not respond to those questions, as did some physicians, 46. Inquiries for 1900 were scaled back, but the courts upheld a broader census inquiry in 1901 and applied legal penalties to those refusing to answer, 53.

157. McCoy, *Policing America's Empire*, 24, 26. This was the "golden age of private detective work." See Frank Morn, *"The Eye That Never Sleeps": A History of the Pinkerton National Detective Agency* (Bloomington: Indiana University Press, 1982).

158. Simon A. Cole, *Suspect Identities: A History of Fingerprinting and Criminal Identification* (Cambridge, MA: Harvard University Press, 2001), 20.

159. Thomas, "Making Darkness Visible," 136. See also Allan Sekula, "The Body and the Archive," in *The Contest of Meaning: Critical Histories of Photography*, ed. Richard Bolton (Cambridge, MA: MIT Press, 1989), 353–375.

160. McCoy, *Policing America's Empire*, 24.

161. McCoy argues that U.S. counterinsurgency and policing in the Philippines following occupation in 1898 paved the way for a national surveillance state at home and created the template for World War I, including "massive surveillance, vigilante violence, and the formation of a permanent internal security apparatus." *Policing America's Empire*, 8. For histories of the Bureau, see Rhodri Jeffreys-Jones, *The FBI: A History* (New Haven, CT: Yale University Press, 2007); Frank J. Donner, *Age of Surveillance: The Aims and Methods of America's Political Intelligence System* (New York: Knopf, 1980); and Fred J. Cook, *The FBI Nobody Knows* (New York: Macmillan, 1964). It would be renamed the Federal Bureau of Investigation in 1935.

NOTES TO PAGES 48-49

162. Beverly Gage, *The Day Wall Street Exploded: A Story of America in Its First Age of Terror* (New York: Oxford University Press, 2009), 96. Particularly important were the Haymarket bombing of 1886, the attempted shooting of Henry Clay Frick of the Carnegie Steel Works in Homestead, Pennsylvania, in 1892, and William McKinley's assassination in 1901. For an analysis of the importance of the assassination on attitudes toward the working class and anarchism, see Eric Rauchway, *Murdering McKinley: The Making of Theodore Roosevelt's America* (New York: Hill and Wang, 2003).

163. Peter Conolly-Smith details early domestic surveillance by the U.S. Bureau of Investigation, including the creation in August 1919 of its General Intelligence Division, headed by a 24-year-old J. Edgar Hoover, in "'Reading between the Lines': The Bureau of Investigation, the United States Post Office, and Domestic Surveillance during World War I," *Social Justice* 36: 1 (2009): 7–24.

164. Mary Graham, *Presidents' Secrets: The Use and Abuse of Hidden Power* (New Haven, CT: Yale University Press, 2017), 50–79. See also David Kennedy, *Over Here: The First World War and American Society* (New York: Oxford University Press, 1980); and John Whiteclay Chambers II, *To Raise an Army: The Draft Comes to Modern America* (New York: Free Press, 1987).

165. Christopher Capozzola, *Uncle Sam Wants You: World War I and the Making of the Modern American Citizen* (New York: Oxford University Press, 2008), 201.

166. Gage, *The Day Wall Street Exploded*, 127. See also Paul L. Murphy, *World War I and the Origin of Civil Liberties in the United States* (New York: Norton, 1979).

167. McCoy, *Policing America's Empire*, 39.

168. Gage, *The Day Wall Street Exploded*, 112. As Michael Kazin writes, by 1918 "it was getting hard to tell the difference between 'seditious speech' and the sort of grievances Americans had normally voiced about public authorities without risking a felony indictment." To express displeasure with war "had become a perilous act—for avowed radicals and ordinary citizens alike." *War against War: The American Fight for Peace, 1914–1918* (New York: Simon & Schuster, 2017), 245. See also Kennedy, *Over Here: The First World War and American Society*, 43–92; David Rabban, *Free Speech in Its Forgotten Years* (Cambridge: Cambridge University Press, 1997), 248–341; and Murphy, *World War I and the Origin of Civil Liberties*.

169. Mark Ellis, *Race, War and Surveillance: African Americans and the United States Government during World War I* (Bloomington: Indiana University Press, 2001), xvi; on the monitoring of equal rights activities specifically, see pp. 101–140. He notes that the Wilson administration was content to defer to the views of the white South. For Wilson's racial policies within the federal government and civil service, see Eric S. Yellin, *Racism in the Nation's Service:*

Government and the Color Line in Woodrow Wilson's America (Chapel Hill: University of North Carolina Press, 2013).

170. Writes Mark Ellis, "One of the most striking features of day-to-day reports on racial matters by domestic intelligence agents across the United States was how little insight they yielded about their subjects." *Race, War, and Surveillance*, 228–230.

171. Lisa McGirr, *The War on Alcohol: Prohibition and the Rise of the American State* (New York: W. W. Norton, 2016), 221, 199. She notes that, unevenly enforced, Prohibition subjected less privileged Americans to high levels of scrutiny. Law enforcement agents' attention to home distilleries rather than upscale speakeasies, for example, meant that "as never before in U.S. history . . . the government invaded private homes, mostly of poorer citizens, in a widespread, systematic, and coercive campaign," 71, 89. See also Wesley M. Oliver, *The Prohibition Era and Policing: A Legacy of Misregulation* (Nashville: Vanderbilt University Press, 2018) on criticisms of police misconduct that were both triggered and limited by Prohibition.

172. Richard Polenberg, *Fighting Faiths: The Abrams Case, the Supreme Court, and Free Speech* (New York: Viking, 1987); Rabban, *Free Speech in Its Forgotten Years*; Murphy, *World War I and the Origin of Civil Liberties*; Capozzola, *Uncle Sam Wants You*, 144–172 (see especially his discussion of the shift in the standard from "responsible" to free speech as a result of the war).

173. See Cole, *Suspect Identities*, 32–59.

174. Cole, *Suspect Identities*, 2. Lawrence M. Friedman notes that the "culture of mobility and the culture of criminal justice were deeply intertwined" in the late nineteenth century, prompting a new corps of professionals: "police, detectives, prison officials, medical examiners, forensic scientists, and, in general, a growing army of criminal justice workers." *Crime and Punishment in American History* (New York: Basic Books, 1993), 209.

175. Cole, *Suspect Identities*, 3, 119–120, 197. J. Edgar Hoover, not surprisingly, would seize on universal fingerprinting as "the key to a national web of individualized surveillance, under his personal control," 247.

176. Robert L. Duffus, "U.S. Builds Greatest Fingerprint Bureau," *New York Times*, August 24, 1924, p. XX7.

177. "Fingerprints Cause Strike: Cleveland Chauffeurs Object to Requirement in New Law," *New York Times*, May 27, 1920, p. 4. Christian Parenti discusses citizens' resistance to being fingerprinted in *The Soft Cage: Surveillance in America: From Slavery to the War on Terror* (New York: Basic Books, 2003), 43–60.

178. Henry Fitzgerald, Letter to the Editor, *New York Times*, October 7, 1922.

179. Gurstein, *Repeal of Reticence*, 152; Glass, *Authors, Inc.*, 11.

180. Bratman, "Brandeis and Warren's 'The Right to Privacy.'"

181. Seipp, "The Right to Privacy in American History," 85. He argues that the "right to privacy" language was, however, popularized by Godkin in 1890.
182. See, for example, *Schulman v. Whitaker*, 117 La. (1906).
183. Warren and Brandeis, "The Right to Privacy," 214.

2. Documents of Identity

1. "Wiretapping Held Legal," *Literary Digest* 97 (June 16, 1928): 10.
2. *Olmstead v. United States*, 277 U.S. 438 (1928).
3. For the classic work, see Stephen Skowronek, *Building a New American State: The Expansion of National Administrative Capacities, 1877–1920* (New York: Cambridge University Press, 1982).
4. Robert L. Floyd, "Privacy," *Chicago Daily Tribune*, September 27, 1925, p. 8.
5. See Jonathan Levy, *Freaks of Fortune: The Emerging World of Capitalism and Risk in America* (Cambridge, MA: Harvard University Press, 2012); Dan Bouk, *How Our Days Became Numbered: Risk and the Rise of the Statistical Individual* (Chicago: University of Chicago Press, 2015); and Josh Lauer, *Creditworthy: A History of Consumer Surveillance and Financial Identity in America* (New York: Columbia University Press, 2017). The first full-fledged credit card, the Diners Club, appeared in 1949. Lizabeth Cohen, *A Consumers' Republic: The Politics of Mass Consumption in Postwar America* (New York: Alfred A. Knopf, 2003), 124.
6. Lisa McGirr has recently argued for the recognition of Prohibition in 1919–1928 as the "greatest expansion of state building, outside of wartime, since Reconstruction" up to that point in American history. She calls the growth of the state's law enforcement and punitive capacities the "less-examined side of state building," overshadowed by public works and social provisioning. *The War on Alcohol: Prohibition and the Rise of the American State* (New York: W. W. Norton, 2016), 192.
7. David Graeber, *The Utopia of Rules: On Technology, Stupidity, and the Secret Joys of Bureaucracy* (Brooklyn: Melville House, 2015), 13–14.
8. James T. Sparrow, *Warfare State: World War II Americans and the Age of Big Government* (New York: Oxford University Press, 2011), 6. Sparrow estimates that government expenditures quadrupled their 1930s levels during World War II, with "changes in government . . . touching nearly every American": upward of 85 million held bonds, 42 million paid income tax, 17 million labored in war-related industries, and 16 million served in the armed forces. By comparison, New Deal emergency programs reached 28.6 million recipients. For accounts of state growth in this era see also Gary Gerstle, *Liberty and Coercion: The Paradox of American Government from the Founding to the Present* (Princeton, NJ: Princeton University Press, 2016), 185–274; and Anne Korn-

hauser, *Debating the American State: Liberal Anxieties and the New Leviathan, 1930–1970* (Philadelphia: University of Pennsylvania Press, 2015).

9. James Willard Hurst, *Law and the Conditions of Freedom in the Nineteenth-Century United States* (Madison: University of Wisconsin Press, 1956), 9.

10. The Social Security Act established three separate programs, two to be administered by the states (Old Age Assistance and Unemployment Compensation) and one to be administered by the federal government (Old Age Benefits). Histories of the act include Edwin E. Witte, *The Development of the Social Security Act* (Madison: University of Wisconsin Press, 1963); Charles McKinley and Robert W. Frase, *Launching Social Security: A Capture-and-Record Account 1935–1937* (Madison: University of Wisconsin Press, 1970); Arthur J. Altmeyer, *The Formative Years of Social Security* (Madison: University of Wisconsin Press, 1966); Martha Derthick, *Policymaking for Social Security* (Washington, DC: Brookings Institution Press, 1979); Edward D. Berkowitz, *Mr. Social Security: The Life of Wilbur Cohen* (Lawrence: University Press of Kansas, 1995); and Edward D. Berkowitz, *Robert Ball and the Politics of Social Security* (Madison: University of Wisconsin Press, 2003).

11. Jennifer Klein argues that grassroots movements and New Dealers alike "generated an ideology of security" in the mid-1930s, making security "an essential goal in the task of national reconstruction." *For All These Rights: Business, Labor, and the Shaping of America's Public-Private Welfare State* (Princeton, NJ: Princeton University Press, 2003), 78–79.

12. Most notably, the final legislation cast a hoped-for health insurance provision aside. The 1965 Amendments to the Social Security Act finally launched Medicare. The 1972 Amendments made provision for Supplemental Security Income (SSI) federal benefits for the aged, blind, and disabled with limited income and resources. On the decades-long attempt to create a federal provision for health care, see Paul Starr, *Remedy and Reaction: The Peculiar American Struggle over Health Care Reform* (New Haven, CT: Yale University Press, 2011), especially pp. 27–50.

13. Social Security Board, *Why Social Security?* (Washington, DC: Government Printing Office, 1937). Surveys indicate that support for old-age assistance and insurance was especially high across all segments of the population, with support at 68 percent of those polled in 1936 and an astounding 96 percent in 1944. A 1937 poll indicated that "opposition to Social Security seems to be the programs [*sic*] shortcomings—not to Government-provided pensions in principle." Sally Sherman, "Public Attitudes toward Social Security," *Social Security Bulletin* 52: 12 (December 1989): 3. For a compilation of public opinion data on the program in its first three decades, see Michael E. Schiltz, *Public*

Attitudes toward Social Security 1935–1965 (Research Report No. 33), Office of Research and Statistics (Baltimore: Social Security Administration, 1970).

14. See, for example, Jill Quadagno, "Welfare Capitalism and the Social Security Act of 1935," *American Sociological Review* 49: 5 (1984): 632–647; Lizabeth Cohen, *Making a New Deal: Industrial Workers in Chicago, 1919–1939* (New York: Cambridge University Press, 1990); Edward D. Berkowitz, *America's Welfare State: From Roosevelt to Reagan* (Baltimore: Johns Hopkins University Press, 1991); Edward D. Berkowitz and Kim McQuaid, *Creating the Welfare State: The Political Economy of Twentieth-Century Reform*, rev. ed. (Lawrence: University Press of Kansas, 1992); Daniel T. Rodgers, *Atlantic Crossings: Social Politics in a Progressive Age* (Cambridge, MA: Belknap Press of Harvard University Press, 1998); Jacob S. Hacker, *Divided Welfare State: The Battle over Public and Private Social Benefits in the United States* (New York: Cambridge University Press, 2002); Klein, *For All These Rights*; G. William Domhoff and Michael J. Webber, *Class and Power in the New Deal: Corporate Moderates, Southern Democrats, and the Liberal-Labor Coalition* (Stanford, CA: Stanford University Press, 2011), 142–186; and Michele Landis Dauber, *The Sympathetic State: Disaster Relief and the Origins of the American Welfare State* (Chicago: University of Chicago Press, 2013).

15. Weare Holbrook, "Unmistaken Identity," *Atlanta Constitution*, November 15, 1942, p. 11.

16. Holbrook, "Unmistaken Identity," 11.

17. Sophonisba P. Breckinridge, "Home Economics and the Quest for Economic Security," *Journal of Home Economics* 27: 8 (October 1935): 491.

18. Lisa Gitelman, borrowing from Michel de Certeau, writes of an "ever growing, ever more intricate scriptural economy . . . harnessed to the interests of officialdom" in *Paper Knowledge: Toward a Media History of Documents* (Durham, NC: Duke University Press, 2014), ix–x. For accounts of how documentation works (and doesn't), see Annelise Riles, ed., *Documents: Artifacts of Modern Knowledge* (Ann Arbor: University of Michigan Press, 2006); Cornelia Vismann, *Files: Law and Media Technology*, trans. Geoffrey Winthrop-Young (Stanford, CA: Stanford University Press, 2008); Ben Kafka, *The Demon of Writing: Powers and Failures of Paperwork* (New York: Zone Books, 2012); Jane Caplan and John Torpey, eds., *Documenting Individual Identity: The Development of State Practices in the Modern World* (Princeton, NJ: Princeton University Press, 2001); Simon Szreter and Keith Breckenridge, eds., *Registration and Recognition: Documenting the Person in World History* (Oxford: Oxford University Press, 2012); and Ilsen About, James Brown, and Gayle Lonergan, eds., *Identification and Registration Practices in Transnational Perspective: People, Papers and Practices* (New York: Palgrave Macmillan, 2013).

19. Legibility, as Scott defines it, is a central tool of modern statecraft; he uses it to refer to state attempts to organize both land and population, dramatically simplifying them in order to facilitate the "classic state functions of taxation, conscription, and prevention of rebellion." James C. Scott, *Seeing like a State: How Certain Schemes to Improve the Human Condition Have Failed* (New Haven, CT: Yale University Press, 1998), 2. The same insight is the starting premise of recent studies of biopolitics and governmentality inspired by the work of Michel Foucault.

20. I borrow this language from Szreter and Breckenridge, *Registration and Recognition*, who regard recognition and registration as the "infrastructure of personhood" in modern states.

21. On quantification, see Theodore M. Porter, *Trust in Numbers: The Pursuit of Objectivity in Science and Public Life* (Princeton, NJ: Princeton University Press, 1995). On mapping, see Susan Schulten, *Mapping the Nation: History and Cartography in Nineteenth-Century America* (Chicago: University of Chicago Press, 2012).

22. Ben Kafka has argued that "paperwork" is as much frustrating and destabilizing as it is productive of bureaucratic order. As he notes, scholars have had considerable trouble reconciling "our theories of the state's power with our experience of its failure." *The Demon of Writing*, 11.

23. Scott, *Seeing like a State*; Andrea Rusnock, *Vital Accounts: Quantifying Health and Population in Eighteenth-Century England and France* (Cambridge: Cambridge University Press, 2002, 2008); Libby Schweber, *Disciplining Statistics: Demography and Vital Statistics in France and England, 1830–1885* (Durham, NC: Duke University Press, 2006); Mae Ngai, *Impossible Subjects: Illegal Aliens and the Making of Modern America* (Princeton, NJ: Princeton University Press, 2004); Adam McKeown, *Melancholy Order: Asian Migration and the Globalization of Borders* (New York: Columbia University Press, 2008). The history of documentary technologies and their politics is told most soberingly in Edwin Black's *IBM and the Holocaust: The Strategic Alliance between Nazi Germany and America's Most Powerful Corporation* (New York: Crown Publishers, 2001). He notes in particular the importance of IBM's alphabetizer machine, introduced in 1934 and perfected "in conjunction with the Social Security Administration." See his *Nazi Nexus: America's Corporate Connections to Hitler's Holocaust* (Washington, DC: Dialog Press, 2009), 138–139.

24. Matt Matsuda, *The Memory of the Modern* (New York: Oxford University Press, 1996), 121–142.

25. The arrival of a "regime of verification," exemplified by the Passport Control Act of 1918, meant that "documents verified documents," permitting the state to bypass "the individual opinions or memories of its subjects." Craig Robertson,

The Passport in America: The History of a Document (New York: Oxford University Press, 2011), 212.

26. Drew Gilpin Faust, *This Republic of Suffering: Death and the American Civil War* (New York: Vintage Books, 2008), 212–213, 101.

27. Michael Kazin, *War against War: The American Fight for Peace, 1914–1918* (New York: Simon and Schuster, 2017), 210–211; Jeanette Keith, *Rich Man's War, Poor Man's Fight: Race, Class, and Power in the Rural South during the First World War* (Chapel Hill: University of North Carolina Press, 2004), 159.

28. Susan J. Pearson, "'Age Ought to Be a Fact': The Campaign against Child Labor and the Rise of the Birth Certificate," *Journal of American History* 101: 4 (March 2015): 1144–1165. For the fullest account, see Shane Landrum, "The State's Big Family Bible: Birth Certificates, Personal Identity, and Citizenship in the United States, 1840–1950" (PhD diss., Brandeis University, 2014). The coordinated effort to register births began in the mid-nineteenth century with an array of goals: lowering infant mortality, ending child labor, ensuring compulsory education, and barring interracial mixing. It was helped along by Congress, which in 1903 encouraged states to adopt the Model Law for Vital Statistics "to extend the benefits of registration and to promote its efficiency," and became a cause for women's voluntary groups thereafter. Birth certificates by the 1920s would be a local and state-administered program coordinated by the U.S. Children's Bureau. By 1933, officials estimated that 90 percent of every year's infant births were recorded. Landrum, "The State's Big Family Bible," 92, 15, 19.

29. Landrum notes that in this new context, some New York City youths desperate for working papers began to claim they had been born in Passaic, New Jersey, where a courthouse fire had destroyed all records. "The State's Big Family Bible," 51. See also Shane Landrum, "From Family Bibles to Birth Certificates: Young People, Proof of Age, and American Political Cultures, 1820–1915," in *Age in America: The Colonial Era to the Present*, ed. Corinne T. Field and Nicholas L. Syrett (New York: New York University Press, 2015), 124–147.

30. Landrum, "The State's Big Family Bible," 51.

31. "Birth Certificate's Use," *New York Times*, June 8, 1930, p. 87.

32. Landrum, "The State's Big Family Bible," 184, 223. On the problem of lacking identification documents from the perspective of the black press, see "Carry Identification Card," *Chicago Defender*, August 18, 1917, p. 6.

33. "Security Board Accepts Bibles as Proof of Age," *Atlanta Constitution*, March 22, 1939, p. 7; Landrum, "The State's Big Family Bible," 160–182.

34. In the late 1910s and early 1920s, enthusiasm for civilian applications increased, such as fingerprinting schoolchildren and facilitating identity in the case of kidnapping or amnesia. Simon Cole, *Suspect Identities: A History of Finger-*

printing and Criminal Identification (Cambridge, MA: Harvard University Press, 2001), 197–198.

35. See for example, the Miami ordinance requiring the fingerprinting of employees of restaurants and hotels, which was "generally conceded to have been primarily designed to force Race people out" of those well-paying jobs. "Repeal Despised Fingerprint Law in Miami, Florida," *Chicago Defender*, May 15, 1937, p. 2.

36. The main professional society changed its name from the International Association of Criminal Identification to the International Association for Identification in an attempt to erase the "criminal stigma." See Cole, *Suspect Identities*, 196; on various states' efforts around mandatory fingerprinting in the late 1920s and 1930s, see 247–248. "Fingerprint Everybody," *New York Herald Tribune*, February 5, 1930, p. 18; "Finger Print Records," *Washington Post*, July 29, 1931, p. 6; Richard C. Patterson, "Use of Fingerprints Now Widely Extended," *New York Times*, April 3, 1932, p. XX5; "Fingerprinting U.S.," *New York Herald Tribune*, August 31, 1933, p. 20; and Mary E. Hamilton, "Identify Yourself: Everyone Should Be Fingerprinted, Says This Expert," *New York Herald Tribune*, October 1, 1933, p. SM3. In Massachusetts in 1934, for example, the State Bureau of Investigation "invited" all residents to file a fingerprint record, in order "to aid people who are the victims of amnesia or accidents, or for children who have become lost." "Massachusetts Trying to Fingerprint Citizens," *New York Herald Tribune*, August 14, 1934, p. 8. A general who supported the fingerprinting of children was less politic: "We must consider that from the children of today will come the criminals of tomorrow." "Fingerprint School Children, Says Needham," *Daily Boston Globe*, March 18, 1934, p. B1.

37. The American Legion aspired to identification cards complete with both photographs and fingerprints. "To Finger-Print Everybody," *Los Angeles Times*, August 19, 1934, p. 10. See also C. M. Barron, "Voluntary Fingerprinting: Federal Agency for That Purpose Is Suggested," *New York Herald Tribune*, October 17, 1933, p. 16.

38. "May Fingerprint Everyone," *Daily Boston Globe*, November 25, 1934, p. A17.

39. Before this, the State Department had treated U.S. passports as a certificate of citizenship for travelers abroad, a "travel document." They were not used in entry or departure along the national border, a matter left to individual states until the 1870s and then handed over to customs and immigration officials, who again did not rely on the passport. See Robertson, *The Passport in America*, 160; John Torpey, *The Invention of the Passport: Surveillance, Citizenship and the State* (New York: Cambridge University Press, 2000), 93–121; and John Torpey, "The Great War and the Birth of the Modern

Passport System," in *Documenting Individual Identity: The Development of State Practices in the Modern World*, ed. Jane Caplan and John Torpey (Princeton, NJ: Princeton University Press, 2001), 256–270.

40. Robertson, *The Passport in America*, 160–161. See also Amy L. Fairchild, *Science at the Borders: Immigrant Medical Inspection and the Shaping of the Modern Industrial Labor Force* (Baltimore: Johns Hopkins University Press, 2003).

41. Craig Robertson, "Mechanisms of Exclusion: Historicizing the Archive and the Passport," in *Archive Stories: Facts, Fictions, and the Writing of History*, ed. Antoinette Burton (Durham, NC: Duke University Press, 2005), 81. See Kenneth L. Roberts, "Trial by Travel," *Saturday Evening Post* 93 (September 4, 1920): 10; and "Passports Passé," *Nation* 112 (January 19, 1921): 75.

42. Christopher Capozzola, *Uncle Sam Wants You: World War I and the Making of the Modern American Citizen* (New York: Oxford University Press, 2008), 202.

43. See Larry DeWitt, Daniel Béland, and Edward D. Berkowitz, *Social Security: A Documentary History* (Washington, DC: CQ Press, 2008), 4. Also excluded were seamen, federal and state employees, and employees of religious and charitable organizations. Not until 1950 was the act amended to extend coverage to self-employed farmers and workers in a number of other professions, including domestic employees, bringing coverage to about three-quarters of the workforce. The best recent account of Southern Democrats' shaping of the New Deal in order to protect traditional racial hierarchies is Ira Katznelson, *Fear Itself: The New Deal and the Origins of Our Time* (New York: Liveright, 2013). Mary Poole, in *The Segregated Origins of Social Security: African Americans and the Welfare State* (Chapel Hill: University of North Carolina Press, 2006), argues that the racialized nature of welfare was a product of both liberals' and conservatives' interest in preserving a hierarchy of white over black workers.

44. Birchard E. Wyatt and William H. Wandel, *The Social Security Act in Operation: A Practical Guide to the Federal and Federal-State Social Security Programs* (Washington, DC: Graphic Arts Press, 1937), 51. Veterans' pensions and the World War I draft were the two most common comparisons that contemporaries made to the enrollment effort. On the role of veterans' pensions in shaping the U.S. welfare state, see Theda Skocpol, *Protecting Soldiers and Mothers: The Political Origins of Social Policy in the United States* (Cambridge, MA: Belknap Press of Harvard University Press, 1992). Drew Gilpin Faust notes that the creation of a pension system for Union veterans was a challenging task, given the fact that there was "no coherent personnel record for any individual soldier . . . to support a pension claim." It led to the creation of the Compiled Military Service Records, the scale of which led to "the overcrowding of workers and documents" in Ford's Theatre, causing "two

floors to collapse and kill twenty-two employees" in 1893. *This Republic of Suffering*, 255–256.

45. Paul Schor, *Counting Americans: How the US Census Classified the Nation*, trans. Lys Ann Weiss (New York: Oxford University Press, 2017). On the transformation of the United States' patchwork of "indirect, hidden, disaggregated, and partisan import duties and regressive excise taxes" into "a direct, transparent, centralized and professionally administered, graduated tax system," see Ajay K. Mehrotra, *Making the Modern American Fiscal State: Law, Politics, and the Rise of Progressive Taxation, 1877–1929* (New York: Cambridge University Press, 2013); quote on p. 6. Julian E. Zelizer's *Taxing America: Wilbur D. Mills, Congress, and the State, 1945–1975* (New York: Cambridge University Press, 1998) picks up that story in the 1940s.

46. See, for example, Arthur Sears Henning, "Whole Nation Ready for Call to Arms Today," *Chicago Daily Tribune*, June 5, 1917, p. 2. The *New York Times* reported that the draft "machinery" was ready to "take the military census in the shortest time ever allowed for such a huge undertaking—one twelve-hour day." "Preparations for Draft Move Swiftly; 42 States Already Have Their Machinery Organized," *New York Times*, May 21, 1917, p. 1.

47. "Men Newly Twenty-One Must Register Today," *Los Angeles Times*, June 5, 1918, p. II1.

48. In fact, by June 1937, the Bureau had received about 30.3 million applications for SSNs, and a total of 35 million were enrolled in the first eight months of registration. Oscar C. Pogge, "After Fifteen Years: A Report on Old-Age and Survivors Insurance," *Social Security Bulletin* 15: 1 (1952): 5.

49. McKinley and Frase, *Launching Social Security*, 320.

50. For the dense transatlantic traffic of social reform, and the borrowing of European social insurance schemes in particular, see Rodgers, *Atlantic Crossings*, 409–484. The primary international experts were Pierre Tixier, Chief of the Social Insurance Section of the International Labor Office in Geneva, Switzerland, and Ronald Davidson and Ethel Foster, a retired official and staff member, respectively, of the British Ministry of Labour. McKinley and Frase, *Launching Social Security*, 20–21.

51. Wyatt and Wandel, *The Social Security Act in Operation*, 45.

52. McKinley and Frase, *Launching Social Security*, 313–317.

53. Wyatt and Wandel, *The Social Security Act in Operation*, 46. As Simon Cole reveals in *Suspect Identities*, such an assessment overstated considerably the reliability of fingerprints as a means of accurate identification.

54. Wyatt and Wandel, *The Social Security Act in Operation*, 47.

55. Pierre Tixier and R. C. Davison, "Suggestions on the Administration of the Social Security Act and State Unemployment Compensation Laws" (December 14, 1935 with note from May 12, 1938, explaining that the report

was deemed no longer confidential), p. 8, Stanford Ross Papers, private collection of Stanford G. Ross, Commissioner of Social Security, 1978–1979.

56. U.S. Social Security Board, "Summary of Historical Outline of the Development of the Social Security Board Program of Establishing Employers' Identification and Employees' Accounts" (1942), p. 7, Folder: SSN-Numbering System Development, Carrier: 12, Social Security History Archives, Baltimore, Maryland [hereafter, SSHA, with F designating Folder and C the Carrier].

57. Tixier and Davison, "Suggestions on the Administration of the Social Security Act," p. 6.

58. "Aldrich's Views on Social Security Act," *New York Times*, July 11, 1936, p. 26.

59. Minutes on "Assignment of Social Security Numbers," Social Security Board Meeting, April 30, 1936, F: SSN-Initial Registration, C12, SSHA.

60. Memorandum from E. J. McCormack to Mr. H. P. Seidemann, "Use of the Word ENUMERATION," July 6, 1936, F: SSN-Enumeration, C12, SSHA. Pierre Tixier apparently favored the word "matriculation," but this was dismissed as "too academic and 'braintrusty'"; "inventory" was also tested, but fell out of use. McKinley and Frase, *Launching Social Security*, 329.

61. "NOTICE: Deductions from Pay Start Jan. 1," RNC-sponsored notice, F: SSN-Initial Registration 1935–1937, C12, SSHA. The SSB quickly distributed its own pamphlet, titled "Security in Your Old Age." See "Falsehoods on Pay Envelopes," *New Republic* (November 4, 1936): 6–7.

62. "'Forgery' Charged to Security Foes," *New York Times*, November 3, 1936, p. 17.

63. "Here's Proof of Deceit in Payroll Tax," *Boston Evening American*, November 2, 1936, p. 1.

64. "Snooping-Tagging," *New York American*, November 2, 1936; "Benefits of Security Act Called Only Dream," *Boston American*, November 2, 1936; "'Forgery' Charged to Security Foes," p. 17. Alfred Landon, FDR's opponent in 1936, himself warned of "federal snooping." This is from Landon's speech of September 23, 1936; see Brian Balogh, "Securing Support: The Emergence of the Social Security Board as a Political Actor," in *Federal Social Policy: The Historical Dimension*, ed. Donald T. Critchlow and Ellis Hawley (University Park: Pennsylvania State University Press, 1988), 66.

65. McKinley and Frase, *Launching Social Security*, 450–451. Intriguingly, by 1938 the ACLU was accusing antilabor and corporate forces, including the Hearst newspaper empire, of supporting fingerprinting as a mode of "general regimentation of the population"—the same charge that many of these conservative outfits had made about SSNs. American Civil Liberties Union, *Thumbs Down! The Fingerprint Menace to Civil Liberties* (New York, 1938).

66. "Here's Proof of Deceit in Payroll Tax," p. 1.

67. "Hamilton Shows Sample Tag for Workers' Necks," *Chicago Daily Tribune*, November 1, 1936, p. 5.

68. See the Law for the Restitution of the Professional Civil Service, of April 7, 1933. The *Vokskartei* or "Catalog of the People," along with photo identity cards, would be instituted in 1939. Sybil Milton, "Registering Civilians and Aliens in the Second World War," *Jewish History* 11: 2 (Fall 1997): 79–87; see pp. 79 and 81. Milton notes that Bavarian and Prussian laws of 1926 and 1927 had already mandated the fingerprinting and photographing of 8,000 "Gypsies," 82. See also Götz Aly and Karl Heinz Roth, *The Nazi Census: Identification and Control in the Third Reich*, trans. Assenka Oksiloff (Philadelphia: Temple University Press, 2004).

69. Note the reference, for example, to the "Russian passport system" and the "Austrian police registration system" that "have long cumbered the free movements of individuals in Europe," in an editorial opposed to U.S. identification cards. Stephen G. Rich, "Proposals Feared: Identification Systems Seen as Earnest of Worse Things," *New York Times*, February 9, 1936, p. E9.

70. "Hamilton Predicts Tags for Workers," *New York Times*, November 1, 1936, p. N5. "Hamilton Shows Sample Tag for Workers' Necks," p. 5. For Arthur Altmeyer's account of this episode, see *The Formative Years*, 69. What came to be called dog tags were themselves still new in the 1930s, first worn by soldiers during World War I. See Faust, *This Republic of Suffering*, 103.

71. "Snooping-Tagging."

72. "Benefits of Security Act Called Only Dream."

73. "'Dog Tag' Workers May Have under Social Security Act," *Boston Herald*, November 2, 1936; "'Forgery' Charged to Security Foes," p. 17.

74. Indeed, it charged the RNC with fraudulent use of the name of the Board and turned over the campaign materials to the Department of Justice. "Acts to Prosecute on 'Pay Cut' Signs," *New York Times*, October 29, 1936, p. 17.

75. "Social Security Form Condemned as 'Fraud,'" *New York Times*, November 1, 1936, p. 29. The Board's first chairman, John G. Winant, had already resigned in September so that he could reply to political attacks on Social Security.

76. "'Forgery' Charged to Security Foes," p. 17. The spokesperson was Anna Rosenberg, regional director of the Social Security Board.

77. Elwood J. Way, "Development of the Account Number Card Issued by the Social Security Board Together with Notes on the Account Number and Alternative Plans Considered." (November 27, 1941), p. 3, F: SSN-Numbering System Development, C12, SSHA.

78. Memorandum from O. J. Libert to E. J. Way on "Materials for Identification Purposes," April 10, 1936, F: SSN-Enumeration, C12, SSHA.

79. McKinley and Frase, *Launching Social Security*, 329.

80. Memorandum from O. J. Libert to E. J. Way on "Materials for Identification Purposes" detailed the shortcomings even of strong paper as compared to a "metal product." The SSB reportedly issued approximately 5,000 new replacement

cards a day by 1938, triggering "a great deal of unnecessary extra clerical work" as well as introducing "a whole series of frauds." "Little Help Seen in Job Insurance," *New York Times*, June 20, 1938, p. 13.

81. Way, "Development of the Account Number Card"; Minutes on "Assignment of Social Security Numbers," Social Security Board Meeting, April 30, 1936, F: SSN-Initial Registration, C12, SSHA.

82. Social Security's advocates were still worrying about the dog tag story becoming "one of the ongoing myths of the program" in 1982. See D'Vera Cohn, "Early Social Security Plan Called for Dog Tags," *Pittsburgh Press*, May 9, 1982; "Woodlawn Office Displays Social Security Memorabilia," *Baltimore Daily Record*, May 17, 1982; and Letter from Robert J. Myers (Executive Director, National Commission on Social Security Reform) to Abe Bortz, June 1, 1982. All in F: Dog Tag, C8, SSHA. Daniel Patrick Moynihan, "A Counterfeit-Proof Social Security Card, Now," Statement to the Senate, *Congressional Record*, August 4, 1990, p. S12460.

83. In fact, the Treasury Department issued regulations making the SSN mandatory on November 6, 1936. McKinley and Frase note that while the Board claimed that registration was voluntary, "it had been negotiating with the Treasury Department to induce that department to require employees and employers to secure account numbers under regulations carrying considerable penalities." *Launching Social Security*, 346, 351–352, 360. In this, the SSB squares with scholars' descriptions of the early twentieth-century U.S. government as an "improvisational hybrid state that reconciled its coercive and voluntarist elements by concealing the conflict between them." Capozzola, *Uncle Sam Wants You*, 210–211.

84. Wyatt and Wandel, *The Social Security Act in Operation*, 45.

85. Social Security planners traded on Americans' experience with life and group insurance, the "modern private benefits system" through which American employers met the welfare needs of their workers starting in the 1910s and 1920s. The SSB could point to companies such as the Equitable Life Assurance Society and Metropolitan Life, but also to industrial pension plans administered by labor unions and fraternal societies. Klein, *For All These Rights*, 10–11, 16–52, 53–77. On Americans' familiarity with being numbered for life insurance policies beginning in the mid-nineteenth century, see Bouk, *How Our Days Became Numbered*.

86. On this point, see Altmeyer, *The Formative Years*, 70.

87. Kathleen S. Swendiman, "The Social Security Number: Legal Developments Affecting Its Collection, Disclosure and Confidentiality," CRS Report for Congress, updated January 21, 2005, p. 2, n. 5. She notes that from 1946 to 1972, the legend "NOT FOR IDENTIFICATION" was printed on the face of the

card, as a warning that no proof of identity was required to obtain it. "However, the legend was largely ignored and was eventually dropped."

88. Note by contrast the 1940 Smith Act (Alien Registration Act) requirement that all aliens be registered and fingerprinted.

89. Wyatt and Wandel, *The Social Security Act in Operation*, 48.

90. "Old-Age Benefits Enumeration," *Social Security Bulletin* (September–December 1936), F: SSN-Enumeration, p. 42, C12, SSHA.

91. Part I, Sec. 808, Art. 3, 5 of the Social Security Act.

92. Edward Higgs applies this term to modern states that not merely undertake surveillance—a function of all states—but would "cease to function" without the capacity to collect and manipulate information on private citizens. *The Information State in England: The Central Collection of Information on Citizens since 1500* (New York: Palgrave Macmillan, 2004), vii; "The Rise of the Information State: The Development of Central State Surveillance of the Citizen in England, 1500–2000," *Historical Sociology* 14: 2 (June 2001): 175–197.

93. "Historical Summary of Rules, Regulations and Provisions of the Law Relating to Disclosure of OASI Information," undated, F: Confidentiality, C7, SSHA.

94. Memorandum from Executive Committee of the Committee on Assignment of Social Security Account Numbers to the Board, May 5, 1936, F: SSN-Enumeration, C12, SSHA. The Board acknowledged "rare cases" where the applicant did not know the facts regarding his or her parents or date of birth and recommended in those instances supplementing the usual SS-5 form with "a signed photograph, orphans' home record, or endorsement, that might help to identify the person as the one on whose account a benefit might later be paid." See Social Security Board, Bureau of Federal Old-Age Benefits, Enumeration Manual, July 1, 1937, p. 20, F: Enumeration-Manual, C8, SSHA. In 1940, several new pieces of information were requested on the application form, including marital status, the closing date of the last full-time job, and the prior occupation and industry of the worker—all for the purpose of gathering "statistical data"—but these were all omitted in a 1941 revision, the change having proved "unsuccessful." Memo from T. A. McDonald, Assistant Chief, Accounting Operations Division to All Returned Employees, "Accounting Operations Division Procedural Changes," May 14, 1946, p. 2, F: SSN-Process, C12, SSHA; U.S. Social Security Board, "Summary of Historical Outline of the Development of the Social Security Board Program of Establishing Employers' Identification and Employees' Accounts" (1942), p. 1, F: SSN-Numbering System Development, C12, SSHA.

95. Memorandum from E. J. Way to Executive Director, "Proposed letter to be sent to trade associations—Social Security Account Numbers reference made," April 28, 1936, F: SSN-Enumeration, C12, SSHA. McKinley and Frase note

that race was included for "both identification and actuarial purposes" and that most of the debate over its inclusion was about whether to use the word "race" or "color" on the forms; the SSB opted for the latter. *Launching Social Security*, 326. For uses of race in actuarial tables and census taking in the 1930s, see Bouk, *How Our Days Became Numbered*, 41–48, and Schor, *Counting Americans*, 209, 215, 303 n. 16.

96. "Government Will Take First Steps Today to Enroll Workers," *Washington Post*, November 16, 1936, p. X1.

97. McKinley and Frase, *Launching Social Security*, 339.

98. "Running Record of Board Meeting," November 20, 1936, 2:45pm, F: SSN-Enumeration, C12, SSHA.

99. The Mennonite Board of Missions, for example, was willing for its members to pay Social Security taxes, but not to accept the old-age pensions when they became due; "Social Service: Pensioners," *Time* (December 14, 1936). See the brief note about other protests in Social Security Board, Bureau of Federal Old-Age Benefits, Enumeration Manual, July 1, 1937, p. 20, F: Enumeration-Manual, C8, SSHA. Other religious objectors cited the biblical lesson of God's punishment when King David planned to number his people, Chronicles 27:4.

100. "Insulting Our Intelligence," *Pittsburgh Courier*, December 5, 1936, p. 12. The writer scoffed at the explanation, given by a Social Security information officer, that the requirement was put in place to distinguish among applicants with the same name.

101. He continued, "It will be used to penalize us in a thousand ways, just as the photographs attached to civil service applications are used to penalize us today." S. Schuyler, "Views and Reviews," *Pittsburgh Courier*, December 26, 1936, p. 10.

102. Winston Smith, "Social Security Act, Taking in All Races, Explained by Writer, as Post Office Starts Sending out Blanks," *New York Amsterdam News*, November 14, 1936, p. 15.

103. "Running Record of Board Meeting," Friday, November 20, 1936, 2:45pm, F: SSN-Enumeration, C12, SSHA.

104. The study was Claris Edwin Silcox and Galen M. Fisher's *Catholics, Jews and Protestants: A Study of Relationships in the United States and Canada* (Westport, CT: Greenwood Press, 1934). As Kevin Schultz writes of the interwar years, "employment agencies said they found it necessary to secure information concerning an applicant's religion before they sent an applicant to an interview, fearing that a Catholic or Jewish applicant would not have a chance to secure employment at a Protestant-dominated firm." *Tri-Faith America: How Catholics and Jews Held Postwar America to its Protestant Promise* (New York: Oxford University Press, 2011), 23. See also David Sehat, *The Myth of American Religious Freedom* (New York: Oxford University Press, 2011).

105. Altmeyer, *The Formative Years*, 50–51.

106. Frederick Lane, *American Privacy: The 400-Year History of Our Most Contested Right* (Boston: Beacon Press, 2009), 110.

107. Susan Ware, *Holding Their Own: American Women in the 1930s* (Boston: Twayne, 1982).

108. For an argument about disclosure of age as an invasion of privacy, particularly for women (and women workers), see Della T. Lutes, "Why I Don't Tell My Age," *Forum and Century* 97: 4 (April 1937): 244. There were contemporary proposals to remove age information from passports; see Charles S. Taylor, "Passport Data," *New York Times*, June 1, 1934, p. 22.

109. The "Fibbers," "Your Age, Madam," *Chicago Daily Tribune*, November 30, 1936, p. 8. The SSB's answer was that the account holder's information would not in that case be disclosed.

110. "Social Security Board Firm in Guarding Secrets of Files," *Washington Evening Star*, April 29, 1937, p. B14. In fact during early discussions of the format of the SSN, "many persons voiced serious objections" to a number that revealed birth year, "since it gave the employer or prospective employer knowledge of the age of the individual." Way, "Development of the Account Number Card."

111. "Historical Summary of Rules, Regulations and Provisions of the Law Relating to Disclosure of OASI Information." See also historical section of Social Security Administration, "Confidentiality of Information Contained in Old-Age, Survivors, Disability and Heath Insurance Records," February 2 1971, p. 3, F: Confidentiality (Privacy-F1), C7, SSHA.

112. Stephen Meyer, *The Five Dollar Day: Labor Management and Social Control in the Ford Motor Company, 1908–1921* (Albany: State University of New York Press, 1981); Jacquelyn Dowd Hall, "Private Eyes, Public Women: Images of Class and Sex in the Urban South, Atlanta, Georgia, 1913–1915," in *Work Engendered: Toward a New History of American Labor*, ed. Ava Baron (Ithaca, NY: Cornell University Press, 1991), 243–272; and Charles Hyde, "Undercover and Underground: Labor Spies and Mine Management in the Early Twentieth Century," *Business History Review* 60 (1986): 1–27. See also Leo Huberman, *The Labor Spy Racket* (New York: Modern Age Books, 1937), which was based on hearings before the Subcommittee of the Committee on Education and Labor of the United States Senate, also known as the La Follette Civil Liberties Committee.

113. See Social Security Board, "Survey Relative to Requests for Information from the Confidential Board Files," January 1938, F: Confidentiality, C7, SSHA.

114. "Government Will Take First Steps Today to Enroll Workers." The Board discussed options for reassuring employees, including having the Treasury

state that it would not accept returns from employers where there was "any evidence of coercion." One possibility the board weighed was advising employees that "anything they put on the card they turn into the employer is their own business and in those cases where the employers are violating the regulations, they should put such information they wish on that return which goes to him and then write in to the Board in Washington giving the correct information and getting it straightened out." "Running Record of Board Meeting," November 20, 1936, 2:45pm, F: SSN-Enumeration, C12, SSHA.

115. Regulation No. 1: Disclosure of Official Records and Information was adopted by the Board in June 1937. When Congress amended the Social Security Act 1939, it implemented Section 1106, which provided that "information could not be divulged except as the Board by regulation prescribed."

116. McKinley and Frase, *Launching Social Security*, 451–452.

117. "Time Is Extended on Security Form," *New York Times*, December 6, 1936, p. 3.

118. Anna M. Rosenberg, regional director of the Social Security Board, is quoted in "Time Is Extended on Security Form," p. 3. The *New York Times* reported that investigation "substantiated these complaints in the cases of more than fifty concerns."

119. Wyatt and Wandel, *The Social Security Act in Operation*, 57.

120. "Confidential," *Chicago Daily Tribune*, November 15, 1940, p. 28.

121. Unfortunately, the Social Security Board did not retain letters from the public.

122. McKinley and Frase, *Launching Social Security*, 326. They point out, however, that the U.S. Employment Service had previously used "all the items objected to by the state administrators" and "coded union and religious affiliations as well." Regarding the latter, "the Employment Service took the position that it was better to send the employer people he wanted rather than to let an employee begin a job and then be fired because of religious prejudice." As for the inclusion of age and union affiliation, "there had been no protest from the labor unions."

123. United Automobile Workers of America, *Proceedings of the Second Biennial Convention of the International Union* (1941), vols. 2–4, pp. 55–56.

124. Social Security Board, "Survey Relative to Requests for Information from the Confidential Board Files."

125. "Social Security Board Firm in Guarding Secrets of Files," p. B14.

126. Social Security Board, "Survey Relative to Requests for Information from the Confidential Board Files." A few months into this policy, the Board rescinded its policy of forwarding such inquiries, instead advising all inquirers "of the confidential nature of its records."

127. *The Billboard*, June 12, 1943, p. 36.

128. "Lost: One Wife; Clue: Her Social Security Figure," *Atlanta Constitution*, January 7, 1940, p. 11A. See also "Girl Student, 16, Missing for Four Days," *Washington Post*, June 27, 1942, p. 17, which noted not the actual number but the fact that the girl had a Social Security card in her billfold as an identifying detail.

129. "Looking for Someone?" *Baltimore Afro-American*, February 3, 1940, p. 10.

130. "Courier Missing Persons Bureau" (entry for Taylor, Nathaniel Edward), *Pittsburgh Courier*, January 28, 1950, p. 26. A similar entry appears for another man the previous spring, April 16, 1949.

131. "Didn't Want to Lose Picture of His Girl," *Pittsburgh Courier*, January 27, 1940, p. 12.

132. See, for example, Memorandum from Oscar M. Powell and John J. Corson to the Board re: "Revision of Regulation No. 1 to Permit Closer Cooperation with Other Government Agencies," July 9, 1940, F: Confidentiality, C7, SSHA.

133. This was Executive Order 9397, "Numbering System for Federal Accounts Relating to Individual Persons," 8 Fed. Reg. 16095–16097, 3 C.F.R. (1943–1948 Comp.) 283–84 (1943). The specific agencies mentioned in the discussions leading up to the Executive Order were the Bureau of Internal Revenue of the Treasury Department, the Railroad Retirement Board, and the Civil Service Commission. It would not be until the 1960s that federal agencies began to employ the SSN as a general identifier in other contexts. See Swendiman, "The Social Security Number," p. 2.

134. Philippa Strum, *Privacy: The Debate in the United States since 1945* (New York: Harcourt Brace, 1998), 46–47.

135. Notes from Meeting of the Board, March 9, 1937 (dated March 11), F: Confidentiality, C7, SSHA.

136. Social Security Board, "Survey Relative to Requests for Information from the Confidential Board Files." The Board seems to have responded to such requests inconsistently in 1937, sometimes supplying the information, sometimes not.

137. Notes from Meeting of the Board, November 16, 1937 (dated November 19), F: Confidentiality, C7, SSHA.

138. Notes from Meeting of the Board, November 4, 1937 (dated November 6), F: Confidentiality, C7, SSHA.

139. Notes from Meeting of the Board, June 29, 1937 (dated July 1), F: Confidentiality, C7, SSHA. "The Board considered and approved a letter of reply to the Attorney General . . . advising him that because of previous pledges, the Board is estopped from complying with his request."

140. Running Record of Board Meeting, February 23, 1937, 11:15am, F: Confidentiality, C7, SSHA.

141. "Social Security Board Firm in Guarding Secrets of Files," p. B14.

142. Memo from John J. Corson to Oscar M. Powell re: "Disclosure of Confidential Information: For the Consideration of the Board," June 28, 1943, F: Confidentiality, C7, SSHA.

143. "Social Security Board Minutes," July 20, 1943, F: Confidentiality, C7, SSHA.

144. Altmeyer, *The Formative Years*, 70. He stated, "This pledge of confidentiality has been kept throughout the years, the only exceptions having been a very few cases involving person suspected of espionage or sabotage." What this obscured was the expanded definition of those terms during the Cold War.

145. See, for example, correspondence about a Petersburg, Virginia, draft board request for the SSN of a draftee; John J. Corson to V. D. Herbert re: "Social Security Account Number for John Mumford Richardson," December 21, 1940, F: Confidentiality, C7, SSHA. This request was refused.

146. See "Board Minutes" (re: "Disclosing the Existence of a 'Missing Person' to Claimant"), June 22, 1943, F: Confidentiality, C7, SSHA. Interestingly, there were complaints by the late 1950s of the SSA supplying information of this sort (a Cleveland, Ohio, man presumed dead but who had current wage earnings) to the Veterans Administration but not the abandoned family members. See Congressman Charles A. Vanik to Arthur Flemming, Secretary of Health, Education and Welfare, October 14, 1958, F: Confidentiality, C7, SSHA, who charged the SSA "in effect" with sheltering "many likely felons from apprehension, indictment and prosecution."

147. The Board tried to make good on this by reversing course upon the "President's declaration of cessation of hostilities," giving notice to the Department of Justice and the War and Navy Departments that future requests of information would need to establish that "the case involved arose out of the existence of hostilities." Memo from Perrin Lowrey, Memo on "Action Taken by the Commissioner," January 7, 1947, F: Confidentiality, C7, SSHA. This was complicated, however, by the onset of the Korean War and then the ongoing Cold War.

148. O. C. Pogge to W. L. Mitchell, Memo on "Need for Revision of Regulation No. 1, Section 401.3(i)(4)—Disclosure of Information to Federal Bureau of Investigation," February 18, 1952, F: Confidentiality, C7, SSHA. Here the question involved the near-simultaneous termination of World War II and the December 1950 proclamation of a national emergency during the Korean War: "In view of the proclamation and the current unsettled state of world affairs, the Bureau believes that authorization to disclose information . . . should be extended for the duration of the present national emergency."

149. The Immigration and Nationality Act of 1952 required that the Attorney General be informed, "upon request," whenever an alien was issued an SSN and that information as to identity and location of aliens be furnished when requested. See the debate over what this required of Social Security officials in

the Memorandum of J. Lee Rankin, Assistant Attorney General, on "Information from Social-Security Records," February 3, 1955, p. 2, F: Confidentiality, C7, SSHA. Rankin noted that "when the study of our immigration and nationality laws which culminated in the passage of the 1952 Act was undertaken, attention was early directed to the possibility of using social security files as a means to locate aliens illegally in this country."

150. In this case, the answer was a firm "no"; see Memorandum from Victor Christgau to W. L. Mitchell re: "Request by the Department of Justice for Copies of Account Number Applications Cards or for Access to the Bureau Account Number Application Files," October 19, 1959, F: Confidentiality, C7, SSHA.

151. Commissioner's Action Minutes, May 3, 1954, F: Confidentiality, C7, SSHA. A "Request from Immigration and Naturalization Service for Information from our Records to Assist in Locating Certain Chinese Deserters" was granted because of "unusual circumstances" (the possibility that the Chinese had "effected illegal entry into the U.S. for purposes of sabotage or espionage"), but was "not to be considered as a precedent for the continuing program of cooperation between the Bureau of Old-Age and Survivors Insurance and the Immigration and Naturalization Service."

152. This was J. Edgar Hoover's rationale for gaining access to SSA files to track deserters from the Armed Services and violators of the Selective Service Act. He closed his request with the plea, "Without your assistance a heavy blow would be struck at our nation's preparedness." See Letter from Hoover to Charles I. Schottland, Commissioner, November 19, 1958, F: Confidentiality, C7, SSHA.

153. See, generally, F: Confidentiality, C7, SSHA.

154. See "Board, Bureau and Commissioner Decisions, Regulation 1–Disclosure," F: Confidentiality, C7, SSHA. See also Notes from Meeting of the Board, November 30, 1937 (dated December 8) and Notes from Meeting of the Board, August 23, 1940 (dated August 28); both in F: Confidentiality, C7, SSHA. It was not until 1948 that the agency agreed that its information could be furnished to other government departments without the authorization of the interested party in the case of the theft, forgery, alteration, or destruction of a Social Security card. Minutes of Commissioner's Meeting, re: "Proposed Changes in Regulation No. 1," March 3, 1948, p. 8, and Commissioner's Action Minutes, December 13, 1948, F: Confidentiality, C7, SSHA.

155. In 1937, the Board agreed that in cases where an individual died and was unidentified except for name or SSN and officials "can secure no other information from any other source," it would make an exception to its general policy and supply a copy of Form SS-5. It cautioned against advertising this fact except in the form of a "confidential instruction" to SSB employees, since

publicity "would motivate numerous requests and inquiries . . . with which the Board could not comply." Minutes of the Meeting of the Board, April 27, 1937, F: Confidentiality, C7, SSHA. The policy on releasing confidential information from Form SS-5 was expanded a few months later to include "those who are insane or are suffering from amnesia." Minutes of the Meeting of the Board, August 6, 1937 (dated August 12), F: Confidentiality, C7, SSHA. Agency discussions in the mid-1950s took up the question of sharing information in the wage record with the individuals or institutions responsible for institutionalized people or mental "incompetents." See, for example, Commissioner's Action Minutes, March 16, 1953, F: Confidentiality, C7, SSHA.

156. Memo from Victor Christgau to W. L. Mitchell re: "Disclosure of Information for Administration of Public Assistance Programs-Deserting Parents (NOLEO Amendment) in Case of Aid to Dependent Children-Support Responsibility of Relatives," December 30, 1954, F: Confidentiality, C7, SSHA. The memo noted the steady uptick in such requests, with 14,073 in a seven-month period in 1954, and noted some "undesirable newspaper publicity" in which a state official disclosed "how he was able to locate and bring in the missing parent through use of old-age and survivors insurance records." Other accounts suggested that these records were "now available not only for the purpose of locating deserting parents, but (erroneously) also for locating deserting spouses," p. 6. See H.R. 2446, a bill to "amend the Social Security Act to provide that the Secretary of Health, Education, and Welfare shall, under certain circumstances, disclose the current addresses of husbands and parents who have deserted their families."

157. In 1959 the agency noted that the average number of requests from the FBI per year was approximately 3,600, "divided about equally among national security, deserter and Selective Service cases," and that "we are able to provide a good lead as to the whereabouts of the individual sought in the majority of cases." Memo from Victor Christgau to W. L. Mitchell re: "Disclosure of Information to the Federal Bureau of Investigation in Deserted and Selective Service Cases," January 15, 1959, pp. 1–2, F: Confidentiality, C7, SSHA. By the 1970s, Social Security officials noted the "steady increase in the number of requests for SSA assistance (issuing numbers and verifying existing numbers) from non-Federal organizations that wish to structure their recordkeeping systems around the SSN." In the three years from 1968 to 1970, the SSA recorded receiving more than eighty such requests. Social Security Task Force, "Report to the Commissioner, Social Security Administration," May 1971, p. 24, F: SSN-Early History, C12, SSHA.

158. Memo from Victor Christgau to W. L. Mitchell re: "Disclosure of Information for Administration of Public Assistance Programs-Deserting Parents (NOLEO

Amendment) in Case of Aid to Dependent Children-Support Responsibility of Relatives."

159. Already in 1937, false numbers and counterfeit cards were being used by criminals as credentials to set up bank accounts from which to write bad checks, prompting the SSB to issue a warning to banks "not to treat a social security account card as positive identification." "Social Security Board to Issue Fraud Warning," *Wall Street Journal*, April 26, 1937, p. 4.

160. For one potential such instance from 1950, see the recommendation for putting "personal affairs in shape for an emergency," which included placing "old income-tax returns, canceled checks, savings bank books, birth certificate, social security card, and similar papers in a locked file drawer or similar safe place," in Kathleen A. Johnston, "Family Economics—Home Management," *Journal of Home Economics* 42: 6 (June 1950): 462. A similar list appears in "Tips to Wives on Business Management," *Atlanta Constitution*, June 8, 1943, p. 12. But both notices, it seems clear, concerned being able to get to the number and other important documents when needed—rather than worries about theft or public knowledge of the SSN.

161. See, for example, "History Repeats," *New York Times Magazine* (February 9, 1947): 44, in which it was reported that "the shoe number of a pair of red slippers which Annie Ruth Hight, Cedartown, Ga., bought was familiar to her. It was the same as her Social Security number." The paper printed not just this woman's name and number but her location. See also the listing of athletes' numbers by *New York Times* columnist Arthur Daley: "Sports of the Times," *New York Times*, June 10, 1945, p. S2; and April 24, 1950, p. 34.

162. Sonia Stein, "What Became of Banned Giveaways?" *Washington Post*, April 23, 1950, p. L4. "Tower Ticker," *Chicago Daily Tribune*, May 10, 1950, p. 28. Roy Touchet to J. S. Futterman, "Account Number Issuance Procedure—Status Report," November 30, 1959, p. 3, F: SSN-Process, C12, SSHA.

163. "Mercury Sets LP Bonus Plan," *The Billboard*, November 18, 1950, p. 14.

164. William V. Nessly, "Security Board Chairman Hails Court Decisions," *Washington Post*, May 25, 1937, p. 4.

165. Sparrow, *Warfare State*, 11.

166. Wyatt and Wandel, *The Social Security Act in Operation*, 62–63.

167. Letter from Frank Bane, Executive Director to Corrington Gill (Assistant Administrator, WPA), March 19, 1937, F: SSN-Enumeration, C12, SSHA.

168. The proposed Clark Amendment, which would permit employers to opt out if their pension plan matched or exceeded Social Security's, was defeated in 1935. "Social Security Action Urged," *Los Angeles Times*, December 21, 1936, p. A2; McKinley and Frase, *Launching Social Security*, 351–352, 360.

169. "Security Check-Up Uses Tax Returns," *New York Times*, December 16, 1936, p. 32.

170. "Mayor Hartsfield No. 252–12–4939," *Atlanta Constitution*, July 15, 1937, p. 9.

171. The ruling was *Helvering v. Davis*, 301 U.S. 619. "26,000 in Brooklyn Defy Social Security Law," *New York Times*, November 29, 1936, p. 1. This practice was a response to news of legal filings against the Social Security Act and the possibility that failing to note one's protest might imperil the "right to challenge the act or to recover taxes paid under it." The SSB advised, however, that "no added rights accrue to any individual as a result of such a protest."

172. Letter from Frank Bane, Executive Director to Corrington Gill (Assistant Administrator, WPA), March 19, 1937. An SSB Enumeration Manual from 1937 reads, "The employer should realize that the non-possession of an account number is no reason for not hiring a person provided he or she files an application immediately." Social Security Board, Bureau of Federal Old-Age Benefits, Enumeration Manual, July 1, 1937, pp. 19–20, F: Enumeration-Manual, C8, SSHA.

173. "20,000 Old-Age Benefit Checks Going Begging," *Washington Post*, August 3, 1937, p. 8.

174. "Tom McCarthy: Learns It's Tough to Go Straight," *Washington Post*, November 19, 1937, p. 9.

175. "National Affairs: Labor: Social Security," *Time* (November 16, 1936): 25.

176. Ralph T. Jones, "Numerous Possibilities," *Atlanta Constitution*, December 16, 1936, p. 6.

177. Ralph T. Jones, "Silhouettes: Life under a Monarchy," *Atlanta Constitution*, November 5, 1939, p. 18A.

178. "Topics of the Times: Many American Figures," *New York Times*, September 25, 1940, p. 25.

179. "Is It Too Late?" *Atlanta Constitution*, June 16, 1940, p. 10B.

180. "Sermons to Graduates," *Chicago Daily Tribune*, March 27, 1945, 12. For another critique of big government, via Social Security, in this era, see Luther A. Huston, "Social Security Grown to Giant Size in 5 Years," *New York Times*, August 11, 1940, p. 57.

181. See 1936 cartoon in the SSA archives, F: SSN-Initial Registration 1935–1937, C12, SSHA.

182. "The Santa Fe New Mexican . . . came out with full recognition of the Social Security Act today. From E. Dana Johnson down to reporters, social security account numbers were used for bylines. Over the editor's 'Jobs in the Solar Plexus' was: 'By 525–10–9454.' In the personal columns were such items as: 'No. 525–10–9363 is recovering from an attack of the flu.'" Associated Press, "Social Security Figures Are Newspaper By-Lines," *New York Times*, December 11, 1936, p. 29. See also Jones, "Numerous Possibilities."

183. A. G. L (Bloomington, Illinois), "Voice of the People," *Chicago Daily Tribune*, October 2, 1943, p. 12.

184. McKinley and Frase, *Launching Social Security*, 322.

185. Cole, *Suspect Identities*, 249.

186. Letter from John L. Thurston, April 2, 1948; "Information about Birth Number: Order of Events," April 5, 1948. See these and other materials in F: Universal Identifier, C13, SSHA. The Council on Vital Records and Vital Statistics voted on a resolution to create a "uniform birth certificate number" in 1947 and entered into brief discussions in 1947–1948 with the Social Security Administration about coordinating the two numbering systems.

187. Margo DeMello, *Bodies of Inscription: A Cultural History of the Modern Tattoo Community* (Durham, NC: Duke University Press, 2000), 66.

188. See the correspondence in F: Universal Identifier, C13, SSHA.

189. Jack Watson, "Dog Tags of Bureaucracy," *Los Angeles Times*, April 12, 1948, p. A4.

190. "Every Employed Person to Be Given 'Number' by Costly, Cumbersome Security Plan," *El Paso County-Colorado Springs Gazette*[?], November 1936, clipping in F: SSN-Enumeration, C12, SSHA.

191. Memorandum from Mr. Altmeyer to Mr. Way, June 9, 1936, F: SSN-Enumeration, C12, SSHA.

192. "The news that John Smith got $10 by having a social security number will not be slow in getting around, and it will bring in applicants from all unnumbered workers in that area," claimed a Board member. "20,000 Old-Age Benefit Checks Going Begging," p 8.

193. A. M. Wendell Malliet, "'Social Security Is Hope of Negro in America,' Says Cohron," *New York Amsterdam News*, December 24, 1938, p. 4. See also "Negro Democrats Hail Roosevelt as Modern Savior," *New York Amsterdam News*, June 27, 1936, p. 1.

194. For a later example, see "Tips on Checking Social Security," *New York Amsterdam News*, September 11, 1948, p. 5.

195. The amendments were signed into law on August 10, 1939: apart from adding benefits for dependents and survivors of beneficiaries, the start date for monthly benefits was moved up (from January 1942 to January 1940). In the first year of administering monthly benefits, 250,000 individuals became beneficiaries. W. Andrew Achenbaum, *Social Security: Visions and Revisions* (Cambridge: Cambridge University Press, 1986), 3.

196. It continued, "You should consider your card as having the same importance as you do your insurance policies. Neither is handled carelessly: neither should be lost." "Social Security," *New York Amsterdam News*, April 15, 1939, p. 10. See also "Social Security: What It Means—How It Works," Baltimore *Afro-American*, August 16, 1941, p. 9.

197. See, for example, "The New Social Security Act," *The Crisis* 47: 2 (February 1940): 42–43, 59.

198. "Get Your Social Security Number before You Are Unemployed," *American Labor World* (1937): 216.

199. See, for example, "Former Demand for Low Phone Numbers," *Nashville Tennessean and the Nashville American*, December 14, 1911, p. 9; "Urges Car Owners Memorize License," *Washington Post*, July 15, 1923, p. 57. The predecessor of today's zip codes was established in large cities in 1943: "Mail to 178 Cities Soon to be Zoned," *New York Times*, May 6, 1942, p. 44.

200. Major Thomas M. Nial, "Veteran's Postwar Notebook," *Atlanta Constitution*, May 16, 1945, p. 10.

201. North Carolina Employment Security Commission, *North Carolina Employment Security Information* (1941), p. 3.

202. Carolyn Keene, *The Whispering Statue* (New York: Grosset & Dunlap, 1937), p. 56.

203. As reported in Ernest R. Bryan, "America Advances with Social Security," *Health Officer* 4 (May 1939): 104.

204. "Costume Jewelry Requires Art in Wearing," *Washington Post*, August 5, 1939, p. 8. Sheilah Graham, "Colleen Moore Lends Home to Former Film Millionaires," *Atlanta Constitution*, March 27, 1940, p. 16.

205. In fact, workers were cautioned not to carry Social Security cards on their person, given their fragility. See Nina Nazionale, "Tattoo as Memory Prompt," New York Historical Society; http://blog.nyhistory.org/tattoo-as-memory-prompt/.

206. Advertisement, AFL-CIO, *American Federationist* 44: 1 (1937): 570.

207. Advertisement: "Free! Protection for Your Social Security Number," *Chicago Defender*, October 22, 1938, p. 5.

208. Advertisement: "Hurry! Join the Hundreds Who Have Taken Advantage of This Free Gift," *Chicago Defender*, November 12, 1938, p. 5; an ad with the same heading and slightly different wording also ran on December 7, 1938, p. 3.

209. Advertisement: "A Lifetime Gift for You," *Chicago Defender*, October 15, 1938, p. 5.

210. Advertising Section, *Popular Mechanics* 67: 5 (May 1937): 48A. Key Tag Specialty Company, 91 Wall Street, New York City, NY.

211. Advertising Section, *Popular Mechanics* 70: 4 (August 1938): 43A. J. P. Routier Company, 221 Frost Ave, Rochester, NY. A similar product gets a mention as "a gadget which appeared last year" and "turns up again, much improved," in "New Things in City Shops," *New York Times*, March 31, 1940, p. 53.

212. Advertising Section, *Popular Mechanics* 71: 4 (April 1939): 168A. Roovers Bros, Inc. Dept. M41, 258 Broadway, New York, and 3611–14th Ave., Brooklyn, NY. The ad asked potential sellers to "send 10c with your social security number." This was William Hament, 665 W. Lexington Street, Baltimore, MD.

213. See Advertising Section, *Popular Mechanics* 69: 3 (March 1938): 58A. The contact information was listed as Napeus, 1303 Austin St., Wichita Falls, Texas. Another seller, "Stanley-Engraving" of Lansing, Michigan, was listed for similar products in 1944; Advertising Section, *Popular Mechanics* 82: 6 (December 1944): 59A.

214. Advertising Section, *Popular Mechanics* (August 1938): 43A. Company listed was: H. I. Laboratories, 1451 Broadway, New York, NY.

215. Advertisement: "Social Security Record Made Permanent on a Solid Bronze Plate," *Atlanta Constitution*, July 23, 1939, p. 4A.

216. *The Billboard*, November 28, 1942, p. 65. Company was Illinois Merchandising Mart, Dept. 117, 54 W. Illinois Street, Chicago, IL. The same advertisement (this one a full-page ad) appears in *American Legion Magazine* 32–33 (1942); *Popular Mechanics Magazine* 78: 6 (December 1942): 40A; *Popular Science* 141: 5 (November 1942): 21, and various others.

217. "Good-By, Old Pal," *Chicago Daily Tribune*, January 1, 1950, p. 8.

218. Reported by Doe Richards in Arch Ward, "In Wake of the News," *Chicago Daily Tribune*, October 18, 1950, p. C1.

219. See, for example, the scuffle over whether a passport could count for identification at the post office as related in Max Weissbach, "Postoffice 'High Hats' Passport," *New York Herald Tribune*, May 2, 1933, p. 12.

220. Sylvia Weaver, "Shirtwaist Dress Fits Needs of Career Woman," *Los Angeles Times*, January 8, 1942, p. A6. Note also the mention of a movie star favoring "simple dresses with novel belts," one of which had a pocket for a "silver locket engraved with her social security number." Sheilah Graham, "Sheilah Graham Describes Smart Outfits of the Stars: Hollywood Today," *Atlanta Constitution*, July 20, 1937, p. 14.

221. On the encoding of gender dependence in the Social Security Act and other New Deal legislation, see Ruth Feldstein, *Motherhood in Black and White: Sex and Race in American Liberalism, 1930–1965* (Ithaca, NY: Cornell University Press, 2000); Suzanne Mettler, *Dividing Citizens: Gender and Federalism in New Deal Public Policy* (Ithaca, NY: Cornell University Press, 1998); and Alice Kessler-Harris, "In the Nation's Image: The Gendered Limits of Social Citizenship in the Depression Era," *Journal of American History* 86: 3 (1999): 1251–1279.

222. "Shop-Hound around the Town," *Vogue* 89: 10 (May 15, 1937): 118. The disk sold at the Lord and Taylor department store for six dollars.

223. These rings were produced by the S. A. Meyer Company of Washington, Pennsylvania, as advertised in the *Washington Observer*, March 3, 1938.

224. Christine Rosen, "The Flesh Made Word: Tattoos, Transgression, and the Modified Body," *Hedgehog Review* 17: 2 (Summer 2015). See Jane Caplan, ed., *Written on the Body: The Tattoo in European and American History* (Princeton, NJ: Princeton University Press, 2000).

225. Dan Bouk offers the most extended analysis of this image, suggesting that we "consider the ways that some Americans grasped those numbers as their own." *How Our Days Became Numbered*, 210–211. See also David Peeler, *Hope among Us Yet: Social Criticism and Social Solace in Depression America* (Athens: University of Georgia Press, 1987), 103–104. The photograph can be found in Ann Whiston Spirn, *Daring to Look: Dorothea Lange's Photographs and Reports from the Field* (Chicago: University of Chicago Press, 2008), 154. On Lange more generally, see Linda Gordon, *Dorothea Lange: A Life beyond Limits* (New York: Norton, 2009).

226. "Little Help Seen in Job Insurance," *New York Times*, June 20, 1938, p. 13.

227. "Social Security Act Increases Tattooing," *Washington Post*, April 15, 1937, p. 20. See a poem that nods to the "fad" of tattooing one's Social Security number; H. I. Phillips, "The Once Over: Oh, Say, Can You See?" *Washington Post*, May 3, 1937, p. 9. See also the casual mention of "holders of social-security numbers" as customers for tattoos in "Decorative Art," *New York Times*, June 20, 1937, p. 54.

228. "Through the Editor's Specs," *Nation's Business* (December 1937): 7. Several news outlets reported that the favorite design for such inkings was "a fancy spread eagle, tossing a social security number from its beak." See "Social Security Act Increases Tattooing."

229. "Radio Comedians Turn to Mocking Daytime Shows," *Chicago Daily Tribune*, February 11, 1938, p. 28.

230. Margot Mifflin, *Bodies of Subversion: A Secret History of Women and Tattoo*, 3rd ed. (Brooklyn, NY: powerHouse Books, 2013), 35. A San Francisco practitioner averaged "two social security clients a day" in 1937. "Through the Editor's Specs," 7.

231. See other reports of artists "working overtime . . . just tattooing Social Security numbers on the arms and legs of folks who didn't want to be caught without their numbers." C. W. Eldredge, "Identification," *Tattoo Archive* (2000); www.tattooarchive.com/tattoo_history/identification.html.

232. The sign is in the collection of the Patricia D. Klingenstein Library, New-York Historical Society; Nazionale, "Tattoo As Memory Prompt."

233. "Job Applicant Has Social Security Number on Back," *Atlanta Constitution*, August 31, 1939, p. 8.

234. "Tattooed Man Bares His Social Security Number," *Chicago Daily Tribune*, February 16, 1938, p. 8. See also "Miscellany: Red Tape," *Time*, May 16, 1938.

235. "Has Security Number Tattooed on Arm," *Popular Science* 130: 5 (May 1937): 53. Also see note in passing of a Memphis man with his number tattooed on his arm, in Wesley Smith, "The March of Finance," *Los Angeles Times*, January 14, 1937, p. 13.

236. Photograph: "Stamped for Life," *Chicago Daily Tribune*, January 17, 1937, p. SW4. The same man is pictured in the *Washington Post* on January 14, 1937, p. 16, and is referred to as Leon "Roffener" in "Sidelights of the Week: Security Tattoo," *New York Times*, January 17, 1937, p. 60.

237. "Show Girl Keeps Security Secure on Knee," *Atlanta Constitution*, February 10, 1937, p. 22; this is a photograph with the caption: "Apparently fearful of forgetting her social security number, June McNulty, Broadway showgirl, has Doris Donaldson print it indelibly on her knee."

238. "Identified by Tattooing: Musician Had Social Security Number on His Forearm," *New York Times*, August 22, 1943, p. 33; "Tattoo Marks on Arm Identify Florida Man," *Atlanta Constitution*, August 22, 1943, p. 10A. "Body in Lot Starts Slaying Probe Here," *Washington Post*, December 17, 1939, p. 3. See also the mention of murder victims identified by SSN tattoo at http://blog .constitutioncenter.org/2011/08/happy-birthday-social-security.

239. These were the years before serial numbers printed on arms came to be associated with survivors of concentration camps. As Peter Novick and others have observed, the Holocaust loomed much larger in American life starting in the 1970s and after than in the 1940s or 1950s. *The Holocaust in American Life* (Boston: Houghton Mifflin, 1999), 20. Gary Weissman pinpoints 1978 as the year the American public became fully "Holocaust conscious." *Fantasies of Witnessing: Postwar Efforts to Experience the Holocaust* (Ithaca, NY: Cornell University Press, 2004), 8–9. Primo Levi's memoir, *The Drowned and the Saved* (New York: Summit Books, 1988) described the Nazi tattoo as a "pure offense" and a means by which "slaves are branded and cattle sent to slaughter," 12. Comparisons between Social Security numbers and "Nazi tattoos" or "totalitarianism" come from the 1990s and after; see discussions of the dangers of identity cards in "America, Doubled," *New York Times*, April 1, 1990, p. E18, and Robert Ellis Smith, "The True Terror Is in the Card," *New York Times Magazine* (September 8, 1996): 58. Recent critiques of biometrics and identity registration have been articulated most forcefully by Giorgio Agamben in *State of Exception*, trans. Kevin Attell (Chicago: University of Chicago Press, 2005). I have found no reports of new SSN tattoos in the 1950s, but this may also be because tattooing's popularity dropped off in that decade in both the military and the general population. DeMello, *Bodies of Inscription*, 65.

240. Note the considerable doubts in the 1930s that this was in fact a guarantee, however. Brian Balogh cites one insider, Edwin Witte, as claiming that for "nearly two years after the Social Security Act became law, serious doubts continued to exist about its ever coming into full operation." See "Securing Support," 65.

241. Robert F. Lenhart, quoted in Pearson, "'Age Ought to Be a Fact,'" 1165.

3. The Porous Psyche

1. Richard H. Rovere, "The Invasion of Privacy (1): Technology and the Claims of Community," *American Scholar* 27 (Autumn 1958): 413–421.

2. Alfred W. McCoy, *Policing America's Empire: The United States, the Philippines, and the Rise of the Surveillance State* (Madison: University of Wisconsin Press, 2009), 17; see his discussion of "Wilson's surveillance state," which launched a "federal surveillance effort" that endured for fifty years, 293–346. See also Frank J. Donner, *The Age of Surveillance* (New York: Random House, 1980).

3. See Michael Sherry, *In the Shadow of War: The United States since the 1930s* (New Haven, CT: Yale University Press, 1995).

4. K. A. Cuordileone, "The Torment of Secrecy: Reckoning with American Communism and Anti-Communism," *Diplomatic History* 35: 4 (September 2011): 616.

5. Mary Graham, *Presidents' Secrets: The Use and Abuse of Hidden Power* (New Haven, CT: Yale University Press, 2017), 104, 115. She writes that in this era military intelligence "began operating outside domestic restraints and foreign laws. For the next thirty years, secrecy shielded its activities from debate and from integration into the public's understanding of the nation's foreign policy," 82. Michael Schudson notes that "freedom of information" became a U.S. cause after World War II in part because of growing government secrecy, with advocates calling attention "to instances where the Soviets were more open than the Americans in their information policies." *The Rise of the Right to Know: Politics and the Culture of Transparency, 1945–1975* (Cambridge, MA: Belknap Press of Harvard University Press, 2015), 46, 48. See also Daniel P. Moynihan, *Secrecy: The American Experience* (New Haven, CT: Yale University Press, 1998).

6. The internal security acts, respectively, criminalized Communism and allowed the registration and detention of subversive group members. The 1954 Expatriation Act additionally deprived convicted Communists of U.S. citizenship. Stanley I. Kutler, *The American Inquisition: Justice and Injustice in the Cold War* (New York: Hill and Wang, 1982).

7. According to Mary Graham, "more than four million employees were screened during the ten years of the loyalty program, and 27,000 were subjected to detailed investigations" with approximately 1,650 civilian and military employees dismissed while Truman was in office. *Presidents' Secrets*, 105. See also David M. Oshinsky, *A Conspiracy so Immense: The World of Joe McCarthy* (New York: Free Press, 1983); and Ellen Schrecker, *Many Are the Crimes: McCarthyism in America* (Boston: Little, Brown, 1998). For the costs of the

loyalty-security program to suspected homosexuals, see Robert D. Dean, *Imperial Brotherhood: Gender and the Making of Cold War Foreign Policy* (Amherst: University of Massachusetts Press, 2003); and David K. Johnson, *The Lavender Scare: The Cold War Persecution of Gays and Lesbians in the Federal Government* (Chicago: University of Chicago Press, 2006). Johnson estimates that 5,000 federal employees suspected of being gay or lesbian lost their jobs by 1960.

8. Edward Shils, "Privacy: Its Constitution and Vicissitudes," *Law and Contemporary Problems* 31: 2 (1966): 285.

9. Myron Brenton, *The Privacy Invaders* (New York: Coward-McCann, 1964), 12.

10. *Olmstead v. United States*, 277 U.S. 438 (1928).

11. Martin L. Gross, *The Brain Watchers* (New York: Random House, 1962), 13.

12. Abbott Gleason, *Totalitarianism: The Inner History of the Cold War* (New York: Oxford University Press, 1995); Margot A. Henriksen, *Dr. Strangelove's America: Society and Culture in the Atomic Age* (Berkeley: University of California Press, 1997); Timothy Melley, *Empire of Conspiracy: The Culture of Paranoia in Postwar America* (Ithaca, NY: Cornell University Press, 2000).

13. Laura McEnaney, *Civil Defense Begins at Home: Militarization Meets Everyday Life in the Fifties* (Princeton, NJ: Princeton University Press, 2000); Elaine Tyler May, *Homeward Bound: American Families in the Cold War Era* (New York: Basic Books, 1988); Donald R. McNeill, "America's Longest War: The Fight over Fluoridation, 1950–," *Wilson Quarterly* (Summer 1985): 140–153.

14. Samuel A. Stouffer, *Communism, Conformity, and Civil Liberties: A Cross-Section of the Nation Speaks its Mind* (New York: Doubleday & Co., 1955), 87, 69, 59; emphasis in original. Stouffer reported that, given the opportunity to air their worries, respondents cited solely personal and family problems 80 percent of the time, with another 10 percent professing no worries at all; 8 percent mentioned international affairs, 59, 66. Sociologist David Riesman distrusted the finding that only 8 percent of the sample raised political concerns, wondering if the framing of the study pushed respondents to respond to more private concerns. "Orbits of Tolerance, Interviewers, and Elites," *Public Opinion Quarterly* 20: 1; Special Issue on Communication (Spring 1956): 49–73. Stouffer was moderately conservative in his politics, which may help explain his dismissal of anticommunist excesses as a serious concern for the ordinary person.

15. Andrea Friedman, *Citizenship in Cold War America: The National Security State and the Possibilities of Dissent* (Amherst: University of Massachusetts Press, 2014), 28.

16. For Eastern Europeans' own debates over public and private, see Svetlana Boym, *Common Places: Mythologies of Everyday Life in Russia* (Cambridge, MA: Harvard University Press, 1994), especially chs. 1 and 2; and Paul Betts,

Within Walls: Private Life in the German Democratic Republic (New York: Oxford University Press, 2010).

17. As K. A. Cuordileone writes, "Anti-Communism was more than a defense against Communism (or liberalism); in its broadest cultural manifestations and most heated imaginings, it was a defense against America itself." *Manhood and American Political Culture in the Cold War* (New York: Routledge, 2005), xix.

18. Kathleen G. Donohue examines arguments made over government secrecy and the public right to know in "Access Denied: Anticommunism and the Public's Right to Know," in *Liberty and Justice for All? Rethinking Politics in Cold War America*, ed. Kathleen G. Donohue (Amherst: University of Massachusetts Press, 2012), 21–50; Bricker is quoted on p. 40.

19. Nancy Schnog, "On Inventing the Psychological," in *Inventing the Psychological: Toward a Cultural History of Emotional Life in America*, ed. Joel Pfister and Nancy Schnog (New Haven, CT: Yale University Press, 1997), 6. See especially Ellen Herman, *The Romance of American Psychology: Political Culture in an Age of Experts* (Berkeley: University of California Press, 1994).

20. See Andrew Polsky, *The Rise of the Therapeutic State* (Princeton: Princeton University Press, 1991); James H. Capshew, *Psychologists on the March: Science, Practice, and Professional Identity in America, 1929–1969* (New York: Cambridge University Press, 1999); Hamilton Cravens and Mark Solovey, eds., *Cold War Social Science: Knowledge Production, Liberal Democracy, and Human Nature* (New York: Palgrave Macmillan, 2012); and Joy Rohde, *Armed with Expertise: The Militarization of American Social Research during the Cold War* (Ithaca, NY: Cornell University Press, 2013). Psychologists' participation in World War I is described by John Carson in "Army Alpha, Army Brass, and the Search for Army Intelligence," *Isis* 84 (1993): 278–309.

21. May, *Homeward Bound*, 183–207.

22. See W. H. Auden, *The Age of Anxiety: A Baroque Eclogue*, ed. and with an introduction by Alan Jacobs (Princeton, NJ: Princeton University Press, 2011). Schlesinger's title was "Politics in the Age of Anxiety." Historian Ruth Feldstein points out that therapeutic language was "central to renegotiations of liberalism from the New Deal into the Cold War." *Motherhood in Black and White: Race and Sex in American Liberalism, 1930–1965* (Ithaca, NY: Cornell University Press, 2000), 63. See also Peter Sheehy, "The Triumph of Group Therapeutics: Therapy, the Group, and Liberalism in America, 1910–1960" (PhD diss., University of Virginia, 2002). Eric Fromm, Erik Erikson, Daniel Bell, Arthur Schlesinger, and Hannah Arendt were among the intellectuals adopting this language.

23. Ron Robin, *The Making of the Cold War Enemy: Culture and Politics in the Military-Intellectual Complex* (Princeton, NJ: Princeton University Press, 2001), 65.

Robin credits the political scientist Harold Lasswell with opening up the behavioral sciences to psychoanalytic perspectives. Friedman, *Citizenship in Cold War America*, 46.

24. Jonathan Metzl, *Prozac on the Couch: Prescribing Gender in the Era of Wonder Drugs* (Durham, NC: Duke University Press, 2003); Deborah Weinstein, *The Pathological Family: Postwar America and the Rise of Family Therapy* (Ithaca, NY: Cornell University Press, 2013).

25. Ernest Havemann, "The Age of Psychology in the U.S.," *Life* (January 7, 1957): 72.

26. Philip Cushman, *Constructing the Self, Constructing America: A Cultural History of Psychotherapy* (Reading, MA: Addison-Wesley, 1995); Nathan Hale, *The Rise and Crisis of Psychoanalysis in the United States: Freud and the Americans, 1917–1985* (New York: Oxford University Press, 1995).

27. *Life's* series, "Psychology: What It Means in Modern Life," debuted with Havemann's "The Age of Psychology in the U.S.," 68–82; quotes on pp. 70, 79.

28. William A. Creech, "Psychological Testing and Constitutional Rights," *Duke Law Journal* 1966 (1966): 334.

29. James T. Sparrow, *Warfare State: World War II Americans and the Age of Big Government* (New York: Oxford University Press, 2011), 4.

30. Jamie Cohen-Cole, *The Open Mind: Cold War Politics and the Sciences of Human Nature* (Chicago: University of Chicago Press, 2014). See also Andrew Jewett, "Naturalizing Liberalism in the 1950s," in *Professors and Their Politics*, ed. Neil Gross and Solon J. Simmons (Baltimore: Johns Hopkins University Press, 2014), 191–216.

31. This list is culled from Alan F. Westin, *Privacy and Freedom* (New York: Atheneum, 1967), 133–157. Martin Gross instead used the term "psychological espionage," which he borrowed from Jay L. Otis, a former president of the Division of Consulting Psychology of the American Psychological Association. *The Brain Watchers*, 90, 233.

32. George Orwell, *Nineteen Eighty-Four* (New York: Harcourt, Brace, 1949).

33. Hannah Arendt, "The Public Realm and the Private Realm," in *The Hannah Arendt Reader*, ed. Peter Baehr (New York: Penguin, 2000), 212. The anthropologist John L. Locke writes of a long history of human movement toward the opportunity for "personal opacity," which includes the residential walls that allow for certain kinds of personal, marital, and familial relationships. He adds that the search for opacity, however, thwarts the "lifelong quest of all humans to know what is going on in the personal and private lives of others." *Eavesdropping: An Intimate History* (New York: Oxford University Press, 2010), 5–6.

34. Paul Betts, *The Authority of Everyday Objects: A Cultural History of West German Industrial Design* (Berkeley: University of California Press, 2007), 236; Betts, *Within Walls*.

35. Charles Madge, "Private and Public Spaces," *Human Relations* 3 (1950): 187–199; quote on 189.
36. May, *Homeward Bound.*
37. Robert B. Westbrook, "Fighting for the American Family: Private Interests and Public Obligation in World War II," in *The Power of Culture*, ed. Richard W. Fox and T. J. Jackson Lears (Chicago: University of Chicago Press, 1993), 195–221.
38. Andrew M. Shanken, *194X: Architecture, Planning, and Consumer Culture on the American Home Front* (Minneapolis: University of Minnesota Press, 2009).
39. Juliet A. Williams, "Privacy in the (Too Much) Information Age," in *Public Affairs: Politics in the Age of Sex Scandals* ed. Paul Apostolidis and Juliet A. Williams (Durham, NC: Duke University Press, 2004), 215. See Beatriz Colomina, *Privacy and Publicity: Modern Architecture as Mass Media* (Cambridge, MA: MIT Press, 1994); and Victoria Rosner, *Modernism and the Architecture of Private Life* (New York: Columbia University Press, 2005).
40. Margaret Marsh argues that the ideology of domesticity and the suburban ideal were two separate belief systems that fused in the postwar period; but even before this, upper-middle-class men and women "looked to the suburbs as the appropriate place to develop a new kind of family life" such that by the end of the 1920s "suburbanization and domesticity had become seemingly inseparable." *Suburban Lives* (New Brunswick: Rutgers University Press, 1990), 182–183. She argues that by the 1920s, "the owner-occupied, single-family house, set in a community of similar houses, where children were the central focus of family life, and from which families considered 'undesirable' were excluded, had become, not the norm for all families, but very nearly the standard by which one's middle-class credentials were judged," 183.
41. Marsh, *Suburban Lives*, 184–185.
42. Housing starts reached a record 1.65 million in 1955, with fully two-thirds of the construction consisting of private one-family dwellings; Clifford E. Clark Jr., "Ranch-House Suburbia: Ideals and Realities," in *Recasting America: Culture and Politics in the Age of Cold War*, ed. Lary May (Chicago: University of Chicago Press, 1989), 183. See also Gwendolyn Wright, *Building the Dream* (Cambridge, MA: MIT Press, 1981), ch. 13; Kenneth T. Jackson, *Crabgrass Frontier: The Suburbanization of the United States* (New York: Oxford University Press, 1985); Lizabeth Cohen, *A Consumers' Republic: The Politics of Mass Consumption in Postwar America* (New York: Knopf, 2003), 194–256; May, *Homeward Bound*; Dolores Hayden, *Redesigning the American Dream: Gender, Housing, and Family Life* (New York: Norton, 2002); and Rosalyn Baxandall and Elizabeth Ewen, *Picture Windows: How the Suburbs Happened* (New York: Basic Books, 2000).

43. David M. Freund, *Colored Property: State Policy and White Racial Politics in Suburban America* (Chicago: University of Chicago Press, 2007); Thomas J. Sugrue, *Origins of the Urban Crisis: Race and Inequality in Postwar Detroit* (Princeton, NJ: Princeton University Press, 1996). Restrictive covenants and deed restrictions kept most of these communities white until after 1960, even despite the Supreme Court's *Shelley v. Kramer* ruling of 1948. See Jeffrey D. Gonda, *Unjust Deeds: The Restrictive Covenant Cases and the Making of the Civil Rights Movement* (Chapel Hill: University of North Carolina Press, 2015). On the sexual sorting of suburbia, see Clayton C. Howard, "The Closet and the Cul de Sac: Sex, Politics, and Suburbanization in Postwar California" (PhD diss., University of Michigan, 2010).

44. Dianne Harris calls the suburban ethos an "exclusionary discourse" in "Screening Identity: Race, Class, and Privacy in the Ordinary Postwar House, 1945–1960," in *Race and Landscape in America*, ed. Richard Schein (New York: Routledge, 2007), 127–156; quotation on p. 129. See also Wini Breines, *Young, White and Miserable: Growing up Female in the Fifties* (Chicago: University of Chicago Press, 2001).

45. Stephen J. Whitfield, "The Culture of the Cold War," in *The Cambridge Companion to Modern American Culture*, ed. Christopher Bigsby (Cambridge: Cambridge University Press, 2006), 256–274; Clark, "Ranch-House Suburbia," 171–191.

46. Clark writes, for instance, that suburbanites sought to leave the "noise and insecurities" of city life behind. "Ranch-House Suburbia," 188.

47. Housing and Home Finance Agency (Edward Thurber Paxton), "What People Want When They Buy a House: A Guide for Architects and Builders" (U.S. Department of Commerce, 1955), 1. The report was based on a survey by the Institute for Social Research at the University of Michigan and a study by the Small Homes Council of the University of Illinois. *Better Homes and Gardens* conducted a similar survey of new home buyers in 1950.

48. "What People Want When They Buy a House," 8, 15–16.

49. Quoted in Harris, "Screening Identity," 137.

50. Jason Reid, *Get out of My Room! A History of Teen Bedrooms in America* (Chicago: University of Chicago Press, 2017), 39–66. Dr. Benjamin Spock was an important voice in the new science of parenting, beginning with the first edition of his popular manual, *The Common Sense Book of Baby and Child Care* (New York: Duell, Sloan and Pearce, 1946).

51. See Howard, "The Closet and the Cul de Sac," 159–162. Charles Madge noted in 1950s Britain too that the Ministry of Health recommended that every house with three or more bedrooms have not one but two W.C.s. "Private and Public Spaces," 191.

52. Robert Woods Kennedy, *The House and the Art of Its Design* (New York: Reinhold Corporation, 1953), 113; quoted in Howard, "The Closet and the Cul de Sac," 159. Clark likewise notes the division of ranch homes into "living," "housework," and "private" areas. See "Ranch-House Suburbia," 179; on bathrooms, see 181.

53. Howard, "The Closet and the Cul de Sac," 160.

54. Rhonda Y. Williams, *The Politics of Public Housing: Black Women's Struggles against Urban Inequality* (New York: Oxford University Press, 2004), 38–39. Public housing was of a piece with other New Deal welfare programs like Aid for Dependent Children, she notes, in linking eligibility to "middle-class character judgments and state surveillance," 6.

55. Clayton Howard, "Building a 'Family-Friendly' Metropolis: Sexuality, the State, and Postwar Housing Policy," *Journal of Urban History* 39: 5 (2013): 933–955. Compounding this bias, the Servicemen's Readjustment Act of 1944 barred members of the military discharged for homosexual conduct from receiving its low-interest loans. See Margot Canaday, *The Straight State: Sexuality and Citizenship in Twentieth-Century America* (Princeton, NJ: Princeton University Press, 2009), 137–138.

56. As Clark suggests, the "window walls" were meant to signal healthfulness, peace and tranquility by bringing nature and light into the home. "Ranch-House Suburbia," 174, 179.

57. Harris, "Screening Identity," 128–129, 148.

58. Quoted in Harris, "Screening Identity," 139.

59. Harris, "Screening Identity," 143–144. Sandy Isenstadt, "The Rise and Fall of the Picture Window," *Harvard Design Magazine* (Fall 1998): 27–33.

60. Michael Kackman, *Citizen Spy: Television, Espionage, and Cold War Culture* (Minneapolis: University of Minnesota Press, 2005).

61. Westin, *Privacy and Freedom*, 68.

62. Wiretapping was upheld by the Supreme Court during Prohibition in *Olmstead v. United States* (1928), 277 U.S. 438. But it was a contentious practice, regularly provoking federal congressional hearings from 1918 onward and banned (for either public or private entities) by some states—although those bans were also regularly violated and irregularly enforced. See Samuel Dash, Richard F. Schwartz, and Robert E. Knowlton, *The Eavesdroppers* (New Brunswick: Rutgers University Press, 1959), 421.

63. Dash et al., *The Eavesdroppers*, 10.

64. Dash et al., *The Eavesdroppers*, 3–4. On the other hand, they noted, the public was told by the telephone company that "wiretapping does not exist."

65. This contrasted with contemporary portrayals of the anonymity of urban neighborhoods. In Alfred Hitchcock's 1954 film *Rear Window*, a character in Greenwich Village cries out to his apartment courtyard: "You don't know the

meaning of the word 'neighbors'! Neighbors like each other, speak to each other, care if anybody lives or dies! But none of you do!"

66. Quoted in Brenton, *The Privacy Invaders*, 46–47.

67. See Rowena Olegario, *A Culture of Credit: Embedding Trust and Transparency in American Business* (Cambridge, MA: Harvard University Press, 2006); Kenneth Lipartito, "Mediating Reputation: Credit Reporting Systems in American History," *Business History Review* 87: 4 (Winter 2013): 655–677; Josh Lauer, *Creditworthy: A History of Consumer Surveillance and Financial Identity in America* (New York: Columbia University Press, 2017).

68. Brenton, *The Privacy Invaders*, 49.

69. Shils, "Privacy: Its Constitution and Vicissitudes," 285.

70. Brenton, *The Privacy Invaders*, 175–176.

71. Richard Baxter, "The Harassed Respondent: I. Sales Solicitation in the Guise of Consumer Research" (orig. pub. 1965), in *Current Controversies in Marketing Research*, ed. Leo Bogart (Chicago: Markham, 1969), 25. For the growth of opinion and consumer surveys in this period, see Sarah E. Igo, *The Averaged American: Surveys, Citizens, and the Making of a Mass Public* (Cambridge, MA: Harvard University Press, 2007).

72. "That Noise You Hear May Be Pollution," *Business Week*, April 22, 1967: 42, 43; quoted in James E. Hildebrand, "Noise Pollution: An Introduction to the Problem and an Outline for Future Legal Research," *Columbia Law Review* 70: 4 (April 1970): 666.

73. William Burns, *Noise and Man* (London: Murray, 1968), 663.

74. New York Committee for a Quiet City, Inc., Final Report and Recommendations, July 7, 1960, p. 24; quoted in Hildebrand, "Noise Pollution," 656. Later such concerns would extend even to "personality disintegration," as in one Ford Motor Company advertisement: "Studies show that excessive noise can bring on anxiety, bizarre bodily sensations, and personality disintegration. Outside, it's getting noisier and noisier. Inside a 1971 Ford LTD, it's another world. . . . This year take a quiet break." *Newsweek* (October 12, 1970): 52–53; quoted in Gregory F. Houlé, "Toward the Comprehensive Abatement of Noise Pollution: Recent Federal and New York City Noise Control Legislation," *Ecology Law Quarterly* 4: 1 (January 1974).

75. August Heckscher, "The Invasion of Privacy (II): The Reshaping of Privacy," *American Scholar* 28 (1959): 11–20; quote on p. 15.

76. Clark, "Ranch-House Suburbia," 180.

77. Betty Friedan, *The Feminine Mystique* (New York: Norton, 1963), 246. See Deborah Nelson, *Pursuing Privacy in Cold War America* (New York: Columbia University Press, 2002), 86–87.

78. John Demos, *A Little Commonwealth: Family Life in Plymouth Colony* (New York: Oxford University Press, 1970), 46–47.

79. Harris, "Screening Identity," 129.

80. Jackson, *Crabgrass Frontier*; Clifford Clark Jr., *American Family Home, 1800–1960* (Chapel Hill: University of North Carolina Press, 1986); Robert Fishman, *Bourgeois Utopias: The Rise and Fall of Suburbia* (New York: Basic Books, 1987); Marsh, *Suburban Lives.*

81. This was John Keats, *The Crack in the Picture Window* (Boston: Houghton Mifflin, 1956); quoted in Harris, "Screening Identity," 145.

82. Heckscher, "The Invasion of Privacy (II)," 15.

83. See, for example Vance Packard's *The Status Seekers: An Exploration of Class Behavior in America and the Hidden Barriers That Affect You, Your Community, Your Future* (New York: D. McKay, Co., 1959).

84. William H. Whyte, *The Organization Man* (New York: Simon and Schuster, 1956), 389.

85. Whyte, *The Organization Man*, 356, 390; emphasis in original.

86. David Riesman in collaboration with Reuel Denney and Nathan Glazer, *The Lonely Crowd: A Study of the Changing American Character* (New Haven, CT: Yale University Press, 1950).

87. Sloan Wilson, *The Man in the Gray Flannel Suit* (New York: Simon and Schuster, 1955).

88. Riesman, *The Lonely Crowd*, 18; emphasis in original. K. A. Cuordileone argues that "the psychological implications of a mass society, and the difficulty of achieving autonomy—an independent, well-fortified sense of self within that society—became the single most compelling problem for postwar intellectuals and social critics." *Manhood and American Political Culture in the Cold War*, 98–99.

89. See John Seeley, *Crestwood Heights: A Study of the Culture of Suburban Life* (New York: Basic Books, 1956); Keats, *The Crack in the Picture Window*; and William Dobriner, ed., *The Suburban Community* (New York: Putnam, 1958). By the later 1960s, there were critiques of this characterization too, such as Herbert J. Gans's 1967 attempt to correct the dominant view of suburban life as "socially, culturally, and emotionally destructive" in *The Levittowners: Ways of Life and Politics in a New Suburban Community* (New York: Pantheon Books, 1967), 153–184; quote on p. 153.

90. Sidney M. Jourard, *The Transparent Self: Self-Disclosure and Well-Being* (Princeton, NJ: Van Nostrand, 1964), 64–65, 71–72. Elsewhere, Jourard called for an "Education for Private Life" that might counteract Americans' training in the institutions of conformity.

91. Brett Gary, *The Nervous Liberals: Propaganda Anxieties from World War I to the Cold War* (New York: Columbia University Press, 1999); David Greenberg, *Republic of Spin: An Inside History of the American Presidency* (New York: W. W. Norton, 2016); Adam Sheingate, *Building a Business of Politics: The Rise*

of Political Consulting and the Transformation of American Democracy (New York: Oxford University Press, 2016).

92. Historians have covered this territory extensively. For a recent overview see the Special Issue on "Brainwashing: Mind Control, Media, and Warfare," *Grey Room* 45 (Fall 2011): 6–150. See also Catherine Lutz, "Epistemology of the Bunker: The Brainwashed and Other New Subjects of Permanent War," in *Inventing the Psychological: Toward a Cultural History of Emotional Life in America*, ed. Joel Pfister and Nancy Schnog (New Haven, CT: Yale University Press, 1997), 245–267.

93. Susan Carruthers, *"The Manchurian Candidate* (1962) and the Cold War Brainwashing Scare," *Historical Journal of Film Radio, and Television* 18: 1 (March 1998): 75–94; Charles Young, "Missing Action: POW films, Brainwashing, and the Korean War, 1954–1968," *Historical Journal of Film, Radio and Television* 18: 1 (March 1998): 49–74.

94. Edward Hunter, *Brain-Washing in Red China: The Calculated Destruction of Men's Minds* (New York: Vanguard Press, 1951). Hunter first used the term in 1950, and the CIA had used it even before the war began; see Timothy Melley, "Brain Warfare: The Covert Sphere, Terrorism, and the Legacy of the Cold War," *Grey Room* 45 (Fall 2011): 24, 28. See also Joost Meerloo, *The Rape of the Mind: The Psychology of Thought Control, Menticide, and Brainwashing* (Cleveland: Progressive Press, 1956).

95. For the most thorough account, see Charles S. Young, *Name, Rank, and Serial Number: Exploiting Korean War POWs at Home and Abroad* (New York: Oxford University Press, 2014).

96. Robin, *The Making of the Cold War Enemy*, 167. See, for example, Robert Alden, "X-Ray of the Communist Mind," *New York Times Magazine* (December 20, 1953): 12, 34–37; and "The GIs Who Fell for the Reds," *Saturday Evening Post* (March 6, 1954): 17–19. Matthew W. Dunne cites as evidence 231 articles on brainwashing that appeared in the *New York Times* in the decade of the 1950s; he counted 5,391 on the threat of nuclear war and 85 speculating on communist takeover. *A Cold War State of Mind: Brainwashing and Postwar American Society* (Amherst: University of Massachusetts Press, 2013), 39, 243 n. 96.

97. The CIA tried to beat the Communists to the punch by doing their own covert experiments with electroshock, hypnotism, drugs, and sensory deprivation for the waging of "brain warfare" (known as MK-ULTRA and the roots of torture as interrogation) in 1950; Melley, "Brain Warfare," 28–29.

98. Andreas Killen and Stefan Andriopoulos, "Editor's Introduction," Special Issue on Brainwashing: Mind Control, Media, and Warfare, *Grey Room* 45 (Fall 2011): 7, 12.

99. Friedman in *Citizenship in Cold War America* and Matthew Dunne in *A Cold War State of Mind* both make this case. Dunne argues that brainwashing was a

break in the postwar consensus: its move back to the United States allowed a critique of postwar culture, elevating the values of authenticity, individuality, and anti-conformity.

100. The writer is quoting Robert J. Lifton's *Thought Reform and the Psychology of Totalism: A Study of "Brainwashing" in China* (New York: Norton, 1961).

101. Albert Biderman, "The Image of 'Brainwashing,'" *Public Opinion Quarterly* 26 (Winter 1962): 547–563; quotes on pp. 547, 551. See the *Journal of Social Issues* 13: 3 (1957), which is devoted to the "debunking of brainwashing."

102. Anna McCarthy, *The Citizen Machine: Governing by Television in 1950s America* (New York: New Press, 2010); Fred Turner, *The Democratic Surround: Multimedia and American Liberalism from World War II to the Psychedelic Sixties* (Stanford, CA: Stanford University Press, 2013); and Christopher Simpson, *Science of Coercion: Communication Research and Psychological Warfare, 1945–1960* (New York: Oxford University Press, 1994). Part of what historian Ron Robin calls the "canon" of Cold War communications studies was that "propaganda and information management were normative aspects of modern society." This was yet another area of convergence between "Sovietized" and democratic states. Robin, *The Making of the Cold War Enemy*, 91–92.

103. Robin, *The Making of the Cold War Enemy*, 81–82. Studies of mass persuasion from the era stressed its considerable limits as a tactic. See, for example, Alex Inkeles's *Public Opinion in Soviet Russia: A Study in Mass Persuasion* (Cambridge, MA: Harvard University Press, 1950).

104. The 1938 "War of the Worlds" radio broadcast was a prime example. More generally, see Daniel J. Czitrom, *Media and the American Mind: From Morse to McLuhan* (Chapel Hill: University of North Carolina Press, 1982).

105. Robert S. Lynd and Helen Merrell Lynd, *Middletown, A Study in Contemporary American Culture* (New York: Harcourt, Brace and Co., 1929), chs. 8, 9.

106. John Riley, Frank Cantwell, and Katherine Ruttiger, "Some Observations on the Social Effects of Television," *Public Opinion Quarterly* 13 (Summer 1949): 223–334; quotes on pp. 230, 231–232.

107. Lynn Spigel, *Make Room for TV: Television and the Family Ideal in Postwar America* (Chicago: University of Chicago Press, 1992); Cecilia Tichi, *Electronic Hearth: Creating an American Television Culture* (New York: Oxford University Press, 1991).

108. Susan J. Douglas, *Listening In: Radio and the American Imagination* (Minneapolis: University of Minnesota Press, 2004).

109. Frederic Wertham, *Seduction of the Innocent* (New York: Rinehart, 1954). See James Gilbert, *A Cycle of Outrage: America's Reaction to the Juvenile Delinquent in the 1950s* (New York: Oxford University Press, 1986).

110. Daniel Horowitz, *The Anxieties of Affluence: Critiques of American Consumer Culture, 1939–1979* (Amherst: University of Massachusetts Press, 2004); Cohen,

A *Consumer's Republic*. See Frederic Wakeman's *The Hucksters* (1946) and Sloan Wilson's *The Man in the Gray Flannel Suit* (1955) for unflattering presentations of the ad man.

111. One of Dichter's early (1939) successes was a study for Chrysler Corporation that linked convertibles with mistresses and sedans with wives.

112. John S. Sinclair, foreword to Lawrence C. Lockley, *Use of Motivational Research in Marketing*, Studies in Business Policy, No. 97 (New York: National Industrial Conference Board, 1960), 4.

113. Lockley, *Use of Motivational Research*, 23, 9.

114. Cushman, *Constructing the Self, Constructing America*.

115. For a full treatment, see Lawrence R. Samuel, *Freud on Madison Avenue: Motivation Research and Subliminal Advertising in America* (Philadelphia: University of Pennsylvania Press, 2010).

116. Fred T. Schreier and Albert J. Wood, "Motivation Analysis in Market Research," *Journal of Marketing* 13: 2 (October 1948): 172–182.

117. Lockley, *Use of Motivational Research*, 10.

118. Ralph L. Westfall, Harper W. Boyd Jr., and Donald T. Campbell, "The Use of Structured Techniques in Motivation Research," *Journal of Marketing* 22: 2 (October 1957): 134–139; quote on 134. A classic early study (on instant versus drip ground coffee and the motivations of women who purchased each: did the decision signal laziness, care for their families, frugality, etc.) was Mason Haire, "Projective Techniques in Marketing Research," *Journal of Marketing* 14 (April 1950): 649–656.

119. The Rorschach test arrived in the United States in 1924. The difficulty in discerning proper responses to it "left the tester with the final, indeed the only, say in what the test-taker's responses meant." Roderick D. Buchanan, "Ink Blots or Profile Plots: The Rorschach versus the MMPI as the Right Tool for a Science-Based Profession," *Science, Technology, & Human Values* 2: 22 (1997): 168–206; see pp. 175, 177. Also see Rebecca M. Lemov's discussion of the development of projective tests that attempted to "look directly into the mind and heart of a human being," the TAT and Rorchach in particular, in *Database of Dreams: The Lost Quest to Catalog Humanity* (New Haven, CT: Yale University Press, 2015), 19–43; quote on p. 20.

120. See the committee report of a section of the American Marketing Association: Julian L. Woodward, David Hofler, Fred Havilland, Herbert Hyman, Jack Peterman, and Harry Rosten, "Depth Interviewing," *Journal of Marketing* 14: 5 (April 1950): 721–724.

121. Lockley, *Use of Motivational Research*, 15–16, 22, 13; emphasis in original.

122. N. D. Rothwell, "Motivational Research Revisited," *Journal of Marketing* 20: 2 (October 1955): 150–154; quote on p. 150. Calling MR "badly employed and sadly abused" by marketers, this critic painted a "sharp contrast between the

hopeful but cautious clinicians who developed projective testing and the boastful claims made for it by the MR borrowers," 152.

123. Lockley, *Use of Motivational Research*, 24.

124. Lockley, *Use of Motivational Research*, 25, 26. Others made the point that "depth" interviewing and "projective" techniques were vague and unhelpful terms for what marketers were doing. See Robert J. Williams, "Is It True What They Say about Motivation Research?" *Journal of Marketing* 22: 2 (October 1957): 125–133.

125. Jim Montgomery, "Your Automobile Is a Real Tattle-Tale," *Atlanta Constitution*, March 5, 1958, p. 24.

126. Montgomery, "Your Automobile is a Real Tattle-Tale," 24.

127. Marshall McLuhan's *The Mechanical Bride: Folklore of Industrial Man* (New York: Vanguard Press, 1951) had also exposed advertisers' efforts to "get inside the collective public mind."

128. For a full account, see Daniel Horowitz, *Vance Packard and American Social Criticism* (Chapel Hill: University of North Carolina Press, 1994), 102–131. See also his discussion of readers' responses to Packard's books, 158–178.

129. Horowitz, *Vance Packard and American Social Criticism*, 164.

130. Samuel, *Freud on Madison Avenue*, 88–120; James V. McConnell, Richard L. Cutler, and Elton B. McNeil, "Subliminal Stimulation: An Overview," *American Psychologist* 13: 3 (1958): 229–242; Stuart Rogers, "How a Publicity Blitz Created the Myth of Subliminal Advertising," *Public Relations Quarterly* 37 (Winter, 1992–93): 12–17.

131. For popular coverage of the Vicary incident, see Carter Henderson, "A Blessing or a Bane? TV Ads You'd See without Knowing It," *Wall Street Journal*, September 13, 1957, p. 1; "Ads Aimed at Subconscious Criticized by Researcher," *Wall Street Journal*, September 30, 1957, p. 13; "'Invisible' Ads Tested," *Printers' Ink*, September 20, 1957, p. 44; and Gay Talese, "Most Hidden Hidden Persuasion," *New York Times Magazine* (January 12, 1958): 59. See also Ralph Norman Haber, "Public Attitudes regarding Subliminal Advertising," *Public Opinion Quarterly* 23: 2 (Summer 1959): 291–293.

132. Samuel, *Freud on Madison Avenue*, 96.

133. Erving Goffman's work in social interactionism, as well as George Herbert Mead's on the "social self," pointed in this direction. The link between knowing and controlling had also been observed in the literature on experimenter and expectancy effects in psychology and the Hawthorne experiments of the 1930s. See Richard Gillespie, *Manufacturing Knowledge: A History of the Hawthorne Experiments* (New York: Cambridge University Press, 1991).

134. This is why, as Jamie Cohen-Cole has argued, "creativity" was such an important solution to an array of social problems for mid-century social

scientists. "The Creative American: Cold War Salons, Social Science, and the Cure for Modern Society," *Isis* 100: 2 (2009): 219–262.

135. Holmes Alexander, "The Campaign against Intrusion," *Los Angeles Times*, October 21, 1957, p. B5.

136. Signed: Parent, Downey, "State School Test Rapped," *Los Angeles Times*, December 30, 1957, p. B4.

137. In what became known as the Lippmann-Terman controversy, Walter Lippmann and Lewis M. Terman publicly debated the worth of intelligence testing in the early 1920s, Lippmann mounting a sharp criticism of the tests in a series of articles for *The New Republic*. See his "The Mental Age of Americans," *New Republic* 32 (October 25, 1922): 213–215. On the history of intelligence and aptitude testing, see John Carson, *The Measure of Merit: Talents, Intelligence, and Inequality in the French and American Republics, 1750–1940* (Princeton, NJ: Princeton University Press, 2007); and Nicholas Lehmann, *The Big Test: The Secret History of the American Meritocracy* (New York: Farrar, Straus and Giroux, 1999).

138. This is cited in Banesh Hoffman, *Tyranny of Testing* (New York: Crowell-Collier Press, 1962), 37–38. See Oscar Buros, ed., *Mental Measurements Yearbook*, 5th ed. (New Brunswick, NJ: Rutgers University Press, 1959).

139. "Rash of Testing in Schools: Is It Being Overdone?" *U.S. News and World Report* (June 15, 1959); "Testing: Can Everyone Be Pigeon-Holed?" *Newsweek* (July 20, 1959); "What the Tests Do Not Test," *New York Times Magazine* (October 2, 1960): 14.

140. Hoffman, *Tyranny of Testing*. Banesh Hoffman, "'Best' Answers or Better Minds," *American Scholar* 28: 2 (Spring 1959): 195–202, and "The Tyranny of Multiple-Choice Tests," *Harper's Magazine* 222 (March 1961): 37–41. See also Hillel Black, *They Shall Not Pass* (New York: Morrow, 1962), for rising concerns about the discriminatory effects of testing.

141. See Bernice M. Moore and Wayne H. Holtzman, "What Texas Knows about Youth," *National Parent-Teacher* (September 1958): 22–24; and Gwynne Nettler, "Test Burning in Texas," *American Psychologist* 14 (1959): 682–683.

142. Nettler, "Test Burning," 683.

143. Leonard D. Eron and Leopold O. Walder, "Test Burning: II," *American Psychologist* 16: 5 (May 1961): 237–244.

144. On the conservative movement's animus toward what it termed the "mental testing establishment," see Lisa McGirr, *Suburban Warriors: The Origins of the New American Right* (Princeton, NJ: Princeton University Press, 2001); and Michelle M. Nickerson, *Mothers of Conservatism: Women and the Postwar Right* (Princeton, NJ: Princeton University Press, 2012), 103–135. For a contemporary account, see Donald Robison, "The Far Right's Fight against Mental Health," *Look* (January 26, 1965): 30–32. A study of this phenomenon

by psychologists can be found in Richard Schmuck and Mark Chesler, "Superpatriot Opposition to Community Mental Health Programs," *Community Mental Health Journal* 3: 4 (Winter 1967): 382–388. Norman Dain traces psychiatry's critics on the Left and the Right in "Psychiatry and Anti-Psychiatry in the United States," in *Discovering the History of Psychiatry*, ed. Mark S. Micale and Roy Porter (New York: Oxford University Press, 1994), 415–444.

145. Nickerson, *Mothers of Conservatism*, 69–102. A Texas representative from the Daughters of the American Revolution, for example, prepared a list of tests the organization wanted banned, alleging the "possible subversive uses of psychological instruments" and their usefulness to Communists. Nettler, "Test Burning," 683.

146. Nickerson, *Mothers of Conservatism*, 128, 105.

147. Eron and Walder, "Test Burning: II," 237–244.

148. Howard Brick, *Age of Contradiction: American Thought and Culture in the 1960s* (Ithaca, NY: Cornell University Press, 1998), 23–43.

149. Michael Amrine, "The 1965 Congressional Inquiry into Testing: A Commentary," *American Psychologist* 20 (1965): 859–870; quote on p. 859. He noted that on the Right, psychological testing was bundled with attacks on UNESCO, UNICEF, fluoridation and "the mental health conspiracy"; quote on p. 860.

150. Russell Kirk, "Those School Psychological Tests," *National Review* (June 30, 1964): 539. See also Edward J. Van Allen, *The Branded Child: The School Psyche-Snoops Exposed and What Can be Done about Them* (Mineola, NY: Reportorial Press, 1964).

151. Brenton, *The Privacy Invaders*, 165–166.

152. Editorial, "The Test Flunks Out," *Washington Post*, October 4, 1963, p. A20.

153. Monroe H. Freedman, "None of Their Business," letter to the editor, *Washington Post*, October 22, 1963, p. A16. For more, see "College Questionnaires about Parents Burned," *Washington Post*, October 23, 1963, p. B2; and "Testers to Burn Results of Quiz in County Row," *Washington Evening Star*, October 23, 1963.

154. Jacques Barzun, foreword to Hoffman, *The Tyranny of Testing*, 7–8.

155. Dale Tillery, "Seeking a Balance between the Right of Privacy and the Advancement of Social Research," *Journal of Educational Measurement* 4: 1 (Spring 1967): 11–16; quotes on pp. 11, 14, 13.

156. Hoffman, *Tyranny of Testing*, 214. Hoffman proposed a committee of inquiry into the tests, with, as a minimum concern, the quality of the tests and their makers. "For the benefit of defenseless test-takers, it might well formulate a Bill of Rights, among the provisions of which would surely be that difficulty shall not be achieved by means of ambiguity and vagueness."

157. Heckscher, "The Invasion of Privacy (II)," 11.

158. Brenton, *The Privacy Invaders*, 61–62. On lie detectors, see Dwight Macdonald, "The Lie-Detector Era," *The Reporter* (June 8, 1954).

159. Gross, *The Brain Watchers*, 18.

160. The Hawthorne experiments of the 1930s had already turned attention to psychological factors and "morale" in the workplace and had also been subject to some criticism from the Left by those worried about the psychologizing of worker discontent and labor relations more generally; see Gillespie, *Manufacturing Knowledge*. For critics of employer invasiveness by the later 1960s, see Edward Engberg, *The Spy in the Corporate Structure and the Right to Privacy* (Cleveland: World, 1967); and Stanley M. Herman, *The People Specialists: An Examination of Realities and Fantasies in the Corporation's View of People, and the Plain and Fancy Specialties and Specialists That Arise Therefrom* (New York: Knopf, 1968).

161. Creech, "Psychological Testing and Constitutional Rights," 335. Surely these "soft" factors were also resorted to in order to cloak more obvious discriminatory intent.

162. Whyte, *Organization Man*, 108.

163. According to a testing expert, the "first inventory primarily concerned with assessing the individual was the Woodworth Personal Data Sheet," used during World War I to detect "soldiers likely to break down in combat"; even then it used highly personal questions such as "Do you wet your bed?" Lee J. Cronbach, *Essentials of Psychological Testing*, 2nd ed. (New York: Harper & Brothers, 1960), 465.

164. See Herman, *Romance of American Psychology*, 92.

165. Lee J. Cronbach, *Essentials of Psychological Testing*, 3rd ed. (New York: Harper & Row, 1970), 526.

166. Thomas Chappelear, "'Danger! Pseudo-Psychologist at Work!': Psychology and Personnel Management in the Postwar Corporation," unpublished conference paper in author's possession; Gross, *The Brain Watchers*, 6–8.

167. Gross, *The Brain Watchers*, 9.

168. Charles Alex, *How to Beat Personality Tests* (New York: Arco Publishing, 1966). Alan Westin wryly noted Alex's takeaway message to be "always selecting the most heterosexual responses to sex questions, showing no cultural interests, and stressing normality in all inter-personal relations. . . . In regard to ink blots, Alex advises to try to see animals in motion and, above all, to avoid mentioning sex organs." *Privacy and Freedom*, 267.

169. Gross, *The Brain Watchers*, 19–20, 48, 174, 86.

170. Annie Murphy Paul, *The Cult of Personality: How Personality Tests Are Leading Us to Miseducate Our Children, Mismanage Our Companies, and Misunderstand Ourselves* (New York: Free Press, 2004), 57–59.

171. Gross, *The Brain Watchers*, 93–94.

172. See Gross, *The Brain Watchers*, 98–99.

173. Willard Clopton, "Personality X-Rays or Peeping Toms?" *Washington Post*, July 4, 1965, p. E2.

174. Roderick Buchanan, "The Development of the Minnesota Multiphasic Personality Inventory," *Journal of the History of the Behavioral Sciences* 30: 2 (April 1994): 148–161. The interest was in whether the response predicted or had a significant statistical relationship to personal characteristics—or, in the original use of the MMPI, specified clinical conditions.

175. Clopton, "Personality X-Rays or Peeping Toms?" Because the significance of an individual's MMPI responses was derived from statistical aggregates, the MMPI was "more difficult to fake" than some other personality inventories; it meant that its "subjects would have little idea what their responses might mean." See Buchanan, "Ink Blots or Profile Plots," 179.

176. William H. Whyte, "The Fallacies of 'Personality' Testing," in *Readings in Psychological Tests and Measurements*, ed. W. Leslie Barnette (Homewood, IL: Dorsey, 1964), 312.

177. This was especially true of tests like the "biographical index," which took successful company executives as the standard and measured test takers responses' against it. Charged Gross, the tester "sees himself as a self-appointed bastion of normality." *The Brain Watchers*, 92.

178. Gross, *The Brain Watchers*, 78–79.

179. Alan Westin asked, for instance, "whether employers or the government should be allowed to require individuals to have their inner processes probed through . . . test measurements." *Privacy and Freedom*, 134.

180. Whyte, "The Fallacies of 'Personality' Testing," 312.

181. Philip Vernon, *Personality Assessment: A Critical Survey* (London: Methuen, 1964), 257.

182. Cronbach, *Essentials of Psychological Testing*, 2nd ed., 459–460. Similarly, two social scientists acknowledged that "some personality tests induce the subject unwittingly to reveal more about himself than he wishes to," trapping the individual "into making public those facts and feelings about himself or others that he would not wish to disclose." Oscar Ruebhausen and Orville Brim, "Privacy and Behavioral Research," *Columbia Law Review* 65 (November 1965): 1196.

183. Cronbach, *Essentials of Psychological Testing*, 2nd ed., 459.

184. Wilson, *The Man in the Gray Flannel Suit*.

185. Whyte, *The Organization Man*, 405.

186. Jourard, *The Transparent Self*; as cited in James Neal Butcher and Auke Tellegen, "Objections to MMPI Items," *Journal of Consulting Psychology* 30: 6 (1966): 527.

187. Butcher and Tellegen, "Objections to MMPI Items," 527–534; quote on p. 534. They reported on which items seemed offensive, including 22 percent of those on the Psychopathic Deviate scale and 18 percent of those on the Masculinity-Femininity scale.

188. Butcher and Tellegen, "Objections to MMPI Items," 529–530, 533.

189. Butcher and Tellegen, "Objections to MMPI Items," 533–534. They also acknowledged that purging the MMPI of offensive items would not notably "reduce objections in an employment situation."

190. "The 'I Love My Mother Tests,'" *Washington Star*, May 19, 1965. Ashbrook as quoted in Westin, *Privacy and Freedom*, 250. See also John Ashbrook, "Brain-picking in School: A Study of Psychiatric Testing," *Human Events* 19: 46 (1962): 883–886.

191. These are representative MMPI items classified by Philip Marks and William Seeman in *The Actuarial Description of Abnormal Personality: An Atlas for Use with the MMPI* (Baltimore: Williams & Wilkins, 1963, p. 24); adapted in Cronbach, *Essentials of Psychological Testing*, 3rd ed., 528.

192. Art Buchwald, "A Head Start on Brain Inventory," *Los Angeles Times*, June 19, 1965, p. B1.

193. The hearings were on: Psychological Tests and Constitutional Rights (1965); Special Inquiry on Invasion of Privacy (1966); The Computer and Invasion of Privacy (1966). See Cornelius Gallagher, "Why House Hearings on Invasion of Privacy," *American Psychologist* 20: 11 (November 1965): 881–882; and Sam J. Ervin Jr., "Why Senate Hearings on Psychological Tests in Government," *American Psychologist* 20:11 (November 1965): 879–880.

194. Deborah Nelson charts the "sudden visibility of privacy" and a new and "measureable density" to privacy fears in the 1950s United States in *Pursuing Privacy*, xi–xii, 6.

195. Brenton, *The Privacy Invaders*, 171.

196. Alan Westin set out to research and write *Privacy and Freedom* (1967) to alert Americans to invasions of their privacy, but by the time he completed it, "the need to warn the American public about the threats to personal privacy that had motivated his book no longer existed." Nelson, *Pursuing Privacy*, 19.

197. Brenton, *The Privacy Invaders*, 163.

198. Vance Packard, *The Naked Society* (New York: D. McKay, 1964).

199. There were dissenting voices—those who argued that Americans' clamor for privacy was misplaced or symptomatic of other problems—but they were in the distinct minority. See Granville Hicks, "The Invasion of Privacy (III): The Limits of Privacy," *American Scholar* 28: 2 (Spring 1959): 185–193; and Margaret Mead, "Our Right to Privacy," *Redbook* 124 (April 1965): 15–16.

200. Edward V. Long, *The Intruders: The Invasion of Privacy by Government and Industry* (New York: Praeger, 1967), 3.

201. Creech, "Psychological Testing and Constitutional Rights," 336. "Never before in our history has the Government been so concerned with the personalities of its citizens," he declared.

4. A Right to Be Let Alone

1. The nonbinding Universal Declaration of Human Rights passed in December 10, 1948.
2. Elizabeth Borgwardt, *A New Deal for the World: America's Vision for Human Rights* (Cambridge, MA: Harvard University Press, 2007), 242.
3. Universal Declaration of Human Rights, Article 12, 1948.
4. Historians of the Declaration make little to no mention of its inclusion of privacy. See for example, Mary Ann Glendon, *A World Made New: Eleanor Roosevelt and the Declaration of Human Rights* (New York: Random House, 2001). Even when Glendon analyzes the Declaration part by part, she skims over the mention of privacy and notes no debate over the article or language; 181–183. Morsink's discussion of Article 12 indicates that the primary debates involved not the right to privacy, which was assumed, but rather (1) the article's initial language of inviolability (e.g., was the home truly "inviolable" if there were those who "had every right to enter the home and read the gas meter"?, 136); and (2) the positive vs. negative mode of expression (whether these rights were protected or were simply not to be interfered with). Johannes Morsink, *The Universal Declaration of Human Rights: Origins, Drafting, and Intent* (Philadelphia: University of Pennsylvania Press, 2000), 130–156.
5. According to Samuel Moyn, there existed a general consensus as to the content of the rights; thus, debates centered more on specific language than the spectrum of rights to be included. *The Last Utopia: Human Rights in History* (Cambridge, MA: Harvard University Press, 2012), 44–83.
6. According to Carol Anderson, despite the "politics of moral outrage the Holocaust engendered," the federal government and prominent liberals "steadfastly refused to make human rights a viable force in the United States or in international practice." Eisenhower and Dulles even announced that human rights declarations "threatened basic liberties protected in the constitution." Anderson, *Eyes off the Prize: The United Nations and the African American Struggle for Human Rights, 1944–1955* (New York: Cambridge University Press, 2003), 4, 6. Moyn too argues that the impact of the Declaration and human rights in the 1940s and for decades after was negligible, vague, and certainly not intended to bind states. He claims that the human rights idea became irrelevant because it could not determine the choice between a welfarist and a communist scheme and thus did not serve as an effective ideological paradigm during the Cold War. *The Last Utopia*, 44–83. See also

Mark Bradley, *The World Reimagined: Americans and Human Rights in the Twentieth Century* (New York: Cambridge University Press, 2016).

7. Growing numbers of jurists were also inclined to see privacy rights as implicit in the provisions of the Bill of Rights.

8. See Mary Ann Glendon, *Rights Talk: The Impoverishment of Political Discourse* (New York: Free Press, 1991).

9. Note that these rulings were not typically concerned with intimate relations, making *Griswold* an outlier. Michal R. Belknap, *The Supreme Court under Earl Warren, 1953–1969* (Columbia: University of South Carolina Press, 2005); Morton J. Horowitz, *The Warren Court and the Pursuit of Justice* (New York: Hill and Wang, 1998).

10. Bruce J. Schulman, *Lyndon B. Johnson and American Liberalism*, 2nd ed. (Boston: Bedford / St. Martin's, 2007), 90. For a helpful discussion of mid-century liberals' understanding of "qualitative liberalism," see Kevin Mattson, *When America Was Great: The Fighting Faith of Postwar Liberalism* (New York: Routledge, 2004), 140–171; and Brian Balogh, "Making Pluralism 'Great': Beyond a Recycled History of the Great Society," in *The Great Society and the High Tide of Liberalism*, ed. Sidney M. Milkis and Jerome M. Mileur (Amherst: University of Massachusetts Press, 2005), 145–182. James T. Patterson describes a duty-bound consciousness giving way to a rights consciousness in this era, shaped by postwar consumer culture and the promises of personal happiness that it offered, as well as by the postwar civil rights movement. *Grand Expectations: The United States, 1945–1974* (New York: Oxford University Press, 1996).

11. Peter Clecak, *America's Quest for the Ideal Self: Dissent and Fulfillment in the 60s and 70s* (New York: Oxford University Press, 1983), 6.

12. The flurry of essays on the ruling's fifty-year anniversary in 2015, including the special issue "Reproductive Rights after Griswold: A Fifty Year Retrospective," *Connecticut History Review* 54: 2 (Fall 2015), celebrated its significance for reproductive freedom and for "break[ing] the connection between sex and procreation." Linda Greenhouse, "From *Griswold* to *Roe* and Beyond," *Connecticut History Review* 54: 2 (Fall 2015): 275. But recently there has been a recuperation of other meanings of *Griswold*, with the ruling understood as more than just the starting point of reproductive rights. See, for example, the essays devoted to *Griswold* in the *Yale Law Journal* 124 (2015). For the disappointments of *Roe* and some critique of that narrative, see Linda Greenhouse and Reva B. Siegel, "Before (and after) *Roe v. Wade*: New Questions about Backlash," *Yale Law Journal* 120 (2010–11): 2028–2087.

13. *Griswold v. Connecticut*, 381 U.S. 479 (1965).

14. The federal Act for the Suppression of Trade in, and Circulation of, Obscene Literature and Articles of Immoral Use, also known as the Comstock Act, was made law in 1873; it prohibited sending information about contraceptives and other so-called obscenities through the mail. Connecticut's statue was one of the many "little Comstock" state laws enacted on its model. By the time the Supreme Court heard the case, birth control remained illegal only in Connecticut and Massachusetts.

15. Barbara Sicherman, "Introduction: *Griswold v. Connecticut," Connecticut History Review* 54: 2 (Fall 2015): 256–259. See Helen Lefkowitz Horowitz, *Rereading Sex: Battles over Sexual Knowledge and Suppression in Nineteenth-Century America* (New York: Alfred A. Knopf, 2002); Donna Dennis, *Licentious Gotham: Erotic Publishing and Its Prosecution in Nineteenth-Century New York* (Cambridge, MA: Harvard University Press, 2009); Sharon R. Ullman, *Sex Seen: The Emergence of Modern Sexuality in America* (Berkeley: University of California Press, 1997); and Andrea Tone, *Devices and Desires: A History of Contraceptives in America* (New York: Hill and Wang, 2001). The Connecticut courts upheld the criminal ban in the 1940s (in *Tileson*) and 1950s (*Poe*).

16. *Poe v. Ullman,* 367 U.S. 497 (1961).

17. Linda Gordon, *The Moral Property of Women: A History of Birth Control Politics in America* (Urbana: University of Illinois Press, 2002) and *Woman's Body, Woman's Right: A Social History of Birth Control in America* (New York: Penguin Books, 1977). Rickie Solinger writes that by the late 1920s, fertility control had shifted for many from being a "guilty secret" to a "matter of privacy." *Pregnancy and Power: A Short History of Reproductive Politics in America* (New York: New York University Press, 2005), 102. The federal appellate judiciary in 1936 ruled that the Comstock law could not be used to prevent the transport of contraceptives for medical use in *United States v. One Package of Japanese Pessaries* 86 F.2d 737 (2d Cir.1936). Nancy F. Cott, *Public Vows: A History of Marriage and the Nation* (Cambridge, MA: Harvard University Press, 2000), 182.

18. Lawrence Friedman, "Review of Griswold v. Connecticut: *Birth Control and the Constitutional Right of Privacy," Journal of Interdisciplinary History* 37: 1 (Summer 2006): 161–163.

19. See David Allyn, *Make Love, Not War: The Sexual Revolution, an Unfettered History* (New York: Routledge, 2001). There had also been political advocates for freer sexual expression, most notably the American Civil Liberties Union, which had raised the issue in obscenity, nudism, and censorship cases from the 1930s onward. See Leigh Ann Wheeler, *How Sex Became a Civil Liberty* (New York: Oxford University Press, 2013).

20. David Allyn, "Private Acts / Public Policy: Alfred Kinsey, the American Law Institute and the Privatization of American Sexual Morality," *Journal of American Studies* 30 (1996): 405–428; Nancy Cott, *Public Vows*, 196.

21. Although most states regulated contraceptives in some fashion, Connecticut's law was considered the most restrictive in the nation, followed by that of Massachusetts. Donald T. Critchlow, *Intended Consequences: Birth Control, Abortion, and the Federal Government in Modern America* (New York: Oxford University Press, 1999), 59.

22. The Supreme Court mooted three cases in 1961, citing lack of enforcement and stating, "This Court cannot be umpire to debates concerning harmless, empty shadows."

23. Griswold and Buxton were arrested, convicted, and fined $100 each. David J. Garrow's is the most trustworthy account of the road to *Griswold*. See his *Liberty and Sexuality: The Right to Privacy and the Making of Roe v. Wade*, updated ed. (Berkeley: University of California Press, 1993), 196–269. See also John W. Johnson, Griswold v. Connecticut: *Birth Control and the Constitutional Right of Privacy* (Lawrence: University Press of Kansas, 2005). Estelle Griswold declared, "We don't wish to impose birth control on anyone," but would "welcome prosecution by the state" so that the "absurd and antiquated" 1879 law could be stricken from the books. Garrow, 196.

24. Arthur E. Sutherland, "Privacy in Connecticut," *Michigan Law Review* 64: 2 (December 1965): 283–288; quote on p. 285.

25. Johnson, Griswold v. Connecticut, 224.

26. *Boyd. v. United States*, 116 U.S. 616, 630 (1886).

27. Caroline Danielson argues that *DeMay v. Roberts* was "the earliest case in the United States explicitly to name a right to privacy." "The Gender of Privacy and the Embodied Self: Examining the Origins of the Right to Privacy in U.S. Law," *Feminist Studies* 25: 2 (1999): 311–344, quote on p. 311. Danielson raises a number of intriguing issues regarding alternative lineages for the legal right to privacy in the United States, including, in this early instance, the gendering and embodying of privacy rights in the form of a woman delivering a child.

28. According to Charles Reich, the first statement regarding the special sanctity of a private residence was in *Agnello v. United States* (1925): "the search of a private dwelling without a warrant is in itself unreasonable and abhorrent to our laws." "Midnight Welfare Searches and the Social Security Act," *Yale Law Journal* 72 (1963): 1354.

29. *Olmstead v. U.S.*, 227 U.S. 438 (1928).

30. 262 U.S. 390 (1923); 268 U.S. 510 (1925). Martha Minow has argued, however, that these cases are part of an "invented tradition of continuous constitutional protection for the family" that is quite contradictory and as much about

regulation as protection. "We, the Family: Constitutional Rights and American Families," *Journal of American History* 74: 3 (1987): 962.

31. In 1944, although in a case that affirmed the power of the state over the parent, *Prince v. Massachusetts*, the Court acknowledged the existence of constitutional protections for a "private realm of family life which the state cannot enter."

32. These were *On Lee v. US* (1952), regarding a federal agent gathering incriminating testimony via a concealed radio transmitter; *Beauharnais v. Illinois* (1952), on free expression; and *Public Utilities Commission v. Pollak* (1952), on the right to privacy from music on streetcars.

33. Anita L. Allen views the case's holding—that "Alabama could not compel revelation of the names and addresses of NAACP members"—as central to the development of data privacy. See her "Associational Privacy and the First Amendment: NAACP v. Alabama, Privacy and Data Protection," *Alabama Civil Rights and Civil Liberties Law Review* 1 (2011): 1–13; quote on p. 7. Deborah Nelson writes that in NAACP v. Alabama, the Court broke its "thirty-six-year refusal to establish a right to privacy by concluding that a political organization had the right to keep its membership private." *Pursuing Privacy in Cold War America* (New York: Columbia University Press, 2002), 280–281.

34. John Johnson bundles all of these together as "tantalizing references to privacy emanations from the fringes of the Bill of Rights"; see Griswold v. Connecticut, 71–76; quote on p. 71.

35. William L. Prosser, "Privacy," *California Law Review* 48: 3 (August 1960): 383–423. Prosser's essay was an influential attempt to catalog and classify privacy damages into four distinct torts.

36. ACLU leaders suggested as early as 1932 that laws against birth control might be unconstitutional because of due process rights; as with the case of Prohibition, attempts to suppress birth control devices and literature involved unlawful searches and seizures. Wheeler, *How Sex Became a Civil Liberty*, 53.

37. See Wheeler, *How Sex Became a Civil Liberty*, ch. 4. Sanger in the 1940s viewed civil liberties as encompassing not just freedom of press, speech, and worship but also the "right of free men and free women to control . . . their own destiny on earth," 96. The ACLU was slow to adopt this interpretation, maintaining throughout the 1950s that civil liberties applied only to the dissemination of birth control information.

38. Wheeler, *How Sex Became a Civil Liberty*, 103.

39. Garrow, *Liberty and Sexuality*, 196.

40. I thank Leigh Ann Wheeler for pointing me to this image; see *How Sex Became a Civil Liberty*, 97.

41. Wheeler, *How Sex Became a Civil Liberty*, 103.

42. In his *Poe* dissent, Harlan wrote that the plaintiffs' "most substantial claim . . . is their right to enjoy the privacy of their marital relations."

43. Garrow, *Liberty and Sexuality*, 245. Jamal Greene explains that Douglas's first draft had "treated the intimacies of the marital relationship as protected by the First Amendment right of association." "The So-Called Right of Privacy," *University of California, Davis Law Review* 43 (2010): 715–747, quote on p. 722.

44. Donald Critchlow calls the first draft of the opinion "lackadaisical" and notes that Douglas's attempt to derive the right to use contraceptives from the First Amendment freedom of assembly was met by Justice Hugo Black's objection that "the right of a husband and wife to assemble in bed is a new right of assembly to me." It was at that point that a law clerk, Paul Posner, suggested that the statue violated the right to privacy implied in the Third, Fourth, and Fifth Amendments. *Intended Consequences*, 59. Garrow notes that Justice Brennan pushed Douglas to argue for a right of privacy. *Liberty and Sexuality*, 246.

45. See Gary Gerstle's discussion of the Court's broader move to "break the power of the states" in the 1960s in areas of marriage, religion, voting, and the like. *Liberty and Coercion: The Paradox of American Government from the Founding to the Present* (Princeton, NJ: Princeton University Press, 2015), ch. 9.

46. On the novelty of invoking the Ninth Amendment, see for example, "Constitutional Law: Supreme Court Finds Marital Privacy Immunized from State Intrusion as a Bill of Rights Periphery," *Duke Law Journal* 1966: 2 (Spring 1966): 562–577.

47. Del Dickson, ed., *The Supreme Court in Conference, 1940–1985: The Private Discussions behind Nearly 300 Supreme Court Decisions* (New York: Oxford University Press, 2001), 800. Justice Clark was more certain, saying, "There is a right to marry, to have a home, and to have children. . . . This is an area where I have the right to be let alone," 801.

48. Garrow, *Liberty and Sexuality*, 249.

49. Emerson named five possibilities: equal protection, the First Amendment, substantive due process, right of privacy, and the Ninth Amendment. "Nine Justices in Search of a Doctrine," *Michigan Law Review* 64: 2 (December 1965): 219–234; quote on p. 220.

50. Emerson claimed after the fact that the statute "invaded the sacred realm of marital privacy, and for all practical purposes denied to married couples the right of deciding whether or when to have children." "Nine Justices in Search of a Doctrine," 219.

51. The population control argument in particular was forceful in the mid-1960s. As Emerson saw it, the Connecticut statute "was fantastically in conflict with the clearly perceived need to deal with the world's second most critical problem—the population explosion" (he did not say what the first problem

was). "Nine Justices in Search of a Doctrine," 219. See Matthew Connelly, *Fatal Misconception: The Struggle to Control World Population* (Cambridge, MA: Belknap Press of Harvard University Press, 2008); and Alison Bashford, *Global Population: History, Geopolitics, and Life on Earth* (New York: Columbia University Press, 2014), 305–327.

52. Emerson, "Nine Justices in Search of a Doctrine," 219.

53. Robert G. Dixon Jr., "Griswold Penumbra: Constitutional Charter for an Expanded Law of Privacy," *Michigan Law Review* 64: 2 (December 1965): 215. He noted that "privacy was handled only in the fictional context of bedroom invasion."

54. Melissa Murray argues that the *Trubek* case framed birth control as centrally about women's equal citizenship—a "precondition for structuring marriage along more egalitarian lines" and also for a woman's career—even as it also spoke to marital privacy. "Overlooking Equality on the Road to *Griswold*," *Yale Law Journal* 124 (2014–2015).

55. Cary Franklin, "Griswold and the Public Dimension of the Right to Privacy," *Yale Law Journal* 124 (2014–2015). Franklin argues that *Griswold* was "part of a series of Warren Court decisions that suggested the Constitution, properly understood, was concerned with certain forms of material deprivation and material injustice"—and thus "the way *Griswold* has been categorized and canonized" as a reproductive rights case has obscured other sorts of issues at play in 1965.

56. Quotations are from the analysis provided in Dickson, *Supreme Court in Conference*, 802.

57. *Griswold v. Connecticut*, 509. Garrow, *Liberty and Sexuality*, 255. Stewart also failed to find a constitutional guarantee that the law infringed.

58. Freedom from the government is, of course, one of the classic or "natural" American constitutional rights, but as Mary Ziegler has suggested to me, privacy in the more expansive sense may not have aligned well with these sorts of rights.

59. Dixon Jr., "Griswold Penumbra," 199.

60. Garrow, *Liberty and Sexuality*, 263.

61. The relationship between public aspirations and law is explored in the literature on popular constitutionalism. See Larry D. Kramer, *The People Themselves: Popular Constitutionalism and Judicial Review* (New York: Oxford University Press, 2004); Robert Post and Reva Siegel, "Popular Constitution-alism, Departmentalism, and Judicial Supremacy," *California Law Review* 92 (2004): 1027–1043; and David Cole, *Engines of Liberty: The Power of Citizen Activists to Make Constitutional Law* (New York: Basic Books, 2016).

62. *Griswold v. Connecticut*, 485.

63. See Marc Stein, *Sexual Injustice: Supreme Court Decisions from* Griswold *to* Roe (Chapel Hill: University of North Carolina Press, 2010), 30.

64. Dixon Jr., "Griswold Penumbra," 218. He called this playing "charades with the Constitution."

65. Glendon, *Rights Talk*, 56. She writes that there was "nothing in *Griswold* to suggest privacy as individual right." Instead, "*Griswold* seemed at the time merely to consolidate . . . the kind of protection for marriage and family life that, by 1965, was the subject of express provisions in more modern constitutions."

66. Cott, *Public Vows*, 197–198.

67. On state economic support for marriage, see Cott, *Public Vows*; and Alice Kessler-Harris, *In Pursuit of Equity: Women, Men, and the Quest for Economic Citizenship in 20th-Century America* (New York: Oxford University Press, 2001).

68. See Deborah Weinstein, *The Pathological Family: Postwar America and the Rise of Family Therapy* (Ithaca, NY: Cornell University Press, 2013).

69. Franklin, "Griswold and the Public Dimension of the Right to Privacy."

70. See, for example, Rickie Solinger, *Wake Up Little Susie: Single Pregnancy and Race before Roe v. Wade* (New York: Routledge, 1992); and Margot Canaday, *The Straight State: Sexuality and Citizenship in Twentieth-Century America* (Princeton, NJ: Princeton University Press, 2009). Peggy Pascoe examines intricate state laws that grew up in the years after Reconstruction to ban various combinations of white-other marriages, which increasingly restricted even privileged white men's liberty to choose a spouse. *What Comes Naturally: Miscegenation Law and the Making of Race in America* (Oxford: Oxford University Press, 2009).

71. Solinger, *Pregnancy and Power*, 63. On the other hand, she notes in reference to the decriminalization of condom use during World War I the "cultural recognition that sexual intercourse, at least for white males (at least those serving their country), was a private act," 98. Condoms were also readily available in Connecticut at this time: at issue in *Griswold* was female contraception and poor women's access to birth control. See Tone, *Devices and Desires*.

72. Leslie J. Reagan's study of abortion during the criminal era reveals how poor women's bodies and decisions about their bodies were often the objects of public scrutiny, whereas women of means could, for example, keep abortions private. Reagan also documents how the state built and retained its power to intervene into the lives of women through reproductive regulation, sometimes in concert with physicians. *When Abortion Was a Crime: Women, Medicine, and Law in the United State, 1867–1973* (Berkeley: University of California Press, 1997). See also Khiara M. Bridges, *The Poverty of Privacy Rights* (Stanford, CA: Stanford University Press, 2017), which argues that poor mothers in particular have been denied privacy rights by the state.

73. See Rhonda Y. Williams, *The Politics of Public Housing: Black Women's Struggles against Urban Inequality* (New York: Oxford University Press, 2004).

74. Reich, "Midnight Welfare Searches and the Social Security Act"; Solinger, *Pregnancy and Power*, 147. As she notes, protection against search and seizure was a racial and class benefit.

75. Stein, *Sexual Injustice*, 77. Noting that U.S. law supported the deportation of homosexual aliens in this era, he writes that such men "were not just excluded from the privileges of privacy; they were subject to the demands of compulsory publicity."

76. The Court, Stein argues, "constructed normative heterosexuality, non-normative heterosexuality, and deviant homosexuality in dynamic and hierarchical relationships to one another," *Sexual Injustice*, 18.

77. *Griswold v. Connecticut*, 498–499; 505–507; Stein, *Sexual Injustice*, 29–34.

78. This remained true in *Eisenstadt v. Baird* of 1972, which was often hailed as extending sexual liberty to single adults. Although it struck down a birth control ban aimed at the unmarried, it was decided narrowly, not on grounds of privacy but of equal protection: single people were deemed to have been treated differently as a class than married ones under the law in question. The Court, in Marc Stein's words, did not endorse libertarian notions about the freedom of consenting adults in private, but rather "special rights and privileges for adult, heterosexual, marital, monogamous, private, and procreative forms of sexual expression." *Sexual Injustice*, 18. This regime of heterosexual and reproductive normativity would not end until 2003, when the landmark *Lawrence v. Texas* was handed down, striking down anti-sodomy laws. See also Michael J. Karman, *From the Closet to the Altar: Courts, Backlash, and the Struggle for Same-Sex Marriage* (New York: Oxford University Press, 2013).

79. Most recently, *Griswold* was cited in Justice Kennedy's majority opinion in *Obergefell v. Hodges* (2015), which recognized same-sex marriage as constitutionally protected.

80. Cott, *Public Vows*, 199.

81. *Eisenstadt v. Baird*, 405 U.S. 438, 453 (1972): "The marital couple is not an independent entity with a mind and a heart of its own, but an association of two individuals each with a separate intellectual and emotional makeup." Mary Ann Glendon argues that it was at this moment, in 1972, that the Court "abruptly severed the privacy right from its attachment to marriage and the family and launched it as a full-fledged *individual* right." *Rights Talk*, 57; emphasis in original. This was the moment that marked a shift from privacy as freedom from surveillance or disclosure to the freedom to engage in certain activities and make choices without government interference.

82. *Roe v. Wade*, 410 U.S. 113 (1973); although note that *Roe* spoke to a joint right of the "woman and her doctor." Deborah Nelson observes that this expansion of

the right was also its first contraction, which she links to its gendering as female. See "Beyond Privacy: Confessions between a Woman and Her Doctor," *Feminist Studies* 25: 2 (Summer 1999): 279–306. Nelson explains elsewhere that "*Griswold*'s zone of privacy quickly expanded beyond the home and domestic autonomy" to encompass the right to personal decision-making. *Pursuing Privacy in Cold War America*, 20. This tilt toward protecting "choices central to personal dignity and autonomy" would persist in the Court's later jurisprudence around reproductive rights, notably in *Planned Parenthood of Southeastern Pennsylvania v. Casey*, 505 U.S. 833, 851 (1992).

83. Some attorneys thought it might be possible to use *Roe* or *Eisenstadt* or *Griswold* outside the context of sexuality and reproduction, especially until the later 1970s. See Mary Ziegler, *After* Roe: *The Lost History of The Abortion Debate* (Cambridge, MA: Harvard University Press, 2015). The coupling of privacy and reproductive rights also subjected all those cases to critique, famously by Judge Robert Bork, who called *Griswold* an "unprincipled" usurpation of democratic authority unauthorized by the Constitution's text.

84. Vincent Vecera writes that while "discussion of public health did not disappear immediately . . . the rise of a language of rights was stark and sudden." He argues that "as the conception of an abortion right founded on privacy rose to rhetorical dominance during the 1970s, advocates found themselves writing of an abortion decision no longer made in consultation with a physician but instead by a lone woman, in the privacy not of a medical office but instead the solitude of her conscience." It meant that abortion advocates' arguments "came to be situated in three rhetorical frameworks: privacy, choice, and autonomy." "The Supreme Court and the Social Conception of Abortion," *Law & Society Review* 48 (2014): 345–374.

85. As Mary Zeigler writes, "The legal academy has not been kind to the privacy rationale set forth in *Roe v. Wade*." "The Price of Privacy, 1973 to the Present," *Harvard Journal of Law & Gender* 37: 2 (2014): 285–329; quote on p. 285. Most writers have argued that reliance on liberty or equality, rather than privacy, would have garnered better and less "political" results. Justice Ruth Bader Ginsberg has memorably suggested that the privacy claim was an error. Reva B. Siegel has instead suggested that the very fact that privacy is "one of the most fiercely contested rights in the modern constitutional canon" has "helped to entrench the right to privacy, to make it endure, and to imbue it with evolving meaning." "How Conflict Entrenched the Right to Privacy," *Yale Law Journal* 124 (2014–2015).

86. Johnson, Griswold v. Connecticut, 4. This trajectory may have come to an end. As Jamal Greene argues in "The So-Called Right of Privacy," "privacy" has been abandoned by the Court in recent decisions on these topics, in favor of "liberty." Jill Lepore has also suggested that reproductive rights based on

445

privacy arguments and gay rights based on equality arguments have diverged, with gay rights in much better shape for forsaking the privacy strategy. "To Have and To Hold: Reproduction, Marriage, and the Constitution," *New Yorker* (May 25, 2010).

87. Johnson, Griswold v. Connecticut, 206.

88. Quoted in Stein, *Sexual Injustice*, 211.

89. Paul G. Kauper, "Penumbras, Peripheries, Emanations, Things Fundamental and Things Forgotten: The *Griswold* Case," *Michigan Law Review* 64: 2 (December 1965): 235–258; quote on p. 258.

90. Robert B. McKay, "The Right of Privacy: Emanations and Intimations," *Michigan Law Review* 64: 2 (December 1965): 63–86; quote on p. 77.

91. Dixon Jr., "Griswold Penumbra," 205.

92. Emerson, "Nine Justices in Search of a Doctrine," 233.

93. Dixon Jr., "Griswold Penumbra," 197.

94. Harry Kalven Jr., "Privacy in Tort Law—Were Warren and Brandeis Wrong?" *Law and Contemporary Problems* 31: 2 (1966): 326–341; quote on p. 327.

95. Clark C. Havighurst, foreword, *Law and Contemporary Problems* 31: 2 (1966): 251.

96. Glenn Negley, "Philosophical Views on the Value of Privacy," *Law and Contemporary Problems* 31: 2 (1966): 319–325; quote on p. 320.

97. William M. Beaney, "The Right to Privacy and American Law," *Law and Contemporary Problems* 31: 2 (1966): 253–271; quotes on pp. 255, 258–259.

98. Dixon Jr., "Griswold Penumbra," 202, n. 22.

99. Emerson, "Nine Justices in Search of a Doctrine," 229.

100. Beaney, "The Right to Privacy and American Law," 271. As Edward Shils put it in the same issue, "Privacy has become a problem because it has become engulfed in the expansion of the powers and ambitions of elites and in the difficulties that they encounter in attempting to govern and protect and please vast collectivities." "Privacy: Its Constitution and Vicissitudes," *Law and Contemporary Problems* 31: 2 (1966): 281–306; quote on p. 305.

101. Negley, "Philosophical Views," 320.

102. Beaney in fact discounted the importance of the 1890 essay for forwarding privacy as a right, believing it had not "effected any significant change in American life." In his view, "The approximately 350 decisions handed down between 1905 and 1965, many of them under New York's statute prohibiting intrusive conduct 'for the purposes of trade,' have had the effect of proscribing some of the more blatant, thoughtless, or intentional invasions of privacy, especially where a materialistic motive is evident, but we can only speculate as to a possible wider social effect of the right." "The Right to Privacy and American Law," 258.

103. Milton R. Konvitz, "Privacy and the Law: A Philosophical Prelude," *Law and Contemporary Problems* 31: 2 (1966): 272–280; quotes on pp. 277, 279–280.

104. Shils, "Privacy: Its Constitution and Vicissitudes," 286.

105. Few in the 1960s and early 1970s "mentioned abortion at all in the context of the right of privacy." Johnson, Griswold v. Connecticut, 197. The case for a link between *Griswold* and abortion rights is often attributed to an influential 1968 essay by Roy Lucas: "Federal Constitutional Limitations on the Enforcement and Administration of State Abortion Statutes," *North Carolina Law Review* 46 (June 1968): 730–778.

106. Johnson, Griswold v. Connecticut, 196–197.

107. Emerson, "Nine Justices in Search of a Doctrine," 232.

108. Stein, *Sexual Injustice*, 208. He argues that a kind of popular constitutionalism wound up reshaping these decisions so that even the Court would misread its earlier rulings by the time *Lawrence v. Texas* was decided in 2003. Distorted reportage and the commentary of many legal scholars, lower courts, and even the gay and lesbian media, eager to see the Court as a protector and supporter of sexual rights, all presented a more sexually liberal view.

109. Stein, *Sexual Injustice*, 217.

110. McKay, "The Right of Privacy: Emanations and Intimations," 82–83.

111. Beaney, "The Right to Privacy and American Law," 256.

112. W. T. R., III, "The Fourth Amendment Right of Privacy: Mapping the Future," *Virginia Law Review* 53: 6 (October 1967): 1315.

113. Charles A. Reich, "Police Questioning of Law Abiding Citizens," *Yale Law Journal* 75: 7 (1966): 1170.

114. *Olmstead v. United States*, 277 U.S. 438 (1928). In 1933, Congress banned wiretapping in Volstead Act investigations; a 1934 Act of Congress formally prohibited the interception and divulging of telephone communications. See Samuel Dash, Richard Schwartz, and Robert Knowlton, *The Eavesdroppers* (New Brunswick, NJ: Rutgers University Press, 1959), 386–389.

115. "Constitutional Law: Supreme Court Finds Marital Privacy Immunized from State Intrusion as a Bill of Rights Periphery," *Duke Law Journal* 1966: 2 (Spring 1966): 577 and n. 62 on that page. He noted prohibitions against miscegenation as well.

116. Emerson, "Nine Justices in Search of a Doctrine," 232–233.

117. *Lopez v. United States* 373 U.S. 427 (1963), concurring opinion. The case concerned a cabaret owner whose bribe of an Internal Revenue Agent was captured on that agent's "pocket wire recorder."

118. Sidney E. Zion, "Wiretap v. Privacy: Court's Recent Ruling on Birth Control Seen as Wedge against Eavesdropping," *New York Times*, June 15, 1965, p. 25.

119. A California court in 1970, for example, invoked *Griswold* to support the right of a psychiatrist to refuse to provide evidence about a patient, noting that "the

retention of a degree of intimacy in interpersonal relations and communications lies at the heart of the broad rationale of *Griswold*." Stein, *Sexual Injustice*, 237.

120. McKay, "The Right of Privacy: Emanations and Intimations," 278.

121. Zion, "Wiretap v. Privacy," 25. Others were certain the case would have an impact on wiretapping and electronic eavesdropping, and, perhaps, data gathering by computers. See Beaney, "The Right to Privacy and American Law," 196.

122. FBI agents "attached a [stereophonic] tape recorder on top of the roof of the middle telephone booth" he frequented on Sunset Boulevard. See David A. Sklansky, "*Katz v. United States*: The Limits of Aphorism," in *Criminal Procedure Stories*, ed. Carol S. Steiker (New York: Foundation Press, 2006), 223–260; quote on pp. 223–224.

123. As Sklansky observes, the attorneys for Katz made the point that the physical location of communication was a factor, but only one among several other factors, in assessing its intended confidentiality. "The point of the Fourth Amendment was to protect 'the right to privacy,' and that right 'follow[ed]' the individual.' . . . Equally if not more important was 'the activity engaged in by the enforcement officer'—the lengths to which the officer had to go in order to overhear the conversation." "*Katz v. United States*," 243.

124. As Lawrence Lessig writes of the case, "In the framers' context of 1791, protecting against trespass to property was an effective way to protect against trespass to privacy, but in the *Katz* context of the 1960s it was not. In the 1960s much of intimate life was conducted in places where property rules did not reach (in the 'ether,' for example, of the AT&T telephone network)," *Code: And Other Laws of Cyberspace, Version 2.0* (New York: Basic Books, 2006), 164. See also Orin S. Kerr, "The Fourth Amendment and New Technologies: Constitutional Myths and the Case for Caution," *Michigan Law Review* 102: 5 (2004): 801–888.

125. John Neary, "The Big Snoop: Electronic Snooping: Insidious Invasions of Privacy," *Life* (May 20, 1966): 38–43.

126. The bugged martini olive appeared in sources from *Life* magazine, to the *Los Angeles Times* (Arthur Miller, "The Computer Threat to Privacy," July 20, 1969, p. F7), to Senator Edward V. Long, *The Intruders: The Invasion of Privacy by Government and Industry* (New York: Praeger, 1967), photo after p. 54.

127. John Neary, "On an Assignment with the Ace of the Bugging Business," *Life* (May 20, 1966): 44–47.

128. Alan F. Westin, *Privacy and Freedom* (New York: Atheneum, 1967), ch. 8.

129. Westin, *Privacy and Freedom*, 69–80. Westin attributed the accelerating use of such devices to the booming private-detective trade since World War II, the marketing of voyeurism, and a culture enamored of "Superspy and scientific

wizardry," 90, 98, 101. Myron Brenton offered a similar laundry list in *The Privacy Invaders* (New York: Coward-McCann, 1964), 9.

130. See Sklansky, "*Katz v. United States*," 223–224.

131. His remarks came in lectures at the University of Kansas School of Law on September 26 and 27, 1974, which were then written up in William H. Rehnquist, "Is an Expanded Right of Privacy Consistent with Fair and Effective Law Enforcement? Or: Privacy, You've Come a Long Way, Baby," *University of Kansas Law Review* (1974): 1–23. See also "Rehnquist on Privacy," *Privacy Journal* 1: 1 (November 1974): 4; and Christopher Slobogin, "Rehnquist and Panvasive Searches," *Mississippi Law Journal* 82: 2 (2013): 310–311.

132. Naomi Murakawa argues that conservative versions of law and order but also racial liberal ones ("liberal law-and-order") solidified the criminalization of race and built the carceral state. This would defeat or limit many of the Warren Court reforms. *The First Civil Right: How Liberals Built Prison America* (New York: Oxford University Press, 2014), 2. See also Michelle Alexander, *The New Jim Crow: Mass Incarceration in the Age of Colorblindness* (New York: New Press, 2010); Elizabeth Hinton, *From the War on Poverty to the War on Crime: The Making of Mass Incarceration in America* (Cambridge, MA: Harvard University Press, 2016); and Heather Ann Thompson, *Blood in the Water: The Attica Prison Uprising of 1971 and its Legacy* (New York: Pantheon, 2016).

133. See Shils, "Privacy: Its Constitution and Vicissitudes," 291, 301; Arthur Selwyn Miller, "Privacy in the Corporate State: A Constitutional Value of Dwindling Significance," *Journal of Public Law* 22: 3 (1973): 3–35; and Barry Schwartz, "The Social Psychology of Privacy," *American Journal of Sociology* 70 (May 1968): 743.

134. Beaney, "The Right to Privacy and American Law," 261–262.

135. Rebecca Zietlow describes these rights as ones that "promote an inclusive vision of who belongs to the national community and facilitate equal member- ship." "The Judicial Restraint of the Warren Court (and Why It Matters)," *Ohio State Law Journal* 69: 2 (2007): 255–301; quote on p. 257.

136. In her study of challenges to vagrancy laws and the regulating of people "out of place," for example, legal historian Risa Goluboff argues that the Court's decisions in this era were "part of a process of dismantling the criminal law as a method of social control," effectively constitutionalizing a "new pluralism." *Vagrant Nation: Police Power, Constitutional Change, and the Making of the 1960s* (New York: Oxford University Press, 2016), 329–330.

137. This set of developments is often termed the "modern criminal procedure revolution," with key cases including: *Mapp v. Ohio* (1961), *Brady v. Maryland* (1963), *Gideon v. Wainwright* (1963), *Escobedo v. Illinois* (1964), *Miranda v. Arizona* (1966), and *United States v. Wade* (1967). See A. Kenneth Pye, "The

Warren Court and Criminal Procedure," *Michigan Law Review* 67 (1966): 249–268. See also John Hart Ely, *Democracy and Distrust: A Theory of Judicial Review* (Cambridge, MA: Harvard University Press, 1980). Legal historians have begun to reassess the "rights revolution" narrative, either by suggesting that the courts recognized some rights much earlier than we think or by arguing that the importance of the protections created by the Warren Court have been overstated.

138. On the sensibility and rhetoric of the New Left, see Doug C. Rossinow, *The Politics of Authenticity: Liberalism, Christianity, and the New Left in America* (New York: Columbia University Press, 1998).

139. Boston Women's Health Book Collective, *Our Bodies, Ourselves: A Book by and for Women* (Boston: Women's Health Collective, 1971). See Jennifer Nelson, *More than Medicine: A History of the Feminist Women's Health Movement* (New York: New York University Press, 2015). A similar impulse lay behind the health clinics established by the Black Panthers. Alondra Nelson, *Body and Soul: The Black Panthers and the Fight against Medical Discrimination* (Minneapolis: University of Minnesota Press, 2011). Edward Berkowitz documents the way minorities, women, and individuals with disabilities recalibrated their interactions with the medical establishment, writing that "in general, people felt more free to challenge doctors in the seventies than they had in the postwar era." *Something Happened: A Political and Cultural Overview of the Seventies* (New York: Columbia University Press, 2006), 8–9.

140. Lt. Colonel Arthur A. Murphy, "The Soldier's Right to a Private Life," *Military Law Review* (Dept. of the Army Pamphlet), 27–100–24 (April 1964): 97–99.

141. At issue were warrantless searches of GIs' surroundings and bodies for drug use in the U.S. Army European Command; the court upheld those searches. As far as reasonable expectations of privacy, the court ruled, "military inspections have been traditionally accepted and are expected by soldiers." *Committee for GI Rights v. Callaway*, No. 74–1285 (September 2, 1975).

142. Paul Ramsey, *The Patient as Person: Explorations in Medical Ethics* (New Haven, CT: Yale University Press, 1970), xiii. There was a precedent in earlier twentieth-century movements to restore the study of the "patient as a person," in reaction to the perceived depersonalization of scientific medicine. George Rosen, "Approaches to a Concept of Social Medicine: A Historical Survey," *Milbank Memorial Fund Quarterly* 26: 1 (1948): 7.

143. Dorothy W. Smith, "Patienthood and Its Threat to Privacy," *American Journal of Nursing* 69: 3 (March 1969): 508–513; quote on p. 509.

144. Smith, "Patienthood and Its Threat to Privacy," 509–510, 513.

145. Smith, "Patienthood and Its Threat to Privacy," 510–511.

146. American Hospital Association, "Patient Bill of Rights," adopted 1973.

147. Albert M. Bendich, "Privacy, Poverty, and the Constitution," *California Law Review* 54: 2 (May 1966): 407–442; quotes on pp. 414, 440–441; emphasis in original.

148. McKay, here quoting William Ball, "The Right of Privacy: Emanations and Intimations," 281. Emerson wrote that "the whole field of social welfare legislation and administration may be forced into procedures and practices more compatible with human dignity and integrity." "Nine Justices in Search of a Doctrine," 233.

149. At the very least, it paved the way for a good deal of scholarship on poverty and privacy. See John Gilliom, *Overseers of the Poor: Surveillance, Resistance, and the Limits of Privacy* (Chicago: University of Chicago Press, 2001); Christopher Slobogin, "The Poverty Exception to the Fourth Amendment," *University of Florida Law Review* 55 (2003): 391–412; and Bridges, *The Poverty of Privacy Rights.*

150. See Charles Reich, "The New Property," *Yale Law Journal* 73: 5 (1964): 733–787. The title reveals how indebted privacy still was to property rights, perhaps especially regarding the poor who do not have "personal rights."

151. Charles Reich, "Individual Rights and Social Welfare: The Emerging Legal Issues," *Yale Law Journal* 74 (1965): 1245, 1246.

152. Reich, "Individual Rights and Social Welfare," 1254, 1256. He argued that although *Griswold* was "a major forward step, the law has not yet developed a constitutional theory of privacy fully adequate to the present-day interdependent world." See William E. Forbath, "Constitutional Welfare Rights: A History, Critique and Reconstruction," *Fordham Law Review* 69: 5 (2001): 1821–1891.

153. Reich looked to *Frank v. Maryland* (1959), a case that concerned health inspectors investigating homes for unsanitary conditions without a warrant. The Court upheld the law (5–4) in part because it made "the least possible demand on the individual occupant" and caused "only the slightest restriction on his claims of privacy," 1350. Reich believed that it could not apply to welfare searches that frequently came with the very "midnight knock on the door" that the *Frank* ruling had condemned.

154. Reich, "Midnight Welfare Searches and the Social Security Act," 1355.

155. Reich, "Midnight Welfare Searches and the Social Security Act," 1359. Reich's concern was that growing dependence on government enabled state coercion, the price of government largesse coming in the form of restrictions on speech, association and privacy. See William H. Simon, "The Invention and Reinvention of Welfare Rights," *Maryland Law Review* 44: 1 (1985): 23–28.

156. See Williams, *The Politics of Public Housing*, 155–228; Premilla Nadasen, *Welfare Warriors: The Welfare Rights Movement in the United States* (New York: Routledge, 2005); Annelise Orleck, *Storming Caesars Palace: How Black*

Mothers Fought Their Own War on Poverty (Boston: Beacon Press, 2005); Felicia Kornbluh, *The Battle for Welfare Rights: Politics and Poverty in Modern America* (Philadelphia: University of Pennsylvania Press, 2007); and Karen M. Tani, *States of Dependency: Welfare, Rights, and American Governance, 1935–1972* (New York: Cambridge University Press, 2016), 113–150.

157. Williams, *The Politics of Public Housing*, 6.

158. Between 1964 and 1966, the rule had resulted in the removal of 15,000 black children from the rolls and the rejection of another 6,400; 97 percent of the children were black. Tani, *States of Dependency*, 261. See the discussion of the case in Kornbluh, *The Battle for Welfare Rights*, 67–68.

159. Walter Goodman, "The Case of Mrs. Sylvester Smith: A Victory for 400,000 Children," *New York Times Magazine* (August 25, 1968): 28.

160. In fact, Smith argued that she was being punished for her sexual behavior as well as her political views.

161. *King v. Smith*, 392 U.S. 309 (1968); Goodman, "The Case of Mrs. Sylvester Smith." Kornbluh explains that "the Court ruled based on the regulations themselves, and not on constitutional grounds." *The Battle for Welfare Rights*, 67–68.

162. Goodman, "The Case of Mrs. Sylvester Smith."

163. Kornbluh, for example, suggests that other welfare activists staked out claims to "sexual privacy" as well and that it would no longer be routine by the late 1960s for welfare departments to catalog clients' sexual behavior or make decisions based on it, at least formally. *The Battle for Welfare Rights*, 71–73.

164. Kornbluh, *The Battle for Welfare Rights*, 79.

165. Joel F. Handler and Margaret K. Rosenheim, "Privacy in Welfare: Public Assistance and Juvenile Justice," *Law and Contemporary Problems* 31: 2 (1966): 377–412; quotes on p. 377. While they examined the "suitable-home" policy and bedroom prying under AFDC, their focus was more on the information procured to administer these programs than on the raids themselves.

166. Handler and Rosenheim, "Privacy in Welfare," 378. Indeed, they believed that "tension between insistence on detailed punitive eligibility procedures and emphasis on elevation of public support programs to the position of 'rights' is inevitable." See Gilliom, *Overseers of the Poor*, on this point.

167. Handler and Rosenheim, "Privacy in Welfare," 379. They noted further that money payments, rather than food stamps or other badges of relief, were therefore "highly valued in any welfare scheme that strives to protect the privacy of the poor."

168. Handler and Rosenheim, "Privacy in Welfare," 391.

169. Handler and Rosenheim, "Privacy in Welfare," 404, 406, 410. For an instructive parallel from the early twentieth century, see Michael Willrich, *City of Courts: Socializing Justice in Progressive Era Chicago* (New York:

Cambridge University Press, 2003). Willrich writes that the result of the effort to "humanize" criminal justice for the poor "was often an intensified scrutiny and control of individual offenders and their families rather than the radical reconstruction of society that Progressive ideology at times seemed to demand," 320.

170. For an influential treatment of the tension between Fourth Amendment privacy and the state's need to gather information for regulatory purposes, see William J. Stuntz, "Privacy's Problem and the Law of Criminal Procedure," *Michigan Law Review* 93: 5 (1995): 1016–1078. He notes that "a privacy value robust enough to restrain the police should also prevent a great deal of government activity that we take for granted—activity that, at least since the New Deal, is unquestionably constitutional," 1017.

171. Warren W. Willingham, foreword to "Forum on Invasion of Privacy in Research and Testing," *Journal of Educational Measurement* 4: 1 (Spring 1967): 1; he expected continuing tension between "the desire to minimize personal distinctions (which protects privacy) and to equalize opportunity (which requires investigation of inequality" (1). Giving substance to civil rights, in other words, could entail novel ways of keeping track of them. See David A. Hollinger, *Post-Ethnic America: Beyond Multiculturalism* (New York: Basic Books, 1995; 2000), 19–50; and John D. Skrentny, *The Minority Rights Revolution* (Cambridge, MA: Belknap Press of Harvard University Press, 2002).

172. Legal scholar Robert McKay noted the irony that a contraceptive launched the right, since its "very existence was little recognized in the polite society whose privacy Brandeis and Warren sought to protect." "The Right of Privacy: Emanations and Intimations," 64.

173. Glendon, *Rights Talk*, 48. She sees this as not new, but as an old and deep aspect of American legal and popular culture.

174. My thanks to Mary Ziegler for these points.

5. Codes of Confidentiality and Consent

1. Edward Shils, "Social Inquiry and the Autonomy of the Individual," in *The Human Meaning of the Social Sciences*, ed. Daniel Lerner (New York: Meridian, 1959), 117. "In 1950 . . . the suggestion of having a fellow-psychologist pose as a patient in a group therapy situation, so that the therapy process might be studied with greater control, gave one an uneasy feeling." But in 1966, it was "almost *de rigueur*." Erasmus L. Hoch, "The Privacy Issue and a Professional Response at the Departmental Level," *Journal of Educational Measurement* 4: 1 (Spring 1967): 18.

2. Shils, "Social Inquiry and the Autonomy of the Individual," 117. Elsewhere Shils wrote, "What was once prurience and voyeurism has now become

'scientific curiosity.' What was once 'exhibitionism' is now cooperation in 'scientific research.' What was once regarded as the subject of 'blue films' and 'circuses' is now called a 'research situation.' The result is the same—an invasion of personal privacy of an extreme character, more elaborate and naturally better documented than its pre-'scientific' predecessors." "Privacy: Its Constitution and Vicissitudes," *Law and Contemporary Problems* 31: 2 (1966): 299.

3. John M. Shlien, "Mental Testing and Modern Society," in *Readings in Psychological Tests and Measurements*, ed. W. Leslie Barnette (Homewood, IL: Dorsey, 1964), 343.

4. In the same vein were Edward Gross, "Social Science Techniques: A Problem of Power and Responsibility," *Scientific Monthly* 83: 5 (1956): 242–247; and Margaret Mead, "The Human Study of Human Beings," *Science* 133 (January 20, 1961): 163.

5. See Julie A. Reuben, *The Making of the Modern University: Intellectual Transformation and the Marginalization of Morality* (Chicago: University of Chicago Press, 1996); Rebecca S. Lowen, *Creating the Cold War University: The Transformation of Stanford* (Berkeley: University of California Press, 1997); Margaret O'Mara, *Cities of Knowledge: Cold War Science and the Search for the Next Silicon Valley* (Princeton, NJ: Princeton University Press, 2005); Christopher P. Loss, *Between Citizens and the State: The Politics of American Higher Education in the Twentieth Century* (Princeton, NJ: Princeton University Press, 2012); Hamilton Cravens and Mark Solovey, eds., *Cold War Social Science: Knowledge Production, Liberal Democracy, and Human Nature* (New York: Palgrave Macmillan, 2012); and Mark Solovey, *Shaky Foundations: The Politics-Patronage-Social Science Nexus in Cold War America* (New Brunswick, NJ: Rutgers University Press, 2013).

6. See Brian Balogh on the emergence of the "prominstrative state" and the "courtship" between professionals and the federal government that began in the Progressive era and would be consummated by 1950. *Chain Reaction: Expert Debate and Public Participation in American Commercial Nuclear Power, 1945–1975* (New York: Cambridge University Press, 1991), 21–59.

7. Warren W. Willingham, foreword to "Forum on Invasion of Privacy in Research and Testing," *Journal of Educational Measurement* 4: 1 (Spring 1967): 2.

8. On Humphreys's activism, see his biography, as well as David Kraslow, "Movement to Counter Rightists Being Revived," *Los Angeles Times*, March 28, 1965, p. 14, in which Humphreys is named as the possible next executive director of an anti-rightist national organization. Humphreys later served a three-month jail sentence for draft board resistance. His activism (starting with his civil rights agitation) was tracked by the FBI, who used people close to him as informants. John H. Galliher, Wayne H. Brekhus, and

David P. Keys, *Laud Humphreys: Prophet of Sociology and Homosexuality* (Madison: University of Wisconsin Press, 2004), 71.

9. Glenn A. Goodwin, Irving Louis Horowitz, and Peter M. Nardi, "Laud Humphreys: A Pioneer in the Practice of Social Science," *Sociological Inquiry* 61: 2 (1991): 139–147. They note that this blend of theology and sociology was not unusual, especially at Washington University in the mid-1960s and was "especially fruitful at a time when moral concerns and empirical investigations cross-fertilized with such fierce potency," 140.

10. Goodwin et al., "Laud Humphreys," 140. Humphreys named his own influences as Becker, Goffman, Mead, Simmel, the Chicago School, John Dollard, the Lynds, William F. Whyte, Polsky, Malinowski, Firth, Oscar Lewis, Jules Henry, Elliot Liebow, Marx, C. Wright Mills, Paul Goodman, Edgar Friedenberg, Michael Harrington, Irving Horowitz, and Christian Bay. See Myron Glazer, "Impersonal Sex," Appendix to *Tearoom Trade: Impersonal Sex in Public Places*, enlarged ed. (New York: Aldine, 1975), 219.

11. See Greg Smith, "Introduction: Interpreting Goffman's Sociological Legacy," in *Goffman and Social Organization: Studies in a Sociological Legacy*, ed. Greg Smith (New York: Routledge, 1999), 1–18. See also Michael John Pettit, "The Con Man as Model Organism: The Methodological Roots of Erving Goffman's Dramaturgical Self," *History of Human Sciences* 24: 2 (2011): 138–154.

12. This was Alfred Lindesmith, who turned to studying drug addicts instead; Galliher et al., *Laud Humphreys*, 26. Only a handful of others had studied the "homosexual scene," notably Evelyn Hooker in "The Homosexual Community," in International Congress of Applied Psychology, *Personality Research* (Copenhagen: Munksgaard, 1962), with an introduction by Stanley Coopersmith, 40–59.

13. Laud Humphreys, *Tearoom Trade: Impersonal Sex in Public Places*, enlarged ed. (New York: Aldine, 1975), 218; Galliher et al., *Laud Humphreys*, 24. The department, after many run-ins with the administration, was "phased out" beginning in 1989 and shuttered in 1991; it was only reestablished in 2014.

14. Personal correspondence between Laud Humphreys and Myron Glazer, reprinted in Glazer, "Impersonal Sex," 219.

15. As Humphreys related it, his advisor's question was, "But where does the average guy go just to get a blow job? That's where you should do your research"; as for the derivation of "tearoom," Humphreys explained that it came from British slang, "tea," for urine. *Tearoom Trade*, 16, 2. On tearooms earlier in the century, see George Chauncey, *Gay New York: Gender, Urban Culture and the Making of the Gay Male World, 1890–1940* (New York: Pantheon, 1994), 179–206.

16. Lee Rainwater, foreword to *Tearoom Trade*, xi–xii. As he put it, "For a significant number, the tearooms seem to represent their only contact with a deviant sexual setting, and these individuals could not be considered social deviants in Goffman's sense," xiii.

17. David Sklansky, "One Train May Hide Another: *Katz*, Stonewall, and the Secret Subtext of Criminal Procedure," *U.C. Davis Law Review* 41: 3 (2008): 924. He adds, that, with publicity widely seen as a cure for vice, disclosure was the ruling fear of homosexuals in this era.

18. Humphreys, *Tearoom Trade: Impersonal Sex in Public Places* (Chicago: Aldine, 1970). See also his 1970 account of the research findings, reprinted in William L. Leap, ed., *Public Sex/Gay Space* (New York: Columbia University Press, 1999), 29–54. A useful commentary on the study appears in the same volume: Peter M. Nardi, "Reclaiming the Importance of Laud Humphreys's 'Tearoom Trade: Impersonal Sex in Public Places,'" 23–27.

19. Martin B. Duberman, *Stonewall* (New York: Dutton, 1993).

20. See Howard S. Becker, "Becoming a Marihuana User," *American Journal of Sociology* 59: 3 (1953): 235–242, and *Outsiders: Studies in the Sociology of Deviance* (London: Free Press of Glencoe, 1963); and William Foote Whyte, *Street Corner Society: The Social Structure of an Italian Slum* (Chicago: University of Chicago, 1943).

21. See Rainwater's summary, "The Lessons of Pruitt-Igoe," *National Affairs* 8 (Summer 1967): 116–126.

22. Galliher et al., *Laud Humphreys*, 18.

23. Galliher et al., *Laud Humphreys*, 28.

24. Laud Humphreys, "Tearoom Trade: Impersonal Sex in Public Places," *Transaction* 7: 5 (January 1970): 10–25.

25. For Humphreys's detailed account of his methods and research design see chapter 2 of *Tearoom Trade*: "Methods: The Sociologist as Voyeur," 16–44.

26. Humphreys, *Tearoom Trade*, 4.

27. There was some contemporary attention to these findings, especially among sociologists of deviance. But many of these findings would await the 1990s and the advent of queer studies to be appreciated and reframed as a key origin point of studying public gay sex. See, for example, Leap, *Public Sex/Gay Space*.

28. Humphreys did secure the cooperation of a dozen informants, whom he called the "intensive dozen."

29. Humphreys, *Tearoom Trade*, 30.

30. Humphreys, *Tearoom Trade*, 38. He later clarified that these were campus police; Laud Humphreys, "Social Science: Ethics of Research," *Science* 207 (February 15, 1980): 712.

31. Glazer, "Impersonal Sex," 217.

32. These were the working-class and middle-class men whom Humphreys cataloged as "trade" and "ambisexuals."

33. Humphreys, *Tearoom Trade*, 139.

34. Humphreys, *Tearoom Trade*, 135–136.

35. In this he followed in the footsteps of others like Alfred Kinsey, but in a more narrative and less statistical fashion.

36. Humphreys, *Tearoom Trade*, 11, 13–14.

37. This was the profile of the mid-century homophile movement as well, in which middle-class respectability and discretion were paramount. Marc Stein provides an account of the need for homophile organizations to keep a low profile, given the propensity of local officials to raid their offices, in *City of Sisterly and Brotherly Loves: Lesbian and Gay Philadelphia, 1945–1972* (Chicago: University of Chicago Press, 2000), ch. 8.

38. With public spaces risky, private spaces and churches became key sites for sociability and community formation for southern African Americans. Robin D. G. Kelley, "'We Are Not What We Seem': Rethinking Black Working-Class Opposition in the Jim Crow South," *Journal of American History* (1993): 75–112. In another parallel to Humphreys, Kelley notes the use of stool pigeons for surveillance in black communities, 102. Michel Foucault's 1967 lecture, "Other Spaces: Utopias and Heterotopias," spoke to new theories of the ways spaces for nonconformity were carved out from the dominant society; it appears in *Architecture/Mouvement/Continuité*, trans. Jay Miskowiec (October 1984): 1–9.

39. Sklansky, "One Train May Hide Another," 911–912.

40. On the Jenkins affair of 1964, see Lee Edelman, *Homographesis: Essays in Gay Literary and Cultural Theory* (London: Routledge, 1994), 148–151.

41. Sklansky, "One Train May Hide Another," 915.

42. John J. Gallo et al., "The Consenting Adult Homosexual and the Law: An Empirical Study of Enforcement in Los Angeles County," *UCLA Law Review* 13 (1966); see "Part III: Enforcement Techniques," 689.

43. Sklansky in "One Train May Hide Another" calls this "virtually the unanimous view of scholars at the time, and of the organized bar as well." He speculates that attention to protecting a particular sort of privacy in *Katz* was a mark of concern about the policing of homosexuality and a way of reining in the police and their tendencies to "proto-fascism." This relates, he argues, to modern criminal procedure's emphasis on "informational privacy," what William J. Stuntz calls "the individual's ability to keep some portion of his life secret, at least from the government," 918–919. See Stuntz, "Privacy's Problem and the Law of Criminal Procedure," *Michigan Law Review* 93 (1995): 1034.

44. Within a year of the investigation, postal surveillance collapsed; Leigh Ann Wheeler, *How Sex Became a Civil Liberty* (New York: Oxford University Press, 2013), 154–155.

45. Sklansky, "'One Train May Hide Another.'"

46. Edward Sagarin, Review of *Tearoom Trade, Journal of Sex Research* 6: 4 (November 1970): 337. "The real harm of public sex," a later writer summarized, "was putting these men at risk for blackmail, payoffs, and destroyed reputations at the hands of the police." Nardi, "Reclaiming the Importance of Laud Humphreys's 'Tearoom Trade,'" 25.

47. Humphreys, *Tearoom Trade*, 32.

48. Fred Cohen, Review of *Tearoom Trade, Criminal Law Bulletin* 7 (1971): 67–69; quote on p. 69. On the ways gay men created privacy in public earlier in the century, see Chauncey, *Gay New York*, 179–206.

49. Although the issue did not come up at the time, in retrospect, some have suggested that Humphreys blurred the line between researcher and subject. His biographers speculate that his findings could only have come from his active participation in the tearoom action, his involvement "more than he was able to report" given "institutional and disciplinary" but also legal norms. As they put it, "Laud may have been even closer to his data than anyone could have imagined. His behavior was his data." Galliher et al., *Laud Humphreys*, 29–30.

50. Humphreys later mused over why the legal issues didn't loom larger: "By observing, perhaps facilitating, and failing to report some 200 acts of fellatio, was I not guilty as an accomplice to the acts? Stated in that form, the answer may appear obvious. Strangely enough, I don't think the question even occurred to me until late in my research." *Tearoom Trade*, 228.

51. Certainly, Humphreys's subject of inquiry—furtive, gay sex—cannot be separated from his methods. His biographers suggest that "the controversy his research methods generated probably had as much to do with what he studied as with how he studied it." Galliher et al., *Laud Humphreys*, 7. While it seems obvious that the study attracted more scrutiny because of its controversial subject matter, none of the published reviews of the book shied away from the contents. The one reviewer who admitted his aesthetic distaste for what he called "a very dreary and dingy sexual outlet," also wrote that he had "little sympathy for those who would object to the subject of Humphreys's work because it is felt to be sordid." David E. Lavin, Review of *Tearoom Trade, Annals of the American Academy of Political and Social Science* 398: (November 1971): 200.

52. Donald P. Warwick, "Tearoom Trade: Means and Ends in Social Research," *Hastings Center Studies*, Institute of Society, Ethics and the Life Sciences 1: 1 (1973): 27–38.

53. These criticisms are similar to those of Stanley Milgram for potentially causing his subjects great distress. See Gina Perry, *Behind the Shock Machine: The Untold Story of the Notorious Milgram Psychology Experiments*, rev. ed. (New York: Free Press, 2013).

54. The Commission was created by the 1974 National Research Act; Dennis M. Maloney, *Protection of Human Research Subjects: A Practical Guide to Federal Laws and Regulations* (New York: Plenum Press, 1984).

55. "Informed consent" was recognized in the law as early as 1957. Michael Schudson, *The Rise of the Right to Know: Politics and the Culture of Transparency, 1945–1975* (Cambridge, MA: Belknap Press of Harvard University Press, 2015), 12. Minors as well as adults were covered by the new regulations, which granted subjects "the ability to assent to research from the age of seven up." Tamar W. Carroll and Myron P. Gutmann, "The Limits of Autonomy: The Belmont Report and the History of Childhood," *Journal of the History of Medicine and Allied Sciences* 66: 1 (January 2011): 82–115. See also Heather Prescott, "Using Student Bodies: College and University Students as Research Subjects," *Journal of the History of Medicine and Allied Science* 57 (2002): 3–38. Such changes did not necessarily mean that researchers adopted a more autonomous or dignified vision of their subjects. Laura Stark has argued compellingly that human rights took a distinct second place to legal self-protection in the new research regime and that IRB regulations were put in place precisely to enable rather than constrain human investigation. *Behind Closed Doors: IRBs and the Making of Ethical Research* (Chicago: University of Chicago Press, 2012).

56. See Susan Lederer, *Subjected to Science: Human Experimentation in America before the Second World War* (Baltimore: Johns Hopkins University Press, 1997); Andrew Goliszek, *In the Name of Science: A History of Secret Programs, Medical Research, and Human Experimentation* (New York: St. Martin's Press, 2003); and Paul Julian Weindling, *Nazi Medicine and the Nuremberg Trials: From Medical War Crimes to Informed Consent* (New York: Palgrave Macmillan, 2004). Stark writes that its principles were deemed "appropriate for moral monsters, not for democratically minded American physicians." *Behind Closed Doors*, 104. Jill Morawski too claims that Nuremberg "heightened attention" but "produced no consensual lesson." "Epistemological Dizziness in the Psychology Laboratory: Lively Subjects, Anxious Experimenters, and Experimental Relations, 1950–1970," *Isis* 106: 3 (September 2015): 583.

57. Stark, *Behind Closed Doors*, 125.

58. Henry K. Beecher, "Ethics and Clinical Research," *New England Journal of Medicine* 274 (June 16, 1966): 1354–1360. On Beecher's 1966 exposé and its impact, see David J. Rothman, *Strangers at the Bedside: A History of How Law and Bioethics Transformed Medical Decision Making* (New York: Basic Books,

1991), 15–29; and Lederer, *Subjected to Science*. Stark argues that Beecher's revelations did not effect the change. Rather, "American moral and medical sensibilities in the late 1960s lifted the article to prominence." *Behind Closed Doors*, 160.

59. Stark, *Behind Closed Doors*, 77–78; Zachary Schrag, *Ethical Imperialism: Institutional Review Boards and the Social Sciences, 1965–2009* (Baltimore: Johns Hopkins University Press, 2010), and "How Talking Became Human Subjects Research: The Federal Regulation of the Social Sciences, 1965–1991," *Journal of Policy History* 21 (2009): 3–37. It was in a memo of 1966 that the Surgeon General clarified that the new requirement covered social and behavioral scientists as well as medical researchers. Writes Laura Stark: "Tellingly, the U.S. Surgeon General wrote to university administrators in 1966 regarding the new ethics committees that 'the wisdom and sound professional judgment of you and your staff will determine what constitutes the rights and welfare of human subjects in research, what constitutes informed consent, and what constitutes the risks and potential medical benefits of a particular investigation.'" "Victims in Our Own Minds? IRBs in Myth and Practice," *Law and Society Review* 41: 4 (2007): 781. See also Hunter Crowther-Heyck, "Patrons of the Revolution: Ideals and Institutions in Postwar Behavioral Sciences," *Isis* 97 (2006): 420–446; and Ruth R. Faden and Tom L. Beauchamp in collaboration with Nancy M. P. King, *A History and Theory of Informed Consent* (New York: Oxford University Press, 1986).

60. Allan M. Brandt, "Racism and Research: The Case of the Tuskegee Syphillis Study," *The Hastings Center Report* 8: 6 (December 1978): 21–29; James H. Jones, *Bad Blood: The Tuskegee Syphilis Experiment* (New York: Free Press, 1992). A Commission on the Protection of Human Subjects in Biomedical and Behavioral Research was also established. The Belmont Report of 1978 would define ethical guidelines for medical research.

61. American Psychological Association, *Ethical Standards of Psychologists* (Washington, DC: APA, 1953), 113–124, and *Ethical Standards for the Distribution of Psychological Tests and Diagnostic Aids* (Washington DC: APA, 1954). See Irwin A. Berg, "The Use of Human Subjects in Psychological Research, *American Psychologist* 9 (1954): 108–111; and C. R. Rogers, "Persons or Science? A Philosophical Question," *American Psychologist* 10 (1955): 267–278. See also American Psychological Association, "Ethical Standards of Psychologists," *American Psychologist* 18 (1963): 56–60.

62. Comment, "Legal Implications of Psychological Research with Human Subjects," *Duke Law Journal* 2 (Spring 1960): 265–274; quote on pp. 267–268.

63. "Infrequently used before the war, deceiving subjects about the 'real' nature of the experiment or experimental stimuli became increasingly common after 1948." Morawski, "Epistemological Dizziness in the Psychology Laboratory," 580.

Similar questions were raised among anthropologists, although not usually framed as privacy questions, perhaps because their subjects were typically non-U.S. populations. On the history of deception in American psychology, see Michael John Pettit, *The Science of Deception: Psychology and Commerce in America* (Chicago: University of Chicago Press, 2013).

64. Stanley Milgram, "Behavioral Study of Obedience," *Journal of Abnormal Psychology* 67 (1963): 371–378. Useful interpretations of the experiments can be found in Perry, *Behind the Shock Machine*, and Ian Nicholson, "'Torture at Yale': Experimental Subjects, Laboratory Torment, and the 'Rehabilitation' of Milgram's 'Obedience to Authority,'" *Theory and Psychology* 21 (2011): 737–761.

65. See especially Diana Baumrind, "Some Thoughts on Ethics of Research: After Reading Milgram's 'Behavioral Study of Obedience,'" *American Psychologist* 19 (1964): 421–423. Milgram's reply was "Issues in the Study of Obedience: A Reply to Baumrind," *American Psychologist* 19 (1964): 848–852.

66. Stanley Milgram, *Obedience to Authority: An Experimental View* (New York: HarperCollins, 1997; 1974), 219, 212–215. Milgram noted that "for some critics . . . the chief horror of the experiment was not that the subjects obeyed but that the experiment was carried out at all," 211. Perry's recent history, *Behind the Shock Machine*, challenges Milgram's characterizations of the effect of the experiment on participants.

67. Some of the skepticism came from recognition of the self-serving claims of scientific authorities—for example, chemists on the safety of DDT pre-*Silent Spring*. For a retrospective account of Milgram's work and influence, see Thomas Blass, ed., *Obedience to Authority: Current Perspectives on the Milgram Paradigm* (Mahwah, NJ: Lawrence Erlbaum, 2000).

68. For Zimbardo's own account see Philip G. Zimbardo, *The Lucifer Effect: Understanding How Good People Turn Evil* (New York: Random House, 2007).

69. Constance Holden, "Ethics in Social Science Research," *Science* 206 (November 2, 1979): 538. Herbert C. Kelman also charged that the experiment involved "entrapment and degradation" and that "unsought self-knowledge" was not morally defensible. He raised the possibility of a subjects' bill of rights and subject unionizing in "The Rights of the Subject in Social Research: An Analysis in Terms of Relative Power and Legitimacy," *American Psychologist* 27 (1972): 989–1016.

70. For accounts of Project Camelot, see Mark Solovey, "Project Camelot and the 1960s Epistemological Revolution: Rethinking the Politics-Patronage-Social Science Nexus," *Social Studies of Science* 31: 2 (2001): 171–206; and Joy Rohde, *Armed with Expertise: The Militarization of American Social Research during the Cold War* (Ithaca, NY: Cornell University Press, 2013): 63–89.

71. Boas was prompted to write by the fact that several anthropologists had been implicated in state-sponsored espionage in Central America during World War I.

He argued that any scholar "who uses science as a cover for political spying, who demeans himself to pose before a foreign government as an investigator and asks for assistance in his alleged researches in order to carry on, under this cloak, his political machinations, prostitutes science in an unpardonable way and forfeits the right to be classed as a scientist." Boas, "Scientists as Spies," *The Nation*, December 20, 1919. Boas would be censured by the American Anthropological Association for this statement. For the entanglement of anthropology and the state in the postwar era, see David H. Price, *Cold War Anthropology: The CIA, the Pentagon, and the Growth of Dual Use Anthropology* (Durham, NC: Duke University Press, 2016).

72. Alexandra Rutherford, "The Social Control of Behavior Control: Behavior Modification, Individual Rights, and Research Ethics in America, 1971–1979," *Journal of the History of the Behavioral Sciences* 42 (2006): 203–220. See the entire issue of *American Sociologist* 13: 4 (1978) on the protection of human subjects.

73. Nancy D. Campbell and Laura Stark argue that this process was at work in the self-description of biomedical research subjects in the 1970s. "Making up 'Vulnerable' People: Human Subjects and the Subjective Experience of Medical Experiment," *Social History of Medicine* 28: 4 (2015): 825–848.

74. Orville G. Brim Jr., "Reaction to the Papers," *Journal of Educational Measurement* 4: 1 (Spring 1967): 29.

75. Brim, "Reaction to the Papers," 30.

76. Bernard Berelson, introduction to "Forum on Invasion of Privacy in Research and Testing," *Journal on Educational Measurement* 4: 1 (Spring 1967): 5. The issue summarized a 1966 symposium devoted to the issue.

77. Oscar Ruebhausen and Orville Brim, "Privacy and Behavioral Research," *Columbia Law Review* 65 (November 1965): 1184–1211; quotes on pp. 1184–1185, 1190. Ruebhausen was chairman of the Special Committee on Science and Law of the Association of the Bar of the City of New York.

78. Ruebhausen and Brim, "Privacy and Behavioral Research," 1201.

79. Ruebhausen and Brim, "Privacy and Behavioral Research," 1208, 1192, 1194, 1201.

80. Oscar Ruebhausen and Orville Brim, "Privacy and Behavioral Research: Preliminary Summary of the Report of the Panel on Privacy and Behavioral Research," *Science* 155 (February, 3, 1967): 535–538; quotes on pp. 535, 536.

81. Ruebhausen and Brim, "Privacy and Behavioral Research," 1208.

82. Ruebhausen and Brim, "Privacy and Behavioral Research: Preliminary Summary," 537.

83. See Laura Stark, "The Science of Ethics: Deception, the Resilient Self, and the APA Code of Ethics, 1966–1973," *Journal of the History of the Behavioral Sciences* 46: 4 (2010): 337–370.

84. Ruebhausen and Brim, "Privacy and Behavioral Research," 1200.

85. Comment, "Legal Implications of Psychological Research with Human Subjects," 270.
86. See Samuel Messick, "Personality Measurement and the Ethics of Assessment," *American Psychologist* 20: 136 (1965): 140. Surely for some subset of subjects, however, the desire to advance scientific knowledge was a factor in their participation, and a kind of benefit.
87. Ruebhausen and Brim, "Privacy and Behavioral Research," 1198 and n. 49 on that page.
88. Morawski, "Epistemological Dizziness in the Psychology Laboratory"; Pettit, *The Science of Deception*; Stark, *Behind Closed Doors.*
89. Ruebhausen and Brim, "Privacy and Behavioral Research: Preliminary Summary," 537. The panel instead recommended establishing a "partnership" between the "scientist and his subject": if full consent could not be obtained, the scientist had to ensure a trusting fiduciary relationship and also arrange a possible exit from the research for the subject.
90. Hoch, "The Privacy Issue and a Professional Response," 19–20.
91. Eugene J. Webb, Donald T. Campbell, Richard D. Schwartz, and Lee Sechrest, *Unobtrusive Measures: Nonreactive Research in the Social Sciences* (Chicago: Rand McNally, 1966), vii.
92. See Morawski, "Epistemological Dizziness in the Psychology Laboratory."
93. This was research conducted by Edward H. Peeples Jr. and reported in *Community Nutrition Institute Weekly Report* 5: 45 (November 13, 1975): 4. See "Dormant Data," *Privacy Journal* 2: 3 (January 1976): 5–6. Peebles estimated that pet food was a significant part of the diet in 225,000 American households, and the issue had recently attracted the attention of the Senate Nutrition Committee. See the report in the Port Huron, Michigan, *Times Herald*, December 23, 1975, p. 20.
94. William A. Creech, "Psychological Testing and Constitutional Rights," *Duke Law Journal* 1966 (1966): 369. See also G. Cooper, "Legal Implications of the Use of Standardized Ability Tests in Employment and Education," *Columbia Law Review* 68 (1968): 690–744.
95. George K. Bennett, "Testing and Privacy," *Journal of Educational Measurement* 4: 1 (Spring 1967): 9.
96. Willingham, foreword to "Forum on Invasion of Privacy in Research and Testing," 1.
97. Herbert S. Conrad, "Clearance of Questionnaires with Respect to 'Invasion of Privacy,' Public Sensitivies, Ethical Standards, etc.: Principles and Viewpoint in the Bureau of Research, U.S. Office of Education," *Journal of Educational Measurement* 4: 1 (Spring 1967): 25.
98. Conrad, "Clearance of Questionnaires with Respect to 'Invasion of Privacy,'" 27.

99. Robert O. Carlson, "The Issue of Privacy in Public Opinion Research," *Public Opinion Quarterly* 3: 1 (1967): 1–8.

100. Carlson, "The Issue of Privacy in Public Opinion Research."

101. Carlson, "The Issue of Privacy in Public Opinion Research."

102. Charles S. Mayer and Charles H. White Jr., "The Law of Privacy and Marketing Research," *Journal of Marketing* 33: 2 (April 1969): 1–4.

103. Mayer and White, "The Law of Privacy and Marketing Research," 3.

104. Leo Bogart, "The Researcher's Dilemma" (1962), in *Current Controversies in Marketing Research*, ed. Leo Bogart (Chicago: Markham, 1969), 9.

105. Mayer and White, "The Law of Privacy and Marketing Research," 3. At the same time, the writers pointedly observed that existing privacy rights were not identical to the rights citizens imagined that they were entitled to.

106. "Census Programs Attacked as Invasion of Privacy," *American Statistician* 22 (April 1968): 12–13.

107. Roderick D. Buchanan argues, for example that the congressional personality test hearings were managed in the end by experts. "On Not Giving Psychology Away: The Minnesota Multiphasic Personality Inventory and Public Controversy over Testing in the 1960s," *History of Psychology* 5: 3 (2002): 284–309.

108. Goodwin et al., "Laud Humphreys," 142; Alvin Gouldner, "The Sociologist as Partisan: Sociology and the Welfare State," *American Sociologist* 3: 2 (May 1968): 103–116.

109. Galliher et al., *Laud Humphreys*, 21.

110. Galliher et al., *Laud Humphreys*, 20. Institutional Review Boards were modeled on the Clinical Research Committee of the National Institutes of Health, established in 1953. On the history of this model of research clearance (based on "review procedures rather than ethics principles"), see Stark, *Behind Closed Doors*.

111. Galliher et al., *Laud Humphreys*, 19–20. These were actually physical blows, although there are conflicting accounts of what actually happened. "Sociology Professor Accused of Beating Student," *New York Times*, June 10, 1968, p. 25; Goodwin et al., "Laud Humphreys," 142–143. The *Times* reported that the dispute concerned Gouldner's personal attacks on sociologists (including his colleague Lee Rainwater) who studied deviant behavior, "suggesting that these researchers were more interested in their own professional advancement than in the plight of the drug addicts and other deviants they studied, and that some of their methods were dishonest and immoral." According to Gouldner, the dispute stemmed from Humphreys's anger about the article. Gouldner, "The Sociologist as Partisan."

112. This account comes primarily from Galliher et al., *Laud Humphreys*, 21, 27.

113. At some point, Humphreys had been offered a teaching position in the department. Following this series of events, there was a public protest,

published in the *St. Louis Post Dispatch*, by seven sociologists against the administration for replacing the department chair, delaying Rainwater's grant, and questioning the legitimacy of Humphreys's dissertation. Galliher et al., *Laud Humphreys*, 21–22, 27.

114. Two *Transaction* articles followed, including a cover-page feature in 1970.

115. Humphreys, "Social Science: Ethics of Research," 714. In a letter to Myron Glazer in 1971, however, Humphreys did say that even despite the fact that there was "plenty of precedent for my research strategies," he worried about publishing the research and that he and his advisors "agonized over every move, every step of the research." See Glazer, "Impersonal Sex," 219.

116. Likewise, in a 1970 defense of Humphreys, Rainwater and Irving Horowitz would underscore their support, as editors of a sociological journal, of "the right to privacy of the researcher over and against the wishes of established authority." Irving Louis Horowitz and Lee Rainwater, "On Journalistic Moralizers," *Transaction* 7: 7 (May 1970): 4–10, reprinted in Appendix to *Tearoom Trade: Impersonal Sex in Public Places*, enlarged ed. (New York: Aldine, 1975), 189.

117. Lee Rainwater and David J. Pittman, "Ethical Problems in Studying a Politically Sensitive and Deviant Community," *Social Problems* 14 (1966–1967): 357–366; quote on p. 361. They went on to write, "Being aware of the possibility of having our records subpoenaed . . . we can take precautions. We can arrange to obliterate identifying information on records. We can obtain a clear legal definition of who can and who cannot subpoena us and exactly what kind of control they can exercise over our records. Also, it seems to us, we must face up to the necessity if all else fails of having to engage in one or·another kind of 'hanky panky' to preserve the informant's anonymity where the courts will not sustain that right," 364. Worries over the confidentiality of research sources from subpoena were a live topic for social scientists in this era. See James D. Carroll and Charles R. Knerr, "The APSA Confidentiality in Social Scientific Research Project: A Final Report," *PS* 9: 4 (Autumn 1976): 416–419. They argued that increasing public sensitivities about misuse of personal information, the greater volume of "relevant" and interventionist research, the "increased dependence of public decision makers upon social and behavioral research," and the increase in "naturalistic" and "interactive" research, had combined to make confidentiality and other legal and ethical problems more present in social research in recent years, 418.

118. Rainwater and Pittman, "Ethical Problems in Studying a Politically Sensitive and Deviant Community," 361.

119. Lee Rainwater, *And the Poor Get Children: Sex, Contraception, and Family Planning in the Working Class* (Chicago: Quadrangle Books, 1960). One of the conclusions was that the new oral contraceptives would be a difficult method

for working-class women to use conscientiously, and one that they also might distrust. To overcome this challenge, the study recommended mobile units, caseworkers, and discussion groups at women's homes, 172–173. (This perhaps suggested that contraception was not seen as a particularly "private" matter in the years prior to *Griswold*). Because Rainwater's study was then used to support the idea that working-class women didn't want help limiting their families, Rainwater and Pittman used it as an object lesson in researchers needing to guard against misuse and misinterpretation of their results. "Ethical Problems in Studying a Politically Sensitive and Deviant Community," 362.

120. Moynihan lifted his most controversial phrase, "tangle of pathology," from psychologist Kenneth Clark's "Youth in the Ghetto" report. In historian Daniel Geary's framing, Moynihan, Rainwater, and Clark all represented a "prevalent social-scientific school known as 'pathologism' that stressed how racism damaged African American social life," using a medical term to describe social ills affecting the community. But Clark would by 1970 become one of Moynihan's detractors. Geary, *Beyond Civil Rights: The Moynihan Report and Its Legacy* (Philadelphia: University of Pennsylvania Press, 2015), 61–62, 114. For Clark's critique of Moynihan, see p. 203.

121. Rainwater was "Moynihan's staunchest supporter," writing with a graduate student, William Yancey, a book in 1967 on the affair. Rainwater and Yancey, *The Moynihan Report and the Politics of Controversy* (Cambridge, MA: MIT Press, 1967). The book defended "social scientists' autonomy to portray African American social life" and thereby "upheld the intellectual authority of a white-dominated profession." See Geary, *Beyond Civil Rights*, 116–118. Rainwater would be sharply criticized for his stance, with charges by black power intellectuals such as Julius Lester that Moynihan and his colleagues believed that they were "greater authorities on blacks than blacks themselves," 121. Other correctives were offered by sociologist Carol Stack and the historians Herbert Gutman and Eugene Genovese.

122. This was Rainwater's *Behind Ghetto Walls* (1970), which analyzed the "pathologies" of public housing and portrayed the lives of his subjects quite harshly. See Geary, *Beyond Civil Rights*, 116–118. There are some striking resonances to the recent controversy over Alice Goffman's ethnography, *On the Run: Fugitive Life in an American City* (Chicago: University of Chicago Press, 2014). On the politics of white scholars writing on African Americans in this era, see Gary T. Marx, "Reflections on Academic Success and Failure: Making It, Forsaking It, Reshaping It," in *Authors of Their Own Lives: Intellectual Autobiographies by Twenty American Sociologists*, ed. Bennett M. Berger (Berkeley: University of California Press, 1990), 260–284.

123. Geary, *Beyond Civil Rights*, 115.

124. Rainwater and Pittman, "Ethical Problems in Studying a Politically Sensitive and Deviant Community," 363; emphasis in original.

125. Rainwater and Pittman, "Ethical Problems in Studying a Politically Sensitive and Deviant Community," 365; emphasis in original. Here they were referring to confidentiality vis-à-vis politically powerful informants and the "publicly accountable," it should be noted.

126. Humphreys, "Tearoom Trade."

127. This information comes from personal correspondence between Humphreys and Myron Glazer. See Glazer, "Impersonal Sex," 215. Humphreys allowed that "memories of that time of panic have helped me understand, though not approve, the procedures of some White House conspirators in the Watergate cover-up." *Tearoom Trade*, 229.

128. Strikingly, given Humphreys's own experience being tracked by the FBI for his civil rights work, it did not seem to occur to him to worry that he might lead law enforcement right to the door of tearoom users. See Galliher et al., *Laud Humphreys*, 71.

129. Humphreys, *Tearoom Trade*, 170–171.

130. See especially his postscript in the reissued 1975 edition of *Tearoom Trade*, offering "a Retrospect on Ethical Issues," and the commentaries that follow; Humphreys, "Postscript: A Question of Ethics," 167–173. Fifty-seven pages of the reissued book were devoted to the ethics controversy. See also Donald O. Granberg and John F. Galliher, *A Most Human Enterprise: Controversies in the Social Sciences* (Lanham, MD: Lexington Books, 2010).

131. Kenneth Plummer, Review of *Tearoom Trade*, *British Journal of Criminology* 12: 2 (April 1972): 190.

132. Warwick, "Tearoom Trade: Means and Ends in Social Research." Warwick's long list of the sociologist's deceptions included passing as gay (although of course, in some sense, Humphreys wasn't); disguising his identity by posing as a watchqueen; making an oral record of his observations by hiding a tape recorder in his car; deceiving police about the nature of his study to gain access to automobile license registers; changing his appearance so he could conduct interviews; and misrepresenting the social health survey and "random sample," which may have thereby distorted the social health survey results, 199.

133. Glazer, "Impersonal Sex," 217.

134. Glazer, "Impersonal Sex," 220–221.

135. E. B. Eiselein, Review of *Tearoom Trade*, *American Anthropologist* 73: 4 (August 1971): 861. As it turned out, Humphreys was not exactly taking on the "guise of the gay guy," but was keeping his sexual identity hidden from his colleagues.

136. Lawrence Rosen, Review of *Tearoom Trade*, *Journal of Marriage and Family* 34: 2 (May 1972): 382.

137. Glazer, "Impersonal Sex," 217. Stanley Milgram was similarly criticized for not providing adequate debriefing and follow-up in his obedience study; see Gina Perry, *Behind the Shock Machine.*

138. Warwick, "Tearoom Trade," 204–205. "This concern should be especially great when a researcher imposes himself on others for his own ends, without their knowledge. The men in the tearoom did not, after all, *ask* to be studied or helped," 205; emphasis in original.

139. Warwick, "Tearoom Trade," 202–203.

140. Warwick, "Tearoom Trade," 204.

141. Barry Krisberg, Review of *Tearoom Trade, Issues in Criminology* 7: 1 (Winter 1972): 126. Krisberg considered Humphreys a practitioner of "hip sociology," along with Becker and Goffman. Similar charges of "pornography" and "ghetto tourism" were used to criticize Lee Rainwater's work, as well as Kenneth Clark's.

142. Edward Sagarin, who also wrote under the name Donald Webster Cory, was the author of the influential 1951 book, *The Homosexual in America: A Subjective Approach.* He was famously "outed" by Laud Humphreys at the 1974 meeting of the American Sociological Association. Sagarin, Review of *Tearoom Trade,* 337–338.

143. Sagarin, Review of *Tearoom Trade,* 338.

144. Warwick, "Tearoom Trade," 207.

145. Warwick, "Tearoom Trade," 207.

146. Glazer, "Impersonal Sex," 222.

147. Glazer, "Impersonal Sex," 222.

148. This was via excerpts published in the sociological monthly, *Transaction.* See *Transaction* 7: 5 (January 1970): 10–25. Rainwater and Irving Horowitz, both Humphreys's advisors, were editors of the journal and would defend his work in it pages later that year.

149. Nicholas von Hoffman, "Sociological Snoopers," *Washington Post,* January 30, 1970, pp. B1, B9.

150. See, for example, Herbert C. Kelman, *A Time to Speak: On Human Values and Social Research* (San Francisco: Jossey-Bass, 1968); and Myron Glazer, *The Research Adventure: Promise and Problems of Field Work* (New York: Random House, 1972).

151. Kai T. Erikson, "A Comment on Disguised Observation in Sociology," *Social Problems* 14: 4 (Spring 1967): 366–373; quotes on pp. 367–369, 373. Erikson lambasted the presumption of the sympathetic researcher who thinks he knows how his actions will affect others, "particularly when, as is ordinarily the case, he has elected to wear a disguise exactly because he is entering a social sphere so far from his own experience." Erikson's article directly followed Rainwater and Pittman's essay on "Ethical Problems" in that issue of *Social Problems.*

Interestingly, Humphreys wrote in 1975, "It may provide some insight into my lack of doubt about the ethics of my observations to know that I spend an hour discussing my research with Erikson at about the same time his paper on ethics was published. Neither of us recall that he raised any ethical objections at that point; we were both more interested in the nature and quality of the data being gathered." *Tearoom Trade*, 227.

152. Humphreys linked the new worries over these issues to Watergate plumbers and domestic surveillance, and he hoped his material on ethics would help social scientists "clarify their research posture in a post-Watergate society." *Tearoom Trade*, 175.

153. Robert T. Bower and Priscilla de Gasparis, *Ethics in Social Research: Protecting the Interests of Human Subjects* (New York: Praeger, 1978). See also the *American Sociologist* symposium on the topic in 1978.

154. Bower and de Gasparis, *Ethics in Social Research*, 4.

155. Bower and de Gasparis, *Ethics in Social Research*, 12–35; quote on p. 26. Joan Cassell made the additional distinction that while subjects of behavioral experiments may be at risk during data collection, the risk to subjects of observational study is often deferred until data and analysis are made available. Joan Cassell, "Risk and Benefits to Subjects of Field Work," *American Sociologist* 13 (August 1978): 134–143.

156. Zachary Schrag observes that presumed dangers to social scientific research subjects—as opposed to medical ones—centered especially on the "unwarranted invasion of privacy." *Ethical Imperialism*, 8. Bower and de Gasparis commented here on the ethics of unobtrusive measures, which were in part espoused for their avoidance of risks of coercion, embarrassment, or imposition. "Most strenuous objections" to such studies, they noted, "come under the heading of invasion of privacy, with privacy defined as the individual's right to decide what of himself he will expose, to whom, and in what circumstances." Both the problem and the benefit of this kind of research were that the subject was unaware of being observed. *Ethics in Social Research*, 35.

157. Bower and de Gasparis, *Ethics in Social Research*, 14. Privacy concerns would of course soon come to the biomedical domain in fears of genetic databases and the like. Other writers would also distinguish social research in terms of the difficulty in securing true consent. By the 1980s some social researchers even reversed the presumption that their inquiries were less risky or at least more amenable to consent than the biomedical ones: "Since what may happen in social interaction is never fully predictable and often quite unanticipated, there is a very real sense in which truly informed consent is more illusory in social research than in biomedical research with the latter's sometimes even life-threatening dangers." This writer also noted that "social science folk literature is rich with tales of inadvertently blown covers and identification of

disguised and supposedly anonymous individuals, institutions, and communities." Allen D. Grimshaw, "Whose Privacy? What Harm?" *Sociological Methods and Research* 11: 2 (November 1982): 244, 242.

158. Bower and de Gasparis, *Ethics in Social Research*, 19.
159. Bower and de Gasparis, *Ethics in Social Research*, 35. They noted the usefulness of such studies for probing deviant behavior. But they remarked that "the brave researcher that undertakes them nowadays can expect the vocal opposition of many of his peers on the ground of deception and invasion of privacy." This was true even if his use of unobtrusive techniques "may get the applause of others . . . because of their very unobtrusiveness."
160. Bower and de Gasparis, *Ethics in Social Research*, 22, 46.
161. Horowitz and Rainwater, "On Journalistic Moralizers," 185. Horowitz would continue to defend Humphreys through the 1970s, protesting in a letter to *Science* a "moral hard-liner" approach to deception in social research and praising that "courageous band of scholars who continue to believe that research priorities and protection through discussion have their own moral imperatives." Irving Louis Horowitz, "Social Science Research Ethics," *Science* 206 (November 30, 1979): 1022.
162. Horowitz and Rainwater, "On Journalistic Moralizers," 181, 188–189. They pointed to "a key contradiction in the contemporary position of the liberal: he wants to protect the rights of private citizens, but at the same time he wants to develop a welfare system that could hardly function without at least some knowledge about these citizens," 189. See also Irving Louis Horowitz, *The Decomposition of Sociology* (New York: Oxford University Press, 1993).
163. Humphreys, *Tearoom Trade*, 188.
164. Humphreys, *Tearoom Trade*, 17. See Gallo et al., "The Consenting Adult Homosexual and the Law," 804. They cite a Mansfield, Ohio, study, in which sixty-five men were caught in two weeks of police surveillance.
165. Humphreys, "Tearoom Trade"; emphasis in original.
166. Humphreys, *Tearoom Trade*, 231. For social scientists' worry about lost knowledge due to research regulations, see Schrag, *Ethical Imperialism*.
167. Humphreys, "Social Science: Ethics of Research," 714. Stanley Milgram made an identical claim about the benefits of his obedience study to participants.
168. This was the Committee of Concern about Institutional Review Board Practices. "Social Scientists Form Committee to Protest Proposed Regulations," *IRB: Ethics & Human Research* 1: 8 (December 1979): 7. See *Federal Register*, August 14, 1979; and *IRB*, November 1979, pp. 1–5, 12.
169. Susan C. Lawrence, *Privacy and the Past: Research, Law, Archives, Ethics* (New Brunswick, NJ: Rutgers University Press, 2016), 47.
170. Holden, "Ethics in Social Science Research," 538.
171. Humphreys, *Tearoom Trade*, 175.

172. Holden, "Ethics in Social Science Research," 537. She was reporting on the proceedings of an NSF-funded conference on the topic. See Humphreys's reply, "Social Science: Ethics of Research."

173. Peter Nardi, for example, notes this framing of the study in the 1996 textbook *Sociology* (Belmont, CA: Wadsworth) by David Ward and Lorene Stone. "Reclaiming the Importance of Laud Humphreys's 'Tearoom Trade,'" 23.

174. Laura M. MacDonald, "America's Toe-Tapping Menace," *New York Times*, September 2, 2007, p. C10.

175. Galliher et al., *Laud Humphreys*, 47.

6. The Record Prison

1. In 1974, Seymour M. Hersh reported in the *New York Times* that Nixon's CIA had conducted secret surveillance of antiwar protesters and other dissidents, despite prohibitions in the 1947 National Security Act; a host of other revelations would soon arrive about assassination plots, civil rights surveillance, mail opening, NSA watch lists, and secret LSD experiments. Hersh, "Huge CIA Operation Reported in U.S. Against Antiwar Forces, Other Dissidents in Nixon Years," *New York Times*, December 22, 1974. Mary Graham, *Presidents' Secrets: The Use and Abuse of Hidden Power* (New Haven, CT: Yale University Press, 2017), 143–146; Seth Rosenfeld, *Subversives: The FBI's War on Student Radicals, and Reagan's Rise to Power* (New York: Farrar, Straus and Giroux, 2013).

2. For the background on the plan, see Priscilla Regan, *Legislating Privacy: Technology, Social Values, and Public Policy* (Chapel Hill: University of North Carolina Press, 1995), 71–77; see also Arthur R. Miller, *The Assault on Privacy: Computers, Data Banks, and Dossiers* (Ann Arbor: University of Michigan Press, 1971), 71–82.

3. "Privacy and Efficient Government: Proposals for a National Data Center," *Harvard Law Review* 82 (1968): 400–417.

4. Raymond T. Bowman, "Crossroad Choices for the Future Development of the Federal Statistical System," *Journal of the American Statistical Association* 63 (1968): 810.

5. Richard Ruggles, Richard Miller, Edwin Kuh, Stanley Lebergott, Guy Orcutt, and Joseph Pechman, "Committee on the Preservation and Use of Economic Data," Report presented to the Social Science Research Council of the American Economic Association (1965), 6–7. Carl Kaysen, Charles C. Holt, Richard Holton, George Kozmetsky, H. Russell Morrison, and Richard Ruggles, "Report of the Task Force on the Storage of and Access to Government Statistics," *American Statistician* 23: 3 (1969): 15–16.

6. See, for example, Nan Robertson, "Data-Center Aims Scored in Inquiry," *New York Times*, July 28, 1966, p. 24; "Bureaucracy: Chains of Plastic," *Newsweek* (August 8, 1966): 27; Anthony Prisendorf, "National Data Center: Computer

vs. the Bill of Rights," *The Nation* 203 (1966): 449–452; "A Government Watch on 200 Million Americans?" *U.S. News & World Report* (May 16, 1966): 56; and "The National Data Center and Personal Privacy," *The Atlantic* (November 1967): 53. For the scholarly response, see E. S. Dunn Jr., "The Idea of a National Data Center and the Issue of Personal Privacy," *American Statistician* 21 (1967): 21–27; and Jack Sawyer and Howard Schechter, "Computers, Privacy, and the National Data Center: The Responsibility of Social Scientists," *American Psychologist* 23: 11 (1968): 810–818. Jerry M. Rosenberg devoted a chapter of his 1969 book, *The Death of Privacy* (New York: Random House, 1969), to the threat of a proposed national data bank, 22–40.

7. Sawyer and Schechter, "Computers, Privacy, and the National Data Center," 811.

8. This last was the Government Accounting Office's blueprint for a center called FEDNET. Helen Nissenbaum, *Privacy in Context: Technology, Policy, and the Integrity of Social Life* (Stanford, CA: Stanford Law Books, 2010), 39. See also Robert Ellis Smith, *Ben Franklin's Website: Privacy and Curiosity from Plymouth Rock to the Internet* (Providence, RI: Privacy Journal, 2000), 309–312. "A detectable trend toward increased public criticism of the plans of organizations and their personal records" was also obvious in Britain, according to Malcolm Warner and David Stone, *The Data Bank Society: Organizations, Computers and Social Freedom* (London: George Allen & Unwin, 1970), 20.

9. They noted that "credential systems became an object of wide-ranging protest in the 1960s," prompting challenges "to the authority of established public and private institutions" and to the "criteria of individual evaluation" that many organizations employed. Alan F. Westin and Michael A. Baker, *Databanks in a Free Society: Computers, Record-Keeping and Privacy* (New York: Quadrangle Books, 1972), 343.

10. FOIA was signed, with reservations, by President Lyndon Johnson, and went into effect in 1967. Cornelia Vismann writes that "public debate over the decisive power of records found immediate confirmation in the official information politics of the Vietnam War." *Files: Law and Media Technology*, trans. Geoffrey Winthrop-Young (Stanford, CA: Stanford University Press, 2008), 147. On the longer battle over the public's "right to know," see Kathleen G. Donohue, "Access Denied: Anticommunism and the Public's Right to Know," in *Liberty and Justice for All? Rethinking Politics in Cold War America*, ed. Kathleen G. Donohue (Amherst: University of Massachusetts Press, 2012), 21–50; and Michael Schudson, *The Rise of the Right to Know: Politics and the Culture of Transparency, 1945–1975* (Cambridge, MA: Belknap Press of Harvard University Press, 2015). Mary Graham writes that so many exceptions were built into FOIA by Johnson and others that by the time it was approved in committee, "it sparkled like a Christmas tree, its worthy purpose obscured by

glittering exceptions"; nine exceptions "took back much of what the disclosure requirements promised the public." Graham, *Presidents' Secrets*, 127, 131.

11. On the distrust of experts and authorities in the 1970s see Peter Carroll, *It Seemed like Nothing Happened: America in the 1970s* (New Brunswick, NJ: Rutgers University Press, 1990), 235. Edward Berkowitz argues that this was a "crisis of competence" that "defined the seventies." *Something Happened: A Political and Cultural Overview of the Seventies* (New York: Columbia University Press, 2006), 6.

12. *The Parallax View* (1974), dir. Alan J. Pakula, and *Three Days of the Condor* (1975), dir. Sydney Pollack. Francis Ford Coppola's *The Conversation* (1974), in production when Watergate broke, had as its protagonist a surveillance expert who suffers a crisis of conscience.

13. CCTV came into regular use in urban areas in the 1970s as a technology of "public safety" and grew to become so important that it was dubbed the "fifth utility" in some cities. Clive Norris and Gary Armstrong, *The Maximum Surveillance Society: The Rise of CCTV* (New York: Oxford University Press, 1999). Here the "target hardening" theories of architect Oscar Newman were influential. See his *Defensible Space* (New York: Macmillan, 1972) and *Architectural Design for Crime Prevention* (Washington, DC: Department of Justice, 1973). Magnetic stripes were first used on transit tickets in the early 1960s by the London Transit Authority and on credit cards in 1970.

14. Michel Foucault, *Discipline and Punish: The Birth of the Prison*, trans. Alan Sheridan (New York: Pantheon, 1977) was the first American edition of Foucault's work. See Francois Cusset, *French Theory: How Foucault, Derrida, Deleuze, & Co. Transformed the Intellectual Life of the United States*, trans. Jeff Fort with Josephine Berganza and Marlon Jones (Minneapolis: University of Minnesota Press, 2008), 54–75.

15. Alan F. Westin, *Privacy and Freedom* (New York: Atheneum, 1967). See, for example, Westin's *New York Times* obituary from 2013. Margalit Fox, "Alan F. Westin, Who Transformed Privacy Debate before the Web Era, Dies at 83," *New York Times*, February 23, 2013, p. D7. A second important, early intervention in debates over privacy and data banks was Miller's *The Assault on Privacy*.

16. Westin, *Privacy and Freedom*, 7. For a similar definition of privacy as "control over information about oneself," see Charles Fried, "Privacy," *Yale Law Journal* 77 (1968): 483.

17. Stanton Wheeler, "Problems and Issues in Record-Keeping," in *On Record: Files and Dossiers in American Life*, ed. Stanton Wheeler (New Brunswick, NJ: Transaction Books, 1969), 23.

18. "The Computer and Invasions of Privacy," *Hearings before the Subcommittee on Government Operations, Special Subcommittee on Invasion of Privacy*,

U.S. House of Representatives, 89th Congress, Second Session, July 26–28, 1966; "Computer Privacy," *Hearings before the Subcommittee on the Judiciary, Subcommittee on Administrative Practice and Procedure,* Parts I and II, U.S. Senate, 90th Congress, First and Second Session, March 14–15, 1967, and February 6, 1968; "Federal Data Banks, Computers and the Bill of Rights," *Hearings before the Subcommittee on Constitutional Rights of the Committee on the Judiciary,* U.S. Senate, 92nd Congress, First Session, February–March, 1971. See also "Computerization of Government Files: What Impact on the Individual?" *UCLA Law Review* 15: 5 (1968): 1371–1498.

19. Among these were Wheeler, ed., *On Record*; Westin and Baker, *Databanks in a Free Society*; and James B. Rule, *Private Lives and Public Surveillance: Social Control in the Computer Age* (New York: Schocken Books, 1974).

20. Robert Wallace, "What Happened to Our Privacy?" *Life* (April 10, 1964): 10. The article noted that "private business and industry are even more heavily engaged [in dossier-keeping] than the federal government, and often with less reason."

21. U.S. Congress, Senate Committee on the Judiciary, Subcommittee on Administrative Practice and Procedure, "Government Dossier: Survey of Information Contained in Government Files" (Committee Print) (Washington, DC: U.S. Government Printing Office, 1967), 7–9. Todd Robert Coles, "Does the Privacy Act of 1974 Protect Your Right to Privacy? An Examination of the Routine Use Exemption," *American University Law Review* 40 (1991): 957–958, n. 2. See also "Records Maintained by Government Agencies," *Hearings on H.R. 9527 and Related Bills Before a Subcommittee of the House Committee on Government Operations,* 92d Congress, 2d Session 22 (1972), which estimated that the "average American is [the] subject of [an] estimated 10–20 files compiled by the federal government on private organizations."

22. Nan Robertson, "Data Center Held Peril to Privacy," *New York Times*, July 27, 1966, p. 41.

23. Richard Harwood, "There's a Dossier on You," *Washington Post*, May 29, 1966, p. E1.

24. The *Washington Post* described the center as a "harbinger of Big Brother," while the *LA Times* warned that "Big Brother May be a Computer." The *New York Times* later characterized the National Data Center as "an Orwellian threat to privacy" and "a Big Brother in Washington with an eye on all of (the public)." George Lardner Jr., "Data Center Hearing Warned on Privacy: Hearing on Data Center Cautioned on Privacy," *Washington Post*, July 27, 1966, p. A1; Viewpoint of the Times, "'Big Brother' May be a Computer," *Los Angeles Times*, October 8, 1967, p. M7; Nan Robertson, "Data Bank: Peril or Aid? The U.S. Central Data Bank: Would It Threaten Your Privacy?" *New York Times*, January 7, 1968, p. 1. James Rule noted that "my first sensitivity to these

issues came on reading Orwell's *1984*." *Private Lives and Public Surveillance*, 15. *Cancer Ward* (1968) was distributed in samizdat in 1966 in the Soviet Union, with versions available outside the USSR appearing beginning in 1968.

25. U.S. Congress, House of Representatives, Committee on Government Operations, *Privacy and the National Data Bank Concept*, 90th Congress, 2nd Sess., July 1968 (Washington, DC: U.S. Government Printing Office, 1968), v.

26. Thomas Haigh, "How Data Got Its Base: Information Storage Software in the 1950s and 1960s," *IEEE Annals of the History of Computing* (October–December, 2009): 6–25.

27. Jack Star, "The Computer Data Bank: Will it Kill Your Freedom?" *Look* 32 (June 15, 1968): 29.

28. Lasswell used the term in writing about the potential of using audiovisual media as "social observatories" for social science research: "The archives that contain this material provide a 'data bank' available for instructional purposes." See "Technique of Decision Seminars," *Midwest Journal of Political Science* 4: 3 (1960): 213–236; quote on p. 218.

29. Warner and Stone, *The Data Bank Society*, 28, n. 12; emphasis in original. Rex Malik, "The Databank Society: Can We Cope?" *New Scientist and Science Journal* (March 4, 1971): 498. Among other things, Malik's article warned of "government by electronic caprice." By 1975, the Very Large Database Conference had been organized to share "research and development results in the field of database management." See www.vldb.org/conference.html.

30. See, for example, Westin and Baker, *Databanks in a Free Society*, 229.

31. Warner and Stone, *The Data Bank Society*, 24.

32. COINTELPRO was created by the FBI in 1956 under J. Edgar Hoover as a vehicle to disrupt the Communist Party U.S.A., and it then moved on to other targets. It was exposed in 1971 through a burglary at an FBI field office in Media, Pennsylvania, organized by a group calling itself the Citizens' Commission to Investigate the FBI. Nelson Blackstock, *COINTELPRO: The FBI's Secret War on Political Freedom* (New York: Vintage, 1976); David Cunningham, *There's Something Happening Here: The New Left, the Klan, and FBI Counterintelligence* (Berkeley: University of California Press, 2005); David Garrow, *The FBI and Martin Luther King, Jr.*, rev. ed. (New Haven, CT: Yale University Press, 2006); Tim Weiner, *Enemies: A History of the FBI* (New York: Random House, 2012); Betty Medsger, *The Burglary: The Discovery of J. Edgar Hoover's Secret FBI* (New York: Alfred A. Knopf, 2014).

33. Miller, *The Assault on Privacy*, 54–55.

34. Donohue, "Access Denied," 29, 46. See also Rosenfeld, *Subversives*.

35. Josh Lauer argues that commercial surveillance in the United States has from its beginnings outpaced state surveillance systems. For the whole sweep of this

history see his *Creditworthy: A History of Consumer Surveillance and Financial Identity in America* (New York: Columbia University Press, 2017).

36. "New Service Uses Computers to Supply Fast Credit Checks," *New York Times*, July 10, 1966, p. 1; Westin, *Privacy and Freedom*, 305–309.

37. "Retail Credit's Day in Court," *Privacy Journal* 1: 2 (December 1974): 1; "Retail Credit Co. on Trial," *Privacy Journal* 1: 11 (September 1975): 4. Intriguingly, Retail Credit attempted to use FCRA against the Federal Trade Commission, arguing that the federal agency should not be privy to its customer files. On the Retail Credit Company, see the exposé "Anything Adverse?" *New Yorker*, April 21, 1975, as well as *Roemer v. Retail Credit Co.* of 1975. The company would soon, as a result of all this bad publicity, rename itself Equifax.

38. Even after the passage of FCRA, James Rule reported that the Associated Credit Bureaus "still stipulates that information contained in credit reports 'must not be revealed to the subject reported on.'" *Private Lives and Public Surveillance*, 212.

39. Robert C. Goldstein and Albert S. Dexter, "Privacy Regulation and Your Computer," *Business Quarterly* 40: 4 (Winter 1975): 31.

40. FCRA was passed in 1970 as an amendment to the Consumer Credit Protection Act of 1968.

41. "Under Surveillance: CBS Looks at How People Are Watched," CBS Television broadcast, December 23, 1971.

42. "Assault on Privacy," ABC Television broadcast, January 8, 1972. From the program summary: "A penetrating bit of research turns into a most revealing documentary on the ways you're being checked out by credit investigators and law enforcement agents. It is a story of expanding invasion of privacy, of official surveillance and credit company peeping, perhaps intended to help but often abused or intentionally misused."

43. Robert Ellis Smith founded and edited the journal, an outgrowth of his work as associate director of the Privacy Project of the ACLU. Subscribers seem to have been those in data-processing fields, business management, government, library work, educational institutions, banking, insurance and credit, as well as civil liberties, public interest, and press groups, with individuals making up 10 percent of the subscription base. The list of subscribers, of course, was "not made available to others." See "Who Reads *Privacy Journal* Anyway?" *Privacy Journal* 1: 9 (July 1975): 8.

44. "Bucking the System," *Privacy Journal* 2: 8 (June 1976): 3.

45. *Privacy Journal* 1: 11 (September 1975): 6; *Privacy Journal* 1: 6 (April 1975): 3.

46. Sharon Biederman, "Privacy at the Check-Out Counter," *Privacy Journal* 1: 3 (January 1975): 1.

47. "American Way," *Privacy Journal* 1: 7 (May 1975): 7.

48. Biederman, "Privacy at the Check-Out Counter," 2.

49. "The Snooper's Walking Tour," *Privacy Journal* 2: 2 (December 1975): 4–6.

50. Paul Armer, "Keeping Your Bills Secret in an Electronic Age," *Privacy Journal* 1: 5 (March 1975): 1. The article discussed National Science Foundation funding to explore cashless technologies, including the question of "how deep and how broad the concern for privacy is and how it will impede change in the payments system," 6. The author explained that "the extreme case, in which all transactions go through the system in real time, obviously represents the greatest threat to privacy" but he thought it unlikely that "we'll get to the extreme case in the near future, if ever." There is a mention of a "cashless society" in the notice on "Electronic Funds," *Privacy Journal* 1: 1 (November 1974): 2.

51. See the run of *Privacy Journal* for 1974 and 1975. On cable television see "In the States," *Privacy Journal* 1: 6 (April 1975): 5; on the increased rate of wiretapping (conservatively estimated at 1,052 taps intercepting 1.9 million conversations in 1974; these figures did not include unknown illegal taps or unreported ones, wiretaps with the consent of one party, or "service monitoring" by telephone companies), see "The Wired Nation: Wiretaps," *Privacy Journal* 1: 9 (July 1975): 1, 6.

52. These are all from *Privacy Journal* for 1974–1976.

53. See *Privacy Journal* 1: 4 (February 1975): 5.

54. Vance Packard, "Don't Tell It to the Computer," *New York Times Magazine* (January 8, 1967): 44–45, 89–92.

55. Robert Ellis Smith, *Privacy: How to Protect What's Left of It* (Garden City, NY: Anchor Press, 1979). Other titles were Stephen W. Leibholz and Louis D. Wilson, *Users' Guide to Computer Crime: Its Commission, Detection & Prevention* (Radnor, PA: Chilton Books, 1974); and a guide book for teenagers, Gerald S. Snyder, *The Right To Be Let Alone* (New York: Julian Messner, 1976). See also "Government Snooping—How to Fight Back," *U.S. News & World Report* (September 22, 1975): 21–23. There were also countervailing how-to guides for snooping, such as John M. Carroll, *Confidential Information Sources, Public and Private* (Los Angeles: Security World, 1975).

56. Robert A. Wright, "For Privacy from Cranks, Creeps and Crooks, Millions Getting Unlisted Phone Numbers," *New York Times*, December 22, 1971, p. 18.

57. National Research Council, *Privacy and Confidentiality as Factors in Survey Response* (Washington, DC: National Academy of Sciences, 1979), vii.

58. Miller, *The Assault on Privacy*, 73. For the longer view of the computer revolution, see Martin Campbell-Kelly and William Asprey, *Computer: A History of the Information Machine* (New York: Westview Press, 1996).

59. Matthew Wisnioski, *Engineers for Change: Competing Visions of Technology in 1960s America* (Cambridge, MA: MIT Press, 2012). Some experts did warn early on of the dangers of computer power, including Bernard Benson,

president of the Benson-Lehner Corporation; Richard Hamming, a Bell Laboratories researcher; and the author David Bergamini. See Westin, *Privacy and Freedom*, 299–305.

60. Inventory of Automatic Data Processing Equipment in the United States Fiscal Year 1971, General Services Administration; cited in Sam Ervin, Jr., "The First Amendment: A Living Thought in the Computer Age," *Columbia Human Rights Law Review* 4 (1972): 25. Westin and Baker give a similar accounting in *Databanks in a Free Society*. Jerry Rosenberg estimated that there were 45 computers in government use in 1954, 1,946 in 1965, and 2,600 in 1967 in *The Death of Privacy*, 24.

61. Rosenberg, *The Death of Privacy*, 24.

62. Miller, *The Assault on Privacy*, 66.

63. Star, "The Computer Data Bank," 28.

64. These were the Dunn and Ruggles reports. See Westin, *Privacy and Freedom*, 317; and Dunn, "The Idea of a National Data Center," 23.

65. Kaysen et al., "Report of the Task Force on the Storage of and Access to Government Statistics," 19.

66. Dunn, "The Idea of a National Data Center," 23. Despite assurances, there were significant worries about individual identification. In follow-up discussions, privacy safeguards of several kinds were proposed, including standards for consent and confidentiality, penalties for transgressors, independence from other agencies, guidelines for secure input and processing, cryptographically coded output, a Public Advisory Committee to oversee operations, and a "devil's advocate group" that would attempt to acquire data illegally. Sawyer and Schechter, "Computers, Privacy, and the National Data Center," 815–816. A *Harvard Law Review* article proposed further safeguards, including the scrambling of individual identifications according to a secret program and the establishment of specific variable boundaries and sample sizes. "Privacy and Efficient Government," 413–414.

67. Star, "The Computer Data Bank," 28–29.

68. Roger Piper, *The Story of Computers* (New York: Harcourt, Brace, 1964), 11.

69. Martin L. Ernst, "What Else Will Computers Do to Us?" *Wall Street Journal*, October 21, 1970, p. 18.

70. "Federal Data Banks, Computers and the Bill of Rights," *U.S. Senate Hearings* (1971), Part I, 24–25. Warner and Stone, although they wrote in this register themselves, derided the "mythology" propagated by "science-fiction writers and ill-informed press articles" about electronic brains. For them, the power of computers was not mythical but "real, and urgent, because they reflect the very substantial information-processing power of present-day machinery." *The Data Bank Society*, 29.

71. On the computer as metaphor in American culture more broadly, see Paul N. Edwards, *The Closed World: Computers and the Politics of Discourse in Cold War America* (Cambridge, MA: MIT Press, 1996), especially 303–351. See also Wisnioski, *Engineers for Change.*

72. Other novels cited by privacy scholars of the day include Michael Frayn, *The Tin Men* (1965), Robert A. Heinlein, *The Moon Is a Harsh Mistress* (1966), Dennis Feltham Jones, *Colossus* (1966)—the basis of the *Colossus* film—and Olof Johannesson, *The Tale of the Big Computer* (1968). Films include *Hot Millions*, dir. Eric Till (1968) and *The Computer Wore Tennis Shoes*, dir. Robert Butler (1969). David Burnham's *The Rise of the Computer State: A Chilling Account of the Computer's Threat to Society* (New York: Vintage, 1984) is a later, nonfiction work in this vein.

73. Steven Lubar, "'Do Not Fold, Spindle or Mutilate': A Cultural History of the Punch Card," *Journal of American Culture* 14 (1992): 43–55.

74. IBM cards, Fred Turner notes, were employed symbolically to protest the intertwining of "the corporate world, the university, the military, and the punch-card universe of information." *From Counterculture to Cyberculture: Stewart Brand, the Whole Earth Network, and the Rise of Digital Utopianism* (Chicago: University of Chicago Press, 2006), 12. Protests occurred at U.C. Santa Barbara, University of Pittsburgh, George Williams University-Montreal, University of Maryland, Howard University, State University of New York at Stony Brook (twice), New York University (where a computer was held for ransom), Fresno State College, University of Wisconsin-Madison (twice), University of Kansas-Lawrence, and Stanford University. David P. Julyk, "'The Trouble with Machines Is People.' The Computer as Icon in Post-War America: 1946–1970" (PhD diss., University of Michigan, 2008), 214.

75. Star, "The Computer Data Bank," 27.

76. Warner and Stone, *The Data Bank Society*, 13, 15.

77. Political mailing lists and direct mail campaigns, pioneered by Richard Vigurie, date from the early 1970s.

78. Isaac Asimov, "The Individualism to Come," *New York Times* advertising supplement, sec. 11, January 7, 1973, pp. 12, 13.

79. "A National Survey of the Public's Attitudes toward Computers" (December 1971); see Ervin, "The First Amendment," 50. Creative Computing conducted another of the early surveys in 1975; see "Public Attitudes about Computers," *Privacy Journal* 2: 4 (February 1976): 1. In a 1983 survey, 48 percent of those polled voiced strong concern about threats to personal privacy from technology, a twofold increase from 1978. Fully 60 percent believed that their privacy required limitations on the use of computers. Louis Harris, "The Road after 1984: A Nationwide Survey of the Public and Its Leaders on the New

Technology and Its Consequences for American Life," 1983. For privacy surveys, see www.privacyexchange.org/iss/surveys/surveys.html.

80. Westin and Baker, *Databanks in a Free Society*, 343.

81. "FTC Is Assailed on Tax Checking," *New York Times*, June 20, 1964, p. 29.

82. "The Paper Prison: Your Government Records," *ABC News Close-Up* broadcast, April 25, 1974. Congressional scrutiny led the Department of Defense to discontinue the use of SPNs that year, to stop providing the number to employers, and to enable veterans to have the form reissued without the SPN classification. Two years later, however, the numbers were still being used "extensively" by employers, most certificates still carried the code, and those certificates that had been reissued absent an SPN were "instantly suspect." "The Codebreakers," *Privacy Journal* 2: 10 (August 1976): 7. Note also "blue papers" and the long-standing practice of using discharges to deny benefits to homosexual service members. Margot Canaday, "Building a Straight State: Sexuality and Social Citizenship under the 1944 G.I. Bill," *Journal of American History* 90: 3 (2003): 940–941. In both cases, the paperwork followed the ex-soldier into civilian life.

83. Advertisement for "The Paper Prison: Your Government Records," *Chicago Tribune*, April 25, 1974, p. B10.

84. " 'Paper Prison' Captivating," *Chicago Tribune*, April 25, 1974, p. B10.

85. Philippa Strum, *Privacy: The Debate in the United States since 1945* (New York: Harcourt Brace, 1998), 46–47.

86. This was the Social Security Number Task Force of 1970. See Nissenbaum, *Privacy in Context*, 117–118. Social Security Task Force, "Report to the Commissioner, Social Security Administration," May 1971, F: SSN-Early History, C12, Social Security History Archives, Baltimore, Maryland [hereafter, SSHA].

87. Memo from Commissioner of Social Security to the Secretary of Health, Education, and Welfare, "Social Security Number Misuse—Possible Congressional Interest," February 15, 1977, F: SSN-Process, C12, SSHA. This included "identifying information on 256 million peoples . . . earning histories for 90 percent of the work force; family, financial, and in some cases, medical details on the 38 million people who are entitled to a benefit under one of the programs administered by SSA."

88. Jack Star, "The Computer Data Bank," 28.

89. "Social Security Numbers," *Privacy Journal* 2: 5 (March 1976): 1.

90. "Social Security Numbers," *Privacy Journal* 2: 3 (January 1976): 4. See Flavio Komuves, "We've Got Your Number: An Overview of Legislation and Decisions to Control the Use of SSNs as Personal Identifiers," *John Marshall Journal of Computer & Information Law* 16 (1998): 529–577.

91. Milton R. Knovitz, "Privacy and the Law: A Philosophical Prelude," *Law and Contemporary Problems* 31: 2 (1966): 272–280.

92. Legislative History of the Privacy Act of 1974, Senate and House Committee(s) on Government Operations, CMP-1976-OPS-0021 (September 1, 1976), 932; see Meg Leta Jones, "A Right to a Human in the Loop: Political Constructions of Computer Automation and Personhood," *Social Studies of Science* 47: 2 (2017): 216–239; quote on p. 228.

93. Michael A. Baker, "Record Privacy as a Marginal Problem: The Limits of Consciousness and Concern," in *Surveillance, Dataveillance and Personal Freedoms*, ed. Staff of the Columbia Human Rights Law Review (Fair Lawn, NJ: R. E. Burdick, 1973), 100, 101, 108–109, 111; emphasis in original.

94. Miller, *The Assault on Privacy*, 65.

95. See also, for example, Charles A. Reich's worry about the wiping away of second chances in "Police Questioning of Law Abiding Citizens," *Yale Law Journal* 75 (1966): 1161.

96. Arthur Miller, "Computers, Data Banks and Individual Privacy: An Overview," in *Surveillance, Dataveillance and Personal Freedoms*, ed. Staff of the Columbia Human Rights Law Review (Fair Lawn, NJ: R. E. Burdick, 1973), 18–19.

97. Miller, *The Assault on Privacy*, 65.

98. This figure appeared in debates over the National Data Center as well. U.S. Congress, *The Computer and the Invasion of Privacy*, 2.

99. See "Double Jeopardy," *Privacy Journal* 1: 1 (November 1974): 5.

100. Testimony on Fair Credit Reporting Act–1973, Subcommittee on Consumer Credit, Senate Committee on Banking, Housing and Urban Affairs, October 1–4, 10, 1973; quoted in Jones, "A Right to a Human in the Loop," 226. Attempts to amend the law in 1973 to permit consumers to perform a physical inspection of their credit information did not succeed.

101. Frank Askin, "Surveillance: The Social Science Perspective," in *Surveillance, Dataveillance and Personal Freedoms*, ed. Staff of the Columbia Human Rights Law Review (Fair Lawn, NJ: R. E. Burdick, 1973), 87.

102. Edward V. Long, *The Intruders: The Invasion of Privacy by Government and Industry* (New York: Praeger, 1967), 55.

103. Wheeler, "Problems and Issues in Record-Keeping," 24. Wheeler noted that records carried more formal legitimacy and authority than the people they represented; had permanence, with a "life far beyond the life-span of given individuals"; were transferable, with a "career independent from that of the person to whom it refers" and indeed had "a life of their own"; were separable from those who supplied their information in the first place and thus had a facelessness "missing from interpersonal communication"; and could be combined, "often without the knowledge of the person whose fate they may be helping to determine," the composite picture potentially bearing "little resemblance to the person it purports to describe," 5.

104. Miller, *The Assault on Privacy*, 65.
105. Miller, *The Assault on Privacy*, 64–65.
106. U.S. Department of Health, Education, and Welfare, *Records, Computers, and the Rights of Citizens* (Cambridge, MA: MIT Press, 1973), 92, 167, 111. Helen Nissenbaum calls the report "ground-breaking" in its attempt to balance the benefits of record-keeping systems with protection for citizens. *Privacy in Context*, 38.
107. Rule, *Private Lives and Public Surveillance*, 13, 7–8.
108. Rule examined police record systems, vehicle and driver licensing, and National Insurance in Britain along with consumer credit reporting and the BankAmericard system in the United States. He argued that if these systems did not yet constitute a "total surveillance society" a la Orwell—the costs of continuous mass surveillance were simply too high—he argued that they "now monitor some of the most important junctures between private individuals and the major institutions of modern society." *Private Lives and Public Surveillance*, 30–31, 36.
109. Rule, *Private Lives and Public Surveillance*, 39, 42, 331. Rule acknowledged that centralization of personal data in electronic form could lead to enhanced rather than diminished protection of that information, 334, 336. He also raised the issue of sophisticated techonologies of "evasion" arriving in step with new technologies of "control," such as benefits fraud or "the plastics business," 342. He believed in particular that the last few decades of increasing mass surveillance had brought the "relaxation of many forms of small-scale surveillance" such as gossip and social shaming and that the very impetus for modern surveillance systems "stems at least partly from the breakdown of their traditional counterparts," 332.
110. Orville G. Brim Jr., foreword, *Databanks in a Free Society*, xvii.
111. Westin and Baker, *Databanks in a Free Society*, 222–223. They argued that the major surge occurred between 1940 and 1955, which they attributed to increased affluence, spending, and travel; the expansion of social programs; the increasing number of students in higher education; and the like.
112. Westin and Baker, *Databanks in a Free Society*, quote on p. 233.
113. Westin and Baker, *Databanks in a Free Society*, 237, 249.
114. Westin and Baker, *Databanks in a Free Society*, 263, 269, 341. In this report (see especially pp. 242–243), Westin backtracked from some of the speculations in his 1967 *Privacy and Freedom*. Most who wrote from the point of view of business or marketing practices agreed with these assessments, not surprisingly. See Goldstein and Dexter, "Privacy Regulation and Your Computer," which concluded that "most authorities now agree that information in a computerized system is potentially easier to protect than that in a traditional, manual one," 30.
115. Westin and Baker, *Databanks in a Free Society*, 256.

116. Rule, *Private Lives and Public Surveillance*, 7–8.

117. This was in reference to the new Privacy Act. David S. Broder, "Ford Vows to Enforce New Law on Privacy," *Washington Post*, September 22, 1975, p. A2; Philip Shabecoff, "Ford Sees Peril of 'Big Brother,'" *New York Times*, September 22 1975, p. 13. In fact, Ford, advised by then-Justice Department official Antonin Scalia as well as Richard Cheney and Donald Rumsfeld, had vetoed the Privacy Act out of fears that it would compromise intelligence and FBI information. A sign of the high pitch of privacy concerns in 1974 was that his veto was easily overridden.

118. Richard M. Nixon, Radio Address, February 23, 1974. John T. Woolley and Gerhard Peters, *The American Presidency Project* [online], www.presidency .ucsb.edu/ws/?pid=4364.

119. Francis W. Sargent, "Politics of Privacy, the View from Massachusetts," *Privacy Journal* 1: 6 (April 1975): 1. In fact, Sargent believed the "biggest political problem associated with privacy is not the lack of public support, but the opposite." He thought it might lead to hasty and poorly conceived remedies.

120. Mary Margaret Penrose, "In the Name of Watergate: Returning FERPA to its Original Design," NYU *Journal of Legislation and Public Policy* 14: 1 (February 2011): 75–113. She writes that the scandal bred "a climate of fear, perhaps even paranoia, of 'private' information and 'secret data collection' attended by an equally compelling desire to know precisely who had what information in their possession," 83.

121. James Rule, Douglas McAdam, Linda Stearns, and David Uglow, *The Politics of Privacy: Planning for Personal Data Systems as Powerful Technologies* (New York: Elsevier Press, 1980), 101. In the 92nd and 93rd Congresses alone there were almost 300 bills introduced focused on access to and dissemination of personal data. Jerome J. Hanus and Harold C. Relyea, "A Policy Assessment of the Privacy Act of 1974," *American University Law Review* 25: 3 (1976): 567.

122. FOIA was initially enacted in 1966, taking effect in 1967.

123. The privacy of records was a bipartisan issue, although one could see the fissures. Liberals' faith in the effectiveness of data in attacking social problems put them at odds with an emerging conservative position that attacked data collection itself: the meddling of the IRS, for example, and racial record keeping, which 1960s civil rights legislation and affirmative action made mandatory. The new Supreme Court justice William Rehnquist, for example, was willing to speculate in 1973 that the cleanest solution to the problem of regulating the personal data used in running government programs might be to dismantle some of the programs. William H. Rehnquist, "Is an Expanded Right of Privacy Consistent with Fair and Effective Law Enforcement? Or: Privacy, You've Come a Long Way, Baby," *University of Kansas Law Review* (1974): 1–23. "Rehnquist on Privacy," *Privacy Journal* 1: 1 (November 1974): 4.

124. *Freedom of Information Act Guide and Privacy Act Overview* (Washington, DC: Office of Information and Privacy, Office of Policy and Communications, U.S. Dept. of Justice, 1992–). The Privacy Act of 1974 would be just one in a series of laws and initiatives addressing the security of data records, including the Social Security Number Task Force of 1970, the Fair Credit Reporting Act of 1970, The Family Educational Rights and Privacy Act of 1974, the Video Privacy Protection Act of 1987, the Computer Matching and Privacy Protection Act of 1988, and the Drivers Privacy Protection Act of 1994. This profusion of bills illustrates what is known as the "sectoral approach" in U.S. privacy law.

125. The period between 1961 and 1979, Alan Westin noted, witnessed the "rise of information privacy as an explicit social, political, and legal issue of the high-technology age." "Social and Political Dimensions of Privacy," *Journal of Social Issues* 59: 2 (2003): 435. In a review of privacy legislation, two experts noted in 1975 that "there now seems to be an irreversible trend in the Western, industrialized world toward recognition of a right of personal privacy, and greater control by individuals over information about them." Goldstein and Dexter, "Privacy Regulation and Your Computer," 35–36.

126. David H. Flaherty, *Protecting Privacy in Surveillance Societies: The Federal Republic of Germany, Sweden, France, Canada, and the United States* (Chapel Hill: University of North Carolina Press, 1989).

127. The HEW report, for example, included reports from Canada, Great Britain, and Sweden. *Records, Computers, and the Rights of Citizens*, preface (x).

128. This was the Privacy and Protection of Personal Information in Europe report. See Jones, "A Right to a Human in the Loop," 228.

129. George Sirgiovanni, "The Buckley Amendment," Freedom of Information Center Report no. 373, School of Journalism, University of Missouri at Columbia (June 1977): 2.

130. The amendment was named for its sponsor, the conservative Republican senator James Buckley of New York, the brother of conservative intellectual William F. Buckley. FERPA was enacted on August 21, 1974, with an effective date of November 19, 1974. It was attached to the omnibus Elementary and Secondary Education Act of 1974 and was amended in January of 1975. The lack of congressional debate may have signaled a rough consensus compared to other provisions regarding school busing and distribution of funds. See Richard D. Lyons, "Senate Backs Access of Parents to School Records of Children," *New York Times*, May 15, 1974, p. 29.

131. The NCCE was a grassroots membership organization with affiliates all over the country, funded in part by Ford Foundation monies and assisted on this issue by the Russell Sage Foundation. In 1973 the NCCE replaced the National Citizens Commission for the Public Schools, established in 1956 to lobby for improvements in the public schools; the organization was defunct by

1996. One of President Ford's staffers noted that advocates of the amendment feared that "school administrators are testing, experimenting, and classifying their children to their detriment" and viewed the legislation "as part of a set of issues which involves neighborhood control of the schools." Memorandum from Robert R. Belair to David Lissy, "President's Position on Buckley Amendment," May 4, 1976, Domestic Council on the Right to Privacy, David H. Lissy Files, 1975–1977, Ford Papers, Gerald R. Ford Library, Ann Arbor, Michigan [henceforth, Ford Papers]. See Albert Shanker, "In the Public Good: A Second Look at the Privacy Law," Display Advertisement, *New York Times*, November 24, 1974, p. 213; Eric Wentworth, "Changes Sought on Student File Inspection," *Washington Post*, December 9, 1974, p. A2.

132. Wentworth, "Changes Sought in Law on Student File Inspection." For example, Shirley A. Chisholm, liberal Democrat of New York, and John Ashbrook, conservative Republican of Ohio, were both supporters of the legislation on school files.

133. Michael J. Zdeb, "A Student Right of Privacy: The Developing School Records Controversy," *Loyola University Law Journal* 6: 2 (1975): 430, 432–433.

134. Quoted in Diane Divoky, "Cumulative Records: Assault on Privacy," *Learning* 2 (September 1973): 18–21.

135. This was the characterization of Katherine Ludlipp, Georgetown Law Center Right of Privacy Seminar. See also Wentworth, "Changes Sought on Student File Inspection."

136. "The Nation: Open Sesame Street," *Time* (December 16, 1974).

137. "School Files: The Law Went too Far," *New York Times*, December 15, 1974, p. 235.

138. Sirgiovanni, "The Buckley Amendment," 2.

139. Diane Divoky, "How Secret School Records Can Hurt Your Child," *Parade Magazine* (March 31, 1974). Divoky was approached by the NCCE to write the article for *Parade*.

140. Divoky, "How Secret School Records Can Hurt Your Child."

141. Diane Divoky, "Cumulative Records."

142. Quoted in Divoky, "Cumulative Records." As Representative Jack Kemp put it, the NEA recommended in 1925 that "health, guidance and psychological records be maintained for—on—each pupil"; the American Council on Education in 1941 developed record forms "that gave more attention to behavior description and evaluations and less to hard data on subjects and grades." "Student Records: A Proposed Strategy for Preventing Abuses of the Right to Privacy," Congressional Record, 93rd Congress, second session.

143. She noted that guidance counselors, who produced the most "sensitive and inferential records," were the staunchest opponents to parental access to student records. Divoky, "Cumulative Records."

144. Divoky, "How Secret School Records Can Hurt Your Child." On the centrality of the family dynamic to understandings of psychological development in the postwar era, see Deborah Weinstein, *The Pathological Family: Postwar America and the Rise of Family Therapy* (Ithaca, NY: Cornell University Press, 2013).

145. Zdeb, "A Student Right of Privacy," 430, 443. He is quoting *Doe v. McMillan*, 459 F.2d 1304, 1325 (D.C. Cir. 1972).

146. Zdeb, "A Student Right of Privacy," 434.

147. This is the difference between the intrusion and the trace; see Dan Bouk, "The History and Political Economy of Personal Data over the Last Two Centuries in Three Acts," *Osiris* 31: 1 (2017): 85–106. Indeed, a colleague of the inventor of the MMPI predicted in 1966 that "the invasion of privacy issue is going to be with us for a long time. Centralized computer storage and retrieval of personal information is going to be the next arena." Roderick D. Buchanan, "On Not Giving Psychology Away: The Minnesota Multiphasic Personality Inventory and Public Controversy over Testing in the 1960s," *History of Psychology* 5: 3 (2002): 294.

148. At that time the organization's name was the National Committee for Public Schools; it had reconstituted itself as the NCCE by 1974. It described itself as "the only national organization dedicated to redressing the imbalance of power in public school governance" and the "only mass membership organization devoted to increasing citizen participation in the educational decision-making process"; emphasis in original. See letter from Katharine L. Auchincloss to Mr. Guzzardi, April 22, 1974; National Committee of Citizens in Education records, Box: 1, Folder: 16, Pennsylvania State Special Collections Library [hereafter NCCE].

149. See test mailing material, titled "Denial of Access and Invasion of Privacy: A Test Mailing in Two Parts," Box: 1, Folder: 15 (and prior draft in Box: 1 Folder 16), NCCE.

150. "Denial of Access and Invasion of Privacy: A Test Mailing in Two Parts," Box: 1, Folder: 15, NCCE. The mailer pointed readers to an article for inspiration: Jeremiah S. Gutman, "The Right to Know," *Hastings Center Report* 3: 5 (November 1973).

151. National Committee for Citizens in Education, *Students, Parents and School Records* (Columbia, MD: 1974), 45–50. Key to the question of parents' rights was the "in loco parentis" doctrine. See memorandum from Sarah C. Carey to Stuart Sandow, "The 'In Loco Parentis' Doctrine and Parents' Right to School Records," December 7, 1973, Box: 1, Folder: 15, NCCE. See also Sarah C. Carey, "Students, Parents and the School Record Prison: A Legal Strategy for Preventing Abuse," reprinted in *Students, Parents and School Records*, 23–43; and Alan H. Levine, Eve Cary, and Diane Divoky, *The Rights of Students: An American Civil Liberties Union Handbook* (New York: Avon Books, 1973).

Advocates of parents' rights often drew from the 1925 *Pierce* case holding that "the child is not the mere creature of the state; those who nurture him and direct his destiny have the right, coupled with the high duty, to recognize and prepare him for additional obligations." Cases, such as *Merriken v. Cressmen* (U.S. District Court for Eastern Pennsylvania), placed limits on the nature and extent of information collection on children's relationship to their parents; other cases suggested rights of parents to inspect records, such as *Van Allen v. McCleary*, which turned on a parent's wish to review the findings of a school psychologist.

152. NCCE, *Students, Parents and School Records*, vi.

153. Quoted in NCCE, *Students, Parents and School Records*, 96, 103, 177 (I believe but am not certain that this letter is from a mother), 188, 247 (emphasis in original), 220.

154. Wentworth, "Changes Sought in Law on Student File Inspection." This detailed language about the range of documents on file was removed when the Act was amended the following year.

155. Melvin J. Goldberg to John Duggan, Vassar College, November 30, 1974, Box: 8, Folders: 2–3, NCCE.

156. Mrs. Alexandria Castagnaro [sp?] to J. William Rioux, February 28, 1975, Box: 8, Folders: 4–6, NCCE. Grateful to NCCE for advice, she explained, "I cannot afford to give anything as yet, but *as soon as I can save $15.00 you will be the first to get it.*" Emphasis in original.

157. "The Buckley Privacy Amendment Two Years Later," *Congressional Record-Senate*, June 3, 1976, S8483. Eric Wentworth, "Unlocking School Files: The Buckley Amendment," *Washington Post*, November 17, 1974, p. C5. See also Peter B. Edelman, "Children's Rights Coming to the Fore," *New York Times*, January 15, 1975, p. 71. David Schimmel and Louis Fischer, *Rights of Parents in the Education of Their Children* (Columbia, MD: National Committee for Citizens in Education, 1977); and the Children's Defense Fund pamphlet, "Your School Records: Questions & Answers about a New Set of Rights for Parents & Students," October 1975, Ford Papers.

158. Bowen speech notes on FERPA, Educational Staff Seminar, December 18, 1974, Box: 7, Folder: 26, NCCE.

159. Quoted in Wentworth, "Unlocking School Files."

160. *Milwaukee Journal*, November 19, 1977; quoted in Sirgiovanni, "The Buckley Amendment," 3.

161. These other organizations included the National Urban League, the National Council of Jewish Women, the Urban Policy Research Institute, the Child Welfare League, and the National Council of Catholic Women. NCCE documents indicate an average of one thousand calls a month to its toll-free telephone number; on dialing the callers would be asked for their address so

as to receive a card for recording their experiences attempting to access their child's records; "Hot Line Opened for Citizens in Education Privacy Info," *Education Daily*, October 7, 1974, p. 2, Box: 8, Folder: 17, NCCE. On the volume of calls, see notes from the "Women in Community Service" meeting, May 7, 1975, in Box: 8, Folder: 17, NCCE. "News Briefs," South Carolina School Boards Association, November 20, 1974, Box: 8, Folders: 2–3, NCCE.

162. Memo from NCCE to Thomas McFee, "Recommendations for Final Regulations for the Family Educational Rights and Privacy Act of 1974," March 4, 1975, Box: 8, Folders: 4–6, NCCE.

163. *Louisville Courier-Journal*, November 5, 1974; quoted in Sirgiovanni, "The Buckley Amendment," 3.

164. Memo from Brandon B. Sparkman to Board of School Commissioners, "An Act Passed by Congress—'Protection of the Rights and Privacy of Parents and Students,'" October 30, 1974, Box: 8, Folder: 1, NCCE.

165. "Public Notice," per order of the Providence School Committee, *Providence Journal*, November 19, 1974; Box: 8, Folder: 2, NCCE.

166. On the other hand, the executive secretary of the National Association of Secondary School Principals opposed the "panic-button purging of files" since it "suggests that school officials have something to hide and overlooks the fact that records are kept for one purpose only, i.e., to assist the student." Wentworth, "Unlocking School Files," C5.

167. *Louisville Courier-Journal*, November 5, 1974; quoted in Sirgiovanni, "The Buckley Amendment," 3.

168. Letter from J. William Rioux, April 5, 1974, Box: 8, Folder: 1, NCCE. In Maryland's case, for example, there was an attempt to distinguish "pupil records" from "pupil nonrecords," the latter a form of personal property created by a staff member and kept in his or her own files, intended to be "an extension of memory"; "Proposed Draft Bylaw Revision," Box: 8, Folder: 1, NCCE. And some school administrators applauded, including one from Park Ridge, Illinois, who wrote to the NCCE in thanks for their effort in tackling the issue. "School records," he lamented, "have grown like topsy." Merlin W. Schultz to NCCE, November 18, 1974, Box: 8, Folders: 2–3, NCCE.

169. Sirgiovanni, "The Buckley Amendment," 6. At UCLA, for example, student records could be "scattered in as many as 200 offices around campus." "Abuse of Educational Records Probed by Privacy Commission," *Access Reports*, October 18, 1976, p. 1; "Repeal of Education Privacy Act Urged by Spokesman for Colleges," *Access Reports*, November 15, 1976, p. 5.

170. Memo, Robert R. Belair to David Lissy, "President's Position on Buckley Amendment," May 6, 1976, folder "Buckley Amendment," Box 1, Domestic Council, David H. Lissy Files: 1975–1977, Ford Papers. All letters of recommendation were originally made accessible by the law, but FERPA was

amended on December 31, 1974, to protect the confidentiality of existing letters and to permit students to waive the right to see their letters. See Edward B. Fiske, "Colleges Ask Students to Forgo Right to See Files," *New York Times*, December 3, 1980, p. A1; Alfred Fitt, "The Buckley Amendment: Understanding It, Living with It," *College Board Review* (Summer 1975). Fitt, a special adviser at Yale, in a letter to the NCCE leadership, purported to be "dumbfounded" by the legislation: "The act intended to strengthen the rights of parents of school children has, without the slightest consideration of the matter, destroyed the rights of parents of college students"; it had also given students unwise access to their medical records, etc. See Alfred B. Fitt to J. William Rioux, November 4, 1974, Box: 8, Folder: 2–3, NCCE.

171. "School Records," *Privacy Journal* 2: 9 (July 1976): 6.

172. Liz Roman Gallese, "Student Job Referrals by Teachers Hit Snags Due to a Privacy Law," *Wall Street Journal*, January 14, 1977, p. 1. Others warned of an increase in "bland recommendation letters" because of the risk of students gaining access to them, with "objective" measures like grades and test scores correspondingly gaining more weight. The chancellor of the University of Wisconsin predicted that faculty would wind up "going to the telephone more" to keep their assessments off the record. Sirgiovanni, "The Buckley Amendment," 5–6; Bart Barnes, "College Entrance Problem: Law Leads to Bland Recommendations," *Washington Post*, December 1, 1975, p. A1. Edward B. Fiske, "Access to Students' Records Still Burdening Schools," *New York Times*, February 1, 1976, p. 33.

173. Memo, Robert R. Belair to David Lissy, "President's Position on Buckley Amendment," Ford Papers.

174. "College Records," *Privacy Journal* 1: 2 (December 1974): 5.

175. Memo from NCCE to Thomas McFee, "Recommendations for Final Regulations for the Family Educational Rights and Privacy Act of 1974," March 4, 1975, Box: 8, Folders: 4–6, NCCE. Similar complaints would be lodged about the Freedom of Information Act, as Michael Schudson notes in *The Rise of the Right to Know*, 30–34.

176. A congressional report two years after FERPA's passage noted that there had been some "purging" of student files, "cleaning out material which is irrelevant, and perhaps damaging, to a student's education"; it also suggested that the law "has given some educators a much sought-after basis for refusing to turn over files to police, the armed services, or the FBI." "The Buckley Privacy Amendment Two Years Later," *Congressional Record-Senate*, June 3, 1976, S8483. An education news service noted in 1976 that "there hasn't been a rush by students and parents to look at school records" and that "those who do . . . seem more bored than titillated by what they find." "Buckley Law Not So Burdensome after All, Lawyers Say," *Education Daily* 9: 59 (March 24, 1976): 1.

Estimates of the use of the act varied widely, with some universities claiming hundreds of requests for files and others dozens; Fiske, "Access to Students' Records." A *New York Times* survey of the early impact of FERPA on fourteen college campuses indicated that small numbers of students were taking advantage of their new rights—and those "mainly out of curiosity about items such as their I.Q.'s or their high school letters of recommendation"—and found that parental response in secondary schools had also been modest. Edward B. Fiske, "Law Opening School Files Has Slight Impact so Far," *New York Times*, February 17, 1975, p. 22.

177. The other sponsor was Senator Sam Ervin. Edmund Muskie, "The Federal Government and Your Right to Privacy," *Congressional Record-Senate*, September 26, 1975, p. 30496; "Government Snooping—How to Fight Back," 21–23.

178. The Privacy Act was passed on December 31, 1974.

179. Hannah Arendt, *Eichmann in Jerusalem: A Report on the Banality of Evil*, rev. ed. (New York: Viking, 1964), 289.

180. Miller, *The Assault on Privacy*, 54.

181. "Focusing on Federal Files," *Washington Post*, September 19, 1975, p. A26. See also Jerry Oppenheimer, "Bureaucracy's Molasses-Like Reluctance to Disclose," *Washington Star*, April 1, 1976, p. A1.

182. "Now: Access to Your Own Records," *Privacy Journal* 1: 11 (September 1975): 1.

183. Linda Mathews, "Privacy Law Now in Effect," *Los Angeles Times*, September 27, 1975, p. 1A.

184. Mathews, "Privacy Law Now in Effect."

185. Miller, *The Assault on Privacy*, 71.

186. These were the statements of Mary Lawton, deputy assistant attorney general in the U.S. Justice Department, as quoted by John Painter Jr., "Well-Meant Information, Privacy Acts so Loosely Knit Administrators Going Ape," *Portland Oregonian*, March 28, 1976. She was referring here both to the Privacy Act and the newly amended Freedom of Information Act.

187. Mathews, "Privacy Law Now in Effect."

188. Privacy Act requests were most common for the Department of State, the FBI, and the CIA. Oppenheimer, "Bureaucracy's Molasses-Like Reluctance to Disclose," A1. The article notes that the number of lawsuits had climbed significantly as well. "The Buckley Privacy Amendment Two Years Later," *Congressional Record-Senate*, June 3, 1976, p. S8483.

189. "The Price Tag," *Privacy Journal* 1: 4 (February 1975): 1.

190. Baker, "Record Privacy as a Marginal Problem," 102.

191. "Inventory of Uncle Sam's Data Banks," *Privacy Journal* 2: 10 (August 1976): 1.

192. Mathews, "Privacy Law Now in Effect." The advocate was Douglass Lea, counsel to the Senate Judiciary Subcommittee on Constitutional Rights. The U.S. Office of Management and Budget estimated a start-up cost of $100

million and then $200 to $300 million annually for the first four to five years to implement the privacy provisions in the 1974 legislation. See "The Price Tag," 1. The OMB did expect some savings, however, because of "disincentives to collecting personal data inherent in the legislation."

193. "Routine use" was interpreted to mean disclosure "compatible with the purpose for which it was collected." Even as President Ford signed the Privacy Act, he criticized this section as weak. See "In Congress," *Privacy Journal* 1: 3 (January 1975): 2.

194. Arthur Miller put it this way, writing about the failure of the proposed National Data Center: "even though public debate and outrage can be successful in a particular case, total reliance on counterattacking against individual information gathering activities will not reverse the growing risk to personal privacy created by an ever-increasing level of federal data collection." *The Assault on Privacy*, 82.

195. Myron Brenton, *The Privacy Invaders* (New York: Coward-McCann, 1964), 10. The exception to this pattern was FCRA, the only law in place at this time to regulate private data banks. Of FCRA, James Rule noted that although it did "involve the consumer more in the processing and selling of information about himself," it "virtually ratifies the position of credit bureaus with respect to the main patterns of their operations." As he summarized, the "intent of the Act is clear: to remove some of the popular objections to credit reporting in the interests of making it work as efficiently as possible," *Private Lives and Public Surveillance*, 215–216.

196. Edmund Muskie voiced these hopes in "The Federal Government and Your Right to Privacy."

197. The Privacy Act set up a seven-member commission, "equipped with sub-poena power and a budget of $1.5 million to examine for two years privacy issues not included in the act." Mary Ann Kuhn, "Americans Worry over Growing Loss of Privacy," *Washington Star*, September 22, 1975. Originally intended to have broad rulemaking and investigatory powers, it was reduced to a study group. The upshot was that the private sector was mostly exempted from legal scrutiny, except when singled out for regulation, as with FCRA and the credit industry. The failure to regulate the private sector set the stage for future battles over commercial data mining. The contrast to European privacy law, which rigorously regulates corporations' data collection, is instructive. James Q. Whitman, "The Two Western Cultures of Privacy: Dignity versus Liberty," *Yale Law Journal* 113 (2004): 1153–1221.

198. *Privacy Journal* reported that HEW, which had done so much to inspire privacy legislation through its report on *Records, Computers and the Rights of Citizens*, had by 1976 "become the battleground for crucial bureaucratic decisions on confidentiality, all of them losses for the remaining privacy

advocates in the department." "New HEW," *Privacy Journal* 2: 7
(May 1976): 2.

199. *Final Report of the Privacy Protection Study Commission*, July 12, 1977, quoted
in Jones, "The Right to a Human in the Loop," 228.

200. See Rule, *Private Lives and Public Surveillance*, 348.

201. Meg Leta Jones, following Westin, sees the 1980s as a "quiet period" regarding
data privacy, with far less commentary and action, even as personal computers
were becoming more commonplace. She notes that the Reagan administration
was not particularly interested in oversight. Jones, "The Right to a Human in
the Loop," 225, 228. Also see John Shattuck, "In the Shadow of 1984: National
Identification Systems, Computer Matching, and Privacy in the United States,"
Hastings Law Journal 35 (1983–1984): 997–998. In the 1980s the Electronic
Communications Privacy Act extended wiretapping restrictions to the
computer transmission of electronic data. The Computer Matching and
Privacy Protection Act of 1988 protected subjects of Privacy Act records from
being automatically matched with records across agencies. Neither of these
laws was particularly stringent or effective, but did mark the beginnings of our
current conversation about big data correlations and discrimination.

202. Named for Idaho Senator Frank Church, the formal name of the investigatory
body was the Select Committee to Study Governmental Operations with
Respect to Intelligence Activities of the United States Senate. It was one of
several investigations of intelligence abuses in the 1970s, including the
Watergate hearings themselves, the Rockefeller Commission, and the Pike
Committee. The outcome would be a "long process of surrounding intelligence gathering with layers of oversight and other legal limits," yielding bans
on assassinations, CIA and NSA surveillance within the United States, mail
opening, and agencies' examination of tax returns, for example. An Intelligence Oversight Board and new Foreign Intelligence Surveillance Court were
created as well. Graham, *Presidents' Secrets*, 146. For a contemporary perspective on the developing debate, see Richard H. Blum, ed., *Surveillance and
Espionage in a Free Society* (New York: Praeger, 1972).

203. The American Hospital Association had recently specified legitimate users of
medical records in *Hospital Medical Records: Guidelines for Their Use and the
Release of Medical Information* (Chicago: American Hospital Association,
1972).

204. *Whalen v. Roe*, 429 U.S. 589 (1977). The district court had concluded, "An
individual's physical ills and disabilities, the medication he takes, the frequency of his medical consultation are among the most sensitive of personal
and psychological sensibilities. One does not normally expect to be required to
have to reveal to a government source, at least in our society, these facets of

one's life." Donna C. Parratt, "Developments in the Right of Privacy: *Whalen v. Roe* and the Extent of the Right to Anonymity in the Doctor-Patient Relationship," *Congressional Research Service* 76–204A (November 1, 1976): 9–10. Also see *Doe v. MacMillan* on junior high school student records being used by officials in a review of the Washington, DC, schools.

205. Note, however, a set of recent cases that have come before the Court on GPS devices and location tracking ("cell site" information) via mobile phones. See *U.S. v. Jones*, 132 U.S. 945 (2012), where Justice Sotomayor specifically worried about the aggregation of data, and *U.S. v. Carpenter* (currently pending), which is likely to address the kind of information accessible through databases. Privacy concerns were also raised about DNA databases in *Maryland v. King* 569 U.S. (2013).

206. Arthur Miller, "The Surveillance Society: Just How Far Can It Go?" *Los Angeles Times*, September 6, 1970, pp. C1–2. Miller in this article was most concerned with U.S. Army surveillance of domestic political activity. On dating the term, see David Murakami Wood, "The 'Surveillance Society': Questions of History, Place and Culture," *European Journal of Criminology* 6 (2): 179–194. Wood notes that it is usually credited to sociologists Gary Marx, Oscar Gandy, and David Lyon, in particular.

207. Oscar H. Gandy Jr., *The Panoptic Sort: A Political Economy of Personal Information* (Boulder: Westview Press, 1993); David Lyon, *The Electronic Eye: The Rise of Surveillance Society* (Minneapolis: University of Minnesota Press, 1994), and *Surveillance Society: Monitoring Everyday Life* (Philadelphia: Open University, 2001); Gary Marx, "What's New about the 'New Surveillance'? Classifying for Change and Continuity," *Surveillance & Society* 1: 1 (2002): 9–29. David Alan Sklansky notes a telling shift in the uses of Orwell's *Nineteen Eighty-Four* in privacy debates over the last several decades: "today, the book is generally seen as a warning not so much about privacy in general as about surveillance," which he takes as indicative of an overall shift in attention away from physical and toward informational privacy. "Too Much Information: How Not to Think about Privacy and the Fourth Amendment," *California Law Review* 102: 5 (2014): 1077, n. 27.

208. Again, Foucault's writings on discipline, classification, and panopticism may have been influential for these analyses, but it is also quite possible that a grassroots grasp of surveillance preceded its formal theorizing. Certainly, Gilles Deleuze's notion of the database as the "exemplary new control mechanism *in itself*" and of individuals as "*dividuals*, and masses, samples, data, markets, or '*banks*,'" aligns with many of the ideas about record systems circulating in the United States in the 1960s and 1970s. Gilles Deleuze, "Postscript on the Societies of Control," *October* 59 (Winter 1992): 3–7; emphasis in original.

209. Daniel Rodgers describes the effort by academics in this period to find "a language for power adequate to the era" in *Age of Fracture* (Cambridge, MA: Belknap Press of Harvard University Press, 2011), 102. See especially his discussion of the intellectual currents undergirding the "dematerialization of power," 77–110.

7. The Ethic of Transparency

1. The revised Freedom of Information Act, FERPA, and the Privacy Act of 1974 were all examples of the former; the Church Committee, the Rockefeller Commission, and the Pike Committee examples of the latter.

2. Mary Graham notes that the efforts in Congress to pull back the secrecy of the executive branch and to promote access to government information were always partial and flawed. *Presidents' Secrets: The Use and Abuse of Hidden Power* (New Haven, CT: Yale University Press, 2017), 130. See Archon Fung, Mary Graham, and David Weil, *Full Disclosure: The Perils and Promise of Transparency* (New York: Cambridge University Press, 2007).

3. As already noted, closed-circuit television, or video surveillance, grew to become so important that it was dubbed the "fifth utility" in some cities. Clive Norris and Gary Armstrong, *The Maximum Surveillance Society: The Rise of CCTV* (New York: Oxford University Press, 1999). See the writings of architect Oscar Newman: *Defensible Space* (New York: Macmillan, 1972) and *Architectural Design for Crime Prevention* (Washington, DC: Department of Justice, 1973).

4. Christian Parenti, *The Soft Cage: Surveillance in America from Slavery to the War on Terror* (New York: Basic Books, 2003), 195. See Mike Davis, *City of Quartz: Excavating the Future in Los Angeles* (New York: Verso, 1990), 221–264; and Neil Smith, *The New Urban Frontier: Gentrification and the Revanchist City* (New York: Routledge, 1996).

5. Bruce J. Schulman, "The Privatization of Everyday Life: Public Policy, Public Services, and Public Space in the 1980s," in *Living in the Eighties*, ed. Gil Troy and Vincent J. Cannato (New York: Oxford University Press, 2009), 167–180; quote on p. 168. He notes that in the 1980s, what had been a "secession of the rich" from public services and public life "spread downward," 169. For broader trends in political culture see his *The Seventies: The Great Shift in American Culture, Society, and Politics* (New York: Free Press, 2001); Bruce J. Schulman and Julian E. Zelizer, eds., *Rightward Bound: Making America Conservative in the 1970s* (Cambridge, MA: Harvard University Press, 2008); and Beth Bailey and David Farber, eds., *America in the Seventies* (Lawrence: University of Kansas, 2004).

6. Schulman, "The Privatization of Everyday Life," 171. See also Mike Davis, *City of Quartz*, ch. 4. The privatization of residential communities had its counterpart in enclosed, privatized commercial spaces in the form of shopping

malls. See M. Jeff Hardwick, *Mall Maker* (Philadelphia: University of Pennsylvania Press, 2003); and Michael Sorkin, ed., *Variations on a Theme Park* (New York: Hill and Wang, 1992).

7. As Michael Schudson argues, "Openness was a key element in the transformation of politics, society, and culture from the late 1950s through the 1970s." The phrase "right to know" was voiced as early as the Constitutional Convention, but did not appear in Supreme Court rulings or "even in popular rhetoric" until 1945 when journalists began to organize around it. *Rise of the Right to Know: Politics and the Culture of Transparency, 1945–1975* (Cambridge, MA: Harvard University Press, 2015), 5–6.

8. Samantha Barbas traces the longer history of this tendency in the news industry, starting in the late nineteenth century, in *Laws of Image: Privacy and Publicity in America* (Stanford, CA: Stanford University Press, 2015).

9. *Stanley v. Georgia*, 394 U.S. 557 (1969). There was pushback, however, including the pronouncement of "legitimate state interests at stake in stemming the tide of commercialized obscenity" in *Paris Adult Theatre I v. Slaton*, 413 U.S. 49 (1973).

10. As Leigh Ann Wheeler summarizes it, a civil liberties approach "tilted toward freedom *to* and against freedom *from*." This meant that "constitutional sexual privacy played a major role" in the visibility of sex in public. *How Sex Became a Civil Liberty* (New York: Oxford University Press, 2014), 92, 7–8, 177; emphasis in original. Wheeler traces these developments to the ACLU's campaigns on behalf of sexual expression, leading to an emphasis on decriminalization of "victimless crimes," including prostitution and even public solicitation, versus unwanted sexual display.

11. See E. Wayne Karp, *Family Matters: Secrecy and Disclosure in the History of Adoption* (Cambridge, MA: Harvard University Press, 1998); and Ellen Herman, *Kinship by Design: A History of Adoption in the Modern United States* (Chicago: University of Chicago Press, 2008).

12. See, for example, Doug C. Rossinow, *The Politics of Authenticity: Liberalism, Christianity, and the New Left in America* (New York: Columbia University Press, 1998); and Russell Rickford, *We Are an African People: Independent Education, Black Power, and the Radical Imagination* (New York: Oxford University Press, 2016).

13. Two key works are Sara Evans, *Personal Politics: The Roots of Women's Liberation in the Civil Rights Movement and the New Left* (New York: Knopf, 1979); and Ruth Rosen, *The World Split Open: How the Women's Movement Changed America* (New York: Viking, 2000).

14. As Robert O. Self writes, "What lived in the shadows of the 'private'—abortion, rape, homosexuality, sexual harassment and abuse—activists pushed into the public realm." In this sense, "secrets became public, and then the basis of rights." *All in the Family: The Realignment of American Democracy since the*

1960s, repr. ed. (New York: Hill and Wang, 2013), 11. Also see Deborah Cohen, *Family Secrets: Living with Shame from the Victorians to the Present Day* (New York: Viking, 2013).

15. See Sissela Bok, *Secrets: On the Ethics of Concealment and Revelation*, repr. ed (New York: Pantheon, 1983).

16. Kenneth Cmiel, "The Politics of Civility," in *The Sixties: From Memory to History*, ed. David Farber (Chapel Hill: University of North Carolina Press, 1994), 263–290; Maurice Isserman and Michael Kazin, "The Failure and Success of the New Radicalism," in *Rise and Fall of the New Deal Order*, ed. Steve Fraser and Gary Gerstle (Princeton, NJ: Princeton University Press, 1989), 212–242.

17. Nancy F. Cott, *Public Vows: A History of Marriage and the Nation* (Cambridge, MA: Harvard University Press, 2000), 202.

18. Sam Binkley, *Getting Loose: Lifestyle Consumption in the 1970s* (Durham, NC: Duke University Press, 2007), 3–4.

19. Bruno Bettelheim observed as early as 1968 a "changing attitude of the younger generation toward privacy," focused on communality "even in times that they are alone." Bettelheim, "The Right to Privacy is a Myth," *Saturday Evening Post* (July 27, 1968): 8–9. For a dramatic case of "loosening," see Gay Talese, *Thy Neighbor's Wife* (Garden City, NY: Doubleday, 1980).

20. Abigail McCarthy, *Private Faces/Public Places* (Garden City, NY: Doubleday, 1972), 3–4.

21. McCarthy, *Private Faces*, 399.

22. McCarthy, *Private Faces*, 399–400, 405, 407–408, 409–10. She referred to Eisenhower's hospitalization for a heart attack; Lyndon Johnson had also publicized his scar after gallbladder surgery in 1965, which took many commentators aback. See Schudson, *The Rise of the Right to Know*, 9.

23. McCarthy, prologue, *Private Faces*. Her title was taken from a poem by W. H. Auden.

24. McCarthy, *Private Faces*, 435.

25. This was Myra McPherson.

26. See Schudson, *The Rise of the Right to Know*, especially ch. 4.

27. Campaign contribution disclosures were enacted in 1974 as an amendment to the 1971 Federal Election Campaign Act and required the disclosure of the names, addresses, and places of business of all citizens who made political contributions over $100. A strange set of bedfellows, including conservative senator James Buckley of New York, former senator Eugene McCarthy, and the New York Civil Liberties Union, along with nine other parties, argued that the provision violated contributors' political privacy. Lesley Oelsner, "12 Criticize New Vote Law in High Court," *New York Times*, September 20, 1975,

p. 10. In *Buckley v. Valeo* (1976), the Supreme Court ruled that disclosure of voters' information did not violate First or Fourteenth Amendment rights. See Julian E. Zelizer, "Seeds of Cynicism: The Struggle over Campaign Finance, 1956–1974," *Journal of Policy History* 14: 1 (2002): 73–111.

28. The *Chicago Tribune* reported that "most members who have moved on their own to disclose their finances say they did so in an attempt to restore the credibility of government, especially in light of Watergate." "60 in Congress out of 534 Offer Financial Data," *Chicago Tribune*, May 7, 1974, p. B7.

29. This was Representative Louis Frey Jr., Republican of Florida. See "Invasion of Privacy," *Congressional Record* 7790 (1974): 7822.

30. Schudson, *Rise of the Right to Know,* 104.

31. These developments were propelled by a desire to weaken powerful committee chairs and clear the way for liberal legislation. Important in this effort was a liberal coalition, the Democratic Study Group, dedicated to adding "anti-secrecy" amendments to the Legislative Reorganization Act of 1970, a major revision of Congress's procedural operations, which had not been altered in a significant way since 1946. Schudson persuasively argues that credit for transparency measures properly belongs to those in Congress in the 1960s, not the "Watergate babies" elected in 1975 and 1977. *Rise of the Right to Know,* 105–134.

32. Schudson, *The Rise of the Right to Know.* Ralph Nader's *Unsafe at Any Speed* was published in 1965. On consumer watchdogs, see Daniel Horowitz, *The Anxieties of Affluence: Critiques of American Consumer Culture, 1939–1979* (Amherst: University of Massachusetts Press, 2004), 166–176.

33. Eagleton had been treated for depression three times in the 1960s; the concern was about the mental stability of a man "with a finger on the button." Joshua M. Glasser notes that while rumors had swirled around Eagleton's drinking problems and hospitalizations, these did not initially doom his candidacy. *The Eighteen-Day Running Mate: McGovern, Eagleton, and a Campaign in Crisis* (New Haven, CT: Yale University Press, 2012); see p. 131.

34. This is what John B. Thompson calls the "trouble that can afflict politicians in an age of mediated visibility—phenomena such as the gaffe, the leak, the outburst and the scandal." He notes that "while the 19th century was the birthplace of mediated scandal, the 20th century was to become its true home." See "The New Visibility," *Theory, Culture and Society* 22 (2005): 31–51, and also his *Political Scandal: Power and Visibility in the Media Age* (Cambridge: Polity, 2000), chs. 2 and 4.

35. John Robert Greene, *Betty Ford: Candor and Courage in the White House* (Lawrence: University Press of Kansas, 2004), 28. The scrutiny was in part thanks to the 25th Amendment (ratified in 1967), which made Ford subject to congressional investigation and approval. As Mary Graham notes, his tax

returns were scoured, his associates interviewed, and his more than two decades of votes and statements in Congress reviewed. *Presidents' Secrets*, 134.

36. This is taken from Ford's inaugural address, delivered on August 9, 1974.

37. Betty Ford with Chris Chase, *The Times of My Life* (New York: Harper & Row, 1978), 151.

38. Greene, *Betty Ford*, xiii. Paul Healy, "Betty Ford: Candor with a Capital C," *Chicago Tribune*, January 5, 1975, p. D1.

39. She had a predecessor in Marvella Bayh, wife of the Democratic senator from Indiana, Birch Bayh, who also talked publicly about her surgery. The *New York Times* reported that a mastectomy was often seen as the "operation that women fear most" and that "up until a few years ago, mastectomy was a subject that was only whispered about outside of doctors' offices." Bayh, along with Shirley Temple Black, brought the "once taboo subject into the open." Judy Klemesrud, "After Breast Cancer Operations, a Difficult Emotional Adjustment," *New York Times*, October 1, 1974, p. 46.

40. James T. Patterson observes that early in the twentieth century, patients often refused to reveal diagnoses even to close friends. By mid-century, patients were becoming more open about talking about cancer in particular, as cures appeared on the horizon. *The Dread Disease: Cancer and Modern American Culture* (Cambridge, MA: Harvard University Press, 1987). Emily K. Abel notes the appearance of a handful of published statements in the mid-1950s with titles like "I Had Breast Cancer" (1954). That particular essay argued, "A deplorable curtain of silence hangs about this subject and it is time we lift it." Patients were not the only ones to keep a cancer secret. Physicians often withheld information from patients and their families, either a cancer diagnosis or the disease's extent. "When treatment was necessary, doctors gave just enough information to obtain compliance." The writer John Gunther discovered the nature of his son's brain tumor, for example, "only after he 'peeped' at the medical records lying on a technician's desk." *The Inevitable Hour: A History of Caring for Dying Patients in America* (Baltimore: Johns Hopkins University Press, 2013), 92–94.

41. Siddhartha Mukherjee, *The Emperor of All Maladies: A Biography of Cancer* (New York: Scribner, 2011), 26–27.

42. Greene, *Betty Ford*, 51.

43. Greene, *Betty Ford*, 51.

44. Suzanne Loebl, "A New Way Must Be Found to Safeguard Medical Privacy," *New York Times*, December 7, 1974, p. 29.

45. Greene, *Betty Ford*, 51–52.

46. See Brenda Stone, "Thousands Seek Breast Cancer Examinations and Information," *Chicago Tribune*, October 3, 1974, p. A1. A Chicago Cancer Prevention Center was reported as "being bombarded with calls" after Ford's

surgery. See also Jane E. Brody, "Inquiries Soaring on Breast Cancer," *New York Times*, October 6, 1974, p. 21; "'Thank God for Betty Ford': U.S., U.K. Women Flock to Cancer Clinics," *Toronto Globe and Mail*, October 19, 1974, p. 15; Ronald Kotulak, "Can the Mass of Publicity Push a Cure for Cancer?" *Chicago Tribune*, October 24, 1974, p. B9; and Dorothy Collin, "Many Saved by Telling of Surgery," *Chicago Tribune*, January 28, 1975, p. 1. Breast cancer advocates would by the later 1970s rely on such personal testimonies to publicize the need for funding and research, such as Rose Kushner's memoir, *Why Me?* (1979) and Betty Rollin's *First You Cry* (1976).

47. Stuart Auerbach, "Mrs. Ford a Little Tired but Otherwise Doing Well," *Boston Globe*, September 30, 1974, p. 1. Judy Ross, letter to the editor, *Los Angeles Times*, October 3, 1974, p. C4.

48. Loebl, "A New Way Must Be Found to Safeguard Medical Privacy," p. 29.

49. Mary McGrory, "First Lady Is 'Everywoman' Now," *Boston Globe*, October 2, 1974, p. 19. An editorial noted that some Americans "soundly criticize the plethora of publicity about First Lady Betty Ford's breast cancer as an invasion of privacy," but took the opposite view. Editorial, *Hartford Courant*, October 18, 1974, p. 18.

50. Ellen Goodman, "The Doctor's Code of Silence," *Boston Globe*, October 1, 1974, p. 30.

51. "Her malignancy has no bearing whatsoever on the 'state of the nation,' nor might I add, is it anyone's business whether or not President Ford toasts his own English muffins for breakfast and shares a room with his wife." A. R. Franco, "Allow First Family a Private Life," *Hartford Courant*, October 4, 1974, p. 18.

52. Peter Gordy, "What Price News?" *Atlanta Constitution*, October 7, 1974, p. 5A.

53. For accounts of her comments about "how often she sleeps with the President," see *McCall's* September issue with Myra MacPherson. "They've asked me everything but how often I sleep with my husband, and if they'd asked me that I would have told them . . . as often as possible." "Betty Answers the Only Question Left Unasked," *Atlanta Constitution*, August 21, 1975, p. 1A; "Pillow Talk by Mrs. Ford," *Boston Globe*, August 21, 1975, p. 1; "Betty Ford Speaks Her Mind—Again: Secrets of the White House Bedroom," *Los Angeles Times*, August 21, 1975, p. B18.

54. Betty Ford, *60 Minutes*, July 21, 1975. See also Greene's account in *Betty Ford*, 75–79.

55. "Betty Ford Would Accept 'an Affair' by Daughter," *New York Times*, August 11, 1975, p. 16.

56. Sheila Rabb Weidenfeld, *First Lady's Lady: With the Fords at the White House* (New York: G. P. Putnam's, 1979), 162.

57. Weidenfeld, *First Lady's Lady*, 162.

58. Healy, "Betty Ford: Candor with a Capital C."

59. The White House received 28,000 letters in response to the show, the majority critical. Greene, *Betty Ford*, 78.

60. Greene, *Betty Ford*, 83. Greene notes that polls also showed majorities favoring her comments on both her reaction to her daughter's hypothetical "affair" and the Equal Rights Amendment. See Louis Harris, "Survey Reveals Betty Is a Big Asset for Ford," *Atlanta Constitution*, August 9, 1976, p. 2A.

61. Sociologist Michael Schudson argues that after the 1960s, the press became more critical of and adversarial toward established power, billed itself publicly as "aggressive," and engaged in longer-form, more contextual reporting. *Rise of the Right to Know*, 150–164. He cites the 1960 scandal over President Eisenhower's deception about the U.S. downing of a U-2 spy plane over Russia, the Kennedy-Nixon debates, confrontations between journalists and military spokesmen over Vietnam, underground publications, and maverick reporters along with deeper changes in the culture of journalism, governance, and the culture at large—including the rise of a more "critical culture" with the expansion of higher education—as behind this shift. *Rise of the Right to Know*, 141–143. Throughout the Watergate scandal, Nixon had also been "scrutinized for clues" as to the stability of his mind and marriage. There were rumors of problems with drugs and alcohol, the use of sleeping pills, and "secret visits to a New York psychiatrist" during the 1968 campaign. Andreas Killen, *1973 Nervous Breakdown: Watergate, Warhol, and the Birth of Post-Sixties America* (New York: Bloomsbury, 2006), 48–49.

62. Schudson, *Rise of the Right to Know*, 143–144.

63. The heroic role of the *Washington Post*'s investigative reporters during Watergate was important here. See Carl Bernstein and Bob Woodward, *All the President's Men* (New York: Simon and Schuster, 1974).

64. Thompson, "The New Visibility," 45.

65. Edward Berkowitz, *Something Happened: A Political and Cultural Overview of the Seventies* (New York: Columbia University Press, 2006), 217.

66. Greene, *Betty Ford*, 76. Greene notes that neither Lady Bird Johnson nor Pat Nixon had been asked to give such an interview. This is not to say that earlier First Ladies had been silent about life in the White House. Lady Bird Johnson, for example, published the rather decorous *A White House Diary* (New York: Holt, Rinehart and Winston, 1970).

67. Weidenfeld, *First Lady's Lady*, 168.

68. Greene, *Betty Ford*, 86.

69. Weidenfeld, *First Lady's Lady*; Greene, *Betty Ford*, 107.

70. See Larry J. Sabato, *Feeding Frenzy: Attack Journalism and American Politics* (Baltimore, MD: Lanahan, 2000); and Suzanne Garment, *Scandal: The Crisis of Mistrust in American Politics* (New York: Times Books, 1991).

71. Berkowitz, *Something Happened*, 102. "Such behavior might have been routine in previous years, but it was also well hidden from public view," Berkowitz notes. This was, he writes, just one of the "intimate Washington conversations that the public savored during the seventies."

72. Susan Wise Bauer, *Art of the Public Grovel: Sexual Sin and Public Confession in America* (Princeton, NJ: Princeton University Press, 2008), 98–99. Bauer notes that the comments were credited with wiping out Carter's significant lead in the presidential race. She argues that he simply hadn't mastered the new and requisite "language of public confession."

73. Marion Winik, "The Neighbor, d. 1978," *The Glen Rock Book of the Dead* (Berkeley: Counterpoint, 2007).

74. Emily Nussbaum, "The Great Divide: Norman Lear, Archie Bunker, and the Rise of the Bad Fan," *New Yorker* (April 7, 2014). See Saul Austerlitz, *Sitcom: A History in 24 Episodes from 'I Love Lucy' to 'Community'* (Chicago: Chicago Review Press, 2014); and Donna McCrohan, *Archie & Edith, Mike & Gloria: The Tumultuous History of All in the Family* (New York: Workman, 1987).

75. For the fullest account, see Jeffrey Ruoff's excellent *An American Family: A Televised Life* (Minneapolis: University of Minnesota Press, 2002). See also Laurie Rupert and Sayanti Ganguly Puckett, "Disillusionment, Divorce, and the Destruction of the American Dream: *An American Family* and the Rise of Reality TV," in *The Tube Has Spoken*, ed. Julie Anne Taddeo and Ken Dvorak (Lexington: University Press of Kentucky, 2010), 83–97; and Andreas Killen's discussion of the series in *1973 Nervous Breakdown*. There were precedents, including a Canadian documentary, *The Things I Cannot Change* (1966–1967), which tracked an impoverished family, the Baileys, and led to much critique of the filmmakers.

76. Commentators on this aspect of the show have often referred to Lance "coming out" during the filming, but that is not quite accurate. His mother, referring euphemistically to "the life Lance was leading," simply noted that "for the first time I knew what was going on with Lance in New York." Pat Loud with Nora Johnson, *Pat Loud: A Woman's Story* (New York: Coward, McCann & Geoghegan, 1974), 96.

77. Paula Rabinowitz, *They Must Be Represented: The Politics of Documentary* (New York: Verso, 1994), 136. Jackie Kennedy's eccentric cousins, meanwhile, became the subjects of a documentary, *Grey Gardens* (1975).

78. See Mark Andrejevic, *Reality TV: The Work of Being Watched* (Lanham, MD: Rowman & Littlefield, 2003); and Taddeo and Dvorak, eds., *The Tube Has Spoken*.

79. Rabinowitz, *They Must Be Represented*, 131. See also Jim Lane, *The Autobiographical Documentary in America* (Madison: University of Wisconsin Press, 2002).

80. Jeffrey Ruoff, "Conventions of Sound in Documentary," *Cinema Journal* 32: 3 (Spring 1993): 24–40; quote on p. 26. He cites Joyce Chopra's *Joyce at 34* (1972), Amalie Rothschild's *Nana, Mom, and Me* (1974), and Jill Godmilow's *Antonia: Portrait of a Woman* (1974), all of which explored personal issues in the growing women's movement. See also Ed Pincus's autobiographical *Diaries, 1971–76* (1981), which "turned the camera on his own marriage and family life for more than five years"; he edited the twenty-eight hours of footage into a three-and-a-half-hour film in 1981. William Yardley, "Ed Pincus, Documentary Filmmaker, Dies at 75," *New York Times*, November 8, 2013, p. A33.

81. Ruoff quotes the former president of NET as saying that the transitional moment between NET and PBS was likely the only moment that the documentary could have been made "in the history of public TV." *An American Family*, 5.

82. Ruoff, *An American Family*, xii.

83. Ruoff, *An American Family*, xviii.

84. Margaret Mead, "As Significant as the Invention of Drama or the Novel," *TV Guide* (January 6, 1973): A61.

85. It registers as #32 on TV Guide's "50 Greatest Shows of All Time" list.

86. Sam Binkley writes that it appeared "to confirm the obsolescence of the nuclear family itself—a sign of increased liberty to some, but a frightening indicator of larger processes of social uprootedness and moral confusion to others." *Getting Loose*, 63.

87. See, for example, John Carmody, "'American Family': Shattered American Dream," *Washington Post*, December 1, 1972, p. D1; Stephanie Harrington, "An American Family Lives Its Life on TV," *New York Times*, January 7, 1973, p. 141; "Future of the Family," *Atlanta Constitution*, March 17, 1973, p. 4A; and Pat Colander, "One Man's Family—The Norm Exposed," *Chicago Tribune*, April 3, 1975, p. B1. See also Shana Alexander, "The Silence of the Louds," *Newsweek* (January 22, 1973): 28.

88. Tom Shales, "On Camera Again," *Washington Post*, February 22, 1973, p. C1. One critic pointed out that the filmmakers were not subjects of the film, though at times they outnumbered the family and "must have constituted a major feature of life in the household during the filming." Bernard Beck, "Ghost in the Family," *Society* 11 (January / February, 1974): 80.

89. Paula Rabinowitz cites the influence on the documentary of 1960s *cinéma vérité*: "Its reality, authenticity, spontaneity, unmediated truth, and direct access to emotion signaled a break with both Hollywood and the overt theatricality of 1930s documentary forms." *They Must Be Represented*, 133–134.

90. Ella Taylor, *Prime-Time Families: Television Culture in Postwar America* (Berkeley: University of California Press, 1989), 44. In the 1970s, "family became a forum of rare articulation of social conflicts of all kinds," 65. She points out that television families in the 1970s were either "troubled" (with

divorced or single parents) or "intact" but set in the past, as in *The Waltons* or *Little House on the Prairie*, 50.

91. See Jason Landrum and Deborah Carmichael, "Jeffrey Ruoff's An American Family: A Televised Life—Reviewing the Roots of Reality Television," *Film & History: An Interdisciplinary Journal of Film and Television Studies* 32: 1 (2002); Killen notes that 1973 was a "uniquely creative year" in film. *1973 Nervous Breakdown*, 76.

92. Killen, *1973 Nervous Breakdown*, 76.

93. Among the changes were of course the reproductive rights rulings handed down by the court from *Griswold v. Connecticut* to *Roe v. Wade*.

94. According to Ruoff, phone taps were installed by Susan Raymond. *An American Family*, 46. As Killen observes, the filming in effect "entailed an extensive bugging operation—from telephone taps to the mikes installed throughout the house . . . to the numerous cameras, all positioned to provide maximum coverage." *1973 Nervous Breakdown*, 57. Nixon in 1971 installed a voice-activated recording system that secretly recorded all conversations in the Oval Office. It was more sophisticated than the systems of his predecessors, but not a major departure. FDR had recorded press conferences via a microphone in a lamp on his desk in the Oval Office. JFK used concealed microphones that transmitted to a reel-to-reel recorder in the White House basement. Johnson had secretaries listen in on phone calls when he was Senate majority leader and secretly recorded some phone calls as vice president; as president, he installed microphones in the Cabinet Room, Oval Office, his secretaries' desks, the Situation Room, his White House bedroom, and his ranch in Texas. See Bruce J. Schulman, "Taping History," *Journal of American History* 85: 2 (September 1998): 571–572.

95. Allen D. Grimshaw, "Whose Privacy? What Harm?" *Sociological Methods and Research* 11: 2 (November 1982): 234.

96. Loud, *Pat Loud*, 125. Pat claimed that she was persuaded to tell Bill on camera by both Gilbert and the Raymonds: "Craig wanted me to because he said it was real and inevitable and everything led up to it." She added, "Alan and Susan concurred that Bill should be told of my decision on camera unprepared," 128.

97. Loud, *Pat Loud*, 116–117.

98. Laurie Winer, "Reality Replay," *New Yorker* (April 25, 2011).

99. Ruoff, *An American Family*, 26–27. Bill Loud was able to have a few lines of his removed from an episode, for example; Loud, *Pat Loud*, 134.

100. Ruoff, *An American Family*, 27.

101. Loud, *Pat Loud*, 96, 108, 91.

102. Note that the editors, though they did not spend time with the Louds in person, themselves became enmeshed with the family, feeling that their lives were "becoming more real than our own." Ruoff, *An American Family*, 42.

103. See Loud, *Pat Loud*, 111.
104. Loud, *Pat Loud*, 122. She also said it made the event "less stark a horror," 181.
105. Loud, *Pat Loud*, 122.
106. Loud, *Pat Loud*, 133, 135.
107. Anne Roiphe, "Things Are Keen but Could Be Keener," *New York Times Magazine* (February 18, 1973): 292.
108. Loud, *Pat Loud*, 137.
109. Ruoff, *An American Family*, 105.
110. Shales, "On Camera Again."
111. Pat Loud, Letter to the *Forum for Contemporary History*, February 23, 1973; reprinted in Ron Goulart, *An American Family* (New York: Warner Paperback Library, 1973), 237. As Jeffrey Ruoff writes, it was "the broadcast, not the shooting," that "radically transformed their private lives." *An American Family*, 38.
112. See Ruoff, *An American Family*, xviii, 115.
113. Harrington, "An American Family Lives Its Life on TV," 141.
114. Grimshaw, "Whose Privacy? What Harm?" 239, 234. See *Galella v. Onassis*, 487 F.2d 986 (1973), an early paparazzi case.
115. Calvin Pryluck, "Ultimately We Are All Outsiders: The Ethics of Documentary Filming," *Journal of the University Film Association* 28: 1 (Winter 1976): 21–29; quotes on pp. 21, 23.
116. Pryluck observed that documentarian Frederick Wiseman finds, "as did Allen Funt, of Candid Camera—that few people do object." He noted that Funt would boast that "we get 997 out of every thousand releases without pressure." But that did not surprise him, because he believed the method for obtaining consent to be stacked in the filmmaker's favor: the "initiative and momentum of the situation favor the filmmaker," as did the very presence of the film crew. "Ultimately We Are All Outsiders," 22.
117. Pryluck wrote, "In our society there is a profound social respect for the right to decide for one's self how to live one's life," which includes the right to be free from "harassment, humiliation, shame, and indignity." "Ultimately We Are All Outsiders," 24–25.
118. Shales, "On Camera Again."
119. Elizabeth Jensen, "Lance Loud's Last Testament," *Los Angeles Times*, January 6, 2003, p. E1.
120. Quoted in Ruoff, *An American Family*, xv.
121. Roiphe, "Things Are Keen but Could Be Keener."
122. Pat Loud, Letter to the *Forum for Contemporary History*, 234.
123. See, for example, Harrington, "An American Family Lives Its Life on TV," 141.
124. Ruoff, *An American Family*, 110.

125. Two scholars argue that "the empathy built throughout the series for Mrs. Loud's marital dilemma, the choice between preserving a dysfunctional family or ending the charade of the typically 1950s style ideal family" echoed the "doubts and shifting values" of those watching. Landrum and Carmichael, "Jeffrey Ruoff's An American Family," 68.

126. Abigail McCarthy, "'An American Family' and 'The Family of Man,'" *The Atlantic* (July 1973): 72–76. As she and others noted, Gilbert had searched for a family "already in trouble," one in the mold of the fictional characters in Ross Macdonald's detective novels, also using as a contact Santa Barbara family therapists.

127. Loud, *Pat Loud*, 16, 170. See excerpts of clippings and also letters to Pat, 164–172.

128. Stephanie Harrington noted "the compulsion" with which "you find yourself sticking with the Louds," likening the show to "your favorite soap opera." "An American Family Lives Its Life on TV," 141.

129. Roiphe, "Things Are Keen but Could be Keener."

130. McCarthy, *Private Faces*.

131. McCarthy, "'An American Family' and 'The Family of Man.'"

132. Loud, *Pat Loud*, 92. She added, "Crowds gather around television crews everywhere."

133. Pat Loud, Letter to the *Forum for Contemporary History*, 234. She repeats this in "An American Family: Real-Life Louds Recall Their Days as TV's Louds," *Chicago Tribune*, April 22, 1973, p. A2.

134. Pat Loud, Letter to the *Forum for Contemporary History*, 238.

135. Beck, "Ghost in the Family," 80. See also Richard Schickel, *Intimate Strangers: The Culture of Celebrity in America* (Garden City, NY: Doubleday, 1985).

136. As for herself, "I dragged a bit at first." *Pat Loud*, 90, 109.

137. Harrington, "An American Family Lives Its Life on TV," 141.

138. Less "typical" was the family's size, with five children. Ruoff notes that this exasperated PBS, given that following all seven members of the family would make the filming more expensive than anticipated.

139. See Ruoff, *An American Family*, 67.

140. Loud, *Pat Loud*, 174.

141. Ruoff, *An American Family*, 89.

142. Roiphe, "Things Are Keen but Could be Keener"; Rabinowitz, *They Must Be Represented*, 140–141.

143. Shales, "On Camera Again." On the other hand, both parents at times decried the influence of television on their children. Pat described it as every parent's problem, and Bill remarked that he wished he'd thrown the family's TV set "into the Pacific." Ruoff, *An American Family*, 107.

144. Loud, *Pat Loud*, 125–129. At another point she described the argument in which she confronted Bill with his infidelities as "probably my best scene." Shales, "On Camera Again," p. C10.

145. Loud, *Pat Loud*, 16. Lance too talked about his parents' separation as "a scene" that had been rehearsed many times.

146. Shales, "On Camera Again."

147. Loud, *Pat Loud*, 48.

148. Beck, "Ghost in the Family," 80. A writer for *The New Republic* had made a similar analysis. Roger Rosenblatt argued that "the Louds were born a TV program waiting to be discovered. They had always thought of themselves as a family show." See Killen, *1973 Nervous Breakdown*, 63.

149. Lynn Spigel, *Make Room for TV: Television and the Family Ideal in Postwar America* (Chicago: University of Chicago Press, 1991); Cecilia Tichi, *Electronic Hearth: Creating an American Television Culture* (New York: Oxford University Press, 1991). Andreas Killen sees the series as a response to the "'reality deficit' that TV had itself produced" in vehicles like *The Brady Bunch*. *1973 Nervous Breakdown*, 5. Ella Taylor calls network TV the "uncrowned queen of popular entertainment," with 4.4 million families owning TV sets by 1950 and 50 million sets sold by 1960. *Prime-Time Families*, 20.

150. Taylor, *Prime-Time Families*, 1. She writes that during the first two decades of its history, the "episodic series established itself as television's characteristic genre"; this made for a "continuous chronicle of domesticity that has provided a changing commentary on family life," 17.

151. T. Coffin, "Television's Effects on Leisure-Time Activities," *Journal of Applied Psychology* 32 (1948): 550–558.

152. Vincent M. Rue, "Television and the Family: The Question of Control," *Family Coordinator* 23: 1 (January 1974): 73–81; quotes on 73, 78, 79. For the statistics, see *Television Factbook*, 1969–1970.

153. *Candid Camera* began as a radio show (called *Candid Microphone*) in 1947 and by 1960 was a hit show for CBS (1960–1966), garnering in 1960–1961 the seventh highest ratings in the nation. See Wolfgang Saxon, "Allen Funt, Creator of 'Candid Camera,' is Dead at 84," *New York Times*, September 7, 1999, p. 9. See Fred Nadis, "Citizen Funt: Surveillance as Cold War Entertainment," in *The Tube Has Spoken: Reality TV & History*, ed. Julie Anne Taddeo and Ken Dvorak (Lexington: University Press of Kentucky, 2010), 11–26.

154. Allen Funt, *Eavesdropper at Large: Adventures in Human Nature with 'Candid Mike' and 'Candid Camera'* (New York: Vanguard Press, 1952), 23, 205.

155. Allen Funt and Philip Reed, *Candidly, Allen Funt: A Million Smiles Later* (New York: Barricade Books, 1994) 11.

156. Funt himself noted that up until this point "concealed microphones had been used a good deal in criminology, to some extent by secret government agents, but hardly at all in broadcasting." *Eavesdropper at Large*, 17.

157. Erving Goffman, *The Presentation of Self in Everyday Life* (Garden City, NY: Doubleday, 1959); Daniel J. Boorstin, *The Image: A Guide to Pseudo-Events in America* (New York: Harper & Row 1964).

158. See "An American Family Fights Back," *Boston Globe*, and "Art Is Talking back to Life—The Nelsons Are Hitting the Neilsens," *Chicago Sun-Times*; cited in Ruoff, *An American Family*, 162.

159. John O'Connor, "Mr. & Mrs. Loud, Meet the Bradys," *New York Times*, March 4, 1973, p. 137.

160. Shales, "On Camera Again."

161. This episode of the *Dick Cavett Show* aired February 20, 1973.

162. Warner Paperback Library published a printed version of series, with commentaries appended, to transcripts of twelve episodes plus photos. The back cover read, in all caps, "never before has television probed so close to human truth."

163. O'Connor, "Mr. & Mrs. Loud, Meet the Bradys," p. 137. To another critic, however, Craig Gilbert appeared "distraught—more visibly shaken by the experience than any of the family members." The Louds' criticism "has reportedly driven Gilbert back into psychoanalysis." Shales, "On Camera Again."

164. Ann Japenga, "'An American Family' 8 Years Later," *Los Angeles Times*, January 6, 1980, p. I1.

165. Shales, "On Camera Again."

166. O'Connor, "Mr. & Mrs. Loud, Meet the Bradys."

167. Loud, *Pat Loud*, 162.

168. O'Connor, "Mr. & Mrs. Loud, Meet the Bradys." He noted that the Louds "almost doubled ratings for the Cavett show."

169. Loud, *Pat Loud*, 19.

170. "The Broken Family: Divorce U.S. Style," *Newsweek* (March 12, 1973): 45–57; Tom Donnelly, "The Loud Phenomenon," *Washington Post*, July 1, 1973, p. F1.

171. Donnelly, "The Loud Phenomenon."

172. Harry Shearer, "An American Family: A Televised Life," *Wilson Quarterly* 26: 3 (Summer 2002): 118–119.

173. See Rabinowitz, *They Must Be Represented*, 141. Lance had corresponded with Andy Warhol even before *An American Family* arrived on the scene; afterward he would report for Warhol's *Interview* magazine. Andreas Killen notes Lance's "infatuation with Warhol," dying his hair and beginning a correspondence with him before the series began. *1973 Nervous Breakdown*, 71.

174. Thomas J. Lueck, "Lance Loud, 50, Part of Family Documentary," *New York Times*, December 29, 2001, p. D7.

175. Donnelly, "The Loud Phenomenon." Indeed, journalists kept an eye on the Louds, reporting in 1976 for instance that Pat was reading manuscripts for a New York literary agency; that Bill, now 55, had remarried; and that Lance was appearing in New York nightclubs with his rock band. Tom Bronzini, "Postscript: The Continuing Saga of an American Family," *Los Angeles Times*, October 22, 1976, p. D1; Japenga, "'An American Family' 8 Years Later"; John Carman, "Ho Hum, the Loud Family Is Back," *Atlanta Constitution*, August 11, 1983, p. 7B. A whole series of retrospectives began in 1978, including the film *Five Years Later*, for ABC; the HBO broadcast of Susan and Alan Raymond's *An American Family Revisited* in 1983; and *People's* profile of the family in 1993 to mark the twentieth anniversary of the series. In 1982, one reporter announced, "The surprise ending" was that "the Louds have turned out just fine." The parents had made new lives for themselves on opposite coasts and the five Loud children were out on their own. Lance, at 30, was—almost too neatly—attending the School for Television Arts. Bill said that his former wife was "probably the best friend I have" and that they regularly talked on the phone. The article concluded that the Louds were in better touch with each other, and healthier, than most families. Scott Kraft, "Family Broken on TV Heals in Real Life," *Chicago Tribune*, April 4, 1982, p. B1.
176. Shearer, "An American Family: A Televised Life."
177. Ruoff, *An American Family*, 123.
178. Ruoff, *An American Family*, 106.
179. Pat appeared on TV to promote her autobiography, in which she wrote (some) about appearing on TV. Ruoff, *An American Family*, 123.
180. Harrington, "An American Family Lives Its Life on TV," 141.
181. "American Family: Real-Life Louds Recall Their Days as TV's Louds," p. A2. Bill and Pat had write-ups, and the children were all interviewed separately.
182. As the *New York Times* noted in Lance's obituary, "Perhaps most shocking to an audience that had rarely witnessed frank portrayals of homosexuality on television, were scenes of Mr. Loud himself coming out. He was shown wearing blue lipstick, and, after moving to the Chelsea Hotel in Manhattan, introducing his mother to a world of transvestites and hustlers." Lueck, "Lance Loud, 50, Part of Family Documentary."
183. O'Connor, "Mr. & Mrs. Loud, Meet the Bradys," p. 137.
184. Roiphe, "Things Are Keen but Could be Keener."
185. Here, Roiphe admired Pat's bravery and self-control rather than her emotiveness—her ability to hide her feelings from the camera and maybe from herself.
186. Roiphe's visceral language provoked a strong counter-response from the Gay Activist Alliance and set the wheels turning regarding attention to representations of gays on commercial TV. Killen, *1973 Nervous Breakdown*, 71.

187. Harrington, "An American Family Lives Its Life on TV," 141.
188. Eve Kosofsky Sedgwick, *Epistemology of the Closet*, rev. ed. (Berkeley: University of California Press, 2008), 67.
189. Jenifer Dodd notes that "egoistic" homosexuality remained in the DSM, a kind of compromise measure that allowed some forms of homosexuality to remain pathologized. The American Psychiatric Association specified that those "who are either bothered by, in conflict with, or wish to change their sexual orientation" could still be diagnosed as ill under a new category called "sexual orientation disturbance." "'Compulsive Rapism': Psychiatric Approaches to Sexual Violence in the 1980s" (PhD diss., Vanderbilt University, 2016).
190. Ruoff, *An American Family*, 127–128. The second critic is columnist Frank Rich. Killen calls the series a "touchstone for gay culture." *1973 Nervous Breakdown*, 75.
191. Ruoff, *An American Family*, 127.
192. Catharine A. MacKinnon, "Privacy v. Equality," in *Feminism Unmodified: Discourses on Life and Law* (Cambridge, MA: Harvard University Press, 1987), 100.
193. George Chauncey has argued that "gay people in the pre-war [pre-WWI] years . . . did not speak of coming out of what we call the gay closet but rather of coming out into what they called homosexual society or the gay world, a world neither so small, nor so isolated, nor . . . so hidden as 'closet' implies." *Gay New York: Gender, Urban Culture and the Making of the Gay Male World, 1890–1940* (New York: Pantheon, 1994), 7. Psychologist Evelyn Hooker has been credited with introducing the use of the term "coming out" to the academic community in the 1950s.
194. The homosexual rights movement began to form allegiances with "sympathetic heterosexual liberals" in this period and was in accord about "the right to sexual freedom in private." Larry Gross, *Contested Closets: The Politics and Ethics of Outing* (Minneapolis: University of Minnesota Press, 1993), 146. This is not to say that gay life was marked by "silence, invisibility, and isolation," as John D'Emilio points out in *Sexual Politics, Sexual Communities* (Chicago: University of Chicago Press, 1983)—only that communities often found a logic in keeping their sexuality hidden from outsiders. Marc Stein, *City of Sisterly and Brotherly Loves: Lesbian and Gay Philadelphia, 1945–1972* (Chicago: University of Chicago Press, 2000).
195. Self, *All in the Family*, 78. As Gross notes, after gay liberation came on the scene, "there was no longer any consensus among either homosexuals or their allies that gay rights should be confined to the right to privacy." *Contested Closets*, 146.
196. See William N. Eskridge Jr., "Privacy Jurisprudence and the Apartheid of the Closet, 1946–1961," *Florida State University Law Review* (1997): 703–840; and "Challenging the Apartheid of the Closet: Establishing Conditions for Lesbian

and Gay Intimacy, *Nomos*, and Citizenship, 1961–1981," *Hofstra Law Review* 25 (1997): 817–970.

197. Self, *All in the Family*, 78. In this way, Self argues, sexual freedom "pushed against liberalism's insistence of the sanctity of the line between public and private," 100.

198. Many social movements were coming to terms with lack of visibility as a potentially greater harm than scrutiny in this period. As Kenneth B. Clark had observed in his study of Harlem, African American respondents freely talked about crimes they had committed, which he took as their response to someone actually listening to them. *Dark Ghetto: Dilemmas of Social Power* (New York: Harper & Row, 1965), xviii–ix. The Black Panthers also launched an analysis of social neglect as the other side of the coin to overt oppression. See Alondra Nelson, *Body and Soul: The Black Panthers and the Fight against Medical Discrimination* (Minneapolis: University of Minnesota Press, 2011), 11, 64–65.

199. Humphreys accused Edward Sagarin, a well-known sociologist of homosexuality and critical reviewer of *Tearoom Trade*, of homophobia and came out himself. See Glenn A. Goodwin, Irving Louis Horowitz, and Peter M. Nardi, "Laud Humphreys: A Pioneer in the Practice of Social Science," *Sociological Inquiry* 61: 2 (1991): 145. Sagarin had written one of the earliest calls for homosexual civil equality as a gay man in 1951, under the name of Donald Webster Cory (*The Homosexual in America: A Subjective Approach*). But by the 1970s he was "well known within sociology as a fierce opponent of gay liberation." See Gross, *Contested Closets*, 16–17.

200. *Time's* cover for its September 8, 1975, issue read, "'I Am a Homosexual: The Gay Drive for Acceptance." The issue included two articles, "Gays on the March" and a brief profile of Leonard Matlovich titled "The Sergeant v. the Air Force."

201. "Gays on the March."

202. Laud Humphreys had been chastised for imperiling the collective privacy of men in the tearooms, an instructive contrast.

203. "Gays on the March."

204. William Cooney, "Ex-Marine Probably Saved Ford," *San Francisco Chronicle*, September 23, 1975; Frank Del Olmo and Daryl Lembke, "Ex-Marine Deflects Weapon as Woman Shoots," *Los Angeles Times*, September 23, 1975, p. 3; Daryl Lembke, "Hero in Ford Shooting Active Among S.F. Gays," *Los Angeles Times*, September 25, 1975, p. 3; Fred W. Friendly, "Gays, Privacy and a Free Press," *Washington Post*, April 8, 1990, p. B7. See Elizabeth A. Armstrong, *Forging Gay Identities: Organizing Sexuality in San Francisco, 1950–1994* (Chicago: University of Chicago Press, 2002). *Sipple v. Chronicle Publishing Co.*, 154 Cal. App. 3d 1040 (1984) 201 Cal.Rptr. 665.

205. Goodwin et al., "Laud Humphreys," 144.

206. Goodwin et al., "Laud Humphreys," 146.

207. Irving Louis Horowitz, *Tributes: Personal Reflections on a Century of Social Research* (New Brunswick, NJ: Transaction, 2004), ch. 20. See also Peter M. Nardi, "'The Breastplate of Righteousness': Twenty-Five Years after Laud Humphreys' *Tearoom Trade: Impersonal Sex in Public Places*," *Journal of Homosexuality* 30: 2 (1995): 1–10. Another scholar found that Humphreys's findings held up well two decades later, both the demographics of participants in tearooms and their specific manner of interaction. See Frederick J. Desroches, "Tearoom Trade: A Research Update," *Qualitative Sociology* 13: 1 (1990): 39–61. Phillip Brian Harper praises Humphreys's closing chapter on "What's Wrong with Public Sex" as "an extremely lucid and cogent explication of the problem." *Private Affairs: Critical Ventures in the Culture of Social Relations* (New York: New York University Press, 1999), 74; for the entire discussion, see pp. 73–77. See also Janice M. Irvine, "'The Sociologist as Voyeur': Social Theory and Sexuality Research, 1910–1978," *Qualitative Sociology* 26: 4 (Winter 2003): 429–30.

208. As William Leap wrote, "The regulatory power of the state has *already* established all of these locations [where gay sex occurs] as *public* locations," and that "claims to sexual (and other) privacy are constructed in spite of public regulation." Public and private were thus "relative, almost subjective interpretations of local terrain." He noted the fiction of claims to privacy since they came always with the possibility of intrusion, supervision, and disruption. "In this sense, *all* sites of sexual practice are public locations, and any claims to privacy which unfold there are *fictional* claims." Discussions of "sex-in-public-places," he argued, raise "questions about the meaning of public, and the sources which give the term its regulatory power." Leap, ed., *Public Sex / Gay Space* (New York: Columbia University Press, 1999), 4, 9, 14; emphasis in original. See also Dangerous Bedfellows and Ephen Glenn Colter, eds., *Policing Public Sex: Queer Politics and the Future of AIDS Activism* (Boston: South End Press, 1996).

209. Leap, ed., *Public Sex / Gay Space*, 14. See also Zachary Schrag, *Ethical Imperialism: Institutional Review Boards and the Social Sciences, 1965–2009* (Baltimore: Johns Hopkins University Press, 2010), for more recent arguments about the harm of IRB regulations to research in history.

210. Larry Gross writes, "The gay movement of the early 1980s . . . had placed the right to privacy at the center of its agenda. Flying the same banner liberalizing movements had used to secure the right to contraception and abortion and to force back the forces of sexual censorship, the reformist wing of the gay movement used the rhetoric of privacy rather than the more subversive language of sexual liberation." *Contested Closets*, 33–34.

211. A critic describes the ruling as an example of the way "privacy rights have been gerrymandered by the courts," functioning as "an instrument used by

government to promote socially desirable ways of life, rather than a source of protection for those seeking relief from official coercion." Juliet Williams, "Privacy in the (Too Much) Information Age," in *Public Affairs: Politics in the Age of Sex Scandals*, ed. Paul Apostolidis and Juliet A. Williams (Durham, NC: Duke University Press, 2004), 219–220.

212. Peter Clecak characterized the 1960s and 1970s as ushering in a revolution in the "culture and politics of everyday life" such that "individuals began to conceive of themselves as possessing equal rights to self-fulfillment and to a greater measure of control over their inner and outer lives." *America's Quest for the Ideal Self: Dissent and Fulfillment in the 60s and 70s* (New York: Oxford University Press, 1983), 212–213.

213. The 1970s gay liberation movement, writes historian Heather Murray, "marked a moment of hope that gay individuals would no longer just be faintly—or even pruriently—imagined figures in North American life." This early, ebullient moment passed fairly quickly. *Not in This Family: Gays and the Meaning of Kinship in Postwar North America* (Philadelphia: University of Pennsylvania Press, 2010), 78.

214. This was Scott Tucker, quoted in Gross, *Contested Closets*, 146. See Scott Tucker, *The Queer Question: Essays on Desire and Democracy*, with a foreword by Sarah Schulman (Boston: South End Press, 1997).

215. Gross, *Contested Closets*, 146.

216. *Bowers v. Hardwick*, 478 U.S. 186 (1986). The ruling aligned with a neoconservative definition of privacy that was explicitly normative and aimed to preserve a certain version of heterosexual privilege even as it enlisted a libertarian understanding of privacy in the economic sphere.

217. Conservatives referred to it derisively as the "so-called right of privacy" and skepticism about privacy rights had helped torpedo Robert Bork's Supreme Court nomination; by the 1980s, this was "becoming something of a secret handshake on the right," Jamal Greene notes. "The So-Called Right to Privacy," *UC Davis Law Review* 43 (2010): 715–747.

218. Marc Stein, *Sexual Injustice: Supreme Court Decisions from* Griswold *to* Roe (Chapel Hill: University of North Carolina Press, 2010). *Lawrence v. Texas*, 539 U.S. 558 (2003).

219. Richard D. Mohr, *Gay Ideas: Outing and Other Controversies* (Boston: Beacon Press, 1992), 17.

220. Deborah Nelson, *Pursuing Privacy in Cold War America* (New York: Columbia University Press, 2002), 158. See also Kendall Thomas, "Beyond the Privacy Principle," *Columbia Law Review* 92 (1992): 1461–1467; Janet Halley, "Reasoning about Sodomy: Act and Identity in and after *Bowers v. Hardwick*," *Virginia Law Review* 79 (1993): 1721–1780; and Lauren Berlant, *The Queen of*

America Goes to Washington City: Essays on Sex and Citizenship (Durham, NC: Duke University Press, 1997).

221. The disease was initially referred to as "gay related immune disorder"; by 1982 it had been renamed "acquired immunodeficiency syndrome" by the Centers for Disease Control. Steven Epstein, *Impure Science: AIDS, Activism and the Politics of Knowledge* (Berkeley: University of California Press, 1996), 46–48. Heather Murray gives the figure of 5,600 deaths by 1984 and nearly 50,000 by 1988. *Not in This Family*, 137, citing Sean Wilentz, *The Age of Reagan: A History, 1974–2008* (New York: HarperCollins, 2008), 186. See also John D'Emilio and Estelle B. Freedman, *Intimate Matters: A History of Sexuality in America* (New York: Harper and Row, 1988), 354–355. Reagan would not discuss AIDS publicly until 1987. See Dennis Altman, *AIDS in the Mind of America* (Garden City, NY: Doubleday, 1986), 118.

222. Carol Sanger, *About Abortion: Terminating Pregnancy in Twenty-First-Century America* (Cambridge, MA: Belknap Press of Harvard University Press, 2017), 223. As Fairchild et al. write, "By writing and speaking publicly about their experiences, women with cancer sought to remove the stigma and silence they saw as surrounding the disease; they challenged existing treatment paradigms and demanded a great role in medical decision making." They also "demanded to be counted," for both symbolic and political reasons. As would be the case with AIDS visibility, activists claimed that "the government was devoting paltry financial resources to a problem of unrecognized magnitude. Surveillance thus became a lever in a struggle for greater government funding that would drive research agendas." The Cancer Registries Amendment Act was signed into law in 1992. See Amy L. Fairchild, Ronald Bayer, and James Colgrove with Daniel Wolfe, *Searching Eyes: Privacy, the State, and Disease Surveillance in America* (Berkeley: University of California Press, 2007), 135.

223. Mohr writes that "it is no accident that the outing movement . . . came into being almost simultaneously—in the early spring of 1990—with the coming into being of the social and political movement Queer Nation," which was committed to the visibility of gay life. *Gay Ideas*, 47.

224. See Randy Shilts, *And the Band Played On: Politics, People, and the AIDS Epidemic* (New York: St. Martin's, 1987); Martin Duberman, *Cures: A Gay Man's Odyssey* (New York: Dutton, 1991); and Epstein, *Impure Knowledge*.

225. There was strong opposition by privacy and gay rights activists to the reporting of HIV-infected people to state public health registries, despite pledges of confidentiality from health officials. This was unlike the case of cancer registries in this period, where "many people with illness would demand the right to be counted so that the extent of their afflictions could serve as a prod for social reform and ameliorative legislation." Fairchild et al., *Searching Eyes*,

137, 228–229, xix. See their more general discussion of the right to privacy and patient advocacy, 83–112.

226. Quoted in Michelangelo Signorile, *Queer in America: Sex, the Media, and the Closets of Power* (Madison: University of Wisconsin Press, 1993; 2003), 87.

227. Joshua Gamson, "Silence, Death, and the Invisible Enemy: AIDS Activism and Social Movement 'Newness,'" *Social Problems* 36 (1989): 351–367.

228. Lee Edelman, *Homographesis: Essays in Gay Literary and Cultural Theory* (New York: Routledge, 1994), 82. Edelman criticized the slogan for its "insistence upon the therapeutic property of discourse without specifying in any way what should or must be said. Indeed, as a text produced in response to a medical and political emergency, 'Silence=Death' is a stunningly self-reflexive slogan," 87.

229. By deliberate contrast, the national project of an AIDS quilt publicized names of those who died of the disease. On press treatments of AIDS, see Gross, *Contested Closets*, 53. He notes that the *San Francisco Chronicle* was the only major newspaper to report AIDS deaths as such, but that gay readers became astute decoders of obituaries.

230. Murray, *Not in This Family*, 192.

231. Gross, *Contested Closets*, 34.

232. Signorile, *Queer in America*, 70. Note his reference to *Bowers v. Hardwick* as a "crushing blow," 86–87. See also Vito Russo, *The Celluloid Closet: Homosexuality in the Movies* (New York: Harper & Row, 1981).

233. Gross, *Contested Closets*, 35; Signorile, *Queer in America*, 73.

234. Signorile, *Queer in America*, xv.

235. Michelangelo Signorile, "The Secret Gay Life of Malcolm Forbes," *OutWeek* (March 18, 1999): 40.

236. See Kenji Yoshino, "Covering," *Yale Law Journal* 111 (2011): 769–939.

237. Signorile, *Queer in America*, 73. Roger Rosenblatt characterized outing as a logical contradiction that implied "homosexuals have a right to private choice but not to private lives." "Who Killed Privacy?" *New York Times Magazine* (January 31, 1993): 24–28.

238. Signorile, *Queer in America*, xv.

239. Signorile, *Queer in America*, 68; see also 192.

240. Richard Mohr noted in 1992 that outing was almost universally opposed in the gay press and within gay political and legal organizations. *Gay Ideas*, 11–12. Andrew Sullivan, gay conservative and editor of *The New Republic*, was among those who denounced what he called "queer revolt" and liberationist homosexual politics, exemplified by celebrity outing. Sullivan argued that outing "depends upon the kind of discourse in which something hidden is revealed, something shameful exposed, something secret stigmatized," *Virtually*

Normal: An Argument about Homosexuality (New York: Alfred A. Knopf, 1995), 78–79. See also Harper's discussion in *Private Affairs*, 89–124.

241. See Margot Canaday's discussion of "blue" or undesirable discharges, between honorable and dishonorable, which allowed the impression "that there is something radically wrong with the man in question"—"something so mysterious that it cannot be talked about or written down but must be left to the imagination." "Building a Straight State: Sexuality and Social Citizenship under the 1944 G.I. Bill," *Journal of American History* 90: 3 (2003): 949. She notes that some preferred dishonorable discharge to the implication of homosexuality; indeed, going AWOL was a lesser stigma than being known as a homosexual, 952.

242. Signorile, *Queer in America*, 76, 313–315, 163.

243. Signorile, *Queer in America*, 75.

244. Gross, *Contested Closets*, 57.

245. Signorile, *Queer in America*, 80; emphasis in original.

246. Adding to the sensation was the fact that the Starr Report was made available online. Office of the Independent Counsel, Referral to the U.S. House of Representatives pursuant to Title 28, United States Code § 595(c), September 9, 1998, accessed at http://thomas.loc.gov/icreport/. For interpretations, see Lauren Berlant and Lisa Duggan, eds., *Our Monica, Ourselves: The Clinton Affair and the National Interest* (New York: New York University Press, 2001); and Paul Apostolidis and Juliet A. Williams, eds., *Public Affairs: Politics in the Age of Sex Scandals* (Durham, NC: Duke University Press, 2004).

247. Renata Adler described Lewinsky as "not one to understate" her reported nine "in-person" sexual encounters with the president. "Decoding the Starr Report," *Vanity Fair* (December 1998): 118. See Lauren Berlant, *The Female Complaint: The Unfinished Business of Sentimentality in American Culture* (Durham, NC: Duke University Press, 2008); Thompson, *Political Scandal*; and Wesley O. Hagood, *Presidential Sex: From the Founding Fathers to Bill Clinton* (Secaucus, NJ: Carol Publishing Group, 1998).

248. William J. Clinton and Hillary Clinton, "Governor and Mrs. Bill Clinton Discuss Adultery," *60 Minutes*, NBC, January 26, 1992.

249. See Joan Didion, "Clinton Agonistes," *New York Review of Books* (October 22, 1998): 16–23.

250. As Dave Tell notes, many applauded this performance. A. M. Rosenthal, the conservative columnist, wrote that the Clintons gave the American people "a gift" by treating them "as adults." He added: "we can at least treasure the hope that Americans would be fed up with the slavering inquisition on politicians' sexual history." Dave Tell, *Confessional Crises and Cultural Politics in Twentieth-Century America* (University Park: Pennsylvania State University Press, 2013), 162.

251. Bauer, *The Art of the Public Grovel*, 178. The 50 percent figure is for the time between January 21 and April 20, 1998.

252. Bauer, *The Art of the Public Grovel*, 244.

253. Adler, "Decoding the Starr Report," 116–24, 128–36; quotes on pp. 116 and 118.

254. Didion, "Clinton Agonistes," 22.

255. William Bennett, *The Death of Outrage*; quoted by Tell, *Confessional Crises*, 163.

256. As many noted, partisans would reverse the positions they had taken in the Clarence Thomas–Anita Hill controversy that erupted with Thomas's nomination to the Supreme Court in 1992.

257. All quoted in Tell, *Confessional Crises*, 168, 162.

258. Adler, "Decoding the Starr Report," 116.

259. Adler, "Decoding the Starr Report," 134.

260. Bauer, *Art of the Public Grovel*, 162.

261. Nancy Cott argues that public acceptance of Clinton's affairs demonstrates that "his sexual transgressions were between him and his wife" and that a decoupling of marriage from public morality had been effected, such that marriage was no longer a "pillar of the state." *Public Vows*, 199–200. Didion, "Clinton Agonistes," 20. See also Barbara Leah Harman, "In Internet Age, Not Even President Has Privacy," *New York Times*, September 19, 1998, p. A14. Noting Clinton's high levels of support from African Americans in particular, Orlando Patterson argued that "one reason African-Americans have so steadfastly stood by the President, in spite of his having done so little for them, is that "their history has been one long violation of their privacy." "What is Freedom without Privacy," *New York Times*, September 15, 1998, p. A27. Some cultural critics noticed that, no matter how beleaguered the president, his assumption that it was public office that had revoked his privacy marginalized the daily violations of privacy suffered by minorities in the United States. By insisting that "even Presidents have private lives," Clinton implied that ordinary citizens did have that privilege, "for whom it remains unproblematically inviolate so long as they do not voluntarily, altruistically, assume the responsibilities of public office." Harper, *Private Affairs*, x.

262. Peter Brooks, *Troubling Confessions* (Chicago: University of Chicago Press, 2000), 167.

263. Susan Bauer argues that Clinton's first statement was not contrite enough and too legalistic for many commentators, but an August statement to the public and a "confession" at a September prayer breakfast in Washington, DC, fit the bill much better. See her discussion of Clinton's multiple confessions in *The Art of the Public Grovel*, 152–182. Tell argues that by this point there was a battle over "which standards should govern public confession." *Confessional Crises*, 153.

8. Stories of One's Self

1. Others have used the phrases "the society of self-disclosure" or "the expository society." See John B. Thompson, "The New Visibility," *Theory, Culture and Society* 22 (2005): 38–39; and Bernard E. Harcourt, *Exposed: Desire and Disobedience in the Digital Age* (Cambridge, MA: Harvard University Press, 2015).

2. David Bromwich, "How Publicity Makes People Real," *Social Research* 68: 1 (Spring 2001): 145. This entire issue of *Social Research* is devoted to privacy, concluding with a discussion of the question, "Is Privacy Now Possible?" A sign of the times, just a year earlier, *Social Philosophy and Policy* 17: 2 (Summer 2000) also dedicated an entire issue to privacy.

3. Anita L. Allen, *Unpopular Privacy: What Must We Hide?* (New York: Oxford University Press, 2011), xi, xii. She cites some moves already made in this direction, such as the Children's Online Privacy Protection Act of 1998, designed to prevent children under 13 from disclosing personal data to websites. Why not, she asks, extend such restrictions to adults?

4. For example, *Whalen v. Roe*, 429 U.S. 589 (1977).

5. Peter Brooks, *Troubling Confessions* (Chicago: University of Chicago Press, 2000), 4. Brooks provides a capsule history of criminal and Catholic confession. He and other scholars point to Augustine's confessions and spiritual autobiography as the oldest published form of confessional speech. These would be modernized by writers like Daniel Defoe and Jean-Jacques Rousseau in the eighteenth century, which is sometimes seen as the first "memoir boom."

6. Brooks, *Troubling Confessions*, 4, 140, 9.

7. Brooks, *Troubling Confessions*, 89.

8. One scholar of the confessional turn, for example, states merely that it is "well known and well documented" that we live in a "confessional culture." Dave Tell, *Confessional Crises and Cultural Politics in Twentieth-Century America* (University Park: Pennsylvania State University Press, 2013), 1. For many, the point of departure is Michel Foucault's statement: "We have become a singularly confessing society. . . . One confesses in public and in private, to one's parents, one's educators, one's doctor, to those one loves; one admits to oneself, in pleasure and in pain, things it would be impossible to tell to anyone else, the things people write books about. One confesses—or is forced to confess." *The History of Sexuality*, trans. Robert Hurley, vol. 1 (New York: Pantheon, 1978), 59.

9. Gini Graham Scott, *Can We Talk? The Power and Influence of Talk Shows* (New York: Insight Books, 1996).

10. Susan Harding, *The Book of Jerry Falwell: Fundamentalist Language and Politics* (Princeton, NJ: Princeton University Press, 2000), especially 153–182;

Susan Wise Bauer, *The Art of the Public Grovel: Sexual Sin and Public Confession in America* (Princeton, NJ: Princeton University Press, 2008).

11. Mari Boor Tonn, for example, notes that the 1990s saw "increasing casting of social controversies such as affirmative action, escalating crime, and welfare reform in the language of 'conversation,' 'dialogue,' and the therapeutic talk of healing, dysfunction, coping, self-esteem, and empowerment." "Taking Conversation, Dialogue, and Therapy Public," *Rhetoric & Public Affairs* 8: 3 (2005): 405–430; quote on p. 405. See Wendy Kaminer, *I'm Dysfunctional, You're Dysfunctional: The Recovery Movement and Other Self-Help Fashions* (Reading, MA: Addison-Wesley, 1992); Leslie Irvine, *Codependent Forevermore: The Invention of Self in a Twelve-Step Group* (Chicago: University of Chicago Press, 1999); and Eva S. Moskowitz, *In Therapy We Trust: America's Obsession with Self-Fulfillment* (Baltimore: Johns Hopkins University Press, 2001), 218–278.

12. The uptick of the "apology phenomenon" in the later 1990s is the subject of Aaron Lazare, *On Apology* (New York: Oxford University Press, 2004), 6–7. He views pseudo apologies as part of "so many trash confessional and forgiveness programs on television," 9.

13. See Tell, *Confessional Crises*, 146–179

14. Bauer, *Art of the Public Grovel*, 159.

15. Brooks, *Troubling Confessions*, 167.

16. Leigh Ann Wheeler, *How Sex Became a Civil Liberty* (New York: Oxford University Press, 2013), 168. At mid-decade, the ACLU received letters from all over the country complaining of this practice, a response to an era of unprecedented sexual visibility in books, magazines, and movies, 165. Others insisted that there is "no right of privacy for people in the public arena" and there could be no restrictions on speech under the First Amendment, 168. While the emphasis would be on free speech, there was a successful campaign for protections of postal privacy following complaints (200,000 in 1966 alone) about unsolicited sexual mailings. In 1970, the Supreme Court announced that "a mailer's right to communicate" must "stop at the mailbox of an unreceptive addressee" in order to "protect minors and the privacy of homes," 87.

17. Gary T. Marx, *Windows into the Soul: Surveillance and Society in an Age of High Technology* (Chicago: University of Chicago Press, 2016), 30.

18. Daniel Mendelsohn, "But Enough about Me: What Does the Popularity of Memoirs Tell Us about Ourselves?" *New Yorker* (January 25, 2010).

19. See Alan F. Westin, *Privacy and Freedom* (New York: Atheneum, 1967), 53.

20. Brooks, *Troubling Confessions*, 9, 4, 140.

21. Tell, *Confessional Crises*, 2. He notes that *True Story* was not classified as a "confession magazine" until the 1950s, however; 21.

22. See, for example, John F. Kasson, *Amusing the Million: Coney Island at the Turn of the Century* (New York: Hill & Wang, 1978); Kathy Peiss, *Cheap*

Amusements: Working Women and Leisure in Turn-of-the-Century New York (Philadelphia: Temple University Press, 1986); Claude S. Fischer, *America Calling: A Social History of the Telephone to 1940* (Berkeley: University of California Press, 1992); Philip Cushman, *Constructing the Self, Constructing America: A Cultural History of Psychotherapy* (Reading, MA: Addison-Wesley, 1995); Deborah Nelson, *Pursuing Privacy in Cold War America* (New York: Columbia University Press, 2002), who describes confessional poetry as part of a "general personalizing of public discourse in the cold war era," 31; and Sam Binkley, *Getting Loose: Lifestyle Consumption in the 1970s* (Durham, NC: Duke University Press, 2007).

23. Peter Brooks observes that Catholic confessions began as public acts. *Troubling Confessions*, 91.

24. Bauer, *The Art of the Public Grovel*, 5, 63, 68–69, 122. In 1960, the Federal Communications Commission changed its policy from allotting time for free to recognized mainline religious groups to selling airtime to fulfill public service programming, 70. On Graham's influence, see Grant Wacker, *America's Pastor: Billy Graham and the Shaping of a Nation* (Cambridge, MA: Belknap Press of Harvard University Press, 2014); and George M. Marsden, *Fundamentalism and American Culture*, 2nd ed. (New York: Oxford University Press, 2006).

25. Bauer, *The Art of the Public Grovel*, 118. She writes that the Bakkers' show was "a confessional program not primarily because of the Bakkers' religious bent, but because the talk shows of the 1980s were fundamentally confessional." Implicated in scandals, the Bakkers quit their television program in 1987, thirteen years after it was first aired.

26. Ellen Herman, *The Romance of American Psychology: Political Culture in an Age of Experts* (Berkeley: University of California Press, 1994).

27. Essayist V. S. Pritchett, for example, noted the "tremendous expansion in autobiographical writing" already in 1956, ascribing it in part to the "dominant influence of psychological theory." Quoted in Ben Yagoda, *Memoir: A History* (New York: Riverhead Books, 2009), 238.

28. On the therapeutic, see Elisabeth Lasch-Quinn, "Liberation Therapeutics: From Moral Renewal to Consciousness Raising," in *Therapeutic Culture: Triumph and Defeat*, ed. Jonathan B. Imber (New Brunswick, NJ: Transaction, 2004), 3–18. She writes of the "belief in primacy of personal authenticity, now associated with emotional disclosure" and the retreat from politics to psychic solace or self-help such that the therapeutic self triumphs over the citizen. Also see James Nolan, *The Therapeutic State: Justifying Government at Century's End* (New York: New York University Press, 1998); Lauren Berlant, *The Female Complaint: The Unfinished Business of Sentimentality in American Culture* (Durham, NC: Duke University Press, 2008); and Elizabeth

Lunbeck, *The Americanization of Narcissism* (Cambridge, MA: Harvard University Press, 2014).

29. Est (Erhard Seminars Training), for example, was a two-weekend course that offered personal transformation, accountability and possibility. See Sheridan Fenwick, *Getting It: The Psychology of est* (New York: J. B. Lippincott, 1976).

30. Jessica Grogan chronicles the movement in *Encountering America: Humanistic Psychology, Sixties Culture, and the Shaping of the Modern Self* (New York: Perennial, 2013), 19; on encounter groups specifically, see 189–208. For some participants, she writes, "These unconstrained opportunities for self-expression were wildly liberating," expressing an "extraordinary desire for emotional intensity." Encounter groups came out of academia and corporate training. T-groups of the 1950s and early 1960s had emerged at National Training Laboratories in Bethel, Maine, and were focused on working together; analyzing experiences, feelings, perceptions, and behaviors; and the realm of interpersonal dynamics rather than personal transformation, 192–193.

31. Joy Gould Boyum, "Cinema Verite's Orwellian Aspect," *Wall Street Journal*, May 4, 1973, p. 10.

32. Boyum, "Cinema Verite's Orwellian Aspect," 10. Boyum was reviewing John Whitmore's 1973 documentary on encounter groups, *Here Comes Every Body*.

33. The *Oprah Winfrey Show* aired from September 8, 1986, to May 25, 2011, and remains the highest-rated talk show in television history. In 2009 its viewership was estimated at 42 million a week in the United States alone. See Kathryn Lofton, *Oprah: The Gospel of an Icon* (Berkeley: University of California Press, 2011), 2–3; and Franny Nudelman, "Beyond the Talking Cure: Listening to Female Testimony on The Oprah Winfrey Show," in *Inventing the Psychological: Toward a Cultural History of Emotional Life in America*, ed. Joel Pfister and Nancy Schnog (New Haven, CT: Yale University Press, 1997), 302. See also Micki McGee, *Self-Help, Inc.: Makeover Culture in American Life* (New York: Oxford University Press, 2005).

34. Jeremy Green, "Jonathan Franzen, Oprah Winfrey, and the Future of the Social Novel," in *Late Postmodernism: American Fiction at the Millennium* (New York: Palgrave Macmillan, 2005), 88. See also Adrian Jones, "Oprah on the Couch: Franzen, Frey, Foucault, and the Book Club Confessions," in *Compelling Confessions: The Politics of Personal Disclosure*, ed. Suzanne Diamond (Madison, NJ: Fairleigh Dickinson University Press, 2011), 94–109.

35. Lofton, *Oprah*, 8, 4. As she notes, Winfrey's turn from TV as entertainment to TV as transformation in the mid-1990s was a response to her weariness with the exhibitionism of "trash TV." Janice Peck details the program's "configura-

tion of self, illness, and technology of healing," in *The Age of Oprah: Cultural Icon for the Neoliberal Era* (Boulder, CO: Paradigm, 2008), 39.

36. Many observers have blamed these developments on the "personal politics" of the 1960s and 1970, and especially the feminist movement. See Jean Bethke Elshtain, "The Displacement of Politics," in *Public and Private in Thought and Practice*, ed. Jeff Weintraub and Krishan Kumar (Chicago: University of Chicago Press, 1997), 166–181; and Christopher Lasch, *The Culture of Narcissism: American Life in an Age of Diminishing Expectations* (New York: Norton, 1978), 3–30.

37. Nancy Fraser, "From Redistribution to Recognition? Dilemmas of Justice in a 'Post-Socialist' Age," *New Left Review* 212 (July–August 1995): 68–93.

38. Anthony Giddens, *Modernity and Self-Identity: Self and Society in the Late Modern Age* (Stanford, CA: Stanford University Press, 1991), 225.

39. Heather Murray, *Not in This Family: Gays and the Meaning of Kinship in Postwar North America* (Philadelphia: University of Pennsylvania Press, 2010), 183. Murray explains that parents and children were urged to talk through these matters together and that parents themselves began speaking more publicly about their relationships with their gay and lesbian children in the 1990s; see p. 189. She links this trend to the coincident rise of the "tell-all biography genre." See Evan Ember-Black, *Secrets in Families and Family Therapy* (New York: W. W. Norton, 1993); and Jeffrey Weeks, "Intimate Citizenship and the Culture of Sexual Story Telling," in *Sexual Cultures: Community, Values and Intimacy*, ed. Jeffrey Weeks and Janet Hollands (New York: St. Martin's, 1996), 34–52.

40. Blanche Wiesen Cook writes about the continuing "romance of the closet" in the 1980s and 1990s. "Outing History," in *The Seductions of Biography*, ed. Mary Rhiel and David Suchoff (New York: Routledge, 1996), 70.

41. Murray, *Not in This Family*, 193–195. Revealing how far the scales were tipping toward disclosure, Murray writes that "discretion was a scarcely acknowledged strategy or value" within gay culture and politics in this period.

42. Pat Loud with Nora Johnson, *Pat Loud: A Woman's Story* (New York: Bantam Books, 1974). Jeffrey Ruoff, *An American Family: A Televised Life* (Minneapolis: University of Minnesota Press, 2002), 135.

43. Loud, *Pat Loud*, 15; emphasis in original.

44. Quoted in Andreas Killen, *1973 Nervous Breakdown: Watergate, Warhol, and the Birth of Post-Sixties America* (New York: Bloomsbury, 2006), 61; Ruoff, *An American Family*, 106.

45. Stephanie Harrington, "An American Family Lives Its Life on TV," *New York Times*, January 7, 1973, p. 141.

46. Loud, *Pat Loud*, 56.

47. Even those who saw the genre as very old thought there was something new afoot, although they couldn't always put their finger on it. As Daniel Mendelsohn noted, "Confessional memoirs have been irresistible to both writers and readers for a very long time, and, pretty much from the beginning, people have been complaining about the shallowness, the opportunism, the lying, the betrayals, the narcissism. This raises the question of just why the current spate of autobiography feels somehow different, somehow 'worse' than ever before—more narcissistic and more disturbing in its implications." "But Enough about Me."

48. Yagoda, *Memoir*, 226–227.

49. Mendelsohn, "But Enough about Me." Sven Birkerts employs the term "traumatic memoir" to describe "a distinct subgenre" in which the memoirists engage in "private salvage operations." *The Art of Time in Memoir: Then, Again* (St. Paul, MN: Graywolf Press, 2008), 145.

50. Sidonie Smith, *Subjectivity, Identity, and the Body: Women's Autobiographical Practices in the Twentieth Century* (Bloomington: Indiana University Press, 1993), 159.

51. Ann Fabian, *The Unvarnished Truth: Personal Narratives in Nineteenth-Century America* (Berkeley: University of California Press, 2000).

52. See Henry Louis Gates Jr., ed., *The Classic Slave Narratives* (New York: Signet, 2002).

53. Yagoda, *Memoir*, 2.

54. Tom Donnelly, "A Life Story Mighty like a Novel," *Washington Post*, April 9, 1974, p. B1.

55. Robert Kirsch, "Pat Loud a Part of the Age of Exposure," *Los Angeles Times*, April 28, 1974, p. O62.

56. Kirsch, "Pat Loud a Part of the Age of Exposure." Indeed, a film scholar calls Pat's chapters on *An American Family* "the most remarkable testimony by the subject of a documentary in the history of the medium." Ruoff, *An American Family*, 125.

57. Loud, *Pat Loud*, 19.

58. Bill Loud claimed that his ex-wife received $150,000 for writing the autobiography.

59. She referenced her shared fate with McGovern's short-lived vice presidential running mate in 1972: "Me and Eagleton, with our brief flashes of fame," Loud, *Pat Loud*, 214.

60. In 1980, the rest of the Louds were still talking to the press but Pat, wrote a reporter, "simply doesn't want to talk about the series anymore. 'I'm a literary agent,' she says. 'I just work. My family is very ordinary.'" Ann Japenga, "'An American Family' 8 Years Later," *Los Angeles Times*, January 6, 1980, p. I1.

61. The same article also quotes Lance as saying that while he has views on the series, "I'm through giving them away." Scott Kraft, "Family Broken on TV Heals in Real Life," *Chicago Tribune*, April 4, 1982, p. B1.

62. Loud, *Pat Loud*, 216.

63. Loud, *Pat Loud*, 218; emphasis in original.

64. Ruoff, *An American Family*, 123. For the particular modes and impulses behind women's autobiographies, see Smith, *Subjectivity, Identity, and the Body*.

65. Betty Ford with Chris Chase, *The Times of My Life* (New York: Harper & Row, 1978), 187–189, 193.

66. It was known for instance, that Ford was prescribed muscle relaxants; see "Betty Ford Faces Surgery," *Chicago Tribune*, September 28, 1974, p. N1.

67. John Robert Greene, *Betty Ford: Candor and Courage in the White House* (Lawrence: University Press of Kansas, 2004), 112–113; Betty Ford with Chris Chase, *Betty: A Glad Awakening* (Garden City, NY: Doubleday, 1987).

68. Greene, *Betty Ford*, 111.

69. Greene, *Betty Ford*, 113.

70. Yagoda cites Mary Jane Ward's *The Snake Pit* (1946) and *The Final Face of Eve* (1958); Sylvia Plath's *The Bell Jar* (published as Victoria Lucas, 1963); and Joanne Greenberg's *I Never Promised You a Rose Garden* (published as Hannah Greene, 1964). Anne Sexton's "confessional" poems of the same era were the exception rather than the rule.

71. Yagoda, *Memoir*, 215.

72. Yagoda, *Memoir*, 220.

73. Yagoda, *Memoir*, 282. *The Diary of Anne Frank* was first published in English in 1952, and Elie Wiesel's *Night* was translated into English in 1960 (and was variously classified as a novel, memoir, nonfiction account, and "autobiographical novel"). Gary Weissman notes that the new attention paid to the Holocaust by the American public occurred circa 1978, the year Jimmy Carter established the President's Commission on the Holocaust and a major miniseries was aired; he notes that the term "the Holocaust" became widely used in the United States in the 1960s largely through memoirs and anthologies. *Fantasies of Witnessing: Postwar Efforts to Experience the Holocaust* (Ithaca, NY: Cornell University Press, 2004), 8–9, 24.

74. Yagoda, *Memoir*, 226–227.

75. See Yagoda's catalog of titles from 1989 to 1997. *Memoir*, 227–228. Peter D. Kramer observed in 1996 that across the twentieth century there was about "one book per decade" on melancholy or depression ("a bit more if chronicles of mania are included"), but that the 1990s had thus far produced a flood of such accounts. "Bookend: The Anatomy of Melancholy," *New York Times* Book Review, April 7, 1996, p. 27.

76. William Styron, *Darkness Visible: A Memoir of Madness* (New York: Random House, 1990); Kramer, "Bookend: The Anatomy of Melancholy"; James Atlas, "The Age of The Literary Memoir Is Now," *New York Times Magazine* (May 12, 1996): 25. Atlas cited approximately 200 memoirs published in the prior year.

77. Styron is quoted in Victoria Glendinning, "A Howling Tempest in the Brain," *New York Times* Book Review, August 19, 1990, p. 1.

78. Mendelsohn, "But Enough about Me."

79. Joshua Gamson, "Taking the Talk Show Challenge: Television, Emotion, and Public Spheres," *Constellations* 6: 2 (December 2002): 190–205; quote on p. 195.

80. Yagoda, *Memoir*, 238–239.

81. One scholar argues that documentaries appeal to viewers through "the pleasure in knowing" that comes from the "closer indexical relation to the real" and "more intimate connection to the real world" they offer as compared to fiction. This scholar is Bill Nichols, as referenced in Barry Keith Grant and Jeannette Sloniowski, eds., *Documenting the Documentary: Close Readings of Documentary Film and Video* (Detroit: Wayne State University Press, 1998), 20.

82. Bennett Cerf as quoted in Yagoda, *Memoir*, 239.

83. Leigh Gilmore, *The Limits of Autobiography: Trauma and Testimony* (Ithaca, NY: Cornell University Press, 2000). She notes that this impulse has sometimes led to the mislabeling of fiction as memoir.

84. Atlas, "The Age of The Literary Memoir Is Now"; emphasis in original.

85. Atlas, "The Age of the Literary Memoir."

86. This phrase was found in Amazon's review of *The Kiss*; see discussion below.

87. Yagoda, *Memoir*, 228.

88. Kathryn Harrison, *The Kiss* (New York: Random House, 1997). Like many memoirists of the 1990s, Harrison got her start as a novelist, alluding to these same themes in her fiction, including *Exposure* (New York: Random House, 1993).

89. Review of *The Kiss*, Amazon.com: https://amazon.com/Kiss-Memoir-Kathryn -Harrison/dp/0812979710/ref=sr_1_1?s=books&ie=UTF8&qid=1502124018&sr=1 -1&keywords=the+kiss+harrison.

90. Lisa Schwarzbaum, "Did Kathryn Harrison's New Memoir Go too Far?" *Entertainment Weekly* (March 21, 1997). Schwarzbaum asked her question with regard to the living people the memoir implicated: Harrison's father, spouse, and two young children.

91. Harrison, book notes, *The Kiss*, 227, 231, 233.

92. As Carol Sanger notes, this silence around abortion persisted even as strictures about other taboo topics—cancer, depression, divorce, homosexuality—

loosened. *About Abortion: Terminating Pregnancy in Twenty-First-Century America* (Cambridge, MA: Belknap Press of Harvard University Press, 2017), xiii, 22. She notes that courts treat abortion, like mental illness, personal safety, homosexuality, transsexuality, and illegitimate or abandoned children in welfare cases, as a justification for anonymity, 46. She also notes some moves toward disclosure, such as a recent "abortion voices project" and #ShoutYour-Abortion, 227.

93. E. L. Godkin, "The Census Questions," *Nation* 50 (June 5, 1890): 445.

94. William Grimes, "We All Have A Life: Must We All Write about It?" *New York Times,* March 25, 2005, p. E27.

95. Mendelsohn, "But Enough about Me." Some memoirists in fact compared the work of writing to the psychological process of therapy; see Birkerts, *The Art of Time in Memoir,* 115, 145–146, 155.

96. Atlas, "The Age of The Literary Memoir Is Now." See also William Gass, "The Art of Self: Autobiography in an Age of Narcissism," *Harper's* (May 2014).

97. Susanna Kaysen, *Girl, Interrupted* (New York: Turtle Bay Books, 1993). See Andrea Sachs, "Books: The Unconfessional Confessionalist," *Time* (July 11, 1994): 60. The memoir was the basis for a 1999 film.

98. Review of *The Camera My Mother Gave Me* in *Publishers' Weekly;* www .publishersweekly.com/978-0-679-44390-2.

99. Kaysen, *Girl, Interrupted,* 94.

100. Yagoda, *Memoir,* 228.

101. Similarly, Kathryn Harrison's novel *Exposure* raised many of the issues of her later memoir about incest. In it, the father is a photographer and Harrison inserts in the text excerpts from newspaper articles, letters, museum catalogs, court proceedings, and so on: "as if Ann [the protagonist] can characterize herself only as a series of documents in her father's never-ending documentary," David Shields writes. *Enough about You: Adventures in Autobiography* (New York: Simon & Schuster, 2002), 126.

102. Timothy Garton Ash, *The File: A Personal History* (New York: Vintage Books, 1998), 12.

103. Kaysen, *Girl, Interrupted,* 147–149, 150–159.

104. Carl Kaysen, Charles C. Holt, Richard Holton, George Kozmetsky, H. Russell Morrison, and Richard Ruggles, "Report of the Task Force on the Storage of and Access to Government Statistics," *American Statistician* 23 (June 1969): 11–19. See also Westin, *Privacy and Freedom,* 317.

105. Kaysen, *Girl, Interrupted,* 167.

106. This theme resonates in another memoir of depression from this period, Elizabeth Wurtzl's *Prozac Nation: Young and Depressed in America* (Boston: Houghton Mifflin, 1994). For an interpretation of Wurtzl's self-display and

disclosure as a meditation on the dangers of invisibility, especially for the addict whose life depends on "being seen," see Kathy Farquharson, "Escaping the Panopticon: Vision and Visibility in the Memoirs of Elizabeth Wurtzel," in *Compelling Confessions: The Politics of Personal Disclosure*, ed. Suzanne Diamond (Madison, NJ: Fairleigh Dickinson University Press, 2011), 68–75; quote on p. 71.

107. Memoirs of depression and medication by Wurtzl in 1994's *Prozac Nation*, and later by Lauren Slater in *Prozac Diary* (New York: Random House, 1998), also fueled this demand.

108. Sachs, "Books: The Unconfessional Confessionalist," 60.

109. "Author Q & A: *The Camera My Mother Gave Me* by Susanna Kaysen," Penguin Random House; www.penguinrandomhouse.com/books/90575/the -camera-my-mother-gave-me-by-susanna-kaysen/9780679763437/.

110. Cheryl Strayed in *Why We Write about Ourselves: Twenty Memoirists on Why They Expose Themselves (and Others) in the Name of Literature*, ed. Meredith Maran (New York: Plume, 2016), 210–211.

111. Ayelet Waldman in *Why We Write about Ourselves*, 228–229.

112. In an interview with the *Austin Chronicle* Kaysen stated, "But I tell you, this is the end of memoirs for me. There are too many of them. People think they're real but they're not. They're just as full of self-deception and occlusion as a novel." Marion Winik, "Susanna Kaysen Lays it on the Line," *Austin Chronicle*, October 19, 2001; www.austinchronicle.com /books/2001-10-19/83325.

113. Peter Kramer uses "autopathography," a modification of "pathography," a term coined by Joyce Carol Oates. Atlas, "The Age of The Literary Memoir Is Now." Others used "pathobiography." See Cook, "Outing History," 70. Cook criticizes the term as part of the high culture backlash against "the contradictions and textures that actually make humans so interesting."

114. See www.publishersweekly.com/978-0-679-44390-2. The jury is out on the origins of the phrase, which the *Oxford English Dictionary* defines as "too much information (used to indicate that someone has revealed personal information of an embarrassing nature)." It was the title of a Duran Duran song of 1993 and also of a 1981 song of The Police. Others have suggested military or virtual community roots.

115. BookPage review, October 2001; brooklyn.bibliocommons.com/item/show /10580183062_the_camera_my_mother_gave_me.

116. *Bonome v. Kaysen*, 17 Mass. L. Rptr. 695 (Mass. Super. Ct. 2004).

117. Paul Schwartz and Karl-Nikolaus Peifer, "Prosser's *Privacy* and the German Right of Personality: Are Four Privacy Torts Better than One Unitary Concept?" *California Law Review* 98 (2010): 1925–1988; quote on p. 1961.

118. *Bonome v. Kaysen.* For a precedent, see *Haynes v. Alfred A. Knopf and Nicholas Lemann*, 8 F.3d 1222 (7th Cir. 1993); the case concerned a man whose life appeared in a historical account of the Great Migration by author Nicholas Lemann, *The Promised Land* (New York: Vintage, 1992). Lemann used the man's actual name and the court ruled this appropriate, since a pseudonym would not have hidden his identity and because changing details about him would have amounted to writing fiction.

119. Eugene Volokh, "'You Are Also Ordered Not to Post Any Further Information about the [Plaintiff],'" *Washington Post*, August 24, 2015; see also Volokh, "Freedom of Speech and Information Privacy: The Troubling Implications of a Right to Stop People from Speaking about You," *Stanford Law Review* 52 (2000): 1049–1124. Websites now offer assistance to writers in navigating the legal issues of "telling their own story." See www.rightsofwriters.com/2011/01/can-you-tell-your-own-true-story-even.html. See also Sonja R. West, "The Story of Me: The Underprotection of Autobiographical Speech," *Washington University Law Review* 84 (2006): 905–967. She argues that "the time-honored practice of talking about yourself has been ignored by legal scholars," with the consequence that "current free speech principles protect the autobiographies of the powerful but leave the stories of 'ordinary' people vulnerable to challenge," 905. She compares Kaysen's case to that of the blogger "Washingtonienne" (Jessica Cutler), who was sued for disclosing sexual escapades with men online.

120. Samantha Barbas, "The Death of the Public Disclosure Tort: A Historical Perspective," *Yale Journal of Law & the Humanities* 22 (2010): 171–215.

121. Neil Richards, "The Puzzle of Brandeis, Privacy, and Speech," *Vanderbilt Law Review* 63: 5 (2010): 1343.

122. Since the 1960s courts have nearly always found for the media in invasion of privacy suits. The public's "legitimate interest" in the information has been treated as quite expansive, generally overriding privacy concerns. See Amy Gajda, *The First Amendment Bubble: How Privacy and Paparazzi Threaten a Free Press* (Cambridge, MA: Harvard University Press, 2015); and Samantha Barbas, *Newsworthy: The Supreme Court Battle over Privacy and Press Freedom* (Stanford, CA: Stanford Law Books, 2017).

123. This is from the most recent edition of William Prosser and Page Keeton, *Handbook of the Law of Torts*, 5th ed. (1984), quoted in Lawrence, *Privacy and the Past*, 55. There were countercurrents, however. Celebrities gained new protections from the intrusive press after the passage of California's pioneering 1999 paparazzi law, lobbied for by celebrities and the Screen Actors Guild, as well as victims' rights groups. It created tort liability for "physical" and "constructive" invasions of privacy through photographing, videotaping, or

recording a person engaging in a personal or family activity. Shay Sayre and Cynthia King, *Entertainment and Society: Audiences, Trends, and Impact* (New York: Routledge, 2003), 216.

124. Schwartz and Peifer, "Prosser's *Privacy* and the German Right of Personality," 1927.

125. As noted in Chapter 1, that vision of individual dignity has been much more at home in Europe in the form of a "right of personality." See, for example, James Q. Whitman, "The Two Western Cultures of Privacy: Dignity versus Liberty," *Yale Law Journal* 113 (2004): 1151–1221. Edward J. Bloustein defended the "inviolate personality" concept in "Privacy as an Aspect of Human Dignity: An Answer to Dean Prosser," *New York Law Review* 39 (1964): 962–1007.

126. Rochelle Gurstein argues that casting privacy as an individual right "was ill-fated from the start" because it "made it virtually impossible to take account of the sweeping damages to taste and judgment or address the coarsening tone of public discussion, matters that were central to the debate about privacy." *The Repeal of Reticence: A History of America's Cultural and Legal Struggles over Free Speech, Obscenity, Sexual Liberation, and Modern Art* (New York: Hill and Wang, 1996), 148–149.

127. See the essays in *The Seductions of Biography*, ed. Mary Rhiel and David Suchoff (New York: Routledge, 1996), 118–172. In the same volume, Blanche Wiesen Cook writes of the "extraordinary resistance" she faced when narrating the intimate lives and relations of famous women, beginning in the 1970s. "Outing History," 70. For a full treatment of the issues, see Susan C. Lawrence, *Privacy and the Past: Research, Law, Archives, Ethics* (New Brunswick, NJ: Rutgers University Press, 2016).

128. Literary theorist Barbara Johnson uses this phrase in *The Seductions of Biography*, 119.

129. Diane Wood Middlebrook, "Telling Secrets," in *The Seductions of Biography*, 124. On confessional poetry see Deborah Nelson, "Beyond Privacy: Confessions between a Woman and Her Doctor," *Feminist Studies* 25: 2 (Summer 1999): 279–306; and Hugh Stevens, "Confession, Autobiography and Resistance: Robert Lowell and the Politics of Privacy," in *American Cold War Culture*, ed. Douglas Field (Edinburgh: Edinburgh University Press, 2005), 164–184.

130. Diane Wood Middlebrook, *Anne Sexton: A Biography* (Boston: Houghton Mifflin, 1991).

131. Middlebrook, "Telling Secrets," 124, 126; Alessandra Stanley, "Poet Told All; Therapist Provides the Record," *New York Times*, July 15, 1991, p. 1. Janna Malamud Smith on the other hand wrote of planning to destroy the papers of

her famous father, Bernard Malamud. As she put it, "I was not eager to have my private father—the one I knew and carried with me—tampered with by someone else's appraisal. In the aftermath of his death, as he made his way from real to remembered, I wanted him left alone. Not only did I feel myself vulnerable, but I felt he was." Smith added, "I felt uneasy about the kind of biography anyone could receive in a publishing climate that often favored sensational books." Prologue, *Private Matters: In Defense of the Personal Life* (Reading, MA: Addison-Wesley, 1997).

132. Diane Wood Middlebrook, *Her Husband: Hughes and Plath—A Marriage* (New York: Viking, 2003).

133. Hughes kept quiet, even though he knew, as he wrote to yet another biographer, that "my silence seems to confirm every accusation and fantasy. I preferred it, on the whole, to allowing myself to be dragged out into the bull-ring and teased and pricked and goaded into vomiting up every detail of my life with Sylvia for the higher entertainment of the hundred thousand Eng Lit Profs and graduates who—as you know—feel very little in this case beyond curiosity of quite a low order, the ordinary village kind, popular bloodsport kind." Janet Malcolm, *The Silent Woman: Sylvia Plath and Ted Hughes* (New York: Alfred A. Knopf, 1994), 165, 140–141.

134. Malcolm, *The Silent Woman*, 8–9.

135. This was Edward Butscher's *Sylvia Plath, Method and Madness* (New York: Seabury Press, 1976).

136. Malcolm, *The Silent Woman*, 164–165. Here she referred also to the willingness of acquaintances to talk.

137. William H. Honan, quoted in David Shields and Shane Salerno, *Salinger* (New York: Simon & Schuster, 2013), 511. Ian Hamilton, *In Search of J. D. Salinger* (New York: Random House, 1988); Joyce Maynard, *At Home in the World: A Memoir* (New York: Picador, 1998); Paul Alexander, *Salinger, a Biography* (Los Angeles: Renaissance Books, 1999); Margaret Ann Salinger, *Dream Catcher: A Memoir* (New York: Washington Square Press, 2000); Kenneth Slawenski, *J. D. Salinger: A Life* (New York: Random House, 2011); Shields and Salerno, *Salinger*. As a reviewer of the Slawenski book wrote, "J. D. Salinger spent the first third of his life trying to get noticed and the rest of it trying to disappear. He would have hated . . . [this] reverent new biography, which comes to us just a year after the writer's death and creditably unearths and aggregates the facts and reads them into the fiction—reanimating the corpse without quite making it sing." Jay McInerney, "Salinger's Love and Squalor," *New York Times* Book Review, February 10, 2011, p. A1.

138. Malcolm, *The Silent Woman*, 111.

139. Malcolm, *The Silent Woman*, 110. The case was *Salinger v. Random House, Inc.*, 811 F.2d 90 (2d Cir. 1987).
140. Hamilton, *In Search of J. D. Salinger*.
141. Salinger "had to register all seventy-nine disputed letters at the Copyright Office, where any person willing to pay $10 can peruse them." Phoebe Horan, quoted in Shields and Salerno, *Salinger*, 498.
142. Loren Glass, *Authors Inc.: Literary Celebrity in the United States, 1880–1980* (New York: New York University Press, 2004), 199.
143. Maynard, *At Home in the World*, 199.
144. Margaret Salinger, *Dream Catcher*, 395.
145. Peggy Salinger's book, for example, "of all the private documents that have lately found their way into print under the abused publishing category known as 'memoir,'" was described as "so unequivocally removed from the realm of literature—so inward-looking, so ungenerous, so artless—that it achieves a perfect state of irrelevance, the nadir, if you will, of the autobiographical practice, revealing falsehood where it seeks to expose the 'truth,' and truth where it reveals the hollows of the secret-teller's damaged little heart." Benjamin Anastas, quoted in Shields and Salerno, *Salinger*, 536.
146. In Maynard's account: "With my younger children heading off to college, and the challenge before me of footing the bills—I decided to sell J. D. Salinger's letters to me, written over a quarter century ago." As she explained, "I did not sell the letters as an act of vengeance, but neither did I feel compelled not to sell them, as some sort of act of exaggerated loyalty. I believed the letters were better entrusted to a person whose appreciation of Salinger found its origins in an understandable love of the writer's prose, rather than one who made the costly mistake of trying to live out fictions best left on the page." (Peter Norton, a software developer bought the letters and returned them to Salinger.) See Phoebe Hoban in Shields and Salerno, *Salinger*, 531.
147. Larissa Macfarquhar, "The Cult of Joyce Maynard," *New York Times Magazine* (September 6, 1998): 32–35; quote on p. 34.
148. Macfarquhar, "The Cult of Joyce Maynard," p. 34; Maynard, *At Home in the World*, xi. For a recent and similarly cutting profile of Maynard, see Caitlin Flanagan, "The Queen of Oversharing: The Personal Essay May be Over—but Joyce Maynard Isn't," *The Atlantic* (October 2017).
149. Maynard herself presents this as progress from her earlier literary career, during which she wrote entire books about herself that left out items that were too personal or shameful, such as her alcoholic father. *At Home in the World*, 163.
150. Influential memoirs by men followed as well, including Augustus Burroughs's *Running with Scissors* (2003) and James Frey's *A Million Little Pieces* (2003).

Both of these became controversial for their alleged fictionalizing of autobiographical events. (Also note Binjamin Wilkomirski's *Fragments: Memories of a Wartime Childhood* [1996], which was celebrated until it was discovered to be an entirely fictional Holocaust memoir.)

151. See Berlant, *The Female Complaint*; Lauren Berlant and Lisa Duggan, eds., *Our Monica, Ourselves: The Clinton Affair and the National Interest* (New York: New York University Press, 2001); and Paul Apostolidis and Juliet A. Williams, eds., *Public Affairs: Politics in the Age of Sex Scandals* (Durham, NC: Duke University Press, 2004).

152. Jonathan Yardley, "J. D. Salinger's Holden Caulfield, Aging Gracelessly," *Washington Post*, October 19, 2004, p. C01.

153. Jonathan Yardley, as quoted in Shields and Salerno, *Salinger*, 537.

154. Maynard characterized the attacks "not only on my book but on my character" as "brutal, intensely personal and relentless." See afterword, *At Home in the World*. But she had anticipated the criticism, writing in her author's note, "While I have no doubt that some will view my choice to tell this story honestly as an invasion of others' privacy, I have tried hard to describe only those events and experiences that had a direct effect on the one story I believe I have a right to tell completely: my own." *At Home in the World*, xi.

155. Both are quoted in Macfarquhar, "The Cult of Joyce Maynard," p. 35.

156. Margaret Salinger, *Dream Catcher*, xi, 420.

157. Maynard, *At Home in the World*, 302.

158. Jean Miller, quoted in Shields and Salerno, *Salinger*, 524.

159. See Shari Benstock, ed., *The Private Self: Theory and Practice of Women's Autobiographical Writings* (Chapel Hill: University of North Carolina Press, 1988); Peter Gilmour, *The Wisdom of Memoir: Reading and Writing Life's Sacred Texts* (Winona, MN: St. Mary's Press, 1997); Judith Barrington, *Writing the Memoir: From Truth to Art* (Portland, OR: Eighth Mountain, 1997); and Tristine Rainer, *Your Life as Story: Writing the New Autobiography* (New York: G. P. Putnam's Sons, 1997). Albert E. Stone observed that "in this century, and particularly in the years since World War II, no other mode of American expression [autobiography] seems to have more widely or subtly reflected the diversities of American experience," *Autobiographical Occasions and Original Acts: Versions of American Identity from Henry Adams to Nate Shaw* (Philadelphia: University of Pennsylvania Press, 1982), 1.

160. Similarly, author Joyce Carol Oates wrote of the controversy: "Though Joyce Maynard has been the object of much incensed, self-righteous criticism, primarily from admirers of the reclusive Salinger, her decision to sell his letters is her own business, like her decision to write about her own life. Why is one 'life' more sacrosanct than another?" Quoted in Shields and Salerno, *Salinger*,

530–531. Similar convictions underwrote critical theory about the confessional mode in this period. Literary theorist Deborah Nelson argues that "privacy rights rest on a foundation of visibility" and that "confession in fact underwrites privacy—especially for those with the most fragile claims on citizenship." *Pursuing Privacy*, 26.

161. Maynard, afterword, *At Home in the World*.

162. Killen, *1973 Nervous Breakdown*, 159.

163. Don DeLillo, *Mao II* (New York: Viking, 1991); see Glass, *Authors Inc.*, 197.

164. Yardley, "J. D. Salinger's Holden Caulfield."

165. Yardley, "J. D. Salinger's Holden Caulfield."

166. Shields and Salerno, *Salinger*, xiv, xv, xvii.

167. Shields and Salerno, *Salinger*, xiii.

168. Shields and Salerno, *Salinger*, 569–570. They write that Salinger, drawing on his World War II experience, "never stopped living his life like a counterintelligence agent."

169. Larry Gross, "What is Wrong with This Picture? Lesbian Women and Gay Men on Television," in *Queer Words, Queer Images: Communication and the Construction of Homosexuality*, ed. R. Jeffrey Ringer (New York: New York University Press, 1994), 143. See also Bruce Robbins, ed., *The Phantom Public Sphere* (Minneapolis: University of Minnesota Press, 1993); Richard Schickel, *Intimate Strangers: The Culture of Celebrity in America* (Garden City, NY: Doubleday, 1985); and Bromwich, "How Publicity Makes People Real," 145–172.

170. Joshua Gamson, *Freaks Talk Back: Tabloid Talk Shows and Sexual Nonconformity* (Chicago: University of Chicago Press, 1998), 4, 18. He pegs talk shows as "an absurd, hyper enactment of what Michel Foucault called the 'incitement to discourse.'" See Gamson, "Taking the Talk Show Challenge," 190–205.

171. For a trenchant analysis of American uses of narcissism in cultural criticism, see Lunbeck, *The Americanization of Narcissism*.

172. Deborah Nelson argues for the collapse of a dominant (elite and patriarchal) view of privacy starting in the late 1950s, which yoked together private property, bodily integrity, sovereignty over family members, and the proprietary interest in family name as one coherent interest. *Pursuing Privacy in Cold War America*, xiii. I would argue that this process began long before the 1950s, though it may have only become fully evident at mid-century.

173. One of the most acclaimed memoirists of recent times, Leslie Jamison, argued in 2014 for the outward-looking and empathetic face of confessional writing, in *The Empathy Exams: Essays* (Minneapolis: Graywolf Press, 2014).

174. See, for instance, Jill Hamburg Coplan, "Moved to Write Memoirs," *Newsday*, March 13, 2004.

175. Yagoda, *Memoir*, 7. These figures come from Nielsen BookScan, which tracks 70 percent of book sales in the United States.

176. Yagoda, *Memoir*, 28.

177. See memoirsbyme.com, cited by Yahoda, *Memoir*, on p. 20. According to Yahoda, there has been approximately one scandal a year over "autobiographical fraud" during the last four decades. The most recent series began in 2006. This was the year that James Frey's memoir, *A Million Little Pieces* (2003) was exposed as playing fast and loose with the "facts" of the author's life. Intriguingly, Frey had tried unsuccessfully to sell his book as a novel. But it was immediately optioned when he reclassified it as a memoir, and it became a bestseller with help from Oprah Winfrey. For the contretemps over Frey, see Mary Karr, "His So-Called Life," *New York Times* Book Review, January 15, 2006, p. D13; and Michiko Kakutani, "Bending the Truth in a Million Little Ways," *New York Times*, January 17, 2006, p. E1. Regarding fraudulent memoirs, Yagoda notes, "in any society where a particular currency has high value and is fairly easily fashioned, counterfeiters will quickly and inevitably emerge," 243.

178. Maran, ed., *Why We Write about Ourselves*, dedication page.

179. Birkerts, *The Art of Time in Memoir*, 3.

180. Mendelsohn, "But Enough about Me."

181. Shields, *Enough about You*, 6.

182. Shields, *Enough about You*, 162; emphasis in original.

183. Birkerts, *The Art of Time in Memoir*, 7.

184. Birkerts, *The Art of Time in Memoir*, 9, 190.

185. See the essays by Leslie Jamison and Charles McGrath, "In the Age of Memoir, What's the Legacy of the Confessional Mode?" *New York Times* Book Review, October 4, 2015, p. 31. Jamison, somewhat wearily, observed, "These days, American literary culture features both a glut of so-called 'confessional' work and an increasingly familiar knee-jerk backlash against it."

186. danah boyd, *It's Complicated: The Social Lives of Networked Teens* (New Haven, CT: Yale University Press, 2014), 6.

187. Deborah Lupton, *The Quantified Self: A Sociology of Self-Tracking* (Malden, MA: Polity, 2016), 61.

188. boyd, *It's Complicated*, 62.

189. Janet Murray, *Hamlet on the Holodeck: The Future of Narrative in Cyberspace* (New York: Simon & Schuster, 1997), 252.

190. Dave Sifry, "State of the Blogosphere, February 2006," Technorati.com; http://technorati.com/weblog/2006/02/81.html.

191. "Buzz in the Blogosphere: Millions More Bloggers and Blog Readers," Nielsen Online, March 8, 2012; www.nielsen.com/us/en/insights/news/2012/buzz-in-the-blogosphere-millions-more-bloggers-and-blog-readers.html.

192. West, "The Story of Me," 910. At that writing, there were 50 million web logs in existence. West notes that two-thirds of bloggers "almost never" ask permission

before writing about another person by name, according to a survey coming out of the Massachusetts Institute of Technology. Predictably, the survey found that "bloggers are starting to come up against a range of privacy-related issues varying from minor embarrassments with family and friends to termination of their employment," 911. Emily Nussbaum, "My So-Called Blog," *New York Times Magazine* (January 11, 2004): 33–34. Nussbaum theorized that this new desire to talk publicly about personal experiences, particularly among the young, "has multiple roots, from Ricki Lake to the memoir boom to the AA confessional, not to mention thirteen seasons of 'The Real World.'" These modern speakers learned that revealing personal experiences had its rewards and that "exposure may be painful at times, but it's all part of the process of 'putting it out there,' risking judgment and letting people in." In return, the payoff for this openness is "a new kind of intimacy, a sense that they are known and listened to. This is their life, for anyone to read."

193. Emily Nussbaum, "Say Everything," *New York Magazine* (February 12, 2007). This was partly a caricature. As Nussbaum acknowledged, given that "your life is being lived in public whether you choose to acknowledge it or not . . . it may be time to consider the possibility that young people who behave as if privacy doesn't exist are actually the sane people, not the insane ones."

194. William Haefeli, *New Yorker* (October 11, 2010).

195. Nussbaum, "Say Everything."

196. Mary Madden et al., "Teens, Social Media, and Privacy," Pew Internet and American Life Project, May 31, 2013; www.pewinternet.org/Reports/2013/Teens -Social-Media-And-Privacy.aspx; danah boyd and Alice Marwick, "Social Privacy in Networked Publics: Teens' Attitudes, Practices, and Strategies," A Decade in Internet Time: Symposium on the Dynamics of the Internet and Society, September 2011. For a detailed investigation, see boyd, *It's Complicated*, especially ch. 2. Based on her ethnographic research, boyd argues that "instead of signaling the end of privacy as we know it, teens' engagement with social media highlights the complex interplay between privacy and publicity in the networked world we all live in now," 57. She also amply documents teens' frustration "with adult assumptions that suggest that they are part of a generation that has eschewed privacy in order to participate in social media," 54–55. See also Christopher Jay Hoofnagle et al., "How Different Are Young Adults from Older Adults When It Comes to Information Privacy Attitudes and Policies?" SSRN 1589864, 2010; papers.ssrn.com.

197. See Jason Reid, *Get out of My Room! A History of Teen Bedrooms* (Chicago: University of Chicago Press, 2017).

198. boyd, *It's Complicated*, 60.

199. John Gilliom and Torin Monahan, *SuperVision: An Introduction to the Surveillance Society* (Chicago: University of Chicago Press, 2013), 43.

200. See boyd, *It's Complicated*, 75–76. "Achieving privacy in networked publics," as she notes, has led to a host of creative tactics: switching platforms and working around technical affordances but also encoding messages, or what she calls social steganography (e.g. "subtweeting"), which recognizes that "limiting access to meaning can be a much more powerful tool for achieving privacy than trying to limit access to the content itself," 69.
201. Gilliom and Monahan, *SuperVision*, 52.
202. Gilliom and Monahan, *SuperVision*, 51; emphasis in original.
203. Julia Angwin, *Dragnet Nation: A Quest for Privacy, Security, and Freedom in a World of Relentless Surveillance* (New York: Times Books, 2014), 154.
204. Julian Dibbell, "My Modem, Myself," *Village Voice Literary Supplement* (October–November 2000).
205. On this general theme, see James Livingston, *The World Turned Inside Out: American Thought and Culture at the End of the Twentieth Century* (Lanham, MD: Rowman & Littlefield, 2010).
206. Mendelsohn, "But Enough about Me."
207. Two film scholars called *An American Family* significant for its creation of a new genre "that finds its ultimate expression in an age of cable television when factual and fictional modes have blurred and merged." Jason Landrum and Deborah Carmichael, "Jeffery Ruoff's An American Family: A Televised Life—Reviewing the Roots of Reality Television," *Film & History: An Interdisciplinary Journal of Film and Television Studies* 32: 1 (2002): 66–70; quote on p. 67. The form of the series was also returned to regularly. The series was spoofed in a *Saturday Night Live* skit in 1978, and actor-director Albert Brooks took the series as inspiration for his film *Real Life* in 1979. See the reflections of the writer for the Brooks film in Harry Shearer, "An American Family: A Televised Life," *Wilson Quarterly* (Summer 2002): 118–119.
208. Shearer, "An American Family."
209. The show is now called *Real World*. There were also by the early 2000s, some pronouncements of the death of the genre. "Reality TV Cools its Jets," *USA Today*, March 29, 2002. Noted two scholars, "within a two-year period, twenty-five shows dedicated to the lives of ordinary people vanished from the airwaves, leaving CBS's *Survivor* and MTV's *The Real World* as the only consistent ratings-draw." The glut made clear that two styles were emerging: game shows and serialized shows with developed, real-life characters. Landrum and Carmichael, "Jeffery Ruoff's An American Family," 66.
210. More than 6,100 people applied to be on *Survivor*, a competitor. Sales of webcams were pegged at one-third of a million in 1997 and 2.5 million by 2000. See James Poniewozik, "We Like to Watch," *Time* (June 26, 2000): 56–61; quote on p. 60; Jon Dovey, *Freakshow: First Person Media and Factual Television* (London: Pluto Press, 2000).

211. *An American Family Revisited: The Louds 10 Years Later,* dir. Alan Raymond and Susan Raymond (Home Box Office, 1983); the film would air on PBS in 1991.
212. This was reportedly aggravated by drug addiction.
213. Elizabeth Jensen, "Lance Loud's Last Testament," *Los Angeles Times,* January 6, 2003.
214. Pat Loud released a book about her son with the help of a collaborator in 2012. Full of photographs, scrawled notes, and postcards written by Lance, as well as testimonials from friends, it can be seen as another attempt to preserve a particular version of Lance for the public eye. Pat Loud, *Lance out Loud,* ed. Christopher Makos (New York: Glitterati, 2012).
215. A two-hour anniversary edition of the original series was, however, released on DVD in 2011 by Alan and Susan Raymond.
216. Jensen, "Lance Loud's Last Testament." Pat Loud in a 2013 profile confirmed that she was again living with her ex-husband. Philip Galanes, "The Mother of All 'Housewives,'" *New York Times,* June 16, 2013, p. ST1.
217. Jensen, "Lance Loud's Last Testament."
218. The *Times* piece went on: "'Because of the series, some of the more militant gays wanted Lance as their spokesman,' said Kristian Hoffman, a friend since childhood. 'That wasn't his objective,' Mr. Hoffman said. 'Lance used to tell them that being gay was only one finger out of 10, not a be-all and end-all.'" Thomas J. Lueck, "Lance Loud, 50, Part of Family Documentary," *New York Times,* December 29, 2001, p. D7.
219. Jensen, "Lance Loud's Last Testament."
220. Laurie Winer, "Reality Replay," *New Yorker* (April 25, 2011). The piece was triggered by the production of a new docudrama by HBO, "Cinema Verité," about the making of *An American Family.* Controversy persisted: Gilbert protested HBO's "fallacious" script and hired a lawyer to represent his and the Louds' interests. (The Louds accepted a financial settlement in exchange for not discussing the script publicly.)
221. Winer, "Reality Replay."
222. "Greetings from the Fishbowl," *New York Times Magazine* (April 4, 1999): 18.
223. See, for example, the essays in Jamison, *The Empathy Exams.*
224. Glen Bowersock, "GWM Seeks Classical Greece, Sex, Jewish Roots, Paternity" (Review of Daniel Mendelsohn's *The Elusive Embrace: Desire and the Riddle of Identity*), *New York Observer,* June 14, 1999.
225. Felix Stalder, "Opinion: Privacy Is Not the Antidote to Surveillance," *Surveillance & Society* 1: 1 (2002): 120.

Conclusion

1. Emily Dreyfuss, "Privacy Isn't Dead. It's More Popular than Ever," *Wired* (July 27, 2017). This writer's assessment was drawn from the expanding popularity of an encrypted messaging app, WhatsApp, and the declining popularity of an unsecured one, Twitter. "Twitter is public. WhatsApp is private. Twitter has a huge problem with safety, while WhatsApp has made privacy and security the center of its mission. And it's now more clear than ever that people have made their choice."

2. Paul M. Schwartz and Daniel J. Solove, "The PII Problem: Privacy and a New Concept of Personally Identifiable Information," *NYU Law Review* 86: 6 (December 2011): 1814–1894.

3. See for example David Brin, *The Transparent Society: Will Technology Force Us to Choose between Privacy and Freedom?* (Reading, MA: Addison-Wesley, 1998), which projected a society of mutual surveillance, and Adam Tanner, *What Stays in Vegas: The World of Personal Data—The Lifeblood of Big Business—and the End of Privacy as We Know It* (New York: Public-Affairs, 2014).

4. The CEO of Sun Microsystems, Scott McNealy, stated, "You have zero privacy anyway. Get over it"; Polly Sprenger, "Sun on Privacy: Get over It," *Wired* (January 26, 1999). See also columnist Thomas Friedman, "Four Words Going Bye-Bye," *New York Times*, May 21, 2014, p. A29; and Martin Enserink and Gilbert Chin, special section on "The End of Privacy," *Science* 347: 6221 (January 30, 2015). These last writers declare, "Privacy as we have known it is ending, and we're only beginning to fathom the consequences," 491.

5. Anupam Chander, "Youthful Indiscretion in an Internet Age," in *The Offensive Internet: Speech, Privacy, and Reputation*, ed. Saul Levmore and Martha C. Nussbaum (Cambridge, MA: Harvard University Press, 2010), 124–125.

6. Anita L. Allen, *Unpopular Privacy: What Must We Hide?* (New York: Oxford University Press, 2011), xv; Chris Jay Hoofnagle et al., "Behavioral Advertising: The Offer You Cannot Refuse," *Harvard Law and Policy Review* 6 (2012): 273–296. See also Joseph Turow, *The Daily You: How the New Advertising Industry Is Defining Your Identity and Your Worth* (New Haven, CT: Yale University Press, 2011).

7. Konstantin Kakaes, "Drones Can Photograph Almost Anything. But Should They?" *Columbia Journalism Review* (April 21, 2016).

8. Most infamously, Facebook founder Mark Zuckerberg claimed in 2010 that "the age of privacy is over" and that privacy was no longer a "social norm." Bobbie Johnson, "Privacy No Longer a Social Norm, Says Facebook

Founder," *The Guardian*, January 10, 2010; Marshall Kirkpatrick, "Facebook's Zuckerberg Says the Age of Privacy Is Over," *New York Times*, January 10, 2010. See also Dan Fletcher, "How Facebook Is Redefining Privacy," *Time* (May 20, 2010); Jenna Wortham, "Facebook and Privacy Clash Again," *New York Times*, May 6, 2010, p. B1; Stephanie Clifford, "Tracked for Ads? Many Americans Say No Thanks," *New York Times*, September 30, 2009, p. B3.

9. Joseph Turow, *The Aisles Have Eyes: How Retailers Track Your Shopping, Strip Your Privacy, and Define Your Power* (New Haven, CT: Yale University Press, 2017), 12–13. He cites a 2015 study indicating that Americans give up personal information in exchange for discounts or other benefits primarily because "they are resigned to the inevitability of surveillance and the power of marketers to harvest their data," 254.

10. Julie E. Cohen, "The Biopolitical Public Domain: The Legal Construction of the Surveillance Economy," *Philosophy & Technology* (2017): 1–21. Shoshona Zuboff describes this as "surveillance capitalism," a system marked by "illegible mechanisms of extraction, commodification, and control that effectively exile persons from their own behavior while producing new markets of behavioral prediction and modification." "Big Other: Surveillance Capitalism and the Prospects of an Information Civilization," *Journal of Information Technology* 30: 1 (March 2015): 75–89.

11. Mary Madden et al., "Public Perceptions of Privacy and Security in the Post-Snowden Era," Pew Research Center, November 12, 2014; www .pewinternet.org/2014/11/12/public-privacy-perceptions/.

12. Omar Tene and Jules Polonetsky, "A Theory of Creepy: Technology, Privacy, and Shifting Social Norms," *Yale Journal of Law & Technology* 16: 1 (2014): 59–134; quote on p. 61. See also Ryan Tate, "Creepy Side of Search Emerges on Facebook," *Wired* (February 15, 2013). This unease also greeted what Mark Andrejevic has termed "lateral surveillance" or peer monitoring, wherein individuals act like law enforcement agents or marketers in attempting to gather information on social interactions. "The Work of Watching One Another: Lateral Surveillance, Risk, and Governance," *Surveillance & Society* 2: 4 (2005): 479–497.

13. This is what Erving Goffman called "civil inattention" in *Behavior in Public Places* (New York: Free Press of Glencoe, 1963).

14. Dave Eggers, *The Circle* (New York: Knopf, 2013), 303, 485. See also the near-futuristic imaginings of a fully transparent world in Gary Shteyngart's *Super Sad True Love Story: A Novel* (New York: Random House, 2010).

15. "CIA's 'Facebook' Program Dramatically Cut Agency Costs," *The Onion*; www.theonion.com/video/cias-facebook-program-dramatically-cut-agencys -cos-19753.

16. Meg Leta Jones, *Ctrl+Z: The Right to Be Forgotten* (New York: New York University Press, 2016), 23.

17. Gary T. Marx, *Windows into the Soul: Surveillance and Society in an Age of High Technology* (Chicago: University of Chicago Press, 2016), 29, 47–48. He writes, "The new technologies probe more deeply, widely, and softly than traditional methods, transcend the barriers—both natural (distance, darkness, skin, time, microscopic size) and constructed (walls, sealed envelopes, incompatible formats)—that historically protected personal information."

18. Glenn Greenwald, "NSA Collecting Phone Records of Millions of Verizon Customers Daily," *The Guardian*, June 6, 2013; Barton Gellman and Laura Poitras, "U.S., British Intelligence Mining Data from Nine U.S. Internet Companies in Broad Secret Program," *Washington Post*, June 7, 2013; Jennifer Granick and Christopher Sprigman, "The Criminal NSA," *New York Times*, June 27, 2013. For a concise summary, see Raymond Wacks, *Privacy: A Very Short Introduction*, 2nd ed. (Oxford: Oxford University Press, 2015), 5–9. See also Ronald Goldfarb, ed., *After Snowden: Privacy, Secrecy, and Security in the Information Age* (New York: Thomas Dunne Books, 2015).

19. Bernard E. Harcourt, *Exposed: Desire and Disobedience in the Digital Age* (Cambridge, MA: Harvard University Press, 2015), 77.

20. James Vlahos, "Surveillance Society: New High-Tech Cameras Are Watching You," *Popular Mechanics* (October 1, 2009): 64–69. See also Aaron Doyle, Randy K. Lippert, and David Lyon, eds., *Eyes Everywhere: The Global Growth of Camera Surveillance* (New York: Routledge, 2012).

21. Ari Melber, "About Facebook: As the Old Concept of Privacy Fades and a New One Arises Online, What Is Being Lost?" *The Nation* (December 20, 2007): 20–24; Siva Vaidhyanathan, *The Googlization of Everything (and Why We Should Worry)* (Berkeley: University of California Press, 2011). The 800 million figure is from John Gilliom and Torin Monahan, *SuperVision: An Introduction to the Surveillance Society* (Chicago: University of Chicago Press, 2013), 49.

22. For figures on identity theft, see Wacks, *Privacy*, 24. Also see Steven Levy and Brad Stone, "The Scary New World of Identity Theft," *Newsweek* (July 4, 2005): 41.

23. The Privacy Rights Clearinghouse maintains a chronology of data breaches: see www.privacyrights.org/data-breach. At this writing, the most recent major breach was at Equifax in May 2017, affecting some 143 million Americans. Sarah Igo, "The Equifax Breach Has Potentially Catastrophic Consequences, But We Can't Let It Obscure the Bigger Problem," *Washington Post*, September 26, 2017.

24. Gilliom and Monahan, *SuperVision*, 43.

25. David Lyon has argued that consumer surveillance easily outstrips the surveillance capacities of most modern nation states. "Surveillance

Technology and Surveillance Society," in *Modernity and Technology*, ed. Thomas J. Misa, Philip Brey, and Andrew Feenberg (Cambridge, MA: MIT Press, 2003), 172.

26. Daniel J. Solove, *The Digital Person: Technology and Privacy in the Information Age* (New York, 2004).

27. Natasha Singer, "When No One Is Just a Face in the Crowd," *New York Times*, February 2, 2014, p. BU3. Plans for the iPhone 8 in 2017 included facial recognition technology "to see its owner in just a few hundred milliseconds." Andrew Griffin, "iPhone 8: Facial Recognition Unlocking the Main Feature of New, Premium Apple Phone, Report Claims," UK *Independent*, August 22, 2017.

28. Wacks, *Privacy*, 9.

29. Marx, *Windows into the Soul*, 116, 48.

30. Viktor Mayer-Schönberger and Kenneth Cukier, *Big Data: A Revolution That Will Transform How We Live, Work, and Think* (Boston: Houghton Mifflin Harcourt, 2013); Erez Aiden and Jean-Baptiste Michel, *Uncharted: Big Data as a Lens on Human Culture* (New York: Riverhead Books, 2013); Rob Kitchin, *The Data Revolution: Big Data, Open Data, Data Infrastructures and Their Consequences* (Los Angeles: Sage, 2014); Christian Rudder, *Dataclysm: Who We Are When We Think No One's Looking* (New York: Crown, 2014); Alex Pentland, *Social Physics: How Good Ideas Spread—The Lessons from a New Science* (New York: Penguin Press, 2014).

31. For example, Steve Lohr, *Data-ism: The Revolution Transforming Decision Making, Consumer Behavior, and Almost Everything Else* (New York: Harper-Collins, 2015).

32. For example, Bruce Schneier, *Data and Goliath: The Hidden Battles to Collect Your Data and Control Your World* (New York: W. W. Norton, 2015).

33. Caroline Perry, "You're Not So Anonymous," *Harvard Gazette*, October 18, 2011.

34. Legal scholar Anita L. Allen, for example, describes privacy as "a condition of inaccessibility of the person, his or her mental states, or information about the person to the senses or surveillance devices of others." Allen, *Uneasy Access: Privacy for Women in a Free Society* (Totowa, NJ: Rowman & Littlefield, 1988), 15.

35. See Randolph Lewis, *Under Surveillance: Being Watched in Modern America* (Austin: University of Texas Press, 2017).

36. Julia Angwin, "The Web's New Gold Mine: Your Secrets," *Wall Street Journal*, July 30, 2010. As Joseph Turow documents, traditional physical retail outfits have similar ambitions, certain that they must "trace, quantify, profile and discriminate among shoppers as never before" if they are to survive in a digital

environment, with personalization and smartphones the tools. *The Aisles Have Eyes*, 3.

37. Charles Duhigg, "How Companies Learn Your Secrets," *New York Times Magazine* (February 16, 2012); Kashmir Hill, "How Target Figured out a Teen Girl Was Pregnant before Her Father Did," *Forbes Magazine* (February 16, 2012); Gus Lubin, "The Incredible Story of How Target Exposed a Teen Girl's Pregnancy," *Business Insider*, February 16, 2012. Those in the predictive analytics industry described the story as inaccurate and sensationalized, lamenting its "viral outbreak." See www.kdnuggets.com/2014/05/target-predict-teen-pregnancy-inside-story.html. Target itself recognized the "creepiness factor" as Tene and Polonetsky point out in "A Theory of Creepy," 67.

38. Pricewaterhouse Coopers, "The Wearable Future," cited in Turow, *The Aisles Have Eyes*, 223.

39. Turow, *The Aisles Have Eyes*, 224.

40. Gilliom and Monahan, *SuperVision*, 12, 17, 19.

41. Marx, *Windows into the Soul*, 117.

42. Gilliom and Monahan, *SuperVision*, 108–109.

43. Turow, *The Aisles Have Eyes*.

44. Eli Pariser, *The Filter Bubble: What the Internet Is Hiding from You* (New York: Penguin Press, 2011).

45. Raymond Wacks notes the disintegrating "divide between the state and business" as an important feature of the present privacy landscape in *Privacy*, 15.

46. See, for example, David Rosen, "Four Ways Your Privacy Is Being Invaded," *Salon.com*, September 11, 2012; Dave Gilson, Alex Park, and AJ Vicens, "How We Got from 9/11 to Massive NSA Spying on Americans: A Timeline," *Mother Jones* (September 11, 2013).

47. Chris Jay Hoofnagle, "Big Brother's Little Helpers: How ChoicePoint and Other Commercial Data Brokers Collect and Package Your Data for Law Enforcement," *North Carolina Journal of International Law and Commercial Regulation* 29 (2003): 595–637.

48. David Lyon, ed., *Surveillance as Social Sorting: Privacy, Risk, and Digital Discrimination* (London: Routledge 2003); Oscar H. Gandy Jr., *The Panoptic Sort: A Political Economy of Personal Information* (Boulder, CO: Westview Press, 1993).

49. Frank Pasquale, *The Black Box Society: The Secret Algorithms That Control Money and Information* (Cambridge, MA: Harvard University Press, 2015), 1, 9.

50. David C. Gray and Danielle Keats Citron, "The Right to Quantitative Privacy," *Minnesota Law Review* 98 (2013): 62–144. Frank Pasquale, "Reputation Regulation: Disclosure and the Challenge of Clandestinely Commensurating

Computing," in *The Offensive Internet: Speech, Privacy, and Reputation*, ed. Saul Levmore and Martha C. Nussbaum (Cambridge, MA: Harvard University Press, 2010), 107–123. Jaron Lanier, *You Are Not a Gadget: A Manifesto* (New York: Alfred A. Knopf, 2010).

51. This was Andreas Weigend, a physicist turned e-commerce expert. He termed data the "most important raw material of the twenty-first century." *Data for the People: How to Make Our Post-Privacy Economy Work for You* (New York: Basic Books, 2017), 13, 177.

52. The movement announced itself in 2007. See http://quantifiedself.com; Gary Wolf, "Know Thyself: Tracking Every Facet of Life, From Sleep to Mood, to Pain, 24/7/365," *Wired* (June 22, 2009); and Gary Wolf, "The Data-Driven Life," *New York Times Magazine* (May 2, 2010): 38–45.

53. Natasha Dow Schüll, "Data for Life: Wearable Technology and the Design of Self-Care," *BioSocieties* (2016): 317–333; quote on p. 320. She notes that the online marketplace Amazon has launched a specialty shop for "Wearable Technology" featuring approximately 800 products and that the Fitbit tracker alone had generated profits of almost $2 billion annually by 2015.

54. Deborah Lupton, *The Quantified Self: A Sociology of Self-Tracking* (Malden, MA: Polity, 2016); Rebecca Lemov, "On Not Being There: The Data-Driven Body at Work and at Play," *Hedgehog Review* 17: 2 (Summer 2015).

55. Lupton, *The Quantified Self*, 4–5.

56. Kate Crawford, "When Fitbit Is the Expert Witness," *The Atlantic* (November 19, 2014). As the subhead summarizes, "An upcoming court case will use fitness-tracking data to try and prove a plaintiff's claim, bringing us one step closer to the new age of quantified self incrimination."

57. Lupton *The Quantified Self*, 20.

58. Julie E. Cohen, "The Surveillance-Innovation Complex: The Irony of the Participatory Turn," in *The Participatory Condition in the Digital Age*, ed. Darin Barney, Gabriella Coleman, Christine Ross, Jonathan Sterne, and Tamar Tembeck (Minneapolis: University of Minnesota Press, 2016), 207–226.

59. Lupton, *The Quantified Self*, 61.

60. Simon A. Cole, *Suspect Identities: A History of Fingerprinting and Criminal Identification* (Cambridge, MA: Harvard University Press, 2001), 3–4. Although there has been steady U.S. opposition to a universal ID, for example the Real ID Act of 2005, many observers have pointed out that the capacity already exists in the form of data aggregators that merge data sets and sell individuals' profiles to others; see Gilliom and Monahan, *SuperVision*, 29, 40–43.

61. Richard H. Thaler and Cass R. Sunstein, *Nudge: Improving Decisions about Health, Wealth, and Happiness* (New Haven, CT: Yale University Press, 2008).

62. Charles Duhigg, "What Does Your Credit-Card Company Know about You?" *New York Times Magazine* (May 17, 2009): A40–45.

63. David Lyon and Zygmunt Bauman, *Liquid Surveillance: A Conversation* (Oxford: Wiley Blackwell, 2013).

64. Christopher Slobogin, "Panvasive Surveillance, Political Process Theory, and the Nondelegation Doctrine," *Georgetown Law Journal* 102 (2014): 1721–1776. See also Barry Friedman, *Unwarranted: Policing Without Permission* (New York: Farrar, Straus and Giroux, 2017).

65. The journal *Surveillance & Society* debuted in 2002, run by the UK-based Surveillance Studies Network. For key works see Sean P. Hier and Josh Greenberg, eds., *The Surveillance Studies Reader* (New York: McGraw-Hill, 2007); David Lyon, *Surveillance Studies: An Overview* (Cambridge: Polity Press, 2007); Kirstie Ball, Kevin D. Haggerty, and David Lyon, eds., *Routledge Handbook of Surveillance Studies* (New York: Routledge, 2012); Gilliom and Monahan, *SuperVision*; and Marx, *Windows Into the Soul*.

66. Kevin D. Haggerty and Richard V. Ericson, "The Surveillant Assemblage," *British Journal of Sociology* 51: 4 (2000): 605–622. See Dan Bouk, "The History and Political Economy of Personal Data over the Last Two Centuries in Three Acts," *Osiris* 32: 1 (2017): 85–106.

67. Harcourt, *Exposed*, 103.

68. Harcourt, *Exposed*, 215.

69. Julie E. Cohen, *Configuring the Networked Self: Law, Code and the Play of Everyday Practice* (New Haven, CT: Yale University Press, 2012).

70. Viktor Mayer-Schönberger, *Delete: The Virtue of Forgetting in the Digital Age* (2009). Jeffrey Rosen, "The Web Means the End of Forgetting," *New York Times Magazine* (July 21, 2010): 30–37, 44–45; Jeffrey Rosen, "The Right to Be Forgotten," *Stanford Law Review Online* 64 (2012). Calls for a right to forget or delete (or even "reinvent") have, however, been countered by those who argue that this might amount to censorship, the violation of free expression, or even rewriting history.

71. Jones, *Ctrl+Z*, 2. As Jones recounts, Article 17 of the European Union Data Protection Directive of 2012 addressed "the right to be forgotten and to erasure," a novel legislative right that could force deletion of personal data held by data controllers, 10. The relevant ruling European case is the 2010 suit by a man against a Spanish newspaper (and then Google) that publicized his insolvency proceedings; in the 2014 case, *Google v. AEPD*, Google was ordered by the Court of Justice of the European Union to edit the results retrieved when his name was searched. Jones offers an analysis of the gulf between U.S. and European law on this point in "A Right to a Human in the Loop: Political Constructions of Computer Automation

and Personhood from Data Banks to Algorithms," *Social Studies of Science* 47: 2 (2017): 216–239. See also Megan Garber, "How Google's Autocomplete Was . . . Created / Invented / Born," *Atlantic Monthly* (August 23, 2013).

72. See Daniel Solove, *The Future of Reputation: Gossip, Rumor, and Privacy on the Internet* (New Haven, CT: Yale University Press, 2007); and Danielle Keats Citron and Mary Anne Franks, "Criminalizing Revenge Porn," *Wake Forest Law Review* 49 (2014): 345–391.

73. Jones, *Ctrl+Z*, 3.

74. A noted example was wrestler Hulk Hogan's 2016 suit against the gossip website Gawker for publishing a sex tape without his consent in *Bollea v. Gawker*; the successful suit wound up bankrupting Gawker.

75. Gilliom and Monagan, *SuperVision*, 49.

76. Marx, *Windows into the Soul*, xv.

77. The show was a creation of Dutch television in 1997.

78. Julie Anne Taddeo and Ken Dvorak, introduction, *The Tube Has Spoken: Reality TV & History*, ed. Julie Anne Taddeo and Ken Dvorak (Lexington: University Press of Kentucky, 2010), 5. In the same volume, see Lee Barron, "From Social Experiment to Postmodern Joke: *Big Brother* and the Progressive Construction of Celebrity," 27–46.

79. Jones, "A Right to a Human in the Loop," 229.

80. Carol Sanger, *About Abortion: Terminating Pregnancy in Twenty-First-Century America* (Cambridge, MA: Belknap Press of Harvard University Press, 2017), 55.

81. On the overall expansion of laws and policies that limit and regulate collections of personal information, see Colin J. Bennett and Charles D. Raab, *The Governance of Privacy: Policy Instruments in Global Perspective* (Burlington, VT: Ashgate Publishing, 2006).

82. Pasquale, *The Black Box Society*, 143; he asks, "What better way to mark oneself out as a 'someone to watch' than to bargain with a boss for an unmonitored work computer?" See Daniel J. Solove, "Introduction: Privacy Self-Management and the Consent Dilemma," *Harvard Law Review* 126 (2013): 1880–1903.

83. Gilliom and Monahan, *SuperVision*, 6.

84. Gilliom and Monahan, *SuperVision*, 128; they earlier argue that the very term "privacy" is "out-of-date" and "not well suited to helping us make sense of" contemporary conditions, 7, 25.

85. Weigend, *Data for the People*, 47, 19, 41; emphasis in original. He continues, "Building up the idea of privacy and dismantling it all happened in the span of just a couple centuries—a blip in human history," 47.

86. Electronic Frontier Foundation: https://ssd.eff.org/en; Pasquale, *Black Box Society*, 53.

87. J. J. Luna, *How To Be Invisible: Protect Your Home, Your Children, Your Assets, Your Life* (New York: Thomas Dunne Books, 2012).

88. Haggerty and Ericson, "The Surveillant Assemblage," 619.

89. Pasquale notes, however, that "the ability to hide . . . is so comprehensively commodified" that only the wealthy can truly benefit from it. *The Black Box Society*, 56. There is also software designed to this end, such as AdNauseam and TrackMeNot, which create digital noise, ghost queries, and false information trails.

90. One example is the iSee app; Harcourt, *Exposed*, 275.

91. Surveillance Camera Players, *We Know You Are Watching* (New York: Factory School, 2006).

92. Finn Brunton and Martha Nissenbaum, *Obfuscation: A User's Guide for Privacy and Protest* (Cambridge, MA: MIT Press, 2016).

93. Fred Stutzman and Woodrow Hartzog, "Obscurity by Design: An Approach to Building Privacy into Social Media," CCSW'12 (February 2012, Seattle, Washington); Woodrow Hartzog and Evan Selinger, "Obscurity: A Better Way to Think about Your Data than 'Privacy,'" *Atlantic Monthly* (January 17, 2013).

94. Mary Graham, *Presidents' Secrets: The Use and Abuse of Hidden Power* (New Haven, CT: Yale University Press, 2017), 199. This became a hotly contested political issue when the FBI sought a court order in 2016 to force Apple to develop software to defeat the password protection on a phone used by an alleged terrorist. Eric Lichtblau and Katie Benner, "As Apple Resists, Encryption Fray Erupts in Battle," *New York Times*, February 18, 2016, p. A1.

95. Weigend, *Data for the People*, 166–171.

96. This idea has been floated by Latanya Sweeney, computer scientist at Harvard, and her collaborators. See Perry, "You're Not So Anonymous."

97. On micro-payments, see Jaron Lanier, *Who Owns the Future?* (New York: Simon and Schuster, 2013).

98. John B. Thompson, "The New Visibility," *Theory, Culture and Society* 22 (2005): 31–51; quote on p. 38. Thompson has noted that information in the present media environment is not just more extensive and intensive. It is also "*less controllable* in the sense that . . . it is much more difficult for political actors to throw a veil of secrecy around their activities, much harder to control the images and information that appear in the public domain, and much harder to predict the consequences of such appearances and disclosures," 48–49; emphasis in original.

99. Michael Schudson, *The Rise of the Right to Know: Politics and the Culture of Transparency, 1945–1975* (Cambridge, MA: Belknap Press of Harvard University

Press, 2015), 239–240, 243. He cites GovTrack.us as a model of "legislative transparency" that has been borrowed by other nations.

100. Megan Garber, "Doxing: An Etymology," *Atlantic Monthly* (March 6, 2014).

101. Marx, *Windows into the Soul*, 141. One response has been to "close" and regulate the Internet, leading to a new battle over net neutrality.

102. David Leigh and Luke Harding, *WikiLeaks: Inside Julian Assange's War on Secrecy* (London: Guardian Books, 2011).

103. Harcourt, *Exposed*, 267.

104. Graham, *Presidents' Secrets*, 188.

105. Steve Mann, Jason Nolan, and Barry Wellman, "Sousveillance: Inventing and Using Wearable Computing Devices for Data Collection in Surveillance Environments," *Surveillance and Society* 1: 3 (2003): 331–355. Gary Marx describes sousveillance as "watchful vigilance from below," possible in a society defined by dense social interactions, material resources, and civil liberties. *Windows into the Soul*, 22.

106. See I-Witness Video; http://iwitnessvideo.info/. Dean Jonathon Wilson and Tanya Serisier, "Video Activism and the Ambiguities of Counter-Surveillance," *Surveillance and Society* 8: 2 (2010): 166–180; and Bijan Stephen, "Get up, Stand up: Social Media Helps Black Lives Matter Fight the Power," *Wired* (November 2015).

107. Aida Hurtado, as quoted in Sidonie Smith, *Subjectivity, Identity, and the Body: Women's Autobiographical Practices in the Twentieth Century* (Bloomington: Indiana University Press, 1993), 159. Simone Browne frames slavery as a prehistory of modern surveillance practices, beginning with slave ships, the Book of Negroes, slave passes and runaway notices, lantern laws, branding and biometric identification, the one-drop rule, and synoptic power at auction blocks all the way to passports, stop-and-frisk, CCTV, and mass incarceration; see *Dark Matters: On the Surveillance of Blackness* (Durham, NC: Duke University Press, 2015). See also Khiara M. Bridges, *The Poverty of Privacy Rights* (Stanford, CA: Stanford Law Books, 2017); and Michele Estrin Gilman, "The Class Differential in Privacy Law," *Brooklyn Law Review* 77: 4 (2012): 1389–1445.

108. Virtual invasions and data records were examples of what one scholar called "thin" surveillance, which monitored individuals without constraining their mobility. "Thick" surveillance, in contrast, including physical confinement, disproportionately affected "lower-status and marginal groups, such as the institutionalized." John Torpey, "Through Thick and Thin: Surveillance after 9/11," *Contemporary Sociology* 36: 2 (2007): 116–119; Marx, *Windows into the Soul*, 44.

109. David Sklansky, "Too Much Information: How Not to Think about Privacy and the Fourth Amendment," *California Law Review* 102: 5 (2014): 1069–1121.

110. For an influential analysis of the carceral state, see Michelle Alexander, *The New Jim Crow: Mass Incarceration in the Age of Colorblindness* (New York: New Press, 2010). Birth control has in the early twenty-first century again become controversial. In *Burwell v. Hobby Lobby Stores, Inc.* (2014) the Supreme Court exempted certain corporations from adhering to a federally mandated contraceptive provision of the Affordable Care Act if the owners objected on religious grounds—establishing a protection of conscience that collided with the kind of privacy granted in *Griswold*.

111. The case for privacy is made well by Colin J. Bennett, "In Defence of Privacy: The Concept and the Regime," *Surveillance & Society* 8: 4 (2011): 485–496.

Acknowledgments

Work on a book for long enough and you risk the acknowledgments section becoming a book in itself. But, as I'd like to stay on my editor's good side, these few paragraphs will have to do the job. I hope they will convey something of the depth of my gratitude for the backing of so many friends, family members, colleagues, students, and institutions over the past decade. Let me begin with those who pulled this book over the finish line, most especially Joyce Seltzer, editor extraordinaire. She has my thanks for her confidence in this project, her ability to see it whole when I couldn't, and her sage advice every step of the way. The crack team at Harvard University Press, led by Kathi Drummy and Stephanie Vyce, handled my many queries with equal parts grace and efficiency. Late in the game, Mario Rewers took time out from his own doctoral research to puzzle through thorny permissions and copyright questions, going far beyond the call of duty. Kim Giambattisto steered the book through the production process surely and smoothly.

Support for my scholarship flowed first and foremost from Vanderbilt University and its fabulous history department. It has been my good fortune to work with a series of terrific chairs who are also friends—Liz Lunbeck, Jim Epstein, and Joel Harrington—and in a program kept humming by an extraordinary administrative staff (with particular thanks on that score to Heidi Welch). Time, space, and funding also came from the Whitney Humanities Center at Yale, the Max Planck Institute for the History of Science in Berlin, and the Andrew W. Mellon Foundation. I am especially grateful for a Mellon New Directions Fellowship, which allowed me to spend a year at Berkeley's Law School and Center for the Study of Law and Society. The tremendous group of scholars there—including Melissa Murray, James Rule, Paul Schwartz, Jonathan Simon, and David Sklansky—offered a warm welcome and lessons in legal thinking; Chris Jay Hoofnagle introduced me to the vibrant intellectual community that he and Dan Solove have created through the Privacy Law Scholars Conference. Two spring stints at Rivendell Writers' Colony supplied the best kind of solitude (thank you, thank you,

Carmen Toussaint!), leavened by the companionship of a remarkable group of novelists, essayists, and poets.

Time and funds were critical to this book, but for its substance I'm indebted to the staffs of numerous libraries and archives, including the Social Security Administration Historian's Office (with thanks to Eric DeLisle and Richard Gabryszewski), the Gerald R. Ford Library and Museum, the Special Collections Library at Penn State, and Vanderbilt's Jean and Alexander Heard Library. Several skilled undergraduate research assistants—Leslie Bruce, Caley Caito, and Abigail Miller—were immensely helpful in gathering and analyzing research materials.

I was seriously lucky in the people—and the brainpower—around me as I produced this tome. A raft of friends and colleagues shared ideas, read drafts, commented on conference papers, volunteered cites, and cheered this book along, including Brian Balogh, Samantha Barbas, Casey Blake, Dan Bouk, danah boyd, Howard Brick, Jessica Burch, Jamie Cohen-Cole, Jeff Cowie, Katie Crawford, Dirk Hartog, Ellen Herman, Chris Hoofnagle, Dan Horowitz, the late Michael Katz, Chris Loss, Liz Lunbeck, Heather Murray, Kathy Peiss, Neil Richards, Stanford Ross, Edward Rubin, James Rule, Jeffrey Ruoff, Bruce Schulman, Barbara Sicherman, David Sklansky, Chris Slobogin, Mark Solovey, Amy Dru Stanley, Kim Welch, Michael Willrich, and Mary Ziegler. Conversations over the years with Leslie Butler, Jennifer Ratner-Rosenhagen, and Dorothy Ross—along with their trenchant scholarship and critique—invigorated my work. Dorothy in particular has kept a close eye on this project and kindly helped me think through many of its angles. Invitations to give talks at institutions too numerous to list sharpened my arguments, regularly reminding me of the profound generosity undergirding academic life.

One of the saving graces of writing a book is the fellow travelers on the journey. At Vanderbilt, I had the inspiring company of Dominique Béhague, Paul Kramer, Terry Maroney, Dan Sharfstein, Ganesh Sitamarin, and Laura Stark as they crafted fascinating research projects of their own. I thank each of them for dissecting chapters, and for plenty of commiseration along the way. For moral support at the sentence level, I'm not sure what I would have done without Ruth Rogaski and Arleen Tuchman (and the many Nashville coffeehouses we camped out in). What began as an experiment became an indispensable weekly ritual, and I'm so grateful for their collective wisdom about work, words, and much else.

And then there are those hardy souls who read all, or nearly all, of a sprawling manuscript. I thank my lucky stars that Dan Rodgers still agrees to read my work after all these years, never failing to deepen and transform my understanding of what I've written. I am forever grateful to have been his student—and for a conversation that now spans two decades. Whether down the hall or across the Atlantic, my dear friend Gary Gerstle offered incisive commentary on just about every piece of the manuscript, and the book is much better for it. Ole Molvig had no choice but to play the role of in-house critic. Fortunately for me, he did so with characteristic virtuosity and verve. Two anonymous readers, whom I am delighted to thank publicly here, floored me with their thoroughgoing, searching reviews of an early draft. I can only hope that I've done justice to the time and investment others have poured into this book.

A critical, if less visible, infrastructure of scholarship is the network of family and friends that sustain it. I can't possibly name all the people who organized carpools and sleepovers, dinner parties and camping trips, and generally made Nashville such a great place to live and work for almost a decade now. But the short list must include Lauren Clay, Leor Halevi, Dominique Béhague, Ann Mikkelsen, Dan Sharfstein, Adriane Seiffert, Frank Tong, Traci Nordberg, Peter Nordberg, Anne Fentress, and Tim Nichols. Although further afield (alas!), my extended family has been just as critical to the enterprise. My parents, John and Mittie Igo, took us in for a memorable year in the Bay Area. They have, more importantly, been an unflagging source of support and encouragement in all things. Dianne Molvig and Randy Korda's willingness to make the drive from Madison made research trips easier to contemplate and much happier for my children. Precious time spent with my sisters and brothers-in-law on the West Coast—Susan and Nigel Forman, Kate and Greg McClain, Becky and Matt Sniffen, and Jennifer Igo, along with Claire, Scott, Charlotte, Emmie, Benjamin, and Ian—has fortified what my kids call our "little family," as have our Wisconsin sojourns with Ariel Molvig, Anna Momont, Olaf, and Aren. Pixel helped too, by dragging me away from my desk and taking me on lots of walks.

There are still others to thank. Though my topic has been privacy, my most heartfelt appreciation goes to those who have—hands down—invaded mine most thoroughly. My three remarkable daughters were all born during the time that I labored on this book, and they have grown up alongside it. From a tender age, each in her way seemed to understand and forgive the time required of this project. Eleanor: thank you for your loyalty and insight, your interest in other people (including your mom), and your wonderful way with words. Greta: thank you for your laughter, your joyful nature, and for making our life together so fun. Hattie: thank you for your independent spirit, your big-heartedness, and for always asking about my day. In the end, my children's precise mix of patience and impatience with this book was just what I needed to get it done—and I am so pleased, at long last, to be able to give them incontrovertible evidence of its completion.

Finally: I knew when I married Ole Molvig that I was hitching myself to a charming and brilliant historian of science. What I could not know, then, was that this was a man who would be utterly unfazed by a ten-hour solo drive with three young children (not to mention a brand-new puppy) if that's what it took for me to squeeze in a few extra days of writing. And that is just to begin to recount his dazzling array of talents—and my truly incalculable debt to him. It is to him and our children that I dedicate this book, with love.

Credits

1.1 Kodak Brownie Camera advertisement, 1900. Courtesy, Ellis Collection of Kodakiana (K0430), David M. Rubenstein Rare Book & Manuscript Library, Duke University.

1.2 Samuel D. Warren and Louis D. Brandeis, "The Right to Privacy," *Harvard Law Review* 4, no. 5 (December 15, 1890): 193. Republished with permission of Harvard Law Review Association, Cambridge, MA; permission conveyed through Copyright Clearance Center, Inc.

2.1 Social Security Files, Candler Building, Baltimore. Courtesy, Social Security Administration History Archive, Baltimore, MD.

2.2 Advertisement for Social Security plate, *Chicago Defender* (October 29, 1938). Courtesy, Chicago Defender, Chicago, IL.

2.3 Advertisement for "Personalized" Social Security number ring, *Observer-Reporter* (March 3, 1938). Courtesy, Observer-Reporter, Washington, PA.

3.1 "Functional Diagram of the Telephone System with a Tap." Figure 5 from *The Eavesdroppers* by Samuel Dash, Robert Knowlton, and Richard Schwartz. New Brunswick: Rutgers University Press, 1959. Copyright © 1959 by the Pennsylvania Bar Association Endowment. Reprinted by permission of Rutgers University Press.

3.2 Claude Smith suburb cartoon for *The New Yorker*, February 11, 1956. Claude Smith / The New Yorker Collection / The Cartoon Bank.

4.1 "A POLICEMAN IN EVERY HOME IS THE ONLY WAY TO ENFORCE THIS LAW . . . .passed in 1879." Cartoon by Robert Osborn. Planned Parenthood League of Connecticut, "Special Legislative Edition," Spring 1955. Courtesy, American Civil Liberties

Union Records, Box 771, Folder 18 (MC001.02.03); Public Policy Papers, Department of Rare Books and Special Collections, Seeley G. Mudd Manuscript Library, Princeton University.

4.2 "Women's Rights Defenders Celebrating." Mrs. Estelle Griswold and Mrs. Ernest Jahncke, on the day *Griswold v. Connecticut* was decided, June 7, 1965. Bettmann Collection/Getty Images.

4.3 "The Big Snoop," LIFE *Magazine*, May 20, 1966. Arthur Schatz/The LIFE Premium Collection/Getty Images.

5.1 Laud Humphreys's "systemic observation" form. Republished with permission of Taylor and Francis Group LLC, from Laud Humphreys, *Tearoom Trade: Impersonal Sex in Public Places* (Chicago: Aldine Pub. Co., 1970), © 1970 R. A. Laud Humphreys; permission conveyed through Copyright Clearance Center, Inc.

5.2a "Victim is strapped into chair." Published in *Obedience to Authority: An Experimental View* by Stanley Milgram (New York: Harper & Row, 1974; London: Pinter & Martin, 1997), fig. 3, p. 25. Copyright © 1974 by Stanley Milgram. Reprinted by permission of Pinter & Martin via PLSclear in the United Kingdom and Commonwealth, and HarperCollins Publishers throughout the rest of the world. Photograph reproduction courtesy of Stanley Milgram Papers (MS 1406), Box 145, Folder 12, Manuscripts and Archives, Sterling Memorial Library, Yale University.

5.2b "Learner demands to be shocked." Published in *Obedience to Authority: An Experimental View* by Stanley Milgram (New York: Harper & Row, 1974; London: Pinter & Martin, 1997), fig. 13, p. 91. Copyright © 1974 by Stanley Milgram. Reprinted by permission of Pinter & Martin via PLSclear in the United Kingdom and Commonwealth, and HarperCollins Publishers throughout the rest of the world.

6.1a LOOK *Magazine* 32, no. 13 (June 25, 1968), front cover. Look Magazine Photograph Collection, Prints & Photographs Division, Library of Congress, Washington, DC. Gift; Cowles Communications, Inc. (DLC/PP-1972:282).

6.1b Jack Star, "The Computer Data Bank: Will It Kill You?," LOOK *Magazine* 32, no. 13 (June 25, 1968). Photograph by Phillip Harrington for Look Magazine. Look Magazine Photograph Collection, Prints & Photographs Division, Library of Congress, Washington, DC. Gift; Cowles Communications, Inc. (DLC/PP-1972:282).

6.2 Cover of *Records, Computers, and the Rights of Citizens*, 1973. US Department of Health, Education, and Welfare, *Records, Computers, and the Rights of Citizens: Report of the Secretary's Advisory Committee on Automated Personal Data Systems*, scan of cover image. © 1973 Massachusetts Institute of Technology, by permission of The MIT Press.

7.1 President Gerald R. Ford with First Lady Betty Ford, President's Suite, Bethesda Naval Hospital, October 2, 1974, Bethesda, MD. David Hume Kennerly/Hulton Archive Collection/Getty Images.

7.2 Advertisement for *An American Family.* Courtesy of WNET, New York.

8.1 Facsimile of Susanna Kaysen case record folder at McLean Hospital. Published in *Girl, Interrupted* (New York: Turtle Bay Books, 1993), frontispiece. Copyright © 1993 by Susanna Kaysen. All rights reserved. Permission is granted by the author through Harold Matson Co., Inc.

8.2 "What was the point of writing a blog that nobody else could read?" *The New Yorker,* October 11, 2010. William Haefeli/The New Yorker Collection/The Cartoon Bank/Condé Nast.

Index

Abortion, 149, 150, 158, 262, 268; and "choice," 158–159; clinics, 362; criminalization of, 147; political controversy over, 276; and public health, 149, 159; rights, 272; secrecy, 323, 331

Acquired Immunodeficiency Syndrome (AIDS), 298, 300–301; advocacy, 300; HIV status as private, 300; Reagan Administration neglect, 300; visibility, 300

Acxiom, 354

Administrative state, 56–57, 97; "information state," 71

Advertising: postal, 116; and "right to privacy," 33, 41–44; subliminal, 128, 142, 194; and the "unwilling audience," 310

"Age of Anxiety" (Auden), 106

AIDS Coalition to Unleash Power (ACT UP), 300

Aid to Dependent Children, 175

Alcoholics Anonymous, 215

Alex, Charles, 136

Algorithms. See Big data

All in the Family, 277

Altmeyer, Arthur, 68, 73, 80, 83, 88

American Anthropological Association, 196

American Civil Liberties Union (ACLU), 49, 51, 100, 147, 150, 157, 363

An American Family, 277–293, 315; audience, 284–285; critical response, 279, 282–286; and desire for publicity, 288–289; family ideals,

279–280, 286; innovation of, 278–279; as invasion of privacy, 283, 288–289; Louds' reaction, 282–283; making of, 280–281; as precursor of reality TV, 344–345; as product of an "image society," 291. See also Television

An American Family Revisited, 345

American Law Institute, 147

American Protective League, 48–49

American Psychiatric Association, 332

American Psychological Association, 107, 196

American Sociological Association, 196, 296

American Telephone & Telegraph, 26

Amrine, Michael, 132–133

Anonymity, 364–365, 368; "obscurity by design," 364

Anonymous (hacker collective), 366

Anthropology, 196

Anti-Communism. See Communism

Antisemitism, 73

Apple corporation, 353, 365

Arendt, Hannah, 109–110

Armed Services Vocational Aptitude Battery, 135–136

Army General Classification Test, 135

Ash, Timothy Garton, 325

Ashbrook, John, 141

Asimov, Isaac, 238, 244

Assange, Julian, 366

557

Freudianism. *See* Psychoanalysis
Friedan, Betty, 117
Frisking. *See* Policing
Funt, Allan, 291

Gallagher, Cornelius, 205
Garfinkel, Harold, 185
Gated communities, 265
Gay and Lesbian Alliance against Defamation (GLAAD), 300
Gay liberation movement, 186, 266, 294, 298–301; "coming out," 295, 314; freedom of sexual expression, 295–296; and right to privacy, 295, 298–301; visibility, 296, 298–299
Gilbert, Craig, 278–279, 280, 284, 288–289, 291–292, 347
Gilman, Charlotte Perkins, 23
Girl, Interrupted (Kaysen), 324–328; medical documents in, 325, 327
Glendon, Mary Ann, 181
Global positioning system, 354; and tracking, 350
Godkin, E. L., 10, 34, 37, 38, 39, 40, 46–47
Goffman, Erving, 185, 291
Goldberg, Arthur, 152, 157
Goldmark, Alice, 40
Google, 351, 353–354, 365
Gossip, 20, 28, 32
Gouldner, Alvin, 206
Graham, Billy, 312
Great Depression, 55, 57, 59, 74, 92, 96, 109
Great Jones Street (DeLillo), 337
Great Society, 145, 175
Greenbelt towns, 110
Grimshaw, Allen, 283
Griswold, Estelle, 147–148, 150, 152, 161, 166
Griswold v. Connecticut, 7, 146–159, 262; and anti-totalitarianism, 155; application to wiretapping, 166–167; criticism of ruling, 152–154; dissents, 153–154; due process argument, 152; equal protection argument, 152, 153; free speech argument, 153; influence on reproductive rights, 156, 158–159, 164; and "penumbras" of the Bill of Rights, 152; precedents for, 148–149; privacy rationale, 152–154; protections for "marital privacy," 150, 154–156, 158, 160, 164, 185, 190; represen-

tations of, 165; social context for, 154–155; speculation as to effects, 159–170; and women's rights rationale, 153; and "zones of privacy," 158, 163, 164, 167, 170, 182, 190, 262
Gross, Martin, 136, 138

Hamilton, Ian, 333–334
Hamilton, John D. M., 66–68
Handler, Joel, 178–179
Harlan, John Marshall II, 150, 152, 157
Harrison, Kathryn, 322–323
Harvard Law Review, 35–36
Havighurst, Clark, 162–163
Hayes, Wayne, 276
Health Insurance Portability and Accountability Act, 362
Hearst, William Randolph, 66
Heckscher, August, 117
Hidden Persuaders, The, 127–128, 142
Hill, Anita, 304, 335
Hitler, Adolph, 68, 93, 109
Hollerith card puncher, 46
Holocaust: memoirs, 320; and tattooed numbers, 97
Home Owners Loan Corporation, 110
Homophile movement, 191, 300; and the closet, 295; role of discretion, 295
Hoover, J. Edgar, 79, 81, 215
Horowitz, Irving L., 207, 282
House Un-American Activities Committee (HUAC), 100, 102, 104, 134, 228
How to Beat Personality Tests (Alex), 136
Hughes, Ted, 332. *See also* Plath, Sylvia
Human rights, 6, 283. *See also* Universal Declaration of Human Rights
Humphreys, Laud: attitudes toward homosexuality, 191–192; biography, 185, 206–207, 297; "coming out" as gay, 296; ethics questions, 192, 211–218, 219–220; influence on sexuality research, 297–298; research methods, 186–189; training, 185–186. See also *Tearoom Trade* (Humphreys)
Hunter, Edward, 122

Identity documents. *See* Documentation practices
Identity theft, 82, 354

561